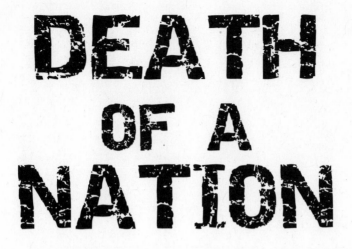

DEATH OF A NATION

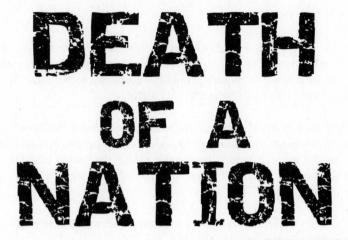

DEATH OF A NATION

9/11 AND THE RISE OF FASCISM IN AMERICA

GEORGE W. GRUNDY

FOREWORD BY DYLAN AVERY

Skyhorse Publishing

Skyhorse Publishing books may be purchased in bulk at special discounts for sales promotion, corporate gifts, fund-raising, or educational purposes. Special editions can also be created to specifications. For details, contact the Special Sales Department, Skyhorse Publishing, 307 West 36th Street, 11th Floor, New York, NY 10018 or info@ skyhorsepublishing.com.

Skyhorse® and Skyhorse Publishing® are registered trademarks of Skyhorse Publishing, Inc.®, a Delaware corporation.

Visit our website at www.skyhorsepublishing.com.

10 9 8 7 6 5 4 3 2 1

Library of Congress Cataloging-in-Publication Data is available on file Jacket.

Jacket design by Michael Short
Jacket photograph: iStockphoto

Print ISBN: 978-1-5107-2125-8
Ebook ISBN: 978-1-5107-2126-5

Printed in the United States of America

To Nelly, to my dear Mum,
and to Bill Hicks, who set me on this road.

CONTENTS

CONTENTS

CONTENTS

CONTENTS

FOREWORD

9/11 was my introduction to The Real World.

I was 18 years old and finishing up high school when the twin towers fell on September 11, 2001. My best friend Korey Rowe had enrolled in the US Army in August and recently left for Basic Training. We had all joked before he left that there wouldn't be a war any time soon. It was funny at the time.

With hindsight it became funny again, but there was a period when I would read a headline about a downed helicopter in Afghanistan and worry that the red and blue-bordered envelopes from overseas would stop showing up. That's what made the "War on Terror" very real for me, and one of the reasons I fought to seek the truth behind the event that led to its creation.

Despite not losing anyone close to me on 9/11, it was the fear that I might lose my best friend to its aftermath that kept me going.

It was this fear, combined with anger, that led to the creation of *Loose Change*. Originally intended as a narrative film in which the protagonists expose a cover-up regarding the events of September 11, it morphed into a documentary that wound up dominating the charts of Google Video (YouTube's predecessor) in 2006, and was labeled "the first Internet blockbuster" by *Vanity Fair*.

The years after the attacks were confusing, angry, and scary. Americans were quick to hide under the 9/11 blanket and attack those who questioned the central premise of the government's version of that day's events. Thankfully, many have found their way to more rational thinking.

I think we'll be arguing for a very long time about what happened that day. Nevertheless, people should continue to seek information about this seismic event that continues to affect America's foreign and domestic policies in a very real way.

While there are other books about 9/11, if you're interested in an examination of the effects of 9/11 on America, George W. Grundy has you covered. This book provides a comprehensive profile of events and participants in 9/11 and the context of the attacks. But I'm particularly interested in his analysis of how 9/11 remains vitally relevant to this day. Without 9/11, there would be no drones; millions of Americans wouldn't be living in poverty in the wake of the largest real estate crisis in history; and we would not face the frightening possibility of an authoritarian leader presiding over the collapse of American democracy.

July 4, 1776 was the birth of a nation. If we continue to be afraid of an honest conversation about the truth, September 11, 2001 will prove to be the *Death of a Nation*.

Dylan Avery
Long Beach, California, 2017

INTRODUCTION

At 10:06 on the morning of September 11, 2001, the fourth and final plane hit the ground in rural Pennsylvania. The attacks were over. Twenty-two minutes later, the collapse of the South tower of the World Trade Center provided the final horrific act in 102 minutes of unprecedented mayhem in the Northeastern United States. Thousands were dead, and it was clear that the greatest act of terrorism in history was going to mark September 11 as a line in the sand for America. The most powerful nation in the world would not recoil wounded for long.

Although I remember exactly where I was on September 11, I'm not so sure when or where it was that I first saw footage of the collapse of Building 7 at the World Trade Center. It had fallen some seven hours after the second twin tower. Most of those not in the Eastern Time Zone hadn't seen it happen, and many Americans remained (and remain) unaware of a third building collapse that day.

It seemed strange. The tower hadn't been struck by a plane, and yet Building 7 fell in a straight line down and collapsed at what looked like free-fall speed. I'd occasionally seen buildings demolished on the nightly news. It looked like that.

So I looked into it, genuinely expecting to find a simple explanation for why a tall building might collapse so suddenly in that way. September 11 had been the very definition of chaos. There must be a reason.

But there wasn't one, and there isn't one, and despite hugely flawed government "investigations," nobody has been able to provide a satisfactory explanation as to what happened to Building 7.

Unless there were explosives placed inside the building. That would provide a perfect explanation, a perfect fit.

And so began a slow, initially casual examination of the wider story. What I found was that Building 7 was just one of a bewildering number of confusing—even *impossible*—anomalies in the official narrative of 9/11. How could you explain the widespread testimony of explosions throughout the twin towers before they collapsed? Why were those first on site in

Shanksville unable to find any evidence of a plane? Did the official explanation, that the soft ground had swallowed the plane whole, seem plausible?

At some point I found the weight of the evidence overwhelming, and was forced to contemplate the awful idea that perhaps the whole event was falsely portrayed. What was initially a mind-boggling proposition—that someone other than Osama bin Laden had been behind the attacks—was supported by so much evidence that it became untenable to retain belief in the official story.

It took some time to swallow, because to question 9/11 is to question your entire belief system. Governments don't attack their own people. Surely their role is to look after them. If the US government was involved in 9/11, what light does that shine on subsequent developments? I was happy to accept that the Bush administration had lied in order to take the world to war against Iraq. I knew his neoconservative colleagues were a bellicose, belligerent bunch. But 9/11? It was too big. It was too much.

Over time, I began to assemble a body of evidence casting grave doubt on the official story of 9/11. It became almost impossible to resist the notion that the whole thing was a pack of lies.

Death of a Nation argues that the events of September 11, 2001 were falsely portrayed, and in fact carried out by entities within the United States government and military in order to further their own goals and to provide profit for their paymasters.

It's a very serious charge, but I contend that the evidence is overwhelming, and in fact surprisingly obvious.

The implications are hard to overstate. The idea that the American government was willing to sacrifice thousands of their own citizens' lives is something that many people find impossible to believe.

The true nature of 9/11 means that many of the events that followed are based on one very big lie. Wars in Afghanistan and Iraq, domestic surveillance, Guantanamo, drones, ISIS, and the rise of Donald Trump were all spawned by the events of that terrible day. The full consequences may still lie ahead of us.

The changes in American society caused by the reaction to 9/11 have, I contend, unbalanced America's already fragile political system and left its citizens facing authoritarianism and a proto-fascist government that risks ending its 240-year-old democracy. The dangers we face cannot be overstated, and it is for this reason that I have tried to write a book that is accessible and easy to understand.

To those (and there are many) who say that to question 9/11 is an insult to those who died that day, I counter that the biggest insult would be to blindly accept what the government told us all, and to keep quiet and not ask questions. That would be a true betrayal, and runs counter to the values of freedom that America espouses.

Death of a Nation is far from the first book on the subject. Some support the official story. Some focus on specialty subjects, like the melting point of structural steel. Some cater to the "lizard people and the Illuminati-control-the-world" corner of the market. My goal has been to write a holistic account of both the events of 9/11 and those that followed, so as to illustrate my conclusions.

As such, we move at a quick pace. Amazon has 8,741 books listed about the Iraq War. I've given it one chapter. This is not to skimp on detail; it's just that there are so many subjects to discuss that brevity is an unfortunate necessity.

The book is not referenced. I have not tried to write an academic document, and it's hard to avoid the contradiction that would be inherent in referencing the 9/11 Commission report (for example) then going on to say that its conclusions were a transparent sham. *Death of a Nation* has been researched almost exclusively through open-source media. If you disagree or want to check something, almost all of it can be simply found.

A word about suspension of disbelief: in writing this book, I have on occasion found it necessary to use disbelief suspension like a light-switch that is turned on and off. In Chapter 1, I describe the final moments of American Airlines flight 11 before it hit the north tower, yet later in the book I suggest that the plane that hit the tower may not have been American 11. I refer to the nineteen Arab men accused of the crime as "hijackers," when it is clear that they were idiotic patsies, placed at the scene of the crime to take the blame. I've found it hard to avoid doing this, but trust that the intelligent reader will understand.

When possible, I have also tried to avoid drawing conclusions without evidence. *"So what do you think really happened?"* is a question you often get asked when voicing doubts about the official 9/11 story, but not knowing what happened to flight 77 does not stop us from observing that the hole in the side of the Pentagon was a fraction of the size of a commercial jet. It is not necessary to have all of the answers to every question in order to see that what we have been told is a lie. At the very least, the story of 9/11 contains dozens and dozens of quite extraordinary coincidences and anomalies. Taken as a whole, I posit that these strain credulity well beyond breaking point.

America now possesses a mighty military machine, as well as a huge industry behind it that demands endless war and death; surveillance powers that dwarf any in human history; a militarized police; corporate-controlled media; a broken body politic; and a concentration of power in the executive branch that has only been made possible through the attacks of 9/11. This fine country, filled with fine people who greet you warmly and are among the most hospitable on earth, has become the most overtly fascist nation the world has seen since the 1930s. Americans are disgusted with their politicians, and that anti-politics sentiment has boiled over into a widespread rejection of the entire system. The potential consequences for humanity are more serious than my mere words can express.

PART ONE
SEPTEMBER 11, 2001

CHAPTER ONE

WORLD TRADE CENTER

American Airlines Flight 11

From 8:14 to 10:06 on the morning of September 11, 2001, America's air defenses failed completely. For one hour and fifty-two minutes, every civilian and military protection surrounding New York City and Washington, DC suddenly stopped working.

112 minutes seems like a short space of time, but for a nation that had spent most of the previous fifty years imagining Russian fighter jets or nuclear missiles coming over the horizon, every second counted.

Prior to the collapse of the Soviet Union and the downgrading of the overall Soviet-US military posture, America's doomsday scenario had been an unexpected nuclear attack on Washington or New York. Although the air above the eastern seaboard of the United States might seem like a playground filled with cattle moving from A to B and businessmen drinking gin and tonics, it is in fact the most highly restricted and well-defended airspace on Earth.

Domestic and international flights around Washington and New York are closely monitored by numerous parties, including the Federal Aviation Administration (FAA), the airlines themselves, and the US military (with a budget larger than that of the next largest ten nations combined). Defense protocols had been written, gamed, tested, re-tested, and used on numerous occasions. Nothing was faulty, until the morning of 9/11.

At dawn, Mohamed Atta and Abdulaziz al-Omari flew from Portland to Boston, departing at 6 a.m. Their flight was right on time, arriving in Boston at 6:50 a.m. Had the Portland flight been just thirty minutes behind schedule, Atta and al-Omari would have missed the connecting flight from Boston that they intended to hijack, and would have been unable to mount the first World Trade Center attack. No explanation has been forthcoming as to why the two

2

lead hijackers chose to take this preposterous risk, and put the entire mission in peril for seemingly no benefit.

As it was, both men boarded American Airlines flight 11 on time, meeting fellow hijackers Waleed al-Shehri, Wail al-Shehri and Satam al-Suqami onboard. All sat in Business or First Class. The plane left Boston's Logan Airport at 7:59 a.m. with ninety-two people onboard, bound for Los Angeles.

At 8:14 a.m., flight 11 failed to respond to a standard in-flight order from the FAA, and at 8:21 its radio and transponder were turned off.

When a plane is over land, its transponder gives air traffic controllers on the ground detailed information on the flight's location and altitude. Without a functioning transponder, those on the ground can use primary radar to see where the plane is, but not its altitude or other information.

Transponders are also used when a distress code is broadcast, known as a "squawk." Pilots unable to use radio can punch in a four-digit code and issue an automated distress message, but no such message was sent from flight 11. None of the pilots on 9/11 managed this relatively standard action. At the time, some newspapers speculated that there must have been a hijacker in the cockpit before each hijacking began. But experienced pilots questioned how it could possibly be that four separate hijackings occurred and not one of them involved an emergency code transmission that takes seconds to perform.

At 8:23, a radio announcement was heard. The voice is widely assumed to have been Mohamed Atta on flight 11, pressing the wrong button while trying to communicate with the passengers. "We have some planes. Just stay quiet and you'll be OK. We are returning to the airport." Two similar announcements were heard as the minutes passed.

At 8:24, the plane went radically off its course, turning one hundred degrees to the south, toward New York. Boston flight controllers never lost sight of the plane. What they heard was garbled and intermittent radio transmissions from the cockpit. Controllers suspected the captain, John Ogonowski, was surreptitiously pressing the talk button on the radio. The voices that could be heard spoke with heavy accents or in Arabic. More than one FAA controller said they heard the words "we have more planes."

Flight attendants Betty Ong and Amy Sweeney used onboard phones to contact those on the ground. Sweeney called Boston's Logan Airport and quickly gave controllers information on the seat numbers of the hijackers. American Airlines officials would have known within minutes that these seat numbers corresponded with a series of Middle Eastern sounding names, and assumed immediately that a hijacking was taking place.

In fact, the forty phone calls received from the four flights on 9/11 are the only direct evidence we have of what happened on the hijacked planes, since no information was broadcast by the pilots.

Ong and Sweeney reported that fellow flight attendants had been stabbed, and that a passenger, Daniel Lewin, had been killed. Lewin, an American-Israeli, was an ex-officer in Israel's Sayeret Matkal special forces unit, which specializes in anti-hijacking actions and is highly trained in combat.

The majority of the eleven men described by the press as the "muscle" hijackers (those charged with overpowering the crew and passengers) were by no means physically imposing—being between 5'5" and 5'7" in height, and slight in build. It is unclear how the small Arabic terrorists over-powered Lewin, unless a gun was involved, as was reported in an FAA memo written on the evening of 9/11.

Flight 11 tracked south uninterrupted for another twenty-three minutes, and hit the north tower of the World Trade Center complex at 8:46 a.m. Seismic records pinpointed the impact at 8:46 and 26 seconds. The plane had roughly ten thousand gallons of fuel on board, and was travelling around 470 mph. Thirty-two minutes had elapsed between the hijacking and the building impact.

Most of the damage was between the ninety-third and ninety-eighth floors of the 110-story building. Horrifically, no one above the crash impact survived. Approximately 1,360 people were killed. Everyone on the ninety-second floor was killed; everyone on the ninety-first floor survived. Below the impact line, approximately seventy-two people died, with four thousand escaping to survival. At least two hundred people plunged to their death to escape the fires. Cantor Fitzgerald, a financial services firm with headquarters on the 101st to 105th floors of the tower, lost 658 employees.

Although 2001 seems so recent, technologically it was another age. Smart-phones like the iPhone were still six years away. Today we would expect an almost unlimited number of smartphone pictures and videos, but on the morning of 9/11 the first impact was recorded by just one camera, held by French film-maker Jules Naudet. Jules and his brother Gedeon were filming a documentary about New York City firefighters, heard the plane flying low and heading south across Manhattan, and captured the last second before the plane crashed into the north tower.

Accordingly, we have very little photographic evidence of any aspect of the above story, except to know that a large plane hit the building at 8:46 a.m. Oddly, there was some kind of bright flash moments before the plane hit the building, but with only one distant recording of the impact, this can't be further examined.

CNN began their coverage within three minutes of the first impact. Rapidly, the entire world turned on their televisions.

United Airlines Flight 175

United Airlines 175 left Boston for Los Angeles with fifty-six people on board. With 168 seats, it was only a third full. The plane departed sixteen minutes late, at 8:14 a.m., which was just as the FAA was learning that flight 11 was possibly hijacked.

Although American 11 and United 175 departed from the same airport with the same destination, Los Angeles International Airport (LAX), 175 was routed indirectly, and further south than the normal "Great Circle" route, which is the fastest way of getting from Boston to LA. This meant that when 175 left its flight path, it was much closer to Manhattan than would have normally been the case, significantly reducing the time it took to reach the World Trade Center (twenty-one minutes, compared to flight 11's thirty-two minutes) and the amount of time American defenses had to intercept the plane. This also means that the two hijacked planes almost simultaneously crossed each other's paths at 8:36 a.m., right over Stewart Air National Guard Base.

Flight controllers asked flight 175's pilots to look for American flight 11, which was around ten miles to their South and had stopped responding. The pilots answered that they could see the plane at around thirty thousand feet, and were told to stay away from it. They were not told of a possible hijacking.

At 8:42 a.m., the pilots of flight 175 told ground control they had heard suspicious radio transmissions from flight 11 and suggested a possible hijacking might be taking place. Seconds later, 175 itself stopped responding.

As with flight 11, the official story is that five Middle Eastern hijackers took control of the plane, with pilot Marwan al-Shehhi in the cockpit. Two of the men had such poor English that they had trouble answering the standard security questions at the check-in, and the questions had to be repeated slowly, word by word, so they could respond before being allowed to board the plane.

At 8:47 a.m., the plane's radio and transponder frequencies were changed twice in a minute, and it radically changed course. At 8:50 the plane made a U-turn and headed northeast, toward New York. By this point the FAA, and presumably those along the chain of command, knew that a large plane had hit the tallest tower in Manhattan. Now, a second hijacking was clearly taking place.

Flight 175 nearly collided with a Delta plane as it headed North, missing by only one hundred meters. Calls were made from the plane to the ground, including by passenger Peter Hanson, who told his father that an airline hostess had been stabbed and that the plane was being hijacked. Brian Sweeney called his mother and told her that the passengers intended to do something about the hijacking. He said the Middle Eastern men appeared to have bombs and mace, and that he suspected the plane might be piloted into a building.

From 8:58 a.m., the plane descended rapidly, dropping more than twenty-four thousand feet in five minutes, an unheard of rate of descent. The plane came steeply out of the sky toward Manhattan.

Every network in the US was showing live pictures of the north tower in flames. The FAA and the North American Aerospace Defense Command (NORAD) both knew a second hijacking was taking place, and that the plane was heading towards Manhattan. According to normal hijack response times, fighter jets should have intercepted the plane. Instead, twenty-one minutes after being hijacked, the plane crashed into the south tower, six seconds before 9:03 a.m. Seventeen minutes had elapsed since the first strike on the north tower.

With the world's eyes already on the Manhattan skyline, the last few seconds of the flight were recorded from a wide number of angles by television cameras, and seen live by countless people. Unlike the first plane, which had crossed Manhattan in a straight line, the second plane made a steep, diving, banking corrective maneuver that brought it out of the skies and into the side of the building quickly and accurately. A technically stunning move.

Both World Trade Center (WTC) impacts were remarkably accurate, with Boeing 767–200 planes with a wingspan of 156 feet hitting buildings just 208 feet wide dead-on. Commercial aircraft have very poor maneuverability. They're big buses in the sky. At well over 400 mph, just a tiny error would have caused the planes to clip or miss the buildings entirely.

The plane struck between the seventy-eighth and eighty-fourth floor of the 110-story building. It is estimated that one hundred people in the building were killed instantly, with another five hundred dying in the south tower. Eighteen people made it to safety from above the crash zone.

Now no one was in any doubt. The largest terrorist attack in history was taking place.

The Pod

There was much confusion on the day as to the nature of the second plane itself. Some witnesses, unsighted by the building, said they had seen no plane at all. Some said they saw no markings on it, or no windows, or that it was "definitely not a commercial plane." Others said it looked "like a military plane." One Fox reporter said he saw a blue logo on the front of the plane, but no windows on the sides. Despite all the camera angles, the plane's steep descent made it nearly impossible to make out markings. The plane was the right size, and appeared a similar color, but none of the video footage definitively identified the plane as a United Airlines aircraft.

Several shots were taken from directly underneath the plane's path, in the seconds before it struck the World Trade Center, and it's here that we find cause for concern, because there appeared to be a strange attachment on the underside of the plane.

Although the bottom of a 767's fuselage has fairings that contain the landing gear, this "pod" appeared much more pronounced. The images are quite distinct. Spanish newspaper *La Vanguardia* published a study in 2002 showing that the pod seen on the belly of plane was a 3D object, not a shadow, as had been claimed.

This unexpected addition to the fuselage could be a number of things. The pictures might indicate that this was extra equipment added to United 175, but it seems very unlikely that pilots and ground staff would not have noticed something so large attached to the plane's underbelly before takeoff. Another possibility that has to be considered is that this was not United 175.

Global Hawk

While there is footage of both crashes, the only evidence we have to confirm that the two planes that hit the World Trade Center towers were indeed the flights hijacked out of Boston are the in-flight calls made by flight attendants and passengers, limited radar information, and the supposedly mistaken broadcast by Mohamed Atta, saying that he had "some planes."

Some of the in-flight phone calls were long and detailed. Most were brief and only lasted a couple of sentences. Flight attendant Betty Ong's call was said to have lasted twenty-three minutes, but only four minutes were recorded. Hers is the only call whose audio has been publicly released.

We also have no way of knowing who was in control of the planes. No one identified themselves as the new pilots, and apart from Atta's "mistaken" announcement, we don't know who was in the cockpit. The established narrative supposes that the Middle Eastern hijackers did a superb job of flying these large planes under exceptional pressure directly to their targets, hitting them pretty close to dead center. But in truth we have very little concrete information to confirm that the planes that hit the buildings were indeed the flights that we were told, and no evidence at all as to who was controlling the planes.

As will be shown in this chapter, the collapse of the twin towers was caused by controlled demolition, so it's impossible to imagine that those responsible would have left the matter of the aircraft strikes on the buildings (without which there would have been no cause for building collapses) to a ragtag bunch of amateur pilots under the most exceptional pressure imaginable. Had the planes crashed before making it to Manhattan, or missed their targets, the entire scheme would have failed, the explosives in the buildings been found, and the greatest treason in modern history exposed. The planes had to hit the buildings.

So the question of who controlled the planes is one worth considering. Was there technology available that allowed the precise remote control of such large vessels, because remote-controlled planes, as fanciful as that may sound, would have allowed an outside agency to ensure that nothing was left to chance.

As it transpires, there was.

Raytheon

The late 1990s saw huge advances in remote-controlled flight. Global Hawk was a prototype drone that was developed primarily for the Pentagon by the Defense Advance Research Projects Agency (DARPA) at the Air War College at Maxwell Air Force Base, Alabama. Maxwell was not just the home of Global Hawk. Mohamed Atta had been an enrolled student there.

Raytheon is one of America's biggest defense and weaponry manufacturers, and the largest producer of guided missiles in the world. The company made significant advances with its Global Hawk and flight termination technology in the months before 9/11, flying a pilotless drone across the Pacific in April 2001, and in August 2001 landing a 727 six times at a military base in New Mexico without any pilots or passengers on board. Ironically, the new technology was promoted as making hijackings impossible in the future, allowing those on the ground to take control of airborne hijacked planes.

Flight Termination Systems (FTS) allowed the remote control of multiple aircraft from the ground or air, and could also take over or disable transponder channels and radio communications. This might explain why none of the 9/11 pilots (eight of them, two per plane) issued the standard four-digit 7500 emergency squawk.

The story becomes even more intriguing as a number of Raytheon employees involved in their electronic warfare division were among the passengers on all three planes that hit their targets on 9/11. Overall, a surprisingly high number of passengers, especially on flight 77, had military connections. Raytheon itself had an office on the ninety-first floor of 2 WTC (the south tower), but no employees died in their offices that day. Raytheon was also one of the defense companies involved in suspicious share trading the day before 9/11 (an unusually large number of bets were placed that Raytheon's share price would go up, which it did, following the attacks). Raytheon also had access to the A3 fighter jet, the aircraft that many suspect was the object that hit the Pentagon.

Dov Zakheim

Which brings us to the curious figure of Dov Zakheim, a Jewish rabbi, dual Israeli citizen, and senior US intelligence career officer. Zakheim served as a foreign policy adviser to George W. Bush during the 2000 election, as part of a group led by Condoleezza Rice that called themselves "the Vulcans." He was also a signatory to the Project for the New American Century strategy documents (published by leading neocons before George W. Bush took office) that hoped for a new Pearl Harbor to effect a transformation of the US military and the Middle East. As such, Zakheim counted as one of the most hawkish senior political figures in the United States.

By May 4, 2001, Zakheim was comptroller of the Pentagon, the man in charge of the entire Pentagon budget. All was not well in the budget office; on September 10, 2001, Zakheim (alongside Donald Rumsfeld) announced that the Pentagon had "lost" $2.3 trillion in transactions. Even by US military standards, this was a staggering sum. However, the story was never pursued, overtaken by the events of the next day. Perhaps by chance, when the Pentagon building was struck on 9/11, the area hit was Wedge 1, the budget analyst offices where staff were investigating Zakheim's missing trillions.

Prior to taking up his role at the Pentagon, Zakheim had been CEO of a company called Systems Planning Corporation International (SPC), which developed a Flight Termination System (FTS) for the US military, providing the user the power to remotely control a variety of airborne vehicles. Using the FTS, multiple large planes could be remotely controlled, at a range of hundreds of miles, from the ground or the air.

Zakheim's SPC secured a contract to test the FTS on at least thirty-two Boeing 767 aircraft at MacDill Air Force Base in Florida. The FTS equipment was placed on the underside of a plane's fuselage, and was cylindrical in shape, as was the curious pod on the underside of the plane that hit the second World Trade Center tower.

A subsidiary of SPC (the Tridata Corporation) had also overseen the investigation of the 1993 World Trade Center bombings. This meant that they had complete access to blueprints, maps, and other information showing the structural details of the World Trade Center buildings.

To briefly summarize, Dov Zakheim had:

- Access to the structural details of the World Trade Center towers.
- Access to Boeing 767 aircraft through a deal he brokered with the Pentagon, where he subsequently took up one of the most powerful roles.
- Cutting edge remote control aviation technology which allowed the user to take control of multiple flights in real time.
- Membership of an extremist right-wing sect that called for the restructuring of world geopolitics, to be ushered in by a "new Pearl Harbor."

Perhaps you find it hard to accept that the planes that struck the World Trade Center towers might not have been those we were told they were. Inside the twin towers that day, there was plenty more to raise suspicion.

Before Collapse

Fifty thousand people worked in the twin towers of the World Trade Center. If the attacks had come an hour later, the death toll might have been many multiples of the 2,606 that died there. As it was, the first strike at 8:46 a.m. occurred just as many people were arriving for work. Even then, there were around six thousand people in each of the two towers when the first plane hit.

Curiously the overall death toll on 9/11 was remarkably light, given the terrible events that took place. Consider:

- The first impact at the WTC took place before 9:00 a.m., at which time many more people would have been at their desks.
- At the Pentagon, the section that was struck was the only reinforced area of the building, and sparsely populated due to renovations taking place in that particular section. Striking the side of the building also caused a fraction of the number that a plummet into the roof from above would have achieved.

- All four of the planes involved were unusually empty, most being around 30 percent capacity.

Although the death toll was utterly devastating, at every turn it could be argued that a much higher body count could have been achieved had the attackers been smarter, luckier, or more timely. Other targets, such as the Three Mile Island nuclear reactor nearby could have produced tens or hundreds of thousands of deaths if impacted by a plane.

The north tower (1 WTC) was hit first and hardest, as the plane struck the building dead center. It collapsed 102 minutes later. 2 WTC was struck second, and off center. Incongruously, it collapsed first, just fifty-six minutes later.

Workers in the south tower heard an announcement on the building's PA, instructing them to consider an orderly evacuation, just one minute before the building was struck. Prior to that, public announcements had said that the building was secure, and that people should return to their offices. Despite this false assurance, around two-thirds of those in the south tower began evacuating in the seventeen minutes between the plane strikes, saving thousands of lives.

Both towers wobbled considerably for up to two minutes after being struck so hard from the side, but after that the buildings were, from a structural perspective, sound.

That was not the case found by those who came to help.

William Rodriguez

In the period between the plane impacts and the building collapses, a whole swathe of testimony points toward explosions taking place inside the buildings, in the lobby, around the elevators, in the basement, and on floors much lower than those damaged.

Janitor William Rodriguez, who had worked at the World Trade Center for twenty years, reported that a large explosion rocked the service levels below the ground floor (the building had six sub-levels) just prior to the impact of the first plane.

After hearing two loud explosions in quick succession, one below him and one far above, Rodriguez ran down to one of the sub-levels, and saw a huge steel door ripped from its hinges and crumpled up like a piece of tin. His co-worker had been badly burned, and had skin ripped from his arms. Four witnesses reported explosions in the basement before the impact of the first plane, including Rodriguez and Evalle Sweezer. Rodriguez's colleague Mike Pecoraro was in the north tower's sixth underground basement level when he heard an explosion. Making his way to C-level, which was still well underground, he found a machine shop and garage entirely destroyed.

The official explanation given to William Rodriguez for the explosions in the sub-levels was that gas tanks in the kitchens had exploded due to the impact of the plane far above. But the kitchens were all electric. There was no gas. And Rodriguez said the explosions took place before the plane hit the building, some ninety stories above where he was working.

Rodriguez's testimony matches with an audio record made by Ginny Carr, a businesswoman who was recording a meeting being held at One Liberty Plaza, a block away from the World Trade Center. A loud boom is heard, and remarked upon by a colleague, but seven seconds later a much louder crash rings through the room. At that point the colleague says, "Sounds like something crashed."

William Rodriguez held a full set of building access keys, and bravely made his way to the thirty-ninth floor, helping dozens of people escape, before being turned around. He was the last person alive to exit the north tower, and later personally decorated for his bravery by President Bush.

However, when Rodriguez was called to testify to the 9/11 Commission, they insisted his particular testimony was heard behind closed doors. His name doesn't even appear in the final report, nor does any of the broad and widely reported evidence of explosions in both towers before and after the plane impacts.

The Lobby

Emergency workers arriving at the World Trade Center were puzzled by what they saw. The lobby of the north tower was devastated. Footage shot within the building shows white soot covering everything, huge marble panels ripped from the walls, and all the windows blown outwards, destruction that is hard to reconcile with an impact so many stories above.

Firemen on site one to two minutes after the first plane hit described doors being blown out on the freight elevators (which were in the middle of the building), but the other ones being OK. Each tower had ninety-nine elevators, and a three-tier system, with only three elevator shafts going to the top, so when the elevators exploded at ground level, it wasn't the kerosene from the planes leaking downwards, as the elevator shafts were hermetically sealed.

John Schroeder, a firefighter with Engine Company 10 was on site in the north tower within ten minutes of the first plane impact. He said that it looked like a bomb had gone off in the lobby. Nearly every member of Engine Company 7 described the lobby as looking like a bomb had exploded.

Media reports on 9/11 said the FBI and police were investigating the possibility that a subway train or a van parked in the basement had exploded at the same time as the plane impact.

There can be no doubt at all that there were huge explosions in and around the lobby, given the number of witnesses. However, virtually all the firefighters who escaped and were interviewed on 9/11 reported additional explosions throughout the buildings, long after the initial impacts.

Eyewitnesses

While the 9/11 narrative was established and enshrined as unimpeachable truth in the days and weeks that followed, what could not be controlled was the media reporting on the day, and it often painted a very different picture to the one we are now told to accept.

Nearly everyone in the towers, including reporters, firefighters and the public, said that there had been secondary explosions (a phrase used again and again) caused, they thought, by bombs placed inside the buildings. But by the evening of September 11, the official line had been established and was closely followed by the media. There were no explosions, and the buildings had fallen due to fires.

Those on the ground and in the line of fire told a different story:

- Louie Cacchioli, a firefighter with Engine Company 47, was in the first group to enter the north tower after it was struck. He found the lobby of the north tower completely destroyed. On reaching the twenty-fourth floor, Cacchioli said he found dust and smoke everywhere, which he found confusing since the plane impact was so far above him. Then he said that he "heard this huge explosion that sounded like a bomb," then "another huge explosion . . . this one hits about two minutes later." Then another. Cacchioli thought there were bombs set throughout the building, and that perhaps someone had planted them, like in the 1993 attack.
- Teresa Veliz was a manager working for a software firm on the forty-seventh floor of the north tower. She said, "The explosions were going off everywhere. I was convinced that there were bombs planted all over the place and someone was sitting at a control panel pushing detonator buttons."
- Fox 5 News caught a large white cloud of smoke billowing from the base of the south tower. On air, the reporter said, "There is an explosion at the base of the building . . . white smoke from the

bottom . . . something has happened at the base of the building . . . then another explosion."

- NBC aired a report in which a journalist discussed a conversation he had had with Albert Terry of the Fire Department of New York (FDNY). "[Terry] said there was another explosion that took place in one of the towers here . . . he thinks that there were actually devices that were planted in the building."
- Fireman Paul Isaac Jr. said, "Many other firemen know there were bombs in the buildings . . . but they are afraid for their jobs to admit it because the higher-ups forbid discussion of this fact."

Over 118 New York City firefighters and many others spoke of explosions inside the buildings, including in the lobbies, well before the point of collapse. Interview after interview broadcast on 9/11 (and not since) featured witnesses reporting damage where there should not have been any, and explosions continuing to ring through the lower part of the buildings as they tried to escape.

The twenty-second floor was the control and security center for the building. It was reported to have been totally destroyed, while the twenty-first and twenty-third floors were undamaged. Others spoke of explosions throwing them backward as they made their way through the eighth floor.

Nearly all of the FDNY firefighters' official testimony was retained by the City of New York, until the New York Times won a Freedom of Information lawsuit that forced the release of the records on August 8, 2005.

Looking at the number of television interviews taken on 9/11 in which eyewitnesses report explosions rocking the lower sections of the buildings, it's extraordinary how so very many of them flat out contradict what is now the official established narrative. It's an amazing example of how a broad raft of testimony, broadcast on the day of a major event, can be ignored, and a subsequent story can be propagated and accepted by the public, despite these obvious inconsistencies.

What does match these reports of explosions is the idea of controlled demolition, with explosives cutting the central columns of the buildings and in the basements, preparing them to be brought down.

Reaching the Fires

The official story is, essentially, that the damage caused by the plane impacts and subsequent fires weakened each building's fundamental structure enough to initiate collapse, and that once collapse commenced, the complete destruction of the buildings was inevitable.

This is utter nonsense.

Despite the spectacular fireballs that erupted when the planes impacted the buildings, the jet fuel burned up entirely in a few minutes. What was left to burn was office furnishings (carpet, desks, chairs, paper, etc.). Offices do not provide a huge amount of fuel for a fire, and most materials would have been consumed in a short space of time.

We think of firefighters as brave and rugged individuals, plunging into burning infernos to save souls. They are all that and more, but what they are not is suicidal. Firefighters are trained to take calculated risks, and specifically told not to enter buildings that will imminently collapse. Their role is to be brave, wise, and to stay alive. So it's clear the FDNY did not think the buildings would collapse. As evidenced later in the day when Building 7 of the World Trade Center collapsed, if the chiefs had seen any possibility of complete structural failure, they would have ordered a full evacuation. As it was, the doomed heroes poured into the buildings to put out the fires and rescue the people.

Firefighters are by far the most admired public servants in New York City and when one dies on the job, the grief is long-lasting. The police are known as The Finest, firefighters as The Bravest. On 9/11, 343 lost their lives, more than the total in the previous one hundred years.

Forty-five-year-old Battalion Chief Orio Palmer led a team of firefighters into the south tower and climbed thirty-seven flights of stairs in order to reach the seventy-eighth floor (the crash site) with his colleague Fire Marshal Ronald Bucca. Palmer calmly reported on his radio two isolated pockets of fire, no overwhelming heat, and that he thought they should be able to knock it down with two hose lines. Chief Palmer said he required only two engine companies to fight the fires. It seemed there was a good chance that a full inferno could be avoided, and that the fires could be extinguished.

But then events began to defy expectation. The building collapsed to the ground.

Fire and Energy

To understand the nature of fire and energy, especially in relation to weakening steel, we require a quick physics lesson. A diffuse flame, such as you find in a domestic fireplace, is materials burning in air. Diffuse flames generate the lowest heat intensities of the three types of fire (diffuse, pre-mixed, and jet). A wood fire normally burns at a temperature in the region of 930–1,112°F; however, tests have shown that fires in office buildings usually don't exceed 680°F. Diffuse kerosene (jet fuel) fires might briefly achieve 1,832°, but burn out very quickly and the fire temperature drops, as was witnessed after the plane strikes.

The fires at the World Trade Center were obviously diffuse. They were also oxygen poor, as we can see from the thick black smoke that poured from the buildings. Television pictures showed little or no flames pouring from the windows. Some people trapped above the fires in the south tower managed to pass through the burning area impacted by the plane and make it safely out of the building. Some unfortunate souls stood in the broken windows, waving in the hope of getting help. Yet the fires in the buildings were said to have been strong enough to melt structural steel. These two things simply don't go together.

Not only did the fires lack the requisite heat, they were not large, when compared to recent examples we have of extensive fires burning through many floors of high-rise buildings for long periods. For example:

- On October 17, 2004, a massive fire at the Parque Central Complex, a fifty-story tower (and the country's tallest building) in Caracas, Venezuela, burned for seventeen hours and engulfed the top twenty floors. It stands to this day.
- On February 23, 1991, the thirty-eight-story One Meridian Plaza in Philadelphia burned for eighteen hours through eight floors. A FEMA report into the fire said that some beams sagged and twisted from the intense heat, but that the columns had supported the loads above without obvious damage.
- On February 12, 2005, in Madrid, Spain, the Windsor Hotel, a thirty-two-story skyscraper, burned for twenty hours throughout the entire building. It was described as an inferno. It did not collapse.
- On February 9, 2009, the Beijing Television Cultural Center, a thirty-four-story building which was filled with fireworks for export, caught on fire and burned intensely, creating a genuine towering inferno. Again, it did not collapse.

In these examples the structural steel supporting the buildings was exposed to large, active fires for very long periods, and showed no sign of coming close to collapse. Plenty of tall buildings catch fire, there are on average over one hundred fire emergencies per year in buildings thirteen stories or more. You will search in vain for a steel-framed building that collapsed due to fire. It just doesn't happen.

None of these other building fires involved being hit by planes, you might cry. True, of course. But the twin towers can demonstrably be shown to have survived the plane impacts. After the fireball and some wobbling, the buildings were entirely stable.

The north and south towers of the World Trade Center were unusually robust. An article in *Scientific American* magazine said that nowadays, "they just don't build them as tough." The towers' architect Minoru Yamasaki had known what a symbol and a target these buildings would be. He built the towers to withstand the force of multiple 707 impacts. Frank DeMartini, the construction manager, and the buildings structural engineers all agreed that the impact of fully loaded 707s could easily be sustained. 707s were the largest commercial planes at the time of the World Trade Center construction. 767s are larger, but not by very much.

All tall buildings are over-engineered, meaning they are designed to withstand multiples of the expected normal loads, precisely to avoid any danger of collapse. Steel used in high-rise buildings must be able to hold five times its normal load. Think of the immense lateral pressure that hurricane-force winds place on tall buildings. These have to be resisted.

Each of the towers was 1,300 feet tall. When they were built they were the tallest buildings in the world. To support them, there were forty-seven steel columns in the central core of the building, and 240 around the perimeter (with each column being far thicker at the bottom than at the top, like a tree-trunk).

The floor framing (support) system was complex, and designed to be highly redundant. Redundancy is a basic design tenet of high-rise building construction, and describes a design whereby any damage to one section passes the load evenly to other sections. A simple explanation is as follows: imagine taking a screen door and turning it ninety degrees, so it's flat like a tray. Put a plate on top, then cut five or six of the screen strands. The structure has been damaged, but doesn't collapse and the plate doesn't fall—the weight transfers evenly to the undamaged sections of the screen.

Many respected engineers have said that despite the dramatic fireball, the impact of the planes would have been relatively insignificant because the columns lost on impact would not have been numerous when compared to the overall number, and the load would have shifted to the remaining columns in this highly redundant structure. On 9/11, with little or no wind, the building was probably not encountering even one-third of its base stress capability.

Steel loses half its strength at 1,202° (and melts at 2,800°), but it takes a long time for thick structural steel to reach this sort of temperature. With the building's entire structural strength halved by the steel reaching 1,202° (which simply could not have taken place in the short time during which the buildings were on fire), the over-engineered nature of each tower meant that they still would have had 2–3 times the strength required to support the structure above the damaged area. A much higher temperature and greater reduction in steel strength was required in order for the buildings to collapse.

Steel also conducts heat very well, so not only was a hot fire required, it needed to be applied for a long time in order to raise large enough sections of the structural steel to the temperatures required for collapse. The external façade of the building was made from aluminum, which melts at 1,220°, less than half that of steel. If the fires in the buildings were hot enough to weaken structural steel to the point of collapse, why did we see no evidence of melting aluminum nearby?

Note also the difference between temperature and energy. A flaming match has a high temperature, but low energy. Only a large fire that burned for a long time with very high-heat would have been capable of melting the structural steel in the buildings. And the steel could not have become hotter than the temperature of the fire applied to it.

One simple example of steel at work is the gas cooker in your kitchen. Turn on the heat, and a blue flame of forced gas is fed directly under the steel structure on which you place a pot to cook. This flame is, of course, much hotter than an office fire (natural gas burns at over 3,452°), and it's applied specifically and directly onto the steel, which is just a half inch away. Leave the gas running for an hour. A relatively large amount of heat has been applied directly to a small piece of steel for a long time. But the steel doesn't melt, lose its strength, or collapse. It's not even weakened.

Damaged by a plane's impact or not, how could very thick structural steel, capable of holding up a huge building, lose so much of its strength due to fires that (after the first minute or so) were fed only by office equipment and furnishings?

The very high temperatures required to melt steel can only be produced by special equipment such as a welding torch or cutting charges. Such temperatures absolutely cannot be reached in an office fire. Not even close. If the fires were hot enough to melt steel, firefighter Orio Palmer couldn't have got anywhere near them.

So we're left with a situation where we are told that the intense heat of the fires melted the structural steel, but all evidence suggests that there is no way that could have happened. We're missing nearly a thousand degrees.

What happened next was entirely unexpected and unprecedented. I can find no record of any individual on television or radio that even speculated that the buildings might collapse, even partially, before the first one did. Yet within twenty-nine minutes, both towers collapsed at enormous pace and disintegrated entirely.

Even Robert Shea, who ran the insurance side of FEMA, said, "No one believed that those towers would fall."

Rudy Giuliani

This was not the case with New York Mayor Rudolph "Rudy" Giuliani, who told ABC's Peter Jennings on the morning of 9/11 that he had been in a temporary command and control center at 75 Barclay Street when he was warned that the twin towers were going to collapse, and that the south tower had indeed collapsed before he and his staff could evacuate, leaving them trapped for ten to fifteen minutes.

What is not clear is who told Giuliani of this impending collapse, since firefighters (trained to look for signs of structural failure) were still pouring into the buildings and no one else on site appears to have suggested it could happen. It's also unclear if Giuliani attempted to pass this warning to those most at risk.

When Giuliani testified to the 9/11 Commission in May 2004, his testimony was slightly different, and mentioned no prior warning of the towers imminent collapse.

Memories can change over time, especially of traumatic events, but time also affords people the opportunity, consciously or unconsciously, to shape stories to better fit the way they want things to be remembered. Giuliani's ABC interview on 9/11 is much more likely to have been the unadulterated truth than his testimony two and a half years later, so it is vitally important to find out who told Rudolph Giuliani that the towers were going to collapse.

Senior staff at the FDNY were also apparently in receipt of warnings that the buildings were not stable just minutes before the first collapse; these reports came from the Office of Emergency Management (OEM), which was under Giuliani's control. This leaves us in a quandary. If the warnings came from the OEM, which was under Giuliani's control, and Giuliani himself said he received warnings that the buildings were unstable, who *was* behind this information, since virtually no one else appears to have anticipated collapse as a possibility?

The 9/11 Commission failed to ask these questions.

How The Towers Fell

Most controlled demolition techniques involve the removal of the central core of the building before the floors are blown out one by one. The north tower had a transmission antenna on its roof which was clearly seen to dip and fall, moments before the collapse of the top section (which started much lower than the roof level). This was a phenomenon also seen in the collapse of Building 7, and strongly suggests that the collapse started with the destruction of the central core of the buildings. Had the most likely explanation for the building collapses (that of controlled demolition) been accepted, the antenna dip would have been seen as a classic characteristic of the beginning of a demolition process.

The collapses of both twin towers were virtually identical, despite the plane impacts being at different heights and one being off-center. The collapse characteristics are as follows:

- The collapses started very suddenly. No portion of the buildings appeared to show any sign of failure before collapse commenced.
- Once commenced, the entire structure was destroyed in seconds.
- The buildings collapsed downward, through themselves (they did not topple over).
- Huge dust and debris clouds mushroomed outward during the collapse, indicating forces working laterally as well as vertically.
- Squibs (lateral explosions of air, blowing out windows) were observed during the collapses, much below the area that was disintegrating. These were officially explained as compressed air caused by the collapsing building above, but the structure above was in the process of being destroyed—it had very little capability to contain and compress air. What is much more likely is what was in plain sight: squibs caused by controlled demolition charges ripping through the building cores.
- Enormous clouds of pyroclastic dust were caused, and billowed through the streets.
- The intact portions of the buildings appeared to offer little or no resistance to the falling debris.

Lack of Resistance

Both buildings collapsed at nearly free-fall speed. The lack of resistance from the lower levels of the buildings is possibly the most troubling aspect of their destruction, since there is nothing within the official 9/11 narrative that can explain why such incredibly strong, sturdy building structures failed to stop or even slow the falling sections. This defies the Law of Conservation of Momentum, one of the most fundamental laws of physics.

It is estimated that the tops of the buildings reached the ground in around sixteen seconds, when free fall would have taken around ten seconds. So the entire undamaged sections of these huge structures only slowed the complete destruction of the buildings by six seconds, not just failing to stop the collapses, but not even slowing them down.

Even if each floor had produced only a small amount of resistance (though this makes no sense and is utterly opposed to the rules of engineering and physics)—say each floor slowed the fall by just half of one second—then each building collapse would have taken more than forty seconds.

Suspending disbelief, and assuming that somehow the steel structure was sufficiently weakened to initiate a collapse, the first thing to be expected would have been a partial failure. Whichever part of the building was the most weakened would have crumpled, meaning the top would have buckled, kinked, or fallen in one direction. None of these were observed. The fall was straight down, demolishing all that stood below. One hundred thousand tons of structural steel in each building. Virtually no resistance whatsoever.

Any falling object tries to pass through the path of least resistance, but on 9/11 the buildings fell right through the path of highest resistance—the undamaged structure below.

For the buildings to fall as they did (suddenly, and straight down), failure of the structural steel causing the collapses to commence would have needed to be entirely symmetrical, with hundreds of joints failing simultaneously on all 287 exterior and interior columns. This is clearly an absurd suggestion.

Finally, as the buildings fell, they appeared to be pulverized. What was producing the energy to cause these falling steel and concrete structures to dissolve into dust in midair?

At first glance, the argument that planes hitting the towers caused fires and eventual collapse seems a reasonable proposition, but it only takes a small amount of reason and deduction to understand that:

- The planes clearly did not mortally wound the support structure of the buildings. They withstood the impact and remained stable.
- While the fireballs were shocking, the subsequent fires appear to have been relatively small, relatively brief, and burned at low temperatures.
- To believe that structural steel was melted, we are missing nearly a thousand degrees.

- Theoretically, once the collapses began they required a statistically impossible event to occur: all supports failing at the same time, to make the buildings commence collapsing straight down. In two separate buildings.
- The undamaged structure below offered virtually no resistance to the objects falling from above, entirely contrary to the most basic laws of physics and engineering.
- Something other than gravity provided the energy to throw huge pieces of steel great distances outwards, and to dissolve concrete into dust in midair.

Faced with this, it is impossible not to conclude that there were other forces at work that initiated and sustained the swift collapse of these huge buildings.

Evidence of Explosive Forces

The government's explanation for the building collapses was really just armchair physics, molding theories to a pre-set idea (that the towers fell due to fires), and working backwards to try and make things fit. It was the opposite of science, and not an investigative method worthy of the name.

Even using vast leaps of logic and imaginative stretches of reality, the official explanation is demonstrably nonsense. It is so transparently false that it is remarkable how the story was presented, promoted, and swallowed, when virtually none of it holds water.

Another theory for the building collapses, however unlikely at first glance, provides a much more viable match to the events on the day.

While defenders of the official story have to contort logic and scientific laws to render fire-induced collapse at free-fall speed possible, controlled demolition basks in the simplicity that comes when all the evidence matches the theory. The collapse of the two twin tower buildings matches none of the official explanations and all of the alternate theory, in which pre-placed explosives brought down the towers.

Eyewitnesses also reported precisely what would have been expected during a controlled demolition:

- Fireman Dennis Tardio said, "Floor by floor it started popping out . . . it was [as] if they had detonators and they planned to take out a building . . . *boom, boom, boom.*"

- Ross Milanytch saw the collapse of one tower from the twenty-second floor of a nearby building and said he saw small explosions on each floor as the building came down.
- Paramedic Daniel Rivera said, "Do you ever see professional demolitions where they set the charges on certain floors and then you hear *pop, pop, pop, pop, pop*? I thought it was that."
- An eyewitness told the American Free Press he saw a number of bright lights emitting from each floor between the tenth and fifteenth floors, and heard crackling noises just before the collapse began.
- Assistant Fire Commissioner Stephen Gregory said he saw "low level flashes" and said a colleague had reported the same thing. Both of them told each other, as they wanted to be sure their eyes weren't deceiving them. The flashes they saw were at the lower levels of the building.

Many near the buildings also reported loud explosions in a rapid sequence—*boom, boom, boom*—as the buildings began to fall. Firemen and others nearby reported flashes of light and explosions in upper floors of the north tower, and in lower floors of the south tower, far below the plane impact location, just before collapse.

Controlled demolition is, as the name suggests, a means of destruction that aims to control the collapse of a building (and normally to minimize damage to nearby property). Pre-placed cutting charges or explosives remove all building columns and supports simultaneously, allowing a building to fall quickly and neatly into its own footprint (the shape of the building at ground level).

We are all familiar with the sight of a building being demolished. Demolitions make for good TV and nice spots to end the nightly news. Most demolitions of tall, thin buildings take place with the bottom of the building being taken out and a swift collapse in a straight line downwards. However, there are other methods, used for different structure types (for example, football stadiums, which are wide, not tall), or for when there are different demands on the ground. One such method is called the Verinage Technique, which commences collapse higher up on a tall tower, and allows the top portion of the building to destroy the lower section, without the need for explosives. Look it up on YouTube. The videos all look like the way the twin towers fell.

Although the building collapses started at or near the levels where the planes had impacted, what happened in the subsequent seconds had several bizarre traits that are impossible to square with the idea of fire-induced collapse.

Firstly, while the top sections of the buildings (as they began to collapse) fell straight down, the building structure at and below the plane impacts did not just fall downward, it crumbled to dust in midair.

Although there were hundreds of cameras trained on the buildings, some recorded images from angles most people are less familiar with. In particular, footage taken close to the towers captured both the sound of buildings being obliterated and the impression that the buildings were exploding, or disintegrating, in a rapidly and regularly timed progression, some distance below the area where the collapse was taking place. The best view of this is during a movie produced by the awkwardly named Architects and Engineers for 9/11 Truth. Their movie, available free on the internet, features footage (around the fifty-two minute mark) that I defy anyone to watch without concluding that the buildings were being demolished during the collapse.

As the collapses progressed, the falling debris formed an umbrella shape, as concrete and steel flew outwards from the centers of the buildings. Huge plumes of dust and enormous steel beams were ejected horizontally with such force that nearby buildings were enveloped even before the collapses had finished. Many were badly damaged by large steel girders and building sections that had been ejected laterally. A steel section from one tower weighing three hundred tons embedded itself in the southeast corner of the American Express building, travelling 390 feet.

Gravity works toward the center of the Earth. Something produced the energy to cause these huge beams and dust clouds to move sideways. Especially with the steel, some of which was very substantial, it would have taken huge forces to eject matter laterally.

Pyroclastic clouds are typically seen when volcanoes erupt. These clouds (*pyroclast* is a Greek word meaning "broken into pieces") are caused by the vast amount of energy released during eruption, pulverizing rock and other matter to a fine powder. The clouds have a distinctive billowing shape, and often contain huge amounts of heat, something many of those trapped on the ground on 9/11 spoke of.

Similarly, cutting charges or explosives used in building demolition quickly produce very high levels of energy and heat, and cause the distinctively shaped clouds. What does not cause a pyroclastic cloud is a building collapse initiated by something other than explosives.

When the dust cleared, rescuers found very little intact from the one hundred thousand tons of structural concrete that had been in each building. It had almost all been pulverized to a dust so fine that footsteps on the ground made no sound.

A number of studies have tried to calculate the energy required to pulverize the building's concrete to a sixty-micron powder (many reports indicate the dust was much finer, around ten microns), and reported that over ten times more energy was required than would have been available simply through gravity. Video evidence also showed a great deal of fine dust being ejected very early in the collapse, when the forces at work were much smaller.

In tragic circumstances, such as when an earthquake has caused a concrete building to fall, we generally see the concrete having been broken into large pieces, and very little fine dust. A falling building has a great deal of energy, but there is no historical example of that energy's potential being so great as to convert concrete into dust. Even concrete slabs dropped from one hundred stories up would just break up on impact with the ground. They would not be reduced to dust.

On the ground, each piece of structural steel was found in short sections. Almost every piece had broken at the joints. Only about seven stories of the north tower were still in place, the girders splayed. The south tower was just a two-story heap of rubble. The last survivor was pulled from the wreckage on the morning of September 13. The building collapses killed many, but wounded few. From then on, all that was found was body parts. One firefighter said the parts were so small it was as if everyone had been pulverized. It was a striking feature of the collapse of two one hundred-story buildings that everything inside had been so devastatingly shredded. This may seem logical given the enormity of the event, but it is not something normally found in building collapses.

All of these observations seem impossible to reconcile with a structure falling simply through the effects of gravity. But controlled demolition is a perfect fit.

Mark Loizeaux

The controlled demolition of large buildings is a highly specialized field. There is little evidence that the US armed forces retain this skill. Normally when the army destroys a building it is in the heat of battle, with little thought to the structural consequences of firing bullets and missiles.

In fact, only a handful of civilian companies in the world are skilled enough to carry out controlled demolitions in city areas, given the necessity of minimizing damage to adjacent buildings.

Eleven days after the attacks, Mayor Giuliani accepted a preliminary cleanup plan from Controlled Demolition Inc., the same firm who (with undue haste) had demolished the still standing structure left after the Alfred P. Murrah Federal Building bombing in Oklahoma six years before.

Mark Loizeaux, president of Controlled Demolition Inc., appears to have been one of the only people who predicted the towers would fall. He told John Seabrook at the *New Yorker* that he knew the towers would fall "within a nanosecond" of the plane strikes.

Although cleanup plans for fallen buildings was within Controlled Demolition's scope, the main activity of the business is the safe destruction of tall buildings. In the three years prior to 9/11, the firm set world records for the demolition of large buildings and structures, including the largest single building ever brought down (at the time), in Detroit, Michigan. Had Controlled Demolition been tasked with the destruction of the three World Trade Center towers, it was one of the few businesses in the world with the technical skills to do so.

The company states, "Our DREXS systems segment steel components into pieces matching the lifting capacity of the available equipment," and that cut pieces of steel fit perfectly onto the trucks designated to remove them, as was the case at the World Trade Center. Loizeaux has also stated that the number of different cutting charges now available allow his business to control not just timing, but noise levels and other factors in bringing down buildings.

In 2004, Loizeaux, a man made rich by the attacks, confirmed the existence of molten steel in the rubble at the bottom of the elevator shafts, and said, "If I were to bring the towers down I would put explosives in the basement to get the weight of the building to help collapse the structure." Few men on earth were better placed to have known how to do it.

Thermite

It's important to distinguish here between conventional explosives (such as TNT) and cutting charges. Explosives like TNT make loud, noticeable bangs, and while this noise can be deadened somewhat, it rarely is, as controlled demolitions are always conducted at a known time and place, with people removed a safe distance from the explosions.

Thermite, an incendiary, is the most commonly used cutter in non-TNT demolitions. It is a mixture of iron oxide and aluminum powder, and when ignited reaches incredibly high temperatures, slicing through or even evaporating steel in seconds. Thermite is widely used by the military, as well as in fireworks and underwater welding.

There are other types of similar cutters available. Thermate (which uses thermite with sulfur) works even faster. It produces sulfidation of cut steel, something even FEMA's report said was present in the few recovered steel beams that were not quickly shipped off to China. FEMA called the presence of sulfur a mystery. No explanation was given.

The fastest known cutting charges are superthermites, using nano-aluminum particles to improve cutting to an explosive speed. Superthermites were developed by the US military, and in 2001 there was a very small number of producers of these charges in the world; none of them civilian.

Cutting charges make a large amount of noise, but are not comparable to TNT. Charges are used by controlled demolition companies to slice through multiple floor supports in rapid succession, so as to totally destroy the skeleton of a building and bring it down rapidly, in a straight line.

Although the cleanup around the World Trade Center commenced with indecent haste (within hours of sunset on 9/11), small samples of dust were collected and analyzed by scientists around the world. Many have found residue of thermite and nano-thermite in the dust. Three different dust samples were tested by three independent experts (the United States Geological Survey (USGS), the RJ Lee Group, and Dr. Steven E. Jones). All agreed thermite was present. There can be no logical explanation, except for the obvious and disturbing one. Thermite particles don't feature in building construction, nor does anything remotely like them.

Barium, a toxic metal associated with thermate, was also found in the dust. Due to its toxicity barium is rarely found in civilian settings. There is no reason for such a metal to be present in the WTC dust, unless it was a product of cutting charges.

Removing the Steel

If thermite was indeed used to bring down the buildings, an examination of the structural steel could easily show evidence of its presence through "twinning," a term metallurgists use when two disparate items burn next to each other at high temperatures.

Steel beams from the twin towers held primary evidence to further our understanding of how and why the buildings fell. Given that the two events were the largest building collapses in history, it was vital to understand how such unprecedented events took place, and the chemicals within the steel that held the buildings up could provide incontrovertible evidence as to what was behind their failure.

However, Rudy Giuliani used the excuse that his term as mayor was ending on December 31 to order the removal of the shattered steel as fast as possible, before any examination could take place, defying all norms relating to the investigation of a crime scene. Almost immediately, all 240,000 tons of steel from the three WTC buildings were quickly shipped to the ghoulishly named "Fresh Kills" scrapyard, just ten miles away, then exported on ships to China and Korea for recycling as quickly as they could be loaded. This was in clear violation of engineering and accident codes, and prevented nearly all analysis. It is a federal offense to remove evidence from a crime scene, but the removal of steel at ground zero—a phrase previously used to denote the location of a nuclear explosion—was overseen by federal agents.

There is seemingly no explanation for the haste with which this was done. It was certainly not because there might have been people alive under the wreckage, as the heavy lifting equipment used took no account of possible life beneath. No one died at Building 7, and the steel there was just as quickly removed. On December 25, 2001, the *New York Times* complained that the steel removal meant that "definitive answers" might "never be known" as to what had caused the structural failures.

Ground zero was sealed from the public eye almost as soon as the dust had settled, and Giuliani famously ordered that no photos were permitted. Despite this, several pictures were taken, and showed the massive steel beams that supported the building had been cut in a diagonal manner. Shaped charges cut structural steel at a chevron-shaped angle, ensuring the building falls just as is required. The cut pieces of steel seemed inexplicable if the building had simply collapsed, and entirely consistent with building demolition methods.

Charmingly, some of the small amount of steel that was retained was re-forged into commemorative medallions.

Molten Steel

In the final minutes before the south tower collapsed, an odd thing happened. Molten metal, yellow in color, was observed flowing out of several upper windows. Given the fires inside were burning up filing cabinets, desks, and paper, it's hard to imagine what produced the immense temperatures required to melt metal.

But the real mystery was found after the buildings collapsed.

Huge quantities of molten steel were found at the bottom of the wreckage of all three buildings, and there was an enormous amount of heat left in the smoldering ground.

Despite heavy rains on September 14 and constant water from firefighters that formed a lake on the surface, the underground fires didn't go out until December 13, three months after the attacks. They remain the longest structural fires in history.

Thermal camera images captured from above recorded astonishing temperatures under the ground. Firemen reported the soles of their boots melting seven days after the collapses.

One of the FDNY crews interviewed after 9/11 said, "You would see molten steel [under the wreckage] running down the channel rails, like you're in a foundry." Dr. Keith Eaton wrote in the *Structural Engineer* journal about metal that was still "red-hot, weeks after the event." Leslie Robertson, who worked for the company that designed the towers, said that twenty-one days after the attacks, "molten steel was still running."

Many steel beams pulled from the depths of the rubble had dripping molten steel at their ends. A photograph taken by worker Frank Silecchia shows a beam apparently close to a molten state being removed from the wreckage weeks after 9/11.

The official cleanup crew reported finding most of the hot-spots of molten steel at the bottom of the elevator shafts, down seven (basement levels). This is precisely where hot-spots would be expected if controlled demolition was the cause of the collapses, since the elevator shafts were centrally located next to the structural columns of the towers.

No plausible explanation has been given as to why relatively small office fires and building collapses could have created enough energy to cause this enormous heat, and there was no reason to expect such long-lasting underground fires and molten steel. Buildings that fall down, even huge ones on fire, simply don't have enough energy to melt large quantities of metal, or to keep that metal molten for weeks, especially without oxygen.

The three major official government reports by the National Institute of Standards and Technology (NIST), FEMA, and the 9/11 Commission found one simple way of dealing with the issue. They didn't mention the molten metal at all.

Demolition experts (such as Brent Blanchard, who writes extensively for the explosive demolition industry) have stated that molten metal has never been observed at the site of any building that has collapsed or suffered a major fire, unless thermite or a similar incendiary had been used as part of a controlled demolition.

However, one ready explanation for the extraordinary heat and the molten steel is the use of thermite as a cutting charge. A byproduct of the use of thermite is large quantities of molten iron. The other byproduct, aluminum oxide, provides its own oxygen, requiring no exposure to air to keep burning. The reaction can't be smothered or doused by water.

The molten steel in the wreckage of the three collapsed towers, seen and reported by dozens of people, represents undeniable evidence of the use of cutting charges to bring the buildings down. Nothing else can explain the huge energy and heat required to produce such large quantities of liquid metal, nor water's inability to douse the incredibly long-lasting fires.

How Explosives Could Have Been Planted

To contemplate pre-placed explosives in the buildings takes us to some dark places. These can be uncomfortable to examine.

The twin towers were some of the most secure civilian buildings in America, especially so after the 1993 bombing. They remain the largest buildings ever to have collapsed.

Demolition requires access to the central columns that support a building. These columns are normally next to the elevator shafts, which are mostly located centrally in tall buildings. It takes weeks or months to prepare for a successful controlled demolition, and this was the biggest in human history. If the buildings were brought down deliberately, preparations would have had to be carried out clandestinely, right under the noses of the people working there.

In order to believe that explosives had been placed throughout the buildings, we would need evidence of unusual happenings in the months leading up to 9/11, of work on or near the elevator shafts, of building evacuations (so as to leave the plotters undisturbed at certain points), and of some kind of involvement from insiders, since it is inconceivable that such work could take place without the connivance of those in charge.

All of these have been reported and documented.

Scott Forbes, who worked for Fiduciary Trust in the World Trade Center, wrote a letter that was subsequently published, in which he said, "In 2001 we occupied floors 90 and 94–97 of the south tower, and lost 87 employees plus many contractors [on 9/11]. On the weekend of [September 8–9, just 48 hours before the attacks] . . . there was a power down condition in [2 WTC], the south tower. This power down condition meant that there was no electrical supply for approximately 36 hours from floor 50 up . . . of course, without power there were no security cameras, no security locks on doors, [even while] many, many engineers [were] coming in and out of the tower." Forbes saw what he described as "guys with huge toolboxes and reels of cable" coming in and out of the building that weekend. The power down was corroborated by William Rodriguez, the building's janitor, as well as Gary Corbett, another Fiduciary employee.

Forbes worked all weekend managing the power down, and took September 11 off. When he saw the towers fall from his New Jersey home, he immediately thought of the events of the previous weekend.

Despite the testimony from tenants who were present at the time, no authority has yet acknowledged this power down, which Forbes called unprecedented. Forbes mailed his information to a number of bodies, including the 9/11 Commission, who completely ignored it.

Ben Fountain, an analyst with Firemen's Fund who worked in the south tower, also reported a number of unusual evacuations of the building in the weeks prior to the attacks.

The entire elevator system at the World Trade Center had been upgraded by the ACE Elevator Company from 1994 to 2000, giving workers ample access to the building's infrastructure, both day and night. In the months before 9/11, staff reported several elevators were constantly out of service. This is hardly unusual, but would be expected were final preparations being made for a building demolition.

Some WTC personnel reported heightened security, including twelve-hour shifts for security staff, in the two to three weeks prior to the attacks, which was lifted five days before 9/11. Bomb-sniffing dogs, trained to smell even the tiniest trace of explosives, were removed from the regular security roster in the three weeks prior to the attacks.

The act of drilling and installing explosives and cutting charges in the central columns of the building would have caused a lot of dust to float through the ventilation shafts of the building. Sure enough, tenants have testified that their offices and reception areas were often caked in dust while the elevator work was taking place.

Now, a dusty desk doesn't mean someone is putting explosives in your building, but it is what you would expect if that actually was the case.

What is most interesting is the involvement of Kroll Associates, a security consultancy firm who revamped security at the World Trade Center after the 1993 bombing. The company was closely linked to the CIA and Mossad, and known as the CIA of Wall Street because of the shady kind of people they employed. After the 1993 attack, Kroll was hired to design a new security system, and four contracting companies employed to implement and install it. All four contractors had significant ties to Saudi Arabia.

The firm that handled much of the security at the World Trade Center between 1996 and 9/11 was Stratesec (formerly Securacom). Stratesec installed the new security system in the buildings between 1996 and 2000, and also provided security for United and American Airlines (whose planes were hijacked on 9/11), as well as Dulles Airport, where flight 77 took off.

Marvin Bush, the president's brother, was a director of Stratesec from 1993 to 2000, and Wirt Dexter Walker III, the president's distant cousin, was CEO from 1999 to January 2002, and served as chairman of the board.

Just to recap, a company with two key principles who were related to the president upgraded the fireproofing and security system at the buildings attacked on 9/11, provided security at airports used on 9/11, and for the airlines hijacked on 9/11.

To be sure, none of this represents proof that Stratesec or Kroll were behind the placing of explosives through the World Trade Center, but if you made a list of the various on-site requirements in order to do such a thing, every box here is ticked. And if you wish to look into how murky this nexus of companies really is, read the following.

Stratesec also provided security for Los Alamos National Laboratory, one of the only known places on earth acknowledged to have the technology to produce nano-thermite. Los Alamos was also a world leader in voice morphing technology, which some have suggested was used to fake calls from the hijacked planes

While at Stratesec, Wirt Walker hired several staff from the Carlyle Group, which had bin Laden family members as investors and the President's father on the board. In addition, the Carlyle Group was having a meeting in Washington on 9/11, at which George H. W. Bush, James A. Baker, and Osama bin Laden's brother Shafig were attending.

It's also worth noting that immediately after the attacks, the share price of Stratesec nearly doubled, despite the worst security failures in history. From September 6–10, 2001, Wirt Walker bought fifty-six thousand Stratesec shares. The doubling of the share price just a week after 9/11 netted him a substantial profit. How on earth could the CEO of a company providing security at the World Trade Center buying shares in the most suspicious manner possible not be investigated for insider trading, at the very least?

Despite this security spider web, the power-downs, evacuations, and security changes prior to 9/11 were not mentioned in the 9/11 Commission report. Stratesec's name does not appear once.

Larry Silverstein

"Lucky" Larry Silverstein seemed to lead a charmed life. A successful real estate entrepreneur and dual American-Israeli citizen, Silverstein headed a consortium (including Frank Lowy of Westfield America) that took out a privately held 99-year lease on the previously Port Authority-owned World Trade Center complex for $3.2 billion on July 24, 2001, just seven weeks before 9/11. Silverstein Properties already owned World Trade Center Building 7.

Silverstein immediately negotiated a new $3.5 billion insurance policy on the properties that specifically covered terrorism, doubling the previous coverage and ensuring a huge payout in the event that the buildings were destroyed. Silverstein Properties itself invested only $14 million in the lease deal.

It was a strange investment. The towers were perceived as white elephants, and were losing money for the Port Authority. The so-called "Masters of the Universe" (leaders of the huge banking and brokerage houses of New York) had long since left the World Trade Center complex for more well-appointed offices nearby in lower Manhattan. Though the devastation of 9/11 was profound, the major institutions ruling the financial sector were left mostly untouched.

The buildings were in a poor state of repair, with middle-tier tenants and significant structural issues, such as the huge amount of asbestos in the buildings that required addressing. The cost of fixing the asbestos issues alone was expected to run to over $1 billion.

When asked why he bought the World Trade Center buildings, Silverstein said, "I felt a compelling urge to own them."

Silverstein dined every morning, virtually without fail, at Windows on the World, the restaurant at the top of the north tower. Had he been there, he would have been killed. But on 9/11, "Lucky Larry" claimed to have had an appointment with his dermatologist. It has been rumored that one of his bodyguards said Silverstein in fact received a phone call hours before the attacks, warning him to stay away. The whole family was fortunate—Silverstein's daughter, who worked in Building 7, also decided not to attend work that day.

Silverstein was a very close friend of Israeli Prime Ministers Ariel Sharon and Benjamin Netanyahu, the latter of whom was in New York on 9/11 and in London for the 2005 underground attacks (and on 9/11 quickly said the attacks were of benefit to Israel). They were said to speak by phone every weekend. Silverstein was also extremely well connected with other senior members of the Jewish-American community, as was his partner in the WTC buyout, Frank Lowy.

With our knowledge of the massive Israeli spy ring (see Chapter 9) that at the very least was tailing the hijackers and Silverstein's close connection to the heads of Israeli government, it is by no means a leap of faith to suggest that it was not by chance that Silverstein was absent from Windows on the World on that fateful morning.

After the attacks, Silverstein tried to make two insurance claims against his $3.55 billion policy, claiming the strikes constituted two separate events, and as such he should be remedied with $7.1 billion. By all accounts, he was on the phone to his insurers within hours of the attacks. In 2007, Silverstein's insurers settled the claim and paid out $4.5 billion—the largest individual insurance payout in history. Larry Silverstein also made $500 million in profit from the collapse of Building 7.

Silverstein wasn't finished there. In 2015 he commenced action claiming the two airlines whose planes hit the WTC towers owed him billions more for negligence and monies his insurance firm had claimed from the airlines.

As we will see, Silverstein admitted his central role in allowing the collapse of 7 World Trade Center during a PBS documentary, but has remained entirely above suspicion, despite profiting handsomely from an insurance policy he tailored to match an event that took place just weeks later, from which he and his family members absented themselves.

CHAPTER TWO

PENTAGON

Flight 77

American Airlines flight 77 left Washington's Dulles Airport at 8:20 a.m. At 8:46 (the same minute that the first plane hit the WTC) the flight went significantly off course for several minutes. At 8:50 it got back on course, but without radio contact. No explanation has been given for why a hijacked plane would leave, and then resume its intended flight path.

At around 8:55, while flying over Southern Ohio, the plane abruptly made a U-turn and began heading directly towards Washington. A minute later its transponder was shut off while the plane was out of radar contact, and it failed to respond to an instruction from the ground.

However, unlike the other flights, which lost transponder data but were still visible on the radar, flight 77 appears to have disappeared altogether for at least twenty-nine minutes. For a commercial jet, this is really only possible if the plane lands or is flown at extremely low altitudes. But the plane was not seen flying low by anyone on the ground. This disappearing act means that the plane appears to have been able to fly freely for nearly half an hour, unseen and undetected, or that it returned to the ground, in whatever fashion.

Initially, media reports said the plane had crashed. At 9:09 a.m., an air traffic controller warned that it had crashed in Ohio or on the Kentucky border. FAA head Jane Garvey told the White House that a plane had crashed into the ground.

The idea of a large commercial plane flying across the most heavily monitored airspace in the world for more than half an hour without being detected by any radar system, including those used by the military, during the most traumatic day in modern American history, is utterly ridiculous.

At 9:25 a.m., air traffic controllers at Dulles Airport reported seeing a fast-moving plane appear on their radar, which they thought was headed towards the White House. Some assumed it was the errant flight 77. At 9:27, Dick Cheney, in the White House bunker, was told that an airplane heading towards Washington was being tracked by radar, and was fifty miles out.

At 9:33, radar data showed the aircraft crossing the Beltway and heading toward the Pentagon. However, the plane flew over the top of the Pentagon and White House, and at 9:35 conducted an astonishingly difficult maneuver, dropping seven thousand feet to ground level in two and a half minutes, while conducting a spiraling 270-degree circle descent, before flying so low toward the Pentagon building that it clipped streetlight poles nearby.

Danielle O'Brien, one of the air traffic controllers at Dulles, saw the fast-moving plane enter the Class Bravo controlled airspace over Washington, and later said, "The speed, the maneuverability, the way that he turned, we all thought in the radar room, all of us experienced air traffic controllers, that that was a military plane."

At 9:38 a.m., the Pentagon was hit.

Although never officially confirmed, it is widely known that the Pentagon, the most heavily protected building on the planet, is defended by five ground-to-air anti-aircraft missile batteries stationed on the roof. The Capitol and the White House also have anti-aircraft defenses. As the hub of the most powerful military on earth, the Pentagon's communication and radar systems are at the vanguard of technological capability; systems that "do not miss anything." Yet on the most fraught day imaginable, the Pentagon's occupants appeared unable to notice a 757 flying overhead; or stop it dive-bombing the building.

Central Washington, including the Pentagon, is protected by the most restricted airspace zone in the world, P56, which has three concentric circles of increasing value surrounding the Washington area. It has been called an aviation no-man's land.

The failure to defend the Pentagon at this key moment is particularly surprising, since by the point at which flight 77 approached Washington, it was clear to nearly everyone on earth that the biggest terrorist attack in history was under way. The Pentagon would have been at the highest state of alert. Why was the plane not shot down by the Pentagon's on-site anti-aircraft missiles? Before its spiraling approach, the aircraft also flew right over the White House; why did the missiles there not shoot it down?

The alternate theory that a missile or small plane hit the Pentagon again overcomes this problem, since military aircraft have onboard transponders that indicate "friend or foe" (IFF). An approaching US military aircraft with the correct transponder signal would not have been shot down.

The Pentagon is among the biggest buildings in the world, but it is only five stories high. It took incredible piloting to hit the side facade of the building with a commercial plane. It would have been much easier to crash into the roof, an attack that would have caused a huge amount of casualties. Despite this, a crash into the building's side appears the method of attack that had been anticipated.

On October 24, 2000, the Pentagon conducted a MASCAL (mass casualties) exercise looking at response plans for the scenario of a plane hitting the side of the Pentagon. Less than a year later, the exact scenario took place.

Hani Hanjour

Charles Burlingame was a "Top Gun" ex-fighter pilot and Vietnam War veteran. A weightlifter and boxer, the burly Burlingame was supposed to have been overpowered by the Middle Eastern "muscle" hijackers, who were scrawny and less than 5'8".

Whoever was in control of the aircraft that hit the Pentagon was a supreme pilot, conducting a full-speed controlled downward spiral, then flying so low that the plane clipped streetlights, before finally hitting a building eighty feet high at around 460 mph. And all while under the unique pressure of piloting a hijacked plane in very busy airspace, with the risk of fighters pulling up alongside at any second.

Not only was a turning descent technically challenging, but flying at high speed at such a low altitude and successfully striking a five-story building in a huge commercial plane is close to impossible. Experienced pilots from around the world have described the maneuver as astonishing, at or beyond the boundaries of possibility, both for plane and pilot.

Although the Pentagon is only eighty feet high, the roof covers twenty-nine acres. The attack method chosen was by far the hardest way to do it, and killed the fewest people. So it is curious, to say the least, that the man claimed to have been at the helm of flight 77 is Hani Hanjour, a twenty-nine-year-old Saudi reported to be a truly terrible pilot by all who came into contact with him.

Hanjour had been turned down at flight schools in Jeddah and the US in the 1990s before returning to the US for further flight training. He was viewed as a very poor pilot at every facility he attended. Managers at JetTech flight school in Arizona, which Hanjour attended, reported him to the FAA five times because his English and flying skills were so bad that they thought he should have his license revoked. Peggy Chevrette, the Arizona flight school manager, said, "I couldn't believe he had a commercial license of any kind."

Another employee said, "I'm still to this day amazed that he could have flown into the Pentagon . . . he could not fly at all."

Hanjour tried to hire a plane at Freeway Airport in Maryland in mid-August 2001, just weeks before 9/11, but was refused when he was unable to pilot and control a single-engine Cessna 172. Yet despite this wealth of evidence showing Hanjour to be an incredibly poor pilot, the 9/11 Commission used torture-induced testimony from Khalid Sheikh Mohammed to state that Hanjour had been selected to pilot flight 77 because he was the most experienced and highly trained pilot among the hijackers.

Twin-jet commercial airliners represent a completely different type of flying to that required for smaller planes. The only training Hanjour had on planes this size was on a flight simulator. It is utterly absurd to suggest that someone unable to fly a Cessna could fly a 757 with the precision and skill as is alleged that Hanjour did on 9/11.

Some have suggested that flight 77 may have been piloted by Nawaf al-Hazmi, but al-Hazmi had virtually no flight training and, like others in the plot, a terrible record when he did attempt to learn. His flight instructor had openly scoffed at his request to quickly learn to fly a Boeing jet.

Unlike many of the other hijackers, who were seen as rude or sullen, Hanjour was liked by nearly everyone he met in the US and seemed to integrate relatively well. In mid-2001 this supposedly devout Muslim, whose faith was so strong that he was prepared to pilot a suicide mission, was among a number of future hijackers who visited Las Vegas to drink, gamble, and hire prostitutes.

"Do the Orders Still Stand?"

Billions of people watched the second plane impact at 9:03 a.m., at which point it was clear that this was terrorism on a devastating scale. Yet despite the obvious enormity of the attacks in New York, Washington landmarks remained sitting ducks as flight 77 approached. The Treasury was evacuated just a few minutes before the Pentagon strike, but the Capitol, State Department, and White House were still staffed at that point. The White House was evacuated at 9:45. The Capitol had many Senators and members of Congress in it, and was not evacuated until 9:48. Had the plane's target been the Capitol or White House, many senior political figures would have been killed. Congress was in session, and the Speaker of the House (Dennis Hastert, third in the line of Presidential succession after Bush and Cheney) was in the Capitol building.

Given the possible assassination attempt on President Bush in Florida that morning (see "Bush on 9/11"), a successful strike on the Capitol might have left Dick Cheney the last man standing in terms of Presidential succession. As we will see, Cheney managed to successfully sideline both Bush and Hastert throughout the day on 9/11, and was the most powerful figure in the United States for the key hours of the attacks.

Some reports suggest defense chiefs at the Pentagon had been alerted to an errant aircraft with hostile intent nearby, but no order to evacuate was given until after the building was hit. It seems the headquarters of the most powerful military on earth couldn't see a commercial jet approaching. However, in the White House situation room, the plane had been spotted and tracked for some time.

On May 23, 2003, Secretary of Transportation Norman Mineta was interviewed by the 9/11 Commission. Mineta testified that after arriving at the White House (on the morning of 9/11) he had been escorted to the bunker underneath, where he found Dick Cheney in charge.

Deputy FAA Acting Administrator Monty Belger also testified that Cheney and Condoleezza Rice sat together in the PEOC (Presidential Emergency Operations Center, a nuclear blast-proof concrete bunker under the White House) as they were told by an aide that an unidentified plane was 50 miles outside Washington, and approaching. "We're watching this target on the radar, but the transponder's been turned off, so we have no identification," said Belger.

Mineta testified: "During the time that the airplane was coming into the Pentagon, there was a young man who would come in and say to the vice president, 'the plane is fifty miles out,' 'the plane is thirty miles out.' And when it got down to 'the plane is ten miles out,' the young man also said to the vice president, 'do the orders still stand?' And the vice president turned and whipped his neck around and said, 'of course the orders still stand. Have you heard anything to the contrary?'"

The young man in question was vice presidential military aide Douglas Cochrane.

Mineta inferred that the orders in question were to shoot down the aircraft, but many have suggested that it's more logical to think that the orders were in fact to not shoot down the plane, most obviously because in the end the plane was not actually shot down. All of Mineta's testimony was left out of the 9/11 Commission report.

The official story says that Vice President Cheney didn't give a shootdown order until all four planes had crashed and the attacks had ended. This contradicts the idea that Cheney was being asked if orders to shoot a plane down still stood while two hijacked planes remained in the air. President Bush has said that his first decision onboard Air Force One was to order the shoot-down of any commercial aircraft that did not respond. Cheney's order certainly couldn't have been in relation to flight 93 (which later crashed in Shanksville), which never got within 130 miles of Washington.

So what are we to make of Cheney's actions as he was told a plane was getting closer to Washington? He knew that the FAA had ordered a complete ban on all flights above continental US at 9:26 a.m. Clearly what was approaching had the strong possibility of evil intent, and presented a grave risk to key Washington buildings. Is it not then also possible that the young man at the White House was asking Cheney if an order not to allow military flights to take to the skies (or to engage) still applied, given the rapidly approaching hijacked plane?

This also brings into question how Cheney could have known about the plane for so long, but Donald Rumsfeld, who was at the Pentagon, can continue to claim that he had no idea another plane was coming. If Dick Cheney was aware of an incoming aircraft, why were Pentagon staff not informed? The White House and Pentagon would have been in constant communication.

The blatant contradictions here show that someone is lying. It is unlikely to be Mineta, who was a peripheral figure on 9/11, and whose story goes against the official narrative. What were Cheney's orders that still stood, how could the Pentagon have been unaware of the approach of a commercial airliner, and why didn't the White House (whose staff clearly knew of the plane for some time) at least inform the military at the Pentagon?

Footage

No footage showing a commercial plane over Washington, near or at the Pentagon on 9/11 has ever been released. On the day, the connection between flight 77 and the incident at the Pentagon was not immediately made. The first reports broadcast by Reuters said that a helicopter or private jet had hit the building. A short time later Fox TV said that the Pentagon had been hit by a US Air Force flight.

It was only on the afternoon of 9/11 that unnamed officials, speaking on the condition of anonymity, said that it was flight 77 that had struck the Pentagon. Richard Myers, acting chairman of the Joint Chiefs of Staff, was the first to officially connect the two.

Immediately after the crash, the media was moved back a safe distance, and as a result there is a very limited amount of still and moving pictures showing the impact site and nearby damage prior to the building façade collapse that happened a short time later.

Although no handheld video footage of the plane was taken, a number of nearby buildings had external security cameras that would have recorded the plane flying past. Most notably, the CITGO gas station right next door and the Sheraton hotel nearby are right in line with the plane's approach. The Virginia Department of Transportation also had traffic monitoring cameras pointed right at the impact site.

For obvious security reasons, the Pentagon building itself is covered with CCTV (closed-circuit television) equipment. In total, up to eighty-six civilian and military cameras may have recorded the approach and impact. But workers at nearby businesses reported that the FBI was on site within minutes of the attack to confiscate all CCTV footage. Jose Velasquez, an employee at the CITGO station across the road from the Pentagon, said the CCTV cameras on the forecourt would have captured the moment of impact, but said, "I've never seen what the pictures look like. The FBI was here within minutes and took the film."

On March 7, 2002, the Pentagon released to CNN five frames taken by a nearby parking security camera. These five frames show very little. A small, unidentifiable grey object appears in one corner of one shot, then the building explodes. Officially, the plane was going so fast that it managed to pass between one frame and the next. It is certainly not present in the footage released. The clip also showed white smoke trailing whatever had struck the building, but jet airliners don't emit white smoke at ground level.

The 2002 video release came only three days after the publication of Thierry Meyssan's controversial book *The Big Lie* (which claimed that the Pentagon was not hit by a commercial jet but some kind of missile), and may have been aimed at heading off the negative publicity that the book produced.

Another video was released by the Pentagon in May 2006. It did not show a plane.

The claim that there is no footage of the approaching plane and its crash is clearly absurd. Not only would the tapes confiscated from nearby businesses (with extraordinary haste) almost definitely have shown something, the huge amount of CCTV cameras on the outside of the Pentagon would have recorded the impact from a variety of angles. Why not release the footage? It can't be to show compassion for those killed—footage of the attacks at the WTC has been re-broadcast millions of times. Claiming footage doesn't exist, confiscating external CCTV videos, releasing edited pictures that don't show a plane—all of these strongly suggest that this story is not as it has been presented to us.

Eyewitnesses

While we have no single frame showing a plane, plenty of people saw an aircraft of some sort approaching the Pentagon. Their testimony is highly contradictory and confusing. Below is a sample of the varying statements. For simplicity's sake, testimony has been separated here into those whose impressions support the official story, and those who do not.

Fireman Alan Wallace was with a safety crew at the Pentagon's helipad when he looked up and saw a large commercial plane. The plane was twenty-five feet up, a few hundred yards away, and coming right at him. Wallace dived under a nearby van then used a radio to call his fire chief and report that a commercial plane had hit the Pentagon.

Mike Walter, who worked for USA Today, reported seeing a plane descend as he was stuck in traffic. "I said, 'that plane is really flying low'," he said in an interview. "It disappeared and I heard the explosion and saw a ball of fire. It was an American Airlines plane. You saw a big silver plane and those double A's." He added, "It was like a Cruise missile with wings."

The head flight controller at Washington's Reagan National Airport saw a large plane descending in an area where there should not have been commercial airplanes.

"I saw the tail of a large airliner . . . it plowed right into the Pentagon," was a quote attributed to Dave Winslow, an Associated Press Radio reporter. However, Mr. Winslow's quote has been widely derided as he cannot be located and appears never to have worked for the Associated Press.

Tim Timmerman, a pilot who was in the sixteenth floor of his building in Arlington, said on CNN that he was sure it had been an American Airlines 757. He said the plane had "added power" in its final moments. However, despite saying he had seen the impact, Timmerman claims that the plane had not appeared to crash directly into the building, and that most of the plane's energy had been dissipated when it hit the ground. Subsequent photos show no damage to the ground near or adjacent to the Pentagon building.

Afework Hagos, a computer programmer, was stuck in traffic nearby when the plane flew past. "There was a huge screaming noise and I got out of the car as the plane came over. It was tilting its wings up and down like it was trying to balance. It hit some lampposts on the way in."

Omar Campo, a Salvadorean, was cutting grass by the road when the plane flew over his head. "It was a passenger plane. I think an American Airways plane. I was cutting the grass and it came in screaming over my head. I felt the impact. The whole ground shook and the whole area was full of fire."

Although most of the eyewitnesses saw a plane flying too low in what appeared a final dive towards the Pentagon, virtually none reported having seen the actual impact.

Other eyewitness accounts clearly indicate seeing a plane that was not a 757.

Steve Patterson, seeing the plane from a fourteenth-floor apartment in Pentagon City said the plane looked like a commuter jet, "seemed to be able to hold eight or twelve persons," and "made a shrill noise like a fighter plane." An air-to-ground (AGM) missile does look like a small civilian plane, and produces a distinctive whistling noise similar to that of a fighter aircraft.

The editor of Space News, Lon Rains, said, "I was convinced it was a missile. It came in so fast it sounded nothing like an airplane."

Tom Seibert, a network engineer at the Pentagon said, "We heard what sounded like a missile."

The testimony is so contradictory it is hard to reconcile. We do know of two large aircraft (an E-4B and a C-130) that were definitely in the area. The C-130 was very close to the building in the moments before it was struck. One conclusion that could be drawn is that there were two planes (or a plane and a missile) heading toward the Pentagon, which could explain the disparity in eyewitness evidence.

Extraordinary as this may seem, a second plane could have landed at Reagan National Airport, which is less than one mile from the Pentagon and in the direction in which whatever hit the Pentagon was flying.

Kelly Knowles was in an apartment two miles away and saw "two planes moving toward the Pentagon, one veering away as the other crashed."

USA Today reporter Vin Narayanan said after the building impact he had been "nearly oblivious to a second jet hovering in the skies." The paper's editor Joel Sucherman saw another nearby plane climb steeply and make a sharp turn, "kind of peeling off."

Keith Wheelhouse said he saw two planes approaching the Pentagon, one above the other (which would look like one object on a radar screen). As the lower plane accelerated, the higher one banked off west (which is the direction of Reagan Airport).

The C-130

One of the more interesting eyewitnesses was in the air. At around 9:36 a.m. a flight controller from Reagan National Airport requested a nearby military C-130 that had apparently taken off from Andrews Air Force Base at 9:30

(despite the FAA ban on all civilian and military flights issued four minutes earlier) to find and identify flight 77.

Having sighted a commercial plane, the pilot of the C-130, Lieutenant Colonel Steve O'Brien, was told to turn around and follow it. However, the C-130 did not get close to the (much faster) passenger jet, and O'Brien said he did not see the actual impact.

At least six people on the ground saw a second plane resembling the distinctively shaped C-130 descending sharply as a commercial airliner approached the Pentagon. However, the C-130 came from a different angle to whatever hit the building, and was not above it.

Not only was the C-130 right on the scene at the Pentagon crash, after veering away the same plane found itself just seventeen miles from flight 93 when it crashed twenty-eight minutes later in Pennsylvania.

One further source of intrigue is that the C-130 was one of the plane types that had recently become capable of carrying new technological weapons able to disrupt the mechanical operations of a plane without launching a physical attack upon it, and send it into an uncontrollable dive.

After the Impact

Although we have few reliable sources who saw a commercial plane hit the Pentagon building, within seconds of the crash there were plenty of people on the scene. Despite testimony relating to a plane approaching the building, the physical evidence on the ground was disturbing.

Don Perkal, a war veteran, said, "A bomb had gone off. I could smell the cordite. I knew explosives had been set off somewhere." Cordite has a very different smell to kerosene.

Steve DeChiaro saw the impact site within minutes of the attack, and said, "It only seemed like a small hole in the building. No tail. No wings. No nothing."

In fact, nobody who had *not* seen some kind of plane approaching the building leapt to the conclusion that a large commercial flight must have been behind the explosion. It didn't look anything like that.

A CNN journalist who produced the first reports from the scene told the studio that while the initial word was that a commercial jet may have hit the building, having inspected the scene from close up, he saw no evidence of a plane having crashed anywhere near the Pentagon.

Perhaps the most amazing testimony came from April Gallop, a Pentagon employee in the building, who was about to take her son to daycare when the impact happened. She remembered thinking a bomb had gone off, and miraculously found her son in his stroller unharmed. Gallop reported seeing no evidence of a plane whatsoever, and didn't know that the official story was that of a plane impact until she got to hospital.

Later that day she was visited a number of times by men in suits, who refused to identify themselves but asserted that they were representatives of the government and, while they couldn't tell April what to say, had a number of suggestions, most notably that a plane had obviously hit the building, which they repeated over and over.

The men's advice was for April to take the victim compensation fund money and shut up. April continues to state that she never saw a plane, nor any debris from a plane, and that, "I figure the plane story is there to brainwash people."

Arlington Firefighters

Elsewhere and earlier, after a routine 911 call, Arlington County Emergency Communications Center sent several firefighting units to Rosslyn, Virginia, less than two miles from the Pentagon. The reported fire was in a high-rise building, so nine fire and medical units were sent, but the first one to arrive radioed the others to say the fire had gone out. Within minutes the Pentagon was hit, so by "sheer coincidence," there was a large contingent of fire and medical staff on the road nearby and quickly at the scene.

The Arlington County fire department had been involved in the Pentagon's MASCAL training simulation (of a plane hitting the side of the building) less than a year before, so were uniquely prepared to respond to an emergency that exactly replicated what they had trained for.

On site, the Arlington firefighters were only allowed to fight the fire from the outside of the building, and were kept away from the site of the alleged wreck by a team from FEMA.

Also by chance, the Secret Service were out in considerable numbers. President Bush had been due to visit the Pentagon via helicopter that afternoon, so Secret Service staff were present in numbers at the heliport, a short distance from where the building was struck. Their cars were already blocking the driveways nearby.

Barbara Olson

The key evidence connecting flight 77 to the explosion at the Pentagon came, astonishingly, from the US Justice Department's Solicitor General, Ted Olson.

Mr. Olson told CNN just hours after the attacks that he had received two phone calls from his wife Barbara, who was an author and well-known television commentator. These calls, he said, had been made from flight 77, and received at about 9:25 and 9:30, around ten minutes before the plane crashed. Olson said the first call lasted one minute, the second two to four minutes.

According to Mr. Olson, his wife said nothing about where the plane was or the direction in which it was headed, but that it had been hijacked, that the hijackers had knives and box-cutters, and that the passengers had all been forced to the back of the plane.

Barbara Olson's report of the terrorists having box-cutters is the only reference to these now infamous tools of hijacking on 9/11. It's the reason you've heard that the terrorists had box-cutters.

Another call was made by flight attendant Renee May to her mother, in which she reported that the plane had been hijacked. On all the other flights, telephone calls were made by several passengers and crew. On flight 77, just two on board may have successfully gotten through.

However, Ted Olson's recollection of the phone calls timing and details has changed dramatically over the course of several tellings, in a way that makes his testimony hard to believe, given that the dying words from a beloved wife in a terrifying situation might expect to be burnt upon the psyche forever. In one account, she is in a bathroom, in another near one or maybe two pilots.

There is also significant doubt as to Barbara Olson's ability to make the calls from the plane. The in-flight seatback phones were not working (they had been deactivated earlier in 2001), and at altitude it is doubtful that cellphones would have been able to connect.

Further revealing information came to light during the 2006 trial of Zacarias Moussaoui, the so-called twentieth hijacker. As part of the evidence presented against Moussaoui, the FBI produced detailed reports on phone calls made from the four hijacked planes. In relation to flight 77, their report stated that there was just one phone call attempted by Barbara Olson, which lasted zero seconds.

At the very least, it is yet another amazing coincidence that evidence of the key call connecting flight 77 to the Pentagon strike came from the US Attorney General.

Mr. Olson was a senior insider within the Bush administration, and highly favored, having made George W. Bush's case before the US Supreme Court (that handed Bush the Presidency) following the disputed 2000 election, and having controversially been rewarded with the post of Solicitor General. He hardly had a reputation for candor, having once said that there were an infinite number of situations in which "government officials might quite legitimately have reasons to give false information out" to "protect vital interests." Or to put it another way, it's fine for politicians to lie, especially concerning important issues. This means, without reference to his wife's alleged phone calls, that Mr. Olson is the definition of an unreliable witness.

Protecting Washington

The suggestion that a large civilian airliner was able to simply waltz about the skies above Washington well into the largest terrorist attack in history is absurd. To have that same airliner hit the Pentagon is fantasy.

With Washington being the most heavily defended airspace on earth, the Pentagon—the heart of the US military—is probably the best defended building on the planet. Although the events of the day were at times confusing, it is not credible to suggest that the Pentagon would have been unaware of a commercial plane overhead and closing in. Nevertheless, Donald Rumsfeld claims not to have been informed of the plane's existence, and was still in a meeting with Representative Christopher Cox (a Republican from California) when the impact occurred.

Washington is supposed to be defended by squadrons of combat-ready F-16 fighter jets, on constant alert at Andrews Air Force Base just ten miles from the Pentagon. Their job is to protect the nation's capital from air attack. Yet nearly an hour into the attacks, when the whole world knew what was going on simply by turning on a television, it appears no planes were scrambled. When the F-16s were eventually deployed, they were ordered to fly to nearby Baltimore, in the mistaken belief that this is where they could intercept flight 11, which had already crashed into the World Trade Center. As we will see, a series of war games caused confusion and significantly delayed America's response to the attacks, as well as moving defensive military assets far from the action. However, it remains very hard to believe that under any circumstance, America's capital, and the most highly protected building on earth, could have been left entirely unprotected from the skies so long into a major terrorist attack.

The Doomsday Planes

Up to four E-4B doomsday planes had been scrambled. E-4Bs are converted 747–200s, to be used as airborne command and control centers in the event of a national emergency or nuclear war. This sent some on the ground into panic, as the planes were seen in the sky above Washington (right over the White House) minutes after the Pentagon was struck.

CNN correspondent John King reported at 9:54 a.m. that around ten minutes earlier (so around six minutes after the Pentagon strike) he had seen a white jet circling overhead. Kate Snow, another CNN journalist, confirmed the sighting. A security guard told her that the plane had been the reason for the White House evacuation. The jet was caught on film by a CNN cameraman, and can clearly be identified as an E-4B, flying in a low, circling pattern over Washington.

This is a matter that is in no doubt, but has never been officially confirmed, and again was not mentioned in the 9/11 Commission report.

King's CNN report indicated that the planes were seen above Washington at around 9:45 a.m. The first World Trade Center tower was struck at 8:46 and the second at 9:03, allowing precious little time for the huge E-4Bs to be staffed and airborne in response. What seems more likely, as has been suggested, is that at least one (more probably three) E-4B was in the air already at the time of the attacks, as part of the Global Guardian exercise that so neatly coincided with real events.

What is known is that one of the E4-Bs was en route to Offutt Air Force Base with a high-level group of military brass and business and political leaders such as Brent Scowcroft and Warren Buffett on board, apparently there to observe the exercise. Offutt is the home of Stratcom, America's main nuclear weapons control center. It's the most important military site in the United States.

Had the fourth (and fifth) planes hit their targets, which most believe were the Capitol or the White House, and martial law been declared, having these senior figures at Offutt would have guaranteed continued control of the key military facility in the country at a time of great stress. After all, the key to every coup is to take full control of the military—they're the guys with all the guns.

The Hole, and the Lack of Evidence of a Plane

As it was, not only was the façade of the Pentagon struck, it was struck on the west wing, the only part of the building to have recently been reinforced (at a cost of $258 million), with a sprinkler system and bomb-proof steel columns and bars, as well as blast-resistant windows. The renovations had been managed by Donald Rumsfeld's deputy, Paul Wolfowitz.

It has been estimated that around 4,500 of the twenty-five thousand people working at the Pentagon each day would have normally been working in the area attacked, but on 9/11, because of the renovation work, there was only around eight hundred people nearby, with many of the offices destroyed being temporarily unoccupied. This meant that instead of thousands of casualties, only 125 died in the building, most of whom were civilian contractors. Only one senior military figure, Lieutenant General Tim Maude, was killed. All the key military and civilian personnel, including Donald Rumsfeld, were based in the East Wing, the exact opposite side to where the building was struck.

The official story is that the plane came in almost perfectly level with the ground, but at a forty-five-degree angle to the wall that was struck, bouncing off the grass in front of the building before impact. The hole left in the side of the building was at the bottom of the facade, almost at ground level, but there was no evidence whatsoever that the lawn had been damaged. This makes it hard to explain how the plane's engines, hanging from the wings, would not have plowed into the grass outside the building, leaving clear damage before the final moment of impact. Whatever hit the building came straight through the air and disappeared entirely inside a small circular hole at the very bottom of the building.

The damage to the Pentagon seemed highly inconsistent with the impact of a one hundred-ton commercial craft. The façade of the building was mostly intact. However, the strike packed a heavy punch, penetrating not only the recently reinforced building exterior, but five internal walls. One photo taken from inside the building showed a seven foot hole in the inside wall of the third of the Pentagon's five rings, called the C-Ring, meaning the plane had penetrated six walls, the first one being reinforced. It looked like something small and fast had hit the building at high speed. Unlike the strikes on the twin towers, the attack at the Pentagon did not create a seismic signal that could be detected.

The outer wall of the building collapsed at 10:15 a.m., approximately thirty-five minutes after the impact. A few minutes earlier firefighters had seen signs of structural weakness and pulled back. No firefighters were injured in the collapse. However, in that brief thirty-five minutes, several local photographers were able to get clear pictures of the damage to the building, and these present a very significant problem with the official story of 9/11.

Arguably the most crucial photograph taken on 9/11 was by Tom Horan of the Associated Press, just after the fire-trucks had arrived, but before the firemen had started their work. This photo, and another taken at roughly the same moment, shows a hole in the building façade roughly 15–18 feet in diameter, very near the ground. It shows virtually no damage above or to either side of the hole.

Put simply, the hole in the building was nothing like the size or shape expected from the impact of a 757. At the World Trade Center buildings, the planes had left fearful imprints of their own outline on the side of the towers that were struck. But at the Pentagon, there was no wing or engine damage to be seen around the small, circular impact hole. Although the reinforced side of the Pentagon building may have been much stronger than the (aluminum) World Trade Center building facades, it is very hard to explain where the huge wings and engines can have gone.

Some have suggested that on impact the wings folded back and were dragged into the central hole with the fuselage, but this is counter to the laws of physics. The huge deceleration of impact would have thrown everything forward, rather than backwards. Even accepting this preposterous idea, it's further absurdity to suggest that when the plane struck the building, the wings and engines can have snapped backwards in a fraction of a second, and entered the same hole as the fuselage, leaving no trace.

On September 12, the county fire chief Ed Plaugher said that there were "some small pieces . . . but not large sections" of the plane remaining, and no fuselage sections at all.

In fact, the aircraft appeared to have entirely disappeared. There were no visible plane parts—no seats, no baggage, no bodies—save for some small pieces of indistinct metal, scattered about the lawn, small enough to pick up with your hand. One wrinkled piece of aluminum, apparently bearing the colors of American Airlines, was photographed, but it was alone, and oddly not even singed by fire.

Not only was there no evidence of a plane on the lawn outside the Pentagon, none has subsequently been produced as proof, either physical or photographic.

A Boeing 757–200 has a wingspan of 125 feet. The height from the bottom of the engines to the top of the tail is forty-five feet, with a fuselage made mostly from aluminum, and engines from tempered steel. How did an aluminum and steel plane 125 feet wide and forty-five feet high disappear entirely into a hole eighteen feet wide, leaving no trace. It's absolutely ridiculous.

As with so many aspects of the 9/11 story, the official version has evolved over time. In April 2002 the FBI said that enough of the plane had been recovered to almost completely reconstruct it, without providing any evidence. FBI spokesman Chris Murray said, "The pieces of the plane are stocked in a warehouse and they are marked with the serial numbers of flight 77." But if these large pieces of the plane, including engines and fuselage, were indeed inside the Pentagon, why did none of the people on site see them at the time. And given the hugely controversial nature of the alleged plane strike, why not release photographic proof?

The size of the hole, so entirely and absurdly out of proportion when the outline of a 757 is placed next to the building, has proved one of the more tenacious problems with the official version of the story. It has led to some tortuous attempts at explanation by those charged with maintaining this fiction.

For example, at one point the official explanation for the lack of physical evidence was that the entire plane had been vaporized by the impact and subsequent jet-fuel fires. Yet at the same time it was claimed that investigators had identified 184 of the 189 people who died, many by their fingerprints.

The Armed Forces DNA Identification Laboratory that carried out the identification work on the victims at the Pentagon was the same team who provided identification for the victims of the crash in Shanksville that proved so hard to find for those on the ground.

You do not need to be a scientist to doubt the idea that a plane can have been entirely vaporized, nor that this precludes the identifying of human victims by the skin on their fingers. What fire makes steel disappear but leaves human remains intact? And of course this explanation contradicts the FBI claim that nearly the entire plane was recovered and reconstructed.

The lack of evidence is as evidentiary as anything. Aluminum fuselages and engines made of tempered steel do not vaporize in a hydrocarbon fire. Commercial engines are made from titanium steel alloy. It is utterly absurd to suggest that these could have been vaporized by kerosene jet-fuel. If the fire was that hot, how did the upper floors of the Pentagon survive?

Some photos taken much later in the day do show a closer view of the impact site, and purport to show engine parts, but these are far from conclusive, and many have suggested that the mechanical pieces shown are far too small, or the wrong shape, to have been from a 757. Photographs published allegedly show a turbofan part of a 757 engine, but independent researchers have identified the turbofan as part of a much smaller A3 Skywarrior.

Black boxes stored in the tail of flight 77 were alleged to have been discovered in the Pentagon on September 12, but Donald Rumsfeld said the data from the cockpit voice recorder was unrecoverable, the first time in forty years that a cockpit voice tape, once found, had yielded no data. On the 16th of October 2001 the flight control transcripts were released, but the information ended at least twenty minutes before the plane supposedly crashed.

A Missile

All debate about the incident at the Pentagon could easily be resolved by the release of footage from the numerous CCTV cameras on and near the Pentagon. If pictures supported the government's story, we would expect them to have been released.

As we have seen, the eyewitness accounts of the final moments before the Pentagon was attacked are highly contradictory. Forensic investigators work on the premise that when there is a conflict between the physical evidence and eyewitness accounts, the physical evidence is given more weight.

The hole in the side of the building was far, far too small to have been made by a commercial jet. What could have created this damage, and fits much more with the evidence, is a missile. An AGM Tomahawk cruise missile, with a depleted uranium BLU tip, or a small, remotely controlled A3 Skywarrior fighter plane is most likely to have been what struck the building. Defense company Raytheon owned all the A3s left in America, and are heavily implicated in the events of 9/11. An attack on the Pentagon by these smaller craft would have left exactly what was found—a small, deep hole in the building and a trail of white smoke, as was seen in the limited pictures that have been released. There is simply no possible way that a 757 commercial jet, somehow able to enter Washington airspace and make its way to the Pentagon, could have left such an incongruous hole in the building. It's truly amazing that we were told this story.

CHAPTER THREE

SHANKSVILLE

Flight 93

The fourth plane on 9/11 might have been the biggest story of all, had it hit its intended target. United 93's flight path pointed directly towards Washington, and as we have seen, iconic centers of the US State like the Capitol and White House were sitting ducks. There is little to suggest from the other events of the day that a successful military interception would have been guaranteed before the plane reached its final destination. Shanksville to Washington is just 130 miles, and at 450 mph (well below a 757's top speed), the flight was less than twenty minutes from its likely target.

Worse perhaps, the Three Mile Island nuclear plant was just fifteen minutes of flying time away. A direct hit on the reactor there would have increased the fatality count on 9/11 by a factor of hundreds.

After the attacks, high-ranking al-Qaeda leaders were reported to have claimed that the target was the Capitol, although this is so uncorroborated as to be hearsay. The 9/11 Commission took it upon themselves to consider the scenario had flight 93 not crashed, and concluded that had the plane made it to Washington, air defenses would have failed, as the few fighters in the air lacked the information and authorization to effectively intervene.

Either way, while the images from New York were apocalyptic, it is hard to understate the shock to both the nation and its shattered politicians that an attack on either of these two Washington buildings would have caused. It is not inconceivable that martial law would have been declared. America's politicians were entirely supine to the Bush administration in the two to three years that followed 9/11. Had the Capitol or White House been attacked, we might still be living in a one-party system with an opposition too scared of looking unpatriotic to actually oppose anything at all; with further endless wars raging and democracy all but vanished. It's a sobering thought.

United Airlines flight 93 took off late from Newark Airport at 8:42 a.m. Authorities knew about the hijacking of flight 11 at least eighteen minutes before flight 93 even left the ground. Like the other flights, it was at less than full capacity, with just thirty-seven passengers (including the hijackers) and seven crew.

Before the cockpit was taken over, two planes had already hit the World Trade Center. All four hijacked planes on 9/11 were scheduled to leave at roughly the same time and presumably intended to coordinate their attacks. The other three planes took off within a period of twenty-one minutes, but flight 93 was forty-one minutes behind schedule due to heavy runway traffic. Many have argued that this is the reason the hijackers mission failed on this flight.

It appears staff on flight 93 were very close to having been able to stop the initial hijack. At 9:21 a.m. United Airlines dispatchers were told to warn all their flights to secure cockpit doors. At 9:24 dispatcher Ed Ballinger sent a message to flight 93 reading, "Beware any cockpit intrusion. Two a/c [aircraft] hit World Trade Center." Two minutes later, pilot Jason Dahl replied, "Ed, confirm latest message please Jason."

Within two to three minutes, flight controllers heard sounds of struggling or screaming from the cockpit. Someone yelled "mayday" and "get out of here, get out of here." Then Arabic voices were heard. Later reports from passengers on board indicated two dead bodies outside the cockpit. These may have been the pilots.

At 9:27 a.m., passenger Tom Burnett called his wife Deena to tell her that the plane had been hijacked by men with guns, a passenger had been stabbed, and that there was a bomb on board. He told his wife to call the FBI. Burnett was an avid hunter and had grown up around firearms. It is unlikely he could have mistaken some other object for a gun.

Over thirty more phone calls were made from flight 93 by passengers. Five of them indicated an intent to try to take back control of the plane.

At 9:34 Burnett called his wife again. She told him about the attacks at the World Trade Center, and that a major terrorist attack was taking place.

At 9:36 the plane turned in the direction of Washington.

At 9:37 Jeremy Glick and two other passengers made phone calls and also learned about the WTC attacks.

At 9:40 the transponder on board was turned off. However, Cleveland flight controllers and United Airlines headquarters could still track the plane using primary radar.

At 9:45 Burnett told his wife that he didn't believe the hijackers claim that they had a bomb, and that he and other passengers were making a plan to take back control of the aircraft. At this point, around 21 minutes before the plane crashed, the FBI was listening in on all calls from the plane.

Passenger Todd Beamer began at this point a fifteen-minute conversation with a Verizon staff member that ended at 9:58am with the famous words "let's roll." Lisa Jefferson, the employee speaking to Beamer, offered to connect the call to his wife but, oddly, he declined.

Around 9:47 Glick told his wife that the men had voted to attack the hijackers, who he said only had knives. It is interesting to note that the commonly held view that the attackers used box-cutters is almost certainly wrong—box-cutters were not allowed on planes in 2001, and would have been confiscated, unless of course an insider at the airport placed them on the planes. If knives were used, it's much more likely that switchblades less than four inches long were involved. These were still allowed. But it's strange that despite only having Barbara Olson's second-hand report, we all now associate box-cutters with the terrorists.

At 9:54 Burnett told his wife, "I know we are all going to die. There's three of us who are going to do something about it." Another account had him saying he was confident they could do it.

Incidentally, this marked the moment in history that passive air hijackings ended. For years, hijacked planes had been piloted back to the ground, and passenger instincts were to stay still—not to cause a commotion that might put them in danger—and hope for a safe rescue. Any hijacker now will have to contend with passengers who may believe they have nothing to lose by fighting back.

The passengers known to have attempted to take back control of the plane were all substantially larger, physically, than the hijackers. They appear to have filled containers with boiling water, to be used as weapons, and used food trolleys as crude battering rams.

The passenger revolt story has evolved over time. Initially the FBI line was that the passengers had made it into the cockpit, and the plane had crashed during the struggle. This subsequently changed to the hijackers deliberately piloting the plane into the ground, rather than lose control of the cockpit and the plane.

Whatever happened, compounding the tragedy is the knowledge that the passengers on board held enough experience and skills to perhaps have been able to control and land the plane, had the terrorists been disabled. Donald Greene was an experienced pilot, albeit of single-engine planes. Andrew Garcia was a former air traffic controller, and would have been familiar with use of the onboard radios.

At 9:58 CeeCee Lyles, on the phone to her husband, told him, "They're forcing their way into the cockpit . . . they're doing it, they're doing it." But then her husband heard screaming, followed by a "whoosing sound, a sound like wind," and more screaming before the line was lost.

Passenger Edward Felt, calling from a toilet eight minutes before the crash, said he heard some kind of explosion and saw white smoke coming from the plane. Felt said he thought the plane was going down, seconds before the line was lost. John Shaw, who took Felt's call, was prevented from speaking to the media, and the recording was confiscated by the FBI on 9/11. Strangely, Felt had identified the plane in the phone call by using both the flight number and the plane's tail number, something passengers normally don't notice.

All cell phone calls from the plane stopped at around this moment, leaving eight crucial minutes between the calls ceasing and the plane hitting the ground.

This sudden ending of all passenger phone conversations is curious, given the more than thirty phone calls known to have been made during flight 93's hijacking. Cell phones left on by those attempting to storm the cockpit recorded only silence and strange sounds. Richard Makely, listening to Jeremy Glick's open phone line (after Glick put the phone down to attack the hijackers) described screaming, then a mechanical noise, followed by loud wind sounds.

Fighters Close In

Whether or not the flight was shot down, it's clear that fighter jets were very close by during the plane's final moments. CBS reported before 10:06 a.m. that two F-16s were on the tail of flight 93. Subsequently, a New England FAA air traffic controller contravened the ban on talking to the media, and said he knew that an F-16 had been closely following flight 93 and performed 360-degree turns in order to stay close to the relatively slow moving plane. "[They] must have seen the whole thing," he said.

While the official story has it that, as in the case of the Pentagon, jets arrived narrowly too late, there is just as much chance that fighter jets did in fact catch up with the commercial plane. The FBI have also confirmed there was a C-130 military cargo flight nearby. This was the same plane that had earlier flown very close to flight 77 before it allegedly hit the Pentagon. The fact that this plane somehow managed to be within touching distance of both hijacked flights within a twenty minute period, twenty minutes flying time from each other, is extremely suspicious to say the least. The pilot must have seen the attack on the Pentagon, turned around and somehow managed to fly directly to rendezvous with flight 93 in its last minutes.

If the flight was not shot down, one has to ask how is it possible that US fighter jets were unable to catch and intercept it, nearly one hour and forty minutes after it was known that the first plane had been hijacked. If fighter jets were indeed in touch with flight 93, and the plane crashed due to the actions of the passengers or hijackers on board, it is hard to explain why there have been so many steps taken to promulgate the story that in fact the fighters once again were just moments too late.

Initially at least, several people were told that a plane had been shot down. Major Daniel Nash, a fighter pilot who was returning to base after failing to find flight 175, was told that an F-16 had shot down a civilian airliner in Pennsylvania.

Black Box Evidence

Commercial planes carry two black boxes (they're actually orange). One records flight data, the other audio and conversation from the cockpit. Black boxes can withstand two thousand degrees Fahrenheit for up to an hour, and 3,400 Gs. They are virtually indestructible. When a plane crashes on land, they are always found.

At the World Trade Center, two black boxes were reported to have been found at four in the morning on September 12 and another shortly thereafter. A firefighter called Nicholas deMasi claimed he took FBI agents around the ground zero scene and handed them three of the four boxes. This has subsequently been denied, and the official story is that none of the boxes were recovered. Despite the awesome destruction at the WTC, the loss of all four black box recorders is almost an impossibility. Many other parts of the planes made it through the buildings onto the streets below, damaged but by no means unrecognizable.

At the Pentagon and in Shanksville, the FBI quickly took control of accident investigation. All the black boxes for flights 77 and 93 were reported found. Initially, flight 93's two boxes were deemed irreparably damaged. However, in December 2001 the FBI announced they had recovered the contents, but only released selected parts of the information.

Flight 93 was the only hijacked plane from which a cockpit voice recording was said to have been recovered undamaged. Cockpit recordings work on a thirty-minute loop (sometimes the tape is slightly longer), which means only the last thirty minutes of any flight is recorded.

In the days after the attacks, it was reported that flight investigators listening to the cockpit voice recordings had determined that one hijacker had been invited into the cockpit area prior to takeoff, with the pilots believing their guest was a colleague and extending the typical courtesy of allowing him to sit in the jump-seat. This is lent further credence given that pilot uniforms were reportedly found in Mohamed Atta's luggage (which didn't make it onto flight 11, and carried suspiciously incriminating evidence of Atta's plans).

However, we can't independently assess this, as the black box recordings (the cockpit recordings and the flight data) from flight 93 have never been released to the public, for a series of spurious reasons.

Initially the FBI refused to let even the victims' families hear the recordings. Finally, on April 18, 2002 they relented, but before they could listen to the tape, family members had to sign a waiver stating that they would not sue the government. They were not even allowed to take notes.

The version played to the victims' families began at 9:31 a.m. and ran for thirty-one minutes, ending one minute before the official time at which the plane was said to have crashed. Some of the relatives questioned why, at the peak of the cockpit struggle, the tape suddenly stopped recording voices. Cockpit recordings normally only end at the very point of impact, due to the catastrophic destruction of the plane's systems. But all that could be heard in the last sixty seconds or so was the noise of the engine. How could there have been silence in the cockpit?

The Last Few Moments

Given the controversy surrounding the horrific last few minutes of the ill-fated flight, the timing of the crash is a vital piece of information, so it is hard to understand how there can be such disparity between the official version and the evidence. The 9/11 Commission stated that the plane impacted the ground at 10:03 and eleven seconds, but a seismic study done by the US Army concluded the plane had crashed at 10:06 and 5 seconds. The FAA said the crash was at 10:07. These few moments are an eternity in terms of air disaster, which is often investigated in timelines as accurate as one hundredth of a second.

The sudden ending of the cockpit recordings at 10:02 a.m. left a vital gap of around four minutes that seems hard to explain. However, one simple explanation would be if the plane's systems were destroyed at altitude, rather than at the point of impact with the ground.

On the ground, the scene was even more confusing. Debris was found over an area as wide as eight miles, something not expected from a plane being flown deliberately into the ground. Local residents described finding clothing, books and human remains miles from the official crash site. One half-ton piece of engine was found over a mile away. How could it have got there?

Despite this, the established narrative of a suicidal death plunge was quickly in place. The FBI cordoned off a huge area around the crash scene, as well as at Indian Lake, nearly three miles away, and another area, some six miles from the crash site. Brian Cabell of CNN reported this information live from the scene on 9/11. However, there was little or no wind to spread debris around. Planes falling undamaged from the sky don't leave debris six miles away.

Press helicopters were quickly moved on, but not before they had broadcast images of the impact site from above, which showed a very small gouge in the ground, when compared to the massive size of the airplane, and disturbingly little evidence of anything resembling parts of a commercial aircraft. This lack of physical evidence is perhaps the most disturbing part of the story of flight 93. Huge planes leave devastatingly clear evidence of the trauma suffered. But in Shanksville there was nothing.

Eyewitnesses

It does not necessarily follow that an airborne strike on flight 93 would have been seen from the ground. The area around Shanksville is rural and sparsely populated, and the plane was at considerable altitude (at least ten thousand feet) prior to its plunge from the skies.

However, some local residents gave statements that appeared to confirm the idea of a missile strike.

Ernie Stuhl, the Mayor of Shanksville, said, "I know of two people—I will not mention names—that heard a missile. They both live very close, within a couple hundred yards . . . this one fellow's served in Vietnam and he says he's heard them, and he heard one that day." Mayor Stuhl subsequently changed his story.

Brad Boyer was fishing on Indian Lake, some three miles from the official crash site, and said he heard a huge bang before the sky "rained garbage."

Laura Temyer of Hooversville said, "I didn't see the plane but I heard the plane's engine. Then I heard a loud thump that echoed off the hills and then I heard the plane's engine. I heard two more loud thumps and didn't hear the plane's engine any more after that." She added that people she knew in state law enforcement had privately told her that the plane was shot down, and that the large debris field was due to decompression sucking objects out of the plane.

One witness heard two loud bangs before seeing the plane turn downward. Another heard a sound that was "not quite right" after which the plane "dropped all of a sudden, like a stone."

Many on the ground also reported seeing the plane upside down in the air, testimony that is consistent with a missile strike. The heat-seeking air-to-air Sidewinder missiles carried by an F-16 would have targeted the hottest point on the plane—the engines. After a missile strike, the plane could potentially have flown onward for a short period before beginning to break up in the air. A Korean 747 was hit by two Russian missiles in 1983 and continued to fly (in a fashion) for two more minutes.

On the ground, many people also saw a second, smaller plane flying low at the crash site just seconds before and after the impact.

Lee Purbaugh was just half a mile away, and the sole person to see flight 93 as well as the white jet. He said the plane circled the area twice, then flew off at high speed.

At least six other witnesses on the ground saw the second plane, described as a small, white jet with rear engines and no discernible markings. Among them was Susan McElwain, who stated she saw a small white jet swoop low over her minivan and disappear over a hilltop. She said the plane had no markings but it was "definitely military. It definitely wasn't one of those executive jets." The plane was travelling very fast but barely made any sound. A few seconds after it disappeared behind some trees she heard a huge explosion and saw a fireball. Not knowing about the day's events, McElwain assumed that the small plane had crashed and called 911. It was only later, when authorities claimed that there had been no other planes nearby, that she became concerned.

"The FBI came and talked to me and said there was no plane around . . . but I saw it, and it was there before the crash, and it was forty feet above my head . . . they didn't want my story—nobody here did."

The FBI subsequently said that the plane was a Fairchild Falcon-20 business jet that had been requested, after the crash, to descend to five thousand feet to establish where the crash site was. But none of this corresponds with the type of plane seen by those on the ground, its altitude, or the fact that witnesses saw the jet before flight 93 crashed.

Additionally, if the plane was a business jet, it would be vital to find and interview its passengers and pilots, given that they had the first viewing of the crashed airliner. But these individuals and the plane have never been identified. One could also ask why the private plane was still airborne, given that all US flights had been ordered to land forty minutes previously.

In fact, virtually all eyewitness accounts supported the idea of a missile strike, but if anything, the evidence on the ground provided even stronger information.

On the Ground

Right from the start, there was a problem. Although there was a large gouge in the earth at what the FBI said was the crash scene, there was no plane. No engine, no nose, no wings. No fuselage, no destroyed baggage. No bodies.

Video footage taken from a news helicopter showed a hole in the ground, but there was no evidence of a Boeing 757 crashing anywhere near the site which was cordoned off. The few civilians who were initially allowed on site all told the same mystifying tale; that all evidence of a plane had vanished.

A Fox News reporter interviewed a photographer called Chris Konicki, who had been to the crash site and said he saw "nothing that you could distinguish that a plane had crashed there," and that the hole was "twenty to fifteen feet . . . ten feet wide"; just a fraction of what would be expected.

Assistant Fire Chief Rick King drove the first truck to reach the crash site, but said that when he arrived he thought, *where is this plane, and where are the people?* The local emergency workers he repeatedly sent back into the woods to find the debris came back empty handed, saying, "Rick, there's nothing."

Wally Miller, the Somerset county coroner, said, "It looked like somebody just dropped a bunch of metal out of the sky. It looked like someone took a scrap truck, dug a 10-foot ditch and dumped trash into it. I stopped being coroner after about twenty minutes, because there were no bodies there. I have not, to this day, seen a single drop of blood."

Lyle Szupinka from the Pennsylvania State police geared himself up mentally to see appalling scenes of devastation, but on arrival was "surprised to find that I saw no human remains, none whatsoever."

Patrick Madigan, the head of the Somerset barracks state police said, "It did not, in any way, shape or form, look like a plane crash."

Photographer Scott Spangler said, "I was looking for anything that said tail, wing, plane, metal. There was nothing."

In fact nearly every person who was first on site reported being bewildered by the complete lack of evidence of a plane or its passengers. Local state troopers reported finding no debris larger than a phone book. John Maslak, a

Shanksville resident, said, "There was no way. The hole wasn't big enough, and there was nothing there."

Despite the plane being heavily loaded with jet fuel, those on the ground found no soil contamination or evidence of a huge fire consistent with burning aviation fuel. Soil and water samples showed no contamination from the seven thousand gallons estimated to have been on board.

The FBI line, quickly established, was that the frightening speed of impact had obliterated the plane and buried it into the ground, but this is nonsense, and there is no precedent for such a disappearing act. Nothing like that has ever been seen before at the site of a major plane crash.

Sadly, we have plenty of examples where large commercial airliners have impacted the ground at full speed. All left a trail of destruction that showed obvious signs of what had come from the skies. Fuselage. Engines. Bodies still in their seats.

While an uncontrolled descent from ten thousand feet (which appears to be the altitude at which the flight was cruising) is a terrifying prospect, it does not necessarily make plausible the notion that the wreckage entirely buried itself into the ground. Compare that hypothesis with the well known footage from Lockerbie in 1998. That plane was destroyed by a bomb at thirty thousand feet, yet on the ground there were clearly recognizable large pieces of plane, including the nose, fuselage, and engines. Yet we are told that in this instance the ground had just consumed the plane and, as fire chief Terry Schaffer put it, "the earth literally opened, swallowed the aircraft and closed up."

To say this strains credulity is an understatement. Even if it were true, the hole in the ground was entirely too small. The holes in the side of the World Trade Center were large, and the rough outline of the planes that hit them, but the gouge in the ground at Shanksville was consistently described as being in the region of 15–20 feet long and 8–10 feet deep, absurdly out of kilter with the impact of a commercial airliner.

To believe the official account we have to accept that a plane 125 feet wide, 155 feet long and weighing more than one hundred tons caused a 15–20 foot hole in the ground, and was swallowed (and back-filled) so completely on impact that no evidence of the plane whatsoever was visible to the naked eye by those first on the scene. Utterly absurd.

All that was found by civilian first responders was paper, mostly mail. However, as elsewhere on 9/11, among these effects FBI agents reported finding incriminating items implicating the alleged terrorists. ID and drivers licenses, a passport, and various other identifying items were produced, including a checklist outlining methods of blending in, such as shaving off one's beard. These remarkably resilient items were used as evidence to tie the terrorists to the flight and impact site.

The scene of the crash itself was carefully cleared and cleaned up by the FBI with astonishing and seemingly inappropriate haste. The site was quickly cordoned off and a heavy FBI security presence established. Within twelve days the FBI claimed to have recovered 95 percent of the plane from the impact site. The crater was filled in, and topsoil spread above. Damaged trees were cut down and mulched. Within two weeks the FBI was gone, and so was nearly all evidence of a plane crash.

Other sites near the purported impact location were also cordoned off by the FBI, and those sites were not visited at all by local residents or filmed by the media. Some locals believe that the plane came down just a few miles away, perhaps around Imgrund Mountain Road and New Baltimore Road, an area that matches the distance (6 miles) from Shanksville mentioned by Brian Cabell of CNN in his report on 9/11, in which he said a second area had been cordoned off. The road off route 30 which led to the secondary crash site was cordoned off for weeks after the crash, preventing anyone from accessing the area.

Why Cover Up a Shoot-Down

It is extremely hard to pin down the exact time when orders were finally given to intercept and shoot down commercial jets, especially since these orders appear to have come from a vice president without the authority to do so. However, the best estimate is that the order was given around 9:56 a.m., ten minutes before flight 93 hit the ground.

According to the official account, Dick Cheney was told that there was a plane headed toward Washington, and asked, "There is a fighter in the area, do we engage?" Cheney responded yes. As the fighter got closer to flight 93, Cheney was asked twice more, and confirmed permission to engage. Where the official story diverges from the evidence is the claim that fighter jets did not have the chance to engage the commercial aircraft before it crashed.

Clearly, even according to the official account, fighters were minutes or even seconds away as the passengers tried to wrest back control. Even President Bush knew how close things were—when informed that flight 93 was down, he asked, "Did we shoot it down or did it crash?"

Immediately after the crash, Dick Cheney in particular seems to have been remarkably clear on what had just happened. Despite the Pentagon not confirming whether the flight had or had not been shot down for at least another ninety minutes, and evidence of a passenger revolt coming to light even later on, Cheney, in a bunker under the White House, said on hearing the plane had crashed, "I think an act of heroism just took place on that plane."

He couldn't have had a clue what he was talking about. But his words must have echoed around the room. Cheney was in charge, and if this is what he said had just happened, then we were all agreed that that is how the story had ended.

But Cheney was wrong. The evidence, including debris strewn over a large area, eye-witness accounts and a total lack of what would normally be expected at a crash site on the ground, clearly points towards a missile strike on flight 93, which then broke up in the air. There seems no other rational explanation as to how an intact plane plummeting precipitously through the sky could have left a half-ton piece of engine a mile from the crash site, nor how a site which the FBI said was the location of a major plane crash showed no evidence of such an event whatsoever.

Even if the plane had been flown in such a way by the hijackers that the g-forces caused a catastrophic breakdown, the idea of the plane breaking up in the sky is anathema to the central story we have been told: that what was found in Shanksville was a plane (buried into the earth) that hit the ground in one piece.

In all likelihood, it was Major Rick Gibney who fired one or two Sidewinder missiles at the plane. The impact of the missiles on the plane's engines would have disabled the mechanics of the plane, but may not have mortally wounded the fuselage. The plane may have continued to fly for a few minutes before breaking up in the air, raining debris over a wide area. The plane was downed by the US military, and the media were directed to a small impact area, distracting them from the main crash site that held incontrovertible evidence of a missile strike.

While a shoot-down would have proved an appalling moment for those—political and military personnel—who had to make that decision, it's very likely that given the events of the day, the public would have responded sympathetically in relation to the decisions made. America had, after all, just been the subject of the worst terrorist attack in history. This fourth plane, clearly hijacked, was headed towards the nation's capital with undeniably evil intent. Shooting it down would have been dreadful, but understandable.

Covering up a shoot-down would perhaps be the reflex action of any politician, but to then continue to cover it up, and to go to great lengths to ensure that the cover-up was maintained, smacks of something more than just appalling political cynicism, the kind that in itself should have you removed from office. It suggests there may be other reasons not to simply tell the public the truth.

It is possible to look at this event from another perspective, and to suggest that the flight may have been shot down because the passengers were indeed taking control. If one believes that the other aspects of the 9/11 story indicate a military and political coup, it's easy to suggest that the idea of live hijackers in custody would have been a fundamental risk to the entire narrative of the day.

Even if you believe the official version of events on 9/11, live hijackers facing trial would potentially have had hugely embarrassing stories to tell. As we will see, at the very least these included funding from Saudi Arabia and connections to the Saudi royal family. Additionally, an undamaged plane could have been shown to have flight termination remote control equipment on board.

Shooting 93 down removed those risks.

CHAPTER FOUR

AMERICA'S DEFENSES

FAA Before 9/11

The FAA is the body charged with managing civilian air travel in the United States. In the event of a hijacking it is meant to communicate quickly with NORAD (its military counterpart), to effect a response.

Throughout the 1990s, a cozy relationship with the industry they were meant to regulate meant that the FAA repeatedly failed to force airlines to instigate the FAA's own mandated improvements to security screening, such as reinforcing cockpit doors and improved pre-flight screening, measures that might well have thwarted the 9/11 attacks.

America's lax and ineffective regulatory bodies, and a systemic political culture of industrial lobbying and regulatory compromise meant that this was just another example of public safety taking a back seat to profits.

Scrambling Fighters

Air traffic control over the East Coast of America is a complex network of complementary bodies, running the world's most congested and highly controlled airspace. Commercial airliners with transponders on board have to compete for space with smaller civilian and military aircraft. Small errors can risk unimaginable disaster, so adherence to the rules and procedures is vital, every minute of every day.

Every commercial plane taking to the sky has a flight plan, in which pilots are supposed to hit "fixes" (points on the map) with pinpoint accuracy. If a plane deviates by fifteen degrees, or just two miles, the FAA calls the plane and notifies NORAD, who begin activating emergency measures. Doubt and hesitation are not permitted. FAA hijacking regulations state that if you are in any doubt, handle it as though it were an emergency.

Sometimes planes leave their flight course for a number of reasons. Bad weather occasionally needs to be quickly avoided, but often the issue is minor human error. Radios transmit on the wrong frequency or don't work properly, maps are misread. But in each instance the FAA activates emergency measures and informs NORAD, which begins scrambling fighter jets to intercept the errant flights. Once intercepted, there are a number of escalating measures fighters can take to establish whether the plane is hijacked or just off course.

This is much more commonplace than you might think. In 2000, fighter planes were scrambled 129 times. Between September 2000 and June 2001, it happened sixty-seven times. Most times the fighters don't get off the ground, as the issues are resolved in minutes. However, the processes are there, and regularly used. After 9/11, NORAD spokesman Major Mike Snyder told the *Boston Globe* that fighters routinely intercepted aircraft. It normally takes less than ten minutes for an issue to be identified and passed from the FAA to NORAD.

No approval from the White House or other such agency is required for military interception, so as to remove unnecessary layers of administration. Jets need to be in the skies quickly, and the less people involved the better. This worked well for around thirty years. That was, until June 1, 2001, when Defense Secretary Donald Rumsfeld, apparently at the behest of Dick Cheney, made a curious but crucial change to the long-standing protocols. Where previously the chain of command for launching military aircraft to deal with a domestic hijacking bypassed the secretary of defense, the new document (Joint Chiefs Instruction CJCSI3610.01A) now required any request for the scrambling of aircraft to go to the secretary of defense for approval. This effectively sidelined the generals, who had always had the power to shoot down hijacked aircraft. Now the fighters couldn't scramble without Rumsfeld's say so.

As a result of this change, scrambles fell from their usual number of seven to eight per month to zero between June 1 and September 11 2001.

With the secrecy of the Pentagon, it's impossible to know precisely how this affected America's air defenses on 9/11, but it seems at best a distinctly odd change to have made, given the successful operation of US air defense over the previous three decades. This procedural change in June is especially important in light of the fact that quickly scrambling fighter jets became so very vital to the defense of the nation just three months later.

If Rumsfeld's new protocol was followed (and the army lives and breathes protocol), then the change to the rules and Rumsfeld's own bizarre behavior on 9/11 seem to chime with the idea of a stand-down, as Rumsfeld, now a vital cog in hijacking interception procedures, was initially unavailable and in a meeting that continued despite the carnage unfolding, and then unavailable due to his inexplicable decision to walk around the Pentagon to see the damage to the building, taking himself out of the chain of command for perhaps the most vital hour in modern American history.

At the very least, protocol changes meant that on 9/11, while interception was still possible, Rumsfeld was the most important person in America, and his absence in the key minutes during which the attacks were underway contributed significantly to the failure of previously routine measures providing any kind of defense against the attacks.

On September 12, 2001, they went back to the old scrambling protocol. That's how it's managed today.

FAA on 9/11

If there was as much FAA incompetence on 9/11 as the official account implies, then evidence of regular and institutional incompetence when routine emergencies arose in the months and years prior to 9/11 would have surfaced. There is no such evidence. How could a system that normally worked so well have completely broken down on that one day?

One factor may have been that, as in so many instances on 9/11, most of the agency's senior staff were far away, at a conference in Canada.

In the days following 9/11 the official story changed to indicate that fighters had indeed been sent up quickly, but had arrived at the scene too late. The story then changed again, to suggest that the planes were up in good time but had been sent in the wrong direction, lost in a fog of confusion as to where the attacks were coming from. But there was no confusion—billions were watching the World Trade Center towers burn, Manhattan was clearly under attack. It was obvious where the fighters needed to be.

However, once the attacks began, the FAA was simply not a factor in any of the subsequent events. They knew flight 11 had been hijacked before any of the other three planes had been, and before flight 93 had even left the ground. Yet no measures were taken to alert pilots until it was too late.

There has been a long-running blame-game since 9/11, with the FAA claiming they told NORAD of the hijackings almost immediately, and NORAD claiming inexplicable delays in the FAA reporting the emergencies to them. One of them is lying. However, the headquarters of the airlines involved should also have been reporting to NORAD the moment they knew of the hijackings (which would roughly have been simultaneous with the FAA), and appear not to have done so either.

Thus a crucial period emerges in which the FAA was in receipt of reports that a major terrorist attack was in place, but aircraft were not scrambled. This time period was the difference between the attacks succeeding unchallenged, and the chance of stopping them.

The key military control meeting on the morning of 9/11 was at the National Military Command Center (NMCC) at the Pentagon. The intra-agency teleconference there was meant to coordinate the nation's response. At the NMCC, the FAA's representative Rayford Brooks had no access to the decision-makers at the head of his organization and "no situational awareness." The leadership of the FAA and NORAD appear to have had no contact with each other during the entire time of crisis.

In fact, the only decisive action within the FAA was by a handful of relatively low-level employees, who acted on their own initiative.

If anything, it appears that it was the Secret Service who managed to order the scrambling of fighter jets from the District of Columbia Air National Guard to protect the White House.

At 9:26 a.m., the FAA issued the order to ground all planes over the continental US, including military and law enforcement flights, an order that had never been implemented since the first powered flights in 1903. By 9:45 a.m., just nineteen minutes later, all civilian planes—4,452 of them—had been ordered to land. The order most likely came from Norman Mineta and was passed to either Jane Garvey, head of the FAA, or Ben Sliney, the FAA's National Operations Manager and "the chess master of the air traffic system." Like so many others, Sliney was experiencing his first day on the job. The ban on military flights (that did not include fighter jets) was only lifted at 10:31 a.m.

What Should Have Happened

At 8:24 a.m., as American 11 radically changed direction toward Manhattan, ground control should have concluded that the plane was probably hijacked (the plane was not responding and had turned off its transponder), and handled the matter as if it was definitely a hijacking.

The controller was supposed to immediately contact NORAD, who should have scrambled jets from the nearest military airport. According to NORAD, it takes about one minute from the FAA call to the scrambling of fighters. F-16 fighters go from scramble order to twenty-nine thousand feet in only two and a half minutes and can then fly at 1,850 mph.

However, NORAD did not issue scramble orders until 8:46 a.m., twenty-two minutes after the first hijacking was known, and then inexplicably gave the order to Otis Air National Guard Base in Cape Cod, over 180 miles away, rather than to McGuire Air Force Base in New Jersey, only seventy miles from Manhattan.

Even then, there were seventeen minutes until the south tower was hit—plenty of time to intercept the second plane. But again there was an inexplicable delay as the planes spent nine minutes sitting on the tarmac awaiting orders, not in itself a long time, but in the context of the events of the day the difference between success and failure. One of the pilots remembered sitting in the cockpit, ready to go, and waiting for the order to scramble to arrive.

The two pilots scrambled to track flights 11 and 175 were Lieutenant Colonel Timothy Duffy and Major Daniel Nash. Duffy said in an interview he was in "full blower all the way." Such was the urgency the pilots reported going supersonic while at relatively low altitude, something that is normally avoided. Even allowing two and a half minutes to get into the air and up to full speed, the F-16s should have reached Manhattan in a maximum of eight more minutes—around the time of the second plane attack. Seemingly large distances are no problem for the fastest planes on earth. Yet NORAD's own reports say the planes took nineteen minutes to cover the distance, much longer than would have been expected.

Duffy did arrive over Manhattan in time to see the buildings collapse, but that was a long time after the damage was done. He reported being asked to look at the second tower (some time after the first one collapsed), and saying it appeared to be fine, with no leaning or visible signs of imminent collapse. Moments later, the building fell.

When fighters finally took position over Manhattan, they patrolled the skies for four hours. But by then, like so many other times in this story, it was too late.

FAA after 9/11

On June 4 2004 the FBI allowed a group of victims' families to hear audio tapes of American Airlines managers' and officials' response to the crisis. As with flight 93, the bereaved family members were forced to sign non-disclosure agreements and were not allowed to take notes, but on June 21, Gail Sheehy of the *New York Observer* reported some of the details, including the fact that on the morning of 9/11 American and United Airlines staff had decided to keep information about the hijackings to themselves, rather than inform others. Those who had heard the tapes reported that staff had said things like, don't spread this around, keep it close, and keep it quiet.

Some FAA recordings were not available, however, following the notorious actions of FAA Manager Kevin Delaney.

In the twenty-four hours after the attacks, at least six air-traffic controllers assembled to record their recollections of the day's events. The recordings were specifically made soon after the attacks, to allow law enforcement agencies to hear unvarnished firsthand accounts from those involved.

But before the recordings were listened to or transcribed, Delaney deliberately destroyed the audio tapes, breaking them into small pieces and putting them in several different bins around the New York Air Route Traffic Control Center in Ronkonkoma, where he worked. Delaney was suspended for twenty days, without pay, but filed an administrative appeal.

In the end, no one in the FAA chain of command was even disciplined for the manifest failures on 9/11 that at the very least might have given America a chance of intervening or stopping the attacks.

War Games

Incompetence, however, may be just one of the factors involved in delaying the FAA and NORAD's response. An unprecedented number of war games were taking place on the morning of 9/11 that caused confusion (at best) for those dealing with a situation that suddenly became very real.

A military leviathan like the US conducts drills, training exercises, and war games almost all the time. What was different about the war games on 9/11 was how numerous they were, how many of them mimicked the actual events that took place; how much confusion they caused and how some appear to have been re-scheduled from their originally planned dates to happen on or around September 11, for no obvious reason.

Militarily, war games provide training for personnel using mock real-world scenarios, but historically, war games and military exercises have often been used to provide cover for real plans, such as an invasion, a coup, or an ambush. With all of your assets in the right place, it's easy to switch from game to reality, and to not have to move the pieces on the chessboard at all. Alternately, simulations can provide the perfect means of suppressing a normal response to real-world events, confusing those involved and making key personnel unsure if something is real or a game. Exercises also assist in keeping the number of active participants in a plot very small, since a much larger group of people actively involved believe they are just training.

Many simulations and war games had been conducted in the years preceding 9/11 that closely tracked aspects of the events that day. NORAD had spent the previous few years conducting a number of military exercises positing actions that were startlingly similar to the events of 9/11, often using real aircraft. One war game had simulated the idea of a hijacked aircraft being crashed into the World Trade Center and another into the Pentagon.

These simulations also contradict the outrageous suggestion—made across the board by senior staff in the Bush administration—that no one had ever even imagined scenarios such as planes flying into buildings or an airborne attack on the Pentagon. These exact situations had been imagined and simulated many times. While it is perhaps (and only perhaps) understandable that for political reasons, these senior staff felt the need to profess astonishment that the US had been taken by surprise, it is astounding that they chose to tell such boldfaced lies when information in the public domain so clearly refuted what they said; or that they felt so comfortable telling these lies without fear of ridicule.

It is likely that all of the overlapping exercises around 9/11 were coordinated by senior staff at the Pentagon. Some certainly involved the CIA. Knowing as we do now that the US military and intelligence communities had received numerous credible, timely, and specific warnings about the possibility of a devastating terrorist attack inside the US, the decision to proceed with at least two major annual air training exercises (and many others) was a strange one, considering that the system was "blinking red." These exercises crucially depleted US air defenses in the exact areas where they were needed the most on 9/11.

War games on 9/11 were also unusually intrusive toward the civilian air sector. There are numerous recordings of air traffic controllers, FAA staff, and others receiving the developing news and wondering out loud if this was "part of the exercise."

Some of the war games on 9/11 involved inserting false blips on civilian radars. This made the already highly complex task of managing the East Coast's civilian air traffic much more difficult, as air controllers struggled to work out which readings were real and which were not.

When NEADS (the Northeast Air Defense Sector, who monitor the skies over the US and Canada) was contacted by Boston flight control and told of a hijacked aircraft heading towards New York, the first response was, *is this real world or exercise?* The phone call was handed to Lieutenant Colonel Dawn Deskins, who later said that initially everybody at NEADS thought the call was part of an exercise called Vigilant Guardian. The exercise had covered their radar screens with simulated readings, something unprecedented in civilian air safety. These fake blips weren't removed until after 9:30 a.m., long after the second WTC impact, and minutes before the Pentagon was hit. Frustrated controllers, used to speaking in clipped tones, shouted "Get rid of that crap!" as they tried to decipher real from imaginary.

Many NORAD and military staff also reported that during the initial stages of the attack they thought the real events were part of the exercise, or that the exercise had started early. With so many false blips on their screens, there was much confusion as to how many planes were off course or hijacked, with military and civilian staff claiming that at some points the number ranged from eleven to twenty-nine.

Major James Fox, a fighter pilot, became exasperated in trying to get information on where to fly, saying, "I've never seen so much real-world stuff happen during an exercise."

Whether intentional or not, it's clear that the exercises taking place caused a great deal of confusion at the start of America's response to the events of 9/11. In order for the attacks to succeed, America's air defenses had to fail for a period not much longer than one hundred minutes. Even five minutes lost to confusion over whether events were real or a drill meant five percent less chance of successfully defending the US from attack.

War Games in Progress

Although war game dates and details are mostly kept from the public, the sheer number of war games in progress on or around 9/11 (all under the watch of General Ralph Eberhart, who reported directly to Donald Rumsfeld) appears unprecedented. And although we may never get a full account of the various drills and war games taking place, given the magnitude of events on that day we do now have a broad understanding of the number and nature of many of the war games underway when disaster struck.

These included Amalgam Virgo, which involved the hypothetical scenario of a cruise missile attack by a rogue agency from a barge moored off the East Coast. Osama bin Laden was pictured on the cover of the exercise proposal. The 2002 version of this exercise was to have involved FBI agents impersonating hijackers taking over two civilian aircraft simultaneously.

There was also Vigilant Guardian—a week-long NORAD exercise posing an imaginary crisis to US airspace, which necessitated fighter jets normally defending the East Coast being removed to distant parts of the country, false blips being inserted on radar screens, and military aircraft posing as hijacked civilian flights. The actual events of 9/11 closely mimicked those posed by the training exercise, and although some of the details remain secret, it is suspected that the drill included the idea of a terrorist attack on the World Trade Center. What is clear is that the exercise itself demonstrably confused NORAD's personnel in attempting to respond to events that had quickly become real.

When Richard Clarke (the Bush administration's anti-terrorism "tsar") called Acting Chairman of the Joint Chiefs of Staff Richard Myers at 9:28 a.m., Clarke said he assumed NORAD had already scrambled fighters and AWACs, but Myers replied that it was not a pretty picture, and that because they were in the middle of "Vigilant Warrior" (presumably a mistaken reference to Vigilant Guardian) just two fighters were in the sky, with another two due for takeoff soon.

The "Warrior" aspect may have referred to Amalgam Warrior, another exercise taking place, which included "live fly" exercises where planes were actually in the air pretending to be hijacked.

Northern Vigilance—a NORAD exercise which ran from 9–11 September, deployed an unconfirmed number of fighter jets to Alaska and Northern Canada (as far from the events of 9/11 as possible on home soil) for an exercise repelling a fictional attack from Russia. When NORAD was contacted by the FAA (saying a hijacking was in progress and asking for help), any simulated information (false blips on the radar screen) was ordered to be removed, but this appears to have only taken place after 9:30 a.m. At the very least, it seems likely that false blips on an already crowded radar screen, being frantically scanned by air traffic controllers looking for multiple hijacked aircraft, can hardly have helped reduce confusion.

According to the official account, because of Northern Vigilance, on 9/11 there were just fourteen fighter jets on alert in the whole of North America (two each in seven bases), with no fighters stationed at the bases closest to the most obvious terrorist targets—New York and Washington. America's capital and its largest city were defended by just four fighter jets.

Global Guardian was a nuclear war (or Armageddon) exercise staged annually by Stratcom (United States Strategic Command, the body charged with nuclear weapon control and the military's space and satellite information). The exercise was managed from Offutt Air Force Base, where Brent Scowcroft and Warren Buffett (among others) were arriving on E4-B doomsday planes just as the attacks commenced. The exercise involved a heightened state of alert and readiness for missile operators, as well as planes and submarines at some of America's most significant nuclear installations.

In addition to putting the most integral components of America's military arsenal on high alert at precisely the same time as the attacks, the exercise also meant that at least three of America's four E-4B doomsday planes, specifically built for times of great national crisis, were likely airborne when the terrorist attacks commenced.

Global Guardian was always staged in October or November of each year. In 2001, the date was changed to the week of September 11. By 2002, it was back to its usual October timeslot.

The National Reconnaissance Office (NRO) was running Able Danger, an exercise involving a simulated hijacked plane crashing into the main tower at their headquarters in Chantilly, Virginia. The simulation was run by the CIA's John Fulton and a team of agency colleagues. The exercise was designed to look at the efficacy of not just observing and fighting the terrorists," but manipulating them during the hijacking.

Able Warrior, an exercise run in conjunction with Able Danger, pitted two teams against each other in a terrorism training exercise.

Although the NRO exercise involved a hijacked plane crashing into a building, and began at 9:00 a.m. on September 11, 2001, an NRO spokesman called it "just an incredible coincidence." Coincidence or not, Able Danger meant that NRO offices were being evacuated just as the actual events of 9/11 were taking place. The net effect of this evacuation was to temporarily blind US intelligence to any images from satellites, and to take one of the largest of America's seventeen intelligence agencies entirely out of the picture.

In fact, there is a strong case to argue that the NRO headquarters were the control center for the entire event. The NRO operates many of America's spy satellites, is staffed by the military and CIA, and is based just two miles from Washington Dulles Airport, where one of the hijacked planes took off. This confluence of intelligence and military communities left the NRO perfectly placed to run an operation that involved training exercises designed to confuse and slow normal defenses, and a military response that was designed to fail.

Taken together, the war-games and training exercises taking place on 9/11:

- Evacuated the nation's key satellite and communications hub's headquarters building and staff, just at the moment when they were most required.
- Inserted false blips on civilian radars, confusing air traffic controllers and ensuring that tracking the various threats was nearly impossible
- Moved most of the fighter jets normally charged with defending the East Coast of the US to the most distant possible areas of land within the North American continent.

- Had numerous falsely hijacked military planes in the air at the same time as the attacks took place, in roughly the same locations as the actual hijacked aircraft.
- Put America's nuclear arsenal on a heightened state of alert.

All of these were, you must believe, extraordinary coincidences.

Even assets still in place were hindered. Three F-16 fighter planes stationed at Andrews Air Force Base, just twelve miles from Washington, were on an unusual training mission in North Carolina when the first WTC attack took place. Atlantic City fighters were on a training mission over the Atlantic Ocean. The planes were quickly returned to Washington, but took off without any missiles on board and did not start patrolling the skies until 10:45 a.m., by which point the attack was over.

More key assets were as far from the action as possible on the morning of 9/11. The FBI and CIA were conducting a terrorist training exercise in Monterey, California, meaning that when all aircraft were grounded across the United States, many of the most experienced anti-terrorist and special operations agents were stranded on the other side of the country, and unable to get to the crime scene for the crucial first few days.

Across America, civilian and military telephone and cellphone services failed for most of the day. Although the networks would have encountered more phone traffic on 9/11 than perhaps ever before, even secure lines and those used by the Pentagon worked intermittently at best. This was reminiscent of the events around the assassination of John F. Kennedy; when Washington's phone system failed for at least an hour immediately after the president was assassinated. From one perspective, downing phone networks would allow for the effective control of information in the key few hours during which the attacks took place. One government official said America was "deaf, dumb, and blind" for most of the day. This may have been by design.

CHAPTER FIVE

BUILDING 7

The story of 9/11 contains many contradictions and reasons to suspect foul play, but it is the collapse of 7 World Trade Center that is widely regarded as the single most questionable event of that day—the "smoking gun" of 9/11—since it was entirely without precedent and so closely resembled something we are all familiar with: controlled demolition.

The World Trade Center was a complex of buildings, with the north and south towers (1 WTC and 2 WTC, respectively) being the most prominent by far. The third largest building in the complex was Building 7, completed in 1987 at forty-seven stories high. Despite looking small next to the twin towers, Seven would have been the tallest building in thirty-three states.

Building 7 was set 108 meters from the north tower and even further from the south tower. Because of the distance, it sustained much less damage from the collapse of the two towers than Buildings 3, 4, 5 & 6, all of which were devastated and subsequently demolished, as they were so badly damaged they could not be made safe. However, none collapsed on 9/11, despite enduring raging fires.

Because Building 7 collapsed seven hours after the twin towers (and for various other reasons), the event is much less widely known than the two spectacular disasters in New York that morning, and for the most part remains a forgotten footnote in history. Incredibly, a Zogby poll taken in 2006 reported that nearly half of all Americans were entirely unaware that there had been a third building collapse on 9/11.

Seven was a huge building, with two million square feet of office space. It was informally known as the Salomon Brothers Building, as the investment bank was the major tenant, occupying thirty-seven floors. Dick Cheney and Donald Rumsfeld had been on the advisory board of the company (both resigned ten months before 9/11 to take up their political posts).

As with all modern skyscrapers, the tower was extremely sturdy and highly redundant (if one part failed, the load transferred to the others), with twenty-four huge steel columns and trusses, as well as fifty-seven perimeter columns. Forty thousand tons of structural steel supported the weight of the building.

Not only had Building 7 not been hit by a plane, the office fires that we are told were powerful enough to cause its complete collapse were in fact relatively small (when compared to other large building fires), and did not burn for a long period.

The contortions of logic through which the US government and its agencies have gone, in order to prove something as unlikely as fire-induced collapse, have only served to reinforce the view that we have been told a lie, and that further lies have been concocted so as to sustain the unsustainable.

Early Reports of Collapse

The evacuation of Building 7 began before the second twin tower was hit. There was much confusion and fear that another plane might be closing in—one firefighter arriving on the scene was told that the evacuation was due to a possible third hijacked plane in the area.

The scene around the collapsed twin towers was one of utter devastation, but by the middle of the day it was clear to everyone that the attacks themselves had ended. Building 7 had been damaged by falling debris, and it is thought that office fires were started by the damage sustained during the twin tower collapses. The building's sprinkler system failed to operate.

7 WTC contained electrical generators and five large fuel tanks containing thirty-six thousand gallons of diesel fuel on the first floor and below ground level. These held a great deal of potential energy, but there was no sign of raging diesel fires at any point during the day.

The fires that did burn inside the building (following the twin tower collapses) appear to have burned out by midafternoon. Very little smoke was evident, and no sign of structural weakness was visible, right up to the moment the building began falling. Nevertheless, several media sources predicted the building's collapse prior to it happening, and some reported that the building had actually collapsed well before it did.

CNN reported the collapse of "a fifty story building" at the World Trade Center (7 was the only building that height in the area) at 10:45 a.m. Later, at around four in the afternoon (more than an hour before the building fell), BBC and CNN news began reporting that 7 World Trade Center had collapsed.

The BBC reporter on the scene, Jane Standley, appeared in a live report to London, saying the building had collapsed fully twenty-three minutes before it actually did. The still-standing building was clearly visible over Standley's left shoulder in the live feed. CNN began reporting a possible collapse seventy minutes before it happened. During the next hour CNN's news ticker repeated that the building was "on fire, may collapse." Four and a half minutes before the actual collapse, this message changed to "Building #7 ablaze, poised to collapse." Fox News 5 also carried a report of the collapse around a minute before it happened. Clearly the word was getting out, but the building stood stock still, and showed no sign of structural failure as the news media reported its demise.

This was the most difficult of days for TV news teams. Both CNN and the BBC have explained away the mistake, essentially saying that it was one of a number of errors made in the fog of confusion during a dramatic day. But making a simple reporting error on a crazy day is not the same as making a reporting error, then the event actually happening. That is an entirely different thing. This was not a minor technical error either; this was the collapse of a forty-seven-story building.

It's impossible not to conclude that the broadcasters predicting that the building would come down (or prematurely reporting that it had) were reporting the story because someone had told them that this was what had happened. If that is the case, then it is vital to know who the source of the information was, and how the source knew that the building was going to fall.

Building 7's collapse made engineering history as the first time a steel-framed building had ever collapsed due to fire. However, the structural failures said to have brought the building down happened internally. No visible collapse or sagging was seen from outside the building. This should make us highly suspicious of whoever it was that started propagating the idea of an imminent collapse, as there were no external indications that this might happen.

It is not clear exactly when the area around the building was formally evacuated. The best evidence suggests around 2:00 p.m (three hours before the collapse), and the suggestion that the building was at risk appears to have come from Mayor Rudy Giuliani's Office of Emergency Management, the same office that had earlier told Giuliani that the twin towers would collapse well before they did. Someone in Giuliani's office appears to have had more foresight than most, or known something the rest of us did not.

Between two and three in the afternoon, police chief Daniel Nigro established a clearance zone around the tower. Nigro refused to allow firefighters to enter the building and try to extinguish the fires, apparently because he feared collapse. Assistant Chief Frank Fellini also told a colleague that the building was in danger of imminent collapse.

Around 4:00 p.m., photographer Tom Franklin got near the building and saw firemen falling back in what appeared to be preparation for a collapse. Footage from ground level shows firefighters telling the cameraman to retreat, because "the whole thing is about to blow up," and to "keep your eye on that building, it'll be coming down." MSNBC reporter Ashleigh Banfield recounted that several fire officers had told her that 7 WTC was going to go down next. Hundreds of firefighters were positioned, hours in advance, for the collapse to happen. FDNY firefighter Thomas Donato said that he was in place, waiting for it to come down.

In fact, in interviews after 9/11, sixty firefighters mentioned an early knowledge of the collapse of 7 WTC up to four hours before the building fell.

It is hard to reconcile the confidence with which so many on the scene felt that the collapse was going to happen with the unprecedented nature of the event. If you adhere to the official story, you believe that the damage caused to the twin towers by the planes and fires eventually led to their collapse, but 7 WTC only suffered minor damage from these two collapsed buildings. Virtually no structural damage at all was witnessed, so in the case of Building 7, what officially brought the tower down was fire, and fire alone. This is highly problematic.

On 9/11, many of the news anchors covering the attacks initially remarked how similar it all looked to a deliberate demolition. They would rapidly stop voicing such sentiments. As with the twin towers, there were reports of explosions inside the building many hours prior to its collapse. One man in particular gave compelling evidence.

Barry Jennings

Unlike in the twin towers, the number of people inside Building 7 was very limited. The building evacuation had started before the second tower had been hit, and just two people (outside of firefighters and police) were reported to have been left inside: Michael Hess, an employee of the City of New York, and Barry Jennings, who worked for the New York City Housing Authority.

Both men had headed from the lobby to Rudolph Giuliani's emergency center on the 23rd floor and, finding it unattended, were told by an unnamed person to "leave right away." They started to exit the building via the stairs, but Jennings reported that on reaching the eighth floor there was a huge explosion that caused the floor underneath them to give way. Jennings was left hanging, but managed to climb to safety. They then broke a window and called down for help. The explosion wasn't caused by the nearby tower collapses—Jennings confirmed that when they made it to the eighth floor, both of the twin towers were still standing.

After they were rescued by the fire department, both men were interviewed by the media and recounted their experiences. Both reported seemingly inexplicable explosions in the building. However, Hess subsequently backed away from his statements, and now says there were no such explosions. As an employee of the City of New York, and a senior appointee of Rudolph Giuliani, at the very least Hess's job may have been on the line, and his testimony is unreliable.

Barry Jennings' testimony appears more plausible but has always been problematic, if not devastating to the official story, since it is impossible to explain explosions through Building 7 at this point in the day. Jennings repeated his story to a number of media sources in the following years, and was interviewed for the final cut of the online documentary *Loose Change*, but asked for his testimony to be edited out, as he was concerned about losing his job and, he said, potentially endangering his family.

Barry Jennings died suddenly on August 19, 2008 at the age of 53, just two days before the National Institute of Standards and Technology (NIST) issued its report on the collapse of Building 7. It was a peculiarly timed death, and left Michael Hess as the only witness of events inside Building Seven.

Dylan Avery, the director of *Loose Change*, hired a private investigator to look into Jennings' death, but after a brief time the investigator told Avery that he had concluded that the death was a matter for the police. The investigator returned Avery's fee in full, and said never to contact him again.

As with others whose testimony proved problematic to the official story, Jennings death was untimely, to say the least.

Controlled Demolition

The collapse of Building 7 was caught from at least ten different vantage points, nearly all of them some distance away. In all shots, while the bottom of the building is not visible, most of the upper section is clearly in sight.

What is striking on viewing the footage is how the collapse started in an instant, and how the building came down in a straight line. For most of its journey downwards, the fall was so straight that it follows a ruler placed on a screen. The building had shown no signs of instability whatsoever until the instant the collapse started, so it can be assumed to have been structurally sound until the very moment of collapse initiation. This seems impossible to square with the testimony of firefighters on the scene, who were told to hang back as the building was about to collapse, several hours before it did.

Given that no steel-framed building in history, except on 9/11, has collapsed due to fire, we have to use theoretical calculations to examine the possibility that fire caused the collapse (there are no other examples to compare with), as an alternative to the more obvious conclusion that it was due to controlled demolition. When making a comparison, we find that the collapse had all of the characteristics of controlled demolition, and none of the (theoretical) characteristics of a fire-induced collapse. Namely:

- The penthouse and large roof-level air-conditioning that protruded from the top of the building were seen to kink and collapse a couple of seconds before the building structure began to fall. This clearly shows that the collapse of the building initiated in the center. In controlled demolition, the central columns are the first to be severed, and the roof often collapses inwards. The fires were nowhere near roof level, so could not possibly have caused this internal collapse.

- Squibs (horizontal puffs of smoke) were seen coming from the upper floors of the building, in sequence, just as the collapse began. This is something often seen when explosives are used.

- The building fell at nearly free-fall speed, not encountering any resistance whatsoever from the thousands of tons of steel and concrete below. The roof of the building fell to earth in around 6.6 seconds, when free-fall speed from that height would have been around six seconds. To put it another way, had a stone been dropped from the roof when the collapse began, it would have hit the ground within just half a second of when the roof of the building actually did.

- The building collapsed from the bottom. Most controlled demolition techniques involve severing the steel structure at the bottom, allowing the building to fall in on itself. Again, there is no evidence that there were fires at ground level, let alone the raging fires that would be required to make collapse even a theoretical possibility.

- The building came down in a straight line, almost exactly into its own footprint. The debris field was on average just twenty meters wider than the original footprint, barely damaging surrounding buildings. In controlled demolition, this is normally done to minimize damage to surrounding areas.

- The collapse created huge pyroclastic flows of concrete dust that billowed through the streets, much as had happened when the Twin Towers fell. These clouds again indicate that the structural concrete had been subject to enormous levels of energy that had pulverized and reduced the concrete to a very fine dust. This is not to be expected from an undamaged building structure falling on top of part of a building that has been damaged by fire, but is always seen as part of controlled demolitions. Pyroclastic flows can only be caused by extreme heat and energy—they are seen during volcanic eruptions, or when a space rocket is launched.

- As with the twin towers, molten metal was located in the basement levels of the wreckage. What could have caused metal to become molten, when the fires in the building were burning nothing but office furnishings?

In some ways, the straightness of the building's descent was the most important characteristic. You do not need to be an architect or physicist to realize that in order for the building to have come down in a precise straight line, the entire steel support structure would have needed to fail at exactly the same instant, across the entire breadth of the building. Had fires been more intense in one section of the building, causing beams to melt, the building would have fallen over, rather than come straight down. Given that there were eighty-one steel beams forming the supporting structure of the building, this is fanciful in the extreme.

Dan Rather, watching the collapse, said it was reminiscent of pictures we'd seen before when a building is deliberately destroyed by well-placed dynamite. Many other news anchors live on air said they were not sure if the collapse had been due to the building being weakened or if it had been deliberately brought down as a safety measure.

Those within the demolition industry would have recognized classic signs of their work. Daniel Jowenko, a renowned Dutch demolition expert, was famously shown the clip of Building 7 falling in 2006, without knowing it was footage taken on 9/11. Jowenko said it was obviously a controlled demolition carried out by a team of experts, but was incredulous when told that it was footage of a World Trade Center building on 9/11. He immediately understood the ramifications. The best he could say was, "Then they worked hard." Jowenko stood by his interpretation of the footage in the years that followed, but was killed in July 2011, in a single vehicle accident on a straight road.

All the evidence points toward 7 WTC having been brought down by controlled demolition. Fires, by way of explanation, are laughably inadequate, and make absolutely no sense whatsoever.

Given that the collapse was caused by controlled demolition, which is so obvious as to be entirely irrefutable, we are left looking for a way out, for something that still makes sense. Because without a viable explanation that supports the sacred notion that the 9/11 attacks were a bolt from the blue, the implications of Building 7's collapse lead us down a dark and frightening path.

Suspend disbelief for a moment. Perhaps controlled demolition was used, but the US government decided not to reveal that fact, for reasons involving national security that, we were to learn of, we might accept as something national security had demanded. But if that were the case, work on bringing the building down could only have started after the entirely unexpected airplane attacks that morning. The explosives would need to have been set in less than seven hours, by a qualified team which was at the ready, with a large amount of explosives close at hand, and with detailed maps of the building structure. All this inside a burning building, in an environment that was the very definition of unstable.

Controlled demolitions of large buildings take weeks or months to prepare, and are highly complex operations that only a small number of civilian businesses have the skills to do. All of this makes it completely unrealistic to suggest that explosives were laid during the day on 9/11 by people on our side, with the best intentions of national security and New Yorkers in mind.

All that is left is to conjecture that Osama bin Laden's operatives planted the explosives. But we're grasping at straws here.

What we're left with is increasingly absurd and circular perversions of logic, as we try to come to some—any—explanation other than what is as plain as can be. Building 7 of the World Trade Center was brought down by a controlled demolition, using explosives that had to have been planted before the air attacks on the twin towers earlier that day.

And that places us through the looking glass. Because if that is the case, then, excuse me, but what the fuck is going on? The attacks of 9/11 could not have been carried out by Osama bin Laden alone, and required demolition expertise and access to Building 7's infrastructure in the weeks before the attacks. Something is very, very wrong.

Larry Silverstein and His Tenants

The north and south towers at the World Trade Center were high-profile terrorism targets, and had been known to be so for many years. They were the
symbols of American capitalism and finance, although the buildings themselves were old and the tenant list was no longer stellar. However, Building 7
was much less familiar to people. It's worth asking why this particular building was so important that it needed to be destroyed.

The answer perhaps lies in the tenants that occupied much of the building, because 7 was far from an ordinary commercial tower block. As well
as operating as a command center for the entire WTC complex, tenants
included:

- A large field office for the Secret Service on the ninth and tenth floors.
- The largest CIA office outside of Washington, DC in the United
  States, a secret office only revealed by the disaster.
- Rudolph Giuliani's Emergency Command Center on the
  twenty-third floor, a $15 million hermetically sealed disaster
  coordination center built in 1996, with its own oxygen supply
  and state-of-the-art communications equipment. By all accounts
  it was not used at all, due to Building 7's proximity to the twin
  towers.
- The Securities and Exchange Commission (SEC), home to vast
  records of bank and other financial transactions, on floors 11–13.
  The building's collapse was a major setback in the investigation
  of some of America's largest corporate fraud cases, destroying
  around four thousand files concerning Wall Street crime
  investigations and documents that showed the relationship
  between Citigroup and the Worldcom bankruptcy, as well as
  those relating to the Enron scandal. The Secret Service also lost
  investigative documents, as did the CIA.
- The Department of Defense (DOD)
- The Internal Revenue Service (IRS)
- FEMA also had offices on twenty-third floor and were preparing
  for a biological warfare drill on September 12.

The building's contents were certainly known to be sensitive. After the collapse, the CIA ordered FBI agents to surround the entire building, in order
(they said) to secure secret documents and files.

Pull It

Perhaps keeping the true nature of 7's demise a secret was too much even for the building's owner.

In September 2002, Larry Silverstein participated in a PBS documentary, and while discussing the events of the day, in an unguarded moment said, "I remember getting a call from the fire department commander, telling me that they were not sure they were going to be able to contain the fire. And I said, 'you know we've had such terrible loss of life, maybe the smartest thing to do is pull it.' And they made that decision to pull, and we watched the building collapse."

It was a very strange thing to say. "Pull" is an industry term for demolish, although there is some debate as to whether it means "via explosives." However, without explosives, a building cannot and will not fall straight down. "Pull" was an expression used on 9/11—video captured before the collapse included workers saying they were getting ready to pull Building 7.

Silverstein's company issued a clarification three years later, stating that by "pull it," he had meant to pull the contingent of firefighters back from the building. But that's not what he said at all. Silverstein hadn't mention firefighters, and reports by FEMA and NIST stated that there was no firefighting effort at all at the building after 11:30 a.m., six hours before the collapse.

Why would Silverstein have been involved in the decision-making process in relation to Building 7's structural integrity? He was a property developer. And who started saying that the building was not safe and might collapse? Furthermore, why make a decision to pull, when all the evidence showed only two small areas of the building on fire? Most importantly, given the building collapsed in a straight line downward, how on earth could this have happened absent pre-placed explosives?

Larry Silverstein knows much more than he lets on.

FEMA

Clearly, Building 7's collapse was a problem. Despite much of the public not knowing about it at all, the seemingly inexplicable collapse of a fifty-story building in downtown New York had to be addressed. However, it was completely ignored by the 9/11 Commission, who managed to not mention Building 7 in their entire report; an astonishing omission.

FEMA was the first government body handed the unenviable task of providing an explanation for the building's collapse, and had their own investigative staff onsite in New York City on 9/11. But after the attacks, FEMA staff were denied access to Building 7's wreckage. Staff were given a brief tour of the site, but their movement was strictly controlled and they were not allowed to collect samples. Why would you stop FEMA, a US government agency specializing in fires and emergencies, from collecting evidence?

FEMA investigators were by no means handed a blank sheet of paper. As with other government investigations, the essential premise given to FEMA was "we know that the building fell due to fire, we want you to prove how that happened." So what followed was neither scientific, nor an investigation, as the conclusions had been written before the introduction.

Even then, FEMA refused to play along. Their report dated May 2002 concluded that the sequence of events leading to the collapse of each tower could not be definitively determined, and that "the cause of Building 7's collapse remained unknown at [the] time." They did not dispute the central premise that fires alone had brought down the building, but while "the total diesel fuel on the premises contained massive potential energy, the best hypothesis has only a low probability of occurrence." FEMA called for further investigation.

This was a staggering statement from the government body charged with investigating the first fire-induced collapse of a steel-framed building in history. Essentially, they admitted to not knowing what happened.

The task of putting on a brave face and coming up with palatable lies was handed to the NIST.

The NIST

The NIST took the same approach of reverse-engineering their conclusions in order to find a way of proving that fires did indeed bring town Building 7.

7 WTC's collapse was part of a larger 9/11 investigation by NIST. Finding an explanation problematic, NIST decoupled their reports on the twin towers and Building 7, significantly delaying their report on the latter.

A preliminary report was issued in June 2004, but it took until November 2008, some seven years after 9/11, for NIST to release their final report into the collapse, and from the moment the report was issued by NIST's hapless lead investigator, Dr. S. Shyam Sunder, it was clear that this was another laughable whitewash.

The NIST claimed that while twelve of the building's steel columns had been damaged by debris from the collapse of 1 WTC, the collapse of just one column (number 79) had caused all the others to collapse completely simultaneously.

It was a ludicrous, transparently ridiculous hypothesis.

Sunder proudly proclaimed that the NIST's investigation had concluded that the building had fallen due to fire, and that there had been no proof found of any explosives in the building wreckage, but months later admitted that they had not actually looked or tested for any. Well, it's hard to find proof of something if you don't look for it.

NIST also refused to release details of the computer modeling they had done, declaring that doing so would "jeopardize public safety." They chose not to explain how public safety could be put in danger by the release of computer modeling data. Was not the greatest risk to public safety a huge building collapsing without warning, or (given the explanation that the collapse was due to fire) the risk that it might happen again?

The real proof of the invalidity of the NIST report lies in the commercial sector. If the conclusion of the NIST's final report into the collapse of Building 7 was correct, and fires burning through the building caused a sudden and complete collapse of the steel-framed building, then everything that architects and engineers have assumed in the last fifty years or more needs to be reexamined. Tall buildings across the world need to be reengineered, and insurance policies drastically altered. If fires can cause a steel-framed building to collapse, then thousands of lives are at risk. Fundamental design and engineering considerations in tall buildings are wrong, and there is an urgent public safety requirement that this matter be addressed immediately.

Of course, no such reevaluation has taken place, and the world of engineers, insurers, and architects continues unchanged. The NIST report on Building 7 was a sham and a whitewash, and entirely separate from the reality of how tall buildings operate during fires.

All of this would be greatly clarified, if not cleared up, if the NIST would release the seven thousand photographs and hundreds of hours of footage from 9/11 (mostly privately recorded) which they admit to retaining. But we have been told that our own safety is at risk if we even see the NIST computer modeling data. The government that supposedly works for us uses our own safety as a smokescreen for keeping information secret, and issuing ludicrous reports that a sixth grader could see through.

It's also worth briefly pausing here to dwell on the NIST's final report on the twin tower collapses, as it was equally disingenuous and absurd; and illustrates the garbage, disguised by looking complicated, that this government department was prepared to publish in order to placate a distracted and disinterested public.

The report chose only to look at events leading up to the initiation of collapse, and did not actually include the structural behavior of the towers after the conditions for collapse initiation were reached. This is like finishing your examination of the sinking of the Titanic at the moment when the ship hit the iceberg.

The report took the myopic approach that once the buildings began collapsing, complete structural failure was inevitable, when much of the evidence contradicting the official story occurred after the moment when the buildings began to fall.

The NIST (with a budget of just $16 million) admitted that the building fires had not been sufficiently hot to melt the steel beams, stating that while air (not steel) temperatures could briefly have reached 1,832°F , most of the time the calculated fire temperatures were around 930°.

As with other government agencies, the NIST also completely ignored the written, verbal, and video evidence given by a wide number of witnesses of explosions throughout the buildings well before the collapses began.

The NIST conducted hundreds of computer simulations and extensive laboratory testing, searching for a "scientific" explanation for the sudden building collapses. For this, they engaged Underwriter Laboratories (UL) to model the impacts and subsequent fires, but UL found that in all four tests they conducted (using huge models), the trusses did not fail and the buildings sustained the maximum possible loads without collapse for around two hours. The tests used much higher temperatures and longer fires than had been possible at the World Trade Center. The models did not fall.

Faced with this problem, NIST put together computer simulations, drastically altering parameters at will, and at last found that the buildings fell, due to the curious combination of dislodged fireproofing and subsequent melting of structural steel. But the NIST refused to release the details of their calculations, denying that most basic tenets of research: peer review.

A manager at Underwriter Laboratories, Kevin Ryan, went public with his objections to the assumptions used in their tests. Within a week, he was fired.

The idea that the NIST would find anything other than fire-induced collapse was fantasy. The NIST reports to the Department of Commerce, which was headed by Bush appointees. Any independent thought was structurally precluded. Their reports into the building collapses on 9/11 were transparently a sham.

CHAPTER SIX

A SUCCESSFUL ATTACK

United 23

Just after 9:00 a.m. on the morning of 9/11, the pilots of United Airlines flight 23 received a warning from ground control that a major terrorist attack was in progress. The plane was still on the tarmac at John F. Kennedy International Airport (JFK), having been delayed taking off, so the crew—who could see the smoke from the World Trade Center buildings in the distance—told passengers that there was a mechanical fault and returned the plane to the departure gate.

During the taxi back to the terminal, between three and six Middle Eastern men in First Class argued with flight staff about the change of plan and then refused to get off the plane. Flight staff called security, but the men fled before they arrived. Their luggage was later searched, and said to contain al-Qaeda instruction sheets and box-cutters.

However, law enforcement appear to have been staggeringly disinterested in pursuing the incident, both at the time and subsequently; at one point saying that there was little point in allocating resources to the search, as the chances of finding the men were "rather slim." Because of this, and because the plane never left the ground, the story of flight 23 and the hijacking-that-never-was is not widely known.

The main source of information on the incident aboard flight 23 was the flight's first officer Carol Timmons, who was in the cockpit and used baggage to block the cockpit door. Her male colleague grabbed an axe. Timmons is a highly decorated and respected professional (she was Delaware Air National Guard's first female General), hardly someone with questionable background or motives.

If the story is true, as it seems, then it represents a huge (and hugely under-reported) development to a well-known narrative, as America seems to have escaped attack by a fifth plane only through sheer good fortune.

Despite this, nothing of this story was mentioned by the 9/11 Commission.

Given the potentially devastating possibilities of a fifth attack, the fact that the story was lost smacks more of a cover-up than an event lost in the maelstrom. If the Middle Eastern men on board were potential hijackers, then finding and arresting them should have been the highest possible national priority, since they could rightly have been considered among the most dangerous men in America.

Not only would there have been many eyewitnesses who could identify them, their baggage was left behind, and there would have been many security images taken of them as they passed into and then out of the airport. Why was there not an immediate national manhunt? It's inexplicable.

Over the years, federal officials have, on occasion, hinted that they have evidence that several other flights may have been due to be hijacked, but have proved reluctant to provide any information or oxygen to this startling side to the story. On September 19, 2001, the FBI claimed that there were six hijacking teams on 9/11. Privately, it was reported that they were saying that the number was eight. Further information has suggested that there may have been up to eight hijackings which did not work, or were aborted at the last minute.

Operation Bojinka, the plot hatched by Khalid Sheikh Mohammed in the Philippines (on which the 9/11 attack was supposedly based) involved the hijacking or bombing of twelve planes. Some media reports in the US in late 2001 suggested that up to twenty-seven al-Qaeda operatives had trained at US installations. John Walker Lindh, the American captured fighting for the Taliban in Afghanistan, told investigators that there was supposed to have been a fifth plane, due to crash into the White House.

Several other Middle Eastern men were arrested on or before 9/11, mostly trying to enter the US. Each possessed maps, directions to the World Trade Center, and doctored photos showing them standing in front of the twin towers. Investigators believed the photos were calling cards identifying the men as members of the 9/11 plot. Late on September 11, box-cutters were found stowed under seats on three grounded US planes, including flight 43 from Newark to Los Angeles and flight 1729 from Newark to San Francisco. Time magazine reported that the hijackers probably had accomplices inside the airports.

United 23 may just be the tip of the iceberg. 9/11 may have been a much, much larger plot than we think it was. The ramifications don't bear thinking about. They would have changed the world.

A Stand-Down

America's air defenses, designed to be so efficient that they could counter a ballistic missile attack, all failed in unison. We are seemingly faced with two alternatives—the first, that a broad and disparate group of government departments and workers all became incompetent at the same moment; the second, that a group of the highest level government and military commanders concocted a successful plot that neutered routine defenses.

The fact that the plot did not achieve all of its goals (because one plane was shot down and another didn't get off the ground) does not detract from the likelihood of inside involvement. Given the Iraq War (for example), it's not hard to imagine a world in which senior US officials are belligerent, treasonous, and war-mongering, but at the same time incompetent.

A stand-down seems hard to achieve with such a vast system of national defenses, but in fact the preponderance of responsibility lay in the hands of a very small number of people, and the failure of standard defenses was only required for a very short space of time. It was imperative, for example, that Donald Rumsfeld was at the helm of America's military for exactly eighty minutes (the time between the first plane hitting the WTC and the crash at Shanksville) in order to effect a response to the attacks. If, as it seems, Rumsfeld was absent from his post during those eighty short minutes, the consequences for US government agencies' ability to defend the country cannot be overstated.

The margin of time that allowed the attacks was relatively small. The FAA did nothing for at least eighteen minutes after losing initial contact with flight 11. The fighter jets scrambled to defend American airspace spent precious minutes on the ground, and were sent out across the Atlantic, when everyone on earth knew that Manhattan was under attack. Small increments of time lost here and there amounted to a total failure to defend America. This had not happened before. Systemic failure only occurred on 9/11.

Operation Northwoods

Anyone falling into the "they wouldn't do this to us" camp need only glance at history to see that they most certainly would. We now know that the attack on Pearl Harbor was anticipated and to a great extent provoked by President Roosevelt in order to galvanize US public opinion to join the war.

Another well known example is Operation Northwoods, brought to President John F. Kennedy and defense secretary Robert McNamara in 1962 by high-ranking generals. The document, drafted by the chiefs of staff and signed by Chairman Lyman Lemnitzer, proposed a range of "false flag" incidents (designed to arouse public passions and facilitate an invasion of Cuba), including terrorism on US soil, the fake shooting-down of a US civilian aircraft, or the blowing up of a US ship. In particular, the plan called for the swapping of civilian aircraft for dummy drones, which could then be shot out of the sky with Cuba taking the blame.

Kennedy had the good sense to reject such a plan, apparently shocked that his military officials could even think in such a way. Although a long time ago, never let it be said that the leading military men in America don't think outside the box when it comes to stimulating public opinion.

Declaring the Air Clean

Contempt for public safety was something shown by the Bush administration both before and after 9/11.

George W. Bush finally made it to Manhattan on September 14. Until 9/11, New York City had not been his kind of town. As he drove toward ground zero, New York Governor George Pataki said to him, "See those people? None of them voted for you."

Climbing onto the rubble, his arm around a firefighter, Bush spoke to the large crowd through a megaphone that barely lifted his voice above the throng below. It didn't seem to be going well, but then someone yelled, "Can't hear you!"

Bush shouted back, "Well, I can hear YOU." It was a classic move, one tried many times before, and got the tired group of assembled responders on their feet, chanting for the USA.

However, within days, Bush and his administration betrayed all of those who put their lives on the line to help. The consequences of that betrayal resonate to this day.

Five days after the attacks, the Environmental Protection Agency (EPA) and the Occupational Safety and Health Administration (OSHA) declared the air in downtown Manhattan safe to breathe. Wall Street reopened; schools went back. Though government officials continued to wear hazmat (hazardous materials) suits, workers at ground zero wore paper-thin masks against the dust and smoke.

Perhaps the officials in hazmat suits knew something the rest of us didn't—the press release announcing that the air was clean had been heavily edited by the White House Council on Environmental Quality (CEQ).

In fact, the changes made to the information presented to those working at the World Trade Center wreckage were as radical as changing the message from "the air isn't safe to breathe," to "the air is safe to breathe." Reassuring statements were added, cautionary information changed or removed.

The explosive power of the towers' collapse had pulverized the buildings, leaving a fine dust instead of rubble. The dust and smoke (described as wildly toxic) was contaminated with known carcinogens, including asbestos. Most first responders just dove right in; the paper masks they were subsequently provided were not remotely adequate.

In the years that followed, more and more people began to get sick. It became clear that those who had breathed in the air around the World Trade Center in the hours, days, and weeks after the attacks were facing alarming rates of respiratory diseases and cancers.

In March 2004, residents of downtown Manhattan filed a lawsuit against the head of the EPA, Christine Whitman, accusing her of issuing misleading statements about the air. On September 13, 2001 Whitman had declared the air safe. On September 18 she issued a statement saying she was glad to tell New Yorkers that the air did not pose a health hazard.

But by 2006, a report issued by the Mount Sinai Medical Center indicated that nearly 70 percent of first responders had developed respiratory problems. In 2014, the Mount Sinai Selikoff Centers for Occupational Health reported a total of at least 1,646 cancers in first responders, and 863 more among fire and emergency services personnel.

Marcy Borders, the famous "dust lady" pictured on 9/11 covered from head to toe in fine white dust, died in 2015 at forty-two years of age from stomach cancer, which she went to the grave believing had been caused by the toxins within the building dust.

In 2011, the federal government set up the World Trade Center Health Program (WTCHP). Staggeringly, over thirty-seven thousand people registered with the organization have been declared sick. By mid 2016, over 1,100 had died.

As with so many traumatic and violent events, much of the damage to survivors was psychological. Up to ten thousand people who worked in the 9/11 rescue effort have been diagnosed with post-traumatic stress disorder.

As the scale of the epidemic became clear, the government stepped in, mostly to block any attempts to seek compensation.

James Zadroga

James Zadroga, a New York City police officer who worked for 450 hours at ground zero, developed a persistent cough within weeks of the attacks. Zadroga was a non-smoker, in good health, and had no family history of asthma.

Within months he was unable to walk short distances without gasping for air. In 2004, the 9/11 Victim Compensation fund awarded Zadroga over $1 million, determining that his illness was directly caused by exposure to the toxic dust. Within two years he was dead at the age of thirty-four.

In 2006, New York State enacted legislation relating to first responder illnesses. The act proved controversial, as many types of cancer first responders were suffering from were initially excluded. After much delay and modification, the James Zadroga 9/11 Health and Compensation Act finally made it to the Senate, but Republicans filibustered and blocked the vote. Instead they passed a bill that cut taxes to the wealthy. It took public pressure from comedian Jon Stewart for the Zadroga Act to finally become law in January 2011.

The act initially excluded cancer, as politicians claimed there was no evidence linking cancers to exposure to the toxic dusts. That has since been amended.

In 2015, the act was due to expire. Around thirty-three thousand first responders' health benefits were on the line. It took another concerted media campaign to stop most politicians from looking the other way and leaving the first responders alone in their fight.

The epidemic of respiratory diseases now ravaging first responders, significantly as a result of the government's lies about air quality, is one of the great evils perpetrated by the Bush administration, and an integral part of the tragedy of 9/11. To betray those who acted so bravely on that desperate occasion beggars belief, yet the political system has thrown up large numbers of individuals who have been willing to stand up in front of their contemporaries and argue that ongoing medical help for first responders should be cut. Just imagine doing that.

Sadly, long-term respiratory diseases and cancers related to work at ground zero are predicted to kill more people than the attacks themselves. Given the US government's false declarations that the air in lower Manhattan was clean, and subsequent attempts to block healthcare for those who deserved it the most, it's hard to see how less this qualifies as murder than the events that took place hundreds of meters above.

After 9/11

It's a cliché, but searching for a motive is a method of reasoning used by law enforcement around the world to weed out the guilty. Many parties seemed to directly benefit from the attacks of 9/11, most notably the Bush administration, the Pentagon, the CIA and FBI, military and defense contractor companies and, in the end, Wall Street.

President Bush's fortune began to turn when a resolution passed (with only two dissenting voices) Congress on 14 September 2001, allowing Bush "all necessary and appropriate force" against those nations, organizations or persons that he determined planned, authorized, committed, or aided the terrorist attacks . . . or those who harbored such organizations or persons. This was an unprecedented granting of power to a US president to wage war against anyone he saw fit, whenever and wherever, with no checks and balances, no oversight, and no expiration date.

Bush used this consolidated power to pursue an aggressive militarization of US foreign policy, one that had long been sought by the political and military elites who populated his administration.

The War on Terror terrified Americans into allowing the greatest single heist of taxpayer money in human history to pay for wars based on lies, and the public repaid this daylight robbery by pushing the President's popularity rating through the roof. The CIA, FBI, Pentagon, and military industrial complex received more money than ever before, Wall Street reaped the profits, the media fell silent, and the rich got richer. From their twisted perspective, 9/11 was manna from heaven.

It is stunning to see how failure to defend America was treated. Those who failed the most were promoted. Those who spoke out were threatened or sacked. Intelligence agencies that had managed to miss so much were the ones who received the largest increases in funding. Agency budgets increased by around 50 percent. The airlines received huge financial bailouts. The FAA had their budget vastly increased. No failure went unrewarded. No one took the blame. No one in government (except Richard Clarke) even said sorry.

CIA Director George Tenet wanted authorization and funding for his long sought-after "Worldwide Attack Matrix" of covert operations. Four days after 9/11, he got it, including a 42 percent funding increase. The Pentagon and arms manufacturers received the biggest increase in military spending since the end of the Cold War. When the Pentagon received $48 billion in additional funding, the increase alone was more than any other country spent in total on its military.

For Bush himself, the attacks facilitated a broad consolidation of political power. Before 9/11, Bush was widely perceived as weak and ineffective, with personal ratings in free fall. All of that was reversed by 9/11. In fact, Bush received the highest Presidential approval rating in US history (90 percent) in the immediate aftermath. After 9/11, Bush was described as the most powerful US president in modern times. More than that, the frenzied climate of the next few years allowed Bush a level of political power, courtesy of a cowed media and compliant opposition, of which previous incumbents of the White House could only have dreamed. Outrageous violations of the Constitution engendered barely a murmur of dissent.

It was the Bush administration's response to 9/11 that turned it into the most successful terrorist attack in history. International terrorism is essentially a means of fighting asymmetric warfare on foreign streets, with the simple goal of provoking overreaction. The War on Terror used an attack by non-state terrorists as an excuse to instead attack states on a predetermined list.

Again and again, Bush and Rumsfeld described the attacks as a great opportunity. A year after 9/11, a National Security Strategy paper released by the Bush administration said the events of 9/11 opened vast new opportunities. Ten days after the attacks, the State Department gave Colin Powell a long list of silver linings.

Among a myriad of clear winners from the attacks were major defense logistics companies with close ties to the Bush administration like the Carlyle Group, DynCorp, and Halliburton. The Carlyle Group, which had counted bin Laden family members as investors, made immense profits from the wars that followed and the unprecedented financial bonanza for defense contractors engendered by 9/11.

In just one example, Carlyle bought United Defense in 1997, and sold it for $1 billion in profit. Handy to have the president's father on the board. Indeed, the Carlyle Group was so well connected to the White House that it can fairly be said to have had a direct impact on US foreign policy. Large contributions to George W. Bush's election fund merely cemented that relationship.

President Bush's response to 9/11 only looks wild and irrational through the prism of the official story. If you accept, as you must, that the attack was planned and executed from within the US government and military, then the subsequent trashing of the Constitution and the illegal wars that followed all can be seen for what they are: part of a coup against American democracy that lives on to this day.

Revolution

Just imagine the implications if everything you thought you knew about 9/11 was wrong. The government, the president, the security agencies—what if every single damn one of them had told you a tale that was entirely and completely false? What if the media, who claim to investigate and report fearlessly, do no such thing, and are for the most part mere parrots for the government; too afraid to confront such an earth-shattering reality? What would it say about our society, about its structures of power, and about capitalism and democracy itself if it were proved to you beyond reasonable doubt that the events of September 11, 2001 were in fact carried out by the US government and military? The lie is so overwhelmingly vast and important that its exposure would leave us no alternative but to dismantle and reevaluate our beliefs about the democracy at the heart of this nation. The thought itself is utterly revolutionary.

People often dismiss concerns about government conspiracy with the blithe brush-off that there is no way any large story could possibly be kept secret by a government, as it would involve the simultaneous secrecy of hundreds or even thousands of people. Edward Snowden showed that such a thing is entirely possible. The NSA kept its domestic surveillance program secret for seven years. Thousands, perhaps tens of thousands of people, knew what was taking place, but until Snowden took the brave decision to abandon his life and family, the public was completely unaware.

It is truly preposterous to suggest that Osama bin Laden and his bumbling al-Qaeda friends could have pulled off an attack which on the face of it looked simple, but in fact had a level of complexity and synchronicity suggesting a sophisticated, well-planned and costly military-style operation. Yet we are told that not only was the most successful terrorist attack in history launched from a cave on the other side of the world; not one document or person could be found within or outside of America after 9/11 that told of the plot.

Despite the scale of the attacks, only two men have been convicted for involvement (Mounir el Motassadeq, who was jailed for fifteen years in Germany for his association with Mohamed Atta and the Hamburg cell, and Zacarias Moussaoui).

Bin Laden and his network had been under close surveillance for years by a number of nations. His operatives inside the US were under surveillance. While in America, their behavior was almost comically inept. Many were unable to speak English or fly single-engine planes. All seemed to enjoy alcohol and the company of strippers. Mohamed Atta spectacularly drew attention to himself, actions that were the opposite of those that might be expected from a man secretly masterminding a devastating terrorist attack. The so-called hijackers were scapegoats placed at the scene of the crime to take the blame.

Mainstream media won't even touch the issues raised by the extraordinary anomalies in the official version of events on 9/11. Maybe they will over time. But time can't wait. We can't allow this to become another Kennedy assassination, an event which most have concluded was not a lone assassin's plot, but part of a much wider conspiracy. Fifty years have passed since the only postwar president who spoke of peace and full disarmament took a bullet in the head for his troubles. Kennedy's assassins got away with it. The truth about 9/11 has to be exposed—shocking and painful though that will be—and those responsible need to be arrested and tried.

The results of the attacks have been in the most part profoundly counter-productive to those accused of them. If the goal was to deal America a blow in order to remove US troops from holy lands, or to defend Islam and its people from attack, the results are a disaster. But look at it from a different perspective. If the goal was to concentrate political power within the Bush regime, the attacks could not have worked better. If the goal was to convince the population of the United States to allow military expeditions that might not otherwise receive public support, it was a triumph. If the goal was a staggering increase of America's military budget, nothing could have been better. In fact, from a political, financial, and military perspective in the United States, the attacks were a boon not seen since Hitler's Germany fell.

For most people, even considering the idea that the events of 9/11 have been misrepresented is extremely disturbing. It's simply too much. The concept that the events of that day represent a lie is almost too big to contemplate; the implications too earth-shattering and awful. Many prefer not thinking about it, because subjecting the government story to proper scrutiny is to question "the very foundations of our entire modern belief system regarding our government, our country and our way of life," to quote ex-Pentagon activist Karen Kwiatkowski.

But we already have a lot of information that shows that we have been lied to. No one saw it coming, and the attacks came out of the blue, Condoleezza Rice said. No one, she insisted, had envisaged the idea of flying planes into buildings. But they did, and they had. All sorts of people, including TV producers, had imagined just that, and the attacks weren't out of the blue at all; the system was blinking red with an unprecedented spike in intelligence warnings and activity. Rice lied. For that she was promoted to secretary of state.

To accept the established 9/11 narrative, you need to believe that the Bush administration, one of the most duplicitous and deceptive regimes ever to govern the United States, miraculously acted nobly and honestly, and chose never to lie about one single thing pertaining to the events on that particular day, in a way that makes those events sacrosanct and beyond question.

Their behavior betrays this notion. Bush and Cheney inexplicably refused to testify to the 9/11 Commission, repeatedly said that 9/11 had come out of the blue, and linked the attacks to a series of other unrelated matters—most notoriously to drum up public sentiment for their illegal invasion of Iraq, which was also based on lies. Bush and Cheney lied again and again about 9/11, misrepresenting the events so badly that Americans thought that Iraq had attacked them. They dishonestly took the world into a war against Iraq that killed hundreds of thousands of people, and sacrificed the lives of thousands of US servicemen and women for their own political and financial gain.

The other great coup of the age, the Kennedy assassination, was designed to be concealed from view, and were it not for Abraham Zapruder and his camera we would have no definitive visual record of the event. By contrast, the attack on the twin towers, while of course aiming to have a devastating death toll, was also designed to have great visual impact. Whoever you believe was responsible for 9/11 could have killed many more people by crashing a plane into a nuclear plant, but found it preferable to strike the very heart of America's largest city and its tallest buildings. The primary aim may have been carnage and mayhem, but at least a close second was to provide the most shocking television images of all time. The pictures of buildings exploding into fireballs were a gift for those within the Bush administration who wished to keep the public quiet and afraid, and were ruthlessly used as media propaganda.

There are legitimate concerns as to whether the planes that struck the World Trade Center were indeed the aircraft they were purported to be. While we may never know the truth, the building collapses and subsequent pools of molten metal in the wreckage offer clear evidence of controlled demolitions. The hole in the Pentagon is not even close to being the right size for a 757 impact. The evidence in Shanksville clearly points towards the plane having been shot down. There was no plane at what we were told was the crash site, and the idea that the ground just swallowed a commercial jet is absurdity. Building 7 was obviously, undeniably brought down with explosives that had to have been set before the attacks commenced. 9/11 is a tissue of lies.

Joseph Goebbels said that if you tell a big enough lie and tell it frequently enough, it will be believed. 9/11 is a big enough lie.

The attack was mostly successful, but the biggest success was the selling of the story, however unlikely, of a brilliantly executed attack by a rag-tag group of foreigners who had somehow evaded detection altogether. The official story is, in itself, a conspiracy theory, given that it involves a minimum of nineteen Arabs conspiring to attack the US but apparently leaving no clues or trace of their plot. The alternate narrative involves a conspiracy to execute a coup by the United States government and military. We just have to work out which conspiracy seems more plausible.

"Conspiracy theorist" is a convenient and disparaging label used by the media and those on the right as short-hand for deranged lunatic, but the same Republicans who decry the notion of a fair inquiry into the 9/11 attacks were only too happy to propagate their own conspiracy theories about Barack Obama, his place of birth, his religion, or his plans to take away Americans guns.

Whatever label you care to apply to those who question the official 9/11 story, doubts are much more widely held than you might imagine. A 2004 Zogby Poll found that 49.3 percent of New Yorkers agreed with the statement "some of our leaders knew in advance attacks were planned on or around September 11, 2001, and consciously failed to act." A poll by the *Atlanta Journal Constitution* found that 46 percent of respondents selected the answer "I think officials knew it was coming." A Yougov poll in 2013 found that 38 percent of Americans had some doubt about the official account, with 10 percent not believing it at all.

Bill Doyle, head of the Coalition of 9/11 Families (the largest group of 9/11 families) lost his son on 9/11, but reported that nearly half the families in his group think that the US government was complicit in the attacks.

Yet this public skepticism is not reflected in the media. Those who query the official narrative are routinely shouted down, sidelined, or treated as entirely beyond the realm of rational debate. The sanity of those asking questions is often questioned. Broadcaster Tucker Carlson told 9/11 author David Ray Griffin it was 'wrong, blasphemous, and sinful' to even question the story. Within mainstream American discourse, criticizing the Iraq or Afghanistan wars, the War on Terror, or the conduct of the Bush administration is now acceptable, but 9/11 itself remains, for the most part, a sacred cow. To fundamentally question the events of that day invites derision, and can still be a seriously poor career move.

I suspect that many, if not most people, have nagging doubts about 9/11. Few people doubt that the Bush administration systematically lied to us about all manner of things, including the big lie that Saddam Hussein had weapons of mass destruction. Somewhere in the corner of humanity's psyche is the dark suspicion that perhaps events on 9/11 did not happen in the way we were told that they did. But it's all too much to take in, and for nearly everyone, it's a distant memory of a dreadful day. Besides, life has continued—money needs to be earned, the kids need to be fed, and the washing needs to be done. Some of the more egregious excesses of America's response to 9/11, like wiretapping and mass data retention make us uncomfortable, but for most of us that threat too seems distant and not to affect us.

The truth is that the attacks of 9/11 represent a much more frightening event than that which we saw on our television screens. It was a political and military coup by a secretive, murderous faction willing to risk world peace and nuclear exchange in order to take control of the United States for political, military, and financial gain. The death of a nation.

As I write, kids born around 9/11 are now teenagers. In just a few years they will be adults, and will have known no other circumstance than the bizarre post-9/11 times in which we live. America is a very different country now, but they won't know any better.

PART TWO

SUSPECTS AND THE ACCUSED

CHAPTER SEVEN

NEOCONS AND THE BUSH ADMINISTRATION

History of the Neoconservative Movement

When George W. Bush became the Republican presidential candidate in 2000, he had very little experience of national-level politics or foreign affairs. To assist him in projecting an all-around image of Presidential capability, Bush chose from a highly select group, many of whom had held senior positions in his father's administration. At the central core were the neoconservatives, a group that included Dick Cheney, Donald Rumsfeld, Paul Wolfowitz, Richard Perle and John Bolton. Together, these and other individuals formed an ideological cabal at the highest reaches of the new Bush administration.

Neo-conservatism was a political movement that originated in the 1960s as a counter to the liberal social revolutions of that age. It was mostly based on the ideas of Leo Strauss, a Jewish-American political philosopher. Through the 1970s and '80s, political activists and writers like Irving Kristol applied the label neoconservative to themselves and others to describe an ideology of hard right-wing politics; eschewing compromise and coalition at home, militaristic and skeptical of democracy promotion abroad, and allying with foreign dictators, when prudent, to achieve the desired geopolitical outcomes for the United States.

As with evangelical Christians, neocons were intensely ideological and the two made happy, if strange, bedfellows. An essential part of neocon ideology was the linking of political policy to religious dogma. Central to the rollout of any policy was to say that the direction taken was in line with Judeo-Christian morality and biblical values.

However, above all other belief and ideology, what neoconservatives craved most was political power. Unlike true Christians, neocons were willing to lie and cheat to attain their goals, no matter what the cost. Central to Leo Strauss's theories was the idea that truth is dangerous for the masses, and that responsible leaders often have to lie to the public in order to achieve benevolent societal outcomes. This attitude of duplicitousness prevailed throughout the body of the first true neoconservative administration that entered the White House in January 2001.

Political dishonesty may seem un-Christian, but it's important to remember that the alliance between neo-conservatism and evangelical faith really was a marriage of convenience, as neoconservative ideology contained none of the central messages of Christianity. Religion, and Christianity in particular, plays a huge part in political discourse in the United States, a country where nearly 320 million people (78 percent of the population, more than any other country in the world) still identify as Christian. Had it failed to serve its purpose, neoconservatives would have dumped Christianity in an instant. As it was, evangelical Christians were persuaded that policies like lower taxes for the rich and endless foreign military incursion somehow aligned with the peaceful teachings of Jesus. Just as the modern Republican party plays to the evangelical Christian right in the US while acting in a way entirely contrary to biblical teachings, neoconservatives wore the cloth of Christ while engaging in political skullduggery solely to gain and retain power.

The Clinton presidency was, for all its faults, relatively peaceful. This was regarded by the neocons as weakness. I. Lewis "Scooter" Libby (Dick Cheney's chief of staff) said that the 'cult of peace and prosperity' had made Clinton's foreign policy weak and distracted, and damaged America. Above and beyond any other political goal, the neocons wanted to use the military and war to project US power abroad.

The small clique that advised presidential candidate George W. Bush on foreign policy was made up of neoconservatives who called themselves the Vulcans. Nearly all of them advocated for war, blood, and sacrifice, having avoided it themselves when the call of duty came in younger life.

In the years that followed 9/11, conservatives transformed Bush and Cheney into embodiments of warrior courage; political He-Men during a time of war, even though both had scampered away from combat as young men, avoiding the draft and letting others fight and die for them in Vietnam. The same is true of almost every leading right-wing, super-patriot tough guy: John Bolton, Bill Kristol, Newt Gingrich, Rush Limbaugh, Mitt Romney, Jeb Bush, and Donald Trump. All are shameless warmongers who chose not to serve when their moment came.

To neoconservatives, war itself took on the characteristics of a holy mission. Richard Perle, a senior official (once described by a British politician as the Prince of Darkness), advocated total war against unlimited enemies. In comments that sound like the fanatics he so denounced, he said, "If we just let our vision of the world go forth, and . . . just wage a total war . . . our children will sing great songs about us years from now." This was the man who suggested that the Iraq war could be won with just forty thousand troops.

As America decided whether George W. Bush or Al Gore would lead them in 2000, this militarism was suppressed from view, but the warning signs were there for those who cared enough to look.

Project for the New American Century

In 1997, Bill (the son of Irving) Kristol and Robert Kagan founded the Project for the New American Century (PNAC), a Washington think tank with the aim of promoting what they called a benevolent global hegemony through a more focused US foreign policy vision. Kristol had formerly been Vice President Dan Quayle's Chief of Staff, where he was known by the ignoble title of "Quayle's Brain."

Dick Cheney was a central figure in PNAC, as the project was based broadly on a 1992 document he had drafted in the dying days of the first Bush presidency, outlining his thoughts on how to maintain US preeminence.

PNAC's Statement of Principles was signed by many future members of the Bush administration. Of its twenty-five initial founders, twelve were given high-level positions in the administration of President George W. Bush.

But it was the 76-page document "Rebuilding America's Defenses," completed in September 2000 (a year before 9/11), that has gained the most attention.

"Rebuilding America's Defenses" was commissioned by Dick Cheney, Donald Rumsfeld, Paul Wolfowitz, Jeb Bush and Scooter Libby. It was a strategic document prepared for those managing George W. Bush's presidential campaign, and served as a blueprint for the neoconservatives' foreign and military policies under a theoretical Bush government. Notably, although the document was conceived of well before George W. Bush became president, Bush himself was not involved in its preparation.

Major themes of the document were:

- Defense of the US homeland (an uncommon phrase which has since gained traction).
- The need to place more military bases around the world.

- The need to bring about regime change in countries unfriendly to American interests, and the waging of simultaneous wars.
- Greatly increased military spending, especially for missile defense, enlarging the overall US military budget from 3 percent to around 3.5–3.8 percent of GDP (by 2011, it was running at 4.7 percent).
- Global missile defense deployment, the abandonment of global treaties limiting America's missile program expansion, and the militarization of space.

The PNAC blueprint ambitiously called for regime change in China, supported by increasing the presence of US forces in Southeast Asia.

Among the more egregious discussion items in the document, the report called for the development of advanced forms of biological weaponry that targeted specific genotypes, calling these new weapons a potentially 'politically useful tool'. This insane proposition is particularly ironic given the future American focus on another country's weapons of mass destruction.

Many of the document's items came to pass. Iraq, Iran, and North Korea were identified as deterrents to US hegemony. These same states later became President Bush's famous "axis of evil".

Iraq in particular was identified as a source of malaise, and a roadblock in America's decades-long goal of playing 'a more permanent role in Gulf regional security'.

One key sentence has attracted a lot of attention. "While the unresolved conflict with Iraq provides the immediate justification [for troops in the Persian Gulf], the need for a substantial American force presence in the Gulf transcends the issue of the regime of Saddam Hussein."

The reason the US wanted a permanent role in Gulf "security" was simple—control of the oil. In effect, Bush's cabinet planned to establish direct military control over oil in the Persian Gulf, and Hussein was essentially irrelevant, as his regime could be overthrown if required.

Most striking of all was the lament that the wished-for "process of transformation (of the US military), even if it brings revolutionary change, is likely to be a long one, absent some catastrophic and catalyzing event—like a new Pearl Harbor."

This was an extremely strange thing to have written; that only a national disaster would allow the writers' wishes to be implemented quickly. What lover of the United States would wish a Pearl Harbor-type devastation upon it?

Yet, so it came to pass. 9/11 was widely described as the new Pearl Harbor, even by President Bush. The event took place almost exactly a year after

PNAC's document was published, on the watch of most of the authors, who by then were at the highest levels of political and military power in the US. And of course 9/11 was used to justify many of the measures outlined in the PNAC document, measures that could only have received public approval in the aftermath of such a catastrophic and catalyzing event.

If I wrote a letter to a friend saying that "I'd love to move to the Bahamas but can't do so unless my wife is murdered so I can get the insurance money," you might say that I had a sick imagination. But if she was subsequently murdered and I moved to the Bahamas with the insurance money, the police would come knocking on my door. How different is this—a wish list, which can't be implemented without a catalyzing event—the authors take charge of America, the event happens, and the wish-list is implemented.

The bottom line here is that virtually all of George W. Bush's senior staff planned, before Bush's election, to transform the US military, and for the US to take control of Persian Gulf oil assets, whether or not Saddam Hussein stood in their way, and whether or not he presented a threat to America. As such, the War on Terror, spawned and justified by 9/11, is really a smokescreen for military revolution, political and financial gain, and control of energy resources.

"Rebuilding America's Defenses," the blueprint for the War on Terror, represents evidence of conspiracy. Those involved should be placed under suspicion of involvement in the events that allowed them to implement their long-held plans.

9/11 facilitated the goals of PNAC, allowing America's leaders to manipulate a frightened civilian population into applauding seemingly nonsensical military adventures. A member of the Institute for Strategic Studies said that after 9/11, support for military action [was] at levels that parallel the public reaction after Pearl Harbor.

Despite their extraordinary prescience, the PNAC documents are not widely known outside of 9/11 investigative circles. The US press singularly failed to inform the public that so many senior Bush administration officials had been planning this new anti-terrorism direction for the country since 1992.

Members of the PNAC wished for a new Pearl Harbor. President Bush, before going to bed on 9/11, is reported to have written in his diary, "The Pearl Harbor of the 21st century took place today. We think it's Osama bin Laden." All their dreams had come true.

For those looking to the future, "Rebuilding America's Defenses" also had this to say, "Over the long term, Iran may well prove as large a threat to US interests in the Gulf as Iraq has. And even should US-Iranian relations improve, retaining forward-based forces in the region would still be an essential element in US security strategy given the longstanding American interests in the region." Whatever happens, we're staying in control of the Middle East, and woe betide if Iran gets in our way. This mindset remains at the heart of the Republican party.

The Bush Family

The Bush clan can legitimately be called the most criminal family in the United States. George W. Bush's grandfather, Herbert Walker Bush, was a prominent Nazi sympathizer and financier in the 1930s, and continued to do business with Hitler long after it became clear that he was America's enemy. As Director of the CIA, George H. W. Bush presided over one of the most notorious periods in the agency's history, characterized by paramilitary behavior, the mass importation of drugs into the United States (to pay for clandestine operations), and the support and arming of murderous regimes abroad. Under Bush senior's watch, the CIA turned into an organization barely distinguishable from the mobsters, drug traffickers, and mafia they purported to hunt. George H. W. Bush was also the CIA's lead liaison man with anti-Castro factions when those two groups combined to kill John F. Kennedy in 1963, and was in Dallas on the day of the assassination.

As vice president, Bush narrowly missed out on promotion to the top job when the assassination attempt on Ronald Reagan failed. George Bush Sr. seems to choose his friends unwisely. Time and time again, his family connections seem to end up involved in nefarious deeds. Years later, the Bush family would have to downplay embarrassingly close connections to the bin Ladens. In 1981, their long-standing friendship with the Hinckleys created a flash point that was just centimeters from killing the president.

John Hinckley tried to assassinate Ronald Reagan on March 30, 1981. Hinckley's family, also Texas oil royalty, were financial backers of Bush. Hinckley's brother had a dinner date scheduled with Bush's son (Neil Bush) the day after the assassination attempt.

FEMA had an exercise named Nine Lives that focused on presidential succession scheduled for the day after the attack. Bush, as vice president, was next in line had Reagan died.

A Presidential succession exercise, planned for the day after an actual assassination attempt by a family friend of the man who stood to gain most from the President's death. Yet another of the Bush family coincidences that always seem to break in their favor.

After the shooting, John Hinckley was described as the black sheep of the family, an expression we heard subsequently about Osama bin Laden in relation to the bin Laden family. One might sometimes be forgiven for thinking that world events are just some kind of horrific game of chess for families like the Bushes.

As president, Bush Sr. allowed Oliver North and his cronies to run their clandestine operations—literally—from the basement of the White House.

The Bush family, oil men through and through, had (until 9/11) enjoyed close family ties to the bin Ladens. Bushes and bin Ladens sat on the board of the Carlyle Group until the 9/11 attacks made this untenable. Both families benefitted significantly from the wars in Afghanistan and Iraq, given their involvement in the US defense industry. Despite brother Osama clearly threatening the United States with further terrorist attacks after the USS Cole and embassy bombings in 1998, there appears to have been no cooling in the family friendship until September 11.

The depth of Bush family ties to the Saudi Royal family has been written about extensively, most tellingly in Craig Unger's *House of Bush, House of Saud*. As Unger put it, "Never before has a president of the United States (George W. Bush) been tied so closely to a foreign power that harbors and supports our mortal enemies." It's been said that only a handful of people in the US know the true relationship between America and Saudi Arabia. The Bushes would be among that small number. The Bush family's baleful presence within American polity has been disastrous for all but a tiny number of very rich people, and looks to the future through other members of what is rapidly becoming the premier political dynasty in America.

Before 2000

George W. Bush was a curious character, an unusual mix of supreme self-confidence and absolute certainty in his positions (no matter how wrong they were), yet lacking most people's cognitive processing and questioning abilities, leaving Bush malleable to those in a position to exert influence over him. He proved a tailor-made Manchurian candidate, able to be controlled by a variety of high-power figures, and happy to make public statements selling the unsellable to the masses.

Initially the ugly duckling of the family, Bush Junior appears to have been mostly bored with young life, and took to drink and drugs to fill a void that indolence and affluence could not assuage. Bush's collegiate period of drug use proved no impediment to his later becoming governor of the state that punished more people for marijuana use than any other.

When service came calling, Bush used his family connections to get out of the draft for the Vietnam war. Bush was not alone among his senior administration staff in finding reasons and excuses not to be deployed to Vietnam. Most of the war-mongering neocons didn't like the idea of waging it themselves.

In the court of public opinion, Vietnam draft-dodging has mostly ceased to be seen as a treasonous crime, given it was such an appalling and unnecessary war. What made Bush different to America's other draft-dodgers is that the rest of them did not then cast themselves as brave and fearless wartime leaders, and lie in order to send thousands more to their deaths in another insane war. The term chicken-hawk is meant to sting, and it fits well with Bush, Cheney, et al.

On his graduation from Yale, Bush pursued a diverse business management career that involved mining concerns and football team ownership. Every enterprise he touched was a colossal failure, at least until a more senior (often Saudi) figure stepped in to offer financial rescue. This was not luck. Bush's father, as first oilman and spy chief, then vice president and president of the United States, wielded enormous power, and financial backers strove to gain the favor of America's leading political family.

Three times, George W. was bailed out by friends and investors to stop his businesses going bankrupt.

Bush Jr. made his first $20 million with an oil company funded partly by the bin Laden family's US representatives. Salem (brother of Osama) bin Laden's US representative James R. Bath bought a 5 percent share (probably more) in Bush's company Arbusto Energy. Later, when the company, now renamed Harken Energy, got into trouble, Saudi Sheikh Abdullah Taha Bakhsh purchased nearly 20 percent. Given that Bakhsh's banker Khalid Salem bin Mahfouz was the Saudi who controlled the finances of al-Qaeda under Osama bin Laden, George W. Bush is an American citizen who has done business with both the bin Laden family and those who finance and support terrorism. Under his own explicit terms this made Bush an enemy of America in the War on Terror.

Harken, which had never done any work outside of Texas, subsequently won a large contract in the Persian Gulf and started to make a profit, by chance in the same year that George W.'s father became president.

This was just one of many examples of the quid pro quo that exists between the Bush family and the House of Saud. As leaders, the Bushes have staunchly stood by and defended the rulers of Saudi Arabia, in return for which the Saudis have used their limitless funds to bankroll political campaigns (using creative methods to get around legal bans on political donations from overseas), and to bail out the occasional idiot son who got into trouble.

The major turning point in Bush's life was the decision, unquestionably courageous, to become sober. Like so many seeking solace somewhere other than a bottle, Bush turned to God, which lent him the political power that the modern evangelical movement in the US brings. Right-wing conservatism often practices political policy that is precisely the opposite of the central messages of Christianity, but that has not stopped the evangelical wing of the US population being taken in and voting for candidates aligning themselves with hard-right conservatism and Christian values.

By the time Bush became Governor of Texas, he had become the apotheosis of right-wing Christian politics. He was sober, fit, wore his religion on his sleeve, utterly merciless on the weak, and sported the alternating uniforms of suit and cowboy hat and jeans that denote the Texas gentleman billionaire.

The most striking aspect of his governorship was its murderousness. Bush took life with more enthusiasm than even his predecessors, quite an achievement in Texas. In eight years in power, he pardoned no death penalty clemency application that came before him, even in cases of extreme mental deficiency or questionable convictions.

This combination of strong faith and a complete lack of mercy when it comes to taking life may seem incongruous to any of us vaguely familiar with the teachings of Jesus, but it is standard issue for right-wing American politicians. Christians in power are killers.

The 2000 Election

Bill Clinton presided for eight years over a period of relative peace and stability in the US. As the Clinton presidency neared its end, Vice President Al Gore faced nearly no opposition in his candidacy for the Democratic nomination.

Money colors everything in American politics, and in the 2000 Republican primaries it was used as intimidation. A year out from the election, Bush had raised so much more money than ever before that many other candidates chose to stay out of the race. Sheer weight of money got Bush the nomination, and money would win him the White House. The public had little involvement in these matters. Most of the money came from oil. Six out of the top ten of George W. Bush's lifetime political backers come from or are tied to the oil industry.

In the brief Republican primary battle, George W. Bush faced veteran John McCain, who took an early lead but was set back by a relentlessly negative campaign against him in the South. While Bush campaigned as a compassionate conservative, his supporters (led by Karl Rove) spread innuendo, untruth, and rumors, including suggesting that McCain had fathered an illegitimate child with a black prostitute from New York. Although preposterous and clearly untrue, the tactic worked and the damage was done. McCain's challenge faded. Bush would be the Republican nominee.

In his early appearances as presidential candidate, especially the debates, Bush appeared uncertain, shallow, and out of his depth. However, such is the triumph of style over substance in televised American politics that though Gore appeared much more capable and experienced, his mistake of guffawing at Bush's poor answers turned voters against him, or at least that's what the pundits said.

As the election cycle rolled on, Bush went for the Reagan angle, shortening his statements to folksy sound bites, appearing in a broad-brimmed hat, and sporting a flashy belt buckle at some activity the folks back home could identify with. Virtually all press access was restricted, so as to disguise his lack of political experience (especially internationally) and poor public speaking skills.

Bush portrayed himself as a plain-speaking regular Joe, who the public "might want to have a beer with." Gore was not that type of guy.

The tactics worked, the race tightened.

There was no doubt which candidate money wanted. Corporate donations rolled in on an unprecedented scale.

Bush also portrayed himself as a moderate conservative, championing a humble foreign policy. He surrounded himself with a who's who of veteran neoconservative hawks. These people were (amusingly in light of subsequent developments) portrayed as grizzled experts who would guide the young president towards a foreign policy based on practicality.

Gore waged a weak campaign, out-flanked by the dirty tricks from the right, under-using the still-popular Clinton, and failing to clearly enunciate a vision truly his own. He even lost his home state of Tennessee, due (the NRA claimed) to his stance on guns.

Voter suppression, fraud and intimidation was used against groups known to be leaning heavily towards the Democrats—black and poor people in particular. While dirty tricks have forever been a part of US elections (John F. Kennedy became president after one of the dirtiest elections in history) the sheer scale of malfeasance and electoral law-breaking was unprecedented, and nowhere more than in the state of Florida.

False pamphlets claiming voting had been extended by twenty-four hours were circulated. Others said that anyone with outstanding parking tickets or child support payments would be arrested at the polling booths. False calls were made to Democrat voters saying polling booth addresses had changed—people queued in the rain for hours, only to be told to go back to the correct location. Polling locations in poor or black areas opened late, and had much longer queues than in prosperous white neighborhoods. Bosses threatened staff with the sack if they stayed away from their jobs too long.

With his brother Jeb as governor of Florida, the Bush brothers at the very least managed to disenfranchise a huge number of people of color, using an ancient law and Florida's Secretary of State Katherine Harris to produce a list of 57,000–91,000 purported "felons" who were turned away at the polls. The dirty tricks in Florida proved crucial, swinging the election and changing the course of history.

Despite widespread electoral fraud by the Republican side, the 2000 election ended up as the most closely contested in 124 years. On the day, all major networks called Florida for Gore, based on exit polls, but the numbers coming out of the counting booths were significantly different, something rarely seen.

Katherine Harris excluded 179,855 spoiled votes, mostly the famous "hanging chads," where although it was clear who had been voted for, because the card had not been punched all the way through, the vote was deemed invalid. This, as is so often the case, primarily affected the black vote, with 54 percent of the spoiled and invalid votes having been made by African Americans (with just 15 percent of Floridians identifying as black).

Despite the well-documented voter fraud perpetrated by Jeb Bush and Katherine Harris, the recount was stopped and the result determined not through the ballot box but by a 5–4 Supreme Court decision, based on the idea that manually recounting ballots degraded the physical evidence, risking fraud, and that a proper recount could not be completed in time. It was highway robbery. Bush had lost the popular vote, but he would be president.

President

No US administration has ever been so closely aligned with the military industrial complex as that of George W. Bush. Bush filled his White House with the neoconservatives whose stated goals included the massive expansion of the US military budget and the realignment of the Middle East, including the prosecution of a war in Iraq.

Right from the start it was clear that Bush and his senior staff had a radical agenda for the reformation of government, intelligence, and the military, and that sweeping changes would be made to concentrate power in the hands of a small number of people at the very top of the administration. The compassionate conservatism and humble foreign policy of the election campaign was gone.

Bush's first National Security Council meeting on January 30, 2001 focused extensively on Iraq and ended with Bush ordering contingency plans to be drawn up for war to remove Saddam Hussein. Terrorism wasn't discussed until July, and then only in passing.

The first Bush White House document relating to National Security (in February 2001) made radical changes to the structure of the National Security Council (NSC), the body that oversees all intelligence, security, and foreign affairs in the US. Nearly every intelligence agency except the CIA was abruptly denied the right of automatic attendance at NSC meetings, drastically concentrating National Security policy formation into a few key senior hands, which meant that coordination and communication on key security issues could now be controlled by these players. Interagency Working Groups were abolished. From then on, the agencies charged with national security could communicate with each only when permitted.

Most responsibility for managing this new national security structure was given to Condoleezza Rice, hugely inexperienced in office, whose previous career had been at Stanford University and on the board of Chevron Oil, who named a tanker after her.

Given subsequent events, it is right to ask why intelligence information sharing at the top was abolished. After all, the events of 9/11 are often described as a massive intelligence failure. The procedural changes at the top of the intelligence community surely contributed.

What the new structure also meant was that the flow of information about the terrorism warnings being received in 2001 could be easily manipulated by those at the top of the Bush administration.

This also negates the suggestion that the Bush White House was not aware of the overwhelming warnings that were received prior to the 9/11 attacks. With this new concentration of power, it is absurd that those at the top were the main propagators of the idea that no one had—or could have—predicted using hijacked planes as weapons, or that an attack was perceived as likely. National security information went directly to the top, and 2001 saw an unprecedented spike in warning signs.

Saudi Arabia quickly felt the benefits of having a Bush in the White House. The long relationship between the Bush and Saudi royal families (and the bin Ladens) paid immediate dividends when the new Bush administration instructed US intelligence agencies to back off investigating Saudi state funding of religious extremism, and the bin Laden family in particular.

This abrogation of responsibility was despite the growing chatter of intelligence suggesting something big was in the wings. Although the public were not informed, the state of alert at the G8 summit in Genoa, Italy in July 2001 was deemed so high that when Bush arrived, anti-aircraft guns lined the runway, the airspace was closed, and fighters flew overhead. The CIA had intelligence warnings that Osama bin Laden was planning an attack using an airplane stuffed with explosives. Bush slept each night aboard a navy warship, rather than risk staying on dry land.

Despite the heightened security, Bush decided to take a vacation across most of August 2001, nearly setting the record for the longest US presidential holiday (Bush spent 32 percent of his entire presidency on vacation). Although the August break was billed as a working vacation, it was widely reported that Bush was doing nothing much except attending his daily briefings and cutting timber.

By the end of Bush's August vacation, he had spent 42 percent of his presidency on vacation or en route. Vice President Cheney also spent most of the month at a remote location in Wyoming, his home state.

The primary responsibility of the president, the White House, administration, and staff is to keep America and its citizens safe. By any measure, Bush took a vacation from this responsibility. It would return to haunt him.

Bush on 9/11

Those who belong in the "Bush knew" school of thought have their argument weakened by the sheer feckless impotence of George W. Bush on 9/11. Bush may have been president, but until 8:00 p.m. that day he was essentially a peripheral figure, scooting from one location to another and apparently making no major decisions or interventions that had any kind of effect on the day's events. Bush was effectively sidelined, sent a thousand miles from the action and kept away while the attacks took place and the dust settled, then allowed to return in time to assure the American people that all was well, and that their government was in charge.

That was not the case for most of the day on September 11, 2001.

Bush spent the night of September 10 at the Colony Beach and Tennis Resort in Longboat Key, Florida. The security situation had not cooled since Genoa and the G8 summit. Surface-to-air missiles were placed on the roof.

At around 6:00 a.m., a van containing several men of Middle Eastern descent arrived at the resort, saying that they were a television news crew, and had a poolside interview with the president arranged. The men asked for a

Secret Service officer by name. Another agent told them he knew of no such interview plan, and the men were turned away and left.

Longboat Key fire marshal Carroll Mooneyhan was at the hotel reception while Bush prepared for his morning jog, and overheard a conversation between the security staff and the hotel's receptionist. The incident was reported by the *Longboat Observer*, a local newspaper (which stood by their story when it was disputed). Given the assassination of Ahmed Shah Massoud, the head of the Northern Alliance in Afghanistan, just two days earlier (that so dramatically affected the course of the war that followed), by a bomb hidden in a television camera, it is far from inconceivable to suggest that this was a bungled attempt to assassinate George W. Bush. This fits neatly into the alternative narrative of 9/11, that of a military and political coup. For whatever reason, access to Bush was denied, and the story of what may have been an assassination attempt on the US president on 9/11 has not been pursued.

Sarasota, Florida appears to have been a central location for Saudi terrorists, their government handlers, and the Mossad agents who were observing them, so it is an odd coincidence that Sarasota was also the location chosen for Bush's famous schoolbook reading on the morning of 9/11. The publicity event at the Emma E. Booker Elementary school had been planned since August, but only publicly announced on September 7. On that same day, Mohamed Atta and Marwan al-Shehhi were in the Holiday Inn, Sarasota, just a couple of miles from the resort where Bush stayed on September 10.

This is just one of a dazzling array of coincidences involving seemingly disparate groups involved in the events of 9/11 finding themselves within mere miles of each other.

President Bush was travelling in a motorcade towards the Emma E. Booker elementary school in Sarasota when the first WTC attack occurred at 8:46 a.m. CNN broke into its broadcast three minutes later to show the massive wound on the side of north tower. The Secret Service (responsible for the President's safety) have the best communications equipment in the world—it's impossible to imagine more than another 1–2 minutes elapsing before word was passed to them and on to the president.

Bush's motorcade arrived at 8:55 a.m. Despite knowing that a large plane had struck the World Trade Center, and being in a unique position to know that a major domestic terrorist attack involving hijacked planes had been warned of for many of the preceding months, Bush told the school principal Gwen Tose-Rigell that he would proceed with the "reading thing" anyway. The principal said she first heard of the plane crash from the president himself.

Bush later said that he had seen footage of the first plane crash as he was waiting to go into the classroom and thought, "There's one terrible pilot," but the first crash was only captured by the Naudet brothers and not broadcast until thirteen hours later on CNN. Wild conspiracies aside, we can put this down to the confused memory of a man not known for being particularly intelligent.

Before Bush entered the school, he spoke to Condoleezza Rice on the phone, and was informed that the crash was a commercial airliner. By that time the entire machine of US security—the FAA, NORAD, NMCC, the Pentagon, the White House, and Secret Service—were all aware that three commercial aircraft had been simultaneously hijacked, and that a major terrorist attack was probably underway.

So it is unclear why at 9:03 a.m., seventeen minutes after the first plane impact, Bush was allowed to sit down in a second-grade classroom for a photo opportunity. Given the knowledge of multiple hijackings, the Secret Service's job was to assume that the head of state was a potential target. At around this moment, Dick Cheney was being rushed to the bunker under the White House, yet Bush was left untouched, at this publicized location. This was the moment the Secret Service had spent their professional lives training for. The President's safety is their number one objective.

At almost the same moment as the president sat down in Florida, flight 175 was flown into the south tower of the World Trade Center. After a few minutes, Bush's chief of staff Andrew Card approached him and whispered in his ear, "A second plane hit the second tower; America is under attack."

Any sane leader would have leapt to their feet and left the room immediately. This was not just in Bush's self-interest; this was his duty as commander-in-chief. But Bush didn't even ask for details. Instead, as this generation's Pearl Harbor took place, the president pressed on, listening in silence as the children read him a book called *The Pet Goat*.

As the minutes passed, word of the second attack spread through the assembled press throng of around 150 packed into the back of the classroom, and the cameras focused ever more intently on Bush and his startled face. Bush looked genuinely lost, perhaps terrified. At the back of the room, spokesman Ari Fleischer held up a piece of paper with DON'T SAY ANYTHING YET written on it in thick marker. These moments are captured best in Michael Moore's film *Fahrenheit 9/11*. As the children finished reading their book, Bush seemed to be openly stretching the moment, and took time to compliment the children on their reading skills.

It was only at 9:16 a.m., some thirteen minutes after the world knew that this was a devastating and unprecedented terrorist attack, that Bush left the classroom. As an indictment of his ineptitude, this delay merely adds to a long list, but for the Secret Service to act this way is beyond explanation, because it matters not if the president is a bumbling fool; the Secret Service guarding him are the best of the best. The Secret Service should have run in, picked Bush up by the arms, and dragged him out toward the safety of his bomb-proof limo.

Despite the widely seen footage, the White House relayed a different account in 2002, stating that Bush excused himself politely after Andrew Card's message, and left the room in a matter of seconds. In modern America, even events captured on film can be recast in a better light, and that can become part of an accepted narrative.

Bush would later say that he was trying to project calm and strength, and didn't move faster because he did not want to alarm the children, though the prospect of a suicidal hijacked 757 bearing down on the school may have alarmed some of them, had they known. Calm was the opposite of what was needed at that moment. Instead, Bush looked like a frightened rabbit, trapped in the headlights.

At 9:29 a.m., Bush gave a brief televised address to the nation, again at the exact time and place stated in his publicly announced schedule. No one in the US yet knew how many planes had been hijacked, yet the Secret Service allowed the president to broadcast his exact location.

Bush left the school just after 9:30. Three quarters of an hour had elapsed since a commercial jet struck the World Trade Center. The president had done nothing. Sarasota airport was only three and a half minutes away. Less than ten minutes after the second plane strike, Bush should have been lifting off into the relative safety of the skies. Instead, after these inexplicable delays, his motorcade managed to head in the wrong direction and get lost on that short journey, and had to do a U-turn before finding the airport. Air Force One only became airborne at 9:54 a.m.

The urgency was certainly understood by Air Force One's pilots. After takeoff, the plane gained altitude as quickly as possible, "like a rocket," according to Communications Director Dan Bartlett: "for a good ten minutes, the plane was going almost straight up."

It appears that Air Force One then stayed over Sarasota until a decision was made as to where to go. Reporters onboard sensed the plane was flying in circles, and the signal for a Florida-based TV station remained strong.

Fighters did not appear alongside the president's plane until over an hour and a half later, at 11:41 a.m. With two air force bases in Florida on alert on the morning of 9/11, it is unclear why it took so long for fighters to escort the president.

Barksdale and Offutt

Once the decision had been made not to return to Washington, based on the infamous "Angel is Next" phantom threat to Air Force One (see "Cheney on 9/11," p. 131), Bush flew to Barksdale Air Force Base in Louisiana, arriving at about 11:45 a.m., where he made a brief and somewhat flustered statement.

It appears Bush spent most of his time at Barksdale arguing with Dick Cheney over where he should go next. Further rumors concerning a threat to Air Force One, again communicated to Bush by Cheney, meant that despite the media beginning to ask questions about the President's whereabouts, the decision was made to continue to stay away from Washington.

After about ninety minutes on the ground, Bush left Barksdale on Air Force One, stranding all but five of the White House press corps on the ground. The plane headed toward Offutt Air Force Base, Nebraska, headquarters of US Strategic Command (Stratcom). Offutt is also home to America's most important military nuclear bunker, three stories underground and designed to withstand a direct nuclear blast. Bush arrived at Offutt at 2:50 p.m., and entered the bunny hole entrance to the nuclear bunker at 3:06 p.m. He did not emerge until 4:33 p.m.

At no time in American history have all the pieces been so in place for the possibility of global thermonuclear war. Key defense personnel were in the war room at the Pentagon, the vice president was in the bunker under the White House, the US military was at DEFCON 3, and various other key administration members and officials had been flown to secure locations at Mount Weather and Site R.

Once installed in the conference room of the nuclear bunker, Bush apparently began the meeting by saying, "I'm coming back to the White House as soon as the plane is fueled. No discussion."

At 4:33 p.m., Bush finally left Offutt on Air Force One, bound for Washington, arriving at 6:42 before taking a helicopter flight across the city, to finally make it back to the White House at 6:54 p.m., some ten hours after the attacks had commenced.

On the evening of 9/11, Bush said that immediately following the first attack, he implemented the government's emergency response plans, but in fact, the Interagency Domestic Terrorism Concept of Operations Plan (CONPLAN) was activated by lower level officials. Bush later said that he had given no orders whatsoever until he boarded Air Force One, and in truth Bush was effectively removed from all decision-making throughout the day. There is no evidence that Bush made any meaningful contribution to defending the nation at any point on September 11, and his physical removal from Washington meant that all command and control as events played out was carried out by Dick Cheney in the White House bunker and Donald Rumsfeld at the Pentagon.

Nevertheless, President Bush had value. As head of state, it was vital that he appear on television to reassure the public that all was well, and that the apparatus of government was still in place. Accordingly, Bush gave a brief TV address to the nation at 8:30 p.m.

An hour later, Bush delivered the payload to his military team, saying, "Everything is available for the pursuit of this war. Any barriers in your way, they're gone. Any money you need, you have it. This is our only agenda." The attacks had opened the floodgates.

Putin

Arguably the most important event on 9/11 was Vladimir Putin's phone call. It is widely thought that Putin called the White House personally, and spoke to Condoleezza Rice as President Bush traveled across the country on Air Force One. Rice is reported to have assured Putin that America knew the Russians weren't behind the attack, and that no nuclear exchange would take place. America had made plans to move to DEFCON 2, just one level below all-out nuclear war, for the first time since the Cuban Missile Crisis. This was something the Russians would have been acutely aware of, and their own military would have been put on the highest state of alert.

The risk of accidental nuclear conflagration has always been much greater than the actual risk of war. In Washington, the Nuclear Risk Reduction Center was specifically created (in 1987) so as to exchange information with Russian authorities in times of high emergency, and it was activated on 9/11.

When Bush spoke to Putin later that day, he told him that America was going to invade Afghanistan, something that even Putin would have been hard-pressed to disagree with, given the events of the day. Counter-intuitively, perhaps, the attacks had greatly strengthened America's hand.

Bush after 9/11

As we now know, by the evening of September 11 the White House was a hotbed of powerful Neoconservatives making plans for an invasion of Iraq, sweeping changes to America's military, and a huge raft of legislation that radically scaled back America's relationship with its Constitution, all aimed at governing the US in a new era.

The extraordinary haste with which sorrow was abandoned and opportunity embraced looks astonishingly cynical and cold-hearted, but the neocons saw 9/11 as just that: an opportunity. They said as much on numerous occasions. Their eagerness to embrace this chance to implement pre-planned agendas, before the sun had even set on the wreckage in New York, reveals just how calculating and opportunistic these political operators were.

From the morning of September 12 onward, members of the Bush administration began telling the world that 9/11 changed everything. It was absolutely vital that the public were told again and again that the world had changed forever, because with a changed world, an entirely new set of rules could be written. No matter how badly these new measures subverted the rule of law and the Constitution, when placed in this post-9/11 environment, any means necessary to "keep people safe" seemed acceptable.

Under this new paradigm, anyone questioning the wisdom of their leaders could be told in no uncertain terms that doing so was to risk another 9/11 and betraying the memory of those who died that day. Because of 9/11, we were told, the US could—in fact had to—adopt strategies of preemptive and unilateral war, first use of nuclear weapons, and disregard international treaties and organizations, abandon nuclear proliferation control agreements, use force to extend America's ambitions abroad, torture and imprison America's enemies without trial, and (we would eventually discover) launch a massive program of domestic surveillance at home.

After 9/11 Bush strode tall, his pronouncements delivered with a messianic certainty, safe in the knowledge that no one could question his judgment. That would be unpatriotic, a betrayal of America. Even the way he walked changed to a chest-out type of swagger.

Yet Bush's view of the world was still black and white; a world of good guys and "evil-doers," a place where you were either with us or with the terrorists. This most memorable phrase shows just how facile Bush's take on world affairs was. One questions where Saudi Arabia stood on that monochromatic spectrum.

On September 20, Bush said, "Either you are with us or you are against us. From this day forward, any nation that continues to harbor or support terrorism will be regarded by the United States as a hostile regime." This sort of pronouncement from the leader of the United States of America marked a new era, not because the world had changed, but because America was going to change how it dealt with the world.

Life isn't black and white. Germany had for some time played host to the supposed Arabic terrorists, but was clearly "with us." Saudi Arabia funded terrorists and was the home of the bin Laden family, but for reasons too opaque for us to be asked to consider, they too were judged to be on our side. Iraq, which had no involvement in 9/11 at all, and whose leader offered sympathy to the victims, was most definitely "with the terrorists."

Each of us in our daily lives deal with nuance in our relationships. To simply classify all people as with us or against us is stupid and simplistic, and would lead us to make poor decisions based on such a myopic world-view. However, as the most powerful nation on earth, this declaration was less about how other countries were to be viewed, and more a statement of intent. Do as we say or suffer the consequences.

Resolutions were quickly passed by Congress and the Senate that gave Bush $40 billion and an open-ended license to take action against not only any nation, organization, or person who his administration deemed to have been complicit in the 9/11 attacks, but also against those who opposed the War on Terror. Or anyone who would not do what Bush said. The authorization contained no time limits, no Congressional oversight, and no requirement for the president to come back for additional authority. In other words, it gave the office of the president unlimited power, minus the checks and balances enshrined in the Constitution. Quickly, the tragedy of 9/11 was channeled into unprecedented power for the president and, of course, his administration team.

Bush took time out from his nation's defense to sign an executive order that allowed any sitting or former president to veto the release of personal papers detailing political decision making, meaning Bush's dirty laundry could be kept secret in perpetuity. It would not be the last time his government used the fear of terrorism as a pretext for protecting officials from scrutiny.

The new War on Terror meant color-coded terror alerts on every TV station, wall-to-wall news coverage that portrayed a hysterical country in a constant state of crisis, and the endless repetition of a few key phrases to hammer home what people should be scared of. 9/11 was used as an excuse for any measure, no matter how illegal or unconstitutional, so long as it kept America "safe."

In a country where once a former president declared that the only thing to fear is fear itself, Bush gave his nation a sense that being afraid was the patriotic thing to do. What was unpatriotic was to question the actions of the government, or its leader, a man literally in touch with God. In a speech at Cleveland in 2006, Bush managed to use the word "terror" 54 times. Fear became the lifeblood of his presidency.

A classic Orwellian move by the Bush administration was to take credit for preventing another 9/11 attack, but warn that more domestic terrorism was very likely, or indeed inevitable. Fear was to be mandatory; free thought and inquiry would just hamper the government's War on Terror, and make Americans less safe. No matter that the attacks had taken place on Bush's watch. His people portrayed themselves as brave heroes who kept their nation safe from another devastating attack.

Within weeks of 9/11, Bush authorized the NSA to eavesdrop on US citizens without obtaining the warrants required by law. This action sowed the seeds for the NSA wiretapping program that now looks impossible to roll back. It took four more years for Bush's decision to be made public. The War on Terror was seen, by Bush at least, as something that allowed his administration to do anything and break any rule, sure in the knowledge that he could characterize his actions as having been carried out in the name of national security.

Freed from oversight or opposition, Bush gave notice on December 13 (just nine weeks after 9/11) of America's intention to withdraw from the ABM (Anti Ballistic Missile) Treaty with Russia that had held strong for thirty years. The world's nuclear rules were not going to apply anymore. Bush directed his military to draw up contingencies to use nuclear weapons against at least seven countries (China and Russia included), and to proceed with plans to build much smaller nuclear weapons (mini-nukes) to be used in active battlefield situations. These actions resulted in similar moves by non-US aligned countries, where nuclear brinkmanship is marked by tit-for-tat actions. Supporters of the ABM treaty withdrawal argued that such a move was vital in order for America to pursue its National Missile Defense strategies, including goals specifically sought by members of the Project for the New American Century.

All of this from a man who could not actually say the word "nuclear." Bush pronounced it new-cu-lar. But look on the bright side. Sarah Palin had to have the word spelled phonetically on her teleprompter during 2008 election speeches. The script she read from said "new-clear weapons."

When the Bush administration set up a fund to compensate 9/11 victims relatives, it insisted that those accepting compensation could only sue terrorists, not any other entity, including the government, and that those choosing to sue anyone else would forfeit their compensation. Adrift in a sea of cynicism, this may be one of the most dastardly acts of George W. Bush's eight years in office. One relative, Ellen Mariani, estimated she passed up around $500,000 in cash when she chose to sue the US government for foreknowledge of the attacks. She called the money offered to bereaved relatives the "shut up and go away fund." But the numbers were too much for most people, especially given the devastating loss of a loved one. 97 percent of eligible families applied, and compensation averaged $2.1 million per family.

America's warlike and vengeful response to the 9/11 attacks was not as immediate or as visceral as might be thought. Many New Yorkers sported t-shirts that said "an eye for an eye makes the world go blind," and promoted reconciliation with America's so-called enemies, rather than endless war. The *New York Times* reported that the drumbeat for war was barely audible on the streets of New York. But Bush and his team relentlessly channeled patriotic revenge, anger, and hate through the media to drum up support for their plans.

For those who agreed that the capture or killing of Osama bin Laden was warranted, the invasion of Afghanistan at least seemed logical, but in the early months of 2002 a new strategy began being promoted that seemed distantly related, if at all, to the events of 9/11. Iraq seemed to be preoccupying most of the Bush administration's time and, for reasons that remained unclear, Afghanistan and bin Laden were suddenly less of a priority.

It seems hard to believe now, but this change of focus was so pronounced that in March 2002, just six months after 9/11, Bush felt able to all but dismiss America's nemesis, saying "I don't know where [bin Laden] is. You know, I just don't spend that much time on him."

Bush, now fixated on Iraq (a country with no connection to 9/11), invoked his Christianity selectively. He said that he had not consulted his father when making the decision to invade Iraq, but he did ask his "higher father".

Bush gave Donald Rumsfeld carte blanche when it came to the prosecution of the new War on Terror. The world would soon learn the meaning of new expressions like rendition (kidnap) and enhanced interrogation (torture). Rumsfeld wanted to interrogate prisoners away from the prying eyes of the US legal system, and far from the reaches of international law and the Red Cross, so Bush permitted him to establish the internment camp at Guantanamo Bay, a decision that stains America's reputation to this day.

In his book *Decision Points,* Bush recounted being asked by the CIA whether they could proceed with waterboarding Khalid Sheikh Mohammed, who Bush said was suspected of knowing about pending terrorist plots against the United States. Bush wrote that his reply was "damn right," and that he would make the same decision again.

The widespread use of torture in America's War on Terror was pushed for by Cheney and Rumsfeld, and personally authorized by President Bush after receiving legal rulings from his compliant Justice Department officials John Yoo and Jay Bybee. That legal counsel was far from independent. Yoo and Bybee knew that their job was to come up with answers that the president liked.

But torture isn't legal, under American law or that of many other countries. It's specifically banned by the UN and international law. When Bush visited Canada in 2012, many called for his prosecution under domestic laws that require prosecution of all torturers, regardless of who they are or where they are from. This may explain Bush's virtually non-existent international travel since leaving office.

2004 Election

Much of the disaster that Bush presided over only became apparent during his second term. As the 2004 election approached, moderate but uncharismatic Democrat John Kerry seemed likely to win, given his centrist stance and unblemished personal record, including three Purple Hearts for bravery during the Vietnam war. At the time of the TV debates, 80 percent of Americans said they thought Bush was hiding something or mostly lying about the Iraq war. It seemed like Kerry couldn't lose.

However, Karl Rove and Bush's attack dogs mounted a disgraceful smear campaign against Kerry that somehow managed to cast doubt on his exemplary war record, portraying Kerry as a wimp while ignoring Bush's own cowardly history of finding excuse after excuse to stay home, or often not even turning up during his brief period of domestic service. Apart from being illustrative of how dirty American politics can be, this was an amazing example of how information can be compartmentalized and partitioned out, muddying clear waters and leaving the voter disoriented and confused as to which is the hero and which the villain. Kerry had served bravely and been decorated in Vietnam. Bush had dodged the draft and never shot a weapon in anger. Yet the mood of the day and a belligerent Republican electoral team managed to paint Kerry as the flip-flopper and Bush the war hero commander-in-chief.

During the first televised debate between Bush and Kerry, Bush put in a bizarre, rambling performance. At times he appeared to be responding to someone who wasn't there. Camera angles (taken in contravention of the mountainous set of rules negotiated by the Bush team to protect their man) showed a distinct bulge in the back of Bush's jacket, and many felt this was evidence that Bush was wearing a wire. This should hardly come as a surprise. Bush wore a wire at many press conferences and public appearances. His faltering speaking method was in part a product of parroting the words fed into his ear-piece.

Nearly all of the television adverts for Bush/Cheney in 2004 invoked 9/11. Terror, and the threat of terrorism, was ruthlessly used as a political weapon.

Tom Ridge, the Homeland security secretary, was pressured by Bush's cabinet to raise the terror alert level just before the election so as to guide more fearful voters toward the president who said that he kept them safe. Polls showed that Bush's approval ratings rose in the days that followed a raising of the terror level.

The election day itself was beyond bizarre. Exit polls projected a win for Kerry by five million votes, but the count showed a win for Bush by three million more votes. Kerry lost the crucial state of Ohio to Bush, despite exit polls showing Kerry with a substantial lead. In Virginia and South Carolina, the TV stations held off calling a winner, as exit polls showed things as too close to call, but in the official count Bush won comfortably. No other election in US history has had anything like such a discrepancy. However, the election was also the first truly digital ballot, and the three main companies involved (ES&S, Diebold, and Sequoia) all were tied to the Bush administration. All had significant investments from defense contractors. The result should never have been in doubt.

By 2004 the disaster in Iraq had not entered the public consciousness, and people were unaware of Bush's domestic surveillance programs. The economy seemed to be progressing. There was no outstanding reason to out Mr. Bush, yet he still only got 50.7 percent of the popular vote, and edged the Electoral College by just thirty-five ballots. After the election Bush claimed to have political capital and said he intended to spend it. He certainly did that. His second term was four years of utter mayhem, at home and abroad.

Bush's Legacy

Even in the last days of his administration, Bush's approval rating hovered somewhere just north of 30 percent, the lowest of any president in thirty-five years. Clearly, there was virtually nothing Bush could do that would change the minds of three in ten Americans.

That certainly was the case with Bush's own assessment of his legacy. Bush maintains to this day that the major decisions of his presidency were all correct. With characteristic eloquence, Bush said in 2008 that "removing Saddam Hussein from power was the right decision early in [his] Presidency, it is the right decision now, and it will be the right decision ever."

When George W. Bush took over from Bill Clinton, America was a country in reasonable order: not at war, cutting its military budget, and with a profitable and growing economy. Eight short years later Bush bequeathed a nation in the process of burning itself to the ground; stuck in a seemingly unending war with a hugely increased military budget, a divided populace, the worst jobs record in history and an economy that, in his swansong, threatened to bring capitalism itself to an end. George W. Bush can rightly be considered the most disastrous president in the history of the United States.

But in many ways, the blame really lies with those who controlled Bush.

Dick Cheney

A much more interesting figure than the feckless, moronic, and ineffective Bush is Richard Cheney, the most powerful vice president in American history.

Cheney is accurately portrayed as the ultimate Washington insider, having worked almost exclusively for the federal government since his early twenties, holding senior positions in the Nixon, Ford, and Bush Sr. administrations, and serving as a representative for Wyoming for ten years. His career is inextricably entwined with that of Donald Rumsfeld. They worked together for over thirty years, taking turns as each other's bosses.

In Cheney's only significant period outside the halls of Washington, he worked as CEO and chairman of Halliburton, the oil services and logistics giant.

Like his warmongering president, Cheney found his way to five draft deferments during the Vietnam War, later saying he had "other priorities" in the 1960s. His personal antipathy toward armed service proved no impediment to Cheney enthusiastically sending thousands of his countrymen to fight and die in wars just as pointless and dishonest as that he had sought so hard to avoid as a younger man.

During his eleven years as Representative for Wyoming, Cheney built a reputation as a hard-nosed far-right ideologue, championing causes that most of us would find reprehensible, but happy to change his opinions to fit the prevailing mood of the day. Just a small sample paints an abysmal picture, Cheney opposed government funding for abortion, even in the case of incest or rape. His enthusiasm for guns showed no bounds—he voted against a ban on armor-piercing bullets (so-called cop killers), and against a ban on plastic guns that couldn't be detected by airport security systems. Cheney voted against the creation of the Department of Education, against sanctions for South African apartheid (saying that they almost never work) and against a resolution calling for the release of Nelson Mandela.

As George H. W. Bush's secretary of defense, Cheney oversaw Operation Desert Storm, repelling Iraq's invasion of Kuwait, and was central in the decision not to continue the action once Iraqi troops were routed. His reasoning for not continuing into Iraq makes interesting reading, given subsequent events:

> "Because if we'd gone to Baghdad we would have been all alone. There wouldn't have been anybody else with us. There would have been a US occupation of Iraq. None of the Arab forces that were willing to fight with us in Kuwait were willing to invade Iraq. Once you got to Iraq and took it over, took down Saddam Hussein's government, then what are you going to put in its place? That's a very volatile part of the world, and if you take down the central government of Iraq, you could very easily end up seeing pieces of Iraq fly off."

In 1999, when George W. Bush was putting together his campaign team, he asked Dick Cheney to head up a team to select a running mate. After scouring the country for the right individual and searching through every bin to ensure that those considered had no damaging dirty laundry, Cheney chose himself, and Bush accepted.

As a vice presidential candidate, Cheney had a huge influence over the inexperienced George W. Bush, and was central in the appointment of Donald Rumsfeld and several other key neoconservatives. Behind Bush would be a veritable who's who of leading neocons, with Cheney pulling the strings.

Cheney resigned as chairman and CEO of Halliburton to take up the vice presidential position, for which he received a $36 million severance package, totally disproportionate to the remuneration offered to other senior executives. Halliburton knew on which side their bread was buttered—with an oil man as president and Cheney just a heartbeat away, the $36 million was an investment in the future which would pay rich, rich dividends. Cheney continued to receive up to $1 million per year in deferred payments from Halliburton while in office, and was reported to retain a large stock option holding, the value of which soared from $240K to $8 million in just one year (2004–05). Halliburton's generosity to Dick Cheney also came in handy when they were awarded huge (and hugely profitable) government contracts after 9/11, such as a no-bid (i.e. no competition) $7 billion agreement for work in Iraq.

Once in office, Cheney was tasked by Bush with a holistic review of US energy strategy, and focused much of his behind-the-scenes efforts on a nascent plan to effect regime change in Iraq. Cheney assembled a team called the Energy Task Force to conduct the review, and to assemble a report essentially set up to find out how much oil was left, who had it, and how America could get their hands on it. Work began almost the same day as Bush took office. Staff met in secret. Unusually, no note-taking was allowed.

The report was completed in May 2001. Among its key recommendations was that the US urgently needed to obtain substantial new sources of oil to meet its energy requirements, including from the Caspian Sea region.

On the face of it, such a review might seem reasonable. International oil reserve figures are widely known to be fraudulent and inaccurate, and America depends on a continued flow of oil to keep its economy going. However, the immense secrecy surrounding the task force's activities have given much cause for suspicion. Despite two visits to the Supreme Court, Dick Cheney has successfully kept the workings of his staff a secret from the world.

The focus on oil, energy, and regime change in the Middle East undoubtedly distracted the Bush administration from keeping people safe at home. On January 31, 2001, just 11 days after Bush took office, the final phase of the "US Commission on National Security/21st Century" was released. The report had taken two and a half years to complete, and was the broadest and most important review of national security strategy for over fifty years. The co-chairs of the report personally briefed Condoleezza Rice, Donald Rumsfeld, and Colin Powell, but all fifty of the recommendations on how to combat domestic terrorism were ignored until after 9/11.

In May 2001, Bush put Cheney in charge of an initiative to examine national preparedness for managing a possible attack by weapons of mass destruction, despite the fact that the Commission that had just issued its report had spent the last few years doing exactly that. The order was more about power structure than information. Bush's executive order put Cheney in charge of anti-terrorism, giving him authority over forty-six government agencies anti-terror operations. The task force was just getting underway when the 9/11 attacks occurred.

In the same month, Bush also placed Cheney in personal charge of the new Office of National Preparedness (part of FEMA) to coordinate federal emergency responses and intelligence gathering. Cheney's task force was due to report to Congress on October 1, 2001.

Thus, by the spring of 2001, Cheney was effectively in charge of America's energy and anti-terrorism strategy and operations, two areas that would become central to the Bush presidency.

Prior to 9/11, Cheney also made regular visits to CIA headquarters in Langley. Most of the visits focused on Iraq, a subject that appeared entirely off the agenda at the time.

Cheney on 9/11

Perhaps it was a coincidence, but with President Bush entirely sidelined in a primary school a thousand miles from the action and unable to offer any meaningful contribution, it is striking how Cheney and other key characters were at the center of events on 9/11.

Cheney was at the White House, Rumsfeld at the Pentagon, CIA Director George Tenet was on his way to the White House, and FBI Director Robert Mueller (who had started in the job just a week before) was at FBI headquarters. Meanwhile the president was in Florida, Secretary of State Colin Powell was in Peru, the FEMA director was in Montana, and the chairman of the Joint Chiefs of Staff was on a flight above the Atlantic, headed toward Europe, leaving Richard Myers in charge.

On the morning of 9/11 it appears that every major decision, and the locus of power and command, came from the Presidential Emergency Operations Center (PEOC). Cheney was widely reported to have been in full command. As such, he was the most influential American on September 11 2001.

However, Cheney should have been entirely peripheral. Constitutionally, the vice president has absolutely no chain-of-command role to play in times of crisis. Cheney's taking control on 9/11 was beyond bizarre. It is not acceptable to simply say, well, this was a major crisis, a time of chaos; Cheney intervened in good faith in order to keep America safe. These protocols and the strict chain of command were written specifically for times of great crisis. It's at these moments that their use becomes critical. If Cheney ran America's response to 9/11 from a bunker underneath the White House, and those in the direct chain of command (the president and congressional leaders) contributed next to nothing, then a full investigation into the breakdown of one of the most vital tenets of America's national security would be in order.

As an aside, some might also question what Cheney's wife Lynne was doing at the PEOC. She was repeatedly noted offering her advice and opinions to Cheney during the crisis.

In the chain of command, the decision to engage the military must be made by the president, who gives orders to the secretary of defense (who can also make that decision). The vice president has no place in the chain whatsoever.

In fact, the vice president's only substantial role is to take over if the president is incapacitated (by way of illness or unconsciousness, etc.) or killed. Between 2000 and 2008, Cheney did in fact act as president for two very short periods (a couple of hours) when President Bush was under general anesthetics for routine medical procedures. Other than that, it's an unusually powerless position. Vice President John Garner famously said the office of the vice president was "not worth a bucket of warm piss."

According to standard procedure, with no role to play, Cheney should have been taken by the Secret Service to the secure "Site R" on the border of Maryland and Pennsylvania. It appears that he refused to go.

Vice President Cheney had been conducting routine meetings when the first WTC plane impact occurred. Like many other senior figures that day, Cheney continued with his meeting and did nothing, despite seeing the images from New York on television, and despite knowing of the huge spike in intelligence that had suggested a major terrorist attack was likely.

Scooter Libby, Cheney's Chief of Staff, was even more blasé. Seeing the television footage showing the impact of the first WTC attack, Libby turned the television off to stop him from being distracted from another topic of conversation. As the world turned on their televisions and stared aghast, most of those in charge of the US inexplicably turned away.

Given his intimate knowledge of the heightened security situation, it is astonishing that Cheney would have taken no action on seeing a massive gash in the side of one of the World Trade Center buildings. He had personally received warnings that Osama bin Laden was planning a major terrorist attack inside the US, and that New York City was a particular target.

While it is only just possible to suggest that one senior figure in the Bush administration might have misconstrued events, or had a lapse in judgment and not taken a burning building in New York seriously, the idea that nearly all of the top people in the administration did so at the same time seems incredible, or to be more accurate, impossible. These people had intimate knowledge of the warnings that had been coming in thick and fast. Their job was to defend America. Yet Cheney, Libby, Wolfowitz, Rumsfeld, Myers and others all chose to turn their backs as the world looked on. This action can only reflect a collective decision not to act. *A stand-down.*

Seventeen minutes later, any hint of doubt evaporated when the second attack occurred. Suddenly everyone knew this was terrorism, and the Secret Service would have leapt into action. An unprecedented terrorist attack was taking place, and other planes were unaccounted for.

While some stories have tried to put a more dignified spin on it, it appears four or five members of the Secret Service ran into Cheney's office, picked him up by the shoulders and carried him quickly downstairs to the PEOC bunker. Once there, Cheney was safe from any kind of attack.

The story of Cheney's actions becomes contradictory at this point, and the seemingly insignificant detail of the exact time of his arrival at the PEOC takes on a great deal of importance, given Cheney's clear role in managing the events that were unfolding.

If Cheney was at PEOC early in the course of events, it lends much credence to the idea that he was effectively in control of America's response to the attacks throughout the morning. If Cheney arrived later, then he could not have played that central role. From an establishment point of view, the latter position is something to be desired, as it abrogates Cheney from any involvement in America's response to the attacks, and avoids addressing the clear breakdown in chain of command procedures described above.

Properly informed, perhaps people could see it for what it was: not a breakdown of procedure, but an over-ruling.

It would be expected that the time from the second WTC impact to Cheney's arrival at PEOC would be very small, as he would have quickly been hustled to safety by the secret service. But according to the 9/11 Commission (who repeatedly obfuscated and altered vital timelines to fit their narrative), Cheney was not evacuated from his office in the White House until 9:36 a.m. However, the idea that the Secret Service waited 33 minutes after the second attack to remove the vice president of the United States to safety not only beggars belief, it is contradicted by a wide body of evidence and testimony. Why on earth would the official inquiry have chosen to lie in order to delay Cheney's evacuation for 33 crucial minutes?

Furthermore, the 9/11 Commission admitted that while there was conflicting evidence about when Cheney arrived at the PEOC, it had concluded that Cheney arrived "perhaps" at 9:58, having somehow taken a further twenty-two minutes to move from the White House to the bunker underneath.

Among many eyewitnesses contradicting this, Transportation Secretary Norman Mineta testified to the 9/11 Commission that he arrived at the PEOC between 9:20 and 9:27, and found Cheney in full control. Mineta recounted to the Commission that Cheney was being told every ten miles as the plane approaching Washington got closer (prior to the impact at the Pentagon at 9:38 a.m.). This directly contradicts the 9/11 Commission's assertion that Cheney only made it to the bunker at around 9:58 a.m. Mineta was a respected senior member of the Bush administration, yet his testimony timelines were entirely ignored.

Others also testified that Cheney was at PEOC quickly after the second WTC attack, including Richard Clarke, official photographer David Bohrer, and Condoleezza Rice.

Given the vital nature of every moment during that fateful morning, this disparity in timing is a yawning chasm. In fact, it is clearly a bare-faced lie, given the testimony about Cheney's role in the final moments of flights 77 and 93. As we have seen, as flight 77 approached Washington around 9:25 a.m., Cheney was in the PEOC, repeatedly asked if the orders still stand, and aggressively replied that they did. Yet the 9/11 Commission had Cheney arriving at the PEOC half an hour later, some twenty minutes after the Pentagon was hit. Cheney's barking of orders cannot have been in relation to flight 93, which didn't come close to Washington. How can such an obviously glaring hole in the story have not received closer attention?

Denial can inform you more than the truth on occasions. It's important to understand why it appears to have been so vital to the 9/11 Commission report to alter the chronology of when Dick Cheney arrived at the White House bunker, and what they were trying to obscure.

One clue as to the reasoning relates to the timing of the order to shoot down civilian aircraft. Richard Clarke, another highly credible witness, said he received that order just after 9:45 a.m., but the Commission gave the timing as 10:10, some five minutes or so after flight 93 hit the ground. This deception attempted to close the loop on one obvious line of inquiry—the suggestion that Dick Cheney gave the order to shoot down threatening civilian aircraft, and that flight 93 was shot down based on his orders. The military would not have taken that decision by themselves, so to time Cheney's order at 10:10 a.m. absolves all concerned from the accusation that a civilian aircraft shoot-down was indeed ordered by the vice president (who had no such authority), and carried out on his orders.

The deliberate altering of crucial timelines in relation to Cheney's arrival at PEOC is an extraordinarily obvious falsification, and one that allowed Cheney to claim that he had no role in the final moments of the third and fourth planes, when in fact he clearly did. If such effort was made purely for political reasons (to protect Cheney from responsibility) then it's a revoltingly cynical act. However, it seems just as likely that rather than the avoidance of political embarrassment, the 9/11 Commission falsified timelines to maintain the fiction of the official story.

Angel is Next

A peculiar and vitally important incident took place around 10:30 a.m., half an hour after Air Force One left the runway. In the air above Florida, President Bush received a phone call from Dick Cheney in which Cheney said that a specific and credible threat had been made against Air Force One, including the words "angel is next." Angel was the Secret Service codename for Air Force One.

Accompanying the message, Cheney said, was a series of top-secret code words indicating that the warning came from someone with access to, or even control over, the highest level state secrets within the US government and military, as well as the codes in the "football," the case (always with the president) that allows the launch of America's nuclear missiles.

Colonel Mark Tillman, the pilot of Air Force One, was told of the threat, and an armed guard was posted on the cockpit door. It was Tillman who requested fighter aircraft escorts.

Tillman also said that as Air Force One flew over Florida, air traffic control told him that an unidentified plane above and behind Air Force One was descending toward them, had shut its transponder off, and was not responding to radio requests. Tillman flew Air Force One out into the Gulf of Mexico to see if the other plane followed them. He was later told that the unidentified plane had lost its transponder signal and was not a threat. This unusual story has never been fully explored.

The "angel is next" warning was also confirmed by Congressman Dan Miller and local politician Adam Putnam, both onboard Air Force One on 9/11, who met with Bush in his cabin at the front of the plane. Bush told them Cheney had told him of the threat, which had come from someone credible who knew the plane's codename. Bush also told military aide Lieutenant Colonel Thomas Gould (who was carrying the football suitcase) about the threat.

Conservative *New York Times* columnist William Safire was told by a White House official that the words used in the message had shown a knowledge not only of code words, but of procedures and transponder information that made the threat additionally credible. This story was confirmed to Safire by Karl Rove, and published in the *New York Times* on September 13. It has also been suggested that code word groups of the NSA were among those used.

Major Robert Darling, who was in the PEOC, said, "The talk among the principals in the room quickly determined that the use of a code word implied that the threat to Air Force One and the president could well be from someone with access to the [president's] inner circle, possibly someone who was near the president at that very moment." Some reports suggested the call was made from Sarasota, Florida.

Whatever the nature and credibility of the threat, it was taken very seriously, and was instrumental in keeping the president away from Washington all day on 9/11. On the phone with President Bush, Dick Cheney insisted that with the situation in and around Washington highly unstable, Bush should not return until his safety could be guaranteed, adding that the air was the safest place to be. Bush had wanted to return immediately to Washington, but after Cheney's phone call the plane changed direction and headed for Louisiana. Bush spent the rest of the day crisscrossing the country over a period of eight hours, to destinations apparently suggested by Cheney, only returning to Washington at 6:42 p.m.

At 11:45 a.m., Air Force One landed at Barksdale Air Force Base in Shreveport, Louisiana. At this point it was clear that the attacks were over, and all US airspace had been cleared. But Cheney insisted that there were still credible security threats to Air Force One. The nature and source of these threats has never been addressed. Bush was kept on the move and away from Washington.

In the days that followed 9/11, Dick Cheney, Andrew Card, Karl Rove, and the president's spokesman Ari Fleischer would repeat the story to the media about the "credible" threat made against Air Force One. But by September 27, Fleischer was backpedalling, and the story was quickly allowed to die.

There seems no reason to doubt the accounts of the congressmen, pilot, and others who recounted the Angel story. The incident is of vital importance to the events of 9/11 as it was this one thing, communicated by Dick Cheney to George W. Bush directly, that ensured that the president was kept away from Washington, DC.

For most of the day the high-tech presidential communications equipment on Air Force One failed, or was intermittent at best. Bush struggled to communicate with his key colleagues ("This is intolerable," he shouted as phone and video lines failed), and was forced on several occasions to use an ordinary cell phone.

Bush's itinerancy, a mystifying breakdown in Air Force One's communications, and his absence from Washington led to Bush being effectively sidelined through the entire day on September 11, 2001. Indeed, there is no evidence that Bush made any key decision or issued any major command until the dust was settling and he returned to Washington in the evening. In part as a consequence of the Angel threat, Bush played no role whatsoever as the attacks took place. Vice President Cheney, who delivered the news of the threat, was in full control, at the heart of America's response in the bunker under the White House.

The idea that Cheney wanted to keep Bush away from Washington is given more credence by the fact that the Angel warning was the second Cheney had given to Bush insisting he keep his distance. After the Pentagon was attacked, Cheney phoned President Bush (who was on his way to the airport in Florida) to say that the White House had been targeted. Bush said he wanted to come directly to Washington, but Cheney advised him not to. While it is entirely true that the situation around Washington and New York was unstable and potentially dangerous, there is no information suggesting the White House had been specifically targeted. How did Cheney know this? The White House was an obvious target, but in the years that have followed, no evidence has been produced to suggest that Cheney's warning was prompted by the available information.

On the limited occasions since 2001 that the angel story has arisen, the general line has been that in retrospect what happened was just a misunderstanding, a perhaps natural corollary of the extreme confusion that reigned throughout the day. But the question needs to be asked. Who told Cheney of the threat, and how was it perceived to be credible if it lacked key knowledge of Secret Service code words and procedures? If the code words were indeed used in a warning, how was it then not credible? If that was the case, it represents a supreme national emergency that someone behind the scenes was issuing warnings and threats to the elected leaders of the country.

Only a few key people at the top of the state apparatus have access to the codes that were apparently revealed. If the story is true, then it proves that someone near the head of US politics or the military was actively part of the 9/11 plot.

Further, while it has been assumed that the calls were a threat, it makes no sense for a threat to have been made for no apparent benefit. What makes more sense is the idea that the calls contained an ultimatum. Do this, or that happens. If that is the case, it seems that a deal was made, as no further attacks occurred on 9/11 and the president's life was spared. With government agency code words at their disposal, the callers could conceivably have overridden the president and issued their own orders to the army. Perhaps that's why Bush went to Offutt—physically being at the headquarters of Strategic Command would at least allow him to ensure that his ultimate authority was not usurped.

Cheney has subsequently claimed that the Secret Service passed him details of the threat, but the Secret Service deny this. One of them is lying.

Anyone familiar with military coups knows that the figurehead president or prime minister is normally detained or killed at the start of the event. If arrested, the leader is then kept well away from the action, for his or her own "security." Telling a leader that their security can't be guaranteed is normally code for "stay out of this or we will kill you." The leader is only allowed back to the controls, and to appear on television, when the dastardly deeds are done. Placed in context, the angel story looks like standard operating procedure for a political or military coup.

During those key hours, to see who is actually in charge is revealing.

We Control the Helicopters

Despite the failure (or overruling) of clear chain of command procedures at the White House, other protocols had been followed elsewhere. Senior figures such as Dennis Hastert (Speaker of the House, and next in the line of presidential succession after the vice president) had been taken by helicopter to Mount Weather, a secure location outside Washington.

As the day progressed, Cheney spoke to congressional leaders who wanted to return to Washington immediately, telling them that despite their protestations they were not allowed to return yet, as their safety couldn't be guaranteed. Again, it's important to emphasize that the vice president had no constitutional role whatsoever in these sort of decisions. When Don Nickles, a Republican senator and Cheney's colleague, openly queried why they needed permission from the White House, since they were higher on the chain of command, Cheney replied, "Don, we control the helicopters." Whoever the *we* is in that statement, that is naked political power on display, and it's one of the more remarkable statements made all day.

Later in the afternoon, around five o'clock, the congressional leaders' requests turned to demands, and they were allowed to return. But by then it was all over.

For a very brief and very important period, Dick Cheney managed to circumvent all established chain of command procedures and, with his president redundant and other leaders kept well away, took over the running of America's response to the 9/11 attacks. Once events subsided, normality was restored and key personnel were allowed to return to their posts. It took only a couple of hours, but the damage was done. These are the classic characteristics of a coup.

At around 10:00 p.m. on 9/11, Dick Cheney left the White House by helicopter (violating a long-standing protocol that only the president takes off from the South Lawn) and flew to Camp David. He chose to stay in the Aspen Lodge, long reserved for the president only. Cheney spent many of the following nights at undisclosed secure locations.

Cheney after 9/11

The 9/11 attacks unarguably provided Dick Cheney and his neoconservative friends the opportunity to pursue their publicly stated prior agenda. The new

Pearl Harbor, as many called it, allowed the passage of bills that were counter to the public interest and the US Constitution, and the transfer of huge power to the president and his team. 9/11 created a political environment in which anyone questioning the conduct of the Bush administration could be cast as against America, and national security became a patriotic ideal under which any manner of law-breaking could be hidden or justified. This opportunity was ruthlessly exploited.

Cheney was a center-stage and menacing presence during the unprecedented media blitz of 2002 in which he repeatedly linked Saddam Hussein to 9/11, lied about Iraq's possession of weapons of mass destruction, and spewed forth some of the most irresponsible and deliberately disingenuous rhetoric in American history.

As part of the propaganda push, Cheney established a new Office of Special Plans, which reversed the normal order of intelligence gathering, starting with a premise (Iraq has weapons of mass destruction and is making more) and working backward to find information to match.

Cheney built the case for war with Iraq like no other. He repeatedly claimed that Saddam Hussein was seeking (and had sourced) enriched uranium with the goal of getting a nuclear missile. We now know that this, and nearly everything else they told us about Iraq, was entirely untrue.

When the CIA's researchers came up with nothing, Cheney personally visited their headquarters eight times. Analysts who wrote reports critical of Iraq found themselves at White House briefings; those who continued to write that they could locate no evidence were sidelined.

On September 16, 2001, Cheney was interviewed on NBC's *Meet the Press*. During the interview he said that in order to combat this new threat the government would have to work "the dark side." Few at the time could forecast just how dark America's days ahead would be.

Donald Rumsfeld

As Dick Cheney grimaced through television appearances, Don Rumsfeld seemed happy to take any media criticism head on, grinningly unapologetic about any aspect of the Bush administration's War on Terror. Even as the appalling truth about torture, abductions, secret prisons and detention without trial became public knowledge, each outrage was treated with a smile and a "stuff happens" attitude, protected by a seemingly unbreakable belief that absolutely anything was justified in order to keep America safe, even when those actions palpably did the opposite.

Like Cheney, Rumsfeld had spent most of his life in Washington—as a member of Congress in the Nixon administration, and as secretary of defense for Gerald Ford. His close relationship with Dick Cheney, political and personal, went back over thirty years. They thought much in the same way, were members of the same political groups, and good friends.

Always a scheming ladder-climber and tireless proponent of increased military spending no matter what the political climate, Rumsfeld had an uncanny knack for survival. Henry Kissinger called him a special Washington phenomenon: "the skilled full-time politician-bureaucrat in whom ambition, ability, and substance fuse seamlessly." The Machiavellian Kissinger may have meant it as a compliment.

Rumsfeld combined public service with private sector work from 1977 to 2000, enjoying some success. In late 1983, Ronald Reagan needed someone to cozy up to Saddam Hussein, so he appointed Rumsfeld Special Envoy to the Middle East and dispatched him to Baghdad, reopening a relationship with Washington that subsequently saw financial, intelligence, and arms assistance, most likely including components that were used to create biological and chemical weapons. Strangely, as the Bush administration sold its campaign for a war against Iraq in 2003, the embarrassing picture of Rumsfeld warmly greeting Hussein twenty years earlier was not widely broadcast.

Just before becoming secretary of defense for George W. Bush (at Dick Cheney's recommendation), Rumsfeld finished work as chairman of the Commission to Assess US National Security Space Management and Organization, a body that predictably reported that it considered US space dominance and missile defense vitally important, and a pressing concern for America's national security.

Dubbed the Rumsfeld Commission, one key recommendation was the termination of the 1972 ABM treaty with Russia, under which both sides had agreed to gradually reduce their huge arsenals of nuclear weapons to just one hundred each. The report, published on January 9, 2001 (11 days before the Bush administration took office), demonstrated Rumsfeld's awesome powers of prediction, stating that "history is replete with instances in which warning signs were ignored and change resisted until an external, 'improbable' event forced resistant bureaucracies to take action." As with the Project for the New American Century, it speculated that the only thing that would make the government act would be "a disabling attack against the country and its people". The previously unassailable ABM treaty was indeed dumped by Bush within nine weeks of 9/11, allowing the US to actively commence working on the militarization of space, a measure also desired by PNAC, of whom Rumsfeld was a member.

Donald Rumsfeld is the only member of the Bush administration who published two separate documents expressing the sentiment that only a disastrous attack on America could enable the desired military changes he felt were required. Does this not mean that Donald Rumsfeld is by definition a prime suspect in the attacks of 9/11?

Rumsfeld chose Paul Wolfowitz as deputy secretary of defense, a leading neocon hawk whose outlook closely reflected Rumsfeld's own. It was Wolfowitz who told President Bush that there was a 10 to 50 percent chance that Iraq was involved in 9/11 just four days after the event. This same man mused that within a year or so of the Iraq invasion, grateful Iraqis would name "some fine square" in Baghdad after President Bush.

Curiously, Rumsfeld made an explosive announcement on September 10, 2001, admitting that the Department of Defense had effectively lost $2.3 trillion in transactions. Coverage of this astonishing figure was lost amid the events a day later, and the offices responsible for investigating and tracking down the lost money were the ones attacked and destroyed at the Pentagon on 9/11. There was one off-site backup location for the Pentagon's financial records . . . in 7 World Trade Center.

Rumsfeld on 9/11

The secretary of defense is the chief individual charged with defending the United States and overseeing its armed forces. During the crisis on 9/11, this position was second only to the president. Rumsfeld had the personal authority to order the shooting down of civilian aircraft and the scrambling of fighters to defend America. Given America's response was singularly ineffective, he has much to answer for.

Donald Rumsfeld's behavior on 9/11 was beyond bizarre. He seems to have spent most of the morning ignoring the events and wandering aimlessly around. Without question, his actions did not save a single life.

Rumsfeld was meeting with Deputy Secretary Paul Wolfowitz discussing missile defense as the attacks in New York commenced. Both appear to have seen the second plane impact on television but inexplicably concluded, to quote Wolfowitz, that "there didn't seem to be much to do about it immediately, and we went on with whatever the meeting was."

Ignoring the utterly incredible idea that the US secretary of defense would return to discussing missiles as the two World Trade Center buildings burned, "there didn't seem to be much to do about it'"? Are you fucking kidding me? These men knew of the security situation. They were charged with defending America. It's one of the most inexcusable statements imaginable.

The meeting appears to have continued as the largest terrorist attack in history played out. Staff have spoken of their urgency being stymied because the secretary of defense would not have his meeting interrupted. Representative Christopher Cox said he was still in a meeting with Rumsfeld discussing missile defense just moments before the Pentagon was hit. Fifty-two priceless minutes had elapsed between the first WTC attack and the Pentagon strike and Rumsfeld, uniquely positioned to know of the incredible intelligence spike and warnings of an imminent domestic terrorist attack, appears to have done nothing whatsoever.

Just seconds prior to the Pentagon attack, Rumsfeld had another of his famous moments of clairvoyance, telling Cox, "Believe me, this isn't over yet. There's going to be another attack, and it could be us."

Rumsfeld's office was at the furthest point in the building from where the Pentagon was struck but, rather than walk a mere two hundred feet to the National Military Command Center (NMCC), Rumsfeld decided to stroll two thousand feet from his office, around the Pentagon, and waste at least twenty minutes watching and helping as staff members were carried away on stretchers. This meant that staff at the NMCC teleconference, which was the most important military command center in the US on 9/11, were unable to do their job properly. The secretary of defense was AWOL.

To go and see what had happened might seem like a natural thing to want to do, but for the US secretary of defense to do so was an astonishing abrogation of duty. It is unknown if Rumsfeld had a cell phone or pager. Most think not.

By his own admission, Rumsfeld was outside surveying the damage "for a while". He was photographed assisting carrying a stretcher, but admitted "I don't know what made me do anything I did." Brigadier General Montague Winfield, Commander of the NMCC, said that for thirty minutes, they couldn't find him.

Rumsfeld's disappearing act, when combined with his protocol changes for launching military aircraft in the instance of hijacking just one hundred days earlier, surely contributed to America's defense failure in the skies during the crucial period when interception was still possible. Rumsfeld's June memo meant only he could authorize the scrambling of fighter jets. Without him the chain of command was missing an irreplaceable link.

So it seems the US secretary of defense played no role whatsoever in defending his country during key moments on 9/11. Continuing a meeting when everyone on earth knew America was under attack and then disappearing for half an hour removed a vital cog in America's defense machine, and stopped the entire US armed forces from effecting any kind of response to the terrorist attacks. The singular actions of this singular man left America undefended, and caused the collapse of standard procedures that had previously worked routinely.

Even more bizarrely, Rumsfeld has subsequently claimed that he had no responsibilities that day anyway, reasoning that an attack on US civilian soil was a law enforcement matter. This is despite Rumsfeld telling President Bush on 9/11 that the attacks were not a criminal matter but an act of war.

The NMCC, incidentally, was yet another organization headed by someone on or near their first day on the job. Captain Charles Leidig had taken over the NMCC temporarily on 9/11, at the request (the previous day) of Brigadier General Montague Winfield. Leidig started work in the job for the first time at 8:30 a.m. on September 11. Some first day. As the meeting started, NMCC staff requested that the secretary of defense be patched in (connected via phone), but Rumsfeld was outside, out of reach, and walking around the perimeter of the Pentagon. Despite having initially been inside the Pentagon building and very close to the meeting, Rumsfeld didn't enter the NMCC until 10:30 a.m., by which time the main events of 9/11 were over.

Leidig's inexperience and Rumsfeld's absence are likely the reason for the delayed start to the crisis response teleconference, which began at 9:39 a.m., some thirty-six minutes after the second plane hit the WTC. Brigadier General Winfield took back control immediately after the crash of flight 93 in Shanksville which effectively ended the attacks. Winfield was subsequently promoted to Major General.

After being so spectacularly ineffective and absent during the key moments on the morning of the attacks, Rumsfeld suddenly sprang into action on arrival at the NMCC. Orders were issued, worldwide defense levels raised, fighters scrambled.

Continuity of government plans were officially implemented for the first time, by Vice President Cheney and Defense Secretary Rumsfeld, the two men who had written and refined the plans over thirty years. Cheney and Rumsfeld were a part of the permanent, normally hidden, national security apparatus of the United States, inhabitants of a world in which presidents come and go, but the American state remains relatively unchanged.

Continuity of government protocol moves key government personnel to disparate military command centers, with the idea that if some or many are killed, others will be alive, and their whereabouts known. Around one hundred officials were indeed moved to underground bunkers. However, like Cheney, Donald Rumsfeld refused to be evacuated to Site R, even when the Pentagon started filling with smoke, and instead sent his deputy Paul Wolfowitz.

But all this took place after the attacks had finished.

Sickeningly, the political animal in Donald Rumsfeld appears to have taken just a couple of hours to rise to the surface. At 2:40 p.m., Rumsfeld's aide Stephen Cambone wrote a note based on his boss's dictation, saying he wanted the "best info fast. Judge whether good enough to hit S.H. (Saddam Hussein) at same time. Not only UBL (bin Laden) . . . need to move swiftly . . . go massive, sweep it all up. Things related and not." This was at a time in the day when many had suggested Osama bin Laden and al-Qaeda were responsible, and no evidence whatsoever pointed toward Iraq. Just six hours after the attacks began, Rumsfeld was thinking about how to exploit the deaths of three thousand people to further his own foreign policy aims.

At 7:00 p.m. Rumsfeld held a press conference now famed for its startlingly aggressive politicizing of the day's events, during which he chastised Senator Carl Levin before live cameras, saying, "You and other Democrats in Congress have voiced fear that you simply don't have enough money for the large increase in defense that the Pentagon is seeking, especially for missile defense, and you fear that you'll have to dip into the Social Security funds to pay for it. Does this sort of thing convince you that an emergency exists in this country to increase defense spending, to dip into Social Security, if necessary, to . . . increase defense spending?"

As the sun set on September 11, Rumsfeld was already planning to steal from the old, the poor, and the disabled, so as to spend more money on America's war machine, and was mining the tragedy for political capital.

Funnily enough, the other two key advocates of Rumsfeld's plans for military spending, missile defense, and space dominance were General Ralph E. Eberhart, the commander of NORAD (who was in charge of air traffic control on 9/11), and General Richard Myers, who was acting chairman of the Joint Chiefs of Staff on 9/11 (and shortly thereafter became their chairman). In fact, nearly every top army chief (all of whom failed grievously on 9/11) was promoted rather than reprimanded, a pattern followed by their civilian counterparts.

By the time President Bush made it back to the capital on the evening of 9/11 and met key aides in his underground bunker, there was at least a belated focus on al-Qaeda. But even then, Defense Secretary Rumsfeld was heard to comment, "You know, we've got to do Iraq."

Bush met with his National Security Council at the White House around 9:00 p.m. At the beginning of the meeting he unequivocally stated that America was at war, and that "everything is available for the pursuit of this war. Any barriers in your way, they're gone. Any money you need, you have it." Even Mr. Rumsfeld may have permitted himself a smile.

Late at night on 9/11, Richard Clarke returned to the White House. Expecting the focus to be a response to the terrible events of the day, he wrote in his book, *Against All Enemies*, "Instead, I walked into a series of discussions about Iraq . . . I was incredulous that we were talking about something other than getting al-Qaeda. Then I realized with almost a sharp physical pain that Rumsfeld and Wolfowitz were going to try to take advantage of this national tragedy to promote their agenda about Iraq." This was an agenda that they had been pressing, Clarke said, "since the beginning of the administration, indeed well before."

Clarke was one of a very small number of staff held over from the Clinton administration. His Pentagon colleagues had been telling him for months that the plan was to invade Iraq in 2002. Now it appeared the neocons had a reason, albeit a spectacularly dishonest one.

Clarke and Colin Powell argued against the Rumsfeld and Cheney group throughout the week that followed 9/11, and the policy that emerged was informally called "Afghanistan first." Iraq would be second. Rumsfeld complained that there weren't many valuable targets to bomb in Afghanistan, suggesting Iraq was much more attractive in that regard.

The actions of Donald Rumsfeld during the brief period of the 9/11 attacks are a prima facie indication of a clear stand-down by America's military. Rumsfeld was AWOL when he was needed most, and his absence damaged America's defense capabilities tremendously. His inexplicable behavior has never properly been questioned. It's clear he took every measure to ensure that the Pentagon offered no defense to a nation under attack.

Rumsfeld after 9/11

Before the dust had settled, many senior neoconservatives began publicly ruminating on the positives, or what they called the silver lining of the 9/11 attacks. Rumsfeld said the attacks provided "the kind of opportunities that World War II offered—to refashion the world." On the second anniversary of the attacks, he told Jim Lehrer on PBS that he viewed the attacks as a "blessing in disguise".

Opportunities. *A blessing.*

To Rumsfeld, the attacks provided the opportunity to take advantage of an unprecedented political climate and a devastated and grief-stricken public in order to prosecute the military strategies he had endorsed prior to 9/11. It was something he would ruthlessly pursue. War was coming, and Rumsfeld would be in charge of where, and how.

On September 27, 2001, Rumsfeld wrote an editorial for the *New York Times* in which he laid out the new military priorities for the US and said, this time perhaps with accidental prescience, "Forget about exit strategies; we're looking at a sustained engagement that carries no deadlines." That sentiment would haunt America.

Although the 9/11 attacks were quickly blamed on Osama bin Laden and al-Qaeda in Afghanistan, war with Iraq and a massive increase in American military aggression was Rumsfeld's priority. In the weeks after 9/11, he produced a memo outlining his plans, which were for the US to attack seven countries in five years—Iraq, Syria, Lebanon, Libya, Somalia, Sudan, and Iran, with the overall aim of destabilizing the Middle East and allowing much greater US control over the region.

Cheney is widely rumored to have ordered the Pentagon to draw up plans for the atomic bombing of Iran, should another major terrorist attack have occurred.

Less widely known is the report produced by Rumsfeld's Defense Science Board in 2002 that advocated creating a secret intelligence agency tasked with provoking existing terrorist groups into actions that could then be countered in a way that met with US global-strategic goals. Or, in plain language, getting terrorists to kill innocent people so you can do what you want.

The Iraq misadventure may have exposed the limits of American power, but it is instructive to note that of Rumsfeld's list, only Iran has seen no US (or US-backed) military involvement since 9/11. That exception may not last forever.

It is also worth reflecting on the radical nature of Rumsfeld's memo, since it overtly charged the US military with starting wars, invading countries, and overthrowing governments, rather than deterring conflict. One could argue this had been the case for some time, but until 9/11 the pretense was that the point of the US army was to defend America and stop wars.

Political theorist Hannah Arendt said the history of warfare in the twentieth century was characterized by the growing incapacity of the army to fulfill its basic function: to defend the civilian population. After 9/11, geopolitical power could be wielded by civilians commanding generals, without even a nod to the notion of self defense.

Convincing the public that Iraq was worthy of aggression was just one rung on the ladder to success. Considering this issue, Rumsfeld wrote a memo in November 2001 which concluded, "how start?" How to start indeed. The best way, Rumsfeld felt, was to establish a connection, however tenuous, between the 9/11 attacks and Saddam Hussein. Truth was irrelevant, something had to be found, so on ten separate occasions Rumsfeld asked the CIA to find information linking Iraq to 9/11 (as Cheney did the same, personally visiting CIA headquarters eight times).

Although the CIA repeatedly came back with nothing, it was widely accepted that if Rumsfeld had set out to link Switzerland to 9/11, he would eventually have done so. Richard Clarke's dilemma presents a small sliver of the political pressure put upon the intelligence community. According to Clarke, President Bush never said to make it up, "But the entire conversation left me in absolutely no doubt that George Bush wanted me to come back with a report that said Iraq did this."

When the war in Afghanistan started, Rumsfeld made outrageously pious pronouncements about the precision and humanity of bombing campaigns that were killing thousands of civilians in a deliberate effort to cow and terrify the population. Rumsfeld also estimated that the Iraq war would last six days, and scoffed when told that an army of 380,000 troops would be required to establish control there. Instead, America sent 130,000.

Under Rumsfeld, both wars would also be fought under different rules than before. The attacks, Rumsfeld said, justified throwing out rulebooks, statutes, and conventions, and could be invoked any time his lawless new environment was questioned.

Donald Rumsfeld had a central role in instigating the torture programs. In Rumsfeld's view, torture (labeled as enhanced interrogation techniques) was justified, as it would reveal information that might prevent another 9/11. The nation was scoured for the right people to act as America's torturers, and locations such as Bagram, Abu Ghraib, and Guantanamo were converted into America's torture chambers.

As years passed and details spread of the use of appalling torture by the US, Rumsfeld was entirely dismissive of public concerns over the treatment of America's prisoners. In a memo detailing how Guantanamo interrogators would induce stress in prisoners by forcing them to remain standing in one position for a maximum of four hours, Rumsfeld wrote in the margin, "I stand for 8–10 hours a day. Why is standing limited to four hours?"

Concerning waterboarding, a medieval-era technique, Dick Cheney also wondered how people could consider a splash of water on the face torture.

To take one example from many, rectal rehydration, used as punishment at Guantanamo, was described by doctors as sexual assault masquerading as medical treatment, and of no medical value. As a government veteran, Rumsfeld could have consulted the US Department of Justice's own definition of forcible rape, being "the penetration, no matter how slight, of the vagina or anus with any body part or object . . . without the consent of the victim." Cheney and Rumsfeld, in short, considered the rape of innocent people (the government's own figures show at least 25 percent of Guantanamo inmates to be entirely innocent) to be a price worth paying for America's defense. A veritable river of historical and modern legislation, moralists, and holy teachings beg to differ.

One wonders if Rumsfeld and Cheney would have been quite so blasé about whether the interrogation techniques they approved constituted torture had their dinner been blended and forced up their anus with the widest tube available, or been water-boarded 183 times in a month, or been told that if they didn't cooperate that their wives and daughters would be raped and murdered.

Historically the US has prosecuted many international political figures for the same practice of torture that America, the land of the free, pursued and launched under the watch of Donald Rumsfeld in the wake of 9/11. However, Rumsfeld remains unrepentant, and rarely addresses his role during the eight years of the Bush administration. When pressed, he professes to have been largely ignorant of nearly everything that happened.

It's hard to avoid the impression that Donald Rumsfeld is a man who is prepared to say absolutely anything to defend his position, no matter how nonsensical; safe in the knowledge that America's media consistently let him get away with it. To take another example, in a 2011 Mancow Muller interview, Donald Rumsfeld claimed never to have heard of WTC Building 7 and its collapse. This was utterly astonishing given his role as secretary of defense on 9/11, but perhaps even more so given Rumsfeld had been chairman of the advisory board of Salomon Smith Barney, the main tenant of 7 WTC, occupying thirty-seven of the forty-seven floors. Rudolph Giuliani gave Rumsfeld a personal tour of ground zero weeks after the attacks. It's hard to imagine him not having seen the rubble of a fifty-story building—both men were photographed right across the street from it.

Richard Myers

On the morning of 9/11 Air Force General Richard Myers was the acting chairman of the Joint Chiefs of Staff and the highest-ranked military officer in the United States. As the attacks took place, the chairman Henry Shelton was on a flight over the Atlantic, headed toward Europe. Myers was closely aligned with the neocons and a leading proponent of computer-based and space warfare. He had been nominated as the new chairman eighteen days earlier.

Just as the president and congressional leaders were kept away from Washington, Shelton's plane (which turned around on hearing of the attacks) was denied permission to enter US airspace for several hours, despite it carrying the most senior military man in the country, and despite Shelton being in phone contact with Myers and specifically requesting clearance.

Around 9:00 a.m., Myers was having a routine meeting with Senator Max Cleland, having eaten breakfast with Donald Rumsfeld (at which Rumsfeld had predicted a shocking world event in the near future). Seeing reports of the first plane's impact at the World Trade Center, Myers appears to have concluded it was an accident and continued with the meeting. In his own words, he thought, "Well, whatever." This from a man with a lifetime of military experience that prepares you to do entirely the opposite in such circumstances.

Well, whatever.

Myers' testimony has changed over the years to suggest he sprang into action at the earliest opportunity, but his initial version seemed detailed enough (and incongruous enough) to be plausible.

Even more amazingly, Myers claimed that no one informed him of the second WTC strike and that he remained entirely oblivious of the nature of the attacks for over half an hour more, until the Pentagon was struck at 9:38 a.m.

It's another truly extraordinary claim; that the highest ranking military officer in the United States was unaware of the largest terrorist attack in history while the rest of the world watched CNN and knew exactly what was going on.

Of the senior figures in the Bush administration, it appears that Dick Cheney, Donald Rumsfeld, Paul Wolfowitz, I. Lewis Libby, and Condoleezza Rice all saw the second plane strike and chose to do nothing at all. All kept their jobs or were promoted.

Myers' whereabouts and actions during the next critical period of the attacks are unknown. Like Donald Rumsfeld, he didn't enter the NMCC until around 10:30 a.m., by which time it was too late. His whereabouts in the crucial hour between the Pentagon strike at 9:38 a.m. and entering the NMCC are unclear.

Again, Myers took no action of any consequence whatsoever until well after the Pentagon was hit. Whatever his motives, this scale of negligence amounts to effective complicity.

As punishment for one of the most astonishingly poor performances in military history, Richard Myers was promoted to chairman of the Joint Chiefs of Staff, the highest military rank in the United States, just three days after 9/11.

John Ashcroft

Few in the Bush administration cut as unimpressive a figure as John Ashcroft, the former attorney and governor of Missouri, and a politician so right-wing, unpopular, and slippery that he lost his 2000 Senate election to an opposition candidate who had been killed three weeks previously. Losing an election to a corpse seemed the kind of quality George W. Bush needed in an Attorney General, and at the end of 2000, this once peripheral figure was suddenly the leading lawman in the United States.

Although Ashcroft publicly declared prevention of terrorism to be his number one priority, behind the scenes he systematically stymied and cut programs and budgets for counter-terrorism, even proposing a 50 percent cut to one program on September 10, 2001.

Ashcroft displayed breathtaking disdain for the huge spike in mid-2001 intelligence suggesting a major attack was being prepared. Despite the warnings, he went on a long fishing holiday in July, but took a chartered jet rather than a commercial flight, due to the heightened state of alert. Ashcroft had stopped taking all commercial flights that month, due to the threat assessment. It appears he did not value other traveler's lives as highly.

In August 2001, Ashcroft ranked terrorism as his lowest priority. A few weeks before 9/11, the acting head of the FBI, Tom Pickard, was trying to get Ashcroft to focus on the looming danger, but Ashcroft dismissed him, saying, "I don't want to hear about that anymore. I don't want you to ever talk to me about al-Qaeda, about these threats. I don't want to hear about al-Qaeda anymore."

To the head of the FBI.

On the 13th of September, 2001, David Schippers, the Chief Investigative Counsel for the US House of Representatives Judiciary Committee in 1998 and a well-known attorney, revealed that he had attempted to warn John Ashcroft about the attacks some six weeks before 9/11, in light of information he had received from the FBI.

Not only that, but Schippers said that he had tried to pass on to Ashcroft information from FBI agents that included the hijackers' names, funding, attack dates and the targets of the attacks—information he said was known by the FBI agents months in advance. Hardly an anti-establishment figure, Schippers said it was widely known all over the bureau how these warnings were ignored by Washington.

Having been so blasé about terrorism before 9/11, Ashcroft quickly got on the front foot after the attacks, urging the government to embark on a wartime re-organization of US society. All American Muslims, he felt, fell under suspicion, but specific details weren't required—Ashcroft told FBI and INS agents to question anyone they could find with a Muslim sounding name. Some agents searched for suspicious sounding names in the phone book.

No effort was spared elsewhere. Ashcroft's Justice Department mounted an aggressive effort to persuade the 9/11 Commission to re-write the parts of its report relating to Ashcroft. In the end, there was just one page on John Ashcroft's leadership in the final Commission report. It failed to mention his decision to fly on chartered planes in the period prior to 9/11.

John Ashcroft also used the 9/11 Commission report to argue for greater emergency powers for himself. Since the agencies he oversaw were identified as having had a mass systemic failure that allowed the attacks, this argument was akin to saying that those who had failed most should be rewarded the most.

Across the board, senior Bush administration staff conducted themselves before, during and after 9/11 in a manner that makes the jaw drop. The intelligence they received should have been given the highest priority. Instead, it was ignored. But within intelligence circles, there was also a great deal of inexplicable behavior.

CHAPTER EIGHT

US INTELLIGENCE AGENCIES

There are sixteen official government agencies that make up the US Intelligence Community, with an annual budget of around $50 billion. Most are run on military lines, with top-down command, meaning agents report to directors who make strategic-level assessments. This structure, while sometimes efficient in allowing those at the top to see the big picture, is ripe for politically-motivated agency leaders wishing to pursue their own agenda.

Intelligence experts have long stated that the vast majority of failures occur not because of poor work on the ground, but because good information was ignored by those in power. Although the 9/11 attacks have been portrayed as the biggest intelligence failure since Pearl Harbor, the more we learn about the active blocking of investigators by those at the top of these agencies (and within the Bush administration), the more the impression we get is not of an intelligence failure, but the result of a directive.

The Federal Bureau of Investigation

In a sense, the FBI has never recovered from J. Edgar Hoover. His malevolent and corrupting influence casts a long shadow over the history of the FBI and its modern incarnation. Hoover used the FBI to control the political direction of America, placing his agency beyond the rule of law and projecting power through malevolence, fear, and spite. He collected vast files on the great, good, and fallen, including his own employers, and was extremely effective in doing so, ruling the agency for forty-eight years. J. Edgar Hoover was one of the worst Americans of the twentieth century.

It's been said that Hoover's personality—a combination of narcissism and paranoia—would have made him a perfect high-level Nazi, and this strain of fascism remains in the blood of FBI management.

When the US Attorney General tells the FBI not to bother him with any more information about al-Qaeda, it's hard to know who to blame, but the FBI's performance in 2001 remains surely the greatest intelligence failure in history. Thomas Kean, chairman of the 9/11 Commission, said the FBI had "failed and failed and failed and failed and failed."

However, there is a great deal of evidence that the failure of the FBI to stop the 9/11 attacks was not just incompetence, but that those at the top deliberately chose to obscure and sideline information that clearly pointed to a huge domestic attack.

A number of FBI agents reported suspicious activity by Middle Eastern men to their superiors in 2001. Little or nothing was done.

On July 10, 2001, agent Ken Williams sent FBI headquarters what is now known as the Phoenix Memorandum, warning of suspicious activities involving a large group of Middle Eastern men who were taking flying lessons in Arizona but lacked the normal credentials for doing so. The memo was altered, ignored, and buried, despite Williams' protestations and rising sense of urgency.

Two of the future hijackers lived with a shady FBI informant for seven months while taking their flying lessons. We don't know what information he passed to his FBI handlers—the informant was banned from testifying to the 9/11 Commission.

When Minneapolis agents reported that a Zacarias Moussaoui was taking flying lessons but not learning to take off or land, they were blocked by their superiors from even examining Moussaoui's laptop. One agent complained that Moussaoui might take a plane and fly it into the World Trade Center.

At every turn, agents on the ground were stymied and stopped from investigating clear and obvious suspicious activity—investigations that could well have stopped the attacks of 9/11. The reasons for their efforts being blocked simply make no sense. Again and again, those at the top of the FBI vetoed otherwise routine appeals from their own counter-terrorism experts. Despite around seventy field investigations into bin Laden-inspired terrorism threats within the US in the months before 9/11, none caused the FBI to take action, and most were blocked or otherwise spiked. It's very hard not to conclude that there was a deliberate stand-down coming from the top of the FBI.

One can only imagine the mayhem at the CIA and FBI headquarters on 9/11. Whatever their involvement in the day's events, it was clear that both agencies had failed in their primary responsibilities, and their tracks had to be covered.

The FBI's internal investigation is supposed to have started on the day of the attacks. Having seemingly missed so many warning signs prior to September 11, bureau staff certainly appeared quickly enough at the locations they were needed on the day in order to confiscate security footage near the Pentagon and keep the press back from the curiously plane-free hole in the ground at Shanksville.

The investigation was breathtakingly brief. FBI Director Robert Mueller wound it up on October 10, 2001, just twenty-nine days after the attacks. Mueller had come under intense pressure from President Bush, who opposed and actively worked to thwart all 9/11 investigations, and personally ordered the FBI to curtail theirs. The leader of the FBI's in-house inquiry was Thomas A. Kelley, an establishment man whose previous career highlights included the defense side of the inquiry into the FBI's role in the siege debacle at Waco. Given that the FBI was the agency most responsible for the intelligence lapses that failed to stop 9/11, its investigation of itself was never likely to overcome fundamental conflicts of interest.

As the investigation wound up, Mueller's staff were instructed that they were not trying to solve a crime, and that no further efforts should be made to investigate the events of 9/11. Despite this inquisitorial brevity, Mueller called the investigation the most exhaustive in the FBI's history, adding that as they now had a broad understanding of the events of September 11, it was time to move on.

Like so many investigating bodies, the FBI found that nothing could have stopped the attacks, that no one was to blame, and no new information of import came to light. No liability was accepted whatsoever. One year after 9/11, the directors of the FBI, CIA, and NSA admitted that not only had no individual within their organizations been fired for the intelligence failures that led to 9/11, no one had even been reprimanded.

By April 2002, Mueller was able to report on one of the most fabulously dishonest summaries of flawed investigation, refuted on almost every level by readily available information. Mueller claimed, with a straight face, that the FBI had not found a single piece of paper anywhere in the world that mentioned the 9/11 plot. Despite the fact that we know the hijackers were hiding in plain sight within the US, Mueller claimed that the attackers had used extraordinary secrecy, and because of that there had been no possibility of foiling their plot. It was self-serving dishonest nonsense, but the White House accepted it without comment.

Not for the last time, the Bush administration made clear that because everyone knew what had happened on 9/11, there was no point in wasting resources by investigating things further. Case closed, move on.

Those who had tried to alert authorities to the warning signs they were receiving about a huge upcoming attack found themselves sidelined, or worse.

John O'Neill

Consider the amazing case of John O'Neill, an FBI veteran, counter-terrorism expert and the bureau's leading expert on al-Qaeda, the man known as America's most committed tracker of Osama bin Laden.

O'Neill, who had worked on al-Qaeda and the threat of international terrorism for years, spent the early part of 2001 warning continuously, and with mounting concern, of the rising danger of a domestic terrorist attack mounted by Osama bin Laden and al-Qaeda. But his warnings were ignored, and O'Neill believed he knew why.

He complained that the US State Department, and behind it the oil lobby (which held huge influence within the Bush White House) was blocking all attempts to pursue or capture bin Laden because of al-Qaeda's links to (and funding from) the ruling royal family in Saudi Arabia. O'Neill made this very clear, saying, "All of the answers, all of the clues allowing us to dismantle Osama bin Laden's organization, can be found in Saudi Arabia."

Despite being personally recommended by Richard Clarke as his replacement as US counter-terrorism "tsar," O'Neill's insistence that the funding for al-Qaeda came from Saudi Arabia, and that the main obstacles to investigating al-Qaeda were US oil corporate interests and the role played by Saudi Arabia, earned him powerful enemies within the Bush administration.

Rather than look at the threat posed by Osama bin Laden, those enemies chose to kill the messenger. O'Neill was publicly smeared with leaks about his past. In just one instance, a minor infraction from many years before was leaked to the *New York Times*. O'Neill could clearly see that an internal campaign was being mounted against him and resigned from the FBI in frustration, after 25 years of service. The leaker was right at the top—Tom Pickard, then the interim director of the FBI, who wanted a Bush ally in the post of counter-terrorism tsar. Put simply, O'Neill's refusal to stop making comments about Saudi Arabia's state funding of terrorism precluded him from being viewed as a Bush ally, and ended his long career at the FBI.

On August 23, 2001, O'Neill took the post of Director of Security at the World Trade Center. He moved into his new office on the 34th floor of the north tower on September 10. In a conversation that day with Raymond Powers, the head of security of the Rockefeller Center, O'Neill said that he was sure Osama bin Laden would attack America and target the twin towers. He felt that something big "was brewing."

That night he told Jerome Hauer, "We're due for something big. I don't like the way things are lining up in Afghanistan." When Hauer asked when he thought it would happen, O'Neill said, "I don't know, but soon."

John O'Neill died at the World Trade Center on 9/11, his second day on the job.

Why would the head of the FBI want their leading expert on al-Qaeda forced out, at a time when he was repeatedly warning of a disaster that then in fact did occur, if not because powerful interests, right at the top of the tree, either wanted this information hushed up, or simply did not want to know. In the end, both answers had the same results.

Jerome Hauer

It's worth pausing here to take a look at Jerome Hauer, a nefarious character whose name appears again and again at key intersections of the 9/11 story. Hauer had his fingers in a lot of pies, and each one seemed connected to 9/11.

Hauer was director of New York Mayor Rudy Giuliani's Office of Emergency Management from 1996 to 2000, and established the crisis management center built at great expense in 7 WTC.

A dual American-Israeli citizen and well-known Zionist with connections to the top ranks of the Israeli state, Hauer was also a counter-terrorism expert, and described himself as an expert on building collapse. It was in this role that he appeared prominently on American televisions on the afternoon of 9/11, propagating the idea that the attacks had all the hallmarks of Osama bin Laden, and could not (in his opinion) have had state backing. By that time Hauer was also certain that the buildings had collapsed due to the plane impacts and subsequent fires alone.

Hauer was head of Crisis & Consequence Management Group, a part of Kroll Associates, the firm responsible for security at the World Trade Center. He had been responsible for John O'Neill's appointment at the World Trade Center just days before the attacks. It's worth restating. Jerome Hauer was responsible for hiring the world's leading expert on Osama bin Laden with such astonishing timing that the same man was killed, in attacks purported to have been masterminded by Osama bin Laden, just days later. At the very least, an extraordinary coincidence.

O'Neill had been a fly in the ointment at the FBI, refusing to modify his messages to superiors and make them more palatable. After 9/11, he would have been a much sought after media presence, given his knowledge, and unlikely to have tailored his message to fit the prevailing narrative. As it was, Hauer's appointment removed that possibility.

In addition to these other roles, Hauer was also a member of the US Army Medical Research Institute of Infectious Diseases, the center from which most suspect the post-9/11 anthrax attacks were launched. Hauer managed much of the America's response to the anthrax attacks, and was also the man who advised Bush administration and White House staff to start taking Cipro, the most widely used anthrax antibiotic, on the evening of September 11, 2001.

The man initially accused of the anthrax attacks, Stephen Hatfill had, by coincidence, previously worked for Jerome Hauer at Scientific Applications International Corporation.

Sibel Edmonds

The 9/11 attacks themselves did little to bring sense to the FBI. Reports abound of almost unbelievable cynicism in the wake of national tragedy. Sibel Edmonds, a translator with top security clearance who started work for the FBI in Washington on the 20th of September, 2001, was first harassed then fired after she complained of an intentional slowdown in the translation of vital intelligence documents in order to get a larger budget assigned to the department where she worked.

After Edmonds first raised her concerns internally, then leaked information to the press, the FBI told her that any more leaks would be a risk to the safety of her family abroad, shortly after which a spurious warrant for her sister's arrest was issued in Turkey. The supervisor who told her to slow down was promoted. Edmonds became a whistle-blower and was fired.

The 9/11 Commission initially refused to hear Edmonds' testimony at all, before the 9/11 families group interceded, and Edmonds was finally allowed to testify before a stiff and silent group of Commission staff for over three hours, in a secure private room, giving them specific dates, specific target information, and specific managers in charge. Edmonds told them that during the spring and summer of 2001 many within the CIA and FBI had known the likelihood of terrorist attacks within the US. The Commissioners did not ask her a single question.

Edmonds later told the *Village Voice* that it was common knowledge among her colleagues that an FBI asset in Afghanistan had told the agency in April 2001 that Osama bin Laden was planning an attack in a large American city using planes. It seemed that no one at top of the FBI cared, or took any action to try to keep America safe. In fact, the only actions we know of were aimed at silencing, slowing or stopping those investigating suspicious developments on the ground.

The inaction of the FBI doesn't merit the word failure. It's simply not enough to blame incompetence. This was planned, deliberate inaction, in the face of a system awash with warnings of catastrophe, either resulting from utter indifference to public safety, or a more sinister purpose. A stand-down.

The Central Intelligence Agency

The CIA was created in 1947 by President Truman, with the express purpose of preventing more events like Pearl Harbor. Within fifteen years it had become a sort of Frankenstein's Monster in American life, a semi-paramilitary group funding revolutions abroad and working behind the scenes on the darkest of intelligence arts such as assassinations, coups, and conspiracies. John F. Kennedy perceived an agency entirely out of control, and said he wanted to "splinter the CIA into a thousand pieces and scatter it to the winds," comments that sped his race to an early grave.

Lyndon Baines Johnson thought the CIA would "become camouflage for a private secret army at the personal command of the president." Under the stewardship of the Bush family, that fear became reality. With George H. W. Bush at the helm, the CIA began running guns and other weapons to revolutionary forces in South America, and importing hundreds of tons of cocaine to fund their own black-ops. The CIA funded Afghanistan's mujahedeen, which gave rise to the Taliban. Their malign influence has come back to bite America time and again.

More than at any time in its history, the CIA is now a paramilitary force, responsible for overseas deployments and actions including the droning program. More powerful than presidents, in conjunction with the NSA it is now the most dangerous and uncontrollable organization on earth.

From what we now know, it seems clear that the CIA had a mountain of evidence showing preparations for a major attack in the United States in 2001, but did nothing.

What is undoubtedly true is that the CIA knew a number of Middle Eastern men were in the United States planning terrorist attacks, and failed to tell any other agencies, notably the FBI. The CIA knew that at least one known al-Qaeda terrorist (Khalid al-Mihdhar) was coming to the US at least one year before the attacks, but failed to inform other intelligence organizations. But it's worse than that. CIA officers specifically ordered staff not to tell the FBI what they knew.

What seems likely is that the CIA, echoing many other historical blunders, had decided to try to take control of the situation and turn members of the al-Qaeda terrorist cell into double-agents. This might explain why many of the terrorists were allowed to enter and leave the US freely so many times, despite being known dangerous individuals and despite visa violations which would normally get you turned around and sent home.

When Cofer Black and Rich Blee took over the CIA's Counter-Terrorism Center (CTC) in 1999, this was the direction they chose. Black was the CIA's lead man on terrorism. Blee was the chief of the CIA's bin-Laden unit, whose cover name was Alec Station. At the very least, both failed spectacularly to use the information they had to stop the attacks.

At the beginning of July 2001, a CIA briefing said the following: "We believe that UBL (Osama bin Laden) will launch a significant terror attack against US and/or Israeli interests in the coming weeks. The attack will be spectacular and designed to inflict mass casualties against US facilities or interests. Attack preparations have been made. Attack will occur with little or no warning." This report was prepared for senior government officials, and would have been forwarded to the White House.

Such a warning from an authority like the CIA should have sent shock-waves through the government and put the entire US defense and intelligence apparatus on their highest level of alert. In fact, it seems nothing was done whatsoever.

CIA Director George Tenet appears to have had a particularly loose relationship with the truth. The records show Tenet personally briefed President Bush twice in August 2001, when the system was blinking red (as he put it), but in April 2004, Tenet testified under oath to the 9/11 Commission that he had no direct contact with President Bush whatsoever in August of that year.

By the second briefing in August, Tenet would have known that the FBI had a known international terrorist (Zacarias Moussaoui) in custody, who had been caught learning to fly 747s in the US, during a time of unparalleled intelligence chatter suggesting something huge was coming. Tenet also lied about the CIA's information on the hijackers prior to 9/11.

Imagine lying under oath to such a high-profile investigation as the 9/11 Commission. Imagine lying about such important matters. Tenet's lies suggest a man who knew he was above the law, and that if his lies were exposed there would be no legal consequences. Don't these lies betray the victims of 9/11?

9/11 was the greatest failure in the history of the CIA. George Tenet should have been fired on the afternoon of September 11. Instead, Tenet was awarded the Presidential Medal of Freedom after his well-timed resignation in June 2004.

Tenet's continued control over the CIA after 9/11 also meant that in the run-up to the Iraq war he was in a position to tell his president that evidence of Saddam Hussein's weapons of mass destruction was a slam dunk. Again, a bare-faced lie.

Following the universal pattern of those who failed the most gaining the most, the attacks of 9/11 provided probably the greatest gains in CIA history. Any hint of control or oversight was removed by the Bush administration and its Patriot Act. The CIA became synonymous with secret prisons, extraordinary rendition, kidnap, torture, assassination, Bagram, Guantanamo and Abu Ghraib. The agency went rogue, kidnapping and "rendering" anyone they so wished, anywhere in the world. They tortured and murdered suspects without recourse to international law or facing discipline. There simply was none. The CIA's conduct in the years that followed 9/11 represents one of the most shameful episodes in American history, one that continues to this day. And they have faced no consequences.

A true assessment of the CIA's role in 9/11, both before and after, would demand the wholesale destruction of the agency, or at the very least its rebuilding from the ground up. Instead, their record of 9/11 failure is rewarded with more and more money and power each year.

CHAPTER NINE

STATE SPONSORS

The attacks on 9/11 were allegedly carried out by fifteen Saudis, two Emiratis, an Egyptian, and a Lebanese. The author of the attacks was a Saudi living in Afghanistan, who then fled into Pakistan. While in America, the hijackers were trailed by Israeli spies. International terrorism almost always involves the knowledge or support of sovereign governments and their intelligence agencies. Three states in particular, Saudi Arabia, Pakistan, and Israel, are conspicuous by their involvement, funding or prior knowledge of the impending attacks. All claim to be friends of America.

Saudi Arabia

The absolute monarchy that has ruled Saudi Arabia with an iron fist since 1932 is actually much weaker than it appears, requiring billions in American military aid each year to protect the sprawling royal family from its own citizens.

The dynamic of the kingdom's close relationship with the US has always been that of a loveless marriage, both sides so very different, joylessly dependent on each other and unable to leave. With the advent of fracking and shale deposit harvesting in America, that relationship is changing fast, but for more than half a century the US kowtowed to the Saudis to gain access to their oil, and the Saudis held their noses and dealt with the Great Satan to get the endless dollars and unlimited armaments that ensured the status quo.

Not only is Saudi Arabia absolutely opposed to any notion of democracy at home, it has played a central role in supporting most other Middle Eastern dictators for generations. Because of this, America's rhetorical aspirations concerning democracy in the Middle East should be treated with suspicion. Although the US claims to support a brand of freedom worldwide, often the opposite is true. Even the most pernicious, repressive regimes receive US patronage when these states align with US financial and political goals.

America has tried to overthrow more than fifty governments since 1945, and has bombed civilians in thirty countries. The idea that the US wants democracy abroad is pure bullshit, told to your television screens again and again until it becomes true.

In fact, the idea that America promotes and wishes for democracy abroad is so absurd that, as journalist Glenn Greenwald put it, "it defies belief that people are willing to advocate it in public with a straight face." In 2006, when the Palestinians held a widely praised free and fair election, the US, Israel, and Europe imposed harsh penalties on them for voting the wrong way. Democracy is only praiseworthy when the people choose leaders aligned with America's foreign policies. This is especially true when, like the Palestinians, these people have nothing to offer in terms of wealth, strategic positioning or resources.

Incidentally, the Arab Spring of 2011 (aided by the heroic leaks of Chelsea Manning) shone a bright light on the hypocrisy in America's rhetoric on foreign policy. One of the documents published by WikiLeaks provided details of the lavish lifestyle of Tunisia's President Zine el Abidine Ben Ali, during a period of intense struggle by ordinary Tunisian citizens. Robert Godec, the American ambassador to Tunisia, had spent an evening with Ben Ali's son-in-law, and reported back on the excess he saw. Water poured into the villa's infinity pool from a stuffed lion's head. Ice cream had been flown in from France. They had a pet tiger.

On hearing this, a local shopkeeper named Mohamed Bouazizi set himself on fire in the center square of Tunis, and the riots and protests began that would eventually unseat the governments of Tunisia, Libya, Yemen, and Egypt. The Arab Spring events exposed the lie in America's pious claim to wish for democracy and freedom across the Middle East, while arming and training armies like that of Tunisia and Egypt, who were mostly responsible for quelling civil unrest and keeping dictatorial leaders in power.

The ultimate example of this hypocrisy is, of course, America's relationship with Saudi Arabia (who reacted to the Arab Spring by quadrupling their weapons systems purchases, compared to the previous five years). American and Saudi financial and political interests are often so tightly tied as to be inseparable. This helps explain America's tortuous attempts to shield Saudi Arabia from the overwhelming evidence of state-level involvement in the events of 9/11. The revolting truth is that while the US says it relies intimately on the House of Saud as a partner in the War on Terror, its so-called friend is the chief state-level source of support for radical Islam. It's not unlike calling the Nazis allies in World War II.

Money is the source of this loyalty. The US dollar is the only currency with which you can buy oil, so whoever controls the dollars controls the oil, and vice versa. Every nation on earth needs oil, so every nation needs reserves of US dollars to pay for it. The US dollar's reserve status has allowed America to run up astronomical debt, fund wars, and tax-cuts, and run imbalanced books with impunity. When trouble arises, America has been able to print money without causing inflation (which is what happens in every other economy when you turn on the printing presses).

With American sovereign debt at nearly $20 trillion (the equivalent of every American having $60,000 on their credit card), the vital nature of the greenback remaining the world's reserve currency leaves the US in hock to Saudi Arabia and other OPEC states. Were the Saudis ever to start accepting Euros or the Chinese Yuan, America's currency would rapidly lose value, destroying the world's financial system and bringing worldwide chaos. This perhaps also explains why fifteen Saudis taking part in a devastating terrorist attack within the US elicited no response toward Saudi Arabia whatsoever.

Saudi Wahhabism, that most pernicious brand of conservative Islam, still conducts human rights abuses, state atrocities such as torture and mutilation as well as executions at an alarming rate (and still bans women from driving cars). Strict adherence to Islam is, however, mostly a front for ruling the country with an iron fist in order to guarantee the huge royal family protection. Saudi Arabia has up to fifteen thousand princes, blessed with the wealth of gods, professing their religious dogma in public while indulging in the sins of the flesh—alcohol, cocaine, and prostitution—behind their well-secured doors.

Saudi Arabia produces its own figures on sovereign oil reserves, which are never externally audited. These are vitally important for our understanding of the world's energy resources as reserves slowly dwindle, but Saudi statistics are widely derided as being entirely unreliable cooked books. The idea of vast unlimited reserves allows Saudi Arabia to control the price of oil, increasing or reducing production when they see fit, with the international political power that brings. But published reserves are known to be vastly over-stated—the wells will one day run dry, and even acknowledging the beginning of that slow decline could be the end of the House of Saud.

Survival of the ruling class is paramount. Whether through corruption or sympathy toward the cause, the House of Saud has made countless deals with hardline fundamentalist Muslim groups, mostly as a form of bribery or protection money, to stop terrorist attacks against the kingdom itself. Official and covert support for radical Islam has been a central feature of Saudi governing society for generations, and when in modern times this has spun off into terroristic activity, the Saudis have not distanced themselves with any great alacrity.

The Saudi Binladin Group (spelling of the family name varies, depending on which country is describing them) is the largest construction firm in the world, and the bin Laden family so closely aligned with Saudi royalty that they can be seen as one and the same. The bin Ladens are the second richest family in Saudi Arabia, after the royals.

It is well known that Saudi Arabia's relationship with Osama bin Laden was quixotic. Bin Laden enjoyed widespread support through some sections of the Islamic world, not least in Saudi Arabia. As it became clear through the 1990s that one of the kingdom's leading family's sons had gone abroad to mount a campaign that he saw as a violent defense of Islam, there was debate in Saudi Arabia as to how to manage the issue. While there is no doubt that some Saudi royal family members covertly supported the ideas that Osama espoused and offered financial assistance, many also saw him as a loose cannon, and those near the top of the Saudi regime feared that they themselves would become targets if something wasn't done.

Ever the pragmatists, in 1998 Saudi Arabia made a deal with Sheikh Osama. The Saudis would give the Taliban and Pakistan several hundred million dollars, in return for which bin Laden promised not to mount attacks within Saudi Arabia and—crucially—the Saudis agreed to leave bin Laden alone.

The deal was brokered by Prince Turki, head of Saudi intelligence and a close friend of the CIA. Turki had enjoyed a long relationship not only with the bin Laden family but with Osama bin Laden personally. Before being designated the black sheep of the family, Osama had been regarded as Turki's protégé.

After twenty-four years in the position, Prince Turki resigned as Saudi intelligence chief on August 31, 2001, just twelve days before the attacks, without explanation. He was replaced by Nawaf bin Abdul Aziz, the king's brother, who was described as having no background in intelligence whatsoever. A new face, to manage a situation that was about to change radically.

The deal between Saudi Arabia and Osama bin Laden not only left both parties safe to pursue their own agendas, it meant that the chance of bin Laden's capture or arrest was significantly reduced, given his patronage by the Saudis, and the money that relationship engendered for Pakistan and the Taliban. Bin Laden's arrest might also have exposed the close relationship between Osama, his family, Saudi royalty, and ultimately the Bush family. In short, Osama bin Laden's freedom was expedient to a number of powerful parties.

While playing off one Muslim interest against another to keep themselves rich and safe, the Saudis also sought to maintain a healthy relationship with the US, a country which would be their implacable enemy were it not for the oil beneath their feet. Mutual dependency led to an uneasy but practical alliance. The Saudis wanted the US to keep the market for oil stable and within a certain price range, and to leverage their relationship to continue to receive the huge arms shipments that kept their population cowed and the elite in power. For this they let the US use their air bases for ever more regular actions across the Arab world, and bought off trouble by effectively giving the US control of world oil. Primary access to Saudi oil meant America kept its preeminent place among the world's economies.

Although significant entities within the Saudi royal family supported Osama bin Laden's goals and philosophy, the United States (and the Bush administration in particular) maintained a close and loyal friendship, meaning, as Tariq Ali put it: "Bin Laden and his gang are just the tentacles; the head lies safely in Saudi Arabia, protected by US forces." It was widely accepted within US intelligence circles that this was an impossible contradiction to resolve, and that asking the Saudis for help fighting terrorism was utterly pointless. Despite America's power, its dependence on oil meant that the Saudis had much more leverage on the Americans than the other way around.

This stark conflict of interest would be laid bare after 9/11, but with the evidence we have, Saudi Arabia should long ago have been declared a state sponsor of terrorism. Without oil, Saudi society would be seen for what it is, a country that ranks 160th out of 167 nations on the Economist Intelligence Unit's democracy index. An international pariah state.

But America protects the kingdom, no matter how much evidence it receives of the clear and present danger this relationship presents.

Consider the curious case of Mohamed al-Khilewi, the first secretary at the Saudi mission to the United Nations, who defected to the US more than seven years before 9/11, bringing with him thousands of documents showing the regime's corruption and covert support for terrorism. The US, kowtowing to the Saudis as always, declined to offer al-Khilewi protection and the FBI refused to accept his documents altogether. The Saudis responded by calling for his death.

This would have constituted no more than another rum diplomatic affair between two so-called friends, had it not been for the fact that al-Khilewi said his documents showed that a Saudi diplomat had given money to Ramsi Yousef, the known mastermind behind the first World Trade Center bombing in 1993. That bombing had very nearly brought one of the twin towers down, failing only due to a minor error in the placement of the bomb. Khilewi said his documents proved Saudi intelligence had a direct relationship with Yousef.

The idea that Saudi Arabia was funding terrorism in the United States should have had cataclysmic repercussions but, as was often to be the case after 9/11, the matter was buried.

Prince Bandar, known as Bandar Bush (such was his closeness to the family), was the master Saudi operator in Washington. The moment George Tenet was appointed Director of the CIA in July 1997, the two began regular meetings at Bandar's house near Washington. Tenet didn't share the Saudi information he gleaned from the meetings with his own staff, and the Saudis had the ear of the head of the CIA. Now the two countries had a secret intelligence link, unaccountable to anyone but themselves.

The close relationship between the Bush family and Saudi royalty, including extensive financial relations with the bin Ladens, has been well documented. The Carlyle Group, a secretive Washington investment firm with $14 billion in assets, which employed George H. W. Bush as a Senior Advisor from 1998 to 2003, had an open financial relationship with the bin Laden Group until 9/11, and Bush Sr. met the bin Laden family in Jeddah, Saudi Arabia on a number of occasions. All parties, of course, profited handsomely from events subsequent to 9/11.

Bush denied meetings had ever taken place with the bin Laden family in the years before 9/11, until a thank you note was discovered confirming that they had. His meetings with the bin Laden family continued at a time when Osama bin Laden was the world's most wanted terrorist, and when US intelligence agencies had clearly identified bin Laden family members as being conduits for funding of al-Qaeda and other known terrorist organizations. This makes George H. W. Bush, along with his son, an American citizen who has done business with those who finance and support terrorism. By definition an enemy in the War on Terror.

Such was the closeness of the Bush/bin Laden axis via Carlyle, that on the morning of 9/11, the Carlyle Group was hosting a breakfast as part of its annual investor conference at the Ritz hotel in Washington, where the guests included Shafig bin Laden (Osama's brother), former Secretary of State James A. Baker (who managed the legal team that handed George W. Bush the White House in 2000), and George H. W. Bush. One wonders how the public would react were it more widely known that as the attacks of 9/11 commenced, the President's father was having breakfast with the brother of the man blamed for the attacks.

When a secretive Washington-based defense firm—invested in by Saudis including the bin Ladens, employing the presidents father, and major contributors to his election campaign—goes on to make enormous profits following the attacks of 9/11, you would be a fool not to find the links curious. You could not be called foolish to suggest that there may have been a conspiracy.

Saudi Visas

Four months before 9/11, with the US intelligence system on high alert and widespread intelligence showing that potential Saudi terrorists were training in America, the Bush administration chose to relax the visa regulations pertaining to Saudis wishing to visit the US, and introduced a program called Visa Express. Where previously Saudis wanting to go to America had to attend interviews at the US embassy, suddenly visas were available from travel agents, with little or no background checks involved.

Five of the hijackers received their visas this way from the US consulate in Jeddah (home to the headquarters of the bin Laden Group). In total, thirteen of the nineteen future hijackers received their visas through the Jeddah consulate between April 23 and June 29, 2001. This change, and its potential ramifications, cannot have gone un-noticed by US intelligence—it was an open secret at the Consulate that seventeen of the twenty staff working there were CIA agents.

This would not have been the first time that visa regulation manipulation had been used by the United States as part of clandestine operations.

Michael Springmann, who was head of the Visa section at the US Consulate in Jeddah from 1987 to 1989, reported that he was ordered to issue visas to Saudis of questionable backgrounds at that time. His impression was that the late 1980s visa program was an effort to bring recruits, rounded up by (the CIA and) Osama bin Laden, to the US for terrorist training by the CIA. They would then be returned to Afghanistan to fight against the Soviets. The CIA can thus be shown to have had direct control over al-Qaeda. They used mujahedeen as proxies in Afghanistan and the Balkan wars, and regularly brought them to the United States for training.

Continuing the theme of rewarded failure, those behind the Visa Express program that let in thirteen of the 9/11 hijackers were given outstanding performance awards of $15,000 each after the attacks, while the reporter who was most critical of the program (Joel Mowbray) was detained and pressured to issue a retraction by the State Department.

The Flight Out

The months prior to 9/11 saw US-Saudi relations under unprecedented public strain. America's unqualified support for Israel and that state's dreadful treatment of the Palestinians had always been a source of tension, but in response to further egregious Israeli behavior, Prince Bandar told the US, "Starting today, you go your way and we will go our way," a message delivered just three weeks before 9/11.

However, on 9/11 the Saudis quickly realized the immense ramifications of the attacks, and the risk to their own survival as rulers of the kingdom. Within 24 hours, Riyadh ordered 9 million barrels of oil to be shipped to the US in the following two weeks, a certainty of supply which insured America against a financial crisis.

The US reciprocated.

For two days after 9/11, the skies above America were empty, as an unprecedented total civilian air flight ban remained in place following the devastating attacks. On September 13, some commercial flights resumed, but all private flights remained grounded until the afternoon of September 14.

However, there was an exception allowed to this rule. Small chartered planes crisscrossed the empty skies, picking up Saudi royalty and bin Laden family members, who were quickly spirited back to the safety of Saudi Arabia.

Rich, prominent and royal Saudis in the US on 9/11 had quickly concluded that exiting the country was probably a good idea, and contacted (of all people) the FBI. On September 13, the US government contacted the Saudi government, and arranged for these people to be allowed to leave the United States before the total ban on flying had been lifted. Even Bill Clinton and Al Gore, both overseas, could not get back. But the Saudis made good their escape.

Seventy-five royals and staff were stuck in Las Vegas (that most devout of cities). Some bin Laden family members were driven or flown first to Texas, then on to Washington, under the watchful supervision of the FBI, the very entity that should have been investigating the family and their ties to the recent atrocity. Interviewing relatives of crime suspects is basic policing, and should have been standard operating procedure. Instead, the people who should have been at the top of the list of suspects were given FBI escorts out the country.

One of the passengers on the flights was Prince Ahmed bin Salman, one of the three Saudi princes later alleged to have had prior knowledge of the 9/11 attacks, all three of whom died in mysterious circumstances over an eight day period in July 2002, following the interrogation of al-Qaeda leader Abu Zubaydah.

About 140 Saudis were passengers on the flights, including 24 members of the bin Laden family. At least three bin Laden family members in the US had previously been accused of or investigated for terrorist links. Two of them had their cases re-opened on the 19th of September, right after they left. Another passenger was Saleh Ibn Abdul Rahman Hussayen, a government official who had stayed in the same hotel as three of the hijackers the night before the attacks. He was on one of the first flights out, and the FBI were unable to interview him.

The clues to their malfeasance weren't tenuous or non-specific. Abdullah and Omar bin Laden had strong links to WAMY, a charity known to have been funneling Saudi money to US-based terrorists. Abdullah was both president and director. The bin Laden brothers had lived at 5613 Leesburg Pike in Falls Church, Virginia. Of all the streets in the United States, four of the 9/11 hijackers had chosen to live just down the road, at 5913 Leesburg Pike.

Given the sprawling bin Laden family's well-known connection to terrorism, and that fifteen of the nineteen hijackers had been Saudis, these escape flights are absolutely inexcusable, at a time when smoke still rose from the ashes of the twin towers.

For two years the FAA, FBI, and the White House denied the existence of the flights, and poured scorn on those who asked questions about them, but in 2003 Richard Clarke confirmed they had happened. Clarke said he had signed off on the flights, although many strongly believe it was a decision made at the top.

Clarke claimed that he took the decision after the FBI assured him that no-one on board had connections to terrorism. If this is true, the head of the FBI should have been sacked immediately, as their assurance was a lie, given the knowledge they already had of wider Saudi involvement. But it's impossible to imagine that Bandar Bush would not have used his connection to the president to make sure his citizens were given a red carpet ride out of America.

Why would a US president authorize such a bizarre exodus, given the administration's certainty that Osama bin Laden had orchestrated the attacks, and with the majority of attackers having been Saudis?

This extraordinary tale represents corruption of the highest order. Treason may be the most appropriate word. Allowing clear suspects in the greatest terror attack in US history to board private flights and flee the crime scene? It's as if the US air force formed a guard of honor for Japanese planes after Pearl Harbor. This alone should have been cause for the dismissal and arrest of George W. Bush.

Just a few days later, Bush delivered his famous "you're with us or you're with the terrorists" speech, and a little later he added that the Saudi Arabians had been nothing but cooperative, but this was also a lie. Most reports indicate that on arrival on Saudi soil it was game over for US intelligence gathering. Expressions like "completely unsupportive" and "zero cooperation" were frequently used. America had given 9/11's prime suspects a free ride home.

Bandar Bush

The idea that Saudi Arabia's ambassador to the US was behind the flights out is reinforced by Bush's refusal to cancel or even postpone an evening meeting with Prince Bandar on September 13, just forty-eight hours after the attacks. Photos of the meeting show the pair, along with Dick Cheney and Condoleezza Rice, smiling and enjoying cigars on the Truman Balcony of the president's private quarters at the White House.

Prince Bandar, the Saudi ambassador for twenty-two years, was a Washington institution who smoked cigars and drank cognac with the great and the good. Bandar was thick as thieves with US conservative political royalty, most notably Dick Cheney and the Bush family. But Bandar was also Saudi Arabia's spymaster and master spy, in control of a labyrinth of covert Saudi actions. There could be few stranger people to have sipped cognac with just two days after 9/11.

Bandar Bush later showed his appreciation by donating $1 million to the George W. Bush Presidential Library.

Abu Zubaydah and the Dead Saudis

In March 2002, al-Qaeda leader Abu Zubaydah (a Saudi) was arrested in Pakistan and, after the US paid Pakistan $10 million for him, he was interrogated. Under the influence of sodium pentothal, Zubaydah told his interrogators (Arab-Americans whom he believed to be Saudis) that he was essentially the Saudi government's man within al-Qaeda, and to call Prince Ahmed bin Abdul-Aziz, the king's nephew, who would vouch for his connections. He recalled the prince's telephone number from memory, and claimed that he personally knew many senior Saudi and Pakistani government figures.

When the interrogators suggested that 9/11 must have changed a great deal in relation to the ties between the Saudi government and al-Qaeda, Zubaydah told them that nothing had changed, especially since Prince Ahmed had known in advance of the attacks. He also volunteered from memory the telephone numbers of two other relatives of the king with strong al-Qaeda ties, Prince Sultan bin Faisal bin Turki al-Saud (a nephew of the king) and Prince

Fahd bin Turki bin Saud al-Kabir. He specifically named Pakistani air force chief Mushaf Ali Mir, who was closely tied to the ISI (Pakistan's intelligence service), and recently resigned Saudi intelligence chief Prince Turki.

This was explosive stuff. The head of al-Qaeda apparently intimately connected with the Saudi royal family and Pakistani military.

Then, as is often the case with loose ends, people began to die.

Within months, all of the people Zubaydah named in connection with the funding of al-Qaeda (except Prince Turki) were dead, all killed in unusual circumstances.

Prince Ahmed died on July 22, 2002 from a heart attack at age 43. A day later, Prince Sultan was killed in a single-car accident while driving to Prince Ahmed's funeral. A week later Prince Fahd "died of thirst" while travelling East of Riyadh. Pakistani air-force chief Mushaf Ali Mir later died when his plane crashed in clear weather in February 2003.

Prince Turki, the sole survivor of the group, was made Saudi ambassador to the UK, allowing him immunity from prosecution. When a US lawsuit was filed against Turki and others for their actions in relation to the events of 9/11, the case was dismissed on these diplomatic grounds. Defending the suit, Turki was represented by law firm Baker & Botts, of whom James Baker, former secretary of state under Bush senior, was a senior partner. Baker had been at the Carlyle Group breakfast on 9/11 with the President's father and Osama bin Laden's brother. Sometimes it's hard not to see this world as one where an untouchable elite play a game entirely by their own rules, in which we are just pawns.

Pakistan

The sovereign border between Pakistan and Afghanistan is a relic of an imperial age, drawn with a flourish by Sir Henry Mortimer Durand in 1893, and still called the Durand line. The country is a construct of disparate groups, its name an acronym of Punjab, Afghan, Kashmir, Indus (or Islam) and Sind. This artificial sovereign jigsaw meant that US troops fighting in Afghanistan were almost entirely confined to one side of a non-existent line, and unable to engage within Pakistan, where the madrasas (funded by the Saudis, of course) continually trained and churned out new Taliban fighters.

The invading Americans troops must have wondered why half of the Pashtun people live in Afghanistan and half in Pakistan, yet the war could only take place on one side of this artificial line. In order to win the war, America should first have chosen to fight the right country.

Pakistan has long been an ally to the United States, as a counterbalance to an India that is more friendly with Russia. The US is Pakistan's closest ally, without whom the country would probably collapse. Politics is said to make for strange bedfellows, and never more so than with the ever-tenuous relationship known as AmPak.

The AmPak connection has much history, but came to the fore during the Soviet occupation of Afghanistan in the 1980s. So as to not be seen as arming the resistance to the Soviets, which could have been regarded as an act of war and risked a broader conflagration, Pakistan's army and intelligence organization the ISI became an easy way for the US to funnel billions of dollars in cash and arms to the Afghan mujahedeen.

Most of the money given to the ISI was passed to the Afghans, but the ISI took its share, and worked with the Afghans to mutually profit from the burgeoning trade in illegal drugs.

The ISI began producing heroin, both to make money and to get Russian troops hooked, damaging Russia's fighting force at the instigation of the CIA. When Russia's occupation of Afghanistan ended in 1989, the ISI quickly became the agency most responsible for the import of heroin to the streets of the West. Ten years later, it was estimated that the ISI was making $2.5 billion per year from the illegal drug trade.

Pakistan's drug economy is now regarded as running parallel to the official one, and worth around $15 billion per year. In 2001, Pakistan's official economy was worth a mere $72 billion annually. It doesn't take much imagination to see how corrupting it is to a society when illicit drugs are worth nearly a quarter of the national GDP.

With munificent American patronage, the ISI's power has grown exponentially, and such is its influence many regard it as a state within a state. Without the ISI, it is impossible to gain political control of Pakistan. When General Pervez Musharraf staged his military coup in 1999, it was with the backing of the ISI's Lieutenant-General Mahmud Ahmed, whose own 9/11 connections remain murky and suspicious.

However, trust between the ISI and US authorities has always been minimal, despite the close working relationship. Pakistan is a dangerous place, and political security is touch-and-go at the best of times. When Bill Clinton visited Pakistan in March 2000, Air Force One flew in without him, and Clinton arrived on a small unmarked plane.

The ISI played a key role in the formation and initial success of the Taliban, and had close links to Osama bin Laden. Many suspect that bin Laden's uncanny ability to stay one step ahead of America's bumbling attempts to kill him was due to the ready flow of intelligence and information that came through the ISI, despite their links with the CIA.

The ISI and Osama bin Laden's al-Qaeda were rarely anything other than close. A strong contingent of Pakistanis and their military supported bin Laden. Despite this, the ISI's ongoing relationship with the CIA meant that US intelligence should not have found it hard to find or monitor Osama in the hills of Afghanistan.

Saeed Sheikh

A key connection between the ISI and al-Qaeda was a British student at the London School of Economics who dropped his studies to move to Pakistan and take up terrorism. Saeed Sheikh enjoyed a long career in making mayhem, but each time he was cornered he found help from powerful allies who prevented his long-term incarceration or assassination. In 1994 when he was imprisoned for five years for kidnap in India, the ISI paid for his lawyer. Sheikh eventually escaped his Indian prison in 1999 when passengers on a hijacked plane were exchanged for his (and two partners) freedom.

From there Sheikh moved between Afghanistan and Pakistan, receiving the hospitality and patronage of Osama bin Laden and the Taliban when in the former, and the ISI in the latter. Sheikh became bin Laden's money man, and a crucial go-between for the ISI and al-Qaeda. Despite his known terrorist history, Sheikh lived openly in Pakistan, and appeared to have plenty of money. US authorities concluded he was both an ISI agent and the money man for al-Qaeda, but did little or nothing to address the financial links between Pakistani intelligence and international terrorism. Almost unbelievably, although known as the world's leading terrorist's banker, Sheikh was also able to visit Britain twice to see his family, apparently without a problem.

General Mahmud

Simultaneously an ISI agent and financial conduit for al-Qaeda, Saeed Sheikh wired $100,000 to Mohamed Atta's Florida bank account in August 2001, at the instruction of the Director of the ISI, Lieutenant General Mahmud Ahmed. This was reported on October 9, 2001 by the *Times of India*.

In total, transfers of around $325,000 were made to Atta's account (the last of which was only days before 9/11) by Mustafa Ahmed, widely accepted to be an alias for Saeed Sheikh. Whether the money originated from Osama bin

Laden or the top of the ISI doesn't actually matter—the two were the same thing, interconnected entities funding international terrorism.

Lieutenant General Mahmud, the head of the ISI since 1999, chose the early part of September 2001 to make an extended visit to the US. Pakistani generals aren't a fixture on the Washington scene, nor are they normally afforded access to the full raft of senior figures in US government, but when Mahmud arrived on the 4th of September he commenced a trip in which he met with nearly all major US national security players, including CIA Director George Tenet, officials at the Pentagon, the National Security Council and the State Department, and the chairmen of the House and Senate Intelligence Committees.

Presciently, a prominent newspaper in Pakistan called *The News* reported on September 10 that the General's visit to the US was of particular interest, since "last time his predecessor was [in Washington], the domestic politics turned topsy-turvy within days."

While Mahmud was in the US, Ahmad Shah Massoud (the head of Afghanistan's Northern Alliance) was assassinated. The assassination fragmented the Northern Alliance, removing a man who called for reform and was backed by the Russians, subsequently making the job of invading Afghanistan much easier for America. The Alliance said the assassination had been the work of the ISI. Also while in the US, the ISI was in regular contact with Osama bin Laden and al-Qaeda.

So a straight line of money, information, and communication can be drawn from Osama bin Laden, al-Qaeda, the ISI, CIA, and the Bush administration.

Interestingly, Saudi Crown Prince Abdullah (the ruler of Saudi Arabia) also made a clandestine visit to Pakistan in the late summer of 2001 to visit and meet with ISI director Mahmud.

Mahmud was in Washington on the morning of 9/11, having breakfast with senior intelligence community leaders, including Chairman of the House Intelligence Committee Porter Goss (who would later become Director of the CIA), Senator Bob Graham, chairman of the Senate Select Committee on Intelligence, as well as Senator John Kyl and the Pakistani ambassador to the US. Oddly enough, nearly all of these individuals had been in Pakistan twelve days earlier.

Goss himself was a veteran of the CIA's clandestine operations wing, and as much of an intelligence insider as any American alive. He owed his political career to Graham. Goss and Graham subsequently were chosen as the safe hands to lead the joint house-senate investigation into the 9/11 attacks.

Mahmud's visits with the spine of American security came at the perfect time, as immediately after 9/11 America was able to use his presence to quickly solidify Pakistani support for their nascent war in Afghanistan.

The Bush administration was not keen for the public to know that the head of Pakistan's spy arm had been in meeting after meeting with top US officials prior to and on 9/11. When asked about the meetings between the general and senior intelligence officials on 9/11, Condoleezza Rice gave a disingenuous non-answer ("he certainly wasn't meeting with me"). All transcripts of that particular press conference, save one, blacked out the mention of the name of the ISI chief, indicating that the general's name were the only words that apparently had been inaudible. And the media complied. In fact, the American press barely breathed a word on Mahmud's visit. They had begun to censor themselves.

On October 8, 2001, just twenty-seven days after 9/11, the general was said to have resigned, although in truth the resignation had been requested by the US to avoid publicity and to let the matter of the funding of Mohamed Atta dissipate. Mahmud Ahmed was allowed to quietly disappear from view, effectively blocking any meaningful investigation of the ISI's relationship with al-Qaeda. Pakistan, of course, has benefited hugely (in terms of aid and arms) since the attacks on 9/11.

As with Saudi Arabia, the relationship between the US and Pakistan is that of an awkward, dysfunctional marriage. The Pentagon bankrolls the Pakistani army to fight wars against extremism on their behalf, all the while violating Pakistani sovereignty with virtual impunity, droning at will and killing citizens without any due process or consequence—actions that breed the extremism their proxy war claims to fight.

Yet despite the clear links between the ISI and both Osama bin Laden and the Taliban (and by extension the events of 9/11) the relationship appears unchanged. Pakistan today is a basket case, politically and socially, often on the brink of implosion. Its largest city, Karachi, is a war zone. Rival gangs affiliate with political parties and use violence for political ends.

Pakistan's dysfunctional relationship with its paymasters has been highlighted by Bernard-Henri Levy (the French intellectual), who produced a timeline showing that every Pakistani "capture" of a high profile jihadist just happened to take place the week before a vote in Congress to authorize more funds to the government in Islamabad.

Until this sick relationship is addressed, the Taliban will receive support from the ISI, heroin cultivation and smuggling will continue unchecked, US drones will kill innocents and radicalize survivors, and the whole merry-go-round of death will never be stopped.

Israel

It is impossible to examine any geopolitical picture involving America without including its relationship with Israel, one of the most belligerent nations on earth. America has a tricky diplomatic course to tread in the Middle East, providing unstinting support for their radical friends in Israel while keeping the petrol dollars flowing through the Islamic extremists who rule Saudi Arabia.

Only 1.4 percent of America's population is Jewish, most of whom are politically moderate, yet the Zionist lobby exercises a disproportionately powerful influence over American politics. Even the mildest straying from absolute and unequivocal support for Israel (as was the case under Barack Obama) is treated as heresy. During Obama's presidency, Benjamin Netanyahu openly supported Republican politicians and candidates and repeatedly snubbed Obama, all because of an American approach that was only very slightly critical, especially when compared with the outright condemnation Israel receives from the rest of the world.

The US has assisted Israel in blocking any resolution of the Palestinian issue for nearly forty years. The so-called peace process is nothing of the sort, and just a smokescreen for an ongoing land-grab, a fake process that says that the problem is complicated and intractable and that peace is the ultimate goal, all the while allowing for continued expansion of occupied territories. Since 1973, nearly half a million rabidly right-wing settlers have moved into former Palestinian territory. The number of settlers in the West Bank has sharply accelerated since 2001.

All settlements are illegal under international law. The world calls out for settlement activity to stop, and for Israel to retreat to its pre-1967 borders. Israel entirely ignores this.

The state of Israel could not conceivably carry out its pernicious activities without the unstinting support, both political and military, of the United States. As such, it is rightly seen by most in the Middle East and beyond as a proxy state, an extension (or perhaps fifty-first state) of America. Israeli aggression against Palestinians is permitted and often encouraged by the United States, despite the overwhelming condemnation of nearly all the world's nations. This abusive relationship damages not just Israel's victims (the Palestinians), but America's abrogation of international laws and norms significantly weakens its ability to take the moral lead in world affairs. If anything, Israel's most egregious acts, like extra-judicial assassination and the use of chemical weapons like phosphorus against Palestinian civilians, have been adopted by America.

The US has used its veto forty-two times to stop the UN formally censuring Israel over its treatment of the Palestinians, actions that amount to a generations-long campaign of deliberate and calculated cruelty against millions of people, in order to subjugate an entire ethnic group and achieve Israel's political goals.

Regular military campaigns against the Palestinians are falsely portrayed as being defensive, but the real indignity is in the daily control and rationing of vital resources like food, energy, and medicines. Or a huge wall that cuts off communities. Or snipers killing Palestinian children armed only with stones. Israel threatens the Palestinians with a clenched fist that is permanently raised.

Today, Israel is an apartheid state just as vicious as South Africa was. The government is primarily run by Zionists who thumb their nose at the rest of the world and continue to expand a country based on boundary beliefs sourced from the book of Genesis, which says Israel should run from the brook of Egypt to the Euphrates.

Until America finds itself able to hold Israel to the standards it applies to others (and says it applies to itself), the Israeli nation will be a cancer eating at the heart of America's international affairs, and the Middle East will burn at the outrageous cruelty meted out to millions of Palestinians in the false light of a peace process that aims for no such thing.

Without ever confirming or denying their existence, Israel has managed over the years to put together an underground nuclear missile arsenal of at least eighty warheads (possibly as many as two hundred) as well as chemical weapons systems. President Kennedy sold Israel its first nukes, but countries such as the UK, France, and Germany have, over the years, secretly sold Israel more nuclear materials. That these countries now take a tough line against Iranian nuclear proliferation is, to say the least, ironic.

Israel has also often acquired nuclear technology clandestinely, stealing secrets from its good friend and benefactor America as well as others. Israel's shadowy behavior has led to nuclear proliferation risks elsewhere in the world. Pakistani nuclear physicist Abdul Qadeer Khan sold to Iran and North Korea the same centrifuge blueprints that Israel had stolen from the US. This in turn enabled Israel to create the Stuxnet virus that set back Iran's nuclear progress, safe in the knowledge that Iran's centrifuges were exactly the same design as their own.

Israel's dire warnings about Iran's theoretical nuclear capability have not been muted at all by their possession of an actual nuclear arsenal, supplied and maintained by the US, hidden in secret, never acknowledged, and shielded from any UN or international inspection. Morally, it seems, nuclear weapons are just fine when they are owned by our side, no matter how outside international norms our behavior is in relation to nuclear management and proliferation.

Israel's possession of nuclear missiles is also a major factor behind most Middle Eastern countries refusal to sign a nuclear non-proliferation treaty. Polls across the region consistently rate Israel (and by extension the US) as the greatest threat to peace in the Middle East. Large majorities tell pollsters they believe the Middle East would be more stable if Iran had a nuclear weapon. The greatest danger in the Middle East is the rogue state that is Israel.

The plight of the Palestinians remains the leading cause of Arab resentment of the West, and solving the issue has proved a task beyond two generations of American Presidents. By all accounts, President George W. Bush had made progress on the issue early in his Presidency, and by mid-2001 had privately agreed to the eventual establishment of a separate Palestinian state. The announcement was being drafted when the events of September 11 led to an immediate change in dynamic of the relationship between the US, Israel, and the Saudis. Palestinian independence was forgotten, and Israel gained incalculable traction as the US turned against all things Islamic.

However, there is a great deal of evidence that, at the very least, Israel was fully aware of the impending attacks. It may be worse than that.

In the months prior to 9/11 there was a peak in Israeli intelligence activity within the US, widely seen as the biggest spy operation against America since the Cold War. Multiple Mossad agents posed as art students, conducting covert surveillance of federal and commercial buildings, and keeping close tabs on the hijackers and their associates.

The Mossad is the world's most effective intelligence agency, and very little of import happens in world affairs without them knowing about it. So many people knew so much about 9/11 for so long that it's impossible to imagine the Mossad and Israel having been unaware. More than that, Israel had agents in close physical proximity to many of the key protagonists in the lead-up to the attacks. The Israeli spies followed the hijackers. Some lived just a couple of blocks away from Mohamed Atta and his associates in Florida.

Prior to 9/11, five Israeli agents were arrested for spying in the town of Hollywood, Florida, which just happened to be where four of the hijackers were living. One of the Israelis lived at 4420 Sheridan Street. Mohamed Atta lived at 3389 Sheridan Street, just half a mile away. More than thirty of the

Israelis arrested before 9/11 lived in or close to Hollywood, Florida, which is where fifteen of the nineteen hijackers based themselves at certain points.

In total, more than one hundred Israeli "students" were arrested and deported prior to 9/11, and up to sixty afterwards, all without facing charges. Of course, America's relationship with Israel is absolutely sacrosanct, so there was little media or political follow-up of what was clearly a huge covert action related to the attacks.

On 9/11 itself, Israelis were involved in a number of extraordinary and highly suspicious incidents that lend credence not just to the notion that Israel knew of the pending attacks, but that it was involved in their execution.

Dancing Israelis

Strange things were afoot in and around Manhattan on 9/11. Five young Israeli army veterans who worked for a company called Urban Moving Systems were seen in Jersey City at Liberty Park on the Hudson River, taking photos of themselves with the smoking wrecks of the Twin Towers in the background, and appearing to celebrate. Local residents called the police, disturbed by the incongruous behavior.

The FBI immediately issued the following alert: White, 2000 Chevrolet van with "Urban Moving Systems" sign on back seen at Liberty State Park, Jersey City, NJ, at the time of first impact of jetliner into World Trade Center. Three individuals with van were seen celebrating after initial impact and subsequent explosion. The FBI Newark Field office requests that if the van is located, hold for prints and detain individuals.

Later that afternoon, an anonymous phone call to police led to the closing of all of Manhattan's bridges and tunnels. The transcript of the phone call is extraordinary:

> **Dispatcher:** *Jersey City police.*
> **Caller:** *Yes, we have a white van, two or three guys in there. They look like Palestinians . . . and going around a building. There's a mini-van heading toward the Holland tunnel . . . I see the guy by Newark airport mixing some junk and has those Sheikh uniform.*
> **Dispatcher:** *He has what?*
> **Caller:** *He's dressed like an Arab.*

Given that Palestinians wear Western-style clothing, it seems odd that the caller was somehow able to work out their country of origin on appearance alone. Either way, the police were being directed towards the Holland tunnel and suspicious activity by an "Arab."

Shortly after that, police stopped a truck matching the FBI's description near the New York Giants football stadium on the approach to the George Washington Bridge. When the five occupants were arrested at gunpoint by policeman Scott DeCarlo and colleagues, they found box-cutters in the van, as well as maps of New York with high-profile locations highlighted. One of the men had $4,700 cash hidden in his sock. All those arrested had two passports, one European, one Israeli. Bomb-sniffing dogs detected explosive residue inside the van. As they were being arrested, the driver of the van, Sivan Kurzberg, told police that they weren't the problem; they were on America's side, and that Palestinians were America's problem.

Although it remains unclear if there was a bomb on board, on September 12 the *Jerusalem Post* reported that the van had been packed with explosives. ABC and the *New York Post* reported much the same.

There is some confusion as to whether the van was stopped on the approach to the George Washington Bridge or near the Lincoln Tunnel (7 miles away), leading some to speculate that there were two separate vans driven by Israelis. What is not in doubt is that Israelis were seen celebrating the attacks, and later found driving a van filled with highly suspicious materials on the afternoon of a day when US national security was at its highest level of alert. The anonymous phone call to Jersey City police not only fingered Palestinians as guilty parties, but directed police toward the third major point of crossing to Manhattan. Had attacks on the Lincoln Tunnel and George Washington Bridge taken place, vital police resources would have been diverted away to the Holland Tunnel by the mysterious call.

Two of the five arrested passengers in the van were determined by the FBI to be Mossad agents. The five Israelis were held for seventy-one days then, amazingly, released without charge. The FBI's foreign counterintelligence section, who are responsible for espionage cases, took over control of the suspects but immediately dropped their investigation, and the release of the Israelis was ordered a few weeks later by Attorney General John Ashcroft, following high-level requests from Israeli diplomats and Michael Chertoff, a leading Jewish operator within the Bush administration. The five were quietly deported due to visa violations.

It gets stranger. On their return to Israel in November 2001, the five bizarrely chose to go on a TV chat show to talk about 9/11. As part of a conversation concerning why they were in America, one told the host, "Our purpose was to document the event." We even know their names: Sivan and Paul Kurzberg, Oded Ellner, Omer Marmari and Yaron Schmuel.

It might be possible to argue that the five Israelis were merely spies who by chance found themselves near the scene of the attacks and displayed appalling and astonishingly poorly judged behavior. However, the Israelis had been spotted celebrating immediately after the first plane impact, a point in the day when most thought that perhaps the crash was just a tragic accident, and when the attacks were not yet known to be terrorism. Some local residents saw them positioned at 8:00 a.m., well before the first crash. "Our purpose was to document the event" sounds unequivocally like evidence that the attacks were known to be coming before they commenced.

Urban Moving Systems was a clear Israeli espionage front. Dominick Suter, the Israeli business owner, fled the US in a hurry on September 14, leaving his offices filled with personal effects, cellphones, etc., and a lot of customers in the lurch. Suter was placed on the FBI's wanted list in May 2002, but never formally pursued.

In total, almost two hundred Israelis were deported before and after 9/11. Whatever the reason for their presence, it's clear there was a massive Israeli intelligence operation in place. It's not tenable to suggest that what happened around 9/11 was just a routine intelligence gathering operation—Israel clearly had spies on the ground who were physically very close to many of the alleged hijackers, as well as Mossad agents near New York who knew what was about to happen, and prepared secondary attacks aimed at blaming Palestinians and Arabs for the outrages. As such, this represents the gravest betrayal of America imaginable, and should have caused the US government to cut all ties with Israel, with the seismic ramifications that would have caused.

Israel is supposed to be America's most implacable ally. Its very survival would be in question if the US ever chose to abandon the country politically or militarily. Instead, the entire matter was (and remains) swept under the carpet and, as America's sights turned on the Middle East and demonizing Muslims, Israel became one of the main beneficiaries of 9/11.

Attached to this story is, incidentally, a salutary demonstration of how the US media still works. When Donald Trump was running for the Republican nomination in 2015, he claimed that thousands of Muslim people were seen cheering from New Jersey as the twin towers fell. Trump said he'd seen the footage on YouTube. This revoltingly emotive lie was fact-checked by many and found to be entirely untrue, but the documented, published, and clear evidence of cheering Israelis that day didn't once get a mention.

CHAPTER TEN

THE ACCUSED

International terrorism is incredibly rare. Most terrorists are profoundly disenfranchised and hopeless people, who strike out at some other group in their society which they perceive to be a threat to them or their belief systems. To organize a group of people to travel the world, train in secret, and then circumvent state security takes skill, money, logistics, and a lot of good fortune. On 9/11 we are told that the attacks were conceived of and financed by Osama bin Laden, masterminded (in a way that remains unclear) by Khalid Sheikh Mohammed and carried out by nineteen men from the Middle East, but that nearly no other individuals were involved at all. In addition, the nineteen alleged hijackers are said to have left no trace while inside the US, and not liaised with a single other person in America while there. Every aspect of this story is fantasy.

Osama Bin Laden

Osama bin Laden was one of an incredible fifty-four children sired by his father, Sheikh Mohammed bin Laden, who build the bin Laden group into the largest construction conglomerate in the world.

The decades-long business connections between the Bush family, the bin Laden family, and the House of Saud are well known. George H. W. Bush had long been closely associated with the bin Ladens, staying at the family's private residences on a number of visits to Saudi Arabia. George W. Bush's fortune was built in part doing business with the bin Ladens.

Given that there is no doubt that many senior members of the bin Laden family maintained connections with Osama long after he had been declared America's number one enemy, and the Bush family (most notably via the Carlyle Group) also failed to cut ties with the family, the degrees of separation between the US president and the man alleged to have been behind the 9/11 attacks are not many. At the very least, the business and personal links between the Bushes and bin Ladens make for an extraordinary aspect of the 9/11 story.

The CIA also had ties to Osama bin Laden and al-Qaeda, with whom they worked closely during the Russian occupation of Afghanistan and the war in Bosnia. Osama bin Laden's al-Qaeda was so active in the Balkan Wars that he was given an honorary Bosnia-Herzegovina passport in 1993. The ties between the CIA and al-Qaeda are known not to have been severed following the Bosnian war.

In Afghanistan

Osama bin Laden first travelled to Afghanistan in 1979 to fight the invading Soviets. Given bin Laden's financial clout and membership of such a prominent Saudi family, he quickly became well known across the Islamic world. With the US support for the mujahedeen resistance, it is thought that around this time the first contact was made between bin Laden and the CIA.

Osama bin Laden returned to Afghanistan in 1996, coming from his base in Sudan, where he had lived in exile since 1991 under the protection of the Islamic fundamentalist government. The Sudanese security services had come to think of bin Laden as a liability, and offered to hand him over to the US, but were told America had no problem if he was moved to Afghanistan, and no interest in detaining him.

In early 1988, bin Laden had begun the expansion of a new military group, al Qaeda, meaning "the base" or the foundation. al-Qaeda was a term loosely used to describe US-trained mujahedeen. It may have been coined by the CIA as an Arabic term for a database.

What is undoubtedly true is that since the members of al-Qaeda had been trained and financed using American (CIA) money, the US was far from an uninformed party, nor without influence and communication links to the group.

On February 28, 1998, bin Laden issued a fatwa, demanding that the US leave the holy land (Saudi Arabia). Around twenty thousand American troops had been stationed there since the first Persian Gulf War, to shore up the power and stability of the ruling House of Saud and show US strength within the region.

America's withdrawal from Saudi Arabia was subsequently, quietly, allowed to take place—the same week Bush declared "Mission accomplished" in Iraq. US forces were relocated to Qatar, although secret operations and drone launches continue to this day.

Osama bin Laden has always been portrayed as the black sheep of his family, but BBC Newsnight investigators looking into the funneling of money around the family in 2003 described the bin Ladens as containing "a lot of grey sheep". Although the bin Ladens publicly disowned their rogue son, there is considerable evidence that family ties remained, both in terms of regular contact and substantial financial support.

His family may not have been the only ones shielding Osama from harm. Reading the history of bin Laden's time in Afghanistan, it's hard not to remark on quite how charmed a life he appears to have led. Despite his crimes and intentions, bin Laden was a protected man, not only by his hosts, but also by his supposed enemies.

In the period after the August 7 US embassy bombings in Kenya and Tanzania in 1998, bin Laden was the most wanted man on earth, but opportunities to arrest or incapacitate him were repeatedly missed or spurned. Incidentally, investigators of the two Embassy bombings found that the explosives used were made by the US military, given three years earlier to Afghan Arabs.

Opportunities to kill bin Laden were plentiful. In 1999, CIA director George Tenet turned down three requests to do so, apparently concerned about collateral damage, something that slid down his list of concerns dramatically in the years that followed. No less than Jayne's Intelligence Review (the defense industry's leading publication) concluded that 9/11 was the direct result of a political decision not to act against bin Laden. That decision could only have been taken by very senior US officials.

In early 2001, Defense Intelligence Agency (DIA) analyst Julie Sirrs travelled twice to Afghanistan and returned home with a treasure trove of information about Osama bin Laden's whereabouts and activities. But that information was confiscated by a security officer at the airport, and instead the DIA and FBI investigated Sirrs before removing her security clearance, leaving her no choice but to resign. It's a recurring theme—those conscientiously trying to supply the information that would get bin Laden and his associates were sidelined, stonewalled, or discarded, for reasons that remain unclear.

Bin Laden endured renal deficiency (impaired kidney function) for some years, but this worsened in 2000 and he relied on a dialysis machine and regular medical attention at Peshawar's military hospital in Pakistan, visits facilitated by the ISI.

In July 2001, this most wanted of men spent ten nights (from the fourth to the fourteenth) at the American hospital in Dubai getting kidney dialysis. While there he was treated by an American surgeon (Dr. Terry Callaway), visited by Prince Turki al Faisal (the head of Saudi intelligence) and on July 12 by the local CIA agent Larry Mitchell. Despite being the world's most wanted man, with a $5 million bounty on his head, it appears no attempt was made to arrest bin Laden or even to notify authorities of his whereabouts. On July 15, Mitchell returned to the US to report to CIA headquarters on his meeting with Osama bin Laden.

Why was the CIA meeting with the world's most wanted man, just weeks before 9/11?

It was also reported that bin Laden had dialysis treatment in Rawalpindi, Pakistan, the day before 9/11. Despite bin Laden's clear involvement in international terrorism and attacks on US embassies and staff, it appears Pakistan chose not to arrest or detain him. Instead, Pakistani army forces guarded bin Laden during his treatment.

Bin Laden Videos

"They hate our freedoms" was one of George W. Bush's favorite sayings about his supposed nemesis al-Qaeda, even as Bush and his team worked tirelessly to dismantle the freedoms that US society had fought so hard to gain. Bush's argument was typically facile and reductive, especially given America's tireless support for dictators in the Middle East who ran some of the most repressive societies on earth. But Osama bin Laden's pronouncements, post 9/11, seemed curiously free of comment on societal freedom, and more focused on his perception of the West's outrages against Islam.

Bin Laden's first statement after 9/11 was additionally curious for the angle of its denial. Among other things, bin Laden said, "I was not involved in the September 11 attacks in the United States nor did I have knowledge of the attacks. There exists a government within a government within the United States. The United States should try to trace the perpetrators of these attacks within itself." Had Osama bin Laden been the author of the attacks, this seemed a very odd way of celebrating his greatest triumph.

Bin Laden denied involvement in the attacks three times. On September 16, he sent a statement to Al Jazeera television, in which he again denied being behind 9/11 and said the attacks seemed to have been "planned by people for personal reasons".

Nevertheless, America was sure it had fingered the right man, and as the year came to an end, they seemed to make a breakthrough. On December 13, the US claimed it had found footage of bin Laden admitting his involvement, but the video was the first in a series of increasingly blurred clips, the contents of which were highly disputed. Instead of a "piece to camera," as had been bin Laden's previous form of communication, this one was supposedly recorded without his knowledge and found by chance in an abandoned house in Jalalabad, Afghanistan. Nevertheless, it became a key part of the government's prosecution, the famous confession tape.

Suddenly, bin Laden video recordings began featuring men with distinctly different facial features. One moment his beard was long and grey, the next much shorter and black. Each of them was of exceptionally poor quality, making it hard to definitely say whether the man in the picture was or was not bin Laden. Stills taken from the videos, when placed side by side with earlier pictures, seemed to show bin Laden's beard growing steadily less grey over time and his facial features, such as his long straight nose, changing markedly. Some looked nothing like him.

Frankly, the deceptions were extremely crude. Outside the US, television stations made their own transcripts, and suggested US television translations were inaccurate and misleading. One German television station (Das Erste) translated the so-called confession video and found that those on the tape were just talking about the attacks, and that no responsibility was sought or claimed.

The messages were misleading by omission too, as the Bush White House asked television networks not to show bin Laden's recorded messages unedited. No one was to hear the words verbatim from bin Laden's mouth.

Through 2002 and 2003, fake Osamas popped up regularly, making scratchy video statements, always adding weight to the prevailing story, to be parroted by the unquestioning US television media.

The timing of bin Laden video tape discoveries and releases seemed to match the Bush administration's political requirements too, most notably the tape that was released on October 29, 2004, just three days before the US election, which threatened more attacks. Bush had built his entire campaign on keeping America safe from further terrorism—the threat of more attacks from the mouth of Osama bin Laden was electoral gold dust.

In one video released just before the invasion of Iraq, bin Laden conveniently declared himself in league with Saddam Hussein.

It's not hard to see that what was happening at this time was a concerted media propaganda campaign, with fake videos and misleading translations being used for political purposes. For the most part, Osama bin Laden's video appearances after 9/11 were part of an orchestrated campaign of fakery by the CIA. It has happened many times elsewhere, and would hardly represent the most unusual or outrageous act of media propaganda that the CIA had ever done.

In May 2010, the *Washington Post* reported that the CIA had in fact prepared a fake tape showing a man looking like Osama bin Laden sitting around a fire and swigging alcohol, while discussing his sexual conquests of young boys. The idea of the tape had been to portray bin Laden as a depraved pedophile but, we were assured, the plan had not proceeded. A similar tape was prepared showing a fake Saddam Hussein in an equally unflattering light, using actors drawn from "some of the CIA's darker-skinned employees."

The actual proof of bin Laden's involvement in the attacks of 9/11 was flimsy. On September 19, 2001, the *Wall Street Journal* published an article called "Frail Trail: It's Surprisingly Tough to Pin Terror Attacks on the 'Prime Suspect,'" and the passing of the years has not revealed additional proof. In June 2006, when asked why the September 11 attacks were not listed as the reason for Osama bin Laden appearing on the FBI's most wanted list, the FBI chief of investigative publicity, Rex Tomb, admitted it was because the FBI has no hard evidence connecting bin Laden to 9/11.

Bin Laden's Escape

As the war in Afghanistan commenced, proving the guilt of Osama bin Laden seemed irrelevant, and within an absurdly brief time even his apprehension seemed to slip down America's list of priorities.

Within months of 9/11, the man responsible for the greatest calamity in modern US history seemed unimportant to the Bush administration. Bush's famous 2002 "Axis of Evil" State of the Union speech failed to mention Osama bin Laden at all, just four months after the attacks. In March 2002 (six months after 9/11) Bush said that he wasn't concerned with bin Laden. What he was deeply concerned about, he added, was Iraq.

From March 2002 onwards, Bush actively avoided mentioning Osama bin Laden by name, even when questioned about him directly. On April 6, 2002 Richard Myers, now the most senior military man in America, went even further, saying that in Afghanistan the goal [had] never been to get bin Laden. General Tommy Franks (who led America's invasion of Afghanistan) said the same.

This was in direct conflict with Bush's public pronouncements immediately after 9/11 and his dead-or-alive rhetoric at the time. The goal of the Afghanistan invasion, far from capturing the mastermind of the 9/11 attacks, now appeared to be unseating and replacing the Taliban regime and installing a more compliant government. Although 9/11 could be invoked to justify every military action or domestic legislation, bin Laden had become the unimportant boogeyman.

The hunt for Osama bin Laden was characterized by amazing blunders, blind spots, and ineptitude, including several instances where he appears to have escaped from seemingly impossible positions. One could easily think that the military was trying to let him get away.

On November 12, 2001, bin Laden and his men staged a nighttime exit from Kabul. Given the size of his entourage, this involved a convoy of hundreds of cars and trucks streaming up the main road from dusk to 3:00 a.m. A local businessman said that he didn't understand why the convoy wasn't attacked. After all, America had by then asserted air dominance over the entire country, and the cars drove along the open road with their lights on.

A few days later, a convoy of several hundred cars, including bin Laden and senior al-Qaeda leaders, again escaped by night from the fallen Jalalabad to Tora Bora, without attracting any military attention. Locals said the main road was jammed from 8:00 p.m. to 3:00 a.m. Finally, on November 16, around 600 al-Qaeda and Taliban fighters escaped Tora Bora and Afghanistan on foot, via the long mountain trek to Pakistan. It is well known that there are two routes out of Tora Bora to Pakistan, but for some reason the US bombed only one, leading even the conservative British newspaper the *Daily Telegraph* to write that "the battle for Tora Bora looks like a 'grand charade.'"

Whatever the circumstances, bin Laden and his al-Qaeda team somehow managed to escape en masse from the most sophisticated army on earth, with barely any of them captured. America had, possibly deliberately, once again passed up a golden chance to capture or destroy the accused protagonists in the atrocities of 9/11. They had escaped to the safe soil of America's greatest ally in the war.

Many have questioned to what extent al-Qaeda really is an implacable enemy of the West. Its operatives seem to travel freely despite being known to authorities. Its leader could on innumerable occasions have been extradited or assassinated, but these actions were not just passed up, they were actively blocked. Western intelligence agencies had demonstrably elaborate connections to many of the highest ranked al-Qaeda leaders, but chose not to capture and try them, instead allowing terrorism to continue in a fashion that often gelled with domestic political ambitions and handed them yet more power. Those in charge of the US, in particular, appear to have judged that the geostrategic ends justified the means, regardless of the inevitable loss of human life.

The Death of Osama bin Laden

When bin Laden was allegedly killed on May 2, 2011 ("Obama takes out Osama"), it was not in some remote cave hideout but within a pleasant walled compound in the Pakistani city of Abbottabad, the spiritual heart of Pakistan's military, and home of its most prestigious military academy.

Pakistan was supposedly not informed of the US military's action until it had been completed. However, when army barracks (less than two miles away) heard the helicopters, explosions, and gunfire, they were told by their commanders to hold back. US troops spent forty minutes on the ground in the city that headquarters the Pakistani military, but did not encounter one Pakistani army member. The Pakistanis cannot have been unaware of what was going on.

As the years have passed, however, more and more of the story of Osama bin Laden's death has been questioned and found to be false. The official story was one without any evidential backing or eyewitnesses, and much of the story initially propagated (such as bin Laden having been armed and using women as shields) was exposed as lies within weeks. The CIA's John Brennan, in particular, fed the media a series of wildly inaccurate details about bin Laden's assassination, which were duly and unquestioningly parroted by a compliant media. This was despite Brennan being an inveterate liar who had lied and been proven to have lied at some of the most high-profile stages of his career, including to the 9/11 Commission.

It's now widely accepted that there is simply no conceivable way that bin Laden could have been living at this location without the knowledge of those at the highest levels of the Pakistani military and government, and that the idea of the US successfully carrying out a surprise raid in Pakistan's military stronghold is fantasy. The fact that the US army was able to get so far into Pakistan without being intercepted is highly questionable. Try to imagine how hard it would be for Pakistani helicopters to carry out a surprise raid on West Point Military Academy without being caught.

The lack of photographic evidence and the swift burial at sea add to legitimate questions. It seems extraordinary that the most high-profile execution in decades just happened to leave no photographs and no body. Many of the sailors on board the USS Carl Vinson wrote home saying they had witnessed nothing. It appears no one on board one of the largest ships on earth, with a crew of over six thousand, saw bin Laden being thrown into the sea.

Many of the SEAL team involved in the bin Laden execution raid were killed just three months later in an unusual helicopter crash.

So much of the official tale has been exposed as lies and changed again and again that it is reasonable to ask if the entire story is simply made up. How are we to believe anything we have subsequently been told, when we know how much effort was put into lying to the public. What lunatic would suddenly expect these people to start telling us the truth?

We now know that the original plan was to not acknowledge the raid, and a cover story was to be used in which Obama was to announce that DNA evidence had confirmed that bin Laden had been killed in a drone attack on the Afghan side of the border, allowing both Pakistani and US authorities a clean way out of a sticky situation.

We will probably never know the true story, but you can be entirely confident that more details will eventually emerge that cast further serious doubt on this murky tale of the world's most wanted man, living cheek-by-jowl with Pakistan's military elite, assassinated and then buried with haste at sea just hours later without a single photo being taken.

Seymour Hersh

Pulitzer Prize winning journalist Seymour Hersh has built a career on well-researched exposes of political skullduggery, often furiously denied by authorities on publication, almost always proved accurate. Hersh's May 2015 article in the *London Review of Books* concerning the death of Osama bin Laden suggested that the official story was, in his words, "one big lie, not a word of it is true."

In fact, Hersh alleged, Osama bin Laden had been under house arrest by the Pakistani army and ISI since 2006, with the knowledge and connivance of Saudi Arabia, who as ever provided the funding. Owning bin Laden gave Pakistan control and leverage, and allowed the American government to continue to invoke the scary bogeyman. In the short to medium term, the arrangement suited everyone.

The situation would have continued indefinitely had it not been for a Pakistani intelligence officer (most probably Brigadier Usman Khalid) literally walking into the US embassy in Islamabad and giving them details of bin Laden's whereabouts, in return for a substantial part of the $25 million bounty on offer. The walk-in met with Jonathan Bank, the CIA station chief in Islamabad, and was given a lie-detector test, which he passed.

The US then made a deal with Pakistan, under which the Americans would conduct the raid to kill bin Laden and both sides would deny any knowledge of the event, so as to mollify domestic Pakistani outrage (in a country where America has a popularity rating of just 8 percent).

There was to be no capture. Bin Laden's evidence of Pakistani complicity in his post-9/11 life was too embarrassing for the Pakistanis. His past collusion with the US and CIA clearly could not be aired in public. And, ultimately, his evidence regarding 9/11 itself would have been earth-shattering. Bin Laden had to die. The mission was strictly kill only.

However, once one of the US helicopters carrying out the raid crashed, the public story that was to have later been announced—that a drone strike somewhere vague had got lucky and killed bin Laden—had to be rapidly changed to a covert kill-or-capture mission against an armed coward living secretly in a compound right at the heart of the Pakistani military, that had taken place without the prior knowledge of the Pakistanis.

Bin Laden was not armed, nor did he use anyone as a human shield. A bullet to the head put him down, and was followed up by a barrage that ripped apart much of his face and torso. Most of bin Laden's corpse, badly destroyed by the SEAL team, was thrown out of a US helicopter over the Hindu Kush, and the burial at sea story was entirely bogus.

Rather than a murky and questionable execution in violation of international law, it would have been preferable to have had a trial, with evidence and a verdict. But such a trial would have been a can of worms. Bin Laden could have perhaps mortally wounded the Saudis, Pakistanis, CIA, and the Bush family. The evidence of his involvement in the events of 9/11 was nonexistent. A trial could never have been allowed to take place.

The idea that Osama bin Laden was a CIA asset simply can't be dismissed out of hand. The story of the rise of the bin Laden family is riddled with direct contact and work with Saudi, Pakistani and US intelligence services. The Binladin Group had enjoyed construction contracts with the CIA across the Middle East. As a favored son of the family, Osama was an important figure in the mujahedeen resistance to the Soviets in Afghanistan (bankrolled by the CIA) and maintained close ties to the Taliban, which received the patronage of Pakistan's ISI, which in turn received funding from the CIA. Bin Laden had almost certainly at some point received funding directly from the CIA. The only question was when (or whether) this had ceased.

Khalid Sheikh Mohammed

Khalid Sheikh Mohammed (KSM) was born in Pakistan, lived in Kuwait as a child, and went to college in North Carolina. He first gained worldwide attention through his involvement in the 1993 World Trade Center bombing that so nearly brought down one of the twin towers. Mohammed's nephew, Ramsi Yousef, who was convicted over the bombing, was sentenced (to 240 years in prison, all in solitary confinement) on September 11, 1996, five years to the day before 9/11.

While living in the Philippines in 1995, Mohammed plotted to destroy twelve US-bound passenger jets in an operation called Bojinka, as well as planning an attempt on the life of the pope, and various other attacks. Despite being a renegade terrorist and international fugitive, his lifestyle was known to be extravagant, and many have suggested he was on the payroll of Pakistan's ISI.

Khalid Sheikh Mohammed was publicly declared the mastermind behind the 9/11 attacks in June 2002, and an international manhunt ensued. In March 2003, Pakistan's ISI claimed to have captured him, but video of the capture was widely derided as a crude fake. Despite his ties within Pakistan, it appears the ISI decided to betray Mohammed, following a pattern of behavior in which an asset is protected while useful, then handed over at the moment that most benefits the ISI. Mohammed was given to the Americans, and began an itinerant journey through America's labyrinth of black sites, before ending up in Guantanamo.

We know surprisingly little about Mohammed's role in supposedly masterminding the attacks. Despite this, his testimony was heavily relied upon to form the official narrative of the 9/11 Commission. Mohammed's evidence was taken at face value, despite him having been subject to a ruthless torture program that included being waterboarded 183 times in March 2003. That's six times a day, for a month. It goes without saying that evidence collected this way is entirely compromised and without value. Maybe that was the idea. Mohammed confessed to a bewilderingly long list of plots—at least 31. His testimony may have been that of a man being forced to say what his captors wanted to hear.

Early in his first term, President Obama determined that Mohammed should be tried in a civilian court in New York. A year later, that decision was reversed. The statement made by the President's spokesman, Robert Gibbs, made it clear how free and fair that trial would have been, when he said that Mohammed was "going to meet justice, and going to meet his maker." Now Mohammed faces trial under Guantanamo's military commissions. But the years roll by, and the can is kicked further down the road. After a decade and a half, it is right to question when, if ever, we are going to see this man in a courtroom, giving his own side of the story, and when we are going to see a single piece of evidence tying this man to 9/11.

Many suggest that the huge delays in getting Khalid Sheikh Mohammed to a courtroom in fact indicate that a trial can never be allowed to take place. There's no doubt that Mohammed is a bad person who plotted to do harm to people, but the unprecedented delay in getting the man tried for his crimes only adds to the suspicion that whatever Mohammed has to say is too compromising, contradictory, or embarrassing for those trying him to ever be publicly aired.

Large showpiece terrorism trials are rarely anything other than a media event to placate a distracted public. Not only are there details that the prosecution side wishes to hide, and a media frenzy that demands conviction over and above justice, hard questions can lead to answers no one in power wants to hear. When Khalid Sheikh Mohammed finally comes to trial, expect nothing but a sham.

The Hijackers

On September 14, 2001, the FBI published its list of the nineteen individuals they said had carried out the terrorist attacks. The media, in a fashion, did press administration officials for proof linking al-Qaeda and Osama bin Laden to 9/11. Initially, Colin Powell said that a white paper describing the evidence would be issued. His promise was later retracted, due (he said) to almost all the relevant information being classified. This was the first of countless incidences when Bush (and Obama) officials essentially said, we have this information, it's way too classified to show you, but trust us, it's scary and we need to act and for you to support us. Bush himself said that any white paper would make the war (on terror) more difficult to win.

So what are we to make of the fifteen Saudis and four other Arab men who were apparently able to enter the US and execute the most devastating terrorist attack in history, without any other individual assisting them (in America), leaving no trace—not even a single piece of paper?

The US government and its 9/11 Commission went to great lengths to ensure that the official story involved the smallest imaginable group of plotters, with no apparent support structure whatsoever inside the United States, and no footprints left behind. For whatever reason, it was vitally important that a strong line be held behind the story that the attacks had come out of the blue, with no warning, in a way that could not possibly have been detected, and were carried out by people who left no trail.

While this could be seen as just cynical political management of the story, to hide embarrassing intelligence failures, it is clearly an absurd falsity. International terrorist attacks require supplies, financing, safe-houses, leadership and infrastructure; and 9/11 was the largest attack of its kind ever mounted. Most serious independent researchers have stated that the attacks required a large support network (a minimum of fifty people) inside the US. However, not one accomplice was arrested or charged in the United States following the attacks.

The insistence, in the face of logic, that not one other person even slightly involved could be found or arrested in America after 9/11 hints at a cover-up.

The fifteen hijackers from Saudi Arabia were mostly from wealthy families. Some were well-educated, skilled, middle-class professionals. But others seem to have been hopelessly out of their depth, struggling so badly with English that they found it hard to carry out even the most basic functions associated with living in America. Collectively, their bumbling and un-Islamic behavior was at times almost comically inept, and for people plotting the world's worst terrorist crime, they seemed to hide in plain view. It was all very strange.

Before America

Much of the initial planning for 9/11 was done in 1999 in Hamburg, Germany, where Mohamed Atta and others lived for some time. Atta studied architecture, and was seen with a small model of the Pentagon building at one point. He and his associates were suspicious, and it is widely accepted that they were under CIA and German intelligence surveillance.

Other key decisions took place at an al-Qaeda strategy meeting on the 5–8th of January 2000 in Kuala Lumpur, Malaysia, shortly after which some of the attackers moved to the US. The CIA and other international spy agencies closely monitored this meeting, but did not pass their information on to the FBI.

Mohamed Atta

We are all familiar with the cold, frightening expression on the face of Mohamed Atta (a photo taken from his driver's license). It's an image that has been effective in painting him as a ruthless killer. Less familiar are the numerous other photos of Atta showing him smiling warmly, and looking an entirely different character. For some reason, the scary-eyes picture is the only one most of us have ever seen.

Mohamed Atta had been on the State Department's terrorist watch-list since 1986, but was able to enter and leave the US at will, without questioning. Atta was a man on the move. By all accounts he lived in at least eight locations around the world in the two years before 9/11.

It's amazing how safe the hijackers felt, travelling into and out of America without any problems, and staying in the US for long periods, despite many being on a security watch list. They lived openly in communities, and used their real names on things like credit cards and bank accounts.

To take just one example, Ziad Jarrah, who had been on the terrorist watch list for some time, was at one point interviewed at Dubai Airport on instructions from US agents, and had been monitored by the CIA for nearly a year prior to 9/11, yet he was granted a multiple entry visa to the US and appears to have come and go as he pleased. Although it is sometimes understandable to allow known "bad guys" to move around (in the hope they will uncover further information), to let a known terrorist into the US at a time when the system was picking up huge amounts of chatter about an impending attack smacks of recklessness or complicity.

Ignoring the fact that a number of foreign governments had given the US the names and details of the future hijackers (flagging them as potential terrorists), these men seemed to be above even the basic laws of visa acceptance. Inexplicably, visa applications and renewals by future hijackers, who were being watched by federal agencies, were allowed, despite existing laws which should have denied them entry.

In January 2001, Mohamed Atta was allowed back into the US on a tourism visa, despite being on a terrorism watch-list and telling immigration officials he was taking flying lessons inside the US. Why would Atta have been so honest, when people trying to enter the US without an M-1 student visa were routinely turned back if they admitted anything other than mere tourism as their purpose?

Atta entered the US three times in 2001 alone, despite the fact that his visa had expired in 2000 and his violation of that visa by taking flying lessons. Think back on the last time you entered the US from abroad. Did the immigration people at the airport strike you as the kind of folks who are relaxed about visas? Atta had been under FBI surveillance for some time, including for stockpiling materials for bomb-making, yet he came and went as he pleased.

While in the US, Atta was the opposite of inconspicuous. He was twice arrested for impaired driving and made no attempt to hide his identity. He used his real name constantly, including at the flight schools he attended. Through his flight school contacts, Atta was also in regular email contact with around forty current and former employees of major defense contractors.

In fact, for a man secretly plotting the most devastating terrorist attacks of all time, Atta seemed to go out of his way to be noticed, and to have his presence in certain locations noted. It's impossible not to draw a parallel between Mohamed Atta and Lee Harvey Oswald, who in 1963 took clear steps to get himself noticed at certain times and places. Many suspect that, for one reason or another, there were several men identifying themselves as Lee Oswald, trying to get noticed in the summer of '63.

Atta and his conspirators were so fabulously indiscreet that they were spotted again and again, often behaving in ways that defied their alleged religious extremism, or exposed their plans to anyone who cared to look. There were occasions when Atta, the mastermind ring-leader who somehow took the whole of America by surprise, acted with such abandon that it's very hard not to conclude that he was trying to be seen.

On Boxing Day in 2000, Mohamed Atta and Marwan al-Shehhi stalled a Piper Warrior (a small single-engine plane) that they were learning to fly on the runway at Miami International Airport. Finding themselves unable to re-start the plane, the two got out and walked away, leaving the plane on the run-way and delaying several large commercial passenger airliners behind them waiting to take off. Rudi Dekkers, president of Huffman Aviation (their flight school) said "students do stupid things during their flight course, but this is quite stupid."

Atta met with Johnelle Bryant from the Homestead, Florida offices of the US Department of Agriculture in early 2000 and made a bizarre series of re-quests. During the meeting, Atta:

- Initially refused to speak to a woman.
- Asked for a loan of $650K to buy and modify a crop-dusting plane.
- Said he wanted to build a chemical tank that would take up every spare inch of the plane except for where the pilot was sitting.
- Used his real name, and made sure Bryant spelled it correctly.
- Said he had just arrived from Afghanistan.
- Mentioned he had made trips to Spain and Germany.
- Said he wanted to visit New York.
- Asked about security at the World Trade Center and other landmarks.
- Discussed al-Qaeda and recruiting US members.
- Said Osama bin Laden would one day be known as the world's greatest leader.
- Asked to buy the aerial photo of Washington hanging on Bryant's office wall, and proffered increasingly large sums of cash when she refused.
- When Bryant pointed out a building in Washington where she used to work, said, "How would you like it if somebody flew an airplane into your friend's building?"

Bryant remembered Atta most for his heavily dilated pupils. She thought he must be on drugs. Atta said he had expected to receive cash on the spot, and when the loan was refused, added that he could just get up and break open the department's safe, saying, "What would prevent me from cutting your throat?"

Atta later attempted to get a loan from the same woman, slightly disguised by wearing glasses. Again, remember FBI Director Robert Mueller's testimony: that they gave no hint to those around them what they were about. Yet at this meeting with a representative of a US Federal agency, the only thing Atta could have done more to draw suspicion on himself would have been to say, "I am about to lead a terrorist attack on America."

Why on earth would Atta have risked the entire plot through this ridiculous indiscretion? Either these accused men were diabolical geniuses who left no trace, which is belied by how conspicuous they kept making themselves, or they were blundering idiots who got incredibly lucky again and again. This also strains belief, given the success of the attacks.

Atta on 9/11

On the morning of 9/11, Mohamed Atta flew from Portland to Boston, having driven from Boston to Portland the day before. The risk of compromising the entire mission by taking a connecting flight on the morning of the attacks has never been explained. Luckily for Atta, the Portland flight was on time. Atta's name apparently triggered an alert on Boston airport's security system, but although his bags were not transferred onto the onward flight, he was allowed to board. Because the Portland flight was on time, there was plenty of time to transfer the baggage. No other bags among the 81 passengers on board the Boston to LA flight failed to be loaded onto the plane.

Atta's luggage was quickly discovered and searched after the attacks. The bags were said to contain flight simulation manuals and videos for Boeing planes, a Koran, airline uniforms, a religious cassette tape, a note to the other hijackers on how to mentally prepare for the attacks, and Atta's will and passport. It's hard to imagine a more incriminating set of possessions.

Why would Atta, a suicide pilot, have taken these items (his will in particular) onto a plane he intended to crash into a building? And why risk carrying these highly incriminating documents? Had his bags been searched before the plane took off, the contents would have led to his immediate arrest, risking the entire mission for seemingly no benefit at all. An October 2001 *New Yorker* article by Seymour Hersh said that investigators were speculating that these items were meant to be found for the FBI to chase.

Other hijackers' rented cars were found to contain airline manuals and materials, restricted airport access passes, and lists of the names of the other hijackers. It remains unclear why several of the hijackers took letters and other incriminating items onto planes that they knew would be destroyed.

On September 16, 2001, the text of a five-page handwritten letter, allegedly penned by Mohamed Atta and found in his luggage, was released. It was widely derided as having being written by someone unfamiliar with Islam. Another incriminating letter was found in the wreckage at Shanksville, as was Ziad Jarrah's passport. Attorney General Robert Ashcroft announced on September 12 that Satam al-Suqami's passport had been found in the rubble of the Twin Towers, and IDs for several others were supposedly found at the Pentagon.

This all proved invaluable in tying together the various Middle Eastern men accused of being behind the plot. The story of 9/11 was established, set in stone, and confirmed by the evidence left behind, no matter how illogical or improbable it sometimes seemed.

Many, including this writer, have concluded that the Portland/Boston story concerning the twenty-four hours Mohamed Atta spent before the attacks was entirely made up. The identifying documents that somehow survived horrific plane crash infernos, and in baggage that failed to be loaded onto the doomed flight 11, were extraordinarily incriminating and helped corroborate several aspects of the day's events, for which there was little other evidence. This was convenient to those building the official story.

Omar al-Bayoumi

Khalid al-Mihdhar and Nawaf al-Hazmi, both of whom were experienced jihadi and under CIA surveillance, were able to fly openly from Bangkok to LA and enter the US in January 2000 without comment. Despite their background, neither had visited the West before, and both spoke barely any English whatsoever. Learning to fly a jet aircraft in the United States without support would have seemed impossibly difficult.

At this point the CIA and NSA had enough information on the two to clearly link them to Osama bin Laden, the East Africa Embassy bombings, and the USS Cole attack. Yet they had no problem entering the US.

The two men quickly moved into the San Diego house of a long-time FBI informant, Abdussattar Shaikh, who also had contact with hijacker Hani Hanjour. They lived with Shaikh for seven months.

Shaikh himself had a very questionable background. He was initially said by the FBI to have been a language teacher, then a retired professor at San Diego State University, but none of the schools at which he was supposed to have taught could find a record of him. We will never know what Shaikh learned while living with the hijackers as he was barred from testifying to the 9/11 Joint Congressional Inquiry on the ludicrous grounds that he would have had nothing interesting to say. The FBI gave him $100,000, the contract was closed, and he appears to have disappeared.

How did al-Mihdhar and al-Hazmi come to be living in San Diego with an FBI informant? Well, that's a strange story.

On January 15, 2000, a Saudi named Omar al-Bayoumi travelled from San Diego to LA, where he stopped at the Saudi consulate for an hour-long meeting with Fahad al-Thumairy, an official from the Ministry of Islamic Affairs, before heading to a Middle Eastern restaurant at Los Angeles airport where, he said, he happened to hear Arabic being spoken, and in a kindly gesture invited the two newly arrived young strangers to join him. At his suggestion, the two men decided to move to San Diego where, his hospitality and friendliness unquenched, al-Bayoumi found the two men accommodation in a flat next to his own, co-signed the lease and paid the deposit and first month's rent. He then kept in touch on a daily basis. The next month, al-Bayoumi introduced the pair to Hani Hanjour, future hijacker and pilot of flight 77.

Omar al-Bayoumi was an ex-employee of the Saudi Ministry of Defense and Aviation, headed by Prince Sultan, a man with known al-Qaeda connections who was to die later in a mysterious single-car accident.

In the US, al-Bayoumi worked for a Saudi company called Ercan, which was closely tied to the aforementioned ministry, but he never appears to have turned up for work, and although Ercan attempted to fire him, Saudi Civil Aviation warned (in a letter marked as extremely urgent) that such a move would terminate Ercan's contract with them. Al-Bayoumi continued to be paid for a job he almost never attended, at the Saudi government agency's insistence. Most Saudi ex-pats who knew al-Bayoumi in Los Angeles thought he must be a government spy.

Al-Bayoumi also received a monthly stipend from various Saudi government sources, channeled through third parties to avoid a direct link being drawn. Shortly after the two future hijackers arrived in the US, al-Bayoumi's monthly expense allowance (paid by Ercan) increased from $465 to $3,925. It remained at this level until August 2001, a month before the attacks, when al-Bayoumi left the US. Al-Bayoumi called Saudi government establishments in the US one hundred times between January and May of 2000.

Around this time, $500K of Saudi money was provided for a Kurdish mosque in San Diego, with the proviso that Omar al-Bayoumi was to be paid as the building's maintenance manager. Tax exempt and with charitable status, mosques, and other such buildings are a common way of laundering money. Again, al-Bayoumi almost never showed. The mosque attendees even began proceedings to have him removed from the job.

As al-Bayoumi continued to pay the rent for the two hijackers, money was provided from several sources. Even the Saudi ambassador to the US (the famous Bandar Bush) seems to have been involved, his wife sending regular cashier's checks to a friend of the wife of al-Bayoumi, who signed the checks across to her.

If the Ambassador's wife is writing checks that end up in the hands of a man who is obviously coordinating the actions of international terrorists, that alone should be enough for the US to immediately cease all diplomatic relations with the country. Had the protagonists of this story been Iraqi, this information would have been used to justify war—the US would have needed no further invitation and invaded. However, this was Saudi Arabia. Bandar was so thick with the Bush family that he was nicknamed in their honor. All connections would be ignored.

In August 2001, al-Bayoumi moved to London, and although he was arrested by British agents after 9/11, the FBI released him after a week without charge, accepting his story that he had met the two hijackers by chance, and ignoring the extensive funding he had received from Saudi Arabia (and despite an earlier FBI investigation in 1998 concluding that al-Bayoumi was a Saudi spy).

Prior to 9/11, FBI informant Abdussattar Shaikh reported that he was sure that his two Saudi flatmates benefactor was a Saudi agent. But no action was taken, and his warnings were also ignored.

This is not complicated. The story of Omar al-Bayoumi is one of the clearest possible indications of Saudi involvement in the 9/11 plot. Al-Bayoumi was a Saudi spy, a forward man sent by consulate official Fahad al-Thumairy. He served as a conduit for money from Saudi Civil Aviation to the two future hijackers. But the story was not pursued, and al-Bayoumi was allowed to escape back to Saudi Arabia.

There was clearly a support network for other Saudi hijackers in the US prior to the 9/11 attacks. Several suspects were identified and interviewed after 9/11, but by then most of them were in the safe harbor of Saudi soil. None provided information that was of assistance.

Known terrorists entering the US with ease, being met at the airport by a Saudi spy who sets them up, pays their rent, and introduces them to another hijacker. All the while living with an FBI informant who gets paid off and disappears without testifying in public? And we're told that these people left no trace or clues, and were able to entirely outwit US intelligence. Welcome to the murky world of the alleged hijackers' lives in America before 9/11.

Life in the US

Some Saudis knew what was coming and fled the country (or were ordered to leave) immediately before the attacks, most notoriously the family of Esam Ghazzawi, an adviser to the Saudi king's nephew. Ghazzawi's family abandoned their Sarasota home (in the same town that President Bush was staying on the morning of 9/11) two weeks before the attacks, in such a hurry that they left furniture, a new car in the driveway, an open safe in the bedroom and even a fridge full of fresh food. When suspicious neighbors reported their disappearance, the FBI investigated, but produced no results. The Ghazzawi family home had been used for regular correspondence with (and visits from) Mohamed Atta over the previous year, but none of the information uncovered by the FBI's investigation was passed to the 9/11 Commission, and the disappearing Saudis were not mentioned in the Commission report.

Prior to 9/11, there was a clear pattern of the CIA withholding information from other agencies, the government, the police and even their own departments. Time and again a clear and present danger, in the form of known terrorists acting in highly suspicious manners, was either ignored, buried or secreted. The FBI claim to have finally begun a search for two of the terrorists in August 2001, but despite conducting an investigation which a subsequent internal review characterized by saying that "everything was done that could have been done"; the targets were not found. This is despite the fact that most of the hijackers had used their real names on their bank accounts, driver's licenses, and credit cards. Nawaf al-Hazmi was even in the San Diego phone book.

In April 2001, Hani Hanjour and Nawaf al-Hazmi moved from Phoenix (where they had been for four months) to Falls Church, Virginia. The imam from the mosque they had previously attended in San Diego also moved to Falls Church at this time. His name was Anwar al-Awlaki.

The sleepy city of Falls Church, population twelve thousand, was also by chance the chosen residence of two of Osama bin Laden's brothers, who lived on the same street, in the same town, at the same time as the two hijackers, just four miles away. Although Abdullah bin Laden had been investigated for links to another suspected terrorist group operating within the US, that investigation was closed and the bin Laden family members were left untouched.

Many of the hijackers also chose to live extraordinarily close to the centers of US intelligence agencies. In 1999, Waleed al-Shehri lived in Vienna, Virginia, just three blocks from CIA headquarters. More curious still, at least six of the hijackers (including all those on board flight 77) lived in Laurel, Maryland from August 2001 until a few days before 9/11. Laurel happens to be the home of the NSA. Why would people training for a devastating attack on America choose to live cheek-by-jowl with the intelligence communities they were aiming to surprise?

On the night of September 10, 2001, Hani Hanjour and a two other hijackers stayed at the Marriott Residence Inn in Virginia, near Dulles airport. The attacks were just hours away. The hotel happened that night to also be hosting Saleh Ibn Abdul Rahman Hussayen, a prominent Saudi government official, who moved hotels in order to stay at the Marriott.

Shortly after the attacks, Hussayen was questioned by the FBI, but the interview was cut short when Hussayen feigned a seizure. When taken to a hospital, doctors found nothing wrong with him. FBI agents strongly recommended Hussayen be detained, but instead he was allowed to leave immediately on Bush's famous exodus planes. On arrival back in Saudi Arabia, Hussayen was named a minister in the government.

Training

A peculiar incident took place on November 19, 1999, on an America West flight from Phoenix to Columbus. While airborne, two Saudi students, Mohammed al-Qudhaieen and Hamdan al-Shalawi, asked flight attendants several questions about airport security that made them suspicious. Both then asked about the location of the plane's restroom, but when directed to the back of the plane instead made two attempts to enter the cockpit. The plane made an emergency landing and the two were questioned by the FBI, but later released without charge. Both claimed that the Saudi Embassy had paid for their tickets.

After 9/11, the Phoenix office of the FBI concluded that the incident had been a dry run, a test of airline security for future actions. Saudis were clearly training for 9/11 nearly two years before the attacks.

At least seven of the hijackers took flight training at secure US military installations, including the Naval Air Station in Pensacola, Brooks Air Force Base in San Antonio, Maxwell Air Force Base in Alabama, and the Defense Language Institute in Monterey, California. Three of the hijackers had the naval station at Pensacola listed as their permanent address on their driver's licenses.

In order to gain regular access to military facilities, security clearances are required. These include background checks. Many of the future hijackers had already been identified by multiple international and US agencies as (at the very least) persons of interest. Mohamed Atta had been on a terrorist watch-list since 1986. Yet none of the trainee pilots appear to have encountered problems accessing these secure facilities.

Three of the planes involved in the attacks on 9/11 were allegedly piloted by terrorists who had trained at two flight schools in Venice, Florida, run by Rudi Dekkers and Arne Kruithof. Dekkers' flight school, Huffman Aviation, was notorious for involvement with the CIA, a front company called Brittania Aviation, and the importation of cocaine, facilitated by the CIA whose station was just down the road (as was US Central Command). The place was rotten to the core. Huffman's owner Wally Hilliard had his Learjet seized in July 2001 when it was found to contain forty-three pounds of heroin. Dekkers was a colorful character who was arrested for fraud in 2003 and again for in 2012 for drug trafficking.

So the CIA should have had an intimate knowledge of the hijacker's comings and goings. The absence of what should have been routine impediments to their preparations continued.

On 9/11, FBI officials certainly moved fast when it came to retrieving the hijackers flight training files at Venice. They arrived at 2:00 a.m., just fifteen hours after the attacks ended, to confiscate the student's files.

Many of the hijackers were reported to be very poor pilots. Hani Hanjour was reported to the FAA five times, not for possible terrorism links, but because staff at his flight school said he lacked both the English and flight skills for a commercial pilot's license. One employee said "he could not fly at all."

Hanjour was monitored by American Muslim Aukai Collins while taking his flying lessons. Collins reported to the FBI, and said that the bureau had been fully aware of everything about Hanjour. But Collins also reported that Hanjour was not even moderately religious.

With apparently no support structure in the US at all, these dunderheaded misfits all managed to access secure military facilities despite being known to authorities, lived right next-door to America's key intelligence headquarters, attended a murky CIA drug-running flight school and were reportedly terrible pilots. It hardly seems the record of cunning geniuses, and looks much more like people who were being used and monitored very closely.

Shortly after 9/11, it became accepted that for all the carnage caused, the attack itself was basically simple. This was very far from the case. More and more, when you look at the skills required to carry the attacks out, it looks less like a bunch of bumbling terrorists getting lucky, and more like a superbly executed military operation. It is a significant leap of faith to imagine that these men could have carried out the most devastating terrorist attacks in history. The nineteen Arabs who were blamed don't look remotely capable of having done it.

Financial Backing

In the late stages of Bill Clinton's presidency, thirty industrialized nations made preparations to tighten the screws on offshore financial centers, in part to slow the flow of drug and terrorism funding. America was set to join these efforts, but once George W. Bush was elected, under pressure from the banking lobby (who make fortunes from these illicit and illegal operations), all US cooperation ended, and the US National Terrorist Asset Tracking Center (also created under Clinton) was denied any further budget. Drug and terrorism money could again flow freely with Bush in the White House. His attention was elsewhere.

In the days immediately after 9/11, the question of whether there had been foreign government backing and financing of al-Qaeda was something openly discussed in the media and by some government officials. No less than Donald Rumsfeld, in the week after 9/11, said, "I know a lot, and what I have said, as clearly as I know how, is that states are supporting these people." He may have meant Iraq. But like so many other matters, this line of thinking, and of questioning, quietly disappeared with the passage of time.

When the 9/11 Commission considered state backing of the attacks, the initial focus was on three countries: Iraq, Iran, and Saudi Arabia. For some, the last of these was a surprise, given the Saudi regime is considered a close friend of America, but it had to be included, given that fifteen of the nineteen hijackers had been Saudis.

Strikingly, given subsequent events, the Commission clearly indicated that there was no evidence linking Iraq with the attacks whatsoever. While there was evidence that hijackers had passed through Iranian airports freely, there was very little subsequent focus on Iran's involvement, which appeared negligible or non-existent. Over the years, occasional attempts were made by the Bush administration to link Iran to 9/11, always timed to coincide with the ratcheting up of calls for military action against that country, but nothing approaching proof was supplied.

The Saudi connections were different. With most of the hijackers being Saudis, there was a vast amount of evidence to consider relating to their behavior, their financial affairs, and what the Saudi government and intelligence had known prior to the attacks.

As we know, Omar al-Bayoumi was a conduit of funds from the Saudi government to the hijackers. Pakistan's ISI had sent money directly to Mohamed Atta. But all mention of funding by the ISI was removed entirely by the 9/11 Commission, and the famous twenty-eight pages relating to Saudi funding were cut from the Joint Congressional report, and hidden from public view for fourteen years. The extraordinary lengths the US government has gone to in order to cover up clear evidence relating to the funding of the 9/11 terrorists by Pakistan and Saudi Arabia reveals how important it must be to conceal such explosive information.

Who funded the 9/11 operation is ultimately the most important clue as to how the attacks happened yet, fantastically, the 9/11 Commission concluded that "the question of who financed the operation is ultimately of little practical significance". Little practical significance! This is such an extraordinary statement that it's hard to believe anyone on earth could have delivered it. Yet there we have it. Those charged with the ultimate report into the attacks of 9/11 had no interest in finding out who had provided the funding.

Un-Islamic Behavior

Mohamed Atta and Marwan al-Shehhi lived in the Philippines from 1998 to 2000, learning to fly planes at a local flight school. Locals reported them regularly partying, drinking and sleeping with local women.

Given that these were supposedly fundamentalist Muslims, prepared to sacrifice their lives to defend their faith, much of the behavior by Atta and his team in the years and months before 9/11 seemed un-Islamic, to say the very least. Mohamed Atta made at least six trips to Las Vegas in the months before 9/11, as did many of the other hijackers, drinking, gambling and visiting strip clubs.

While living in Venice, Florida, Mohamed Atta lived with a twenty-two-year-old escort and former stripper called Amanda Keller. She described Atta as a sexually profligate drunk. On one occasion Atta took Keller, whose hair was dyed bright pink, on a three-day orgy of drink, drugs, and sex. He appeared to have (and consume) an endless supply of cocaine, which he said got from the flight schools he was going to. Keller said Atta was a fan of the Beastie Boys, and his favorite meat was pork chops. Atta and his friends, she said, were always drunk and stoned out of their "freaking minds."

Down in Florida, neighbors thought Waleed al-Shehri and Ahmed al-Ghamdi's house was a drug den, such was the profusion of BMWs and

Mercedes coming and going. The parties were so loud and drunken that the police were called on at least two occasions.

Four days before 9/11, Mohamed Atta and two other men stumbled into Shuckum's Oyster Bar in Hollywood, Florida. Atta was clearly wasted, ordered five screwballs, slurred his words, and argued about the bill. Other hijackers were regulars at strip clubs, and known to have taken cocaine.

It's hard to reconcile this behavior. On one hand, it's perhaps tenable to think that those facing certain death would have one last blowout, a sample of life's baser pleasures. But even if you discount the inconsistency of the claim that these men were devout members of the ultra-pious and puritan Salafist al-Qaeda, willing to give their lives for their faith, yet behaved like characters from *The Hangover*, these incidents were spread across many of the hijackers and a long period of time. Their behavior also makes further mockery of FBI Director Robert Mueller's testimony that the hijackers did all they could to stay below the radar.

These were clearly not Islamic fundamentalists. If they were trying to stay out of sight, they were very bad at it.

The Curious Case of the Twentieth Hijacker

In early 2001, a French national called Zacarias Moussaoui started taking flying lessons at Airman Flight School in Norman, Oklahoma, but despite fifty-seven hours of training, dropped out without gaining any qualifications.

In mid-August 2001, Moussaoui relocated and began training at Pan-Am International Flight Academy in Eagan, Minnesota. He was such a suspicious character that within a day of his arrival, most of the staff there suspected he might be a terrorist. Days later they called the FBI.

In keeping with the other hijackers' idiotic actions that seemed almost designed to betray their secret plans, Moussaoui's brief tenure at the flight school was characterized by an almost comical litany of attention-seeking actions:

- He had no aviation background, virtually no flight training and no pilot's license.
- Unlike all the other students, he told staff he didn't want to become a pilot.
- Despite this, he said he wanted to learn a lot about communicating with the flight tower, and the operation of the plane's doors.
- He paid most of his fees using a large wad of cash.
- He seemed determined to learn the requisite basic skills in the shortest possible time.

Rather than learn to fly a small plane first, Moussaoui said he wanted to learn how to pilot a 747, but showed no interest in taking off or landing.

By themselves, these are at the very least the actions of an eccentric or a fool, but the arrival of a French government dossier showing Moussaoui to be a known terrorist suspect should have had bells ringing in all directions. Despite this, the FBI showed little or no interest at all. A staff member at the flight school told agents, "Do you realize how serious this is? This man wants training on a 747. A 747 fully loaded with fuel could be used as a weapon."

Still nothing.

Colleen Rowley

The French government had been tracking Moussaoui for six years, and the substantial dossier they handed the US showed he had clear links to al-Qaeda. This information was passed to FBI agent Colleen Rowley, whose every effort to pursue the case was blocked and stopped. Rowley subsequently became so frustrated that she became a whistle-blower, ending her twenty-four-year career at the FBI.

Rowley and other FBI agents were deeply concerned about the suspicious actions of Moussaoui, and applied for a warrant to search his computer and belongings. The warrant applied for was to be under the Foreign Intelligence Surveillance Act (FISA).

The FISA court is one of the most hidden US government legal entities. It meets in secret. All of its rulings are automatically designated top secret, without exception. Because of this secrecy, the court is widely regarded within government as a rubber stamp.

As would be expected of any institution entirely lacking in oversight, the FISA court almost never rejects applications. The granting of warrants had, until Moussaoui's arrest, been so standard that since 1978, out of twelve thousand requests over more than twenty years, only one had been turned down. But senior FBI staff refused the request from their own agents to apply for a FISA warrant, on the basis that the warnings from France, which explicitly said Moussaoui was probably a terrorist and clearly a threat, were too sketchy.

Minneapolis agents were 'in a frenzy' to find out more about Moussaoui. When FBI headquarters staff scolded the Minnesota supervisor for getting everyone spun up, the supervisor responded that he was trying to get headquarters "spun up" because he was trying to make sure Moussaoui didn't "take control of a plane and fly it into the World Trade Center". But request after request was denied. Local agents joked that someone at head office was a spy or a mole for Osama bin Laden. Such was the incredulity at FBI headquarters setting this up for failure.

Harry Samit, an FBI colleague of Colleen Rowley at Minneapolis, arrested Zacarias Moussaoui in August 2001 for a visa violation. But despite all the evidence and warnings from international sources and their own agents, FBI headquarters insisted Moussaoui could not be connected to known terrorist groups. Beside himself with concern, agent Samit wrote an email to his superiors on September 10, 2001, saying "I am so desperate to get into his computer, I'll take anything."

Based solely on interviews with flight school training staff, Minneapolis agents quickly surmised that Moussaoui was probably a suicide airline attacker, who could be involved in a larger plot. Still nothing happened. The earliest the FBI would give the Department of Defense a meeting at which to present their information was September 12.

After 9/11, Moussaoui's computer was finally searched. It contained various incriminating files, including instructions on how to spray pesticide from a plane.

Giving evidence at Moussaoui's 2006 trial, Samit accused FBI leaders of criminal negligence for ignoring his seventy messages warning about Zacarias Moussaoui.

Seventy messages.

Two individuals in particular at FBI headquarters are known to have been responsible for stopping local agents from progressing their investigations, which quite conceivably could have foiled the entire 9/11 plot. Marion "Spike" Bowman altered the Minneapolis bureau's request for a warrant to search Moussaoui's computer, and was found by a Congressional report to have given Minneapolis agents information that was "inexcusably confused and inaccurate," and "patently false." David Frasca, the head of the Radical Fundamentalist Unit at FBI headquarters in Washington, sabotaged both the warnings coming from the FBI's Minneapolis station and the Phoenix Memorandum (that warned of suspicious activity at flight schools in Arizona), blocking normally routine requests for action.

Frasca knew that suspicious Middle Eastern men, linked to al-Qaeda and already known to the intelligence community, were training at flight schools inside the US during a spike in intelligence warnings relating to domestic terrorism. He knew that one man had been arrested after trying to learn how to fly a 747 without taking off or landing. You did not need to be Sherlock Holmes to put these pieces together and see a serious problem. Yet Frasca went out of his way to block further investigation. This looks like a deliberate action. A stand-down.

There is a compelling case to suggest that David Frasca was a classic mole, stopping vital information from reaching decision points. The chain of command from Frasca's office was to Robert Mueller (head of the FBI), to John Ashcroft (the Attorney General) and then to George W. Bush. But as we know, Ashcroft had made it clear that he didn't want to hear anything more about al-Qaeda, and Bush was on holiday.

On May 21, 2002, Colleen Rowley applied for whistleblower protection and released a two-page memo she had written about the handling of the Moussaoui case. The memo starkly betrayed the statements of CIA Director George Mueller in particular, who repeatedly said that there had been no warning signs whatsoever of the upcoming attacks. The warnings had been numerous, detailed and specific, but had been deliberately altered and ignored by those at FBI headquarters.

As elsewhere, all of the protagonists saw the consequence of their actions. Rowley lost her job and career, but Marion Bowman was promoted by no less than the Director of the FBI, given an award for exceptional performance and a cash bonus of 25 percent of his salary.

Moussaoui wasn't the only lead where the FBI chose to look the other way. In April 2000, Niaz Khan, a British citizen of Pakistani origin, was recruited by al-Qaeda, trained in how to hijack and fly large commercial planes, and flown to the US. However, Khan became afraid, and gambled away the money given to him. Scared he would be killed, Khan handed himself in to the FBI, who were incredulous at his story. They interviewed him using a polygraph test, which he passed. Agents wanted to aggressively continue his interrogation, but then word came from FBI headquarters to return him to London and forget about it. Even Khan was surprised when British officials, on his return to the UK, interviewed him for only two hours and let him go. After 9/11, his case was effectively ignored.

Moussaoui's Trial

Zacarias Moussaoui is the only person to be prosecuted in the United States in relation to the 9/11 attacks. Despite evidence from the FBI in Minneapolis concerning Moussaoui's suspicious activity, it was widely accepted that the case linking Moussaoui to the 9/11 attacks themselves was weak and circumstantial. Investigators found little to no evidence of ties between Moussaoui and the other hijackers. But as the trial continued, a business card allegedly found in the wreckage of flight 93 was produced, which supposedly bore a telephone number used by Ziad Jarrah which Moussaoui had allegedly called once. It's hard to imagine a more flimsy piece of evidence.

Moussaoui indicated that he wanted to testify about the 9/11 attacks in public, before both a grand jury and Congress, claiming he had information that the US government allowed the attacks. The request was refused.

At no point was Moussaoui offered a plea bargain. Although no one was going to give the accused in such a serious case any slack, plea bargaining is almost always used in conspiratorial cases, so as to get the accused to reveal information on his co-conspirators, which a flat sentence would not elicit. One prosecutor said he had never seen a case like it where no plea-bargaining had taken place. This approach was a clear indication that the US government wanted to ensure no awkward information came out. It seemed the primary concern was not for the truth, but as much as possible to keep Moussaoui from speaking in public.

Initially Moussaoui was belligerent, shouting and questioning the legitimacy of the court. But his later appearances were very different in character. During his testimony, Moussaoui was described by the *New York Times* as calm and largely coherent. He testified that some of the people he had met as an al-Qaeda representative included Prince Salman (who in January 2015 became the King of Saudi Arabia), Prince Turki (the intelligence chief), and Bandar Bush, the veteran Saudi ambassador to the USA. This was inconvenient, so say the least.

No chances were taken from then on. During an interview with reporter Pete Williams, MSNBC host Dan Abrams was incredulous at the following exchange:

> **WILLIAMS:** *The old outbursts were gone . . . he was very docile today . . . we believe that he's wearing one of those stun belts, and it may be that he was very worried about doing anything that would cause those Marshals to press the button . . .*
> **ABRAMS:** *A stun belt? They literally have something around his waist? That they can push a button and?*
> **WILLIAMS:** *(Pause) Well . . .*

Moussoui was sentenced to six consecutive life terms. As he was led away, he shouted, "America, you lost and I won!" The wound may have been self-inflicted.

PART THREE
THE COVER UP

CHAPTER ELEVEN

PRIOR KNOWLEDGE

It is not necessary to search for hidden conspiracies, because the conspiracy is right in front of us and all around us; the conspirators are running the country.

—James Ridgeway

No Warnings, Complete Surprise

The three years prior to 9/11 saw a significant increase in activity from Osama bin Laden's group al-Qaeda. The East African embassy bombings in 1998 and the attack on the USS Cole in 2000 demonstrated that al-Qaeda presented a clear and present danger to US assets abroad. Emboldened, bin Laden increasingly called for attacks on the US mainland.

The USS Cole attack was actually preceded by an identical attempt earlier that year in Yemen, targeting USS The Sullivans. In that instance the boat filled with explosives sank under its own weight before reaching its target, and the entire attack remained undiscovered for nearly a year.

Many believe that as US intelligence agencies were monitoring Osama bin Laden's mobile phone conversations through the ECHELON surveillance program prior to the 1998 embassy bombings, they would also have heard detailed plans for 9/11. They were certainly able to intercept phone calls quickly enough after the attacks. Senator Orrin Hatch claimed on 9/11 that the government had already intercepted celebratory calls from bin Laden's assistants in Afghanistan. It's worth noting that much of the evidence provided of Osama bin Laden's guilt also focused on alleged intercepts made by the US and British governments of bin Laden's conversations prior to 9/11. It seems they could monitor bin Laden's phone calls, yet were unable to surmise that he was planning an attack.

The idea that the attacks were mounted by a very small group of people who took America by surprise and left no trace helps to avoid any blame being shouldered by those who abjectly failed to defend America. It also props up the official story against the accusation that the US government was so well-informed of what was coming that they must have actively chosen to do nothing. As such, the "no warnings, complete surprise" line has been consistently held by those in power, despite the overwhelming amount of evidence to the contrary.

In fact, at no time in American history has the government received so many credible warnings of an imminent attack on home soil. It is a bare-faced lie to say otherwise.

George W. Bush and other senior colleagues repeatedly said that no one had even imagined the idea of planes being used as weapons. This again shows an almost unbelievable level of dishonesty in the face of overwhelming evidence. But politicization of the extensive prior warnings happened frighteningly quickly. Within months, Dick Cheney said that any implication that the Bush administration had missed warning signs was "thoroughly irresponsible . . . in a time of war" and that investigating such things would amount to giving aid and comfort to the enemy. In Cheney's view, to suggest the Bush administration had even made errors prior to 9/11 was tantamount to supporting al-Qaeda.

Intelligence Warnings

Condoleezza Rice was given an intelligence summary from CIA Director George Tenet on June 28, 2001, which said that it was highly likely that a significant al-Qaeda attack was in the making within several weeks. It's hard to imagine what sort of person would not act on receiving such a chilling warning, but Rice, staggeringly unqualified to hold her position (and having given Richard Clarke the impression that she had never heard of al-Qaeda at their first briefing), appears to have done nothing at all.

Possibly the best known presidential-level warning came in a briefing dated August 6, 2001—a document requested by Bush himself in light of the warnings America was receiving of a potential domestic attack, and delivered to him during his record-breaking holiday in Crawford, Texas.

Initially kept secret, the memo was a stark warning entitled "Bin Laden Determined to Strike in US." Its contents are so sensitive that they remain classified to this day. The spurious reason for this continued classification is that the memo contains nothing specific. Condoleezza Rice claimed the memo was only one and a half pages long and was fuzzy and thin, but others have stated it ran to more than eleven pages (instead of the usual two to three).

After 9/11, President Bush repeatedly claimed he had received no warning of any kind, until CBS revealed the memo's existence on May 15, 2002.

From the un-redacted information we have seen, the brief revealed the following:

- US intelligence and the president were fully aware that al-Qaeda was present in the US and planning terrorist acts.
- al-Qaeda had powerful backing.
- Osama bin Laden favored spectacular attacks on major US facilities and landmarks, and patterns of activity within the US were consistent with preparations for (multiple) hijackings.
- Osama bin Laden was keen to follow up Ramsi Yousef's attacks of 1993 on the World Trade Center.

Only one terrorist organization was mentioned: al-Qaeda. Only two US cities were named—Washington, DC and New York City. Just one form of attack was listed: hijacking. Just one specific target was on the briefing—the World Trade Center.

To put it another way, the entire 9/11 plot was listed in the document. The memo gave Bush, in clear terms, the who and where, and pointed toward how the terrorist attacks would take place, just thirty-six days later. If that's the information that the administration saw fit to declassify, god only knows what the rest must have said.

Clearly the memo made an impression on the holidaying president, as he responded with a dismissive "alright, you've covered your ass now." Bush spent the rest of the day fishing.

In the instance of clear and present danger, not acting is to invite disaster, and as complicit as being involved. Yet members of the Bush administration, and Bush himself in particular, appear not only to have ignored the warnings, but taken a collective decision to do nothing, no matter what was presented to them.

Nobody Imagined It

The idea that no one had thought of using planes as bombs is laughable. As far back as 1993, a panel reporting to the Pentagon warned that in their estimation planes could be used as flying bombs, to breach national security and attack landmarks. In 1994 one of the panel wrote in *Futurist* magazine that terror-ists would likely consider multiple, simultaneous attacks, and that the World Trade Center would provide "more bang for the buck."

If the attacks looked like something out of a Tom Clancy novel, it's because they were. Clancy published a book in 1994 entitled *Debt of Honor*, featuring a storyline in which Jack Ryan, the hero, is made president after a passenger plane is purposely flown into the US Capitol.

In 1999, a report prepared for the National Intelligence Council (affiliated to the CIA) warned that bin Laden's terrorists might hijack an airplane packed with explosives and crash it into the Pentagon or the White House.

On November 6th 1999, NORAD gamed a scenario in which five terror-ists took over a transcontinental aircraft and tried to crash it into the United Nations in New York, a thirty-nine-story building just three miles from the World Trade Center. On June 5, 2000, another exercise called Falcon Indian included scenarios in which terrorists tried to crash hijacked planes into the White House and the Statue of Liberty (just two miles from the WTC), as well as a scenario where a Learjet flew in close formation with a commercial craft and crashed into the White House.

These exercises came to light during testimony by Richard Myers in August 2004 to the Senate Armed Services Committee. Myers said that five scenarios had been played out in exercises between November 1999 and Octo-ber 2000. All had included the idea of hijacked planes being flown into iconic buildings.

As we have seen, on October 24–26, 2000 (less than a year before 9/11), the Pentagon carried out a detailed emergency drill based on the scenario of a hijacked commercial airliner crashing into the side of the Pentagon. The report on the drill was said to read like an account of what actually happened.

With so much of the official 9/11 story a clear fabrication, it is not unrea-sonable to suggest that rather than scenario planning, these exercises were in fact practice runs or dress rehearsals for the big one to come.

Even TV producers had thought of the idea, and eerily matched the events of 9/11 with their fiction. *The Lone Gunmen* (a short-lived Fox knockoff of *The X-Files*), which aired on March 4, 2001, told the story of a US government agency's plot to crash a remote-controlled 727 into the World Trade Center as an excuse to raise the military budget and then blame the attack on a tin-pot dictator who was "begging to be smart-bombed."

In the program, the plane takes off from Boston's Logan Airport, but there are no terrorists on board, the plane being remotely controlled exter-nally. After those on board manage to overpower the external controllers of the plane and the suicidal flight narrowly misses the World Trade Center, the heroes decide that the terrorist group responsible was actually a faction of their own government. "These malefactors were seeking to stimulate arms manufacturing in the lean years following the end of the Cold War by bringing down a plane in New York City and fermenting fears of terrorism."

In short, not only were prior warnings received, scenarios closely following the events on 9/11 had been extensively imagined, gamed and tested— even broadcast as TV fiction on Fox. Amazingly, however, despite all this freely available evidence, the Bush administration held firm that no one had ever even imagined using planes as terrorist weapons, and the media rarely challenged these lies.

At least six senior government officials predicted the attacks with eerie prescience. Four days before 9/11, General Tommy Franks told his intelligence staff that what worried him most was the thought of a terrorist attack on one of the World Trade Center twin towers, causing it to collapse into the other one, killing thousands.

On September 10, 2001, Charles Nemfakos, deputy under secretary of the US Navy (the number three man in the navy) told a group of civilians in Washington that a terrorist event equivalent to Pearl Harbor would be the only thing to wake America from its state of complacency. Nemfakos knew more about the threat than most other people. He had been a key player in an initiative called New Rule Sets Project that had included war games featuring terrorist attacks on the World Trade Center in the previous twelve months. The initiative was a partnership between a naval war college and (of all people) Cantor Fitzgerald, the brokerage firm devastated in the attacks. Workshops had taken place at Windows on the World, the restaurant at the top of the north tower. When the 9/11 attacks came, the New Rule Sets Project moved from theory to strategy.

As an aside, Cantor's CEO survived 9/11 as, unusually, he decided to take his son to kindergarten that day. His three most senior executives also found reasons not to be in the office on the morning of September 11. Cantor sued American Airlines for negligence (in allowing their plane to hit the building!) and won a $135 million settlement in 2013, the bulk of which was paid out to the shareholders, with $2 per share being paid. Guess who had the most shares in Cantor Fitzgerald. Howard Lutnick, the kindergarten attending CEO. Lutnick, who lost his brother in the attacks, personally made at least $15 million as a result of 9/11.

Warnings

Whether you believe the official 9/11 story or otherwise, the idea that the attacks were planned in secret by a very small group of people, and that no one outside that group had an inkling of what was to come, is refuted by the sheer number of people who clearly knew in advance of parts, details or all of the events that transpired.

Foreign governments and their spy agencies warned America again and again, stock traders took positions showing clear foreknowledge of a devastating and immediate attack. But many other people, even random individuals at a wedding, were warned of a massive terrorist attack to come, in early September, from the skies, in lower Manhattan.

In June 2000, up to twenty highly suspicious web domain names were registered, including attackonamerica.com, attackontwintowers.com, tradetowerstrike.com and worldtradetowerattack.com. The site registrations expired in June 2001. It is unclear if the FBI ever followed up the credit card details of whoever registered the domains.

Mayor Willie Brown of Chicago described how he received a phone call eight hours before the hijackings, warning him not to travel that day (he was booked to fly from San Francisco to New York). The mayor would only say the warning came from his security people, but it has been widely reported that the call came from Condoleezza Rice. Brown cancelled his flight on 9/11, but appears not to have thought to look out for anyone else. Similarly, on September 10, a group of top Pentagon officials suddenly cancelled their travel plans for the next morning, citing security concerns.

The numerous cases of senior political and military figures changing their travel schedules around September 11, in light of warnings received, clearly indicate that those at the top took the security assessments seriously enough to protect themselves. The rest of us were left to our chances.

Internationally, there was a deafening roar of specific, urgent warnings from both America's friends and foes.

In July 2001, Jordan's King Abdullah personally instructed his men to pass on warnings of an imminent al-Qaeda attack to the Bush administration in Washington, stating that the attack would be inside the US and involve commercial aircraft.

A North African head of state was said to have given Washington the precise date, as well as identifying the Pentagon as a target.

In late July 2001, the Taliban's foreign minister told US officials that Osama bin Laden was planning a huge attack inside America that was imminent and would kill thousands. Given the Taliban's knowledge of the impending attacks, it is not a long bow to draw to suggest that Pakistan's ISI would have known too, and the head of the ISI was in Washington on 9/11. It is well known that the ISI is a creation of (and perhaps even a creature of) the CIA. It's a massive circle, and they all knew.

In August 2001 two senior Mossad agents were sent to the US to warn the CIA and FBI of up to 200 Middle Eastern terrorists training for a major attack within the US. Four of the hijackers' names were on their list.

Russian president Vladimir Putin said that in August 2001, "I ordered my intelligence to warn Bush in the strongest terms that twenty-five terrorists were getting ready to attack the US, including important government buildings like the Pentagon". Russia's warning included the possible use of hijacked airliners against civilian buildings. The head of Russian intelligence said, "We had clearly warned them . . . they did not pay the necessary attention."

Moscow Bombings

A quick diversion to look at the key event solidifying Vladimir Putin's quest for power is nothing if not instructive.

Russia made plans to invade Chechnya six months before civilian bombings took place in Moscow in September 1999, killing 293 people and providing the excuse and justification for the war that followed. The bombings have been called Russia's 9/11.

The wave of anger against Chechnya (which was blamed for the bombings) provided the public backing required for an invasion, and gave Vladimir Putin a huge boost in popularity and political power, virtually handing him the Presidency. Putin vowed revenge against the Chechens for the devastating attacks, and his approval ratings went from 31 percent in August to 78 percent in November 1999.

However, the bombings are now widely acknowledged to have been carried out by Russia's state security service, the FSB (formerly the KGB), on the orders of Vladimir Putin.

The key Chechen commanders at the time were not only linked to al-Qaeda and Osama bin Laden, but were simultaneously Russian intelligence assets. This gave Putin control of both protagonists. The whole story should hardly now be surprising, given that Putin (the former KGB agent) has killed opponents at will, and turned Russian into a kleptocracy, the largest mafia state in the world.

Looking back, Russia's 9/11—a false-flag terrorism attack designed to provoke war and consolidate political power—bears striking similarities to America's own.

In all, at least eleven countries provided the US with advance warning of the attacks. The warnings came from governments and intelligence agencies in Britain, Germany, Russia, Israel, Jordan, and Egypt. The Jordanian warning even mentioned al-Qaeda's codename for the attacks, the Big Wedding.

Senator Bob Graham counted twelve instances in which the US had learned of terrorist plans to use airplanes as weapons in the spring and summer of 2001.

One is struck by the fact that despite all these warnings, and measures taken by politicians to keep themselves safe, no one thought to warn the public (who were most at risk), at a time when—in the words of CIA Director George Tenet—"the system was blinking red."

Within US government and intelligence circles there was clear knowledge that something was badly wrong. Porter Goss (Chair of the House Intelligence Committee) said the chatter level went way off the charts . . . and had been for several months. In June 2001, George Tenet told Richard Clarke, "It's my sixth sense, but I feel it coming. This is going to be the big one."

Richard Clarke

Richard Clarke, America's counter-terrorism tsar, appears to have been something of a lone voice in the wind among senior Bush administration staff. According to Clarke, ten weeks before 9/11, US intelligence agencies were convinced a large attack on home soil was imminent. In light of the information he was receiving, Clarke met with all domestic US security agencies around seven weeks before the attacks, warning of the high risk of domestic terrorism. Clarke issued five information circulars to the FAA from June to August 2001. These included direct warnings to beef up security across the board. One of the primary directives was to secure cockpit doors, a measure that could have prevented the attacks entirely. The FAA refused to adopt any of the measures. They also blocked efforts, mostly led by Clarke, to arm pilots or place air marshals on planes.

Clarke became so frustrated by his inability to rouse concern in his colleagues that he considered asking for a transfer in June 2001, later saying:

"If the administration doesn't believe its national coordinator for counter-terrorism when he says there's an urgent problem, and if it's unprepared to act as though there's an urgent problem, then probably I should get another job." Clarke reasoned that if someone else in the job came to the same conclusions that he had, perhaps the Bush administration might finally listen. John O'Neill, the FBI's Osama bin Laden expert (who did resign in frustration and died at the World Trade Center on 9/11), was to be Clarke's recommendation as the man to replace him.

Richard Clarke is the only senior member of the Bush administration to have taken any kind of meaningful action prior to the attacks. On 9/11, unlike so many others (who continued with meetings, went AWOL, or turned off the television so as to not be distracted), Clarke appears to have run as fast as possible to his car while screaming into the telephone. These are the actions of a senior political leader at a time of great crisis. The *Washington Post* said everyone seems to agree that Clarke made the most effective contribution to America's defense on the morning of 9/11.

The immediacy of the threat is illustrated by the fact that just four days before 9/11, the State Department issued a worldwide alert stating that US citizens might imminently be the target of al-Qaeda extremists. US intelligence knew of the warnings and were taking them seriously.

But the information regarding possible terrorism also made it to the civilian sector, in surprisingly varied places.

Shortly before the attacks, people attending a mosque in the Bronx were told to stay away from lower Manhattan on September 11. The FBI interviewed dozens of members of the mosque, who confirmed the story.

Jean-Marie Benjamin, a priest at an Italian wedding just five days before 9/11, was told by a Muslim guest about a plot using hijacked planes as weapons. Benjamin passed the warning on to local politicians.

Odigo Company, an Israeli instant messaging business based in Herzliya (near the headquarters of the Mossad) and with offices near the World Trade Center, reported that two of their employees in Israel had received text messages warning of imminent attacks just two hours before the plane impacts, but not passed them on. This was confirmed by the company's Director, Micha Macover.

When the spotlight of publicity turned on Odigo the company clammed up, stating that releasing details of the warnings would "only lead to more conjecture." Results of the FBI investigation into the story have never been released.

Another Israeli firm, the Zim American Israeli Shipping Company (49 percent owned by the Israeli government), moved out of the sixteenth floor of one of the twin towers just seven days before the attacks, breaking its lease and losing $50,000. The move, which had been announced six months earlier, left just one Israeli company, Clearforest, in the WTC on 9/11. All of Clearforest's employees survived.

In sum, prior warnings received by the United States government were numerous, credible, specific, timely, and accurate. Warnings named names, listed targets, and came from highly credible sources on multiple occasions. Warnings used phrases like "might take a plane and fly it into the World Trade Center."

It would not be an overstatement to say that there has never been a time in US history when so many warnings of a potential domestic attack have been received in such a short space of time. Credible, numerous, authoritative, specific, timely. And ignored.

In the weeks and months following the attacks, information slowly leaked out about the sheer volume of warnings that had been received prior to 9/11. US officials mostly took the line that it wasn't fair to retrospectively cherry-pick items from the vast volume of intelligence that they deal with. However, it's hard to imagine how the warnings the US received could have been any more specific, save for perhaps a note from Osama bin Laden himself saying that he would attack on Tuesday. Not only were the warnings so specific and credible that it beggars belief that they cannot have been acted upon, there is also (as we have seen) a great deal of evidence that US government agencies purposely blocked investigations and leads, for reasons that remain unclear.

How could these warnings have been so catastrophically missed? The answer, of course, is that they weren't.

Bojinka

The genesis of 9/11 lay in a plot hatched in the Philippines some seven years earlier. The plot was foiled and publicly exposed, but from that idea came the seeds that were sown in the largest terrorist attack in history.

Project Bojinka was devised in 1994 by Khalid Sheikh Mohammed and his nephew Ramsi Yousef, who had carried out the 1993 World Trade Center bomb attack and escaped via Iraq and Pakistan.

The two relatives, who lived only a few floors apart in Manila, began planning various assassination attempts on the Pope, Bill Clinton and others, and to place bombs on twelve US-bound commercial airliners, to be exploded simultaneously over the Pacific, causing thousands of deaths. Another scenario considered was the hijacking of eleven planes and flying them into prominent US buildings. Targets included the World Trade Center and the headquarters of the CIA. Even the airlines had been chosen—United Airlines, Northwest and Delta.

The airline bombing side to Bojinka (a nonsense word made up by Yousef) was to be implemented in two stages—a test run and the real thing.

The first part was the test bombing of a Philippines Airlines flight on December 11, 1994. Yousef easily got the small bomb past airport security, assembled it in the plane's toilet, set a timer going that would detonate in four hours, stowed it under seat 26K and got off the plane when it got to Cebu city. On the next leg, as the plane neared Tokyo the bomb exploded, killing a Japanese businessman and injuring ten others, but miraculously failed to bring down the plane.

Back in Manila, Yousef had made over a dozen more bombs, but on January 6, 1995 his accomplice, Abdul Hakim Murad, accidentally set fire to the chemicals in their flat. Yousef fled, but sent Murad back to get his computer (which had Bojinka's details on it), and Murad was arrested.

Yousef had apparently plotted to kill the Pope, who was arriving in the Philippines just four days later. It was a lucky escape. Local police uncovered the plot and reported the details to US authorities. A huge international manhunt began.

Under interrogation Murad admitted another plot; to fly planes loaded with explosives into US landmarks.

On February 7, 1995, Ramsi Yousef was arrested in Islamabad, Pakistan. He was extradited, tried and convicted in New York. When arrested, Yousef had chemical burns on his fingers, US airline flight schedules and had placed components for bombs inside children's toys. America had their man.

Murad and Yousef confessed that their targets had included government buildings in Washington, including the Pentagon. With Bojinka now well known to the CIA and FBI, it would not take a master sleuth to realize that one thing to look out for in the future would be young Middle Eastern men learning to fly American airliners. But neither agency appears to have pursued this line of enquiry, and the investigation ended. No one seems to have thought to look further into Yousef's background, or to try to find whoever was financing his evil plans.

September 11 was merely a refinement of the Bojinka plan. In fact, a Philippine investigator said after the attacks, "It's Bojinka. We told the Americans everything about Bojinka. Why didn't they pay attention?"

Stock Market Activity

Prior knowledge of the 9/11 attacks also made it to the financial community.

In the days leading up to 9/11 a large volume of unusual trades were made on the stock values of United and American, the two airlines whose planes were hijacked, and on some of the larger tenants at the World Trade Center buildings. These highly suspicious trades did not follow other market and industry patterns. Sometimes, of course, the entire market thinks airline or banking stocks are going to go down, and bets that way. That was not the case here.

From September 6–7, 2001, "put" options on United Airlines were bought at a ratio of 10:1 against call options. On September 10, put options on American Airlines were bought at a ratio of 6:1 to calls in Chicago. No similar trading patterns took place on other airlines. Someone was betting that these two airline companies share prices would plummet.

Short-selling and put options are the reverse of most share trades, when you buy stock in a company in the hope of your shareholding going up in value. Puts bet that a share will go down (calls bet they will go up), and allow the placer of the bet to make money through an agreed future sale price with the seller. If you buy a put option and the stock goes down, you sell the shares at an agreed higher price and make a profit.

In the month before 9/11 there was an increase of 40 percent (over the previous month) in short-selling the two airlines involved on 9/11 (compared to just 11 percent for other big airlines). Things accelerated as the day approached. Between September 6 and 10, there was a nine-fold increase in the volume of put options placed on United Airlines. American Airlines saw a six-fold increase.

Morgan Stanley and Merrill Lynch, both large tenants at the World Trade Center, saw similar trades. Put options on Morgan Stanley increased to 27 times the normal level, Merrill Lynch options increased to twelve times normal activity. This too increased as the day approached. Morgan Stanley (who occupied twenty-two floors of the WTC) saw nearly eighty times the normal level of put options bought in the three trading days before 9/11—2,157 contracts in three days as opposed to the average of twenty-seven per day. The options were due to expire on the 30th. Merrill Lynch, whose headquarters were also at the WTC, saw 12,215 put options bought in the four days before 9/11, compared to an average of 252 options per day.

Some trades bet that certain stocks would rise too. There was a six-fold increase in the number of call options on the stock of defense contractor Raytheon the day before 9/11. Raytheon shares soared 37 percent in just one week after the attacks.

Others appear to have been given information detailing a major attack on September 11 and tried to limit their exposure to the shockwaves. Stock advisor Amr Ibrahim Elgindy tried to sell $300,000 of stock on the afternoon of September 10, telling his broker that the value would plunge very soon. It transpired that Elgindy had given $30,000 in cash to an FBI agent for confidential information about Bureau investigations, an illegal act he had done on other occasions. Given what we know of the warnings the FBI had received, it's fair to assume that the agent who took cash from Elgindy knew the likelihood of domestic terrorism attacks on or around September 11. Appallingly, the agent chose to take cash over acting to save the citizens he had sworn to protect.

These put option spikes and other trades indicated foreknowledge of the attacks, and a sickening desire to profit from mass murder. The transactions were widely noted. No less than Ernst Welteke, president of the German Bundesbank, said that he thought the trades represented foreknowledge of the coming attacks, stating they were otherwise inexplicable. Dylan Ratigan, a Bloomberg Business news writer, said of these trades "this would be one of the most extraordinary coincidences in the history of mankind, if it was a coincidence."

Those holding the unusual put options were set to make huge profits from the tragedy. United stocks dropped 43 percent, and American 39 percent on the day the market reopened after 9/11.

The firm used to buy many of the put options was Alex Brown Inc., a subsidiary of Deutsche Bank. Alex Brown had a number of well-known connections to the CIA. Most notably, the company had been headed until three years prior to 9/11 by CEO and Chairman A.B. "Buzzy" Krongard. In March 2001, Krongard had left the world of business, at the behest of President Bush, to take up the post of Executive Director of the CIA, the third most powerful position within the Agency.

The CIA and Wall Street are well known to have a close relationship. Those at the top often move from one sector to the other during their career, with many describing it as a revolving door. It is not a stretch of the imagination to draw a line between the system blinking red with warnings at the CIA, personal relationships between Wall Street and the intelligence community, and the placement of these put options.

Tracking Trades

It is widely known that the CIA and FBI (and the Mossad) use highly sophisticated software to monitor the US stock market in real time for suspicious activity, both to detect commercial crime and for law and order purposes.

In the case of put options, a large bet normally indicates insider trading; the knowledge that a company's value is about to come crashing down before the market has seen the likelihood. This is a crime. Given the trades were so large (and statistical outliers), it is very likely that they would have been quickly identified as indicators of unusual, possibly criminal behavior. Someone was betting that airlines and specific tenants at the World Trade Center were going to experience a very significant downturn in a very short space of time. The intelligence system was blinking red with terrorism warnings. The two had to be connected.

Despite this, the Securities and Exchange Commission (SEC) reported that their investigation had found no evidence suggesting insider trading or suspicious investing by those who had advance knowledge of the September 11 attacks.

The SEC declared that their 9/11 insider trading investigation had been the largest in history, but subsequently destroyed all of the data records relating to it. Because of this we will never know who was betting on disaster just days before 9/11.

The 9/11 Commission, true to form, heavily glossed over the trades, admitting that some unusual trading did in fact occur, but that it all had an innocuous explanation. In fact, the Commission put together one of the most fabulously circular arguments in relation to these trades, stating that they were a blameless coincidence, since 95 percent of them had been bought by a single US-based investor with no conceivable ties to al-Qaeda.

So, because the purchaser was American and not tied to al-Qaeda, and America had no foreknowledge of the attacks, it was (the Commission concluded) logically impossible for the trades to have been suspicious. Case closed.

But the trades were more than suspicious, they were inexplicable, unless you accept what is the most obvious solution—that they showed a clear indication not only of prior knowledge of the coming attacks, but of someone's decision to try to profit from them.

CHAPTER TWELVE

OFFICIAL INTELLIGENCE AND GOVERNMENT INQUIRIES

Every government agency investigating the events of 9/11 came to the same conclusion that the attacks had come out of the blue, and the buildings had fallen due to fires. Despite millions being spent, there were very few notable new findings. But when the government is the prime suspect, and staffs and bankrolls the inquiries, to expect any different would be insanity.

FEMA

FEMA conducted an investigation of the twin towers engineering performance, but it was woefully inadequate. FEMA's investigation was carried out by volunteers, and had a budget of just $600K. Its investigators had no subpoena power and were allowed limited access to ground zero. They saw very little physical evidence, and weren't even allowed blueprints of the buildings.

The illustrations used in FEMA's report were also highly misleading, omitting some beams and core columns, and showing some key supports at half or even one third of their actual size.

It's no wonder then that *Fire Engineering* (the firefighter's trade newspaper) called FEMA's investigation a half-baked farce, and questioned why vital evidence was being removed each day from the crime scene.

Faced with explaining building collapses without mentioning explosives, FEMA chose to fudge the issue. One section of their report concluded that "the specific chain of events that led to the eventual collapse will probably never be identified." Or to put it another way, we don't know why the buildings fell down. That is simply not good enough for the lead government disaster response body when dealing with the largest building collapses in history. Worse was to follow.

The Joint Inquiry of House and Senate Select Committees

Initially, the idea of any government inquiry into 9/11 whatsoever was strongly opposed by the White House. In late January 2002, President Bush and Dick Cheney personally asked Senate Majority leader Tom Daschle not to proceed with any 9/11 investigation. Cheney's tone was described as polite but threatening. Daschle had been on the receiving end of anthrax-laden letters the month after 9/11. He knew to take a call from Bush and Cheney seriously.

But the presiding administration's requests were untenable. September 11 was an earth-shattering event. There was no precedent for something of that magnitude not engendering an inquiry. Nevertheless, Bush asked house and senate leaders Porter Goss and Bob Graham to limit their inquiry to House and Senate Intelligence Committees, whose proceedings are mostly secret. The Bush administration's reasoning was that a broader 9/11 inquiry would unduly burden the defense and intelligence communities, taking away resources and personnel from the War on Terror. This circular, self-serving argument became the prevailing logic of the time: the Bush administration seeking to limit any investigation into the greatest act of terrorism in history in order to fight terrorism.

When stopping any form of 9/11 inquiry became politically impossible, Bush and Cheney put considerable pressure on Congressional leaders (including Daschle) to limit the scope of the inquiry to just potential breakdowns among federal agencies. This was a fabulously narrow remit, and hardly the central story of 9/11.

The co-chairmen, Goss and Graham, publicly declared that their inquiry would not play the blame game, but didn't explain how an examination of one of the greatest disasters in their nation's history could be honest and yet entirely exonerate all those involved. How could they know at the start of the inquiry that their efforts would not uncover evidence of someone unexpected being involved, or at the very least someone having acted so incompetently that some blame had to be apportioned, but this was not to be an open or fair inquiry, and sure enough no disciplinary action against any incumbent federal bureaucrat was recommended.

Goss and Graham, of course, were the men having breakfast with the head of the Pakistani ISI on 9/11—the same man that had arranged for Mohamed Atta to be wired $100K a month earlier. Both men had also travelled to Pakistan for meetings with the ISI in late August 2001, just weeks before the attacks. Both had extensive ties to the CIA and ISI. As such, the two men had as clear a conflict of interest as it is possible to have. This perhaps explains why Pakistan and the ISI were almost completely absent from the Inquiry report they produced.

Goss and Graham were said to have exercised near total control over the investigation and its results. Trust between members seems to have been non-existent. At one point Goss and Graham asked the FBI to investigate whether other members of their panel were leaking information to the press, leading to the bizarre situation where the FBI were investigating people who were investigating the FBI.

Gifted this opportunity to become involved, the FBI used their investigation of inquiry members as a means of intimidation. FBI agents questioned nearly all of the thirty-seven members of the committee about information leaks, and even demanded that Senators and representatives take lie detector tests and release their phone records and diaries. Unsurprisingly, this chilled any real investigative zeal towards the FBI. John McCain said of the FBI's actions, "What you have here is an organization compiling dossiers on people who are investigating the same organization."

The inquiry only involved nine public hearings and thirteen closed sessions. Witness testimony was almost entirely taken at face value and not critically assessed at all.

Given this, and the extraordinarily limited scope afforded the inquiry by the Bush administration, it's not surprising that its findings were laughably inadequate, concluding that US intelligence agencies not only did not receive any prior warnings about the attacks, they had not even contemplated the idea of terrorist attacks within the US. This was preposterous, bare-faced lying.

As elsewhere, the inquiry failed to identify any individuals as having failed, or to hold one person even slightly accountable. They found that the attacks had come out of the blue, and that the devious terrorists had been brilliant in concealing every single aspect of their plans, giving no warnings and leaving no trace of their activities.

The congressional inquiry began its investigation of the performance of various government agencies in February 2002 and reported its findings in mid-December of that year. The report was 832 pages long, but heavily redacted. Most notably, twenty-eight pages that related to foreign funding of the terrorists had been entirely removed. Commenting on all the information that was redacted from the report, Graham (the inquiry's chairman) said Americans would find the information withheld more than interesting. But a government denying its own citizens access to vital information about a generationally defining event was something Americans would have to get used to.

The Missing Pages

The government of the United States has gone to extraordinary lengths to protect Saudi Arabia from blame regarding 9/11. Most prominently, the twenty-eight redacted pages from the Joint Inquiry report remained unpublished and unseen by the public for fourteen years, until their release in 2016.

These pages were kept in a closely guarded basement room under Capitol Hill. They could be read by some politicians, but even these elected officials were severely restricted—they had to make a formal application, were banned from taking notes and watched as they read the report. One official who saw the pages before their redaction said that the nation's relationship with Saudi Arabia would change overnight if the pages were made public.

This grotesque restriction on even limited access to vital public information led to speculation running like wildfire as to the contents of these documents. Yet, on their publication (on July 15, 2016), the story barely made the front page of most newspapers. Perhaps it was a coincidence, but the pages were released on the same day as a highly suspect coup attempt in Turkey, and the day after a horrific terrorist attack in France killed eighty-four innocent people. The pages were lost in the hubbub.

Reading this part of the Inquiry's report, one is struck by two things. First, almost all of the information contained within the document was in the public domain already (although few people were curious enough to have found it). There's very little truly revelatory there. Second though, is how stark and overt the statements are. The first sentence on the first page reads as follows:

> "While in the United States, some of the September 11 hijackers were in contact with, and received support or assistance from, individuals who may be connected to the Saudi government."

One small change of syntax: the substituting of "were" for the words "may be" would make that sentence mean that the Saudi government was involved in attacking America on 9/11. That small change would, surely, leave America no alternative but to sever all ties with Saudi Arabia, and most probably declare war on that country.

The remainder of the document deals mainly with two individuals suspected of being Saudi spies: Omar al-Bayoumi and Osama Bassnan. As we have seen, Omar al-Bayoumi met two of the hijackers at the airport when they arrived in the US, arranged for them to move into the flat next to his own (with an FBI informant), paid the rent and stayed in close contact. He received a monthly stipend from a Saudi company, at the insistence of a Saudi government ministry, for a job that he only attended once. His allowance increased markedly from the moment the future hijackers arrived, and he received funds from a variety of sources, including the Saudi ambassador to the US, who was thick as thieves with the Bush family.

What else could Omar al-Bayoumi have been, except for a Saudi spy? And if a Saudi spy was financing and supporting the alleged terrorists, doesn't that mean that Saudi Arabia attacked America on 9/11?

As such, the 9/11 attacks could or even should be viewed as an act of war, not terrorism. But if the Saudis were so closely involved, and the Israelis knew what was coming, is it possible that the American government, so entwined with Israel as to be inseparable, headed by the scion of America's leading oil family, with close personal ties to both the Saudis and the bin Laden family, had no clue whatsoever?

It's an open secret that the redaction was based on a direct order from President Bush. So if the president of the United States (who flew prominent Saudis out of the country immediately after 9/11) chose to hide information about Saudi government involvement in 9/11, rather than confront an active participant in the murder of three thousand of his citizens, doesn't that make George W. Bush and the senior members of his administration treasonous criminals?

It's hard to overstate the importance here. The Saudis are consistently portrayed as our close friends in the Middle East, a loyal ally in this never-ending war against religious extremism, despite the knowledge that the Saudi regime runs the most extreme Islamic society on earth. It seems that Saudi oil is worth more than three thousand lives.

The words of those who saw the contents of the twenty-eight pages in the years when they were kept secret have proved an accurate portrayal of their import. Even for politicians who parse their words carefully, they were disarmingly frank as to the incendiary contents that were kept from our view.

Walter Jones, (Republican, North Carolina) read the pages and told *New Yorker* in 2014 that there was nothing in them that related to US national security but that they were "about the Bush administration and its relationship with the Saudis" (and the complicity of the Saudis with al-Qaeda in the attacks of 9/11). Congressman Jones said that the twenty-eight pages led him to blame one or more foreign governments for the 9/11 attacks.

Stephen Lynch (D-Mass.) said the pages offered direct evidence, stunning in its clarity, of Saudi complicity in the attacks of 9/11. Lynch said that "those twenty-eight pages tell a story that has been completely removed from the 9/11 Report." This directly contradicted George W. Bush's assertion that the twenty-eight pages contained information that, if released, would make it harder to win the War on Terror.

Even Bob Graham, no bleeding-heart liberal, said that it was as if the President's loyalty lay more with Saudi Arabia than with America's safety. "I think the American people should know the extent of the challenge we face in terms of government involvement . . . there is very compelling evidence that at least some of the terrorists were assisted not just in financing . . . by a sovereign foreign government, and that we have been derelict in our duty to track that down."

That's about as close as a politician could ever come to simply saying that Saudi Arabia financed the 9/11 terrorists.

Graham added that he was convinced that there was a direct line between at least some of the terrorists who carried out the September 11 attacks and the government of Saudi Arabia. Graham said he had found evidence that the Saudis were facilitating and assisting some of the hijackers. He added, "And my suspicion is that they were providing some assistance to most if not all of the hijackers . . . it's my opinion that 9/11 could not have occurred but for the existence of an infrastructure of support within the United States. By the Saudis, I mean the Saudi government and individual Saudis who are for some purposes dependent on the government—which includes all of the elite in the country." He included the Royal family in his views.

Pretty unequivocal stuff.

In referring to the redacted pages, Senator Graham said in August 2014, "None of the people leading this investigation think it is credible that nineteen people—most who could not speak English and did not have previous experience in the United States—could carry out such a complicated task without external assistance."

For fourteen years it seems this was information that the US public (which these people serve) could not be trusted to examine. Yet the 2016 release of official government documents showing a clear link between 9/11 and the Saudi government has somehow been lost, just another piece of world-changing information it seems our press and public servants have no interest in.

It is striking that while the US has bombed and droned Muslim country after Muslim country, the one most likely to have had a hand in the events of 9/11 that triggered this madness remains untouched. To quote journalist Jonathan Schwarz: "The funny thing is I'd bet the Saudi ambassador to the US has closer ties to al-Qaeda than 90 percent of the people we've killed with drones."

The events of 9/11 appear not to have engendered any change of heart at the House of Saud. They have repeatedly cited the virtual exoneration handed to them by the 9/11 Commission report as evidence of their innocence. But Saudi Arabia is a hornet's nest, one America is loath to poke with a stick. The US government deliberately strove to blame a few relatively minor figures for the attacks of 9/11, and entirely ignored and protected the single state that sponsored them. This in and of itself invites further attacks, as the true perpetrators now know they can act with impunity.

Instead of declaring war on Saudi Arabia, the Bush administration went to extraordinary lengths to protect them from blame. George Bush chose to allow Saudis to fly out of the US without questioning after 9/11, and smoked cigars at the White House with the Saudi ambassador just forty-eight hours after the attacks. To those who say that questioning the events of 9/11 is a betrayal of those who died, I would counter that the true betrayal took place on the Truman balcony on September 13, 2001.

Despite America's apparent absence from the Saudi peninsula, it has secretly continued to use Saudi soil for military operations, including launching armed drones for use in Yemen and other nearby countries. Few things could act as a more effective recruitment tool for radicalized Islamists than the knowledge that the most holy of lands is still being used as America's launching pad for the murder of mostly innocent Muslim men, women and children.

Saudi oil remains the single most important factor in keeping the US economy functioning and stable. America's relationship with the Saudis trumps everything, including Saudi support for international terrorism within the United States. This support cost three thousand lives on September 11, 2001.

The level of seriousness with which the Bush administration took the Joint Inquiry is reflected in their subsequent actions. The inquiry made nineteen urgent recommendations to keep the US safe from another terrorist attack. More than a year later, only two of them had been implemented. America was too busy fighting its War on Terror to listen to its elected leaders' advice on how to reduce the risk of domestic terrorism.

Despite this, the inquiry provided enough revelations to leave the Bush administration little alternative but to set up a proper commission. Bush steadfastly refused to set up a full inquiry, but the clamor was becoming impossible to resist.

The 9/11 Commission

In retrospect, it's truly remarkable that the Bush administration was able to offer so much resistance to even the idea of having a commission at all, given the huge and shattering nature of the attacks (the first true attack on national territory since the War of 1812). But the climate of the time allowed Bush to pursue a line of reasoning that argued that since there was in essence nothing to investigate, no investigation was required.

Many Republicans backed Bush's stance. House Majority Whip Tom Delay called the idea of a commission during a time of war "ill-conceived and irresponsible," but there was no historical precedent for such a spurious line of argument. The attacks at Pearl Harbor, for example, were fully and promptly investigated at a time when the entire world was at war. Unlike 9/11, Pearl Harbor also saw people lose their jobs. On December 17, 1941 (ten days after the Japanese attack), President Roosevelt sacked a top general and admiral.

The creation of the 9/11 Commission was significantly due to the lobbying efforts and public opinion whipped up by the 9/11 Family Steering Committee, an organization of twelve bereaved 9/11 victims relatives. Four widows known as the Jersey Girls were the most active within the Steering Committee, and are often credited with having been the factor that made further stalling of an inquiry untenable.

In September 2002, Bush finally relented and agreed to a commission, but initially told its members that he wanted them to focus on border security and visa issues, matters that were, let's face it, not the main issues at play on 9/11.

A comparison of the budgets allocated and delays involved in establishing inquiries into other notable events in modern American history is instructive.

The commission finally started work 411 days after the attacks, and was given an initial budget of $3 million, and eighteen months to report on the biggest attack on America since Pearl Harbor. By comparison, inquiries were ordered:

- Nine days after the attacks at Pearl Harbor.
- Six days after the sinking of the Titanic.
- Seven days after JFK was assassinated.
- Seven days after the Challenger shuttle disaster.

$3 million was a staggeringly small figure for an inquiry of this importance. By comparison:

- The 1986 NASA Challenger disaster inquiry had a budget of $75 million.
- The 2004 NASA Columbia disaster inquiry had a budget of $50 million.
- A 1996 study into legalized gambling was given two years and $5 million.

When Kenneth Starr chose to pursue Bill Clinton for his sexual activities in the Oval office, he managed to appropriate over $40 million in public funds. $40 million for an affair with an intern. The three thousand dead on 9/11 were worth just $3 million to the Bush administration.

The commission got underway in November 2002, and quickly requested a further $11 million in funding, still a miniscule sum given the tasks at hand. The request was turned down. After two more months, an additional $9 million was grudgingly arranged, but the $12 million total budget remained a paltry amount for investigation of such a massive event.

Staffing

Anyone familiar with the history of great commissions of the modern age will be under no illusions as to their composition. We need not delve into the staffing, methods, or conclusions of the fabulously opaque Warren commission into John F. Kennedy's assassination to know that these august bodies are not manned by chance, nor by the natural selection of the great and good. Instead, key positions are awarded by those inheriting great power, in the former case by an assassination, in 9/11 by an epoch-defining event. Each member plays a role, be it mole, straight man, front man, or manipulator.

Allen Dulles was the perfectly nefarious appointment as one of the seven Warren commissioners. Dulles had headed the CIA from its formation. Kennedy had hated the CIA and fired Dulles. The CIA was widely suspected of having been involved in the assassination. Who better to head the assassination investigation than the most influential CIA alumni alive?

Dulles' role at the Warren Commission was to steer the inquiry away from dangerous areas, and to brief star witnesses on what to expect (and what not to say). Those who head major inquiries are not there discover truth; they are to guide the inquiry in the right direction, and to ensure nothing deviates from a central story. The Warren Commission into the death of Kennedy did this and more, finding that a lone (dead) madman was guilty, and that seemingly magic bullets deviated in mid-air to fit their story. This was successfully sold to the public.

Similarly, the 9/11 Commission staff were not chosen because of their great investigative skills or independent approach, but to be insiders, each playing a role. The results could have been written before the first meeting was held.

When signing the 9/11 Commission into law in November 2002, Bush insisted that he appoint the Commission's chairman, and initially selected that champion of transparency and truth Dr. Henry Kissinger, a man widely perceived as one of the leading war criminals of the latter part of the twentieth century, one of US politics most Machiavellian figures, and a man receiving huge consulting fees from corporations heavily invested in Saudi Arabia.

The selection of Henry Kissinger to Chair the 9/11 Commission showed that when it came to appointing astonishingly inappropriate investigation staff, not much had changed in fifty years. The corrupt and compromised Kissinger is scarcely able to travel abroad for fear of arrest, such is the mendacity of his career. His nomination prompted incredulity, not least because of the well known and extensive conflicts of interest in his business concerns.

Among other things, Kissinger had lobbied Congress in favor of Unocal's oil pipeline project through Afghanistan, which prior to 9/11 would have favored working with the Taliban. Given that the Taliban were now America's sworn enemies, this was inconvenient.

In the end, Kissinger resigned (along with his nominated vice chairman, George Mitchell), rather than reveal his business clients and interests, when the Congressional Research Service demanded he do so.

The final straw appears to have come when the Jersey Girls, seeking a proper inquiry, asked Kissinger if he had oil interests that might conflict with his role. Kissinger seemed unable to answer, so they asked if Kissinger had any clients called bin Laden. At that point, reported one of the wives, "he just about fell off his couch".

That Henry Kissinger was prepared to take on the role of 9/11 Commission chairman when he had such close ties to Unocal, the oil industry and the bin Ladens is a searing indictment of the man, and of Bush's extraordinary decision to appoint him. Absurdly, the Commission into the attacks of 9/11 had come close to being chaired by a man with extensive business ties to the bin Laden family.

In the end, Thomas Kean, the former governor of New Jersey, was selected as the chairman, but chose to remain in his post as president of Drew University. This limited the amount of time he would be able to devote to the commission.

Kean had a long record as an establishment man, a national security gatekeeper who didn't upset the applecart, from as far back as Reagan's October Surprise and the Iran Contra trials. What may also have diminished Kean's independence was that he sat on the board of (and was a shareholder in) one of the largest oil companies in the world, Amerada Hess.

In 1998, Amerada Hess had formed a joint venture with Delta Oil, a Saudi oil firm. The new venture was called the Hess Delta Alliance, and registered in the Cayman Islands. Delta Oil was owned by a number of prominent Saudis (one was Osama bin Laden's brother-in-law), some of whom were suspected of have donated millions to Osama bin Laden and his causes. Two partners in Hess Delta were accused as part of the symbolic $1 trillion lawsuit brought by 9/11 victims families. It didn't take six degrees of separation to reach Kevin Bacon—Thomas Kean was essentially business partners with al-Qaeda financers and Osama bin Laden's brother. Twenty-one days before Kean was appointed, the joint venture was ended.

This obvious conflict of interest was not widely publicized, barely criticized, and hardly out of step with the other appointees. Nearly every other member of the commission had clear professional, business or political conflicts of interest. Every single one of them had some kind of connection to the airline, defense, or military industries.

While there were thirty-seven senior figures involved in the 9/11 Commission, the commission board had ten members, plus an executive director. These eleven, along with the chairman and vice chairman, were where the power lay. They set the agenda and ran the show.

After George Mitchell's resignation, Lee Hamilton was named as replacement vice chairman. Hamilton had been a member of Congress for thirty years and was a lawyer by trade (as were six other Commission members). He held a number of key advisory positions within the Bush administration, including with the CIA and Homeland security. He also had a history of political whitewashing, having chaired the Iran Contra Committee, which famously shielded those at the top of the Reagan administration from blame. In all the investigative committees or commissions he had worked on, he had never found serious wrongdoing in any top official.

Executive Director Philip Zelikow was even more of an insider. He had the Bush family to thank for much of his career, had worked with both (senior and junior) Bush presidential administrations and authored a key document used by the Bush White House to justify their doctrine of pre-emptive wars. Zelikow had even authored a book with his good friend Condoleezza Rice.

The Family Steering Committee called on Zelikow to step down when it became known that he had provided Rice with briefings on al-Qaeda ten months before 9/11. Given that the commission's brief was to identify sources of intelligence failure, this was the most obvious conflict of interest possible. It was not the first time the families voiced discontent, nor was it the last when their wishes would be ignored.

Before the investigation even started, Zelikow wrote a detailed outline for the report's conclusions, with chapter headings, subheadings and sub-subheadings. As executive director, Zelikow made clear what the narrative of the investigation would be. He was there to be the representative of the Bush administration, his role to point commission staff in the right direction and to ensure nothing untoward was investigated or made public. Zelikow had control over who could be called to testify, what questions could be asked, and had the final edit over the document to be published. He remained in regular contact with Bush's henchman Karl Rove throughout the hearings. Commissions are not independent when they are headed by such a man.

The 9/11 Commission was created by the institutions it should have been investigating, and its members came from those institutions. Others involved in the commission also had the most obvious conflicts of interest, and careers built on not rocking the boat.

The commission's in-house lawyer was David Marcus, whose law firm Wilmer, Cutler & Pickering boasted among its clients Saudi Prince Mohamed al-Faisal, who was listed as one of the key financiers of 9/11 in the trillion dollar victims' families' lawsuit.

Commissioner Richard Ben-Veniste was widely acknowledged to have made a career out of defending (mostly successfully) political crooks. Ben-Veniste's law firm Mayer Brown represented Boeing, who built the planes destroyed on 9/11, and Deutsche Bank, the firm through which most of the put options (that showed prior knowledge of the attacks) were placed.

Commissioner Fred Fielding's law firm lobbied for United Airlines, whose planes were hijacked on 9/11 (and who subsequently received huge government bailouts). He had been Ronald Reagan's lawyer from 1981 to 1986.

Commissioner Jamie Gorelick served on the CIA National Security Advisory Panel and the President's Review Group on intelligence. Both positions related to the government's policy on the CIA and national security. She was also vice chairman of Fannie Mae—the mortgage lender that benefited massively from Bush's post-9/11 financial policies.

Commissioner James R. Thompson, a Republican from Illinois, was a member of Winston & Straw, a law firm specializing in defending large corporations accused of wrongdoing, including Philip Morris.

Commissioner John Lehman, secretary of the Navy from 1981 to 1987, was an investment banker and senior staff member at the National Security Council, reporting to Henry Kissinger. He was also a director and shareholder in Ball Corporation, which works with the US military and aerospace industry. Ball Corp had extensive defense contracts with the US government, including a laser missile defense program that was resurrected by the Bush administration after the 9/11 attacks. He was also a signatory to a Project for the New American Century letter sent to President Bush on September 20, 2001, calling for a war on terrorism. This put him squarely within the ranks of top Bush administration officials.

The one exception to the insiders rule was the one that didn't last. Max Cleland, the Commission's most outspoken member, grew more and more frustrated, saying that he recognized that the "government knew a whole lot more about these terrorists before September 11 than it has ever admitted." Cleland resigned because of a deal the White House cut with the Commission, limiting access to Presidential Daily Briefings, calling it "a scam . . . absolutely disgusting."

When Cleland resigned from the board, the families again appealed to have their own representative, nominating Kristen Breitweiser (one of the bereaved Jersey Girls). They were to be disappointed. Instead, Bob Kerrey was chosen.

Kerrey was an advisory panel member for the Committee for the Liberation of Iraq, a propaganda front for the Project for the New American Century. He was also a proven war criminal involved in the slaughter of twenty-one Vietnamese civilians in 1969.

Overall, the commission staff contained no one capable of independently assessing evidence, or with the requisite experience to conduct a proper investigation. There were no scientists, no engineers, no independent intelligence experts. Instead the commission staff was filled with employees and close associates of the government, military, White House, FBI, and FAA—the very people whose actions were being investigated.

The team was assembled, and the message from the White House clearly received. Before they even started, Vice Chairman Hamilton said that the focus of the commission would be on the future, and that they weren't interested in trying to assess blame.

How could a commission into the events of 9/11 focus on the future? How could you be sure that no one was to blame for a catastrophic disaster, even before you had started looking into it? President Bush had agreed to authorize the commission solely on the condition that its remit was to report on how to prevent such attacks in the future. With the 9/11 Commission members chosen, not only would blame be avoided—any information contradictory to the official account of the attacks could now be sidelined, ignored, and disposed of.

Hearings

The commission interviewed 1,200 people and reviewed 2.5 million pages of documents. In its public hearings, it took testimony from 160 witnesses. That sounds thorough. But the commissioners called no hostile witnesses, no skeptics, no one outside their sphere of belief. They didn't invite FBI whistleblower Colleen Rowley (who shared *Time*'s Person of the Year award in 2002), so didn't hear testimony about prior intelligence on 9/11 being actively stalled by the FBI. Commissioners often allowed those giving testimony to be accompanied by minders—something no court would ever allow. The Bush White House insisted on having a Justice Department official present during interviews with all federal employees. These are pure kangaroo court tactics.

Organizations such as the FBI and CIA, who provided false or misleading information (or withheld information altogether) were sparingly chastised. The CIA, Justice Department and Department of Defense were publicly castigated by the Commission for not providing documents they had requested, but that was the end of the matter.

The commission formed nine investigative teams. The first investigation was called al-Qaeda and the Organization of the 9/11 Attack, so the truth of what had happened had already been assumed and accepted. What should have been a potential conclusion was instead right at the beginning. No alternate narratives were allowed.

The clock was run down in every way possible. Bush administration employees significantly delayed things as basic as the issuing of security clearances to staff on the commission, while insisting that the report must be completed by May 2004. Because of these delays, by the time commission staff were fully cleared and able to start work in the middle of 2003, they had less than a year to complete the report.

President Bush and Vice President Cheney initially refused to meet the 9/11 commission at all, then haggled over terms before finally agreeing to meet the commissioners, but only in private, with Cheney accompanying Bush, with no notes taken, no transcript of the session allowed, and no public record of any kind issued. Neither of them would testify under oath. Most questions were submitted to the White House prior to their appearance.

People who are telling the truth do not act this way.

Two commissioners took the testimony so seriously that they had to leave early for other engagements.

Having done everything possible to avoid meeting with the 9/11 Commission at all, Bush seemed to feel vindicated by his appearance. After testifying, he said, "I'm glad I did it, I'm glad I took the time."

Condoleezza Rice's testimony, also initially opposed by the White House, was pure filibuster. Every sentence twisted the truth to her own needs and presented a reality that can only have existed in her mind. Rice knew there was a time limit to her testimony, and took every opportunity to run the clock down. When presented with an opportunity for contrition, sorrow, or an apology, Rice had only bluster and wind. It's hard not to conclude, reading her testimony, that this was a woman who did not give a damn about the people who died.

Victims' relatives provided the most damning and insightful testimony of all. Mindy Kleinberg (one of the Jersey Girls) summed up the situation when she testified, saying, "It has been said that the intelligence agencies have to be right one hundred percent of the time and the terrorists only have to get lucky once [but] the 9/11 terrorists were not just lucky once. They were lucky over and over again."

The commission's public hearings were regularly interrupted by angry members of the public demanding more rigorous questioning of those testifying. One man yelled that he wanted to hear about the war games and was dragged out by security. The war games were ignored. That particular hearing threatened to turn into a riot.

There is a spectacular disconnect between Rudy Giuliani's image abroad and that in the US, where he has been and remains a hugely polarizing figure. Nowhere was this more evident than in his appearance at the public hearings of the 9/11 Commission on May 19, 2004. The testimony of "America's Mayor" was marked by booing, abuse, and continued interruptions by family members of victims of the attacks, who called the softball questioning a joke. The commission cut the hearings short after listening to Giuliani's testimony without asking a single probing question.

Some commissioners later found that when they tried to review transcripts from the inquiry, they didn't have clearance to do so, even though they had served on the inquiry itself and read all the material previously. Tortuous arrangements were made to keep simple information away from public view.

In November 2002, Chairman Kean agreed to restrictions imposed by the White House on access to Presidential Daily Briefings (PDBs), such as the one President Bush had received in early August of 2001, entitled "bin Laden Determined to Strike in US." Under the deal, only three of the commissioners could see the briefings, in a guarded room, and only after the White House had been allowed to edit them. Their notes were also subject to censorship by the White House, and the commissioners who read the briefs could not subsequently discuss the information with the other commissioners. Resigning from the commission in protest, Max Cleland called the deal a national scandal.

The FBI went to great lengths to try to prevent several key witnesses from testifying before the 9/11 Commission, including the informant who had lived with two of the terrorists. Those who were likely to provide testimony that would have been embarrassing for the US and Saudi governments were not allowed to testify. Each agency, be it the White House, CIA or FBI (and others) had a corner to defend. Co-operation with the 9/11 Commission was limited and grudging. The idea that the commission would form a complete and independent view of the attacks was fantasy.

What is most striking about the 9/11 Commission is how overtly political an exercise it was. When what was required most was a legal approach, instead the commission was narrowly defined, poorly led, given little time and budget, and staffed with people who had no right to be considered for such a position.

Late in January 2004, the 9/11 Commission asked for more time to complete their report, but were initially rebuffed, with the White House citing an unprecedented amount of cooperation as one reason the inquiry's conclusion could not be delayed. Under different circumstances this statement would be amusing, since the White House had done everything possible to stymie the inquiry.

The Report

A central basis for the 9/11 Commission's conclusions was the unseen testimony of men like Khalid Sheikh Mohammed. NBC found that 441 (over a quarter) of the 1,700 footnotes in the commission's report referenced evidence given by Mohammed, who only began cooperating after being tortured, was water boarded 183 times in a month and told his son would be killed if he didn't talk. Mohammed later told the Red Cross that he had made up things in order to stop the torture. As such, Mohammed's testimony and the subsequent conclusions drawn from it are highly suspect, and put a large hole in the credibility of the 9/11 Commission's already porous conclusions.

The notorious unreliability of evidence given under torture, acknowledged by the US government and universally accepted, means that the key reference point for much of the information used in forming the 9/11 Commission report's conclusions is fundamentally flawed.

The preponderance of the report's conclusions based on torture-induced testimony were in the chapters (5–7) that dealt with the al-Qaeda 9/11 plot. Yet the commission staff were not allowed to meet or question the detainees (or even their interrogators) in order to gain a level of satisfaction that the testimony was accurate or true. They had to just rely on what the CIA told them their detainees had said. And of course, the CIA destroyed their own torture tapes, so we don't even have that option to pursue.

The commission's report, due to be released in January 2004, was delayed six months as staff debated with the White House as to what could and could not be released. As the Commission drew its proceedings to a close, final adjustments were required before the public could see the conclusions, a process characterized as having been made amid discord and tension, most notably from commission members towards the leaders of the group. It became clear that Executive Director Philip Zelikow, in particular, was making major last minute changes and removing key elements of the report, without consulting anyone else on the commission.

By the time Zelikow was through, the report had been thoroughly excised. What was publicly released in July 2004 has been described as an "ad hoc document, absent any critical or complete examination of facts."

The commission's mandate had been to provide the fullest possible account of the events on and surrounding 9/11. But although the commission report is a weighty tome (clocking in at 571 pages) many have focused on what isn't there, rather than what is. For example, the report barely mentioned the extensive war games on 9/11 and, amazingly, didn't mention the collapse of World Trade Center Building 7 at all (media and commission aversion to even mentioning the collapse of 7 WTC is perhaps why polls have found that nearly half of all Americans are entirely unaware of the building and its collapse).

The Bush administration even censored information on Saudi Arabia that was in the public domain and widely known. One staff member, Dana Leseman, was found to have taken a copy of the redacted pages from the congressional report in order to follow up leads relating to Saudi Arabia. Zelikow fired her.

Given the lack of critical assessment done by the various commissions, 9/11 has been called the largest and least-investigated homicide in American history. Despite the passage of time, much of the evidence uncovered during the 9/11 Commission investigation remains classified. Vitally important evidence, such as:

- The flight manifests for the four hijacked planes, the boarding card details of the hijackers, their seat numbers and most video footage of their movements through US airports on 9/11.
- Cockpit recordings from flights 93 and 77 (93's recording was played in private to some victims relatives).
- Confiscated security video footage of the crash at the Pentagon.

It's hard to imagine what national security priority this continued secrecy now serves, and much easier to see how this withheld information stops the official story from being exposed to the gaping holes that blight it.

The 9/11 Commission's starting point was essentially "we know what happened and who did it, now we're going to find out how and why." Positing anything as true before investigating it precludes one from finding out anything new. And that is exactly what happened. The commission's overall conclusion was that there was a systemic breakdown of intelligence, meaning that while everyone was on one level responsible, in practical terms no one was. The commission went out of its way, again and again, to exonerate those responsible for the greatest intelligence and security failure in history. Incredibly, not one single person was found to have been at fault.

The lead protagonists within the 9/11 Commission have for the most part spent the ensuing years complaining about withheld information and being lied to. The chairman, vice chairman, and legal counsel have all said that the commission was set up to fail. Co-Chairmen Thomas Kean and Lee Hamilton used a *New York Times* article in 2008 to denounce the CIA for lying and obstruction, and for destroying evidence that they had wanted to see.

The inquiry completely ignored or redacted any mention of intelligence from (or involvement by) foreign governments, despite the wealth of information we have. The only time Pakistan was mentioned in the report was to praise it for its support in the War on Terror, and to recommend ever-increased funding and foreign aid. Amazingly, despite the wealth of evidence tying the government of Saudi Arabia to 9/11 and Osama bin Laden, the report concluded that no Saudi government institutions or senior Saudi individuals funded al-Qaeda.

On the successful (from the Bush administration's perspective) conclusion of the commission, Zelikow was promoted to the Foreign Intelligence Advisory Board.

In the future, those wishing to find a template for an independent and free inquiry can use the 9/11 Commission as the ultimate example of what not to do. Every aspect of the commission, from its delay, funding, staffing, lines of inquiry, omissions and results, are transparently a half-baked farce, designed to come to a series of pre-set conclusions, with embarrassing or contradictory information censored, buried, or ignored. The commission was a whitewash, a betrayal of those who died on 9/11, and of America.

Christopher Hitchens used to say that the only evidence he found of the possibility that Jesus Christ existed was the cover-up and lies around Christ's story. Lies, when exposed, show a great deal about the truth behind them. Above and beyond all the physical evidence refuting the official 9/11 story, the lengths to which the US government and its agencies went to deny physics, obscure the facts, and lie is the smoking gun to beat them all.

PART FOUR

THE AGE OF TERROR

CHAPTER THIRTEEN

THE DISAPPEARANCE
OF DISSENT

The Media

Maintaining and exploiting the official 9/11 story for political gain relied hugely on the complicity of the media. On the morning of 9/11, CNN was the first to mention Osama bin Laden. By sundown the media were all agreed— only bin Laden, operating on dialysis from a cave in distant Afghanistan, had the wherewithal to carry out the attacks.

It's a rule of thumb that the first twenty-four hours after a major event often provide the most untarnished and illuminating information in the media. Live coverage often produces footage directly contradicting the party line that is subsequently established and rigidly adhered to. On 9/11, almost all of those near or inside the twin towers reported multiple explosions; those near the Pentagon said they saw no evidence of a plane; and first responders who accessed the crash site in Shanksville said they saw no plane or bodies at all. Dan Rather said the collapse of World Trade Center Building 7 looked exactly like a controlled demolition. Yet within a very short space of time, these details were airbrushed from America's television sets, and a very different story was told.

The media was also an integral weapon in the silencing of dissent, as the Bush administration belligerently responded to the attacks. America's television news in 2002 and 2003 began to resemble the sort of propaganda we are more used to seeing from Russia and China. The ease of this manipulation is hardly surprising given the corporate control over virtually all print and screen media in the United States.

Media ownership in America has not always been concentrated. Eighty percent of newspapers in the US were independently owned in 1945. Today, just six corporations own 90 percent of the media seen by the American public's eyes.

In fact, far from acting as skeptical investigators, most of the American media acted as cheerleaders for the new War on Terror (a phrase first used by President Bush on September 20, 2001). The Bush administration directly asked media organizations to refrain from covering certain issues, using the circular argument that as the nation was at war, questioning the administration's conduct was unpatriotic. Almost without exception, the media complied.

Dissent was quickly crushed, and examples made of dissenters. Columnist Dan Guthrie of the *Daily Courier* in Oregon wrote a column criticizing President Bush's actions on 9/11. Tom Gutting, an editor at the *Texas City Sun*, published an article critical of Bush's judgment. Both found themselves out of a job.

On September 14, 2001, the *Washington Post* carried a savage editorial, calling for the suppression of democratic and civil rights, and the permanent transformation of domestic and foreign policy, sacrificing privacy, freedom of movement or other liberties to the needs of domestic security.

So began one of the most disgraceful periods of across-the-board media failure in American history. The press became a slavish mouthpiece for the government. Editors and journalists who toed the line were rewarded with scoops and access to those at the top of the political tree. Those who asked questions were fired. This created a culture of fear and compliance within the US media, one that has far from dissipated to this day.

With very few exceptions, questions about the events of 9/11 disappeared altogether. On the first anniversary of the attacks, the *New York Times* wrote that "one year later, the public knows less about the circumstances of 2,801 deaths at the foot of Manhattan in broad daylight than people in 1912 knew within weeks about the Titanic." Despite this complaint, the *New York Times* did not change its overall approach to this most sacrosanct of events.

A Police State

Not one person in the White House or the Bush administration appears to have been censured or demoted, let alone fired, due to the failings that allowed 9/11 to happen. In fact, it's hard to find evidence that any single person in any government position paid any price at all for the biggest intelligence failure in US history. No one in government resigned, no one apologized—not even to the victims' families, with the exception of Richard Clarke. Clarke's emotional statement included the words "your government failed you . . . and I failed you," a sentiment made all the more poignant by its absence elsewhere. Thousands died, and not one of the people responsible for protecting them was held accountable.

There are, however, a great many examples of firings of those who spoke out, questioned the Bush administration, or generally acted in a way not entirely in step with the accepted narrative, or the goals and mission of the War on Terror.

All the hallmarks of a police state began to manifest themselves. Mass and arbitrary arrests, especially of immigrants and people with the wrong background, the use of torture, disinformation and propaganda designed to cause fear within the populace, a new office of Homeland Security, huge erosions of basic civil liberties and the relaxing or abandonment of many of the constraints law enforcement agencies had on intrusion into public and civic life. 9/11 justified them all. Francis Boyle, an international law professor at the University of Illinois called it a coup d'état against the United States Constitution.

Around 1,200 Muslims were detained as part of the criminal investigation into 9/11, yet two months later federal authorities admitted they had not found any evidence against any of the people arrested. Nearly all were released without charge.

All of US polity united. Wildly unconstitutional laws were passed without a single vote against. Dissent was not tolerated, and anyone who did so was crushed. Legendary CBS anchorman Dan Rather tried valiantly to keep the spirit of journalism alive, in times that were not conducive to such a career move. Rather, in typical fashion, summed things up succinctly. "There was a time in South Africa that people would put flaming tires around people's necks if they dissented. And in some ways the fear is that you will be necklaced here, you will have a flaming tire of 'lack of patriotism' put around your neck. Now it is that fear that keeps journalists from asking the toughest of tough questions."

A career of asking tough questions ended when Rather was unceremoniously sacked, ending forty-four years at CBS, following a story critical of President Bush's scant military service, and pressure from a shadowy right-wing PR group called Creative Response Concepts.

It was becoming very clear what happened to those asking such questions.

The world of academia was targeted. John McMurtry, a renowned philosophy professor at Guelph University in Canada, presented a paper called "Why is there a War in Afghanistan" in December 2001, one of the first academic papers to question aspects of the official 9/11 story. For his efforts, McMurtry was crucified. The redoubtable and normally sober *Wall Street Journal* called him Osama McMurtry, and Fox News and others followed suit. All criticism was aimed at McMurtry personally. None addressed the issues raised in his paper. McMurtry was reported to the FBI and CIA. The university president and McMurtry's department were flooded with emails and letters, all attacking McMurtry for his temerity, and demanding that he be fired. The university bravely retained McMurtry, but the message was clear—deviate from the established line and expect the full throttle of the state's ire. Academics across America took note.

It remains remarkable how little academic or serious critique has been made of 9/11 when so many people have so many questions about the events of that day. Academics and scholars can produce papers questioning the conduct of the Bush administration, the prosecution of the Iraq war or the intelligence failures that led to 9/11, but to actually question the fundamental tenet of 9/11, that America was attacked without warning by nineteen Arab men funded by Osama bin Laden, remains beyond the pale, and a seriously poor career move.

The arts were censored. On the radio, songs were blacklisted. Clear Channel sent a memo to their 1,200 radio stations suggesting 165 songs that were now deemed to contain inappropriate lyrics. The list of banned songs would be comedic, were it not so frightening. "Rock the Casbah" by the Clash. "Imagine" by John Lennon. Because of an Islamic-inspired terror attack, suddenly "Ticket to Ride" by the Beatles was not an acceptable song to play on an American radio station.

Typically, those censored provided some of the most incisive critiques of the absurd new rules. When all songs by Rage against the Machine were deemed (by Clear Channel) questionable, the band was so outraged that (estimable guitarist) Tom Morello was obliged to put out a statement.

"[We are] diametrically opposed to the kind of horrible violence committed against innocent people, which we condemn in the strongest possible terms . . . if our songs are 'questionable' in any way, it is in that they encourage people to question the kind of ignorance that breeds intolerance—intolerance which can lead to censorship and the extinguishing of our civil liberties, or at its extremes can lead to the kind of violence we witnessed."

In March 2003, less than a week before the Iraq war began, Natalie Maines, the lead singer of the Dixie Chicks, said onstage in London that they were ashamed that their president was from Texas. The reaction was instantaneous. Radio stations banned the playing of their songs; supporters of President Bush held rallies and burned Dixie Chicks CDs. They were publicly called traitors, Saddam's Angels, and Dixie Sluts. It was all indicative of a very frightening time.

It's interesting to note the thin skin on display here. In normal times, political dissent is part of a functioning society, and robust debate is allowed, even encouraged. If the Bush administration was confident of its version of the events of 9/11 and their response to the attacks, they could have let it stand or fall in the court of reasonable public debate. Why was it so important that media, academia, and the arts all be so severely censored in the years following 9/11? Why was dissent so harshly treated?

When the low-budget movie *The Interview* came out in 2014, North Korea threatened to launch a nuclear missile at the US. This disproportionate response served only to illustrate the governing regime's pathetic weakness, given that the country was being attacked by a stoner movie with some weak gags. People who are confident of themselves don't act this way.

When control proved not enough, government propaganda took over. The Bush administration actively played a part in not just ensuring media compliance, but writing the news themselves. Donald Rumsfeld secretly established a new Office of Strategic Influence (OSI) shortly after 9/11, whose role was to plant fake news stories in the foreign press and take other secret measures to manipulate public opinion. Many suspect their work was not confined to the press overseas. When the office's existence was leaked, Rumsfeld quickly declared it closed, but no evidence was provided to corroborate his claim. Rumsfeld was probably lying. Defense Secretary Rumsfeld is also known to have continued to create new agencies and positions tasked with information warfare, deliberately blurring the lines between factual information and propagandistic lies.

A fevered atmosphere began pervading America's twenty-four-hour television news cycles, with color-coded terror alert levels, and wall-to-wall coverage that elevated the slightest concern to a screeching fever pitch. Department of Homeland Security chief Tom Ridge disagreed with the political manipulation of color-coded terror, and was replaced by Michael Chertoff, who had no such qualms.

Supporters of the Bush administration repeated the same lines over and over, and over again, creating a siren staccato of lies. The situation, they told us, was absolutely intolerable—an existential threat to the very survival of the United States. Implausible as it now sounds, opinions were repeatedly aired in the media saying that America faced times infinitely more dangerous than at any moment in World War II or the Cold War.

Pronouncements from senior Bush officials reached Orwellian levels of mendacity. John Ashcroft said critics of the administration's actions were fearmongers who "scare peace-loving people with phantoms of lost liberty, and aid terrorists."

Americans of all walks and persuasions got used to a new idea. Criticizing the government was unpatriotic, and could be dangerous to your health.

Questioning aspects of the 9/11 story should not even have been considered dissent. To ask questions is the media's role, and to demand the truth is the true nature of the patriot. Unquestioningly accepting every assertion made by the duplicitous Bush administration was in fact a gross betrayal of the American people.

Overseas, the querying of the 9/11 story did not come from outliers or the insane. Helmut Schmidt, former chancellor of Germany, said that there was no proof that Osama bin Laden was behind the attacks. Francesco Cossiga, a former Italian prime minister, said the attacks could not be accomplished without infiltrations in the radar and flight security personnel. Around the world, many respectable and mainstream organizations and people publicly doubted the official story. This was especially prevalent in the Arab world, which while undoubtedly anti-American, had much more experience of state terrorism than America.

Overall, a world average of polls taken in 2008 suggested only 46 percent thought al-Qaeda was behind the attacks. One survey in Germany suggested nearly a quarter of the people there thought the US government ordered the attacks themselves.

CHAPTER FOURTEEN

FROM 2002 TO 2003

Anthrax

Because of the spectacular nature of the events of September 11, the subsequent anthrax attacks are often overshadowed; forgotten. But the mailing of deadly anthrax powder to various unfortunate recipients in the months that followed 9/11 played a crucial role in maintaining the febrile atmosphere that enveloped the US. This time of national frenzy precluded normal levels of scrutiny and oversight, allowing the passage of previously unthinkable legislation, and the setting of the War on Terror agenda.

The terrifying anthrax attacks that kept the US public in a constant state of fear through late 2001 are so vital a part of the tale that the entire period should be remembered together, as the September 11 and anthrax terrorist attacks of 2001.

As Donald Rumsfeld and others issued dark and apocalyptic warnings about all manner of chemical and biological attacks that might befall America, Dick Cheney and senior White House staff curiously started being given Cipro, the antibiotic used to treat anthrax, on the night of September 11.

Even more strangely, the advice to take Cipro came from Jerome Hauer, the Managing Director of Kroll Associates, the company that had handled security at the World Trade Center. Hauer knew what he was talking about—he was also a member of the army medical center where it's likely the anthrax attacks originated.

By any definition, the anthrax mailings were terrorism, the first biological terrorist attack of the twenty-first century. Anthrax is a potent biological weapon, because it only takes a very small amount to infect a large number of people. The mailing of deadly powder meant that you didn't need to be in a major US city to fear terrorism, it could strike anywhere. Suddenly a trip to the mailbox became a fearful event. America, already on edge, was kept there by anthrax.

The tactic of using small amounts of anthrax to scare an entire population was very effective. Everyone in America has a mailbox, and suddenly all Americans felt exposed to the possibility of becoming a victim of this frighteningly immediate new world of biological terrorism. Suppliers of gas masks and survival gear ran out of stock.

Anthrax-laden letters helped legitimize the politics of hysteria, smoothing the road to war with Iraq and effectively shutting down Congress as a meaningful mechanism of moderation over the White House.

Had it not been for anthrax, the US public might have been in more of a mood to question the stripping of so many rights from their previously inviolate Constitution. What's worse is that these changes, presented as emergency measures when first passed, hardened into law under President Obama.

The Recipients

The first anthrax letters (filled with spores of the bacteria, which cause exposed people to get the disease anthrax) were mailed on September 18, 2001, just a week after 9/11. On October 5, Bob Stevens, photo editor of the *Sun* newspaper, died after a brief and mysterious illness. The *Sun* was a relatively insignificant supermarket tabloid based in Florida, whose main transgression to date had been to publish unflattering reports on the behavior and substance abuse of President Bush's daughters.

Stevens' doctor did not initially considered anthrax as a cause of his illness. After all, in the entire twentieth century there had only been eighteen anthrax inhalation cases in the US, and most of those were from farm workers exposed to animals with anthrax. However, Ernesto Blanco (one of Stevens' colleagues) also tested positive, and the panic began. Stevens was diagnosed on October 3, and died two days later. Terror once again gripped America.

Stevens' editor was Mike Irish, whose wife Gloria was the real estate agent who found apartments for four of the 9/11 hijackers in Florida. Given the odds of finding a connection between these people in a country of 350 million people, one has to consider the possibility that Stevens or Irish were targeted so as to create a connection between the 9/11 hijackers and the anthrax, made more plausible by the Bush administration's concerted effort to blame the anthrax attacks on Osama bin Laden and his al-Qaeda agents in America.

Incidentally, Stevens' wife subsequently sued the US government for negligence, claiming that she could use DNA evidence to show that the anthrax strain had come from the US army facility at Fort Detrick (of which Jerome

Hauer was a member). The government settled the suit and paid her $2.5 million. Her allegation remains untested.

In total, seven letters containing anthrax were mailed. Recipients included NBC, the *New York Post*, Senator Tom Daschle (D-South Dakota) and Senator Patrick Leahy (D-Vermont). The media received the first batch of letters, the senators a second wave.

The total dead was five, with around twenty sickened (some think higher, but mild anthrax symptoms are often not noticed). Two of the dead were postal workers in Washington. The last victim was a ninety-four-year-old widow living alone in Connecticut.

The two letters (that were recovered) accompanying the anthrax were very similar, and contained crude "death to America, death to Israel, Allah is Great, etc." messages, clearly either from a Muslim fundamentalist or designed to be seen as such. All were dated "09/11/01," although Middle Easterners normally write the date with the day first, followed by the month.

Given that we now know the attacks originated from within the US military, the only explanation for the anthrax being accompanied by letters purporting to be from Muslim fundamentalists is that those behind the anthrax terrorism were trying to pin the blame on Osama bin Laden and al-Qaeda.

The timing of the attacks was key. Military action commenced in Afghanistan just two days after Robert Stevens died. The USA Patriot Act was passed nineteen days later, at the peak of the anthrax panic.

It can be assumed that the postal workers and ageing widow were unfortunate collateral damage, in the wrong place at the wrong time. But the high profile recipients—media outlets and prominent politicians—suggest the attacks were meant as both terrorism and explicit warnings, aimed at ensuring no dissenting voices got in the way of the Bush administration's goals. The media in particular was served notice that only complete compliance would now be tolerated, and embraced that ethic.

Senators Daschle and Leahy were prominent Democrats, critical of the Bush administration's initial response to 9/11, and holding up the passage of the Patriot Act due to their profound ethical concerns as to its content. The first draft of the Patriot Act suspended habeas corpus and a number of fundamental democratic and constitutional principles. But following the anthrax-laden letter mailed to his office, Daschle got calls from both President Bush and Vice President Cheney, urging him to drop his opposition to the bill. Daschle dutifully complied.

On October 16 (ten days before the Patriot Act was passed) the Senate was shut, then the entire House of Representatives. The mechanics of government had successfully been shut down.

The Reaction

Initially, a great deal of political noise (amplified by the media) was made by the Bush administration suggesting that the attacks might be being carried out by al-Qaeda. President Bush himself said that he could not guarantee the anthrax did not come from Osama bin Laden.

However, the *New York Times* and *Washington Post* published opinion pieces suggesting that, of all places, Iraq was the most likely source of the anthrax attacks. Despite a total lack of evidence for these claims, both articles urged the US government not to wait on proof before considering a response. For the Bush administration, these reports were political gold. Suddenly the focus could shift from bin Laden and Afghanistan to America's nemesis in the Middle East, who had for some reason chosen this exact moment to launch this curious form of terror attack within US borders.

ABC News' Brian Ross spent a full week in October 2001 telling America that bentonite had been found in the anthrax, that this was a clear sign of Iraq's involvement, and that this information had come from sources within the government. Many leading academics called on ABC to reveal their sources for the story, to no avail. The reports were entirely false, and it remains unclear who fed ABC the bentonite information.

The government scare machine moved into overdrive. A coordinated campaign of fear, lies, and misinformation was conducted, specifically to take advantage of the fevered atmosphere that the anthrax had kept at boiling point. John Ashcroft warned of crop-dusting planes becoming weapons of mass destruction in the wrong hands. In November, Bush warned that America's enemies were seeking not just chemical and biological weapons, but nuclear weapons too. John McCain told David Letterman that the anthrax probably came from Iraq. White house officials repeatedly pressed FBI director Robert Mueller to prove that the anthrax attacks were in fact a second-wave international terrorist assault.

Over the following year, President Bush repeatedly linked the anthrax attacks to the regime of Saddam Hussein. Through 2002 and the early part of 2003, anthrax and Iraq became inseparable in the nation's media dialogue. In his State of the Union address of January 2002 (four months after 9/11, a speech in which Bush did not mention Osama bin Laden by name once), Bush carefully parsed his words in a manner clearly designed to put Iraq, terrorism, and anthrax together in American minds.

This was nothing if not effective. Polls showed large proportions of Americans thought Iraq was behind the anthrax, and involved in the 9/11 attacks. They had not all collectively become mistaken. This was the intended result of a broad political and media campaign.

When Colin Powell went to the United Nations in February 2003 to make the case for war with Iraq, he dramatically held up a vial of white powder. Less than a teaspoon of anthrax had closed the US Senate in 2001, he said, but Iraq (he alleged) could have produced twenty-five thousand liters. Citing the confession of Ibn al-Shaykh al-Libi, a Libyan who had been captured fighting for the Taliban in Afghanistan (and who had been rendered to a secret prison in Egypt—taken there in a coffin—and tortured in the presence of British agents), Powell asserted that there was a direct partnership between al-Qaeda and Saddam Hussein. This was a bare-faced lie.

The unfortunate al-Libi retracted his statement a year later (which he said had been made after being tortured by being locked in a small cage for eighty hours), before spending years being rendered to secret prisons around the world and finally being found dead in a Libyan cell in 2009. Shaker Aamer, Britain's last Guantanamo detainee, was present during al-Libi's interrogation at Bagram. This may explain why America was so reluctant to let Aamer and his embarrassing story leave the confines of Guantanamo.

Powell's speech has been called the most spectacular perjury in UN history. He later said the incident was a blot on his record, and admitted his information had been entirely wrong.

The anthrax attacks also provided the Bush administration with an excuse to further delay and counter the clamor for an investigation into 9/11. Bush said on a number of occasions that an investigation would damage his administration's prosecution of the War on Terror. The anthrax attacks had come at the ideal time (from the Bush administration's point of view) to further their domination over the political mechanics of the nation, and over a population terrified beyond their wits by the threat of domestic terrorism in the mail.

The Grade

Anthrax can enter the body through cuts or eating infected food, but it is most deadly when inhaled. Ninety percent of people who breathe in anthrax will die. However, in a natural environment, anthrax spores clump together and don't float in the air. Infection is extremely rare.

Weaponized anthrax is different, and comes in the form of an incredibly fine dust. Weaponized spores are made to be the right size to be inhaled by a human, and coated, so as not to clump together. Once released in a contained environment, the dust is pervasive, spreading quickly. Tom Daschle's entire office had to be decontaminated after his secretary opened the envelope with anthrax inside of it.

Just eight thousand spores need to be inhaled to constitute a deadly dose. The anthrax used in the 2001 attacks was refined to a trillion spores per gram (a grade that even the US government denied it had the technology to produce). The tested anthrax spores were found to have been made with highly sophisticated milling techniques. They were coated with silica, which is unique to US laboratories.

Given the Bush administration's relentless focus on the weapons of mass destruction allegedly developed and held by the regime of Saddam Hussein, it is irony of the worst kind that the main repository of weaponized anthrax in the world was, in fact, the US. Events in 2015, in which American anthrax was mistakenly mailed around the world to other governments and armies, serve further to illustrate the hypocrisy of America's frantic but false concern that Saddam Hussein might weaponize chemicals, while maintaining the world's largest stockpile of this biological weapon.

Embarrassingly, not only did the strain of anthrax used in 2001 point toward government involvement, but the very existence of weaponized anthrax contravenes US law and the biological weapons treaties to which America is a signatory. American military labs had been claiming for years that this was not something they worked on any more.

Some countries do legitimately conduct research on biological weapons, and could perhaps justify holding weaponized anthrax so as to develop counter-measures for their own civilians and troops. However, as the largest user of chemical and biological (and nuclear) weapons in human history, it would be naïve to suggest an entirely benign reason for America stockpiling this deadly and outlawed weapon.

The 2001 letters contained a particular type of anthrax, known as the Ames strain. It is estimated that around twenty laboratories in the US held the Ames strain, but only four had the technology to weaponize it. The main one was at Fort Detrick, Maryland. No other nation had refined the Ames strain to that extent. This meant that no matter who was sending it, the anthrax used in the attacks had to have come from inside the US.

The decision to use the Ames strain was a strange one, since once discovered it was all but impossible for the government and FBI to continue with the claim that the attacks had originated overseas. Ames was an American strain, and virtually impossible for people outside the military to get their hands on.

Either Fort Detrick, the laboratories at Battelle Memorial Institute, or Dugway Proving Ground (which had existing stores and worked closely with US intelligence agencies) were almost definitely the source.

Manmade anthrax strains normally carry a distinctive signature, so it's possible to work out exactly which batch any sample comes from. It should have been very easy to pinpoint the exact source of the anthrax used in the attacks.

However, best avenues of investigation encountered strange behavior. On October 10 or 11, 2001, following a phone call from the FBI, the University of Iowa (which had a comprehensive collection of every known strain of anthrax) destroyed its entire stock. Had the samples remained, it would likely have been possible to discover the exact batch of the Ames strain which had been sent to the media and senators, and also the paper trail revealing who had been using or moving that strain in the weeks before the anthrax attacks. Why would the FBI, tasked with solving the crime, choose to get the main holders of anthrax samples to destroy their stocks?

At the end of 2001, as the use of the Ames strain became more widely known, the Bush administration changed tack, abandoning its claims of Iraqi or bin Laden-inspired terror, and going with that most favored of options—the lone nut theory.

The Source

Despite the fevered and unquestioning media atmosphere, answers were still required as to where the anthrax had come from, who had sent it and why.

As with so many events surrounding 9/11, someone had considered the possibility of an anthrax mail terror attack before. In 1999, William Patrick, a US army microbiologist (who had invented the process of weaponizing anthrax), wrote a report discussing how to deal with an anthrax terrorist attack in the mail. His paper was extraordinarily prescient, suggesting a dose of 2.5 grams per envelope (the attacks used around two grams). The report was classified, but available to those working with anthrax.

The list of potential sources of the anthrax was very small. Around 200 scientists had worked on the US government anthrax program in the previous five years, but the number with both the practical experience and the access required was less than fifty.

Initially, the perpetrator was identified by the FBI as former army researcher Steven Hatfill, in a report leaked conveniently to the media. Hatfill was subjected to the barbarous personal disintegration tactics that a combination of politicians with an agenda and a compliant media offered. He was harassed with a campaign of political intimidation and media lies, including leaks about his medical records. He was tailed constantly by the FBI, and his home was raided.

However, the case against Hatfill was beyond flimsy, and the evidence non-existent. When it became clear that the identity of the government official leaking information and lies about Hatfill to the media was about to be exposed, the allegations were quickly dropped, and Hatfill was given $5.8 million in damages.

Given that the idea of an orchestrated terror campaign emanating from within the United States military simply could not be contemplated, the lone nut theory, so beloved by those explaining inconvenient events to a docile public, was eventually invoked. The troubled loner story is regularly used to deflect blame from larger conspiracies. From Oswald to Hinckley, a single madman can be used to explain events that otherwise prove too disturbing to contemplate.

All they needed now was to find the one loose cannon that fit. And it took a while.

On August 6, 2008, the FBI finally named microbiologist Bruce Ivins as having been responsible. Ivins was purportedly disgruntled, and had worked at the Army's bio-defense laboratories in Fort Detrick, Maryland. He was an elite government scientist, and among the nation's top experts on anthrax. The case against him looked plausible. Best of all, he was dead.

Conveniently, the FBI announced that they had their man just eight days after Ivins had committed suicide. Ivins was emotionally unstable, and had become more so after being subject to aggressive FBI surveillance. They questioned him at home and at work, and parked day and night outside his house. They even questioned his children. The final straw appears to have been when Ivins learned that the FBI was about to file criminal charges against him in relation to the attacks.

Ivins' death meant he could not defend himself, and the FBI allegations would never be tested in a court of law. Which is lucky, as the FBI have not made public any evidence in relation to their allegations. The case was as good as closed before it began.

However, from the start, the FBI case against Ivins was as flimsy as theirs had been against Hatfill. Despite assurances to the contrary, there was no motive, no gain, very little opportunity and no prior history of behavior that suggested a reason why this scientist might have suddenly decided that right after 9/11 was the time to mail deadly materials to politicians and the media. There was no evidence of a kind that would stand up in a court of law. The allegations were circumstantial, and the logic of the FBI's claims was often ludicrous. So dubious was the case that the *Washington Post*, *New York Times* and *Wall Street Journal* expressed serious doubts, and called for an independent investigation.

Nature magazine published an article called "Case Not Closed." Ivins' attorney Paul Kemp said that all that had been presented was heaps of innuendo, and a staggering lack of real evidence. Dr. Alan Pearson (the respected Director of the Biological and Chemical Weapons Control Program at the Center for Arms Control and Non-Proliferation) called for a full independent investigation.

The media stepped in to help. Various newspapers published uncorroborated leaks from unnamed government sources, designed to convict Ivins in the eyes of the public. ABC ran one of a number of stories in the television media featuring anonymously sourced claims about Bruce Ivins. While the FBI claimed that the anthrax strain alleged to have been used could be traced to Ivins, no evidence was shown to that effect. Ivins didn't work with or have access to the powdered form of anthrax—just the liquid form. His colleagues testified that he didn't have the laboratory skills to make the fine weaponized anthrax that was used. They were unanimous in giving extremely positive character references for Ivins, and outspoken in their belief that he had been framed. Anyone knowing the slightest thing about anthrax would have known not to use their own batch. It didn't seem to make sense.

The characterization of Bruce Ivins (who had no criminal record) as an unstable psychotic with violent tendencies was based on the claims of Jean Carol Duley, a recently graduated social worker with documented drug and alcohol issues. None of Ivins' co-workers corroborated her description of him.

One of the two intended Senate recipients of the letters (Patrick Leahy) stated in September 2008 he did not believe the FBI's case against Ivins, and that he felt there were others involved, who should be charged with murder.

But accusing a dead man worked on one level. Ivins was never charged, tried, or convicted. The government successfully palmed the story off onto a corpse, the media took the bait, and the whole story died.

After the Attacks

Like 9/11, we can't be sure how successful the anthrax attacks really were when we don't know the intentions of the attackers. What can't be excluded is the possibility that the anthrax attacks were meant to be much more widespread, longer, or more effective than the relatively short-term campaign and low level of casualties.

The FBI concluded that all evidence pointed to US government facilities and research laboratories being the source, yet the obvious conclusion—that rogue wings of army and/or government departments deliberately set out to create more terror to further their political and military goals—simply could not be countenanced in the mainstream media.

The attacks used weaponized materials produced and held solely by the US army and government. Surely the US army and government were, by any measure, the most obvious and prime suspect. Yet the FBI investigation took as its initial assumption that it was inconceivable that the attacks could have come from a group within the government and military. With this as their starting point, they searched in vain for years for an individual who would fit the bill. Finally, they found a dead man who they could paint as unstable using the normal tools of character assassination. From there it was all over, the public's tiny attention-span could be sated, and the case closed.

The Media Frenzy of 2002

Historians will look back at America's political and media frenzy, in the eighteen months from 9/11 to the invasion of Iraq, as a textbook example of how a seemingly mature Western democracy can be cajoled, through an orchestrated media propaganda campaign based on the endless repetition of key phrases, into such a state of collective fear that reason and logic entirely vacate the scene. The Bush administration bears direct responsibility for this bizarre period in American history, with the neoconservatives using an unquestioning media to ratchet up the pressure, week by week, day upon day, to the point where Americans seemed to entirely lose the ability to perceive anything beyond their own terror.

Although the behavior was irresponsible and highly propagandistic, much was so over the top that it seems laughable in retrospect.

The concentration of ownership of media in the United States is central to the continuation of political policies that have misinformed and impoverished the majority, and concentrated wealth in the hands of a very small number of people—including the rich people who own the media.

Captured by corporations, and deeply compromised by the Faustian trade between ratings and advertising revenue, television news in the US has long since ceased to perform any kind of investigative or truth-seeking role, but after the events of 9/11 the Bush administration made it clear that any trace of independent thought within mainstream journalism was unacceptable.

Anthrax letters sent to television networks made the blunt point that the media was directly in the firing line. On October 10, 2001, within days of the anthrax story breaking, Condoleezza Rice summoned the directors of all the major US TV networks (CBS, CNN, ABC, Fox, MSNBC), to remind them of their responsibilities in the reporting of news in the nascent War on Terror.

From now on, she made clear, to question the statements made by the Bush administration, or its actions, was to be deemed unpatriotic; treasonous in such a time of war.

Despite complaints of bias (from both sides of politics), the American media's primary role in times of perceived national emergency is not as gatekeepers seeking truth, but subservience to political power. One might have hoped that these media executives, when presented with a senior government official telling them that it was their responsibility to toe the line, would have haughtily declared that this was outrageous interference, and reminded Rice that it was their job to keep politicians honest. In fact, the reverse was the case. The message was taken on board. Investigative reporting could still take place, but the bar on what was now acceptable had been lowered considerably.

The idea that America was now in a time of war transformed normally sane media institutions into belligerent propagandists for the Bush administration's agenda. Insanity took hold.

The PR push (as some genuinely called it) for war with Iraq began in earnest in September 2002. Andrew Card, Bush's chief of staff, said the timing was because "from a marketing point of view, you don't introduce new products in August." The new product (trillions of dollars wasted, a country destroyed and a million dead) was to be sold to the public via the compliant broadcast media.

During the months leading up to the invasion, voicing the idea that America's new war may have been motivated by oil was to open oneself up for savage derision in the press. Bush said the war in Iraq was being waged to save civilization itself. How could someone make a statement like that and the entire room not just break out laughing?

One place America was no longer going to find truthful salvation is the media. CNN is owned by Time Warner, CBS by Viacom, NBC by General Electric, ABC by Disney. Given that General Electric are one of the world's largest manufacturers of weaponized drones, you are hardly going to hear a story critical of drone warfare on NBC's nightly news. In 1983 most US media was in the hands of just fifty corporations. Today that number is five.

You don't need to be a conspiracy theorist to believe that an interconnected web of power controls the flow of information in American society. A team at Sonoma State University conducted a study in 2010 that found just 118 people in total sat on the board of the ten largest US media giants, but that those 118 people collectively sat on the boards of a further 288 corporations. Defense contractors were well represented among the spread. Corporations, media, and defense are entwined. Major public relations companies with a history of doing government work providing propaganda stories that have been shown to be entirely untrue also have their executives sitting on media giant boards. Only a fool would expect the nightly news to be independent of this nexus.

The Scare Campaign

In the months after 9/11, and particularly during the lead up to the 2003 invasion of Iraq, the media began a seemingly endless 24/7 terror cycle, warning of terrifying new weapons that could be deployed in American cities at any moment.

Suddenly it seemed anyone with the intent could make a dirty bomb from materials found inside kitchen microwaves. For a while, dirty bombs were the terrifying new weapon du jour, but almost all evidence suggests that not only has one never been used in a terrorist attack anywhere in the world, the effect of the mildly radioactive materials used would not kill anyone nor make them sick.

Terrorists, we were told, might have access to portable nuclear weapons. The specter of nuclear terrorism was invoked again and again, without proof or reason. At one point in early 2003, George W. Bush explicitly warned Americans to keep enough food and bottled water in the house to be able to stay inside for three days.

The public were intimidated. Weeks after 9/11, Ari Fleischer famously said that all Americans "need to watch what they say; watch what they do".

The color-coding of terror on television was a particularly insidious means of telling people how scared they should be. Viewers got used to a small corner of their TV screens displaying a colored terror alert, designed (it seemed) to help Americans perceive how imminent a new attack might be, and presumably to then take action of some kind. Mostly, it kept the threat of terrorism in the front of everyone's mind.

It's easy to forget the dark days under the Bush administration, when terror was routinely used as a political weapon. Howard Dean, the left-leaning Governor of Vermont, said he was concerned that every time something happened that wasn't good for President Bush, he played his trump card, which was terrorism. The Bush administration used America's greatest tragedy as their most potent political tool. Terrorism, it has been wisely said, is not the bang—it's the fear of the bang. No one used that fear more malevolently than George W. Bush. By any rational definition, this made Bush a terrorist.

Drumbeats for the Iraq War

Nowhere was this more explicit than in the media campaign for war against Iraq. Iraq had not had any involvement in the events of 9/11 or the anthrax attacks, and had not issued any kind of threat against America. The Bush administration had invaded Afghanistan and blamed Osama bin Laden for the attacks. So invading Iraq and drumming up the necessary public support for such a war required a complete change of direction, and a media propaganda campaign without precedent.

The Bush administration's warnings about Iraq were a mixture of outright lies, partial untruths, old information, bad information, information gleaned from torture, and a purposeful blurring of the line between 9/11 and Iraq. Mostly it was just outright lies.

America's media didn't just parrot these lies, they amplified them. Huge holes in logic and fact were left unexamined, and print and broadcast media retreated into a narrow band of discussion that excluded the few dissenting voices who bravely sought to bring sanity to a world gone mad.

The buildup to the war took a long time. For months the drums beat ever louder, and the media campaign was a year-long blitz of misinformation and lies.

In October 2002, George W. Bush said that Iraq was reconstituting its nuclear weapons program. This was entirely untrue. Worse, Bush began making the most egregious and irresponsible links between his planned invasion of Iraq and a nuclear missile attack on the US mainland, despite Iraq possessing no nuclear arms or facilities. "Facing clear evidence of peril, we cannot wait for the final proof, the smoking gun that could come in the form of a mushroom cloud," he said. Again, a disingenuous lie, but taken up by Bush's White House colleagues at the same time, who fed it to the media, who in turn endlessly repeated it to the public. Suddenly Saddam Hussein was not some crank despot half a world away; he was the man who might nuke America. And who can argue with a president warning us of possible nuclear annihilation?

The US Center for Public Integrity published a report in 2008 showing that the eight most powerful figures in the Bush administration (including Cheney, Rice, Rumsfeld etc.) made a total of at least 935 false statements in the two years following 9/11 relating to the threat posed by Iraq, as part of an orchestrated campaign to mislead the public and take the nation to war. These people said unequivocally that Iraq had weapons of mass destruction or links to al-Qaeda on at least 532 occasions.

In fact, the regime of Saddam Hussein was profoundly hostile toward al-Qaeda. There were no links, either to al-Qaeda or to the events of 9/11.

Looking back on what US and British politicians said at the time is to see a toxic world of bluster and dishonesty that brooked no dissent. Those who questioned the wars and strategies were savagely castigated and torn to shreds in the media. Those advocating the party line look as if they were in some kind of parallel universe.

"This is Hitler in 1935," said Newt Gingrich on November 9, 2001. Iraq, he felt, was "a vastly greater threat to our cities than is Afghanistan." Interviewers failed to ask him why the focus had shifted so quickly from bin Laden and Afghanistan, who had attacked America on 9/11, to Iraq, which had not. Nor was there any query as to why Iraq had suddenly become such a vast and urgent threat.

The threat to America from Iraq was routinely characterized as being more than a military or terroristic one—the danger was in fact existential, a threat to the very survival of the United States.

In the run up to the 2003 Iraq invasion, Rupert Murdoch made his feelings known when he opined that war was not just unavoidable, it was desirable, as it would reduce the price of crude oil to $20 a barrel (the price actually went consistently up. By the time the war was through it was $140 a barrel). Murdoch described Bush as acting very morally, very correctly, and added that Tony Blair was being extraordinarily courageous.

Murdoch's News Corporation owns more than 175 newspaper titles, publishing more than forty million papers a week, with an even greater influence and reach in television. Despite consistent claims of editorial independence, it is well known that the dirty digger sets the agenda for his entire media empire. During this fraught period, there was no single example of a Murdoch paper taking an editorial line that went against his views. The *Sun* newspaper in England called those opposing the Iraq war "anti-American propagandists of the fascist left."

With the media acting as cheerleaders and an agenda that painted opposition to the Bush administration as unpatriotic, the Democratic Party collapsed entirely. All opposition vanished, and the normal checks and balances in America's democracy ceased to operate. Legislation which once would have been profoundly opposed was passed with unanimous backing from all sides.

Treason

On January 28, 2003, President George W. Bush gave his State of the Union speech, in which he said, "The British government has learnt that Saddam Hussein recently sought significant quantities of uranium from Africa." This was exposed as a lie by ambassador Joe Wilson, who had been sent to Niger specifically to find out if it was true.

When Wilson saw the State of the Union speech and realized his advice had been ignored in order to further a false political agenda, he wrote a piece for the *New York Times*, entitled "What I Didn't Find in Africa." Enraged by this, and after meeting Dick Cheney, Richard Armitage leaked the fact that Wilson's wife, Valeria Plame, was a CIA operative to the *Washington Post*, as both revenge against Wilson and a warning to others considering speaking out.

The exposing of covert operative identities is a serious federal crime. In other circumstances the leaker might have been sentenced to a decade or more in jail, but in the end just one person, Scooter Libby, Cheney's chief of staff, received a short sentence. He didn't go to jail, of course. Those at the top never do. President Bush commuted his sentence.

Few doubted that the leak had been given the green light at the highest levels, up to and including the office of Richard Cheney, the vice president. The gloves were off, and the leak was intended as a warning—mess with Dick Cheney and his agenda and reap the consequences. Nothing, not even the clear laws of the land, was going to stop the Iraq invasion. The government was acting over and above the law.

The habit of news stations (particularly Fox News) interviewing retired generals was exposed in 2008 by journalist David Barstow's Pulitzer Prize winning exposé, which clearly showed that the generals, supposedly freed up by their retirement from service to talk frankly, were in fact active participants in a concerted propaganda campaign (what Barstow called a media Trojan horse), coordinated by the Pentagon, to comment favorably on the case for the Iraq war and to shape the coverage of terrorism. The generals often also had financial interests in the propagation of the policies they advocated.

When General Barry McCaffrey was outed as being a serial independent television guest (who consistently advocated courses of action that would directly benefit the companies in which he had a financial interest), NBC just ignored the report entirely, and continued to feature the same band of generals.

Worse, McCaffrey (and, it is to be assumed, other generals) was employed as a private consultant to NBC executives, and gave them briefings on a possible war with Iran. The Generals were setting the news agenda, then appearing as independent guests on the shows that followed.

With what amounts to an informal merger between the US media and the military, this is not news, it is propaganda. America's media performed a shameful kowtow to the outright lies of the Bush administration in the lead up to the 2003 invasion of Iraq. Polls consistently showed that the majority of the American public were entirely wrong when it came to basic facts, like Iraq's (non-existent) relationship to 9/11. Even now, many still believe that weapons of mass destruction were indeed found. An informed population is vital to the health of any democracy, but in 2002/03 the public were lied to by a political class that used the media as a megaphone for their warmongering propaganda.

Despite a historically unprecedented media campaign waged by the Bush administration, days before the invasion a relatively modest 62 percent of Americans supported the war. Few now share that sentiment. The US suffered nearly 4,500 deaths and thirty-two thousand wounded, but that pales next to Iraqi casualties, which are impossible to calculate, but certainly in the hundreds of thousands. Iraqis continue to die every day because of the invasion. Iraq, as a country, has all but ceased to exist. Yet no real soul-searching as to what went wrong has been done by the media since the dark days that preceded the Iraq war, and when the next emergency comes along, it can be expected that the same parroting of falsity and misinformation will take place. The frenzy of the lead-up to the Iraq war starkly demonstrated one of the huge flaws in American democracy, and should rightly be considered the greatest failure in the history of US media, when faced with the biggest issue in a generation.

CHAPTER FIFTEEN

EUROPE

As America's focus turned from Afghanistan to Iraq, America sought allies for the invasion in what President Bush called a Coalition of the Willing, a ragged group of disparate countries trying to curry favor with the US, such as Micronesia and Palau. Why Palau might have had a disagreement with Iraq remains unclear.

Discounting these smaller nations (forty-eight countries joined the coalition in total), the key coalition members (and the only ones to send troops) were the UK, Australia, and Poland. Australia and the United Kingdom traditionally line up with America when required. However, the main qualification for countries joining the coalition appeared to be having leaders willing to ignore public opinion.

Across Western Europe (and in nearly every other country in the world), clear majorities opposed the war in such a visceral way that many protest marches through capital cities have never been equaled. In Italy and Spain, 90 percent of the public were against the war. But the pressure to comply from the US was also unprecedented, and applied through every diplomatic, media and political channel imaginable. The response of the two countries bordering the English channel was illustrative of the rewards and perils that faced leaders in their decision-making.

France

Public opinion in France strongly opposed the Iraq War. A Gallup poll in January 2003 showed 87 percent of the French people did not want their country involved, with or without a UN mandate. President Jacques Chirac, facing plummeting popularity ratings and mindful of France's long commitment to egalitarianism, first raised his concerns privately, then announced that France would not be joining the US in invading Iraq without a UN mandate. His decision was based not only on domestic public opinion, but also questions and doubts as to the war's fundamental legitimacy, based as it was on claims about WMDs that no one could prove existed.

The response was a childlike throwing of toys from the American crib. Bush seemed genuinely flabbergasted that a European nation could turn him down. Such was the level of American frenzy around the absolute imperative that the war must proceed, that Chirac's decision not to sign up led to the US subjecting France to a sustained campaign of vilification which seems scarcely credible in retrospect.

We can't believe (the argument went) that France, a country that we saved from Hitler's Germany, won't support us now. Americans had died to free Europe of Hitler, but France wouldn't fight Saddam Hussein, today's Hitler! The comparison was a disgustingly false one. It wasn't France's obligation to support America no matter the cost, and France's leaders were only reflecting the strong sentiment of their people. This is something that the leaders of Britain and Spain (to name just two), failed to do.

Chirac was right. The Iraq war would prove a disaster. It took immense courage to stand up to Bush and his crazed cronies in such a climate but, at the time, Chirac and France were painted as cowardly fools.

For months, Murdoch-owned newspapers used highly emotive and historically insulting language to taunt the French, describing the country as part of the "axis of weasel" in an article accompanied by a photograph of soldiers' graves in Normandy. Jacques Chirac was taunted by the *Times of London* as being consigned to the "un-splendid isolation . . . occupied by history's losers." A subsequent retraction or apology is yet to arrive.

Most memorably, in March 2003, some cafeterias in Washington agreed to a demand by Republican congressman Walter Jones to change the name of French fries to "Freedom fries," as if America had suddenly cornered the market in freedom with their plan to bomb Baghdad from the skies. Anything French went. You could buy freedom toast, or give a patriotic kiss with your tongue; a freedom kiss. America had gone mad, and the French bore the brunt for daring to stick up for their sovereignty.

Britain

Across the English Channel it was a very different story.

Britain's awkward, special relationship with America has historical resonance, but the modern model of economic policies at home and endless military misadventure abroad has been iron-clad since the days when Ronnie and

Maggie danced awkwardly together at his inaugural ball. Reagan and Thatcher genuinely liked each other, and together forged a personal and political alliance closer than that between Churchill and Roosevelt.

As with all political alliances, there was much pragmatism and tangible benefit to augment the personal relationship. Reagan felt that Britain gave his regime the sheen of old-school respectability and an impression of international backing for his radical agenda. Thatcher knew that America's political and military power elevated her role (and that of Britain) on the world stage, hand in hand with the great United States, close at that time to the peak of its powers.

Like so many love stories, in the years since then while ardor has cooled the bond remains, but with each passing year the relationship veers closer to abusive. Britain, the weaker partner, clings to its special relationship in part to hold on to its last few moments of true relevance. Britain used to rule the world, but the truth is now that Britain is saddled with massive debt, a moribund economy propped up solely by a square mile of bankers, and a diminished role on the world stage. It's hard to see what Britain now gains from its devotion to the big friend across the pond. The years following 9/11, and the actions of Tony Blair in particular, laid bare what Britain gains through this relationship—*nothing*—and how far the little island nation was prepared to compromise in order to retain a seat at the big table.

Iraq and Afghanistan constitute the most catastrophic foreign policies pursued by Britain since the 1930s. Britain's national sovereignty has not been remotely threatened since the Second World War, yet it continues to act belligerently and violently on the international stage, particularly toward the Muslim world. This has left Britain's cities in a permanent state of terrorist alert. The comparatively small number of domestic terrorism incidents linked to Britain's involvement in the War on Terror have, without exception, been carried out by individuals who specifically cited Britain's wars in Iraq and Afghanistan as having inspired their own atrocities. For all the billions spent and the lives lost in the War on Terror, it's hard to think of any real gain for Britain, save for the maintenance of its abusive relationship with the United States. Yet Britain goes to war, again and again. If it's not Iraq and Afghanistan, it's Libya, or Syria, maybe Iran next time. Britain's elusive national interest takes its troops from one (Islamic) country to another, without forming any kind of narrative that includes a beginning, middle, and end.

Britain always claims to fight to save a brow-beaten collection of people from another scarcely different group, but it's unclear why this is always in the Middle East, rather than Africa (for example). It's hard to point the finger at a recent intervention that has improved things. We all feel pity towards people enduring insufferable pain, but as Hannah Arendt warned, pity can sometimes possess a greater capacity for cruelty than cruelty itself.

Blair

Upon his election as prime minister in May 1997, ending eighteen years of right-wing conservative party rule, the rejoicing at finally showing the detested Tories the door imbued in Tony Blair the hope that, as his campaign song went, things could only get better. For a short while a breath of fresh air swept through London's political class. Suddenly Britain had a younger man at the helm, a man with an easy way with words and a ready smile, who welcomed Oasis to Number Ten and handled the tragic death of Princess Diana with such aplomb that his personal ratings, for a while, headed close to 95 percent. Such was the level of new hope vested in Blair personally that the tragedy of his downfall was all the more bitter.

Though it seemed unimportant politically at the time, BP's merger with American company Amoco in 1998 meant that one of Britain's most important companies now shared the same interests as the American oil industry. This undoubtedly led to closer political co-operation between Britain and the US, ties that would come into sharp focus when a crisis arrived.

The events of September 11 marked an abrupt U-turn in Tony Blair's outlook, and his political fortunes. Blair's first public pronouncement on 9/11 concluded with the words, "we therefore here in Britain stand shoulder to shoulder with our American friends in this hour of tragedy, and we like them will not rest until this evil is driven from our world." Standing shoulder to shoulder with America, no matter what, would prove Blair's epitaph.

Following the attacks, Blair met with President Bush on September 20 at the White House. When Blair said he wanted to concentrate on Afghanistan, Bush said, "When we have dealt with Afghanistan, we must come back to Iraq." Blair said nothing to disagree, but maintains to this day the lie that the UK's decision to invade Iraq was not made until just days before the war started. We now know the level of the man's deceit. Blair had assured Bush that Britain would be there in private letters a year before the invasion. He lied to his country.

Blair spoke with Secretary of State Colin Powell in March 2002, and privately confirmed Britain would support a US invasion of Iraq. However, it was during Blair's famous meeting with George W. Bush at Prairie Chapel Ranch in Crawford, Texas in April 2002 that matters were set in stone. Despite telling the press that he was "considering all the options [and] not proposing military action at this point in time," the opposite was true. Blair made Bush a commitment to participate in America's invasion of Iraq. This was a year before the invasion; a year Blair spent selling the war to a skeptical public, and lying that he had not yet made up his mind, and that there were options for peace.

As the Bush administration's military sights moved from Afghanistan to Iraq, they initially struggled to put together a plausible coalition that would both avoid excessive international protest and be palatable to the domestic population. Without Britain's help, their next biggest active partner in the war would have been Australia, and the invasion might have been delayed, reduced in size or even conceivably cancelled. The Coalition of the Willing would have been seen for what it was—a small group of countries, cajoled into supporting America's attack on a country that had nothing to do with 9/11.

It was Tony Blair's personal insistence that Britain should be involved, despite overwhelming British public opinion against such a position, that proved crucial in allowing the Bush administration to paint the picture of a broad-based international partnership, when in truth the coalition was exceptionally flimsy and could not command the backing of the United Nations.

Bush wanted war with Iraq at all costs. Blair was to be his facilitator. Any measure could be contemplated. On January 31, 2003, Bush proposed to Blair that a US plane could be painted in UN colors and flown over Iraq, in the hope of getting it shot down. Bush said the faked incident could be used to assist justifying the launch of a war against Iraq. It is believed Blair did not object. Both then held a press conference at which they said that they wanted to avoid war if at all possible.

The Protests

No aspect of society illustrates the disconnect between the people and its ruling class more than war.

At least one and a half million people (probably two million) walked through the freezing streets of London on February 15, 2003, calling for Blair to stop the war. The marches across the country were the largest peace demonstrations ever in Britain. Collectively, marches in eight hundred cities worldwide represent the largest protest in human history.

Days later, an opinion poll showed just 29 percent of Britons backing an invasion. One hundred twenty-one Labor MPs openly revolted, the biggest rebellion against a Prime Minister from his own benches in over one hundred years. But Blair, with typical indifference said, "I ask the marchers to understand this: I do not seek unpopularity as a badge of honor . . . sometimes it is the price of leadership, and the cost of conviction."

Essentially, Blair's point was that he understood the protesters views, but his own convictions meant that no amount of public protest could change the nation's course. Blair insisted that history would be his judge, but even with the benefit of a few short years, it is clear that he was desperately, awfully wrong, and took an unwilling nation into an illegal war. Those marching the streets of London were the ones with better judgment. The limits of British democracy under an intransigent prime minister were exposed.

Blair must have known that the case against Iraq was flimsy, non-existent, or falsified. He refused to let even his own cabinet see the advice he had received on the legality of the war. Faced with this paper-thin case for war, Blair manipulated the information he received, and lied to the British public.

Fabulously speculative claims were made and given a hearing by a supine press. Blair suggested Saddam Hussein had chemical or biological missiles that could be deployed in forty-five minutes, when nothing like that was the case. Right to the end, Blair maintained the fiction that if Saddam Hussein surrendered, the invasion would not take place. It would have been interesting to see what would have happened if Hussein had indeed offered his surrender at the last minute and called their bluff, but Bush and Blair were rightly banking on the Iraqi leader remaining defiant. Although Saddam Hussein did make concessions, such as promising to destroy his long-range al-Samoud 2 missiles, nothing was stopping the invasion.

The Dodgy Dossier

Although it is now clear that he had given private assurances to George W. Bush that nothing would stop Britain's backing of the Iraq war, overwhelming public opposition was a problem Blair needed to address. So a series of reports were published, aimed at convincing a skeptical British public to share the Blair government's viewpoints and support a war against Iraq, a nation correctly perceived as posing no conceivable threat to the UK.

On October 2, 2001, Blair's office at Number 10, Downing Street released a dossier entitled "Responsibility for the Terror Atrocities in the United States." It commenced by saying that the evidence presented was not good enough to use in a court of law, and went on to say that the key evidence was classified, so readers would just have to trust that it was compelling. This tactic was central to the public prosecution of the War on Terror. However, all the evidence that we have subsequently seen into the machinations of the Blair government suggest that this was just an inventive new way of lying to the public.

In September 2002, Blair's government released a dossier assessing Iraq's likely possession of weapons of mass destruction. It was widely seen as speculative and disingenuous, and is today forgotten, over-shadowed by what followed. Every single allegation in it has proved to be false. What is less well known is that MI6 met with Iraq's head of intelligence Tahir Jalil Habbush al-Tikriti in Amman, Jordan, just days before the publishing of the document, and were told in categorical terms that Iraq had no WMDs.

Worse was to come.

In early February 2003, a second report about Iraq's WMDs was released by Downing Street, entitled "Iraq: Its Infrastructure of Concealment, Deception and Intimidation." This was the dodgy dossier, now so infamous in the history of the Iraq war.

Blair, his sinister media guru Alastair Campbell, and the chairman of the Joint Intelligence Committee, John Scarlett, concocted the dossier. Its assembly seems, in retrospect, laughably amateurish.

Entire sections were lifted and copied from older documents already in the public domain, such as parts of articles by journalist Sean Boyne about Iraq, published six years earlier in *Jayne's Intelligence Review*. Boyne was against the war and aghast that his words had been use so dishonestly.

Another source of plagiarized information was a graduate PhD thesis published by Oxford University student Ibrahim al-Marashi, which was published in 2002 but based on documents going back to 1990. Al-Marashi, also opposed to the war, called the use of his document wholesale deception. He asked the British public how they could trust their government after that.

Many of the cut-and-paste jobs were so amateurish that the source documents coded titles, headers, and footers were still visible on the government's website. Within weeks it became clear that much of the information contained in the dossier was years old, taken out of context, or just plain lies.

Although the document was a laughing stock, Colin Powell felt able to reference it in his notorious speech to the UN Security Council. The Iraqi (military) facilities of concern referenced in the dossier were visited at the time by UK journalists in Baghdad and later by UN Weapons Inspectors. There were no weapons to be found.

This sordid tale shows the extraordinary level of contempt Blair's government had for the public, and for the military who served him. In fact, "Concealment, Deception and Intimidation" would have been a title better suited to Britain's role in the forthcoming conflict. The dossier was mostly just amateurishly cobbled together old crap, another perfunctory attempt to placate the public. In the full knowledge that war in Iraq would end the lives of many of his nation's armed servicemen and women, Blair and his friends cut and pasted together a pastiche of lies.

Blair deliberately intimidated the British public for political gain. On February 11, 2003, he sent four hundred troops and tanks to patrol Heathrow airport after receiving what he said was a chilling threat. But more than ten years later no evidence for this claim has been produced, and it's hard to escape the nagging notion that tanks on British streets combined favorably with a political propaganda campaign waged directly by Blair, that was reaching its apotheosis in the last few weeks before war with Iraq commenced.

Dr. David Kelly

On May 29, 2003, BBC radio's Today program broadcast an innocuous story at 6:07 a.m. in which correspondent Andrew Gilligan reported that Tony Blair and Alistair Campbell had personally supervised the assembly of the dossier, sending drafts back to the Joint Intelligence Committee six to eight times to be "sexed up." One of the details subsequently included in the report was Blair's fantastical claim that Iraq had WMD capable of being deployed within forty-five minutes.

In fact, the "forty-five-minute" threat was a story MI6 got from an Iraqi taxi driver, who said he remembered a conversation between two Iraqis about Saddam's weapons in the back of his cab some two years earlier.

Dr. David Kelly, Britain's leading authority on biological warfare (and a man whose expertise was recognized worldwide), was the source of the BBC story. Kelly had told Tony Blair categorically that there were no WMDs in Iraq and, aghast at the false claims subsequently made by Blair in order to manipulate public opinion, he leaked the information to Andrew Gilligan at the BBC.

Kelly, head of biological defense at Porton Down, Wiltshire, had been described as a weapons inspector of unimpeachable competence and integrity. His authority and knowledge gave him the power to single-handedly destroy the Blair government's case for war. The stakes could not have been higher.

Within ninety minutes of the BBC report, a Downing Street denial was issued. Tony Blair responded to the BBC story with a witch-hunt to find out who had leaked the information. The scandal was so huge it eventually brought about the resignation of the BBC's Director General Greg Dyke. Blair's dogged pursuit of an otherwise unremarkable leak put a profound chill on Britain's media, at the precise time when the government was putting out the most mendacious lies about Saddam Hussein. Everyone knows Blair's dossier was indeed sexed up, but people lost their jobs and their lives, and the Blair government continued unabashed.

The Ministry of Defense allowed journalists to read them a list of suspect's names, and confirmed who the guilty party was when Kelly's name was read out, betraying one of their own employees. Kelly was quickly interviewed by British intelligence at a safe house, and his name publicly trashed in the press.

On July 17, 2003, just eight days after the story revealing his identity broke, David Kelly was found dead under a tree, in a forest half a mile from his family home. Kelly had known the risks to his life. David Broucher, a British diplomat, recalled that a month earlier he had asked Kelly what would happen if Blair went through with his plans to attack Iraq. "I will probably be found dead in the woods" had been Kelly's reply.

Although Kelly's death was quickly ruled a suicide, many doubt that claim to this day. Both the circumstances of the man's death and the bizarre events that followed strongly suggest at best a cover-up, at worst state-sanctioned murder.

The day Kelly died, an unopened letter from the government sat on his desk at home, threatening him with the sack if he spoke publicly again. Kelly probably knew the contents without opening the letter. He had already received phone calls to that effect, and was secretly talking to journalists and planning to write a book about his experiences.

Just a few hours before he disappeared, Dr. Kelly sent a series of upbeat emails, including one to his daughter (who was soon to marry), and booked a flight to Iraq. Anyone familiar with suicide knows that there are often very few signs of tragedy ahead, but clearly in this instance there were no obvious indicators of a suicidal frame of mind.

Though not a spy, Kelly was in constant contact with the highest echelons of state intelligence because of his expertise in biological warfare. His home office contained computers able to communicate securely with agencies such as MI5, MI6 and the Mossad. With America and Britain's focus on chemical and biological weapons, the world's leading microbiologists were caught in a very dangerous power struggle between science and politics. Other microbiologists had died in mysterious circumstances around the world in the previous twelve months. It was not a coincidence that Kelly was speculating about being found dead in the woods.

After the death of Dr. Kelly, Tony Blair ordered an inquiry headed by Lord Hutton, which heard testimony suggesting Kelly had died after swallowing painkillers and cutting the ulnar artery in his left wrist, leading him to bleed to death. The ulnar artery is small, not the large one you think of when people cut their wrists. That's the radial artery. A cut to the ulnar artery almost never results in death. Kelly's was the only recorded suicide from ulnar artery wounding that year in the UK. Death by hemorrhage requires the loss of around five pints of blood, a huge amount when seen outside the body, but no such pool of blood was found by the paramedics who attended the scene.

A near empty packet of the painkiller Co-Proxamol was found by Kelly's side, suggesting he had swallowed twenty-nine pills. But he had vomited, and only around one fifth of one pill was found in his stomach, with around one-third the level of painkillers in his blood required to kill someone. The gardening pruner Kelly appeared to have used to cut himself had no fingerprints on it, nor did the bottle containing the pills (or the water bottle and mobile phone next to the body), even though Kelly wasn't wearing gloves.

But the state inquiry moved fast, and was quickly concluded. Kelly had committed suicide, we were told, and there were no suspicious circumstances. Just to be sure, in January 2010, Lord Hutton ordered that all files relating to Kelly's death, including the autopsy documents and photos from the death scene, be kept secret for seventy years. Seventy years! Hutton's justification was to avoid further distress to Kelly's family, but this is absurd, given the public interest.

Lord Hutton himself was out of his depth, having never chaired an inquiry of that size before. As a judge, he had a history of making pro-government rulings, and was widely known as an establishment man. Bizarrely, Hutton was asked to head the inquiry just three hours after Kelly's death was reported, well before the cause of death was suggested, and before the body had even been formally identified. Hutton was appointed as a safe pair of hands by Britain's Lord Chancellor, Lord Falconer, who just happened to be Tony Blair's ex-roommate.

Hutton had been appointed by a government who should have been one of the main suspects in the case. All of these combined to make the Hutton Inquiry a sham, window-dressing to appease the public.

Since David Kelly' death, a number of doctors and experts have voiced disquiet at the suicide verdict, pointing out that it is virtually impossible to die from the wounds he sustained. Those leading the speculation are hardly the sort of conspiracy nuts the media like to demonize. Many are respected surgeons and medical experts. One was Richard Spertzel, former head of the UN Biological Section, who claimed Kelly had told him he was on a hit list.

In 2010, Graham Coe, the detective who found Kelly's body, told British newspaper the Mail on Sunday that the Hutton inquiry had claimed that there was more blood at the scene than he had found, stating that there "wasn't much blood about, if any." Coe was an experienced officer, who had been present at the scene of a number of deaths previously. Paramedics on the scene also reported nearly no blood outside the body. This is dramatically different to what would be expected had Kelly died through hemorrhage and lost five pints of blood. Coe said that despite his evidence to the inquiry, there was in fact a third man with him and his partner (DC Colin Shields) when the body was discovered.

The death of Dr. David Kelly is another example of the mindset that prevails in Western democracies that it could never happen here. Had Dr. Kelly been an Iranian or Russian, for example, we could quite easily stroke our chins and mutter about dirty foreigners killing off their own people, but many in the US and UK think their governments are above such actions, despite the lies we now know were told to justify a war in Iraq that killed thousands of our country's servicemen and women. We collectively suspend our disbelief that governments of all colors and persuasions are not above the idea of killing pesky voices that stand in the way of their larger goals. It has ever been thus through human history, and there is no reason to imagine that we have suddenly entered a more enlightened age.

What is of no doubt is that those who lied and murdered—Tony Blair and his cohorts—retained power and privilege, and were rewarded for their duplicity with directorships of arms companies and the like, while Kelly, who had the temerity to tell the truth about the lies being told, was very quickly dead.

To those who doubt that the Blair government was evil enough to kill one of their own citizens in order to prosecute the Iraqi invasion, consider how many British soldiers also lost their lives for Blair's lies. What was one more death?

On balance, it seems most likely that Dr. David Kelly was murdered by British or US agents, to silence one of the world's leading sources of the kind of information that would have placed the entire Iraqi adventure in peril. The murder was effective, and covered up using the apparatus of state. Blair and his agents of murder got away with it.

A quick story. Cherie Blair once auctioned off a signed copy of the Hutton report (into the death of Dr. Kelly) for £400 to raise money for the Labor party. A truly squalid act, from a truly squalid woman.

After Iraq

Lies begat ever more lies. Having launched an illegal war, which turned into an ongoing occupation that became a disaster, Tony Blair was faced with either falling on his sword and admitting that the entire venture was a catastrophe, or continuing to justify his untenable position and defend what had become indefensible. In both Iraq and Afghanistan, Blair took the position although things were bad, they would become worse if the troops which had caused the disaster now left.

As the horrors of guerilla warfare came home, and the public was confronted with images of torture and death, Blair remained steadfast. No moral depth was beneath his desire to further the nefarious goals of the war on terror.

When Tony Blair visited Afghanistan in January 2002 and was warmly greeted by Hamid Karzai at Bagram airport, the torture chambers were just a few hundred meters away, in clear view. Shaker Aamer, Britain's last Guantanamo inmate, was tortured there. The physical proximity between the politicians who managed the torture regime and those being tortured was striking.

Britain became America's lead partner in the grubby business of kidnap, imprisonment without trial, torture and death, its territories a central hub for the transportation of "rendered" foreigners around the world.

Blair and his home secretary Jack Straw repeatedly denied that Diego Garcia (a tiny atoll in the Indian Ocean somehow owned by Britain) was being used in the global rendition program. In 2005, Straw told parliament, "There simply is no truth in the claims that the United Kingdom has been involved in rendition." This was a lie. Diego Garcia was used extensively, and for a long period. Authorization for the use of Diego Garcia as a hub for rendition was given by Straw and Blair, in clear violation of British law. For this alone, both should be arrested.

In fact, Straw lied so spectacularly, it's worth reprinting: "Unless we all start to believe in conspiracy theories and that the officials are lying, that I am lying, that behind this there is some kind of secret state which is in league with some dark forces in the United States, and also let me say, we believe that Secretary Rice is lying, there simply is no truth in the claims that the United Kingdom has been involved in rendition, full stop."

But he was lying, and so was everyone else. There is a state operating beyond the rule of law in the UK, and it is often in league with dark forces in the United States. The UK was extensively involved in the rendition of men, women, pregnant women, and children to countries where they were hung from the ceiling and had their genitals cut with razor blades. Tony Blair was aware of this, and continued the practice. British territory, airports and airspace were used, and British intelligence agents interrogated people at secret prisons.

Straw personally approved the rendition of British nationals to Guantanamo as early as January 2002, and lied through his teeth about it from then on.

Blair and Straw also introduced anti-terrorism legislation to the UK that mirrored that of their American counterparts. Suddenly civil liberties were under attack, as was the right to protest. At the 2005 Labor Party Conference, Straw gave a blisteringly disingenuous and dishonest speech, which included a tortured justification for an unpopular Iraq war that was already going badly wrong. When Straw said that "[we] are in Iraq for one reason only—to help the elected Iraqi government build a secure, democratic and stable nation," an audience member called Walter Wolfgang shouted out that it was a lie. In full view of the television cameras, and with Straw continuing to speak, security officers waded in and police arrested the eighty-two-year-old Wolfgang under Britain's new Terrorism Act. This was the shape of Britain under New Labor. An octogenarian who had fled Hitler's Nazis, being accused of terrorism for shouting out during a speech.

Britain wasn't alone—more than a quarter of the world's governments (at least 54 of them) secretly offered support to the rendition program. But that doesn't make Straw's lies any less astonishing. How could you believe anything that such a man said after seeing him lie like that?

What is undeniable is that the security apparatus of the state in Britain was acting illegally and entirely out of control during key years of Tony Blair's government. The question is whether this was the action of government agencies gone rogue or whether the agencies were simply reflecting the wishes of their political paymasters. If the latter, then Tony Blair should be arrested for war crimes and stand trial at the Hague.

In February 2008, British Foreign Secretary David Milliband was forced into conceding that Diego Garcia had indeed been used to assist America's rendition programs, but assured parliament that only two planes had landed, and that the detainees had not disembarked. This too was exposed as lies. Diego Garcia was used extensively as part of America's rendition and detention program (there is still a secret US prison there today). These lies were only exposed by a long process of investigation, which was effectively ended in 2014, when documents detailing the renditions were reported to have been accidentally destroyed by water. We will probably never know the full extent of what took place on Diego Garcia, but the cover-up alone suggests that whatever happened there was worse than we have been told.

Blair and Libya

Money trumped all morality in Blair's Britain. In March 2004, when an opportunity for an oil contract came up, Blair decided to become friends with Muammar Gaddafi. This was a man whose staff had shot a police officer (WPC Yvonne Fletcher) on the streets of London with impunity in 1984, and at home was known to be a murderous tyrannical dictator, a borderline psychopath governing an international pariah state. But Blair physically embraced Gaddafi and sold this sudden change of heart as a statesmanlike act of rapprochement.

Relations with Libya had been warming considerably since 9/11, which Gaddafi explicitly condemned, and with the closer ties came cooperation in state abduction and torture.

By way of example, in March 2004, opposition politician Abdelhakim Belhadj and his pregnant wife Fatima Bouchar were abducted at Kuala Lumpur International airport in Malaysia, and taken to one of the CIA's worldwide network of secret prisons, or black sites, in this instance within the boundary of Bangkok's Don Mueang International Airport. Many black sites are located inside or right next to international airports so people can be abducted, detained and transferred easily. You've probably transited through terminals on holiday, just a few hundred meters away from torture cells.

Abdel Belhadj was hung from hooks for hours and badly beaten by CIA agents wearing balaclavas. Eventually both Belhadj and his pregnant wife were bound to stretchers, hooded, blindfolded, and flown to Libya (on a 737 used in many renditions, owned by North Carolina company Aero Contractors, a front for the CIA), via Diego Garcia as a political gift to Gaddafi. Both were imprisoned. Belhadj was interrogated and tortured again, and held in prison for seven years without charge at Abu Salim prison. Libyans say that life in Guantanamo is not even a day in Abu Salim.

British Foreign Secretary Jack Straw claimed to be unaware of the case, saying that no government minister could possibly know details of every single action by his Ministry, before he was confronted with evidence that he had personally signed off on Belhadj's rendition.

Other Libyan exiles faced similar abductions from around the world. Sometimes whole families were rendered, as happened to Sami al-Saadi, whose wife and four children were kidnapped. Their youngest child was a girl aged six.

It was only when the Gaddafi regime fell in October 2011, and the man himself was killed (sodomized with a bayonet before being shot in the head), that documents in Tripoli were discovered in the abandoned offices of Moussa Koussa, the Libyan intelligence chief, that lifted the lid on the extraordinary lengths to which Tony Blair's government had gone to win favor with Gaddafi.

Papers found in Koussa's office proved that Britain's MI6 were behind the abductions and renditions. A March 2004 fax was found from Mark Allen, head of counter-terrorism at MI6, to his Libyan counter-part, congratulating him on the safe arrival of Abdelhakim Belhadj. "This was the least we could do for you and for Libya to demonstrate the remarkable relationship we have built over recent years."

Just to recap, the head of Britain's anti-terrorism division was involved in the kidnap and torture of foreigners around the world, and their delivery to a regime often cited for international terrorism, and notorious for political imprisonment and torture. The purpose, far from being to keep people safe from terrorism, was to curry favor with an oil-rich nation for financial gain. These are actions many would describe as terrorism itself.

The main driver behind these revolting concessions was Gaddafi's agreement to allow oil and gas exploration in Libya. In March 2004, two weeks after Abdel Belhadj had been kidnapped and delivered to Libya, Blair flew to Tripoli for his historic meeting with Colonel Gaddafi. He pronounced that, in Gaddafi, Britain had found a friend, with "a common cause . . . in the fight against al-Qaeda extremism and terrorism." Almost simultaneously, Shell announced it had signed a deal for gas exploration rights in Libyan territory worth hundreds of millions of pounds.

If ever you wonder how we find ourselves in this mess, think about this example. Watch as the War on Terror visits countries conspicuous by their carbon deposit riches or geostrategic locations, and the worst murderers on earth suddenly become friends and allies in this war against terrorism, the moment the money taps are turned on.

The worldwide sale of arms, like the War on Terror, has no moral code. Despite being a known murderous torturing tyrant, America continued to sell arms to Colonel Gaddafi right until the end. In 2009 they sold him $15 million in arms. Gaddafi was known to imprison, torture, and kill his citizens by the score. Imagine what $15 million of arms looks like.

Blair left office to take up a suite of highly paid directorships and advisory roles. Today he remains utterly unrepentant, a death-for-hire merchant of the violent world he helped create. He has made at least £100 million since leaving office, and lives in a cosseted world, apparently believing that his legacy and views remain relevant, and that his contributions to public debate are both welcome and valued, when in fact he is the most disgraced British politician in a century, and can't appear in public for fear of people attempting to effect a citizen's arrest on him for his war crimes.

The London Bombings

As the horrors of Abu Ghraib came to light and the Iraqi invasion became an occupation in the middle of a civil war, Tony Blair sought any means of making sure that the British public remained afraid of the consequences of the violent actions he himself had launched.

Mirroring George W. Bush, Blair strove to remind people that his nation was in a terrifying new war, one waged against a faceless, seemingly all-powerful enemy, both abroad and at home, one that might strike at any time. A day after London won the right to host the 2012 Olympics, that strike arrived.

The London bombings of July 2005 bore some striking similarities to the events of 9/11. Both were blamed on mad Muslims who had somehow escaped the dragnet of surveillance. Both involved training drills on the day of the attacks that somehow mirrored the exact events that took place.

On the morning of July 7, Visor Consultants, a crisis and risk management company employed by the British government, was conducting a simulation drill involving multiple simultaneous terrorist bombings at exactly the same London Underground stations that were actually attacked. The precise entity for which Visor Consultants was running the simulation is unknown. It's vital information, since it was those people who had suggested the times, places, and events on which Visor's simulation was based—which then came to pass with staggering accuracy.

The managing director of Visor, Peter Power, was interviewed on the BBC that day, and professed himself astonished that his company had suddenly had to switch an exercise from fictional to real. Anyone familiar with the training and simulation exercises on 9/11 will be very aware of the extraordinary way in which major terrorist incidents often take place in the middle of training exercises that mimic the exact events that occur.

Visor Consultants was also running an exercise involving mock broadcasts of news reports of bombings in the city. Power said that when news bulletins started coming in, people began saying how realistic their exercise was.

What are the chances that a simulation exercise would be running on the same day as the bombings, simulating the same type of terrorist attack at the exact same places and times that the attacks actually took place? It's astronomically unlikely.

The British government acted as if the attacks came out of the blue and were of profound shock to both them and the nation, when in fact domestic terrorism was something Britain's security services had long warned was all but inevitable following its involvement in the wars in Iraq and Afghanistan. Bombings in London had been envisaged, planned for, and were expected.

Though Blair resigned as Prime Minister in 2007, his successor Gordon Brown pursued such similar foreign policies that the two were indistinguishable. War was, and remains, just another political tool in a British prime minister's armory.

One of the most revolting aspects of Britain's involvement in Afghanistan was how, long after it became clear that the mission was a failure, and that at some point the troop presence would be drawn down, the British government, and Gordon Brown in particular, chose to bide their time until it became politically expedient to make a withdrawal. As Brown waited for the moment that best suited his political requirements, British soldiers fought and died, used as pawns while a Scotsman at 10 Downing Street considered how best to limit the damage to his political career.

The two wars that Blair helped launch and Brown continued were based on lies, and caused incalculable loss, suffering, and death. When the wars became political liabilities, the lives of Britain's armed forces were traded to protect their careers and to maintain power. These people should be seen for what they are, war criminals and mass murderers. Both should be arrested and tried at the Hague, as should Jack Straw, Alastair Campbell, and others involved in this sordid and dark period in British history.

CHAPTER SIXTEEN

THE WAR ON TERROR

The Patriot and Other Acts

Within nine weeks of the attacks on 9/11, a veritable smorgasbord of new legislation was passed, at a speed that would have made previous administrations envious. Secret military tribunals, guilt by association, torture and kidnap programs, arbitrary detention, surveillance of citizens, racial and ethnic profiling, the revoking of habeas corpus and the use of secret evidence—in nine weeks, all these were a part of America's brave new world. Generations of hard-fought liberties were gone in one tidal wave of Constitution trashing.

Just three days (three days!) after 9/11, Congress passed the Authorization for Use of Military Force (AUMF) resolution, which granted Bush unlimited power to use force against anyone in the world that the he said had been involved in 9/11. It was the first in a long line of post-9/11 legislation that was so vague that it allowed the president and his advisors to make virtually any interpretation of the texts they so wished.

The cumbersomely named "Military Order—Detention, Treatment, and Trial of Certain Non-Citizens in the War Against Terrorism" passed two months later, and allowed the president to order the capture of any non-US citizen accused of terrorism (by him) anywhere in the world, and to detain that person indefinitely without access to habeas corpus. Now Bush had the right to arbitrarily accuse anyone on earth of terrorism, attack them, kidnap them and imprison them without trial forever. The non-US citizen restraint has since been removed.

Under these new acts, the Bush administration secured virtually unlimited war powers, with no congressional oversight. They also made law unprecedented curbs on civil liberties and human rights, criminalizing dissent and protest. Many see this as the start of a trend that will inevitably lead the US to one day become a police state. While Bush maintained that the evil-doers hated freedoms, his administration did more than perhaps all previous governments combined to roll back civil rights and social freedom in the United States.

But it was the Patriot Act that proved the most egregious of the raft of open-ended legislation that followed 9/11. Written in the dead of night and passed with little or no time for those who voted on it to have actually read it, the act was mainly the product of Michael Chertoff, the Jewish son of a Mossad agent, a dual Israeli-US citizen and member of one of Israel's preeminent families.

Chertoff, as chief of the criminal division of the Justice department, was the person who had blocked FBI efforts to investigate the Mossad spies arrested before and after 9/11. It was due to the efforts of Chertoff that Israel had escaped any suspicion in the 9/11 attacks. He personally profited handsomely from the War on Terror, sitting on the boards of defense and security firms, and through his involvement with a company called Rapiscan Systems that made a fortune selling metal detector and X-ray machines to US airports. Chertoff relentlessly promoted the use of the machines, but didn't disclose that Rapiscan was a client of his firm. He also maintained a high media profile during the War on Terror years of the Bush administration, consistently fear-mongering, and advocating government courses of action that happily coincided with his private investments.

The 342 pages of the US Patriot Act made an unprecedented number of changes to US Federal law. Many have argued that since the act was introduced only six weeks after the attacks of 9/11, the huge piece of legislation must have been, at least partially, prepared in advance. Most bills of the length and complexity of the Patriot Act can take up to or over a year to write. But the bill was made law just forty-five days after the attacks. It was brought to the floor of the House of Representatives (for a vote) on October 23, the same day it was introduced, and passed the next day by a vote of 357 for and 66 against. The Senate passed it twenty-four hours later. The next day (October 26), Bush signed it into law.

You do not need to be an expert on American politics to know that this was beyond unusual, or that the bill's swift progress meant that no one had the chance to properly consider it. Many who voted for the Act admitted later that they had barely read a word of it. Some said they felt it would have been unpatriotic to subject the law to scrutiny, or to vote against it.

The act was edited just a few hours before being debated, to specifically make foreign companies responsible for security within the US immune from lawsuits. This was immensely beneficial, for example, to ICTS, an Israeli company which was responsible for security in every airport used to launch the 9/11 attacks. It remains unclear why foreign companies providing security services within the US should suddenly have become immune from prosecution.

The Patriot Act is Exhibit A in illustrating the contradiction between an administration that claimed to be engaged in the nation's greatest battle to defend democracy and freedom, and its introduction of anti-democratic laws eroding those same civil liberties and freedoms.

The act was sold as being the vital key to the government's combating of terrorism, but that is not how it has been used. As the years have passed, the Patriot Act has been employed much more regularly for enforcement of issues that don't relate to terrorism or national security than those that do. From 2006 to 2009, for example, Patriot Act provisions were used in 1,618 drug cases, and just 15 terrorism cases.

Among a great many other things, the act removed (already weak) restrictions on the FBI's ability to conduct domestic surveillance, and allowed the removal of such operations from public oversight. It also allowed the government to compel doctors to give up their patients' medical records without a warrant and without explaining why. Now every conversation with a doctor in the US could be monitored by the federal government. It needs no explaining how much power this vested in those able to access such records, or what a radical departure from history this was.

But in many ways the worst aspect of the Patriot Act was the loosely worded Section 215, which in the years that followed was subject to a radical interpretation, allowing the collection of telephone records not just of those under suspicion, but of all Americans (and many other nations), regardless of blame or suspicion, at all times, forever. The Act marked the beginning of the domestic surveillance state that was only exposed by Edward Snowden in 2013.

Other acts didn't even need interpretation. The National Defense Authorization Act affirmed the president's power to hold anyone, including US citizens, without charge or trial for an unlimited period. 9/11 provided both the excuse and the justification for a tidal wave of legislation that tore America's Constitution to shreds, all in the name of preventing another incident that, while terrible, killed just 6 percent of the Americans who died annually because they couldn't get healthcare.

The executive branch of US government now has a range of secret laws, secret budgets, and a worldwide team of assassins. The Patriot Act, once so controversial, was routinely extended by President Obama, almost without dissent. Written purposely to be disingenuous, the act would be dangerous enough as it is, but the way that both the Bush and Obama administrations (mostly secretly) interpreted its provisions threatens the nation's way of life—even its concept of democracy.

Although the authors of the act argued that the new laws were written to improve America's ability to target those who the government suspected were guilty of crimes, in actuality the Patriot Act has been used to put in place programs that target everyone, regardless of their behavior. Legislation passed at a time of national emergency, and sold as temporary measures necessary during those extraordinary times, has hardened into permanent law. The idea of revoking these laws is now barely even discussed among mainstream commentators.

The Patriot Act is the legislative foundation behind all the egregious acts of the NSA, every domestic spying program, and every action of Bush and Obama that demonstrably dismantled the US Constitution. The threat of terrorism, which by definition can never be defeated, means profoundly unconstitutional laws written after 9/11 can never be repealed.

Behind the Patriot Act is 9/11. Without 9/11, the entire thing comes crashing down. If the perpetrators of 9/11 were truly a bunch of Arab extremists hiding in caves in Afghanistan, then with all of them either dead or captured, the smorgasbord of repressive legislation passed in the wake of 9/11 is now entirely unnecessary.

However, the tragedy of 9/11 was swiftly and cynically exploited by the Bush administration to rush through legislation that would never have stood a chance in normal times, and concentrated power in the executive branch of government and the White House that other Presidents could only have dreamed of. This swiftly passed legislation fundamentally undermines US democracy, and appears to have put America on a permanent war footing. It has dragged American politics so far to the right that the word fascism no longer seems inappropriate.

The most obvious comparison, historically, is one that should make us profoundly uncomfortable. In the weeks after the Reichstag Fire of February 27, 1933, that burned down Germany's parliament, Hitler (who had only become Germany's leader four weeks earlier) passed the Enabling Act, which subverted the rule of law and the German constitution, and was used to launch preemptive war, which he justified as vital in order to keep his people safe. The similarities are impossible to deny.

In 2011, Senator Ron Wyden (D-Oregon) tried to amend the Act, demanding that the government end the practice of secretly interpreting law. His words remain compelling:

"It is impossible for Congress to hold an informed public debate on the Patriot Act when there is a significant gap between what most Americans believe the law says and what the government is using the law to do. In fact, I believe many members of Congress who have voted on this issue would be stunned to know how the Patriot Act is being interpreted and applied. Even secret operations need to be conducted within the bounds of established, publicly understood law. Any time there is a gap between what the public thinks the law says and what the government secretly thinks the law says, I believe you have a serious problem."

The problem is that the Patriot Act seems impossible to revoke, despite being clearly redundant. It has spawned a national security and domestic spying apparatus that by its own definition is beyond political oversight, and threatens to turn America into a police state run by unaccountable fascists. Obstacles to stopping this happen have been removed.

The War on Terror

Right-wing, authoritarian, and military dictatorships have long used the concept of terrorism, and the word terrorist, to characterize any kind of opposition to their rule. The more roughshod a government rides over a sovereign constitution and democratic principles, the less space there is for legitimate opponents, and options for rational political debate disappear. This reflexive labeling of those who challenge authority allows a militaristic leader to argue that the only logical, patriotic thing to do is fight to destroy these terrorists, and affords license to paint those who question the government's actions in such a time of crisis as traitors.

In 1946, Hermann Goering said that in order to get an apathetic public to support war, "all you have to do is tell them they are being attacked, and denounce the pacifists for lack of patriotism [. . .]. It works the same way in any country." By such a measure, Goering would have approved of the way the War on Terror was devised, used and manipulated.

A war on terror was not without precedent in America. When Ronald Reagan came to power his foreign policy was explicitly described as a war on terrorism. Reagan's secretary of state, George Shultz, called terrorists depraved opponents of civilization itself, while his president backed and sold arms to groups across the world who, by any measure, were themselves terrorists.

But perhaps even Goering would have struggled to come up with a name so pernicious in its vapid stupidity as the War on Terror. Terrorism is itself a gelatinous concept, ignoring as it does the actions of our side that often close-ly resemble the terrorism which we claim to fight, and the fact that freedom fighters can turn into terrorists (and back again) with one flick of our moral compass. A War on Terror is a war on an abstract, as insoluble as a war on anger, or sadness.

However, looking at it from the Bush administration's perspective, there was an evil genius to the idea of a war which by its own definition cannot and will not ever be completed, since nearly everything counter to the govern-ment's viewpoint can be called terrorism, and the eradication of terroristic human activity is an impossible conceit, especially in a world where the one superpower acts in regular violation of all international laws and norms.

Acts that could be defined as terrorism have been recorded throughout history. Jesus was arrested for blasphemy and tried for crimes against Rome, a typical colonial charge against an agitator. In any calculus, the terrorist has to be small and powerless, the victim immensely strong and powerful. It can-not be otherwise, or it would not be terrorism. To quote Harington: "Treason doth never prosper: what's the reason? Why, if it prosper, none dare call it treason."

One could debate whether terrorism's growth to a twenty-first century global phenomenon is a product of the world's disparity in wealth, producing people who are profoundly disenfranchised and without hope, or perhaps a by-product of the world's richest countries riding roughshod over the poorest, but the idea of a war somehow eradicating all human beings who lose hope and decide to take the ultimate nihilistic choice is laughable.

A war on terrorism wasn't inevitable. It's a mistake to suggest that Ameri-ca's people had an instantaneously warlike response to the horrors of 9/11. In New York, the city that suffered the most that terrible day, there were candle-lit vigils, and people carried banners bearing peace slogans.

President Bush's response required no such introspection or nuance. On September 12, 2001, Bush said he would be leading "a monumental struggle of good versus evil," in which good (the US) would prevail. On September 14, Bush essentially declared war from a church (the national cathedral in Wash-ington), claiming the US would rid the world of evil. Faith, patriotism, right-eousness, and war would hereon be fused, and any questioning of the actions of those seeking to keep America safe was sacrilege.

The War on Terror officially started on September 15, 2001, at Camp Da-vid, when Bush's cabinet met to approve the granting of virtually unlimited powers to the CIA, the agency with primary responsibility for the failures that had led to 9/11. The meeting began as usual with a pause for prayer, led by

President Bush, and with every person attending invited to participate and speak of their hope for divine guidance. A day later Bush first uttered the term War on Terrorism (which he shortened to War on Terror on the twentieth), adding that it was a crusade, a religious term for which he subsequently apologized, realizing its poisonous connotations within the Muslim world.

Facing an enemy without borders, waged by miscreants, held together by an ideology rather than nationalistic fervor, the War on Terror would be the world's first borderless war. The enemy was everywhere, and without a uniform could change from murderous terrorist to innocent civilian in an instant, meaning every male of military age in a certain location could be deemed a potential terrorist. America fought an evil that could never be defeated, because it lived in a person's heart, not their locality. Even the vanquished couldn't surrender and sue for peace, since they had no base to cede. Truly a warmonger's dream.

9/11 should have been the ultimate indictment against Bush and his administration, who were shown to have been asleep at the wheel, ignoring and even subverting those who had warned that an attack on home soil was imminent. Instead, the War on Terror became Bush's ultimate tool for political power, survival, and success.

The circular and endless logic of the War on Terror is, roughly, as follows. The US is fighting a war against terrorism. The battlefield does not have sovereign boundaries, and is thus the entire surface of the earth. Since terrorism, by its very definition, cannot be defeated, the War on Terror means endless war, forever, everywhere on earth, with no restrictions on behavior that might be found in international law, including on US soil. Terrorism is a new kind of crime, one that threatens our society's very existence, and we simply cannot afford to play by the old rules of war and law.

America's president appears to now hold the power to assassinate US citizens without charge or trial, restrained only by the pathetic tenet that this must be when capture is infeasible (which could mean anything—the subject could be armed with a knife, for example). With no recourse to law. Forever.

Bush's new war allowed him unlimited license. Why are you being so secretive? To prosecute the War on Terror. Why won't you testify to the 9/11 Commission? It will distract us from prosecuting the War on Terror. Why are you suddenly spying on all Americans? Because the War on Terror demands that we keep you safe.

George Orwell wrote in his book *1984* (published in 1949), "It's not a matter of whether the war is not real or if it is. Victory is not possible. The war is not meant to be won. It is meant to be continuous. A hierarchical society is only possible on the basis of poverty and ignorance. This new version is the past and no different past can ever have existed. In principle, the war effort is always planned to keep society on the brink of starvation. The war is waged by the ruling group against its own subjects. And its object is not the victory over either Eurasia or East Asia, but to keep the very structure of society intact."

Who among us can say that the War on Terror sounds so very different? The war brings profit to defense contractors and power to politicians, as millions in the richest country on earth live in poverty. It will not be stopped from within.

Various outlandish forecasts have been made as to how long the war will last. In 2013, Michael Sheehan, the Assistant Secretary of Defense for Special Operations and Low-Intensity Conflict, estimated that the war would continue at least ten to twenty years (beyond the twelve years it had already lasted). That ultimate Machiavelli, Donald Rumsfeld, often called the War on Terror "the Long War," and on occasions opined that the war could last for seventy years or more. After all, how can it possibly end? What sane president could claim that war on such a thing as terrorism was concluded? It would only take one madman spraying bullets in public the next day to make him one of history's great fools. But that's OK, the War on Terror's main purpose is to perpetuate its own existence, and waging it produces more terrorism than not fighting it at all. Even internal US army studies have concluded that most terrorism is motivated not by irrational hatred of the West, but by its foreign policies (those of the US in particular), and by violence perpetrated by our side within Islamic countries.

In this way the War on Terror is similar to the war on drugs, which has produced an explosion in trafficking, crime, and drug consumption unseen in human history. Like the war on drugs, it's really not a war at all, but a political calculus.

Though the Obama administration stopped using the term "War on Terror," finding it awkwardly stained with the failures of George W. Bush (and preferring instead the bland cover of "overseas contingency operations"), the central logic of the War on Terror remains—that we are in an epic, historical fight against an unseen enemy that wishes to harm America, for its audacity to free its people. From Bush to Obama, the methods of fighting this so-called war remained virtually unchanged.

Although Obama re-packaged the war, and used drones as a means of mollifying a war-weary public, administration officials widely acknowledged that operations were likely to extend for at least another decade.

It's important to understand that the definition of terrorism is highly fluid, and used very differently by disparate actors. For the US government, terrorism is self-serving, often meaning any non-state entity that opposes the interests of the US. Although predominantly defined as acts of violence against the West by non-white people, violence is not always required. Radical Islamic preachers are now routinely called terrorists. Chelsea Manning, Edward Snowden, even journalist Glenn Greenwald—all have been labeled terrorists. Actions by those on our side (whether individuals or states) which conform with government views and objectives are, it seems, by definition impossible to classify as terrorism.

It's startling to note that this war of generations was launched at a time of almost unprecedented worldwide peace. Indeed, it's been suggested that the last few years are the first in recorded history where no war between two standing armies is being fought anywhere on earth. This is the age of the 9/11 Wars.

So, in our perception of the War on Terror, we face a choice. We can try to find logic in the prosecution of this war, with its immense contradictions and lack of consistency, or we can accept that the War on Terror is a facade, mere window-dressing for something altogether different—a war designed solely to further America's strategic and economic interests; a smokescreen for an empire-building project that knows no bounds.

Terrorism, and the threat of terrorism, has been used time and again to justify troop movements, sovereign invasions, and the establishment of military bases, all with the goal of expanding US control of crucial resources.

This was understood soon after 9/11. Frank Viviano of the *San Francisco Chronicle* wrote on September 26, 2001, that "[the] hidden stakes in the war against terrorism can be summed up in a single word: oil." He continued, "The map of terrorist sanctuaries and targets in the Middle East and Central Asia is also, to an extraordinary degree, a map of the world's principle energy sources in the 21st century."

Control of energy resources seems a more likely true justification for a War on Terror. Curbing worldwide terrorism would require a nuanced approach, and a radical reevaluation of international policy. Instead, the war against terrorism seems absurdly focused on military action, with the day-to-day wellbeing of Americans routinely ignored.

If keeping Americans safe is the goal, terrorism seems a bizarre thing to focus on. The US Department of State reported that in 2011, terrorism killed seventeen Americans worldwide. Yet from 2000 to 2006, 137,000 Americans died because they didn't have health insurance. This, along with America's gun violence epidemic, should be treated as a true national emergency, and given much higher prominence than terrorism.

The War on Terror demonstrably has little do with actual public safety, given its focus on an obscure and almost miniscule threat, while ignoring actual public safety issues like gun control and healthcare.

Victims of the War on Terror have been consistently denied a voice. The federal judiciary, cowed by the enormous pressure placed on it by successive war administrations, has become a roadblock to justice. Not one victim of any US federal crime relating to the War on Terror has been able to sue for damages within the US, even those found entirely innocent. No government official has been held to account. Once the state has labeled you a terrorist, no matter how innocent you are, all of your legal rights disappear.

War should be an unnatural state; something to be avoided at all costs. Enemies should be known, and clear boundaries should be broadly accepted as to what the goals of a war are, how they can be achieved, and how the war can end. The War on Terror fails on all counts.

When we treat terrorism as something special, some new kind of crime that can't possibly be dealt with through regular judicial channels, we pour fuel on the flames of this madness.

Despite definitions that preclude the idea, the state is often involved in terrorism. A July 2014 report by Human Rights Watch concluded that nearly all of the high-profile terrorism plots within the US since 9/11 had included the direct involvement of government agents or informants. The majority of terrorism convictions were for material support rather than carrying out an attack, but the report found that persons working on behalf of the FBI had in some cases suggested or encouraged terroristic activities as part of sting operations.

The obvious risks associated with encouraging potentially unstable people to carry out terrorism (in the hope of then arresting them) need not be spelled out, but Human Rights Watch found several cases where previously law-abiding people had considered or commenced terrorism planning based on an FBI informant inflaming their sentiments by making comments and suggestions using politically sensitive subjects as incitement. The actions also alienated the Muslim-American community, through government informants being placed into law-abiding communities and mosques, and highly questionable convictions of those incited to violence.

We have to live with the fact that our government's actions occasionally kill innocent children. We are told that this is because of the threat that radical Islamic terrorism poses to our own society. But if you just change the words around, you have the precisely same rationalization that Islamic terrorists use to justify their attacks on the West. Just try it. "We have to live with the fact that our actions occasionally kill innocent children, because of the threat that Western military action poses to our society." It's morally indistinguishable—except for the fact that the actions of our side have killed vastly more innocent people than the terrorists.

As then *Guardian* columnist Glenn Greenwald put it in October 2012, "The US does not interfere in the Muslim world and maintain an endless war on terror because of the terrorist threat. It has a terrorist threat because of its interference in the Muslim world and its endless war on terror."

The question is whether this endless war is the unintended result of some very stupid people's failures, or the opposite—the intended result of a deliberate strategy for war and its attending profits, without end, forever. To answer that question, you have to enter the mental calculus of those prosecuting the war, and ask yourself what possible reason they would have for ending it. For belligerent politicians and those involved in the defense and intelligence industries, the end of the War on Terror would be the worst thing that could happen. The war has but one goal—to perpetuate the War on Terror, refueling itself by its own actions.

After 9/11, a distinguished few newspapers and journalists did try to follow up the plaintive "why do they hate us" rhetoric of George Bush. The *Washington Post*, for example, conducted an extensive survey of middle-class US-based Muslims, and found to their surprise that these rational people didn't hate America; they hated its foreign policy of illegal wars, support for dictatorships, the suppression of democracy, and blind allegiance to Israel.

What is abundantly clear is that while the War on Terror guarantees endless military expenditure and adventure, its prosecution has been disastrous for America's ability to maintain its place of worldwide preeminence. In 2004, shortly after George W. Bush's re-election as president, the quadrennial review of US intelligence agencies foresaw continued American global dominance for many years to come. Four years later, it judged that the nation was on the brink of no longer being able to call the shots in a fragmented world.

"The limits of the ability of the USA and its Western allies to impose their will and vision on parts of the world have been very publicly revealed," concluded British journalist Jason Burke.

In the name of state security, America's War on Terror has dramatically compromised its own enduring safety. Insisting that this new war permits America's executive to treat any location where a terrorism suspect is found as a theatre of war gives a green light to other nations to do the same. If the whole world is a battlefield, and our side is permitted to abduct and torture people from the streets of Indonesia, Italy, or any other country, then the other side is, surely, also able to claim that right. By sticking to the long-established rules of war, we could deprive terrorists of legitimacy. By abrogating our own values, we give them a stick with which to taunt us.

America's foreign policy is now almost entirely contrary to its politicians' rhetoric. Actions abroad plainly undermine American national security interests. But here's the thing—the money is so good.

The rise of international terrorism has coincided with the tentacle spread of globalized capitalism. The two are related. Terrorists routinely come from downtrodden states and societies and rebel against the rapacious demands of rich nations that have caused their country so much grief. Every major terrorist attack in Europe since 9/11 (as well as the Times Square bomber and Boston Marathon bombings) has been justified (the attackers have said) by the West's military interventions in the Middle East, which in turn are almost always concerned with control over carbon deposits and wealth. Yet our knee-jerk response always seems to be to double-down on our bombing raids and military actions abroad, fuelling the fire and guaranteeing more terrorism on our streets.

America's hypocritical foreign policy, seen in sharp relief through the appalling and misjudged War on Terror, appears predicated on the notion that, because our side is demonstrably and unquestionably morally superior, nothing we ever do can be immoral, and any resistance to US hegemony is terrorism. Every time we bomb somewhere, allow Israel to do the same, rain death from drones in the sky, or invade a country, ask yourself this simple question: would it be acceptable if the other side was doing this to us? If the answer is no, then what we are doing is almost definitely not moral, or acceptable. America is not at war, despite what foolish political hawks might claim. There is no nation or body that presents an existential threat to the United States. The miniscule risks associated with terrorism should be treated as a law enforcement and intelligence matter, and given no more importance than other types of international crime. By defining terrorism as a special class of crime, and by waging a bogus War on Terror, America is becoming that which it claims to despise.

CIA Torture.

Despite what television programs like 24 will tell you, the CIA's torture program was, for the most part, not aimed at revealing further terrorist plots. Torture was used as a political tool. The 2009 Senate Armed Services Committee Report boldly stated that torture programs were used for exploitation, rather than the gathering of intelligence. Torture has been used throughout history by regimes wishing to solicit false confessions to be used as propaganda.

Despite knowing that information revealed by torture is highly unreliable (people will say anything in order to stop being tortured), the statements elicited by the CIA's torture programs allowed the Bush administration to use all sorts of information to prosecute and maintain their fictitious War on Terror.

Islamic nations and their precious resources were the target. Those who claim that this is not a war on Islam should note that the torture program was aimed exclusively at Muslim men, and that every nation attacked by the United States since 9/11 has been Islamic.

It took years for America to face up to the horrors being conducted in its name. For a long period, use of the word torture was avoided altogether by American journalists—it was called enhanced interrogation, or not mentioned at all. There was rigorous debate as to whether certain techniques qualified as torture, when in fact they had been used since Medieval times as just that.

In recent years the word has become unavoidable, as new and graphic details of the CIA's torture programs have turned even apathetic American stomachs.

In December 2014, the Senate Select Committee on Intelligence (SSCI) released its 524-page executive summary of their long awaited (and long-delayed) report into the CIA's post-9/11 torture program. 90 percent of the report was redacted and the CIA (the subject of the report) had been allowed to lead the redaction process.

Among the report's revelations were facts like:

- Detainees were tortured well before any assessment had been made as to whether they would co-operate.
- At least 25 percent of detainees were innocent, or cases of mistaken identity.
- Detainees were told that their children would be harmed or killed, or their mothers raped.
- Rectal feeding and rehydration was commonplace. Many suffered rectal prolapses as a consequence.
- Some were forced to stand for hours on end with broken ankles.
- Detainees were waterboarded, hung by their wrists, placed in ice water baths, deprived of sleep for up to 180 hours, and placed in coffins.

Most importantly, the report concluded that at no time did torture produce intelligence that averted a terror attack. The report added that at least 26 detainees were wrongly held. Entirely innocent, in other words.

How could this not be a crime in the United States?

The head of the Senate Intelligence Committee, Dianne Feinstein, had for many years been known as the leading defender of government interrogation, secrecy, and surveillance, justified by the inescapable logic of the War on Terror (her enthusiasm for war likely influenced by the fact that her husband was a significant shareholder in major military contracts). Feinstein also long promoted the line that the NSA's collection of US citizens metadata wasn't surveillance at all, as it didn't include any content information, but balked when protesters asked if she would be happy to publish a list of her phone calls, locations, and email recipients.

Feinstein's passion for defending the government waned somewhat when she discovered that the CIA had spied on her and her Committee staff, by hacking into their computers while they were investigating the CIA's torture program. The agency's director John Brennan then lied about the CIA having done so, but faced no censure when his lies were exposed.

At the last minute, Secretary of State John Kerry called Feinstein to discuss the timing of the report's release. His concern was the ongoing safety of American hostages abroad, given the egregious details of America's treatment of Muslim prisoners.

The report found that when torture hadn't provided the information that was required, the CIA took intelligence that the FBI had gained without the use of torture, and pretended they had gotten it through their torture program, in order to justify and extend the torturing. They also ordered that torture be continued on individuals long after they had been told that there was no more information to give.

Torture sessions resulted in false and fabricated information that wasted time and resources, chasing up leads that those being tortured had simply made up. Tortured people will say anything in the hope of ending the agony. Rather than help the US prosecute the War on Terror and keep America safe, torturing people came up with a series of dead ends.

Those behind the torture program continued to defend its efficacy as details of the horror leaked out, claiming torture had saved countless American lives, but evidence relating to their claims was always redacted, due to national security. Those most heavily implicated in the program were routinely rewarded and promoted, rather than being punished or fired.

The architect of the CIA's drone program, John Brennan, was promoted to Director of the CIA in early 2013 by Barack Obama. Brennan was a huge supporter of Bush-era tactics such as torture and rendition, and his appointment symbolic of the refusal of those at the top of American politics to disavow President Bush's CIA torture program.

Thus the CIA raped, tortured, abducted, and killed across the world in a hatred-fuelled rampage, and have faced no consequences whatsoever. This means that any politician wishing to restart the torture can do so, knowing full-well that those who did it before are all still there, ready to go. Without a day of reckoning, America is positioned to begin torturing again, the moment a new commander-in-chief permits it.

Rendition

The license afforded the CIA by President Bush in the days after 9/11 led to the most radical and controversial program in the agency's history. The CIA has always been a murky operation, but after 9/11, a worldwide program of torture and rendition was instituted that is unique in human history in its scope.

Just to be clear, "extraordinary" rendition was the means by which the US kidnapped people from anywhere in the world, mostly without charging them with a crime, and sent their prisoners to compliant countries to be tortured (often by US officials), rather than torture them on US soil, which would be illegal. However, it was a violation of both international and US law, and one of the most overt displays of the Bush administration's utter abandonment of even the pretense of operating within the boundaries of legality.

Following 9/11, a quarter of the world's nations also abrogated their own laws in order to cooperate with America's secret rendition program. Participating countries, including many Western European nations, allowed the use of their airspace, airports and land as part of an international program of abduction, kidnap, detention, and torture.

Like all lawless regimes kept secret from the public, things often went wrong. There are many examples of entirely innocent people with Middle Eastern-sounding names or backgrounds finding themselves suddenly ripped from blameless civilian life into the torturous and psychotic world of post-9/11 justice.

One of the most well-known is the case of Maher Arar, a Canadian telecommunications engineer of Syrian origin, who was transiting through JFK Airport in September 2002 when he was arrested on the suspicion of ties to al-Qaeda. Despite the US being fully aware that Syria routinely tortured its prisoners, Arar was rendered there, without a shred of evidence being offered. On arrival in Syria, he was kept for ten months in a six by three foot cell, and regularly tortured with beatings and electrocution, during interrogations that lasted up to eighteen hours. Arar was asked the very same questions in Syria that he had been asked at JFK Airport, leading him to suspect that the US State Department had supplied the torturers with a list of questions.

On his release in October 2003, entirely cleared of links to terrorism, the Canadian government paid Arar C$10.5 million in compensation. Arar sued the US government, but the Bush administration refused to provide any documents or information whatsoever, and denied any mistakes had been made. They insisted that they had information about Arar that had to be kept secret due to national security, and left Arar's name on the US no-fly list.

Syria, incidentally, was one of the most common destinations for America's kidnapped and rendered prisoners. It seems that Bashar al-Assad's penchant for torture has since become unpalatable.

But in some ways, Arar was luckier than others.

In another instance, CIA agents kidnapped Egyptian cleric Hassan Mustafa Osama Nasr (known as Abu Omar) in broad daylight in Milan, Italy in February 2003, as he walked to his local mosque. Omar was rendered in a Gulfstream jet to Cairo, where he was imprisoned for four years, tortured, beaten, raped, and had electric shocks applied to his genitals.

The Italian government, unhappy with the idea of international kidnapping taking place on its streets, tracked down and charged twenty-three US nationals (all but one were CIA agents) with kidnapping in 2009. The leader of the group and head of the CIA in Milan, Robert Seldon Lady, was convicted in absentia and given an eight-year prison sentence. But when Lady was detained on an international arrest warrant in Panama in 2013, the US made sure the convicted criminal was flown back to the United States without delay. In today's America, convicted kidnappers walk free, and state sanctioned torturers never face prosecution.

As part of the War on Terror, the US established a worldwide network of secret prisons, known as black sites, used specifically for conduct that would not be permissible in America. It's sometimes hard to accept that the nation that so proudly declares itself leader of the free world and moral guardian to humanity can in fact have acted this way. For those in the West, try to comprehend just how unacceptable it would be for, say, Iran to construct a worldwide network of torture camps and begin abducting people from the streets.

A fleet of private aircraft helped the CIA run its clandestine program. Men on these so-called ghost planes were usually sedated through anal suppositories before being dressed in diapers and orange suits, then hooded, muffled, and tied up in the back of the aircraft; treatment that the ASPCA would denounce as cruelty to animals. They were known as "invitees."

It wasn't just men. Women, pregnant women, and families, including children as young as six, were kidnapped and flown around the world to notorious prison sites.

Prisoners of war are supposed to be taken from the battlefield, not abducted from the streets. The twisted logic of the War on Terror may contend that the whole world is a battlefield, but that allows the enemy that same freedom of destruction. America's abandonment of its own laws has led it down a dangerous path.

Guantanamo

The US has maintained control over the Southern part of Guantanamo Bay in Cuba for over one hundred years, courtesy of the 1903 Cuban-American treaty. It's an odd place politically, in that Cuba retains sovereignty but America has possession. Technically, Cuban forces could move in and take control of the area at any time, but a gentleman's agreement of sorts exists between the erstwhile implacable enemies, and America retains its enclave of territory. What was key to Guantanamo Bay being selected as the site for a detention camp was its physical proximity to the United States, and its total lack of the requirement for US law.

Since 2002, this strange little corner of the world has become an American cancer, the ongoing manifestation of all that was wrong with the Bush administration's lawless War on Terror, and America's inexplicable inability to put those dark days behind them.

The original justification for the processing of detainees at a prison camp at Guantanamo Bay was as flawed as everything else that has happened there. Because 9/11 was so huge and unprecedented, we were told, we faced an entirely changed world where the US criminal justice system (which deals daily with murderers and psychopaths) was somehow unfit to cope with the new crime of international terrorism with which the inmates at Cuba were charged.

Terrorists had been successfully tried, convicted, and imprisoned without hindrance by American courts previously, but somehow the awfulness of these new crimes transcended that reality. In any case, those establishing the new facility in Cuba felt little need to mollify the public during the period of shock and outrage that followed 9/11. Habeas corpus could be suspended, no one cared, and pictures of shackled, blindfolded prisoners being led around by six guards at a time matched the prevailing narrative of anything goes.

Guantanamo forms just one part of a broader narrative, where US laws and a Constitution written and enacted over time by very smart men were ripped apart in an instant by very stupid ones, in the belief that one tragic event meant that all this could be pushed aside, and that due process just got in the way. This has been shown to be a terrible error.

The first twenty detainees arrived at Camp X-Ray on January 11, 2002, four months to the day after the attacks, after the Department of Justice assured the Bush White House that the facility was outside US legal jurisdiction, beyond the law. Quickly, the list of detainees grew. Overall, around 780 people have been incarcerated at Guantanamo.

In justifying the camp's existence, Donald Rumsfeld described the inmates as the worst of the worst, almost superhuman in their dastardly evil. However, as the years have passed, it has become increasingly clear that for the most part prisoners were either low-level operatives or sometimes entirely innocent of anything whatsoever. The US government repeatedly labeled inmates at Guantanamo as terrorists, only for us to find out later (or, less often, for a court to find) that the evidence was exaggerated, wrong, or nonexistent. Despite apparently representing the worst of the worst, over six hundred prisoners have been released from Guantanamo without facing trial, mostly under President Bush. According to the US government's own data, 92 percent of the men detained at Guantanamo never fought for al-Qaeda.

Although Guantanamo houses some men likely to be guilty of something, the fact that they've been tortured and imprisoned for so long means that no trial worthy of the name can now ever be conducted. The very system put in place to keep America safe means that those who did participate in actual crimes can never be convicted of them, and must be retained, in defiance of international law, at a facility which has been described by no less than Barack Obama (before he was elected) as "a tremendous recruiting tool for al-Qaeda."

Running roughshod over a domestic justice system that, for the most part, works well put both prisoner and prosecutor in an impossible situation. The CIA was able to keep details of its torture activities classified, or destroy their own records without censure, meaning no free and fair trial could ever take place. Those defending themselves were given limited or no access to details of the crimes they had been accused of, and often claimed that confessions were inadmissible evidence, since they were obtained by coercion. Most prisoners never got the chance to have their day in court anyway.

Every media and public relations trick was tried to sanitize Guantanamo and present the American public with the false story that the incarceration and treatment of inmates there was vital to the ever-present goal of keeping

America safe, despite report after report concluding that the torture camp was a recruiting tool for Muslim extremists, and stating that nearly all inmates were of little or no value. Compliant American newspapers steadfastly refused to use the word torture about the CIA's interrogation techniques for years, despite using the word to describe similar actions by other countries.

Zero Dark Thirty

There is no better example of the years-long public relations campaign that accompanied America's prison camp at Guantanamo than the Hollywood blockbuster *Zero Dark Thirty*, an overt piece of American military propaganda dressed up as gritty realism. The movie portrayed the torturers as heroes, and overtly stated that information gained through torture directly stopped more attacks like 9/11, something almost no one except some former Bush White House officials continue to claim.

The writers and director of *Zero Dark Thirty* were given high-level access to personnel within the military, who briefed them on classified information, so as to make the movie more authentic, although the lack of any subtlety meant it more resembled an episode of *24*. CIA director Leon Panetta committed a federal crime when he revealed classified information to the moviemakers. When that story broke, it was the people who leaked the information that Panetta had leaked information who were investigated.

The extraordinary access granted by the government and lauding of the filmmakers' patriotism resembled a cheerleading squad. Compare that to the treatment of Chelsea Manning, another classified information leaker. It seems it's not the leak that matters but what your intention is. Support the government and the status quo, and you are inviolate, get whatever information you want and can put on a nice gown and go to the Oscars. Reveal something embarrassing and you are a traitor, condemned to spend the rest of your life in jail. This is the twisted approach to truth that Guantanamo spawned.

In time, Kathryn Bigelow and her awful film will be seen in the same light as Leni Riefenstahl, whose 1935 film *Triumph of the Will* is regarded as apologist propaganda for Hitler's Nazis.

Torture at Guantanamo

It's been said that the methods of torture used at Guantanamo were adapted and refined from other torture regimes, but in truth no adaptation or refinement was required. Torture techniques at Guantanamo were direct copies of those used across the world—some since Medieval times. Many had been used by the Nazis.

The horrors of the torture regime instigated at Guantanamo cannot be overstated. For many years, waterboarding had been something US Special Forces were trained to resist, should they fall into the hands of some lawless government. At Guantanamo the tables were turned. Waterboarding was something that US forces inflicted. America had become the lawless government.

It's wrong to suggest that waterboarding simulates the feeling of drowning. It is drowning. It's something the US has prosecuted foreign nationals for. Pol Pot used it as a key torture method in Cambodia. At the center of the genocide museum in Phnom Penh is a waterboarding table. This is not good company to keep.

Although the CIA has maintained that waterboarding was only used on a small number of people, its record of lying, then having their lies exposed, confessing inaccuracies, then having that confession found to also contain substantial lies, is second to none. What sort of a fool would believe anything the CIA says, given their recent history? Much has hinged on technicalities. Some prisoners were found to have been subjected to "water-dousing" rather than waterboarding. Dousing involves naked prisoners being covered in iced water and kept at hypothermic temperatures for long periods. This is torture too.

The moral relativism alive in US society is regularly on show when the legality of torture is debated. Rudy Giuliani, when asked if waterboarding was torture in 2007, said, "It depends on who does it."

Prisoners also faced psychological torture, deprivation of rights, prolonged solitary confinement (itself recognized as torture), beatings, violence, and punishment with extreme heat or cold and ice. Many were told they were about to die, forced to drink salt water, or suffocated and tied in agonizing positions for prolonged periods. Interrogators showed inmates family photos and told them that their wives or children were being hunted down or held, and would be tortured or killed. Mock executions were held. Inmates were threatened with power drills. Just as in Auschwitz, nudity was used to humiliate and degrade prisoners, sometimes for as long as a month. Shower units were built so that they faced the central control atrium, allowing not even the tiniest moment of privacy. Religion was desecrated, beards were shorn and Korans torn up, burned, or flushed down the toilet. Female soldiers smeared fake menstrual blood on themselves and danced near Muslim detainees to try to extract information. Hunger-striking inmates were strapped to chairs and fed by tubes inserted into their nose. Inmates, cleared for release for many years, who wanted to die because they had lost hope, were brutally forced to stay alive so they could continue to be imprisoned. When they rioted, staff used rubber bullets to enforce compliance.

For reasons that need no explanation, rectal rehydration was used on recalcitrant prisoners. Dick Cheney said that rectal feeding was done for medical reasons, though he chose not to comment on why the largest tube available was always used. No one doubts the truth. This was just blending up someone's dinner and sticking it up their ass as punishment. It's been done since medieval times to cause people extreme internal pain.

What is even more terrifying is that this is only the information we have. Given the pattern of lying and deceit practiced by US authorities since the prison camp opened, it is far from a leap of faith to assume that worse treatment has been used and not reported. Guantanamo was just one of a chain of gulag-style facilities around the world, designed to remove prisoners entirely from the prying eyes of the outside world. Many black sites were located in the same torture chambers previously used by the countries the US had "liberated" (such as in Iraq and Afghanistan). At Abu Ghraib, the Iraqi torturers employed by Saddam Hussein moved out, and within weeks America's torturers moved in and employed the same torture methods in the same rooms. Countless examples exist of innocent people imprisoned for years in clear cases of mistaken identity. Many were tortured and beaten, sometimes to death.

All these measures were personally approved by the US secretary of defense, Donald Rumsfeld.

Many of the jailers and torturers at Guantanamo (and elsewhere) were selected based on pre-existing tendencies towards brutality and violence. The worst of the worst were actually many of those running the prisons. For example, Richard Zuley was a Chicago detective and Navy reservist with a violent, abusive reputation within the police force. Domestically, Zuley's methods had included prolonged shackling, threatening family members, death threats, racism, and planting evidence, but at Guantanamo he was able to finally express his cruelty. Zuley's personal design for the interrogation of Mohamedou Ould Slahi (a Mauritian), detailed in a first-person book account by Slahi, has been described as the most brutal in the history of Guantanamo, and was so extreme it was sent to Donald Rumsfeld for his personal approval. Rumsfeld gave it all the green light.

Slahi's book *Guantanamo Diary*, published in January 2015, detailed the prolonged interrogation he suffered at the hands of Richard Zuley. Slahi was forced to drink seawater, sexually molested, beaten, kicked, punched in the face, and subject to a mock execution. A bag was placed over his head that led him to nearly suffocate. While trying to breathe, the guards put bags of ice cubes inside his clothes and added more when the ice began to melt. He was told his mother would be brought to Guantanamo and gang-raped in front of him.

If this is all making you feel rather sick, try to remember that Slahi was, at best, a low-level operative who may (and only may) have been associated with al-Qaeda. Despite never being formally charged with a crime or facing trial, Slahi spent fourteen years incarcerated at Guantanamo Bay (finally being released in late 2016). What kind of country treats its prisoners this way? What interpretation of the word justice is being applied here?

Torture sessions were devised, formalized and supervised by army psychologists who previously had trained elite troops in how to withstand torture at enemy hands. Rather than provide outcomes that improved the health of those in their care, as was their sworn duty, army doctors and psychologists did the opposite, betraying the most fundamental tenets of their profession. These people used their medical knowledge to ensure that the torture didn't kill the victims, but kept them alive and conscious so they could be tortured again, actions that are clear war crimes. Those responsible should be disbarred and prosecuted.

They could start with John Leso, an army psychologist with no training or experience in interrogation, who nevertheless was chosen as the army's first on-site psychologist at Guantanamo. He co-authored a manual on torture techniques borrowing from techniques that China and North Korea had used against American prisoners of war. Leso's manual formed the basis for the entire torture program at Guantanamo. However, in 2014 the American Psychological Association (APA) refused to charge or even rebuke Leso, on the ludicrous grounds of lack of evidence. This was despite official logs from Guantanamo showing that Leso advised the torturers on how to maximize the suffering of prisoners, and was present and an active participant during the infamously brutal interrogation of Mohammed al-Qahtani, the "20th hijacker" (a title bestowed on a number of Middle Eastern men).

However, in 2015, there were signs that a legal process was beginning, with the launch of a lawsuit by the American Civil Liberties Union (ACLU) against James Mitchell and Bruce Jessen, two of the lead psychologists involved in devising the torture program. Both had worked previously on the army's Survival Evasion Resistance Escape program, teaching pilots how to withstand torture if captured. Now the tables were turned.

Money was a significant factor in recruiting people willing to torture—Mitchell and Jessen set up a business (Mitchell and Jessen Associates) that received $81 million in CIA contracts to reverse engineer programs previously used for training, and to turn them into torture methods. Both became rich men, courtesy of torturing Muslim prisoners.

When public accountability and outrage began to rear its head in 2007, the CIA provided Mitchell and Jessen's company with a multiple year indemnity cover, to protect all involved from liability.

The APA was acutely aware of the practices taking place by their associates. An email from CIA psychologist Kirk Hubbard to an executive at the APA in August 2003 said that Mitchell and Jessen were unavailable because they were "doing special things to special people in special places."

The APA vigorously denied any knowledge of this for ten years, pitching itself as an unimpeachable bastion of ethics, and consistent opponent of torture, but revelations in July 2015 showed this to be entirely false. The APA was secretly working with the Bush administration to help ensure the CIA had the legal basis for justifying its procedures, and amended its own ethics rules to allow its members to work more closely with the Department of Defense. Senior members of the APA used their power to stifle dissent within the organization.

In fact, contractors (private sector employees working for companies trying to make a profit) made up 85 percent of those working on the enhanced interrogation program. If the torture stopped, so did the profits.

So egregious was America's behavior that Morris Davis, the former chief prosecutor for the US government at Guantanamo, called it a law-free-zone. He said the US army had been ordered to commit crimes by its civilian political leaders. For a time, even the Red Cross were not allowed to visit.

The CIA justified their treatment of prisoners with torture memos, legal rulings written by the US Deputy Assistant Attorney General John Yoo (documents themselves based on lies and falsification), which allowed the Bush White House to redefine prisoners of war as enemy combatants, a phrase which prisoners legal counsels said they had never heard before. Most checked their legal books to see if they had missed the term.

Not only was the CIA complicit in torture, when cornered they chose to destroy the evidence, as revealed by the ACLU in 2009, who found that at least ninety-two videos of harsh interrogations (waterboarding and other torture) had been deliberately and illegally destroyed. The tapes had also been withheld from the 9/11 Commission. The White House was party to the decision to destroy the tapes, despite the 9/11 Commission and other courts demanding that they be preserved.

The Problem with Using Torture

The use of torture leads a society down a slippery slope. It places US personnel serving overseas at risk. If captured, what is to stop foreign governments from torturing US servicemen and women? Now that the US does it, moral and legal superiority can no longer be claimed.

Torture also opens the door to any other degradation that's available. Populist propaganda like *Zero Dark Thirty* and *24* would have you believe the fictional scenario of a ticking time bomb and recalcitrant evil mastermind who possesses vital information but won't crack under normal interrogation. If you accept that proposition, what else would you do to "save" your people? Would cutting off a prisoner's fingers now be acceptable? Societies that allow limited torture tend to torture people more savagely as the years pass.

The *24* mindset helped many Americans accept that the use of torture was sometimes an imperative to save lives—moral, even—but to date not one example of torture-induced information protecting anyone has been produced.

Conversely, there are countless examples of torture victims saying something—anything—to stop the agony, and valuable time and resources being wasted following up dead-end leads. Torture produces "junk information." Even the CIA admits that much of the "intelligence" they extracted was simply not true. If you pull someone's fingernails out, you can get them to confess to assassinating Abraham Lincoln. That has always been the problem with torture, and why it has been banned by mature societies.

Not only is the information produced through torture unreliable, it's illegal and immoral, and contrary to America's values, a war crime. There is no halfway house here—if torture is a crime, then it must be prosecuted. Torture is and has for decades been a felony in the United States. The military and their torturers were ordered to instigate torture regimes by senior civilian politicians, who should be held accountable. Donald Rumsfeld is a war criminal and must be arrested.

But of course, not one individual has been held accountable for the decade of war crimes at Guantanamo Bay. The US Justice Department says it hasn't prosecuted a single person, because they claim that the evidence would not be sufficient to obtain a conviction. Every civil suit brought by torture victims has been dismissed due to national security. In fact, the only crime that has actually been prosecuted is the leaking of evidence of torture.

Torturing someone and then trying to conduct a legal prosecution against them has put lawyers on both sides in an invidious position. Not only is evidence obtained under torture inadmissible, some of the trials have been declared meaningless, as the government has said that even if the defendant was found not guilty, they would not release him. Many times, confessions obtained during torture have been used as evidence in order to justify continuing to hold a detainee, when no other evidence could be found. Torture an innocent man until he confesses, and then you can keep him.

Inmates

Whether by accident or design, many of America's black site inmates appear to have arrived by simple misfortune. People like Abdul Haleem Saifullah, who was eighteen when he dropped his father off in Karachi for kidney treatment and then vanished. There's Hamidullah Khan, who was just fourteen when he disappeared in Waziristan. It took a year for the Red Cross and their families to find them, both incarcerated without charge at Bagram. To add to this misery, US authorities repeatedly lied about their knowledge as to the whereabouts of these missing people. Some have never been found. Others, lucky or unlucky depending on your perspective, found their way to Guantanamo.

In Afghanistan, US forces offered cash rewards to local militia to hand over captured militants, but instead the militia often appear to have just rounded up random people in order to get the rewards. In a sane world many would have been instantly recognized as frightened civilians and released, but this was the War on Terror, where the enemy is everywhere and the world a battlefield. Sanity was for another day.

Innocent people caught up in the web were tortured and held for years before reason returned to her throne. Bisher al-Rawi, a British-Iraqi citizen, was arrested in 2002 in Gambia while setting up a peanut-processing factory with his brother. For reasons that remain unclear, al-Rawi was considered valuable and taken to Bagram airbase in Afghanistan, where he was tortured, and then on to Guantanamo. Five years later he was released without charge. No evidence has ever been provided as to why al-Rawi was arrested, but for five years he disappeared into an administrative black hole of violence.

Shaker Aamer

Shaker Aamer, a teacher with a wife and four children, was the last British inmate at Guantanamo. His case illustrated the immense and casual cruelty of incarceration at the facility in Cuba, and the almost non-existent benefit Britain receives through its special relationship with America.

Aamer was captured and sold to the US Army by Afghan bounty hunters in November 2001. He was transferred to Guantanamo in February of 2002.

Many other Guantanamo inmates found themselves in Cuba this way, after the US government offered a bounty of up to $5,000 to local warlords, who duly kidnapped anyone they could get their hands on.

The US said Aamer had been fighting at Tora Bora, but no one believes that to be true. At the time of his arrest, his British wife Zin was pregnant with their fourth child. Faris Aamer (born on the day that Aamer arrived at Guantanamo) had to wait until after his thirteenth birthday before he finally met his father.

Much of Aamer's time at Guantanamo was in solitary confinement. Aamer stood up for himself, and was punished for protesting against his treatment, not acting compliantly, organizing hunger strikes, and for not changing the details of his story, which included being beaten while a British intelligence officer was present.

Aamer was originally charged with support for Osama bin Laden and association with al-Qaeda terrorists, but the evidence was spurious or non-existent. His lawyer maintained that the charges would not stand up to the scrutiny of a trial, and after years of imprisonment the Bush administration acknowledged it had no evidence against Aamer that could be presented in a court.

Aamer was cleared for release to Saudi Arabia in 2007 but said he wanted to return to the UK, where he is a citizen, rather than Saudi Arabia. Most suspected that the offer of a release to Saudi Arabia was meant as an effective means of keeping him quiet, as a sham trial and further incarceration would be likely. Aamer was finally released from Guantanamo in October 2015. Despite over thirteen years in jail, he never faced trial.

No Briton released from Guantanamo has been convicted of any offence. In fact, more inmates have died at Guantanamo than have been convicted, and all those who died there had not been charged with a crime. Of 779 detainees imprisoned, only six have been convicted, and many of those cases (like that of Australian David Hicks) were dubious in extreme. Hicks was given the choice of confessing or remaining at Guantanamo. What would you do?

If you want an example of kangaroo courts, look at the treatment of Salim Hamdan, who successfully brought a challenge to the military tribunals system (under which he was to be tried) to the US Supreme Court. The court ruled in Hamdan's favor, but he was then detained under a new law that Congress passed—a law against "material support for terrorism."

Worse, if possible, is the legal limbo into which many inmates at Guantanamo were placed, with the US government clearing them for release but not able to agree on where they should be released to, so continuing to imprison them for years on end. Some were deported to countries that had not pledged not to imprison and torture them anew. As of early 2016, 91 men remained held at Guantanamo, with more than a third cleared for release but retained by an official policy of foot-dragging at the Pentagon, designed solely to limit embarrassment.

Late in Obama's Presidency the total number of inmates at Guantanamo was reduced to sixty, but thirty-five men (the so-called "forever prisoners") remain designated too dangerous to release but not feasible for prosecution, the very opposite of anyone's idea of justice. The reason they can't be prosecuted? Their confessions were obtained under torture, and no judge can be found that will admit their statements as evidence.

In the courtroom at Guantanamo sits a very expensive video system designed to allow links to people around the world who can give testimony for or against an inmate's guilt. It's never been turned on. There are now seventeen guards per inmate, at a cost of $800K per year for each prisoner.

Guantanamo Justice

The detention center on the Southern tip of Cuba is a gulag, a torture prison in defiance of international and US law. Were it run by some South American tinpot dictator we would easily recognize it for what it is: a torture chamber for political prisoners. Guantanamo mocks America's claim of moral superiority, and represents a key recruitment tool for America's enemies. It has become a cancer on American society, yet no-one seems capable of cutting it out.

Barack Obama campaigned on a promise to close Guantanamo, but failed. In his second term, he barely mentioned it. Obama's original plan bears scrutiny, because while the facility in Cuba would have been closed, that was really just window dressing on an issue that had become an embarrassment to the government, and to the country. Obama only planned to move the prisoners to the US mainland (Illinois, to be specific), leaving the doctrine of indefinite detention without trial untouched.

Although Obama signed an executive decree on his second full day in office, stating that the camp would be closed in a year, it remains open. His efforts were desultory at best, and stymied at every turn by the Republican party.

In many ways the high profile of Guantanamo has been at the expense of greater crimes. The CIA still operates black sites around the world, from which even the most basic of oversights are hidden. We know about Poland, Lithuania, and Romania, but there are many more. On the tenth anniversary of Guantanamo's opening, Bagram prison was estimated to have a population of around three thousand, roughly eighteen times the size of that in Cuba. Although this has been significantly drawn down since then, detainees at Bagram faced, if anything, a much worse set of prospects than those at Guantanamo. The US never named its inmates, they had no access to lawyers, and for the most part the US did not explain who they had or why they were keeping them.

On his release from Guantanamo in 2015, Shaker Aamer quickly indicated that he intended to bring proceedings against the British government, alleging that UK intelligence officers interviewed him three times at Guantanamo and were present while he was tortured in Afghanistan. The British government is widely expected to settle the case with a large cash payment, rather than suffer the embarrassment of having the details aired in court, effectively repressing evidence of Britain's involvement in America's sprawling program of torture and international kidnap. This is justice, Guantanamo style.

CHAPTER SEVENTEEN

AFGHANISTAN

Afghanistan before 9/11

Throughout history, Afghanistan has been prized, coveted, and invaded, as a key pivot between East and West. Control of Central Eurasia was known as the great game among the colonial state actors of the nineteenth century. Great powers tried to exert control for a variety of reasons, mostly financial and geo-strategic. The British, Russians, and Americans all attempted to master this wild country, all without success. Afghanistan finds itself at the confluence of major routes, a boundary and a gateway to central Asian land and sea power. Those who question its value are refuted by history, and by the efforts of Alexander the Great, the Moghuls, Genghis Khan, the British (three times), and the Russians. Their historical failure to gain control over Afghanistan should have been examined much more closely by the Americans in 2001.

Most recently, modern Afghanistan is shaped by the Russian invasion of late 1979, and America's misguided attempts to thwart Russia's military success there. Russia's occupation, at the height of the Cold War, sparked the largest covert operation in the history of the CIA.

The CIA and the ISI (Pakistan's equivalent intelligence service) armed, trained, and financed disparate groups of Afghans, loosely grouped together as the mujahedeen, resisting the Soviets. Around ninety thousand Afghans were trained by the ISI during the ten-year Russian occupation.

America couldn't be seen to be directly arming those fighting the Russians—that risked being taken as an act of war. Instead, the CIA used the ISI as an intermediary through which to funnel arms to the Afghan rebels. Madrasas were set up by Wahhabi fundamentalists and financed by Saudi Arabia. It was the beginning of a long and dysfunctional relationship between the United States and Pakistan that continues to this day. The ISI effectively became an instrument of US foreign policy in the region.

It's a matter of record that this funding included not just the supply of arms, but also the financial backing of Islamic schools, centers and teachings. Radicalized young men produced at these institutions made fanatical fighters against the Soviets, and for a while the US embraced the philosophy that "my enemy's enemy is my friend." Estimates suggest that up to $40 billion was funneled to Afghan fighters over the course of the war. Any method of undermining Russia was considered. The cultivation of poppies was encouraged, ensuring poor Russian troops became heroin addicts, weakening the occupying army.

This misguided action led directly and unquestionably to the rise of the Taliban. It was one of many examples through the second half of the twentieth century of the CIA funding wholly unsavory groups for short-term gain, then reaping the harvest of their short-sighted strategies. Worse, arguably, was the decision to dramatically cut US aid to Afghanistan following the Soviet withdrawal, abandoning the broken country to civil war and chaos.

The Taliban came into existence in 1994, banded together under an extremist ideology in the fertile soils of a country in an almost permanent state of catastrophe.

The internal faction most opposed to the Taliban was the Northern Alliance, a murderous, abusive band of thugs scarcely distinguishable from the Taliban themselves, certainly in terms of appalling behavior, including mass rapes, massacres, murder, and pillage. From 1992 to 1996, the Northern Alliance waged a war against women in particular, using rape, abduction and torture as weapons of war. Their time in power was described by the Executive Director of the arms division of Human Rights Watch, Joost Hiltermann, as the worst in Afghanistan's history—quite a statement given the others to choose from.

So rapacious were the Northern Alliance, in fact, that their conduct helped the Taliban come to power. When control of Kabul was ceded to the Taliban in 1996, the Northern Alliance left the city with fifty thousand dead. The fall of the country's capital signified the Taliban's rise to true national dominance, and they spared no measure in vanquishing their beaten foes. When they took control of Mazar-i-Sharif in August 1998, they killed eight thousand Hazaras in a program that was nothing short of ethnic cleansing.

In the failed state that was Afghanistan, the gun was king and no moderate could hope to thrive. There was virtually no rule of law across the entire land until the Taliban took control, and when they did, it was with an iron fist. Schools were closed, music and television banned. Public beheadings and hangings became commonplace. Amputations were regularly used against those found guilty of theft.

Yet, from 1994 to 1998, the US government actually supported the Taliban as the best chance of forming a stable government, largely ignoring human rights abuses and humanitarian issues in favor of negotiating on behalf of strategic and economic national interests. The Northern alliance often had a shoestring budget, but the Taliban controlled the highly profitable narcotics trade and, crucially, received funding from interests as disparate as Osama bin Laden, Saudi Arabia and the oil company Unocal, allowing their grip on power to remain and flourish.

In 1997, Saudi Arabia became the first country to extend formal recognition to the Taliban government. By 9/11, only three countries had done so: Pakistan and the UAE being the other two (all three states implicated in the events of 9/11). This was no surprise, since the Taliban victory itself had been backed and orchestrated by Pakistan's ISI and Saudi oil interests.

By this time, opium poppies had become Afghanistan's largest export. In 2000, the country produced 70 percent of the world's opium. The illegality of heroin, derived from the easily grown poppy, meant that a crop of almost no intrinsic value was worth a fortune, due simply to the pressures of supply and demand from the West. In a broken society like Afghanistan, control of the heroin meant control of the country.

Such was the Taliban's iron grip on Afghanistan that when they banned the growing of opium poppies in July 2000, the annual crop contracted by over 94 percent. Despite a reputation as Islamic purists and extremists, the Taliban were pragmatists, and had no qualms about the revenue that poppies provided. The ban in 2000 was a move of economic warfare to drive up crop prices and reduce world stockpiles, rather than any kind of moral or religious initiative.

The removal of the Taliban by the US caused the immediate skyrocketing of crops once more—an increase of 657 percent from 2001 to 2002. But the ban they had imposed did the trick, and by 2002 the price of opium was nearly ten times that in the year 2000. The billions in drug money started flowing again almost from the moment the Americans arrived.

The Taliban used religion as a fig leaf. Many of their actions directly violated some of the basic tenets of Islam. In many ways, Taliban laws conformed more to brutal local tribal traditions than to Islam. Either way, they were a reflection of the catastrophe that had been a generation or more in Afghanistan. Opium money was vital to keeping them in power.

Despite the narcotic economy and the Taliban's barely believable human rights violations, in May of 2001, Washington was still the biggest donor of aid to the Taliban regime. Amazingly, in 1999, US tax-payers had paid the entire annual salary of every single Taliban government official.

By 2000, US support for the Taliban began to wane, as it became clear that they would not bow to America's demands. Afghanistan had been in a permanent state of war for over twenty years. Its basic infrastructure had been almost entirely destroyed, and a staggering third of its population was gone—either fled as exiles or refugees, or dead. In that period of war, 1.5 million civilians were killed, the equivalent of twenty-four million dead in the US, proportionately.

The mid-90s discovery of what appeared to be huge oil and gas reserves in the Caspian Sea region left world powers scrambling for access and control over these resources, as industry calculated the profits and worked with governments on how to get the assets to market. The oil fields alone were estimated to have a potential value of $6 trillion.

The five former Soviet republics which hold the preponderance of these resources now hold 6 percent of the world's proven oil reserves and 40 percent of its natural gas (original estimates of oil reserves have been substantially revised down), but they are hemmed in by powers with whom America does not hold a dominant relationship. There is China and the Tibetan plateau to the East, Russia to the North, and the belligerent Iran to the West. Afghanistan offered an easy route to Pakistan, and the safety and warmth of the Gulf of Oman. This route was—and still is—highly prized by the oil behemoths that saw untold billions flowing from a supply taking black Caspian gold to port safely and cheaply. What they wanted was a pipeline.

The lead company in the pipeline project was Unocal, a California-based oil consortium which had been negotiating with the Taliban to build a pipeline from Turkmenistan (via Afghanistan) to Pakistan and the Indian Ocean port of Karachi. Amongst others, Unocal hired Henry Kissinger to canvass for the project. Kissinger was later the White House's first pick to chair the 9/11 Commission. He would, after all, have known a great deal about America's dirty laundry in Afghanistan. His selection horrifically tainted the Bush administration's response to 9/11 with the hint of commerce amid tragedy.

Years of Northern Alliance and Taliban atrocities had scarcely attracted a word of censure from the West, but the discovery of energy reserves in the Caspian basin suddenly shone a light on Afghanistan. While quietly rebuking the Taliban for its human rights violations and treatment of women (humanitarian principles only deemed important when aligned with geopolitical interests), successive US governments secretly conducted negotiations with the Taliban for access to their land for pipelines.

Money, like politics, makes for strange bedfellows, and in December 1997 representatives of the Taliban were invited to Texas by Unocal to discuss the pipeline. It appears to have been an eccentric clash of cultures, but that mattered little. After all, the Saudis are extremist religious fundamentalists too, and that has proved no barrier to a relationship built on necessity that has spanned decades.

Such are the close ties and revolving doors in US foreign policy and business that while Unocal was arranging for Taliban ministers to meet State Department officials, the Taliban employed Laili Helms as their spokesperson in New York. She is the niece (by marriage) of Richard Helms, the former boss of the CIA. Helms Jr. told the *Village Voice* in June 2001 that US authorities had repeatedly turned down offers from the Taliban to facilitate the assassination of Osama bin Laden as part of their negotiations. She seemed unconcerned by the Taliban's treatment of women back in Afghanistan.

Energy giant Enron (the criminal investigation of which was badly set back by the collapse of 7 World Trade Center on 9/11) also had huge interests in the region, paying more than $400 million for a pipeline feasibility study, though most of the money went directly as bribes to the Taliban. Enron exerted huge influence in the United States, using Richard Cheney among others to block any government investigation into their immoral dealings with the Taliban.

The Taliban was carefully kept off the State Department's terrorism list, as a declaration that the Taliban were in fact terrorists would have stopped any pipeline deals. This block helped stop the American public from learning more about the diabolical deals being negotiated with a regime that routinely employed rape, torture and execution. Making deals with people like that does not look good in the papers.

The confluence of money and foreign policy can leave you breathless in its contradictory belligerence. By this point it was clear for all to see that the Taliban were a genocidal murderous regime, conducting vast and dreadful human rights abuses, controlling the world's heroin market and hosting a man who had launched terrorist attacks on Americans and continued to do so. Yet Enron and Unocal had other fish to fry, and the political influence to overcome these contradictions.

Indeed, the cooling of the US relationship with the Taliban stemmed not from any moral issues, but from a growing realization that the Taliban were not going to play ball and be the servile government the US required as their entry point to central Asia. By 1999, it was clear that the Taliban would not only not allow a pipeline to be built, but they appeared unable to provide the level of security that was required. Worse, they wanted $100 million per year in rent for the pipeline route, something that was considered unreasonable, despite being common practice elsewhere.

Unocal indefinitely suspended work on the pipeline project in August 1998. It was making no progress, despite company vice president John Maresca being a former US ambassador to the region. US policy began to turn.

In December 2000 it was reported that the US government had quietly begun to align itself with others in calling for military action against Afghanistan. US, Russian, and Indian officials met at this time to discuss what type of government should replace the Taliban. These discussions continued through early to mid-2001. Throughout the year 2000, the US grew progressively more hostile, but even during the early part of 2001, the Bush administration—secretly formulating plans to invade—continued negotiating with the Taliban.

The offers seemed generous. Indeed, with the Pakistani government backing and arming them and the US ignoring their behavior and making cash offers in order to secure access for pipelines, the Taliban's was a charmed existence—a rogue regime whom kindly patrons hoped would one day come into line.

As the relationship with the Taliban foundered, the US repeatedly tried to save it. In July 2001 a further $43 million was given in food aid, though the aid was provided without any accountability, meaning the Taliban could do whatever they liked with it (which almost definitely would not be food). At the same time, the Bush administration gave the Taliban their final warning to pursue stability and allow oil consortiums to build their pipelines, or face destruction. The last offer was made just five weeks before 9/11. At the meeting, Tom Simons, former US ambassador to Pakistan, said, "Either you accept our offer of a carpet of gold, or we bury you under a carpet of bombs." Simons made it clear—cooperate or face "a military operation."

The threat of war and economic strangulation was designed to pressure the Taliban into capitulation. But no progress was made. Something would have to give.

Former National Security Adviser Zbigniew Brzezinski outlined the importance of Afghanistan in cold detail in his 1997 book *The Grand Chessboard: American Primacy and its Geostrategic Imperatives*. Highlighting the value of the vast energy reserves in the Caspian Basin and the overriding necessity of gaining US access to and control of these reserves (and as Middle Eastern reserves began to dwindle), Brzezinski wrote that gaining control of the region required a consensus on foreign policy issues from the American public. He added that "the pursuit of power is not a goal that commands popular passion, except in conditions of a sudden threat or challenge to the public's sense of domestic wellbeing."

To put it another way, military ventures designed to secure geopolitical power do not receive the backing of the American public unless they are scared out of their wits. Brzezinski concluded that the needed consensus on foreign policy issues would be difficult to obtain, except in the circumstance of a "truly massive and widely perceived direct external threat." Three years later, the Project for the New American Century would also voice such sentiments.

Note that there is a big difference between highlighting public attitudes in relation to threats, and including a wish list which suddenly becomes available due to that threat becoming reality.

From 9/11 to the War

The attacks of 9/11 came just in time for the commencement of a war in Afghanistan. The harshness of Afghan winters mean that once much of the country is covered in snow, the options for military progress are limited. This is why the summer is known as fighting season. Had the terrorist attacks taken place on the 11th of November, a ground invasion would most probably have had to have been delayed until the spring.

There is, however, a great deal of evidence that the Bush administration was planning for a war in Afghanistan to commence in October of 2001, well in advance of the attacks of September 11.

Jane's Defense Weekly, the publication of record for that industry, reported in March 2001 that the US planned to invade Afghanistan in October of that year. Niaz Naik, former Pakistani foreign secretary, was told by senior US officials in mid July that military action against Afghanistan would go ahead by the middle of October, "before the snow starts falling." The ultimate objective, he was told, was to remove the Taliban and install a moderate (meaning compliant) government in its place.

This military plan for a US invasion from the North was well known by the summer of 2001 (and opposed by central Asian governments). In light of all the evidence, the best guess is that a war plan had been 'in the works' for at least four years.

As usual, the impression was given that war could be avoided. After 9/11, the US demanded the Taliban hand over Osama bin Laden, and the Taliban said they would do so—if the US could produce conclusive evidence that he was involved in the 9/11 attacks. The Bush administration dismissed this out of hand, calling it a delaying tactic. In truth, international extradition always requires a level of proof be supplied to the host country.

Operation Enduring Freedom (America's codename for the invasion) was largely based on a scenario that had been examined by Central Command in May of 2001. By the end of the summer a full contingency plan for attacking Afghanistan from the North was in place. As a consequence, it took just twenty-six days for the "Allies" to plan, mobilize and launch an attack in distant Afghanistan, after the shock attacks on September 11. Enduring Freedom started on October 7, 2001.

The short space of time between the 9/11 attacks and commencement of the war in Afghanistan was greatly facilitated by the proximity and preparedness of a great deal of army and navy divisions. Once again, by good fortune or otherwise, huge military resources were nearby.

US rangers were on exercises in nearby Kyrgyzstan. Two US aircraft carrier task forces had just arrived in the Persian Gulf at the same time, on rotation. Just before 9/11, the British army put together its largest armada since the Falklands War, as part of a military exercise called Swift Sword II, and had 22,500 air, ground, and naval troops in nearby Oman when the attacks came. NATO moved forty thousand troops to Egypt just before 9/11. An infantryman from the South Carolina National Guard said that in July 2001 all plans for the next two months had been suddenly cancelled, and they were told to prepare for a mobilization exercise on September 14. By the end of August, they were fully prepared for action, with bags and equipment packed; in the highest state of readiness.

Ahmad Shah Massoud

With the Taliban controlling most of Afghanistan, the United Front (another name for the Northern Alliance) was the only substantial domestic opposition force. Sworn enemies of the Taliban, and headed by the charismatic figurehead Ahmad Shah Massoud, the Northern Alliance was the most likely group to take control of the country should the Taliban have been overthrown.

As US negotiations with the Taliban over pipelines and land access progressed, America sought to pacify the Northern Alliance, fearing that a civil war would fracture the fragile peace (of sorts) that the Taliban's rule brought. Bill Richardson and Karl Inderfurth, high ranking members of the Bush administration, both personally visited Afghanistan to discourage various smaller factions from attacking the Taliban. This was one of a number of factors that led to the defeat or surrender of all but one of the Taliban's enemies—Commander Massoud in the North.

Despite its opposition to the Taliban, the Northern Alliance was not the West's darling. The Alliance received backing and arms from Iran and Russia, and showed no sign of wishing to accommodate US demands on Afghan soil. Massoud, a proud and independent nationalist, would not have taken orders from the CIA and the US, nor allowed Western troops into territory he controlled. When surrender was suggested, Massoud threw his hat on the table in front of him and said so long as the Northern Alliance controlled territory as large as the hat, he would never surrender. This was a problem for the United States and their designs on Afghanistan.

However, the Northern Alliance was effectively decapitated just two days before the attacks in the US. On September 9, 2001, General Massoud was assassinated by two Tunisian men posing as Moroccan journalists. They had been trying to gain an interview with Massoud for a number of days, and appear to have grown more agitated and urgent with every passing day. When they finally were granted the interview, a bomb hidden in their video camera exploded, killing Massoud instantly. Both assassins died in the attack.

Massoud had just returned from a trip to Europe, where he had been trying to gain political backing for his group's opposition to the Taliban (who of course hosted al-Qaeda).

Although the assassination was blamed on Osama bin Laden, the accusation was supported by little or no evidence. Bin Laden rarely acted strategically inside Afghanistan, and appeared to care little about defending the Taliban. The ISI, however, was heavily implicated—the Northern Alliance issued a press release the day after the killing saying as much. The timing of the assassination strongly suggests that the ISI knew of the upcoming attacks in America. It is far from drawing a long bow to suggest that if the ISI knew, so did the CIA.

Massoud's death fractured and ended the threat posed by the Northern Alliance. This was extremely convenient for any external army wishing to invade and take control of the country. Only the Taliban would now need to be deposed, with no other internal entity capable of imposing its own wishes on the nation's politics.

Had Massoud lived, he would have been the leading candidate to become Afghanistan's new head of government. The day after the assassination, the BBC commented that with Massoud's death the Northern Alliance was effectively finished, since there was clearly no figure with the skills and popularity to replace him. The US quickly put many of its senior leaders and allies on the CIA payroll.

The Shanghai Five alliance (China, Russia, Kazakhstan, Kyrgyzstan, and Uzbekistan) had threatened US preeminence in the region in the 1990s. Massoud had attended one (or perhaps more) of the regular meetings of this group. His Alliance received their implicit and very powerful support. But all that changed in the three days from the ninth to eleventh of September, 2001. Suddenly America was going to take control of the key to Central Asia, and with Massoud dead, only the Taliban stood in their way.

A Morphing War

When Russia invaded Afghanistan it had to fight not only the Afghans but up to one hundred thousand mercenaries and thugs trained by the CIA and ISI. The US in 2001 faced no such threat, and took on a broken country ruled by the Taliban, who had no formal government or army. Their immediate collapse was never in question.

The goals of Enduring Freedom, as outlined by President Bush in early October 2001, were to destroy terrorist training camps and infrastructure, capture al-Qaeda's leaders, and stop terrorism emanating from Afghanistan. Most of these goals were quickly and painlessly accomplished, as might be expected when the richest nation on earth invades one of the poorest. The Taliban were toppled inside sixty days, at a cost of $3.8 billion and with the loss of just five Allied lives. Many of the known terrorist sites were bombed and destroyed. But capturing al-Qaeda's leaders proved much harder, not least because almost immediately after the invasion commenced, the focus seemed to shift away from the most obvious goal—capturing or killing the man who the US blamed for the devastating attacks on 9/11.

Five months after the war started, President Bush seemed bizarrely disinterested in the whereabouts of Osama bin Laden, saying in March 2002, "I just don't spend that much time on him." It seemed an extraordinary statement—an American president openly voicing apathy as to the whereabouts of the man blamed for the death of three thousand people, just six months after 9/11. We now know that the Bush administration's focus was turning towards Iraq, but the complete disinterest in bin Laden still seems inexplicable.

The war in Afghanistan was always perceived as the good war, especially when placed against the Iraqi debacle. But as time passed, the war being fought to avenge 9/11 became a war to prevent future terrorism, then to liberate Afghans from the Taliban, then to bring democracy, and perhaps finally to preserve our side's credibility by not ending this constantly morphing war. None of these goals were achieved, save for the dubious death of Osama bin Laden and the fracturing of his pathetic band of hoodlums.

The idea that America could somehow have defeated a thousand years of history and transformed this brutalized, broken country into a flower of pro-Western democracy, using their military as freedom missionaries, was beyond absurd. Yet, that notion initially had traction among the American public, fed by righteous anger at the 9/11 attacks and kept misinformed about the likely outcomes by a corporate media who acted as cheerleaders.

Those who knew Afghanistan knew the likely outcome. The *Guardian's* veteran foreign correspondent Jonathan Steele, who had covered the Russian occupation of Afghanistan and subsequent civil war, warned just two days after 9/11 of the folly of a US invasion, offering a prediction that holds good today:

> "You can garrison the cities and deploy your troops in lowland bases. You can rumble up and down between them. But you can never occupy the mountain villages or find, among the hundreds of mutually antagonistic tribal groupings, local leaders to do your bidding for long. The British tried three times to subdue Afghanistan, the Russians once, and if American troops invaded they would no doubt meet the same fate."

It seemed a war entirely absent of strategy. Many of the problems encountered by the occupying troops arose due to a total lack of coherent narrative describing why the US was there, what their goals were, and how the war could be won and concluded. Much the same could be said for the Iraqi war. Instead, the Afghanistan conflict became the longest war in US and Australian history, the longest war Britain fought since the Hundred Years War six hundred years earlier.

With every passing year, the war's central narrative veered further and further from 9/11. But even that was questionable. The Taliban had not attacked the US on 9/11, nor were any of the hijackers Afghans.

The only strategy on show in the early months of the war seemed to be the collective punishment of the Afghan people, which amounted to clear acts of state terrorism. At least five thousand civilians were killed by the bombardment in the space of the first eight weeks, almost double the toll of the 9/11 attacks. This was despite there being nearly no organized opposition whatsoever to the invading Americans.

Several million innocent Afghan civilians fled to the country's borders, fleeing not the Taliban, but the US onslaught. The border to Pakistan was kept sealed for several weeks at US insistence (citing the risk that bin Laden's men would escape this way), leading to further deaths from a lack of water and nutrition. Conditions inside Afghan refugee camps were described by one aid worker as the worst they'd ever seen. Food drops were a tiny fraction of what was required.

As for surgical strikes from the air, US defense officials claimed that there was a lack of hard targets, hardly a surprise given al-Qaeda's training camps were small, entirely undefended, and ramshackle. Despite this, the heavy bombers kept up the barrage, leading many to suggest that the air campaign was a brutal "softening up" process being meted out on the Afghan population to make them more compliant for the coming US proxy rule.

There are several examples from the early stages of the war to support the notion that the civilian population was deliberately targeted. The offices of a UN agency body were bombed October 9, 2001, despite the address having been passed to the US military to avoid being attacked. Whole villages were flattened, despite being known to pose no threat. Later in that month, buildings owned by the International Committee of the Red Cross (ICRC) in Kabul were bombed from low altitude on two separate occasions, despite having large red crosses painted on the roof, and the compounds being only two kilometers from the city's airport.

The US required both Pakistani airspace and cooperation in order to conduct their war on Afghanistan, but throughout the war turned a blind eye to the well-known ties between Pakistan's ISI and al-Qaeda, a contradiction that meant America's main ally in the region was a country that broadly supported the enemy, and provided ongoing and overt support for the people they were fighting.

The commercial interests at play were not hard to discern. On December 22, 2001, just over one hundred days after the 9/11 attacks, the US installed Hamid Karzai as Prime Minister. Nine days later, President Bush appointed Zalmay Khalilzad as America's special envoy.

Karzai and Khalilzad were oil men, both previously on Unocal's payroll. Khalilzad was also a member of the Project for the New American Century. The neocons had their man in Kabul.

Karzai had worked both as lobbyist for Unocal and Deputy Foreign Minister for the Taliban, providing a key link during earlier negotiations between the two. In addition, he was well-known to be corrupt, a CIA asset, regular drug taker, and a crook. With the population displaced, terrified, or dead, the oil men were taking over.

The neighboring countries to the north mostly acceded to American requests to use their soil as launching pads for the Afghan invasion. Thirteen new military tent cities in nine countries now encircled the Afghan border, ensuring not only control of the main gateway for the exploitation of Caspian resource wealth, but a semi-permanent presence of over sixty thousand US troops in the former Soviet and Transcaucasian countries that held these resources.

Uri Avnery, an Israeli writer and former member of the Knesset, said in the daily newspaper *Maariv*, "If one looks at the map of the big American bases created for the war, one is struck by the fact that they are completely identical to the route of the projected oil pipeline to the Indian Ocean." He added, "If I were a believer in conspiracy theory, I would think that Osama bin Laden is an American agent."

By November 2001, bin Laden and his cohorts had disappeared through the hills of Tora Bora and into Pakistan, and the true business of the war—a lengthy occupation of Afghanistan—could begin.

Long guerilla wars inevitably brutalize the occupiers as well as the occupied, exacerbating the problems they came to solve and leading to an unwinnable situation in which both sides misery can only be ended by the withdrawal of the outsiders. This agony tends to continue until it is politically expedient for the occupier's leader (normally a new leader, who can save face) to take the decision to withdraw. Such was the case with Russia's occupation of Afghanistan. Mikhail Gorbachev came to power and quickly saw that Afghanistan was lost, but even this moderate man took four years to find the right time to turn the tanks for home.

America's war in Afghanistan was no different. It began with troops on the ground speaking of winning hearts and minds and working with the Afghans to free their country, and degenerated slowly to the point where Hamid Karzai expelled US Special Forces from certain areas of the country after corroborated accounts of war crimes committed against local civilians. This brutalization of occupying troops is entirely to be expected and the atrocities committed by the occupiers became a cancer, their actions deteriorating the very situation they were trying to control.

Afghanistan is such a disparate society that controlling all of it has been beyond nearly everyone (including Afghans) for a thousand years. Knowing the limits of Karzai's Kabul regime, the CIA and US military organized and trained local paramilitary militias, specifically to operate independently of the Afghan government. Of course, local militias often dealt with local issues, and had little or no accountability. It wasn't long before complaints were received about individuals being abducted, tortured, or killed by those funded by the Americans. Once again, a US military occupation had become synonymous with the arrival of the death squads. The occupier's actions often took on a similar hue to those of the Taliban, from whom they purported to be liberating the people.

Karzai himself has constantly bit the hand that feeds him. He's accused American troops of conniving with the Taliban to set off bomb attacks, called the Taliban his brothers, and said that if there was a war between America and Pakistan, he would support the Pakistanis. In 2015, Karzai questioned the very existence of al-Qaeda, calling the group a myth, and denied that Afghanistan had been the country from which the 9/11 attacks were planned and launched.

The degrading effect of a long occupation was evident in what began being described as isolated incidents—in which allied troops were found to be committing atrocities against Afghan fighters or civilians. This was as inevitable as the rising sun, given the length of the occupation and the often brutal conditions in which soldiers had to operate. In one incident in March 2012, US soldier Robert Bales left his barracks at night and murdered sixteen Afghan civilians, nine of them children. Bales burned the bodies of his victims, but despite committing a crime in Afghanistan whose victims were Afghans, the government of that country was allowed no role in his prosecution. Although eyewitnesses in the villages described multiple attackers, the US insisted Bales alone was involved, and he was quickly whisked out of the country for trial.

Although the Bales story was one of the most egregious, it was far from the only one. Videos were exposed of troops burning the Koran or urinating on dead Afghans. US "kill team" troops were found to be killing civilians for fun, hacking off parts of the dead bodies and taking photos as trophies before leaving weapons in their victims hands, to make it look like they had been engaged in combat. A British guard with a hangover stabbed a ten-year-old in the kidney with a bayonet for no apparent reason. Each time, army officials claimed that these were isolated incidents, but when placed together it's easy to see that, far from isolated, they became a routine symptom of occupiers fighting a long and asymmetric war.

Jeremy Scahill's outstanding investigative reporting allowed us insight into yet another horrific incident in 2010, when US forces attacked a house in a village in Paktia province, killing five civilians who walked unarmed out of their front door to ask what was going on. The five included two Afghan government officials who were working closely with US forces, and two pregnant women. The Pentagon initially released statements blaming the victims, calling the surviving Afghans liars, and saying that the women were already dead on their arrival, victims of "honor killings." The compliant US media followed the party line with scarcely a murmur of dissent. But Scahill's reporting forced the Pentagon to admit that their account was completely false. In fact, soldiers had used knives to dig bullets out of the pregnant women's bodies, to cover their tracks.

These sorts of incidents only exacerbated the civilian population's mistrust of the US army and the information it provided. American behavior was so egregious in some areas that local Afghans called US Special Forces the "American Taliban." In November 2016, it was reported that 42 percent of Afghans said that security was worse than it had been under the Taliban's rule.

Looking back through recent history, at the My Lai massacre in Vietnam, the butchery in Iraq, or any other long occupation (including the Soviets in Afghanistan), it's clear these incidents were the direct result of the corrosive effect that occupying troops encounter when placed in an impossibly dangerous situation for long periods of time. However, in some respects it's hard to blame the soldiers, sent to a distant land to gain revenge for an attack at home, but ending up just as savage as those they sought to avenge. True responsibility lies with those who commanded them.

Under Bush and Obama, the role of JSOC (Joint Special Operations Command) changed dramatically. JSOC is the most covert and secretive unit in the US Army, and the only one that reports directly to the White House. Initially in Iraq, then in Afghanistan, JSOC's size and scope increased exponentially. It's not overstating things to say that that JSOC's expansion has fundamentally changed the way America wages war. JSOC's covert missions, which are almost always capture, kill, render, or torture (or a combination of those) can be directly controlled by the president without any further oversight. This is something unprecedented in US history—a paramilitary private army for the president alone. Death squads, in other words. It's certainly not what you would call a well-regulated militia, and we know from recent history that executive control over unaccountable paramilitary forces eventually leads a society to disaster.

All this took place under the good new president, Mr. Obama (a constitutional law professor), who promised a new way of doing things and much greater oversight. In fact, he did the opposite.

Occupying Afghanistan had nothing to do with Osama bin Laden, and any pretense that it did was quickly dropped. The troops on the ground seemed entirely expendable, in a war that seems to have had a different justification with each year that passes. Afghan civilians saw yet further calamity befall their country.

Those who stayed often tried to survive and make money with the only industry that guaranteed returns.

Opium

It's impossible to tell the story of Afghanistan and America's war there without highlighting the extraordinarily prominent role opium plays in that country's economy and politics. Without the revenue from opium, the Taliban could not possibly have maintained control. The explosion in the cultivation of opium poppies from the moment of America's arrival helps explain the abject failure of that occupation.

Upon taking office, Hamid Karzai announced a total ban on opium cultivation, reasoning that the key to reducing the Taliban's power was to remove the major source of their revenue. But the plan to implement the measure was a laughable sham. Karzai's government offered farmers $500 for each acre of poppies destroyed, but farmers could earn more than $6,000 per acre for an opium crop, so naturally the ban didn't come close to working. National reconstruction projects sped the growth of the opium trade. US taxpayer money built new roads, provided better irrigation, and dug deep new wells. All assisted greatly in increasing the cultivation of opium poppies across the country.

As is so often the case, while this might at first glance look like a terrible failure, not everyone was a loser. The infamous paramilitary company Blackwater and defense behemoth Northrop Grumman both received hugely profitable contracts worth hundreds of millions of dollars to participate in the program of opium poppy eradication. In total, the Pentagon spent over $7.6 billion on poppy eradication from 2002 to 2014. Just look at the results.

Up to 50 percent of Afghanistan's GDP now comes from opium (the country is a war zone; reliable figures are impossible to compile), with over six thousand tons produced in 2013. Annual crops are regularly reported to be breaking all records. Every metric tells a story of failure. Grapes used to be Afghanistan's biggest export, but poppies grow in six months (sometimes less), and the "War on Drugs" guarantees that the illicit demand for these abundant flowers will never drop. Farmers make seventeen times as much from an opium crop than they would if they grew wheat. Faced with such choices, what would you grow? Military personnel knew that eradication was a waste of time and distracting them from engaging the real enemy. Farmers saw crop destruction as the removal of their only viable source of income, turning entire communities against the American occupiers.

The US government grows opium legitimately in Turkey for its domestic painkiller market, but refused to buy the Afghan crops, which would have cut the Taliban off at the knees. Instead the US consistently blamed the Afghan government for the problem, and ignored the demand for heroin from the West that guarantees a source of supply somewhere on earth. The Afghans, in turn, blamed international drug consumers.

What is ironic is that the Taliban's iron grip on the nation, pre-2001, was more effective in regulating the growth of opium poppies than the might of the richest nation on earth and its war machine.

In late 2014, it was reported that the largest opium crop in Afghanistan's history had been achieved. America's long war and huge expenditure had made no impact. Afghanistan remained dominated by warlords and opium money, and produced 90 percent of the world's supply, mostly destined for sale on the streets of Europe and the US. Its political leaders scarcely controlled more than the capital Kabul.

There is a clear and demonstrable link between the production and consumption of illegal drugs and the financing of terrorism, yet it's something that the West refuses to acknowledge or address. If ever there was an example as to why Afghanistan proved an unwinnable war, this is it. Every wasted moment closing down the only income stream of a desperately poor nation by destroying the only thing that grows or sells, was another step towards losing the war.

Denouement

America's decision to withdraw troops from Afghanistan to pursue its Iraqi adventure, as well as its bizarre disinterest in strategy and pursuing Osama bin Laden, meant that within two years of the invasion, the war was lost. Or, to be more precise, it could no longer be won.

The latter years of the Afghan War were characterized by the withdrawal of allied troops to heavily guarded bases, allowing the country to be run by a government named as the third most corrupt in the world. Hamid Karzai's administration was so corrupt and ineffective that many Afghans said they had preferred living under the Taliban.

For those unfortunate Western troops who remained as the years passed, the tragedy grew more acute, as it became clear that young lives were being lost simply because, although the war had long since been accepted to be lost, the time had not yet come for it to be politically expedient to declare as such, so young men and women who chose to serve their country lay dying because Presidents Bush and Obama hadn't yet found the moment which would suit the agenda of their precious political careers, to tell their people the game was up.

The logic of America's decision to stay became more and more tortuous. In 2011, James Bucknall, the deputy commander of NATO forces in Afghanistan, spoke of NATO's "investment in blood." In 2012, British Defense Secretary Philip Hammond uttered the viciously awful line, "We owe it to the all too many who have sacrificed their lives to see this mission concluded." People had to continue to die because others already had.

Successive prime ministers claimed that the actions of British troops in Helmand were vital to Britain's national security, and essential in keeping the streets of Britain safe. This was a bizarre, absurd, and immoral claim, when the truth was the opposite. British operations in Iraq and Afghanistan were recruitment tools for extremists, and cited as justification for Islamic terrorist attacks in Europe. The stupidity, intransigence, and pride of Britain's prime ministers led straight to terror attacks on British soil.

Each of the three notable attacks in the UK—the London bombings, the Glasgow attack, and the murder of Lee Rigby—were perpetrated by people who directly referenced Britain's involvement in the wars in Iraq and Afghanistan as their justification. Conversely, every outrage was cited by British prime ministers as an attack on Britain's way of life. But that too was clearly nonsense. Attacks on Britain's streets were predictable consequences of its government's foreign policies, something domestic security services stated was likely to occur, and for which they extensively prepared. Using the West's logic, if the world is a battlefield, then those striking back can feel justified in taking action anywhere, including on Britain's streets. The only surprise is how limited the attacks have been.

After eight years of fighting in Helmand, British forces held just three of its fourteen districts. At a cost to the British taxpayer of around £6 billion per year, the British held three districts in an area of Afghanistan that contains 3 percent of the population. Poppies, the symbol of British military sacrifice, bloomed unabated in Helmand, with the amount of land being used to grow heroin at record levels, tripling under Britain's watch from 2006 to 2013.

At the beginning of the war in Afghanistan, Tony Blair said that ending the opium and heroin trade was a key objective, saying, "The arms (that) the Taliban buy are paid for by the lives of young British people buying their drugs." Afghanistan now grows more poppies than ever before. It is as decisive a loss as one can imagine.

By the end of the war, the US had spent more on one conflict in Afghanistan than it had on the Marshall Plan for rebuilding Europe after World War II. The cost was around $1 million per soldier per year. Best estimates say that a total of $1 trillion was spent in Afghanistan, enough to give every Afghan over $30,000 each, or seventy-eight years of annual income per person. Imagine what a transformation that might have made to the country. Yet visitors to Afghanistan report a total absence of evidence of this money. Ten percent of the country has electricity. With all this expense and the most sophisticated weaponry and troops on earth, the US was not able to prevail. The money was entirely squandered.

Western leaders love to proudly declare that they don't negotiate with terrorists, yet as the idea of winning the Afghan war receded the US quietly began negotiations with the Taliban, a group whose actions are the very definition of terrorism. In early 2011, the US was reported to be negotiating the release of several high-ranking Taliban leaders incarcerated at Guantanamo Bay, including the former Deputy Defense Minister Mullah Mohammad Fazl Akhund, as part of a deal to hand back control of Afghanistan. In the end, Fazl and four others were swapped for the release of US soldier Bowe Bergdahl. Negotiations continue. The West regularly negotiates with terrorists. To claim otherwise is a lie.

There have been successes. Schools were built, and for a while the most egregious behaviors of the Taliban were rolled back. Briefly, women could walk the streets of Kabul without the full burka. In 2014, 2.9 million girls went to school in Afghanistan. In 2001 that number had been zero. But by 2015, the Taliban were threatening to take back the capital Kabul. It is by no means certain that the number of girls at school will not again drop to zero. But these small successes were an exception to an otherwise depressing rule of diminishing returns. Afghanistan today remains one of the worst countries on earth to be a woman.

If anything, civilian casualty figures went up, rather than down, as the war drew to a close. In 2014, over five thousand Afghan soldiers and two thousand civilians were killed. When sovereignty was handed back to Afghanistan (on December 28, 2014), a whole generation had grown knowing nothing but war. Children of just five in 2001 were now eighteen, and had no recollection of a time when their country was not occupied by Americans with guns. If ever you question how people can act so savagely, eighteen-year-olds in Afghanistan may be able to give you an answer.

Although 9/11 and al-Qaeda were the fallbacks of choice when Western leaders were pressed on a justification for the ongoing action in Afghanistan, President Obama's National Security Adviser, General James L. Jones, suggested in 2009 that there were less than one hundred al-Qaeda members left in the whole country. Most thought the number was closer to fifty. When General David Petraeus took over the war in 2010, his morning briefings almost never mentioned al-Qaeda. In March 2012, *The Nation* magazine reported that allied troops had killed just one person connected to al-Qaeda in the previous ten months, a period during which the Coalition had suffered 466 fatalities. Al-Qaeda, the entity supposedly responsible for the 9/11 attacks, had by all accounts ceased to exist.

Afghans quite reasonably questioned why defeating the Taliban was an objective only addressed in their country, when a seemingly endless supply of radicalized fighters continued to stream from the madrasas through the porous border with Pakistan. Many pertinently asked if perhaps the Americans were actually in the wrong country altogether.

President Obama originally planned to withdraw US troops and air forces completely, but it became clear that the country was not nearly capable of running itself—if the Americans left, the place would implode. So in 2015, Obama announced a reversal of his long-standing promise to end America's military presence in Afghanistan. Around nine thousand troops remained when he left office. If or when they depart, they will bequeath a country in some ways similar to the state it was in when the Russians left. State forces may be able to control the cities, but the rest of the country will be without any clear governance, and mostly run by tribes, thugs, militants, and the gun. The longest war in US history sees no end in sight. As the Taliban make gains across the country, America apparently wishes to stay to slow their progress. Blame Obama if you like, but the Republicans wanted more troops there, not less.

Agreements made between the Obama administration and the Afghan government mean a US and NATO military presence in Afghanistan until 2024 and beyond. This is a permanent occupation, a projection of ongoing military strength in the region. Access to air and land bases mean America will be able to control the region, and continue to kill legitimate opposition to its rule with drones from the skies. The US pays all or nearly all of Afghanistan's security budget. If members of the army stop getting paid, they will go home. It's clear that should American money and troops be withdrawn, the Taliban again will rule Afghanistan. Fifteen years of war will have accomplished nothing.

So, why is America in Afghanistan today? Perhaps it is to project power in East Asia, to surround China, and to protect resource supplies in the region. Perhaps it is simply to save face, to not lose yet another war, something that will rock the confidence of those states who rely on the US to save them should another power threaten their sovereignty. Perhaps it is the knowledge that a failed Afghanistan would lead to a further deluge of asylum seekers across the Western world (Afghans are the second most numerous refugees, after Syrians). Whatever the answer, America faces an invidious choice—leave, lose, and watch the country implode, or continue to pour billions into an unwinnable situation, just to ensure the uneasy status quo.

There was nothing inevitable about the wars that followed 9/11. If it is true that nineteen Arabs perpetrated 9/11, there was little need for a war then and there is no need at all now. To believe that the West was justified in occupying Afghanistan is to agree that the original justifications for the war were a pack of lies. And if that is the case, then the Afghan invasion was a war crime.

In April 2002, FBI Director Robert Mueller admitted during a speech that after six months inside Afghanistan, US forces had not found a single piece of documentary evidence that related to 9/11. In many ways this admission was even more stunning than the failure to find Iraqi WMDs. Consider these words from Mueller:

> "The hijackers also left no paper trail. In our investigation we have not uncovered a single piece of paper—either here in the US, or in the treasure trove of information that has turned up in Afghanistan and elsewhere—that mentioned any aspect of the September 11 plot."

He added that no single person had been found in the United States who knew anything of the plot except the nineteen dead hijackers.

Not a single piece of paper or a single person. We were lied to, and those lies continue today.

CHAPTER EIGHTEEN

IRAQ

In 1821, President John Quincy Adams warned the US, "Go not abroad in search of monsters to destroy, lest she involve herself beyond the power of extrication . . . the fundamental maxims of her policy would insensibly change from liberty to force. She might become the dictatress of the world; she would be no longer the ruler of her own spirit."

As we have seen, spinning a terrorist attack on America that was planned in Afghanistan and carried out almost exclusively by Saudis into justification for an invasion of Iraq took an unprecedented media propaganda campaign. Bush's henchmen were able to drum the phrase "weapons of mass destruction" so incessantly into American heads that by the time of the invasion, most Americans thought Saddam Hussein had personally been involved in the 9/11 attacks.

George W. Bush's speech to the United Nations on September 12, 2002 was perhaps the high point of his administration's arrogance. In a manner that took people's breath away, Bush commanded the UN to vote for a war against Iraq, or risk becoming irrelevant. The message was clear—we're invading Iraq whether you like it or not.

The UN Charter (ratified by the US) is the foundation of international law. Article 2(4) states unequivocally that members should refrain from the threat of or use of force against any state, unless supported by a Security Council resolution. In the absence of an armed attack from Iraq or the threat of one (and there was neither), then an invasion of Iraq by the US was clearly a breach of international law. Kofi Annan agreed, calling the action illegal (but only in September 2004, eighteen months after the war started).

America's launching of a war in Iraq was also a violation of the Nuremberg Principles, set up in the shadow of World War II. It hardly needs repeating that the war against Iraq, launched on a lie, fits the definition of a crime of aggression. Nuremberg called it the "supreme international crime."

Accordingly, warrants for the arrest of Tony Blair and George W. Bush should be issued by the International Criminal Court (ICC). However, the US isn't a signatory to the Rome Statute that established the ICC, and is not a participant in the court, precisely because America's overseas behavior would make it a prime target for prosecutors interested in the even-handed application of international law. The US has actually declared all of its citizens immune from prosecution by the ICC, so international law remains something rich nations apply selectively against poor ones, and flout routinely when it serves their purpose.

Any hope of controlling Afghanistan or capturing Osama bin Laden was drastically reduced by the Bush administration's decision to pivot toward Iraq in 2002. Special forces with Middle Eastern experience were withdrawn from Afghanistan in preparation for an attack on Iraq. Their replacements had expertise in Spanish cultures, something not broadly required in Afghanistan.

For the Bush administration, propaganda not only got them the war they wanted, it was invaluable in stoking domestic political support. An Inter Press Service story in April 2004 found that 57 percent of those who thought Saddam Hussein and Iraq had been involved in 9/11 said they intended to vote for Bush in the upcoming election. Only 28 percent of those who didn't believe the Iraq-9/11 connection were going to vote for him. The more people who thought Iraq was connected to 9/11, the more votes Bush got.

A Total Absence of Strategy

The 2003 Iraq invasion and subsequent war will go down in history as one of the most poorly planned and executed military campaigns of all time. It failed on almost every level, often in ways which would have been comically inept, were it not for the tragedy that blanketed everything. By all accounts, there was virtually no planning whatsoever for the ongoing occupation of the country. The Bush White House apparently expected American troops to be greeted as liberators, and that a stable democracy could be established almost immediately. This scarcely credible insouciance is supported by the lack of documentation showing a comprehensive post-invasion plan. A more cynical view is that Bush and his team didn't care what happened to the country. The war was fought specifically to take control of Iraq's oil fields, and its people simply weren't a consideration.

Saddam Hussein's twenty-four-year reign illustrates the fluid nature of US patronage. During the Iran-Iraq war, Hussein was feted as a bulwark against the Soviet-backed Iranians, and although the US cynically funded and armed both sides in the war, only Hussein received public praise and got to shake Donald Rumsfeld's hand.

It's easy to forget that for many years, Saddam was venerated as a sort of Arab Hugo Chavez, nationalizing the country's oil assets and using the 1973 energy crisis and subsequent huge increases in oil revenues to implement social programs that made Iraq the envy of the Middle East. Public health and education programs improved the lives of ordinary Iraqis beyond recognition, and a raft of standardized public health measures such as literacy, decreases in infant mortality, and life expectancy reflected a society at the vanguard of progressivism in the Arab world.

Iraqis today often say that even though Saddam was a monster, at least you could walk the streets at night without being kidnapped or killed.

This is not in any way to suggest that this murderous tyrant was not an appalling human being. By 1976, Hussein was having enemies and colleagues alike arrested and publicly executed, as his rule became an iron fist. Suddenly the image of Saddam was everywhere—on posters, buses, statues, and murals all over Iraq. To voice dissent was to invite torture and death. The descent into violent dictatorship was swift, but Western support remained steadfast. America, in particular, was happy to sell Hussein arms and chemical weaponry components for use in his eight-year war against Iran, despite clear knowledge of immense human rights abuses.

Although we despise Saddam Hussein for using gas and chemical weapons to kill up to one hundred thousand Kurds in the genocidal Anfal sweep of 1988, or for using mustard gas on Iranian troops, few mention that while he was developing and using weapons of mass destruction, he had the support of America and the West, or that after these awful atrocities "our side" happily gave him more aid and support.

Coming just two years after the end of the war with Iran, Saddam Hussein's 1990 invasion of Kuwait was done in the mistaken belief, widely encouraged by the West, that he would not be challenged. Kuwait was, after all, formerly part of Iraq, and only carved off by Sir Percy Cox in 1922. Kuwait had antagonized Saddam by driving down the price of oil, weakening Iraq's economy. Iraq also claimed that the Kuwaitis were slant-drilling into Iraq's oilfields. The subsequent war to expel Iraqi troops from Kuwait, remembered for its live coverage on our television screens, was in fact a rout, and all over within one hundred hours. The Iraqi army turned and ran, taking television sets and electrical goods with them to be incinerated in the turkey shoot on the road back to Basra. President George H. W. Bush had the wisdom not to pursue the Iraqis back to Baghdad.

Since we're discussing propaganda, let's not forget the tawdry deception mounted to mobilize US public opinion (initially split 50/50) prior to the first Persian Gulf War, in which a young Kuwaiti girl gave tearful testimony to a congressional hearing about the heartless Iraqi troops, who she said had taken newborn babies out of incubators in a Kuwaiti hospital and left them to die on cold concrete floors. The testimony was broadcast around the world, and used as highly emotive propaganda at a time when the American public was apathetic about Iraq's invasion of Kuwait, a country most hadn't even heard of. It later transpired that the testifying girl was in fact the fifteen-year-old daughter of the Kuwaiti ambassador to the US, who had been given acting lessons by a Washington PR firm (Hill & Knowlton). The whole thing was a disgraceful sham, but even its exposure caused little actual damage to those involved. The US government spent $10 million on an extensive PR campaign, got the war it wanted, and Bush Sr. kept his job. The exposure of the sham testimony was quickly forgotten.

The sanctions that followed the Gulf War, instigated by George H. W. Bush and pursued with vigor under Bill Clinton, managed to combine the double failure of punishing the Iraqi people and strengthening the regime of Saddam Hussein. A UN report into Iraq described the country as having been driven back to the Stone Age. Sanctions aimed to further that degradation.

The sanctions ran from 1990 to 2003 and included bans on the import of food and medicine (until oil was swapped for food), in clear violation of international law. Estimated Iraqi fatalities linked to the sanctions during this time are five hundred thousand to one million, mostly infants, children, and the elderly—blameless civilians already suffering, who lived and died in order that US politicians could be seen to be being tough on Iraq. Infants died for lack of medicine before they even knew they were Iraqi, but Bill Clinton's secretary of state, Madeleine Albright, said that she thought the price was "worth it".

Sanctions weakened the intimidated and frightened population, strengthening Saddam Hussein's brutal grip on power. Although Hussein's regime was appalling and murderous, he was responsible for just a fraction as many Iraqi deaths as the sanctions, which killed more than the bombings of Hiroshima and Nagasaki combined.

Report after report clearly showed that while the sanctions were slaughtering Iraqi civilians by the score, they were also strengthening the hand of Saddam Hussein and his family, who lived in luxury, pocketed millions from oil revenues, and killed and murdered with impunity to ensure their grip on power never loosened. Denis Halliday, The UN's Humanitarian Coordinator in Iraq, who resigned in protest in 1998 (after a thirty-year career), said that the sanctions met the definition of genocide. The American author Chuck Sudetic wrote that sanctions had killed more civilians than all the chemical, biological, or nuclear weapons used in human history.

It's ironic that Iraqis knew that US sanctions had killed thousands of their countrymen but Americans did not, because their "free press" failed in its duty to inform them.

By the time of 9/11, the sanctions policy was opposed by most other world powers. The attacks on America changed that entirely.

The West's strategic and military calculus is inextricably linked to oil, although few in power ever have the courage to admit it. As the world's largest consumer of oil, America's future is tightly tied to control of and access to the world's largest producers of oil. But "peak oil," (representing the time when new finds and existing supplies begin to dwindle, and production inexorably declines) may well have passed already. Iraq had the second largest oil reserve in the world, and due to the regime of Saddam Hussein, its reserves had not peaked, so it was not by chance that the Bush administration's leading actors chose Iraq as their wartime target. The rest was a simple exercise in public opinion manipulation, and bare-faced lying about the reasoning for war, so that America could finally take control of the sea of oil beneath the sands of Iraq.

The idea that America would bring democracy to the benighted country of Iraq, and as a consequence a new Arab democracy would flow through the Middle East like a cleansing river, was both delusional and illusionary in that America has no interest in functioning democracies abroad; none whatsoever. If democratization was America's true aim, how could one explain unstinting support for the House of Saud, for Hosni Mubarak, or for a host of other autocrats and dictators (including, formerly, Saddam Hussein), who crush their people's will but bend to the power of the US and allow access to domestic markets and resources?

In any war, the primary political requirement facing a nation's leader is to outline a clear framework of how the campaign will be fought and won, what victory will look like, and (crucially) how it will be concluded. Without these, a country risks being trapped in war without end, and to do that is to lose, pure and simple. America's war in Iraq had none of these parameters, and was inevitably destined for failure. Those who launched it were fools.

Prior Planning

Although it is widely known that resolving the issue of Iraq was a particular focus for the neoconservatives who took charge of the United States following the 2000 election of George W. Bush, there is a great deal of information showing that a war had been planned long before 9/11 provided the bewildering excuse, and that weapons of mass destruction were really an afterthought, justification made on the hoof and simply conjured from thin air in order to provide a casus belli to a bewildered and misinformed American public.

In January 1998, the Project for the New American Century group wrote a letter to then President Clinton, urging him to stop relying on the UN Security Council and take unilateral military action to remove Saddam Hussein. This continued through to the publication in September 2000 of PNAC's "Rebuilding America's Defenses" document, signed by Cheney, Rumsfeld, Wolfowitz, Libby, et al. The document stated, "The United States has for decades sought to play a more permanent role in Gulf regional security. While the unrelated conflict in Iraq provides the immediate justification, the need for a substantial American force presence in the Gulf transcends the issue of the regime of Saddam Hussein."

To put it another way, Saddam and his weapons of mass destruction provided the justification for an invasion, but the goal was a permanent US force in Iraq. The document clearly stated the overall objective to be maintaining American military preeminence in the region.

From the moment George W. Bush took office, Iraq was a pressing concern for those who formed the spine of his administration. In February 2001, a document was published entitled "Plans for post-Saddam Iraq." Another was called "Foreign Suitors for Iraqi Oilfield Contracts." The State Department convened secret meetings to discuss plans for Iraq after Saddam Hussein. The meetings were held at the home of Falah Aljibury, who advised Goldman Sachs, OPEC, and Amerada Hess (on whose board sat Thomas Kean, who headed the 9/11 Commission). The group made it clear that they represented the feelings of the oil industry, and that the US military's primary mission should be resource security.

An article written in the spring of 2001 in the *Army War College* journal by Jeffrey Record, a former member of the Senate Armed Services Committee, advocated shooting in the Persian Gulf on behalf of lower gas prices. The article also advocated presidential-level lying over the real reasons for war, and using some noble veneer to mobilize public support.

In April 2001, a report by James Baker and the Council on Foreign Relations suggested overthrowing the existing regime in Iraq in order to secure plentiful and cheap energy. The report included contributions from what was described as a who's who of oilmen, corporations and political hawks. It was delivered to the hands of Richard Cheney. The report also called for changes to US policy to assist swift and economical export of energy resources from the Caspian basin. The only way out was through Afghanistan.

That same month, at his first deputy secretary-level meeting on terrorism, Deputy Defense Secretary Paul Wolfowitz overruled Richard Clarke and his focus on Osama bin Laden, saying, "Who cares about a little terrorist in Afghanistan?" Instead, Wolfowitz wanted to focus on Iraqi terrorism, of which there was none.

It was the attacks of 9/11 that gave the neoconservatives the excuse and justification to put their plans for regime change in Iraq into action. Donald Rumsfeld in particular seems to have had his dreams come true, and within hours of the attacks was telling staff to find any information they could on Saddam Hussein and Iraq. It takes a special level of cynicism to start making political maneuvers on the afternoon your nation is attacked and three thousand civilians die, but by nightfall Rumsfeld was directing crisis talks at the White House towards a war with Iraq, despite clear knowledge that Iraq had had nothing to do with the day's horrific events.

Others were also quick to move. Admiral James Woolsey was linking 9/11 to Iraq within hours of the attacks. When Woolsey, the Pentagon adviser and former C.I.A. director, appeared on *Nightline* five days after 9/11, and suggested that America had to strike Iraq for sponsoring terrorism, host Ted Koppel rebutted, "Nobody right now is suggesting that Iraq had anything to do with this. In fact, quite the contrary."

Woolsey replied, "I don't think it matters. I don't think it matters." Woolsey also campaigned tirelessly to blame the anthrax attacks on Iraq, despite having no evidence whatsoever.

The justification for the Iraq war has been described as having been reverse-engineered, with the end goal (a war in Iraq) coming first, and then a bunch of information following to justify it.

The key decision to proceed with an invasion of Iraq was made on September 19, 2001, just eight days after the attacks, when members of the Project for the New American Century met with Ahmed Chalabi at the Pentagon, and agreed to write to President Bush calling for the overthrowing of Saddam Hussein. The neocons, led by Dick Cheney, intended to install the compliant Chalabi as the new leader of Iraq. Their letter was published in the name of PNAC, and suggested that failure to act would constitute a decisive surrender in the War on Terror. Less than two months later, Bush secretly told Rumsfeld to draw up plans for an invasion.

Ahmed Chalabi

Ahmed Chalabi has rightly been called the architect of the Iraq war. Chalabi was a former university professor who lived in exile, and led the Iraqi National Council (INC), an opposition group to the regime of Saddam Hussein, based in London.

However, Chalabi was also a convicted bank fraudster who hadn't lived in Iraq since he was thirteen. He found favor in the highest ranks of the Bush administration due to his plausibility and seemingly endless supply of (false) information about Saddam's WMD programs. For a while, he received a $300K per month stipend from the US government, and was specifically tasked with feeding the Bush administration and US media information that would facilitate an attack on Iraq.

Chalabi liked the money, and fed both his political and media masters what they wanted, serving up a fake Iraqi defector called Rafid Ahmed Alwan al-Janabi (codenamed Curveball) to *60 Minutes* in the lead up to the war. Curveball provided a plausible story indicating he had bought components for Saddam's WMD program. Years later, al-Janabi was exposed as an entirely unreliable Iraqi conman. The WMD factories he pointed the American media towards were actually pasteurizing milk. But by then it was too late. He had served his purpose.

Chalabi and Dick Cheney spent hours together at the annual summer retreat of the American Enterprise Institute near Vail, Colorado in the summer of 2002, working on the Iraqi invasion plan, with a particular focus on controlling the oil. Of course, the war would need to be repackaged for public consumption, but that could come later.

Despite being widely discredited as unreliable and a crook, when it was discovered that Chalabi had leaked crucial state secrets to Iran (after the invasion of Iraq), senior neoconservatives (Paul Wolfowitz in particular) did everything possible to dissuade President Bush that Chalabi should be cut loose.

Although Ahmed Chalabi has been described as the man who did more than any other Iraqi to rid the country of Saddam Hussein, he gained no favor from ordinary Iraqis, who voted him 2004's least trusted public figure.

Bush and Cheney worded their public statements in such a way that the mantra of "Iraq and 9/11, Iraq and 9/11" successfully pushed together two things that were clearly unrelated. Here's a classic from Cheney—"If we're successful in Iraq . . . then we will have struck a major blow right at the heart of the base, if you will, the geographic base of the terrorists who had us under assault now for many years, but most especially on 9/11." Fabulously disingenuous and deceptive.

White House rhetoric incessantly pressed a line of argument that, while never directly saying that Saddam Hussein was behind 9/11, blurred the lines so effectively that by the eve of the Iraqi invasion 57 percent of Americans believed that Saddam Hussein had helped the 9/11 hijackers, with 69 percent feeling he had been personally involved. 44 percent thought most or some of the hijackers had been Iraqi, when none had been. In less than six months, the number of Americans agreeing that the War on Terror couldn't be a success without the capture of Osama bin Laden dropped from two-thirds to 44 percent.

The scale of the Bush administration's lies still takes the breath away. Bush and Cheney used forged documents to claim Iraq had bought uranium. They recast testimony by Iraqi defector Hussein Kamel al-Majid concerning weapons that he said had been destroyed years ago, to make it sound like he had said they still existed. They took a National Intelligence Estimate report that said Iraq wouldn't act aggressively unless attacked and said the opposite. They took claims about Iraq's use of aluminum tubes for nuclear weapon manufacture that all their own experts had rejected, and repeated them, saying they were plausible.

At the same time, America's government was receiving highly plausible information indicating that Saddam had no weapons of mass destruction. In September 2002, Naji Sabri, Iraq's foreign minister, told CIA station chief Bill Murray's intermediary that Saddam had virtually nothing related to WMDs.

To put it bluntly, the Bush administration lied, manipulated evidence, planted sources and paid others to lie—in fact, did just about anything they wished, to present the American people with a false picture about Iraq's weapons of mass destruction, so as to launch an illegal war they had wanted well before 9/11. When these virtuosos of deceit were discovered, they remained entirely unrepentant. When Bush was asked by Diane Sawyer in December 2003 about the lack of WMD's, he said, "What's the difference? The possibility that he could acquire weapons, if he were to acquire weapons, he would be the danger."

There was a substantial difference.

Mission Accomplished

In December 2001, victory was declared in Afghanistan, even though the Taliban still controlled much of the country and Osama bin Laden and key al-Qaeda members had neither been killed nor captured. As America's focus turned towards Iraq, Afghanistan—the country that hosted the man they said had attacked America on 9/11—was sidelined.

Despite all the protests, the weapons inspectors, the lack of a UN mandate, and so much controversy, the Coalition of the Willing (the US, UK, Australia, and Poland) launched their attack on Iraq on March 20, 2003. Within days, the Iraqi army was routed and Baghdad fell, as did huge statues of Saddam in town squares, to be attacked and danced on by jubilant Iraqis, many of whom had only known the reign of this one terrible man in their lifetime. Saddam's rule was over, and the Americans were now in charge.

President Bush's May 1, 2003 speech on the deck of the USS Abraham Lincoln, just forty-two days after the war began, was the most delusional moment of his insane presidency. Bush arrived by S-3B Viking fighter jet, and emerged wearing full combat gear, despite his long personal history of avoiding military service. The cheering troops added to a scene that was almost identical to the closing sequence from the movie *Top Gun*. Standing in front of a banner reading "Mission Accomplished," Bush's every word was cheered by the hundreds of sailors that surrounded him.

However, the ship was anchored just off the coast of San Diego. It was made-for-TV war propaganda of the crudest kind, stage-managed by a team of TV producers and veterans from ABC, NBC, and Fox. Every aspect of how the event would look on television was considered. The people visible behind Bush were individually chosen, and wore color-coordinated shirts. Not by chance, Bush's entire speech was made during the magic hour, that time of day when sunset makes everything look golden and warm.

And it worked. Back home, the television media were gushing and breathless in their praise, calling Bush a hero and the "guy who won the war." Much was made of his personal masculinity, swagger, and bravery. Comparisons were made to scenes from *Top Gun* and *Independence Day*. This was not a coincidence.

To ringing cheers, Bush proudly declared a "new era" in warfare, "where with new tactics and precision weapons, we can achieve military objectives without directing violence against civilians." Those words would ring hollow soon enough. Ninety-eight percent of all casualties in Iraq occurred after Bush declared the mission accomplished.

The whole episode was chillingly reminiscent of scenes from Hitler's 1935 propaganda film, *Triumph of the Will*. See if you can spot some similarities.

Hitler's plane comes down from the clouds and lands to a hero's welcome from uniformed troops, who swell around the plane as it comes to a halt.

Hitler is dressed resplendently in army clothing, and later makes a speech in front of banners. Perhaps it's going too far with the comparison to add that at the Nuremberg rallies Hitler asked for support for the accomplishment of the mission.

Saddam's Capture

Regardless of people's profoundly mixed feelings about the launching of the war, it was hard not to take some pleasure in the fall and capture of Saddam Hussein, on December 13, 2003. The tyrant who had killed, gassed, and tortured so many of his own countrymen was found squatting in a hole in the ground, with only mini Mars Bars for company. Photos taken at the scene showed Hussein helpless, weak, heavily bearded, and terrified. He may quite reasonably have expected to be killed the moment he was found.

America's top-value captive was paraded on television just hours later—a clear breach of the Geneva conventions on the use of prisoners of war—and Paul Bremer delightedly declared, "We got him." As a signatory to the Geneva protocols, the US is obliged to prosecute those in breach. Paul Bremer should have been removed from his post for this violation.

For all his faults, Saddam Hussein had successfully kept at bay the forces of radical Islam and al-Qaeda. None meaningfully existed in Iraq prior to the 2003 invasion. George W. Bush changed all that.

L. Paul Bremer was an interesting man. Before being appointed Presidential Envoy to Iraq in 2003 (a post given to him by President Bush, reporting direct to Donald Rumsfeld, and making him the most powerful man in Iraq), Bremer had been chairman and CEO of a subsidiary of Marsh & McLennan (the world's largest insurance brokers), as well as chairman of the Congressional National Commission on Terrorism from 1999 to 2000. He had an extensive history in government counter-terrorism, and had been managing director of Kissinger & Associates.

Marsh & McLennan's offices were on the precise floors struck by the first plane that hit the World Trade Center's north tower on 9/11. Every single person in the company's offices at that time (295 people) died. But on 9/11, Bremer mysteriously failed to show up to work at his office, and within hours conducted a long interview with NBC during which he introduced himself as a counter-terrorism expert and appeared unemotional, despite having lost the staff of his entire company that morning. When it was put to Bremer that Osama bin Laden was the likely individual behind the attacks he agreed, but added that states like Iraq and Iran had to be considered on the list of potential suspects. This was at a time when no-one else was remotely positing that these two countries might be involved.

Occupation

Looking back, it's clear that while the initial attack and over-run of the Iraqi army (hardly the greatest fighting force on earth) was a success, almost every aspect of the war that followed was a debacle.

The laughable notion that Americans would be greeted as liberators was true perhaps for a brief moment, but then the country's infrastructure and civil society collapsed, and America swiftly learned that people want the rubbish collected, police to protect them and light-bulbs to turn on, more than they want democracy.

The top item on the Pentagon's agenda after the invasion was to secure the oil fields in Southern Iraq. Baghdad quickly descended into chaos, and government ministry buildings across the city were smashed, burned, or looted. But at the Ministry of Oil, which housed all the documents outlining Iraq's oil wealth, American tanks and armored personnel carriers surrounded the building, which remained entirely secure.

The US campaign featured so many dreadful blunders and errors, it's hard to see any aspect that was a success. The Bush administration failed to send enough troops, horribly misjudged the mood of the people and their history, and couldn't see that disbanding the military and purging fifty thousand people from the ruling Baath party would decimate civil society and unleash mayhem. The last of those in particular was a breathtakingly naïve tactical error that removed the entire governing infrastructure of the country. Hospitals, schools, government ministries, and rubbish collection all stopped working.

Under Saddam, getting anywhere politically meant joining the Baath party, so a majority of otherwise blameless people were tarred with the brush of his regime and removed from their positions. Iraq's large army was made up mostly from conscripts, but its troops were also armed and trained, and now unemployed in a country rapidly falling apart. It was a recipe for disaster. Within days of their arrival in Baghdad, attacks on US troops began. The country descended into mayhem.

Senior Bush administration officials, and Donald Rumsfeld in particular, could not abide any media coverage from journalists in Iraq that did not follow a script that was rapidly spinning out of control. "Unembedded" journalists (those not attached to the US army and subject to their censorship) took enormous personal risks to bring the world both sides of the story, facing not just the danger of the Iraqi militias but US forces who, by accident or design, seemed unable to distinguish between a camera and a rifle.

Just a few weeks after the war started, Rumsfeld launched blistering verbal attacks on coverage of the war by Arab station Al Jazeera, and just a few days later Baghdad's Palestine Hotel (Al Jazeera's base in Iraq) was targeted by an American tank. It seemed almost impossible that a mistake had been made. The Palestine Hotel was a tall building, and well known among Western occupiers for the role it played in housing international media. The offices hit were precisely those of Al Jazeera. Despite this, the US cleared all those involved, claiming that the tank had come under fire from the hotel. The attack killed three journalists and gave a clear signal that the US occupiers would not allow dissenting voices to be raised.

The Bush administration also hired a Washington-based PR company called the Lincoln Group to insert false news stories supporting the US occupation and troops into the Iraqi media. Hearts and minds could be won with lies.

Prolonged military occupations never end well. Within months of declaring victory, with the situation rapidly deteriorating, the US fell back on counter-insurgency techniques honed in South America, and a bloody factional war began that degraded everything it touched, not least the United States and its armed forces. In another world, civil society would have been maintained, the US occupiers would have ensured that vital services and law and order were kept functional, and Iraq might have had the opportunity to transition to a form of democracy or broader theocracy. These measures would almost definitely have held the country together. As it was, Iraqi society fell apart, and America fell back on its darker military arts.

James Steele

Initially, the US expected no armed uprising whatsoever, and drafted in nonmilitary policemen to try to train around thirty thousand Iraqis to become a domestic police force. When the Sunnis revolted, Donald Rumsfeld decided to arm Shia militias, and that the Iraqi police would now be trained by the US military, in the bizarre hope that this would end the violence, and that the Shias could then be coopted into the new national police force. This was mind-bogglingly wrongheaded. Now armed thugs walked the neighborhoods of Baghdad, backed by America. What was left of the police had little or no control. Civil war was inevitable. It was an extraordinary move.

Almost immediately after the troubles began, the US brought in Colonel James Steele to help set up new police units in Iraq. Steele was an expert in counter-insurgency, and an infamous veteran of America's dirty wars in Central America. He had established the counter-insurgency units that became the notorious death squads in El Salvador and Nicaragua, and was effectively America's most powerful man in those wars. As a Congressman, Dick Cheney had made a number of visits to Central America during the conflict, and was very familiar with Steele and his methods. Now Steele's talents were needed in America's new war.

Under Steele's tutelage, local Iraqi police units set up secret prisons and began torturing and murdering insurgents, or more accurately, anyone who would not do what they wanted. The torture facilities and prisons were mostly funded directly by the US.

Steele and his colleague Colonel James Coffman reported directly to General David Petraeus (a decades-old friend of Steele's). Petraeus, of course, reported directly to Donald Rumsfeld, who is known to have been fully aware of the appalling regime of torture Steele oversaw.

In fact, James Steele was considered so important to America's actions in Iraq that his personal memos were forwarded by Donald Rumsfeld to the president and vice president. This is direct proof that George W. Bush and Richard Cheney knew, approved of, and authorized death squads and torture regimes within Iraq—a clear breach of international law that demands the arrest of those involved, including at the top of the chain of command. The setting up of torture facilities was not an accident; it was deliberate policy, imported by Steele from South America as a means of controlling an out-of-control situation. Steele instigated the regime, knew its main protagonists and what they were doing, supported them and fed them prisoners.

It's worth reiterating. Under America's occupation of Iraq, United States armed forces financed and facilitated the establishment of death squads who abducted, tortured, and murdered their own citizens under the nose of their American paymasters. Reports from the man centrally responsible for this regime reached the highest levels of US politics, including the president.

The Americans also knew about the Iraqi government's secret prisons, and about the torture and murder that took place there. Saddam may have been gone but, if anything, the torture and murder his regime was so famous for became more widespread under the Americans. Steele had, and used, access to these facilities, and daily close contact with those who commanded them. He was often present during the torture sessions.

American troops routinely handed over suspects to the Iraqi police force, in the full knowledge of the consequences those individuals faced. Those who complained to their commanders were told to forget about it and to walk away—a crime in itself. In fact, Frago 242, a US policy leaked by WikiLeaks, directly ordered US troops not to investigate or try to stop abuses and torture by the Iraqis they were funding and training. US forces were allowed to note them.

For a short while, some Iraqi police units even bought cameras (again, paid for by the US), filmed the torture sessions and broadcast them on television as a deterrent to those considering opposition to their rule.

Carnage ensued. At one point, around three thousand bodies were being discarded on the streets of Iraq each month. Many were killed (often after being tortured) by the militias which US forces supported. Death squads once again accompanied a US military occupation. Women and children were not spared. Drills, electricity, dislocations, rape, death. Thousands of bodies in the streets.

For his service, Rumsfeld presented James Steele with a public service medal.

Abu Ghraib

Torture was not just outsourced to the Iraqis. Both the British and US armies set up secret prisons across the country in order to interrogate prisoners away from prying eyes. A number of inmates died at or being transported to these torture camps. We have little information on what happened there, but with what we know from Abu Ghraib, it's very likely to have been horrific. Posters around the bases read "no blood, no foul," a clear indication of the rules being applied. It is not fanciful to suggest that what we don't know would likely be much worse than the small fragments of information we have.

Within months of clearing out Saddam Hussein's notorious torture chambers at Abu Ghraib, US troops were torturing Iraqis there.

As is always the case, the publication of pictures that most saw as horrific (but many US politicians viewed as merely embarrassing) led to the disciplining of a few rotten apples, but no repercussions for those higher up the chain of command who had issued the instructions and overseen the culture that led directly to the horrors that followed. Donald Rumsfeld, more than any other, personified that culture, and escaped any and all official censure. Rumsfeld maintained that rotten apples aside, American troop behavior during internment and interrogation was within the moral standards that the US espouses.

Perhaps one of countless examples will put that to bed. The American Civil Liberties Union obtained documents showing that on one occasion Task Force 6–2 interrogators (later changed to Task Force 145, as unit names are changed to confuse investigators) forced a seventy-three-year-old woman to crawl around a room while a man sat on her back, then forced a broom handle into her anus and broke two of her fingers. There are hundreds of examples of Iraqis treated this way by US interrogators. The apples weren't rotten, the entire orchard was diseased.

Again, the disappearances, torture, and death are all clearly war crimes under the Rome statute of the International Criminal Court. Those responsible must be prosecuted.

In recent years, ISIS leaders have made it clear that much of their organization came about through the experiences of those mistreated at US prisons in Iraq. America's actions in Iraq made ISIS.

Falluja and Weapons of Mass Destruction

The second siege of Falluja (the first was in April 2004, the second in November of that year) was called a war crime by the Red Cross (ICRC), not just because banned weapons such as phosphorus were deployed, but because the use of depleted uranium shells has led to a subsequent public health crisis.

Falluja was an independent nationalist stronghold fifty miles from Baghdad, and the first area to mount an insurgency against US occupiers in 2003, when local residents began arming and defending themselves against the American troops. Falluja had been a model town after Saddam fell, policing itself and willing to work with the occupying Americans. But on April 28, 2003, US troops fired indiscriminately into a peaceful demonstration outside a school, killing seventeen people, and that changed everything. Falluja became a hotbed of insurrection, and the Americans laid bloody siege to the city, twice.

The use of white phosphorus by American troops, long officially denied, was revealed by chance in an article in the March 2005 edition of *Field Artillery*, a magazine published by the US army. In the article, officers boasted about using white phosphorus during "shake and bake" missions, to flush insurgents out of buildings before using explosives to kill them. White phosphorus, when used against people directly, is a banned chemical weapon. On contact with the skin it burns through flesh and continues to do so down to the bone. It can't be washed away and must be cut out of any wound. The US military lied about the use of phosphorus at Falluja until they were exposed. US forces used banned chemical weapons in a war started because of non-existent chemical weapons.

The use of depleted uranium rounds has also become a commonplace battlefield tactic by the US. The substance is extremely dense, meaning it can penetrate armor, and its low melting point means impacts often cause fire or explosions, increasing the devastation. But uranium is a radioactive element, and following the city's siege, and the widespread use of American depleted uranium, the town of Falluja saw an unprecedented spike in birth defects and infancy cancers. Malformations rose to eleven times the normal rate, levels described as an epidemic.

It is estimated over three hundred tons of depleted uranium was used in combat missions within Iraq. Some have called it nuclear warfare by stealth. Those on the ground now dealing with the explosion in cancers and deformed children have little doubt as to the cause.

It seems odd that those Western politicians who were so concerned about Saddam Hussein's possession and use of chemical weapons didn't have a word to say about their own side using them. Israel and the US now routinely use bombs containing depleted uranium. The long-term damage to the health of those nearby (those not killed by the actual bullets and bombs) qualifies these as weapons of mass destruction. The type we were told Iraq had, but didn't.

The consequences of US invasion are now not just borne by civilian populations, but often passed on through generations of malformed infants, and through epidemics of cancers that kill innocent people years after the Americans have left. In time, this public health disaster may be seen for what it is—resembling or exceeding some of Saddam Hussein's most horrific crimes.

Perhaps it is impolite to mention here that the US, also acknowledged to have the largest stored cache of chemical and biological weapons, as well as the largest nuclear arsenal in the world, has consistently refused to allow any international inspection of its weapons stocks. And of course the US was the largest user of chemical weapons in human history during its campaigns against Laos, Vietnam, and Cambodia. In Vietnam it equated to six pounds of dioxin per head of population. The subsequent health disaster that still blights those countries, "fetal catastrophe," as Australian journalist John Pilger calls it, is rarely mentioned in Western media.

Saddam Hussein was charged with mass murder, false imprisonment, torture and chemical weapon use. It is hard to see how those who overthrew him were any less guilty of those offences.

A Lot of Bad Apples

The long war of occupation corrupted everything it touched. Good guys became bad guys, bad guys became worse, and the victims multiplied. Urban asymmetric warfare and the sheer attritional bloodiness and horror of troops living each day under the imminent threat of death made those waging the war lose their moral compass. Rebels fighting the occupiers, or just defending their territory in a land without laws or police, will use whatever methods they can against a much larger and more heavily armed force. In Iraq, incidents abounded showing the degrading cost of war to both sides.

Here's just one. In November 2005, a US marine squad was patrolling the Western town of Haditha when their vehicle was hit by an IED (improvised explosive device), killing one soldier. The squad, enraged, then went on a wild killing spree, firing in all directions at anything that moved. By the time they were finished twenty-four people were dead, including a three-year-old child and seventy-six-year-old man in a wheelchair.

On hearing news of the massacre, the group's commander, Major General Steve Johnson, decided to do nothing. We only know this story because details of the army's internal investigation were found on papers in a rubbish dump in Baghdad, which were about to be used to light a barbeque.

After three years of investigation, charges were dropped against all but one of the troops. The remaining staff sergeant was punished with a rank reduction and a pay cut. Twenty-four dead civilians. A pay cut.

In Ishaqi, eleven people were killed, including five women and four children. The US troops there handcuffed them, then executed each with a bullet to the head. They then bombed the house where it happened, to try to cover the incident up. Countless other similar slaughters occurred. While we know of some of them (perhaps the most egregious), most were never reported or investigated.

In the south, the British attempted to maintain control of the port city of Basra, but with open sewage in the streets and sporadic electricity, society there was imploding under their feet. Many wondered how was it that the area providing Iraq with 70 percent of its oil could be so poor. Mismanagement of civil society led directly to unrest, and then to fighting in the streets, which forced the occupiers to take sides.

Paramilitary militia violently opposed the British occupation, but rather than focus on making the country work, the British used black ops to isolate and demonize the resistance. On September 19, 2005, two British members of the Special Reconnaissance Regiment (the black ops wing of the SAS), disguised as members of the Mehdi Army (the Shia rebels), were pulled over by Iraqi police in Basra and opened fire, shooting police and civilians. When the two were arrested by the Iraqis, their vehicle was found to have been wired to become a car bomb, with weapons and remote controlled detonation equipment.

351

After the arrest, the British sent a column of six tanks, troops and a helicopter to break into the jail and extract the men, knocking down the perimeter wall and allowing 150 other prisoners to escape. A month later the British apologized for mistakes, but made no mention of the details of the operation. This incident was widely known among Iraqis, and gave credence to the broadly held view that the occupiers had no interest in democracy or freedom, but simply wanted to control Iraq's oil.

British troops were involved in the deaths of many ordinary Iraqi civilians. Nearly all were innocent of any crime, and many were tortured or severely abused before their death. Most of the violence was sickeningly mundane. In Basra, a British rifleman shot dead an eight-year-old Iraqi girl in a yellow dress without warning.

After every outrage we were told that this was an isolated incident, one bad apple (a phrase actually used by both the British and US armies), and not representative of the truly moral force that was trying to liberate Iraq. But as the number of incidents multiplied, the idea of this just being statistical outliers grew less tenable. For its part, the US military's tortured logic held that reporting these incidents was counterproductive, as it enraged the locals and caused more issues. This became an excuse for covering up anything unpalatable, which in turn encouraged more bad behavior.

Rarely is the question asked: What would you have done, had you been Iraqi and your police force disappeared, electricity (i.e., refrigeration, food, medicine) stopped, and you faced a choice between militias of your own people or those from the other side of the world, both of whom were abducting, torturing, and killing as your society collapsed?

Stretching Army Resources

Waging two long-term deployments in Iraq and Afghanistan stretched the US army's capabilities, and forced a complete reevaluation of recruitment strategies. Regulations were scrapped to get the numbers required. Where previously those with low IQ's, felons, or people with questionable backgrounds were barred, new regulations welcomed them to the service of the state. In 2006, over a quarter of new recruits were overweight. Over one hundred thousand Americans with criminal convictions (including murder and rape) were allowed to join up. Drug abusers and the mentally ill were also allowed to enlist, and this led directly to atrocities.

The US army's recruitment crisis peaked just as the Iraq war was going through its most disastrous phase. Between 2005 and 2007, recruitment missed its targets by the largest margin since 1979, when the Vietnam war hangover was casting its long shadow over American society. One thousand new army recruiters were added in just one year, aimed at poor urban areas. People under eighteen were deliberately targeted, in contravention of international protocols. One in ten high school kids in Chicago wore military uniforms to school. In a country where education standards were falling and costs of living rising, the army's financial incentives made sense to many poor kids with no other choices. The average bonus for signing up was raised from $14,000 to $17,000. A degraded society was ripe for the picking.

Even Chelsea Manning, with her diminutive figure and fraught personal history was deemed fit to be deployed to Iraq.

This approach, combined with multiple long deployments in areas of utter devastation, badly damaged the esprit de corps of the US army. Across the board, statistics showed unwanted behavior such as drug abuse, violence and alcoholism spiking as the Iraq war descended into mayhem. One in three female soldiers reported being sexually assaulted during their service. Today in the US army a female soldier is more likely to be raped by a male counterpart than killed in action. This was equally true for Iraqi women who came into contact with dangerous American servicemen.

The preponderance of military staff injured or killed in Afghanistan and Iraq were from poorer backgrounds, who had joined the military to pay for college, or just to get a job. At the end of November 2010, Operation New Dawn had seen 4,409 killed and 31,395 wounded. We don't know how many Iraqis died. They had no government to count the dead, and successive US military leaders callously confirmed that they didn't "do" body counts when it came to enemy lives—or foreign lives, to be more accurate, when you consider that the majority of the dead were civilians.

Private Profits

In Vietnam, contractors were mostly back home, making the guns, bullets, and helicopters. By 2003, they were very much on the battlefield.

More so than any other modern theater of war, the Iraqi adventure was privatized, with on-site contractors providing a full range of services, from security to food provision. Many of the privately owned companies providing these services were given no-bid contracts (meaning no tender or other evaluation processes were applied to their appointment). Naturally, this led to a financial free-for-all, in which previously obscure companies like Blackwater received government contracts worth hundreds of millions of dollars (for example, Blackwater won a $1 billion contract for protecting US diplomats and officials in combat zones). In a short space of time, Blackwater became the largest private army on earth.

Halliburton, Dick Cheney's old company, won $35 billion in government work, much of it no-bid contracts that were fabulously profitable. In 2001, Halliburton had defense contracts worth just $427 million. By 2003, contracts totaled $4.3 billion, a third of which were no-bid. What good fortune to have a CEO who leaves office to become vice president of the United States of America.

Of course, there were accompanying issues involved in administering a war zone with a range of non-government actors, many of whom naturally had different priorities to the US army. Army morale suffered too, as grunts in the service realized their mercenary buddies were making 3–5 times more money than they were (sometimes ten times), often for less risky work.

At its peak, there were over one hundred thousand private contractors working for the US inside Iraq, almost one for every American soldier in uniform. As the Bush administration sought to keep the true cost of the Iraq war off the books, it used emergency appropriation funds to bolster the Pentagon's budget. This was one of the main benefits of private contractors playing such a central role in the conduct of the war: the cost of funding them didn't always appear on America's balance sheets.

Worldwide, the ratio of US soldiers in uniform to military contractors is now about one-to-one. During Vietnam it was eight to one. America has privatized much of its war-making machine, and that process has speeded up dramatically since 9/11.

The confluence of corrupt and fraudulent US government entities awash with cash and a private arms industry of (to quote Eisenhower) "vast proportions," often means that the line between private and government defense is hard to distinguish. Positions for security-cleared professionals fill the employment pages of the *Washington Post,* and the move from public to private work is often described as a revolving door. Many leave the public sector to take up more lucrative private jobs, then use their connections to win government work for their new employers. The military's top brass also know that when their service is over they can start the money machine. From 2004 to 2008, 80 percent of three and four-star military leaders who left the service went to work for private contractors.

An industry has sprung up of recruitment firms that service the intelligence community. A search on website intelligencecareers.com shows highly paid jobs around the world, as well as all over the US. Many require "top secret" security clearance. Of those private firms with top secret status, more than a quarter have come into being since 9/11. It is estimated that contractors from more than one hundred firms now make up a third of the CIA. Private firms exist solely to make a profit. So one third of the CIA is now in the business of profitability. It's not hard to see the problem.

Private and public are inexorably entwined. Lockheed Martin made $45 billion in sales in 2010, but 84 percent of its sales came from the US government. This is one area of the economy where the much vaunted free market, so beloved by Republicans, is not on display.

International aid is often no such thing. Client states of the US are obliged to cash in part or all of their aid with purchases of US-built arms. Kuwait wisely bought arms from all five permanent members of the UN Security Council in the years before Saddam invaded in 1990, meaning that there was barely a word of dissent when the UN discussed military plans to liberate the Kuwaitis. Buying American arms is often more about currying favor with the US than the actual arms or a need for them. And the US will sell to nearly anyone. States who receive US military aid are often those with the poorest human rights records. Those in hock to the US become compliant to the wishes of the IMF and World Bank as they try to service sovereign debt, and often privatize national resources at their bidding. The money-men swoop in to clean up.

Put simply, the privately owned arm of the American military-industrial complex is intimately involved in the bare-knuckle world of international business, and an unstable world is the preferred climate for profitability.

Blackwater

The shift from predominantly government troops conducting warfare to a rough 50/50 split between the army and contractors came at a cost. Even in war, structure and accountability are vital means of maintaining control. Contractors in Iraq were essentially offered carte blanche when it came to bad behavior, and this lack of any accountability inevitably led to the violent actions on the streets that were a significant factor in the deterioration in relations between Iraqis and the occupying Americans. Ultimately, this contributed to the occupation ending in failure and civil war.

Contractors were (often correctly) seen as trigger-happy yahoos operating beyond the rule of law. Incidents of malpractice and fraud by contracting firms (who critics call modern-day mercenaries) are legion. But at least fraud does not draw blood. Contractors, and Blackwater in particular, became synonymous with bloodshed on the streets of Iraq, and as the incidents mounted, so did the body count.

One of the most infamous was the Baghdad incident involving Blackwater team Raven 23 in Nisur Square on September 16, 2007. Seventeen Iraqi civilians were killed and more than twenty seriously wounded. Blackwater guards opened fire using machine guns and grenade launchers indiscriminately on civilians in their vehicles, and shot men, women, and children, including a nine-year old boy named Ali Kinani, without any restraint for around twenty minutes. All the civilians were unarmed. Most were shot while fleeing the carnage. Private Blackwater helicopters swooped and fired from overhead. The US army was barely involved.

That was just one event. A 2010 Associated Press investigation listed incidents involving more than two hundred contractors around the world, ranging from drunkenness to sexual assault, and a gunfight outside of a nightclub in Haiti. Blackwater staff were involved in over two hundred shootings in Iraq, but all were deemed immune from prosecution under a ruling (Order 17) signed by Paul Bremer as his last act in Iraq.

The list seems endless. Citizens shot dead because they entered the wrong lane of traffic at the wrong time. Multiple fatalities, on numerous occasions, when car-crashes were caused by contractors driving at high-speeds on poor roads. Guards getting drunk and firing their guns at random into neighborhoods. Nearly all these incidents engendered no investigation or consequences. We only know the extent of the disaster due to releases by WikiLeaks.

Blackwater staff kept weapons in their rooms, where they drank and partied with female guests. They didn't register their weapons, and were often found to be using weaponry they were not qualified to handle. Staff routinely falsified their personnel records and data so as to overbill the State Department. Oversight of contracting was weak, opaque or non-existent—often contracted out, too. One investigation found $4.5 billion of contracts awarded to firms with a history of staff problems and law-breaking. A rare federal audit found contractor International Oil Trading Company had overcharged the Pentagon by $204 million for fuel in Iraq.

The US army was aware there was a problem. Jean Richter, a State Department investigator sent to Iraq specifically to investigate Blackwater, reported in a memo dated August 31, 2007 that Blackwater staff considered themselves above the law, and were facing little or no oversight.

This did not go down well with Blackwater. Daniel Carroll, a senior manager at the company, threatened to kill Richter if he continued investigating the company's clear corruption in Iraq, and added that no one would or could do anything about it, as Iraq was a dangerous combat situation. Then the US government sided with Blackwater, did indeed cease the investigation, and Blackwater continued its ways. Richter was ordered to leave Iraq. His memo was written just seventeen days before the Nisur Square massacre.

The journalist who revealed this story, James Risen of the *New York Times*, was prosecuted by the US Justice Department.

Blackwater (which changes names regularly; it was renamed Xe Services in 2009, then Academi in 2011) paid the US government nearly $50 million in settlements and fines for smuggling arms such as helicopters and automatic weapons, but that pales next to the revenues it received.

The massacre at Nisur Square was so outrageous that it gained the attention of the US press and public, in a way that thousands of other smaller incidents did not. As a result, some eight years later, four Blackwater employees received long sentences. Although this might seem like a win for justice, the larger picture involving mercenaries instead of trained and accountable army troops was all but ignored. There is no reason to think that America's next war will be any different.

What happened on the streets of Iraq and Baghdad was apocalypse-now war Babylon, where the US mercenary was king in a lawless land and the mighty US army kowtowed to their privatized and profitable counterparts. The breakdown of Iraqi society and subsequent loss of the war was due in significant part to the way the US now structures its fighting forces.

But none of this matters if you simply look at profit and loss reports. Far from a disaster, Iraq and Afghanistan were a financial bonanza, and maintaining a permanent state of war is the only way to keep the profits flowing.

Blackwater has, at some points, had over two thousand soldiers on deployment in nine countries at the same time, and has a database of over twenty thousand that could be called upon at short notice. It has helicopters, planes, and the world's largest private military station in North Carolina. Many believe that Blackwater has the military heft to overthrow most governments of the world, if required.

You don't need to be a historian or military expert to know that this is not good at all. It's bad enough a democratically elected leader having access to a private army, but Blackwater's unaccountability means that in theory they could be hired by anyone who has the cash.

PTSD

Some of those who returned from deployment were affected by posttraumatic stress disorder (PTSD), but often deployed again despite being unwell. PTSD is known to be "dose dependent." The more you are exposed to traumatic events, the more likely you are to suffer from the disorder. Those who were deployed to Afghanistan three times suffered double the rate of PTSD than those who went just once. And no modern wars have been fought by the West that employed more multiple deployments than Iraq and Afghanistan. This is not a particularly controversial point—the US army and government deployed soldiers multiple times, knowing full well that this would set off an epidemic of PTSD and leave soldiers psychologically broken.

PTSD now afflicts more than 30 percent of military veterans. Two million War on Terror vets are back on the streets of America. The medical and therapeutic resources available to these ill people who put their lives on the line for their country have improved, but are still threadbare and inadequate, and plagued by delays and administrative red tape.

Veterans have vastly higher incidence of mental health issues, homelessness, drug abuse, and unemployment than the general public. The motto of "no man left behind" is abandoned once service is complete. On average, twenty-two veterans committed suicide each day in the US in the period from 1999 to 2010.

America claims to have a *noblesse oblige* attitude toward servicemen and women. Not only are none left behind, but those who serve are routinely venerated as the bravest and the best. But in 2013, grants for the higher education of children whose parents served and lost their lives were cut by over a third. Benefits due to those returning from war have taken years to be paid out—the average was over nine months, with nearly one million people waiting for the financial assistance often required to build a life back in the civilian world. All this contributes to a society in which these brave people, the bravest and the best, are found homeless, jobless, or mentally ill on the streets of the United States. The sheen of veneration for service is just window dressing. Frighteningly, we already knew this. Vietnam veterans were treated even worse.

Caring for the veterans of Iraq and Afghanistan is going to cost an estimated $20 billion by 2020 alone. This is the hidden cost of these dreadful wars.

The staggering profits available to defense logistics and arms companies in America's seemingly unending wars are in stark contrast to the price paid by the troops sent to wage them. PTSD and suicide has been described as an epidemic, with over sixty thousand ex-servicemen and women (mostly men) now homeless in the United States. In London, 25 percent of those "living rough" have formerly been in the armed services. In 2012, more US soldiers died from suicide (177) than in combat (176). But that was just the active soldiers. A more accurate statistic includes those retired from service. There the suicide figure rises to 6,500 in 2012 alone, one every eighty minutes, a twenty-seven-year high in the US. Many flounder in civilian life after being discharged. The system they joined, and which supposedly reveres their service, spits them out and leaves many for dead.

According to a 2014 survey by the Iraq and Afghanistan Veterans of America (IAVA), 40 percent of post-9/11 veterans know a fellow vet who has died by suicide. This epidemic of suicide and mental illness among US Veterans is the direct result of the lies told by the Bush administration to launch and prosecute these wars. The blood of their citizens is on their hands.

Iraqi Sovereignty

Notional control of Iraq was passed to a transitional government (appointed by the Americans) on June 28, 2004. When a note confirming the renewed sovereignty was passed to President Bush (who was attending a NATO summit), he wrote "let freedom reign" on it, somehow invoking the spirit of Martin Luther King. But to paraphrase Sarah Palin, how's that "freedom-reigny" thing working out for you? An occupation that robbed a sovereign nation of its wealth and caused a civil war that left up to a million dead and destroyed the very notion of the country, was repackaged as a benevolent gift of freedom and democracy.

During Paul Bremer's brief time in charge oil resources were plundered, national institutions collapsed and a torrent of reconstruction money was squirreled away by crooked contractors. $60 billion was spent on reconstruction, but not one project undertaken was completed.

With government institutions destroyed or disbanded, a puppet regime was installed in May 2006, headed by Nouri al-Maliki, a Shia strongman who came highly recommended by Zalmay Khalilzad, oilman and member of the Project for the New American Century. Al-Maliki was one of four men interviewed for the job by the CIA, and carefully vetted to be America's man in Baghdad. However, his taking office as new Prime Minister of Iraq was preceded by the February bombing (by Sunnis associated with al-Qaeda) of the al-Askari shrine. The shrine was a thousand year old mosque in Samarra, one of the most holy Shia sites. With minority Sunnis committing terrorist attacks against the Shia, and a belligerent like al-Maliki in charge, a civil war started that tore the country apart.

Nouri al-Maliki subsequently proved just another sectarian thug, brutally suppressing Sunnis as his country fell apart before him. Al-Maliki's government never held real sovereign power, and battled constantly to hold its ground, using armed militias to intimidate and repress. His governing party never found purchase in a society that was unable to provide basic services like water and electricity. Al-Maliki's prime ministership oversaw the end of his nation.

The Result

When reviewing the devastation, it's hard to see which part of the mission was best accomplished. The US invasion (and the lies that were used to justify it) fatally undermined the legitimacy of the Bush administration's War on Terror and allowed al-Qaeda a foothold in Iraq where once there was none. The occupation left thousands of US men and women dead, tens of thousands injured, perhaps a million Iraqi dead, and multiples of that number displaced, injured, or with lives in ruins. Terrorism and factional violence remains rife, the government can barely function, and the country is torn to pieces by secessionist Kurds in the North, ISIS in the East and regional ascendancy for neighboring Iran (perhaps the only winner of the war), now in a more powerful position than for generations.

Perhaps the real accomplishment was for the war to have sounded the death-knell of America's preeminence in the world, beaten militarily and bankrupted financially by the worst act of military aggression in a generation. If that's mission accomplished, one shudders to think how failure might look.

The personal cost to Iraqis has been unimaginable. One Iraqi ministry estimated that 4.5 million Iraqi children had lost one or both parents. 14 percent of the population are orphans.

Uniquely among American presidents, George W. Bush refused to attend any military funerals or memorials. Most often his team claimed that the president simply lacked the time to be there. It looked bad. It looked like he didn't care. However, Bush did find time to retain the ban (put in place by his father) on media coverage of returning dead soldiers. The press weren't allowed to show the flag-draped coffins being taken off planes (in the middle of the night, to avoid further scrutiny). Bush's priorities, it seems, focused more on media manipulation than mourning his own dead countrymen.

Initial estimates tabled by the Bush administration projected the cost of deposing Saddam Hussein and establishing a democratic government would be $50–$60 billion. It is now estimated that when factoring in the long-term cost of caring for the wounded and the families of those killed, the entire venture will have had a price-tag of $3.7 trillion. All of this expenditure abroad was incurred as America incrementally increased its security industry at home, diverting vital money away from civic services and further impoverishing the citizens it claimed to be fighting for. In 2009, the US spent $661 billion on its military, much more than double the budget from ten years previously.

When the war started, almost 75 percent of Americans supported it. When Obama began removing the troops, over 70 percent supported withdrawal. More than half now think the war was a mistake—formally ending it was one of the most popular moves Obama made.

But perhaps perception really is reality. A poll in 2015 found that 42 percent of Americans (and 51 percent of Republicans) still believed that weapons of mass destruction were indeed found in Iraq.

Although many praise Barack Obama for ending the war in Iraq, it was George Bush who signed the agreement with the Iraqi government that guaranteed the removal of US forces by the end of 2011. The Obama administration actually tried to get American armed forces to be allowed to stay beyond that deadline, in the end withdrawing troops because Nouri al-Maliki's government refused to agree to extend the blanket immunity from prosecution enjoyed by all US forces, after the "Collateral Murder" footage released by WikiLeaks showed the world evidence of clear war crimes.

Despite this, America hasn't really left. The US Embassy in Baghdad remains the largest in the world. The green zone is ten square kilometers, right in the heart of the capital. It's larger than Vatican City, and cost around $1 billion to build. This money was spent in the sure knowledge of a return on investment. Eleven thousand embassy staff are protected by five thousand private security contractors. So although the war is over, there remains a small, menacing army at the center of Iraq's capital city, belying the notion that the US has entirely ceded control of the country to its sovereign government.

As the war drew down in December 2011, President Obama told troops that the country they were leaving behind was an extraordinary achievement, and that they left with their heads held high, but when the US troops left, the consensus in Iraq was that although the departure was welcome, the power vacuum left behind was likely to be hugely destabilizing. This has been the case.

Iraq today exists only in name. It has ceased to exist as a sovereign entity. It has no government (at least, not one that controls the whole country). Militias roam the streets, taking control via the gun. Each disparate faction fights for its own ground. In fact, the entire country is now a proxy battlefield between Iran and the Sunni Muslim world.

ISIS is the direct progeny—the inevitable result of a violent, broken country in a state of civil war. America dismantled Iraq to gain control of its oil. Iraq's people continue to suffer the consequences.

Although the war destroyed the reputations of those who conceived, launched, and waged it, tarnished reputations aside, no one has been held accountable, and none have accepted responsibility. Tony Blair, in particular, still defends his actions despite the overwhelming body of evidence showing that he lied in the lead-up to the war, and despite the calamity that the war has left behind. His late 2015 apology was no such thing—Blair just offered contrition for the fact that the intelligence he had received (about weapons of mass destruction) was wrong, when we all know that he and his colleagues were sexing up whatever they could get their hands on. On the tenth anniversary of the invasion of Iraq, more than half of the British public believed the war was wrong, and that Tony Blair had knowingly misled the public and parliament. 22 percent thought Blair should be tried for war crimes. In time, he may be.

The net may yet close around the Bush administration. In a stunning interview in 2014, Bush's most senior terrorism expert Richard Clarke said that in his opinion the actions of Bush, Cheney, and Rumsfeld "probably fall within the area of war crimes." It's a belief that is more widely held in America than you might expect. The consequences of America facing up to this dark chapter in its history are hard to overstate.

CHAPTER NINTEEN

MONEY AND WAR

The Military Industrial Complex

The debacles of Iraq and Afghanistan weakened the United States. Both wars were hugely expensive and achieved next to nothing. America threw trillions down the drain. A national disaster, right?

You might not think like that if you worked at the Pentagon, or were you a share-holder in one of America's endless list of defense logistics companies. To these giants, 9/11 and the wars that followed represented a once-in-a-lifetime bonanza, the likes of which had never been seen. In fact, nearly everyone involved in war, finance or politics came up a winner.

The Bush administration received public backing for the wars it had long included on its wish-list, and eight years of political power. They used that time to dramatically tear up the Constitution and vest sprawling new powers in both the president and the military, in ways that would have been inconceivable in a pre-9/11 world.

Defense contractors and weapons manufacturers won government contracts worth billions, often without a competitive bidding process and, again often, carried out their work without any formal oversight, making fantastical profits. The security apparatus of the United States saw the dawn of a new Department of Homeland Security, with jobs, money, and prospects that were virtually unlimited.

Every Hellfire missile shot in anger meant another $100K in revenue to Lockheed Martin. Hellfire missiles aren't much fun on the receiving end, but they're a terrific revenue stream for Lockheed.

Lockheed Martin vice president Bruce Jackson made sure the influential Committee for the Liberation of Iraq (CLI) was filled with Lockheed staff and alumni. Then the Committee helped the Bush administration beat the drums for a war with Iraq, then there was a war, and then Lockheed's share-price went up 145 percent, from $41 in March 2003 to $102 in February 2007. Lots of people made lots of money as thousands of Iraqis died.

From 2002 to 2010, sales by the top one hundred arms manufacturers in the world rose 60 percent, totaling $411 billion in 2010. Forty-four of the top one hundred arms companies in the world are American, as are eight of the top ten. Business is concentrated at the top. The top ten companies account for 56 percent of the top one hundred's sales. America has an impregnable monopoly at the top of world arms sales.

Of course, the losers were millions of people in Afghanistan and Iraq, hundreds of thousands of whom were killed, as well as the thousands of dead and wounded US soldiers who fought in those wars, and the three thousand who died on September 11, 2001. If you live in Waziristan these days, the constant sound of weaponized drones overhead might make you wish this all hadn't happened, but from the perspective of the US war machine this is all but irrelevant. The business is death, and the 9/11 wars meant unprecedented profits. 9/11 was a godsend.

A destabilized Middle East may seem bad for all concerned, but if you're a weapons manufacturing country (and the biggest by far is the US), the destabilization of the region is great for business. Funnily enough, the main buyers in the region, including Bahrain, Kuwait, Oman, Qatar, the UAE, and Saudi Arabia (the world's fourth biggest military spender) are all despotic dictatorships or feudal monarchies. The governing regimes in these countries were terrified by the Arab Spring, which our side was supposed to have so warmly supported, given its relative success in toppling murderous dictators and allowing democracy a foothold. After the Arab Spring, all six countries violently cracked down on dissent and protest. Try to remember that the next time an American politician waxes lyrical about how much America loves democracy. This is the same country that sold these Gulf states 50 percent of their arms purchases. From 2010 to 2015, weapons sales to Gulf states increased 70 percent.

We sell the world's leading human rights violators the guns to keep their people at bay. Perhaps that explains why the Middle East is so antipathetic towards the United States and Great Britain. Perhaps that's why the West has been so poor at maintaining peace in the world.

Defense Spending

In the ten years following 9/11, US military and security budgets increased by 119 percent. Even after removing the fabulous sums spent in Iraq and

Afghanistan, the increase was 68 percent. Given America was already (by many multiples) the biggest defense spender on earth, this was a remarkable increase.

Following 9/11, US defense spending for 2002 rose to over $300 billion, not too far short of the entire GDP of Russia. Each year that followed, the spending increased. In 2010 alone, the US spent $687 billion on defense, with $80 billion of that on intelligence, more than double 2001 levels.

The Pentagon saw its budget balloon to levels (proportionate to GDP) not seen since World War II. But in the Second World War, Hitler's Germany and the Japanese posed a real threat to the US and world safety, whereas who can now say that the stated protagonists of 9/11, nearly all of whom are dead or captured, still justify this huge expenditure. Every dollar spent robs the nation of money for food, healthcare, or educating its children, yet from 9/11 to February 2016 the US spent $7.6 trillion on defense. America's military budget is quite completely insane.

While Republican politicians participate in an endless quest to shrink government spending on benefits, education, healthcare etc., the defense budget is almost never mentioned for cuts, despite the fact that savings there would vastly outweigh those proposed in the domestic sector. This may be related to the fact that the already blurred lines between government and industry are further muddied by the huge lobbying sums spent by private defense contractors, so as to shore up their position within the complex. Tens of millions of dollars each year are spent greasing palms.

Because the Department of Defense and Homeland Security are never audited (the only two government departments to enjoy this privilege), they are rife with corruption and fraud. Huge accounting irregularities and massive sums are just lost to thin air in a way that would provoke mayhem in other government departments, but simply comes and goes in the defense sector without a murmur. Private defense contractors often operate overseas in difficult environments, or are so closely tied to government agencies as to be indistinguishable. Corruption and fraud are never far away. It's a racket, and those in charge are laughing all the way to the banks of Wall Street.

Let's not forget: Donald Rumsfeld announced that the Pentagon had lost $2.3 trillion on September 10, 2001. Try to imagine any other government department losing even a fraction of that figure and senior heads not rolling. That announcement was lost in the mayhem that followed the very next day, and post 9/11 even the threat of oversight has been routinely batted away as distracting the government from the War on Terror.

Sometimes the extraordinary scale of wasted money beggars belief. There are so many examples of huge contracts and money simply disappearing that it's hard to know where to start. One of the worst (or best, depending on your perspective) was the Pentagon's decision to spend $297 million on a seven-story high blimp, the size of a football field, at the height of the war in Afghanistan. The idea was to have the blimp permanently floating high over Afghanistan, equipped with the most up to date high-resolution cameras, allowing the army to see nearly the entire country in real-time, 24/7 (except when it was cloudy). Of course, the blimp also needed to be impervious to attack, including from surface-to-air missiles. Hence the price tag. But the armory made the blimp overweight, and the plan was abandoned after one flight. In 2013, the Pentagon sold the blimp back to the company that made it for $301,000.

In August 2011, the bipartisan Commission on Wartime Contracting in Iraq and Afghanistan found that over $31 billion (more than 15 percent of the total monies spent) had been entirely wasted on grants and private contractors over the previous decade. They described the figure as sobering, but conservative, meaning the true number was probably higher.

The report listed many examples of wasted resources, such as $40 million of American money for an Iraqi prison that Iraq had made clear they didn't need or want, and that was never completed; and $300 million for a power plant in Kabul that the Afghan government had neither the resources to run nor the technical expertise to maintain. It too lay in ruins. A separate report by the independent Center for Public Integrity said that $140 billion in defense contracts had been awarded the previous year without any form of competitive tendering—triple the sum in 2001.

The contractor workforce in Iraq and Afghanistan at times exceeded 260,000 people. That's a small city all living high on the US tax dollar. The consequences of 9/11 represent an unprecedented military boom that continues to enrich those lucky enough to be involved.

In China, some people now openly question whether the amazing speed of industrialization enjoyed by that country has been worth it, if the price in the cities is air that people can't breathe. Some in rural American communities have pointed out that the money paid to frack the land doesn't make long-term sense, when the price is ground-water that can't be drunk. Politically, it is right and fair to question whether America's crippled society, with tens of millions under the poverty line, stagnant wages, and a lack of basic provisions like healthcare, is worth the trade for the money spent on national security which hasn't left anyone feeling much more secure.

Homeland Security

The word homeland barely featured in American discourse prior to 9/11, and is a term widely used by Nazi propagandists in the 1930s. It is now disturbingly commonplace.

Those focusing solely on international action undertaken during the War on Terror miss the huge sums being made in the domestic security arena. Across America, new organizations sprang up in the wake of 9/11 as domestic security budgets went through the roof. Just nine days after the attacks, Congress approved $40 billion in domestic anti-terrorism funding. In 2002, they approved $36.5 billion more, and in 2003 a further $44 billion. So it went.

Of the roughly 250 new government agencies created since 9/11, the Department of Homeland Security is the biggest, with 240,000 staff. The department's home is the biggest new building in America since the Pentagon was built. It is sited on the grounds of a former mental asylum.

Five hundred sixty-nine companies registered Homeland Security lobbyists after 9/11. Lobbying money is spent because it guarantees a return. Where once defense behemoths earned nearly all their money fighting wars overseas, 9/11 opened up the biggest market of all—home. The industry has been estimated to already be in the region of $115 billion per year, perhaps more, and exerts a huge influence over government. September 11 allowed the defense industry to leverage unlimited profits in domestic security. Peace, and a return to pre-9/11 normality, would be a disaster for business.

See all that new hardware at airports? What you're seeing is profit. L-3's full-body scanners cost about $200,000 each, and are in nearly every major US airport. L-3 has received nearly a billion dollars of business from the Transport Safety Administration (TSA) alone. When Washington was quibbling about the costs and benefits of the machines, lobbyists brought scanners into the Capitol building to show off how good they were. When the Government Accountability Office reported that it was unclear if the new devices could actually detect a bomb, the report was sidelined and ignored.

In 2007, the TSA spent $20 million on puffers (which tried to detect explosives on clothing), before abandoning the idea. Boeing was given $1 billion to build a virtual fence on the Mexican border, but the scheme was abandoned with only fifty-three miles built. All of these seem like insane wastes of money, but only if you are paying for them. If you're cashing the checks, homeland security is a once in a lifetime opportunity for profit.

Few private industries are more active political lobbyists than defense. On K Street in Washington, lobbying company headquarters physically surround the hubs of state security. From 2006 to 2011, lobbying budgets for private defense companies doubled. Back in 1974 only 3 percent of retiring members of Congress became lobbyists. Now half of them do.

One early justification for this accelerating drift towards the full privatization of war and security administration was that the private sector was more efficient, and would provide better value for money (literally more bang for the buck). But when the Department of Homeland Security conducted a survey in 2008, it found that contractors, who made up 29 percent of their staff, accounted for 49 percent of the budget.

The scale of the expansion of domestic security is without precedent in American history. A *Washington Post* survey entitled "Top Secret America" revealed that there are now 1,271 government entities and 1,931 private companies with operations relating to terrorism, intelligence, or homeland security, all housed in ten thousand locations across the US. In Washington, enough new office space has been taken up to fill three Pentagons. The Pentagon remains the largest employer in the world. America's security apparatus is a state within a state.

Nearly four million Americans now hold top secret security clearance, with around a quarter of them in the private sector, leading some to wonder out loud that if four million people are in on a secret, is it actually a secret anymore?

What is important to remember here is that the millions of people employed and trillions of dollars spent are all there in the name of keeping Americans safe from terrorism, something that kills almost no one, especially when compared to the slaughter each year caused by America's lax gun laws, or the tens of thousands of avoidable deaths associated with not offering citizens free healthcare. It's so vastly disproportionate and out of alignment with the actuality that facts become the elephant in the room, such as that for all this diversion of funds from public benefit to terrorism avoidance, the Boston bombers and San Bernardino terrorists (for example) still slipped through the net.

Money spent elsewhere would save or improve the lives of millions of people. The War on Terror actually impoverishes and kills more people through the misuse of public funds than terrorism itself. Perhaps in time we will gain a perspective on this insane infatuation with safety from terrorism, and the risk this huge "defense" apparatus presents to the long-term freedom—and perhaps even existence—of America.

The United States has faced real threats to its sovereignty and safety before. The Cold War pitted two powerful and heavily armed nations against each other, and in 1962 took the world to the brink of nuclear annihilation. The War on Terror pitches the most dominant military superpower in human history against a disparate group of faraway idiots. It's really not a war at all.

Capitalism and Terrorism

When Gavrilo Princip shot Archduke Franz Ferdinand and his wife in 1914 (sparking the First World War), he was acting as a terrorist. Conduct that could be defined as terrorism has been around as long as human society. Although cross-border terrorism such as the Munich Olympics attack began appearing as commercial air travel made our world smaller, these attacks were usually carried out by small, disenfranchised groups looking to resolve local issues. International terrorism, that of stateless groups funding murder across the globe, has only become a feature of human society in the last three decades.

September 11, and America's response to it, can sometimes make it feel like international terrorism is the biggest issue faced by humanity. However, from the point of view of a body count, international terrorism doesn't even make the top fifty. It kills a very small number of people compared to malaria, malnutrition, or even diarrhea. If you worry about being a victim of terrorism, remember that nephritis kills many more people, and you probably don't even know what that is.

George W. Bush conflated nationalist organizations like Hamas with international terrorism, but al-Qaeda was really the only plausible player, funded by a Saudi billionaire and thus able to plan attacks globally. Now al-Qaeda is all-but gone, and ISIS thugs pose a fraction of the threat. America defeated the Nazis and put a man on the moon. They can handle ISIS.

From a sober perspective, the concept of terrorism should really be divided into three categories.

Starting at the lowest rung: deranged or desperate people commit heinous acts against others for a range of reasons, including hatred, insanity, grief, religious fervor, or for material gain. Individual terrorist acts (those designed to kill total strangers in order to make a point) represent a dark corner of the human psyche, something that every sane person opposes unequivocally.

Second is international terrorism, and it is this area that is of the most interest, as large-scale international terrorist outrages carried out by organized cross-border paramilitary groups (especially against the West) are very unusual, and are almost never carried out without the complicity, knowledge, or even purposeful involvement of the state. Large-scale attacks rarely take place without the apparatus of state having known of the impending disaster on one level or another. The state is often a participant.

It's an extremely uncomfortable thought, but international terrorism also almost always serves a political agenda, most often that of the government which claims to represent those who have been attacked. In fact, the symbiotic relationship between capitalism, geostrategic power, and terrorism is remarkable. The West requires the threat of terrorism, and occasional terrorist outrages, to justify military actions abroad, supposedly in defense of national security. September 11 provided George Bush with a political blank check, but the line between terrorist and protector is blurred at best, and often crossed. Virtually no major international terrorist incident against Western interests in the last twenty years has not been mired by the murky hands of state intelligence nearby.

Consider just a few famous examples:

- In Madrid, the man accused of supplying the dynamite for the 2004 bombings (Emilio Trashorras) was found to have held the private telephone number of the head of Tedax, Spain's Civil Guard bomb squad. Two of the bombers were police informants, and the others were under surveillance.
- Drills were taking place on the same morning as the 2005 London bombings that revolved around the same type of terrorist attacks at the same train stations that were attacked. Like Bush, Tony Blair said calls for an inquiry were a ludicrous diversion.
- TWA 800, a 747 with 230 people on board, was destroyed on July 17, 1996 by a ground to air missile fired from a US military source. The incident was highly effectively covered up by the FBI, using a media campaign that successfully muddied the waters of public opinion, despite the strike having been seen with the naked eye by many on the ground.
- The 1995 bombing of the Alfred P. Murrah federal building in Oklahoma was supposedly caused by a bomb planted by two ex-Green Berets, but the explosive device could not possibly have caused the damage, and secondary explosives were removed from the building wreckage in sight of live TV cameras. During one of the great sham trials in US history, Timothy McVeigh's own lawyer doubted his client's proclaimed guilt, and no witness could even place McVeigh in Oklahoma on the day of the bombing. As on 9/11, explosives had been placed inside the building, which caused the outward explosion so clearly visible to the television cameras on site. As on 9/11, the debris was quickly hidden and taken away, and the building demolished with undue haste by Controlled Demolition Inc. (the company so heavily involved in the cleanup of 9/11). As on 9/11, nearby security camera footage was confiscated and has never been

released. Belief that the government had prior knowledge of the attacks was so mainstream that reports were aired on ABC news program *20/20*.

- The 1993 World Trade Center bombing involved the use of a Ryder truck, the same type of vehicle that was used two years later in the bombing at Oklahoma. The FBI had clear foreknowledge of the attacks through an informant within the conspirators named Emad Salem, whose taped conversations with the FBI indicated that federal agents were trying to foil the case by supplying him with fake explosives.

September 11 was the ultimate international terrorist attack, on a scale never before seen, and was carried out by the United States government and military in order to provide a justification for radical and pre-planned political, military and defense agendas. The sectors attacked—defense (the Pentagon), finance (the World Trade Center), and political (few doubt that the White House or Capitol was the fourth plane's target) were those that benefited the most, and the attacks were used to justify the invasion of an oil-rich country in the Middle East which was the Bush administration's most desired target, and to project further control over the world's remaining carbon deposit areas.

The third category of terrorism is the most misunderstood: state terrorism. This is practiced (for example) by Israel, in its deliberate policy of cruelty and murder against the Palestinians, using violence and the threat of violence as a political tool, and then claiming that Israel is in fact the victim, not the perpetrator. Israel's actions deliberately stoke a culture of instability and insecurity, so as to not have to address the rights and claims of Palestinians, and in order to continue to build and enlarge settlements with impunity.

State terrorism is the most commonly practiced and the most furiously denied, as when the state does it, few dare call it terrorism. But the state and its armies are the most heavily armed and the best funded. The state often has tacit control over the media, who "inform" the public of what has happened. States routinely act as terrorists, attacking whole communities as punishment for the transgressions of individuals, and threatening violence and death against groups of individuals unless compliance is proffered to (often corporate or financial) aggression.

The United Nations has for decades tried to get the world's nations to agree on a definition of terrorism, without success, as has the US Supreme Court. Strangely, the difficulty has been that Western countries want to be exempt from any definition, and the reason is not hard to see. We in the West drop bombs, drone civilians, attack Muslim countries, and start wars based on lies. All of these could and should be defined as state-sponsored terrorism. But we can't have that. So a definition by the highest civilian bodies we have proves elusive.

In fact, states implicitly deny that state terrorism ever happens, or can even exist. If the state does it, by definition it is not terrorism. It's easy for governments to call a poor angry man with a petrol bomb a terrorist, but entirely unthinkable to class the actions of a fighter pilot in the most advanced plane on earth dropping a million-dollar missile on innocents below in the same way.

The strategies employed in the War on Terror undoubtedly engender more terrorism themselves, but national security is not actually the agenda. The essence of the give and take of terrorism (you bomb us, we respond) is the ongoing protection of economic and financial (not sovereign) interests.

It's a mirror image to how matters are commonly portrayed. Black is white, up is down. With trillions of dollars of military spending and profits at stake, terrorists are not liabilities, they are assets. The idea that non-state terrorists are entirely beyond the reach and control of governments is nonsense. Al-Qaeda and ISIS have, time and again, been shown to be sponsored and funded by a range of sovereign nations, all of whom are closely allied with the West—most notably Saudi Arabia. What the public face is an ever-escalating cycle of terrorist danger, never-ending war, and more and more restrictions on civil liberties, through laws supposedly written to protect us from this state-sponsored terrorism. This has been labeled postmodern fascism, and is well advanced in effectively ending democracy in America and the West.

CHAPTER TWENTY

WALL STREET

Before the Crash

The spectacular growth in the size and power of the banking sector in Western democracies (that began with the election of Ronald Reagan) has dramatically altered the structure of Western economies. Banks have become the one indispensible industry. Their role in our society bears scrutiny.

Banking used to be boring. Grey men in grey suits stroked their chins and thought carefully about their customer's circumstances before lending them a cent. Getting a home loan was hard, and a solid case for your ability to make loan repayments had to be made.

Investment bankers and stockbrokers were an entirely different breed, legally separated from retail banking in the United States by the Glass-Steagall Act of 1932. They made money when the market went up, but they lost a lot, often including their jobs, when the market went down.

However, the deregulatory changes commenced by Ronald Reagan and Margaret Thatcher (and continued ever since) have altered this once mundane sector of our national economies beyond recognition. Today banks are exciting, and housed behind tinted windows in high-rise buildings. The profits banks routinely generate make headlines themselves, and their CEOs are revered as economic messiahs, basking in the glow of a system that they control, and which they promise us is the only viable way to run a society. The power of the modern banking sector explains a great deal about how we found ourselves in such a mess in 2008.

From the late nineteenth century until the 1970s, bank assets as a percentage of the UK's GDP remained steady at approximately 50 percent, but from 1980 onwards, the removal of financial regulations allowed banks to balloon in size. By 2006, bank assets as a percentage of UK GDP were over 500 percent. The banks were five times the size of the country.

Because banks are on the other side of the lending equation, loans are considered assets. If you put your money in a bank, the bank considers it a liability, as they have to pay it back when you want it. If you take out a loan or a mortgage, to a bank that is an asset. Banks make huge profits from the interest rates they charge on loans. If the value of the thing behind a bank asset (a house, for example) goes down, that's normally not the bank's problem, as the loan value remains the same. The problem arises if the person paying back the loan runs into trouble and can't make the repayments. That's why banks have traditionally been very skeptical lenders.

Reagan and Thatcher began the process of changing all that by systematically removing the rules and regulations that kept the markets sane. Their argument was that rules for the most part just slowed business down, and got in the way of fair competition and growth. Suddenly, loans for housing could be made more easily, so lots of people in the 1980s took out big loans, and of course house prices went up because there were suddenly so many new buyers. The rules separating investment banks from regular retail banking were also removed, so banks could now use other people's money to invest in shares, or gamble on anything else they fancied. Bank assets exploded. A lot of people who already had money made a lot more. People with no money were mostly left behind. Markets began seeing great periods of booming prices, then huge crashes. As the rules were scrapped, boring banking institutions became exciting, once-conservative bankers became risk-takers, and the stakes grew higher. But these huge bank institutions were still staffed by normal human beings, wanting to make as much money as quickly as possible (just like you and me), so the removal of financial regulations and laws encouraged the irrational banking behavior that eventually brought the world to its knees.

Reagan's idea was that an unrestricted financial sector would have lots of money to lend, and we'd all get a lot richer. Cutting income taxes at the same time would mean that those who got rich would help those who were poor, by investing their money and employing more people, and there would be a trickle-down of wealth. To this day some believe it worked, and that we all got richer. But it was self-serving nonsense, solely designed to make the rich richer. Trickle-down (or supply side) economics has resoundingly been proven wrong, as America's multi-trillion dollar debt and chasm between rich and poor attests.

In fact, the most dramatic improvement in living standards in the US took place in the 1950s and '60s, periods of high income tax and tough financial regulation. The golden age stopped with Reagan. In the twenty-eight years from 1980 to the 2008 crash, the median US household income went up by only 20 percent, while the top 0.01 percent saw their income increase seven times. The baleful influence of money in American politics meant that as the rich got richer, they gained a commensurate increase in political power, creating a vicious cycle where rational economic policy could not be implemented, because rich people had the politicians in their pockets.

Corporations and banks started making unheard-of profits, and while the press lavished praise on the business sector for its newfound genius, millions of working class people saw their lives become more difficult, as prices rose but income remained the same. Social mobility (the ability of people to start poor and become rich through personal ability) collapsed. Today in America, a range of measures of social wellbeing show a country in decline. Perhaps fifty million people in the richest country on earth are living in poverty. Corporate profit is not, it turns out, the best metric by which to measure the health of a society.

Mad Cows

On Wall Street, government alone can set and apply the rules that stop irrational and dangerous banking behavior. When the government lets go the leash, all hell breaks loose.

Much of Western capitalism has evolved to reflect the ugliest side of our character. When examined through the prism of human nature, the truth is that markets and individuals are restrained in their often immoral and greedy quest for wealth only by government, governance, rules, and regulations. Without oversight, there's nothing but fear (of losing money) to stop speculating bankers from taking otherwise unacceptable risks. If they're gambling with someone else's money, there is no risk to the banker. Markets left unchecked always end up acting irrationally.

One of the most fascinating examples of irrational behavior from an unregulated market is from an entirely different sector, but I believe illustrates the insanity that can take hold. It's the story of Britain's mad cow disease outbreak of 1996.

Cows, as you know, live in fields and eat grass. The farmer used to wait until calves grew big enough to slaughter, then sell them for their meat. But as farming became industrialized, market forces came to play just as squarely on farmers and their animals as on any other sector. Fields take up space, cost money to maintain, and sometimes the cows get out. So cows were taken indoors, first into spacious barns, then increasingly crowded ones. When we eat beef, we're eating the cow's muscle, so growth hormones were added to the feed given to cows to reduce the period of time between birth and slaughter, and to increase the size of the animals, both measures improving profits. Over time, antibiotics were added to the feed, so cows would get sick and die less frequently. More money. Muscle growth requires protein, and grass doesn't have a lot of that, so the feed was changed to include high-protein supplements. Faster growing cows, more profits.

Over a number of years, with the industry unchecked, more and more crap was added to the cows' diets until what they were eating and how they were living bore almost no resemblance to traditional farming. Then one day, in an office somewhere in England, a powerful man in a nice suit received a letter on his desk suggesting that, to save money and increase profits, they start feeding cows the ground-up carcasses of sheep and other cows that were left on the floors of the abattoirs. Cheap protein, more profits. It was probably couched in some agreeably neutral language—vertebral residue, let's call it. And suddenly they were feeding cows ground up spinal cord.

In 1986, the cows started getting sick. BSE (bovine spongiform encephalopathy), a disease previously unheard of, was diagnosed. In the '90s, infected meat made the leap from cow to humans, and people started getting CJD (Creutzfeldt-Jakob disease) and dying because they had eaten infected meat.

And when the cows and the people started getting sick and dying, and the newspaper headlines started, most people said something similar. *Don't cows live in fields and eat grass?*

From 2001 to the crash of 2008, the financial markets of the United States operated in a paradigm as insane as this.

9/11 and the Market

The American stock market is the bare-knuckle expression of Western capitalism. Human emotions like confidence, cautiousness, or nervousness are applied to a set of numbers that reflect the collective feelings of the millions of people who invest in stocks, and the thousands who sit atop the power structure. Traders haven't felt the ears of spring corn, or read the studies of new coal deposits—the whole exercise is a never-ending search for just one thing—profit, and a balance between those two most ignoble of human emotions, greed and fear.

America was in recession in early 2001, and George W. Bush's popularity shrank like the profit figures the economists produced. It was 9/11, of all things, that kick-started the economy. Bush cut interest rates to historic lows, starting the day the markets reopened after 9/11 and continuing for two years, sparking a credit and lending orgy that lasted until the great crash. Short-term federal fund rates were cut from 6.5 percent in 2001 to just 1 percent in 2003. From then on, borrowing money would essentially be free. As usual, this made the rich richer, and the poor mostly came away with nothing.

Wall Street and its markets reopened hastily on September 17, 2001, six days after the attacks. Even during a time of disaster, profit can be made. Traders have described seeing the towers fall and feeling guilty because their first thought was, *wow, gold is going through the roof.* There was much concern that the markets would see a period of turmoil after the attacks, but while the political tremors last to this day, on the financial markets the shock was short-lived. The Dow Jones lost 14 percent in that first week, but the losses were quickly regained. A month later the indices were back to pre-9/11 levels.

It was during this period of immense national shock that the Bush administration pushed forward with corporate regulatory reforms that had previously been opposed, but were allowed through in the bipartisan climate of fear that suddenly pervaded American politics. Bush threw billions of dollars at the corporate sector, under the guise of responding to the financial shock caused by the attacks. This massive redirection of public funds may have been bad for the common man, who saw his tax dollar go toward supporting commerce (rather than education and healthcare), but it helped generate billions in profits for a handful of large corporations and banks.

Overall, 9/11 was a blessing for all concerned parties like Wall Street, Washington, the military, the FBI, CIA, NSA, and even the airlines involved. All would regard the years that followed 9/11 as vintage harvests.

The sheer level of political cynicism in Washington was illustrated by the actions of Bill Thomas, chairman of the House Ways and Means Committee, who tried to put through a massive cut in Capital Gains Tax (CGT) just forty-eight hours after the attacks. CGT cuts benefit the wealthy (they are the ones with assets that gain in value and accrue the tax)—80 percent of the benefits of a CGT cut go to the wealthiest 2 percent of tax-payers. Mr. Thomas would have known this well, yet he felt that this was the best way to spend his time, just two days after his nation suffered devastating attack.

A month later a bill was proposed that even the Wall Street Journal admitted would solely benefit corporate profits. The bill was tested on voter focus groups to gauge the likely public reaction, but those in the groups refused to believe that the bill was being accurately described to them. They couldn't believe it could be that cynical.

Bush's proposed stimulus bill offered $25 billion in retroactive tax cuts to corporations that were already highly profitable, and nothing for the unemployed. In this environment, it's hardly surprising that the entire financial sector (including the corporations who own the major media and television stations) uttered barely a word of criticism as Bush set about his prosecution of the War on Terror.

The US airline industry, already in a state of near constant crisis, was left staring into the abyss by 9/11. Understandably, passenger numbers plummeted for a while, and the airlines faced up to the costs and logistics of a new world of transformed security measures. These measures, incidentally, had mostly been called for prior to 9/11, and would almost certainly have helped thwart the attacks, but had been opposed tooth and nail by the airline industry.

Eleven days after 9/11, Bush rushed through a $15 billion airline bailout, but added no conditions on how the money was spent, so CEOs were able to slash 120,000 air-industry workers jobs. The legislation contained no funds for the workers who lost their jobs and their healthcare benefits. Although executives were forced to freeze their pay levels for two years, CEO salaries were already so astronomically high it would, for example, have taken the average American Airlines worker 1,365 years to earn the annual salary of their CEO.

The Sub-Prime Boom

The years that followed 9/11 were to be a period of free money and intense disinterest from regulators. The lax trading conditions under the Bush regime caused American banks and the property market to lose their sanity.

Roughly speaking, it worked like this. With interest rates near zero, the banks could lend money without virtually any cost to themselves, and without regulation they could lend to anyone. Where previously you needed to prove you could make the repayments on your loan, and were financially sound enough to afford to buy large assets like expensive houses, suddenly a postal worker earning $50,000 could get a loan on a half million dollar house. Or two houses. Or five of them.

It didn't matter, because not only were interest rates very low, loans were also offered that had ultra-low interest-only offers for a short introductory period. So-called piggyback loans were made to people who couldn't afford the deposit on a house. With a piggyback, you took out two loans, one for 80 percent of the house's value, the other for the 20 percent deposit. Some loans didn't require a deposit at all. In 2001 those loans made up just 3 percent of the market, by 2005 it was up to 24 percent. Other loans were made at 125 percent of the market value of the house, the theory being you could spend the extra money on renovations, then sell for a guaranteed profit, in a market that never went down.

If you couldn't make the higher repayments once the introductory low-rate period expired (which were often 50 percent more than the initial ones), you could always go and refinance, getting yourself another loan which also featured the ultra-low introductory offer. This could be replicated over and over again, and since loans were always available and house prices were going up so very fast, you couldn't lose. You could make a fortune with almost no money to start with.

But it was debt-fuelled growth, not a natural increase based on inflation and improved value. The financial landscape had changed entirely in a generation. Back in the 1950s, nearly half of all home-owners had no mortgage at all. Suddenly borrowing astronomical sums was not just acceptable, in this market you looked like a fool not to.

The housing boom that ensued in America represents one of the greatest examples of mass public hysteria (or mass myopia, if you will) in recorded history. Everyone bought it. Suddenly construction workers had property portfolios. Those issuing the loans were making fortunes of their own, and anyone in the banking industry who felt uncomfortable with the lending practices on display was in the wrong game. As Upton Sinclair said, "It is difficult to get a man to understand something, when his salary depends on his not understanding it."

Securitization is the practice of packaging loans together, and selling them to other investors wishing to make a steady buck. In turn, those selling the securitized packages can use the money they get to make more loans, ensuring a never-ending flow of debt and the buyers of debt.

With this combination of historically low interest rates, rising property prices, and lenders throwing money in all directions, sub-prime mortgages (those secured with much less capital and paperwork than traditionally required) exploded. From 1993 to 2000, sub-prime had increased as a proportion of all mortgages from 4 percent to 11 percent, and after 9/11 things went even more haywire. Banks made more and more loans to people with less and less money, and no-one had the heart or the courage to point out the insanity.

By 2005, 43 percent of people buying their first home in America were not required to make any deposit at all. Everyone knew this sort of thing was dangerous, but the risks associated with lending huge sums to people without any money could be passed on by the banks through the sale of securitized packages of debt to other investors. Smaller lenders sold bundles of mortgages to Wall Street banks like Lehman Brothers, who in turn repackaged these products and sold them on to some other schmuck. It didn't matter. The market was booming and international investors piled in, keen for a slice of the action.

Ask yourself who could have stopped this. The public was in a frenzy. Lenders were lending more than they ever had, and making fabulous profits from their record transactions. If you think the lenders themselves should have been more careful, imagine the atmosphere around a boardroom table from 2003 to 2007. Try to picture a CEO standing up and saying, "Gentlemen, I think this lending frenzy is unsafe and irrational, and I recommend we stop." The banks were making more money than they ever had before. That CEO would have been standing outside holding a box of family photos before sunset.

Those who make it to the top are by definition aggressive go-getters. Modern business culture only values the next quarter's financial results. We have created a business paradigm where sober assessment of long-term risk is simply outside the boundaries of consideration.

This is what government and ratings agencies are for, and the administration of George W. Bush was spectacularly asleep at the wheel. America's cozy relationship between government and Wall Street meant that the interests of the two were sometimes hard to distinguish. There simply was no one to regulate the insanity.

Now, Wall Street banks may have been acting irrationally, but they weren't totally stupid. Many who worked there knew that these loans were fundamentally crappy, and were aware of the risks if the housing market took a downturn. So they packaged huge tranches of these loans together into more complex products like Collateralized Debt Obligations (CDOs), for sale to anyone who wanted a piece of the action, and insured the CDOs using Credit Default Swaps (CDS). International banks, pension funds, and insurance companies raced themselves to invest. Things got completely out of hand. By the end of 2007, the credit default swap market was worth $62.2 trillion.

Three big ratings agencies (Moody's, Fitch Group, and Standard and Poor's) operate inside the US solely to assess financial offerings and give them rating-grades, based mostly on perceived risk. It was within their power to stop the madness. But like so many other areas of the US financial regulatory sector, they were hopelessly outgunned by the bigger, better connected, and more powerful banks, who had all the best brains in town. No one who wants to make a lot of money joins a rating agency.

The banks knew that outsiders relied on ratings agencies to make an assessment of debt and risk, so they paid huge fees to the agencies, who in turn gave their CDO's and other debt packages triple AAA ratings, the highest available. It was a massive racket.

Now the crappy loans (made to poor people who could barely make the monthly repayments, on house assets that had to go up in price or leave them in trouble) were marked with a gilded badge of safety. Further international money poured in. More money coming in meant more loans going out, which meant more speculation on property, and further increases in house prices. Suddenly every dinner table conversation in America was filled with real estate speculation.

Traditionally, ratings had been based on risk and return. AAA ratings provided lower rates of return, but were supposed to be high-quality loans, offering the buyer much lower risk. BBB category mortgage securities had higher rates of return but were riskier. The banks selling the packages of debt obviously had an incentive to get the highest possible rating for their products, as higher, safer ratings commanded the greatest premium. The idea was that if there was a downturn, the AAA rated investors got most of the money that was still coming in, and those with lower rated products were the first to lose out. But the failure of the ratings agencies meant Wall Street banks were able to successfully use complex methods to repackage junk loans as AAA-rated, and there was no one to stop them.

It was the biggest Ponzi scheme in human history, fundamentally built on sand. The moment the prices stopped going up, everyone was fucked. And it was just a matter of when.

Like a distracted driver who looks up at the road a few seconds too late, the Federal Reserve did eventually see the insanity that was taking place. To calm the market, they raised interest rates, a traditional method of slowing the economy. But by now, US economic growth was heavily predicated on housing and housing loans. Millions of people held debt they could barely afford. Interest rate hikes just added to the list of those on the financial edge. The Fed spectacularly failed to address this, instead raising interest rates by 25 basis points (0.25 percent) seventeen separate times between 2004 and 2006.

Oil was also a significant factor. After 9/11 it had dipped near $20 a barrel, but then the price rose and rose and rose. And then it rose some more. By June 2008, oil had soared to $144 a barrel. Oil is energy, energy is money. The high price of this vital resource put pressure on the entire US economy. The moment house prices stopped going up, the whole edifice collapsed.

During the boom, house prices (which had grown at 1.4 percent per year between 1975 and 2000) went up by 7 percent a year for five years. To get back down to the long-term trend, prices had to go down by 40 percent. However, every previous house price crash had taken values under the long-term average. It didn't take a genius to see that once the party was over, the hangover would be the worst of your life.

By 2006, many people on Wall Street realized that the sub-prime mortgage boom was in fact a disastrous bubble, and began betting the farm on a collapse. Some hedge funds made billions as the market went into free-fall.

A number of Wall Street's biggest investment banks also saw the problem. At the head of the line, as always, was Goldman Sachs, who made billions as the market fell, betting against stocks they had profited from promoting during the market's expansion. As the collapse started, executives lied about how much they had bet on disaster.

For ordinary homeowners, hooked on debt and with precious little equity in their beloved houses, the end of the boom was a disaster. In the summer of 2007, house prices suddenly turned downward, and lenders decided that previously automatic refinancing now wasn't possible. When the sweetener rates expired, tens of millions of people found that they simply couldn't pay the mortgage. The ratings agencies downgraded billions in CDOs and other securities, but it was too late.

The crash that came was much bigger than those before it, but it was also fundamentally different, in that those who had made it happen paid no price.

The System Breaks Down

As Britain's Chancellor of the Exchequer, Gordon Brown famously said that he had abolished the times of boom and bust. He was completely wrong. Just before the crash, Brown made a speech praising London bankers for their efforts in setting up a golden age. He was completely wrong. In the end, Brown presided over the loss of one million manufacturing jobs, and the biggest collapse in British finance since the 1920s. Some golden age.

It's important to understand that the ongoing and increasingly turbulent market booms and crashes we have faced since 1980 have not just been unfortunate accidents but mathematical certainties, with results that were unavoidable (given the behavior of the financial sector) and both predictable and predicted.

The financial paradigm we now have (that of astronomical CEO remuneration and a market focused solely on quarterly results) leads directly to the sort of business practice that causes massive bank asset increases, irrational booming markets, and then disastrous crashes. The disparity between executive pay and everyone else's is one of the primary causes of this risky behavior, yet when inevitable disaster arrives, these same executives are spared the pain.

The culture on Wall Street and in the City of London has changed dramatically since the 1970s, when Gus Levy, then Senior Partner at Goldman Sachs, described investment banking as "long term greedy." Now staff work in an industry where they know that they are constantly only five minutes away from finding their building access card cancelled, and themselves on the street. People act accordingly. If the bank doesn't act in the long-term interests of its staff, staff will only act in their own short-term interests. The idea of staff loyalty to the bank and its customers is a thing of the past.

A downturn in the US housing market caused the 2008 collapse that brought the world to its knees. It wasn't complicated. Home loans were made to people who didn't have the net worth and income to own them. Property values were appraised by valuers who were in the pocket of the banks. Those who gave lower valuations on properties were blacklisted and denied work, so housing valuations went up and up. The abundance of loans further increased the house values, and the pace of the market led more people to borrow to invest, becoming a viciously virtuous cycle. It could only end in disaster.

A significant partner in this crime was the US Federal Reserve and their political masters, mired in thirty years of dogma that said government control and regulation was bad, period. After the crash this dogma remained unchanged, and none of the US statutory, regulatory, or government agencies charged with regulating the financial markets chose to prosecute a single person for wrongdoing. Like 9/11, it seemed that while nearly everyone was at fault, no one was to blame.

Between 2007 and 2010, the median American family lost what has been called a generation of wealth. By 2009, 10 percent of Americans were behind on their home repayments or facing foreclosure. A whopping 30 percent were underwater, holding properties worth less than the debt they had against them.

Worst of all, the number of people who were poor or living below the poverty line dramatically increased. Americans weren't slacking off, nor was industry failing (in 2012, corporations made up the biggest share of the economy since the Second World War), it's just that corporate profits simply don't make it to the average worker any more. For 90 percent of Americans, income since 1973 has risen just 10 percent while healthcare, food, and education costs have soared. A Gallup poll in November 2008 found that one in five Americans had struggled to afford the food they needed in the previous twelve months. *One in five.*

Wall Street had spent a generation arguing that government was the problem, and just needed to get out of the way. They demanded financial rewards as if successful entrepreneurs, and cloaked themselves in the garb of professional risk-takers, but the risks they took were with other people's money. In the blink of an eye these masters of the universe found themselves on their knees, and as their world fell apart discovered that their much-derided government offered them the only way to survive.

Combined, banks, lenders, insurers, auto-makers, and the like were given a $700 billion TARP (Troubled Asset Relief Program) bailout to help them stabilize through the crisis, whereas the 13.1 million Americans who lost their homes were offered nothing. Who could possibly argue that this wasn't entirely the wrong way around? Worse, Wall Street shamelessly demanded public spending cuts to clean up the financial mess that they themselves had made.

As Christopher Hitchens put it:

> "How very agreeable it must be to sit at a table in a casino where nobody seems to lose, and to play with a big stack of chips furnished to you by other people, and to have the further assurance that, if ever anything should chance to go wrong, you yourself are guaranteed by the tax dollars of those whose money you are throwing about in the first place! It's enough to make a cat laugh."

These people were not, in transpired, blessed with the wisdom of Solomon, or some staggering insight into financial affairs, they were just able to take advantage of a broken financial regulatory system and held the right jobs when the boom came along, "standing around with tubas in their arms on the day it began to rain money," to quote journalist Nicholas von Hoffman.

The crash didn't just affect America financially. The systemic financial weakness it exposed marked the end of nearly two decades of unquestioned American world supremacy. The bankers brought the country to its knees.

Glass-Steagall, the Depression-era law passed by President Roosevelt (which was wounded by Reagan and finally done away with by President Clinton after fierce lobbying from the financial sector) had separated investment banks (traders and speculators) from commercial banks (who had local branches and made loans to individuals and businesses). Without the repeal of Glass-Steagall, the investment banks would not have been able to engage in such ridiculous home-loan speculation.

But it wasn't just poor judgment. In fact, since the 1980s, and accelerating with the repeal of Glass-Steagall, much of the global financial sector has become criminalized and fraudulent. These days the biggest Wall Street institutions are a mecca for laundered drug money, assisting tax evasion, the funding of terrorism, and general criminal behavior. International banking houses represent the largest organized crime syndicate in human history, and must be broken apart. Glass-Steagall must be reintroduced, so the gamblers can't again play with your mortgage.

This is unlikely to happen, as government and Wall Street are so entwined as to be one and the same. Charles Ferguson, who directed the documentary

Inside Job, said, "The US political system [and its inability to address the criminal behavior of banks] has become the biggest money laundering operation of all."

Those charged with regulating the madness did nothing as the crash drew close. Alan Greenspan, former chairman of the US Federal Reserve, said that when the sub-prime bubble was approaching, he really didn't "get it" until very late. Greenspan had been given an honorary knighthood by the UK in 2002 for his contribution to global economic stability, but didn't see the largest asset bubble in human history coming. That's a bad one to miss. But I guess many others missed what a fool Greenspan was.

The average bank robbery nets just $7,000. The one in 2008 cost Americans $11 trillion and ten million jobs. That's some bank robbery. And robbery is exactly what it was.

Lehman Brothers

Lehman Brothers, 158 years old and America's fourth-largest investment bank, collapsed on September 15, 2008. Six days previously its shares had suddenly plummeted in value, halving in one day. The bank made a direct plea for assistance to President Bush, but he allowed them to go to the wall. It was the largest bankruptcy in US history, six times larger than the previous record.

Lehman Brothers had no retail banking component whatsoever. No branches, no ATMs. Its collapse should not have made a difference to anyone but Lehman's staff and customers. Instead, Lehman's precipitous collapse led to the disintegration of the global economic system and took capitalism to the brink of calamity.

A nine-volume court examiner's report into the bankruptcy, issued in March 2010, revealed a swathe of extraordinary managerial misjudgments, misleading behavior, and semi-legal (at best) mechanisms employed by senior staff to manipulate Lehman's accounts, in order to hide fundamental issues within the business as it hit choppy waters. All the while, Lehman's top executives had continued to pay themselves stupendous amounts, with CEO Richard Fuld at one point insisting he had taken "only" $310 million in compensation in the seven years prior to the bankruptcy. Lehman's investors were less fortunate, receiving fourteen cents in the dollar.

Lehman Brothers wasn't exceptional on Wall Street. It had just been the unlucky one. All of the major investment houses had been indulging in an unprecedented orgy of risky behavior, dishonesty, and outright fraud that was the hallmark of the Bush administration's laissez-faire attitude to financial regulation. Wall Street's behavior prior to the crash was the clearest example of the folly of letting capitalism run like wildfire.

Lehman failed because (like the others) it massively invested in sub-prime mortgage backed securities, rated AAA by the rating companies. But the actual mechanics of keeping the business afloat when it hit trouble were not especially complicated. Lehman manipulated its balance sheet, using inflated valuations of companies it owned or controlled, fundamentally abusing its fiduciary duty to be prudent and trustworthy with its clients money. This was illegal behavior. Fraud. People should have been arrested, tried, and jailed. Instead, no one was, and for a while it looked like the world's financial system would collapse entirely.

How Close We Came

By September of 2008 we were in a financial shit storm like no other. On the morning of the eighteenth, Hank Paulson told Congress that $5.5 trillion in wealth would be gone within three hours, and the world economy would collapse within a day if they did not act. On September 29, the Dow lost 777 points (7 percent), its biggest one-day drop in history. Market turbulence levels were unprecedented.

In the calm of the passed storm, many economists and politicians have lined up to reminisce about those crazy days when capitalism tottered on the brink of collapse. One thing that is virtually never mentioned is the consequences for us all, had the fundamentals of Western capitalism actually failed. What would that have looked like, how long might it have lasted, and how can we be sure it won't happen in the future?

Make no mistake, the system came just a hair's breadth from disaster. When Tom McKillop, chairman of the collapsing Royal Bank of Scotland, called Alistair Darling (Britain's then chancellor) on October 7, 2008, he said the bank was in desperate trouble. Darling asked McKillop how long the cash reserves would last, expecting an answer of a few days. McKillop told him the bank would be gone in two or three hours. Darling recalled thinking that this was the end for Britain. He likened the effects of complete financial collapse to nuclear war.

Traders on Wall Street have described the atmosphere on the day Lehman Brothers collapsed as having been like the threat of war. Many say they were genuinely terrified. Those in the know called family members to tell them to take all their money out of the bank. City of London workers, interviewed in 2015, recalled talking to their wives and using phrases like hoard food, get as much money from the ATM as you can, or get ready to evacuate the kids to the country.

It's almost impossible to find a cogent description of what would have happened if the global financial system had imploded. Many people say it very nearly did, few seem courageous enough to speculate on the consequences had it done so. But it's not hard to imagine the scene when the entire population of the developed world, reliant on credit cards to pay for things and supermarkets to supply their food, realized en masse that their credit cards had frozen and food deliveries stopped.

The phrase "nine meals from anarchy" was coined to describe how our seemingly placid and safe lives could be turned upside down very quickly in the event of financial or social calamity. The banks don't have all the money we've deposited (they barely have a fraction of it), so if lending and credit froze across the board, within hours the financial system would stop at best, and collapse at worst. ATMs would dispense no cash. Petrol and medical supplies would quickly run out. Worse, the truck delivering food to your supermarket couldn't fill up with fuel, and the driver couldn't work without his pay, so the shelves would quickly empty. Supermarkets are said to stock three days of food for the neighborhoods they support, so within three days hunger would lead us to abandon all social conventions and take to the streets. This may seem apocalyptic, but the economists and bankers smiling comfortably through their interviews knew that this was the abyss into which they had stared.

If this also sounds implausible, ask people in the thirty-seven countries that had food riots in 2008 how it felt. Ask the survivors of Hurricane Katrina in New Orleans, where society almost broke down in a matter of days. Less than forty-eight hours after the hurricane, senior police falsely declared martial law and some officers acted like paramilitary militia, arming themselves with AK-47s and shooting black civilians, whether or not they were committing crimes or looting. Social breakdown can and does happen.

Faced with this terrifying prospect, sanity would demand that we take drastic steps but, systemically and structurally, virtually nothing has changed in the financial world since those dark days. Perhaps the recklessness has being reined in a touch, but only perhaps. Banks that were too big to fail back then are too big to fail now, and threaten us all with their sheer size. If nothing has changed, what is to stop it happening again, and who would bet on us being so lucky next time.

Governments React

What saved us in 2008 was a combination of the hugely expensive nationalization of toxic private assets, printing trillions of dollars, cutting interest rates to zero, and a solid dose of good luck.

Corporations and right-wing governments had, since Reagan took office, insisted that the government and high taxes blocked innovation and free enterprise, and really should only be there for keeping law and order and implementing limited social programs. So it was illuminating to see that philosophy make an abrupt U-turn the moment the banks' own business model fell to pieces. Suddenly it seemed that government and financial intervention wasn't beyond the pale. Not only was it now required, it was (they said) a moral imperative. What became clear in that moment was that this was not a political or business philosophy at all, but a pragmatic system designed to achieve maximum profits, to be ditched at a moment's notice should a crisis arrive.

The people who suffered in New Orleans after Hurricane Katrina also felt that keen need for government assistance, but their skin was brown and their wallets thin, so they suffered a different fate. The taxpayer was instead required to cover private companies that had gotten into trouble; companies so large that they threatened the very system in which they operated.

Over a two week period in September 2008, the US government took control of Freddie Mac and Fannie Mae, the nation's largest mortgage lenders. Both companies' share prices had dropped 90 percent from a year before. Both looked like they were going bust. These two underpinned the entire US mortgage market. They held or offered guarantees on over $5 trillion in debt, and were owned by groups as disparate as the Chinese government and US pension funds. If Freddie Mac and Fannie Mae went under, we were in deep shit.

Insurance behemoth AIG got into trouble and was bailed out with $180 billion in federal funds before the government took over. Astoundingly, six months later they paid their executives a total of $165 million in bonuses.

In November it became clear that Citigroup was insolvent, despite getting $25 billion in TARP rescue funds. Citigroup! Going bust! Can you imagine?

Federal Reserve Chairman Ben Bernanke's response to the crisis (and that of London) was to cut federal interest rates to zero and print money. Lots of money. Quantitative Easing (QEI and QEII), as it was called, was a complicated means of stimulating growth by buying assets from banks. Suffice to say that the Federal Reserve started pumping $30 billion a month into the US economy just to keep it alive.

As the bailouts flowed, the federal government found itself in a position to dictate policy to the financial sector for the first time in a generation. Treasury

Secretary Hank Paulson offered President Obama a proposal whereby the government would quickly distribute a second tranche of TARP funds, in return for which the banks would write down problematic mortgages and save millions of people from being thrown out of their own homes. Obama, whose White House was extensively staffed with Wall Street alumni, turned down the deal.

The expression "too big to fail" was one that Wall Street institutions clung to like a drowning man during the crisis. The US government chose to bail out the banks, no matter what the financial cost, and for the most part ignored the millions of people suffering the consequences of Wall Street's irrational and illegal behavior. That decision was not taken in isolation, but under the most immense pressure from Wall Street's powerful lobbyists, and the decisions themselves were taken by a class of state regulators and rule-makers who were almost without exception products of the revolving door between Wall Street and Washington.

Who paid? Simple. We did.

In the wake of the collapse, and after spending billions of taxpayer dollars propping up bankrupt banks, Western governments imposed austerity measures on their populations, cutting benefits and vital services to the general population, and the poor in particular. These measures were said to have been demanded by the market, which meant the banks and corporations. Fines levied against the finance industry totaled less than 1 percent of the profits the banks had earned during the period in which they were found to have been acting fraudulently.

Charles Ferguson said that the crimes committed by financial services firms included securities fraud, accounting fraud, honest services violations, bribery, perjury and making false statements to US government investigators, Sarbanes-Oxley violations (false accounting), RICO (Racketeer Influenced and Corrupt Organizations Act) offences, federal aid disclosure regulations offenses, and personal conduct offences (drug use and tax evasion etc.). That's quite a list.

What certainly took place was an enormous and explicit breach of RICO. Under this act, not only can the heads of racketeering organizations be prosecuted (with ignorance not an acceptable defense), but personal assets of those accused can be seized before trial. Yet, despite the mountain of evidence of illegal and fraudulent behavior, not one person working at a large US financial institution was arrested, or saw the inside of an American prison cell. This in the country with the highest incarceration rate on earth.

And what is true of most Wall Street banks was doubly so of Goldman Sachs.

Goldman's Chief Executive Lloyd Blankfein said in 2009 that he was do-ing God's work, but most view the company somewhat differently. A few months later, Matt Taibbi at *Rolling Stone* called Goldman a "great vampire squid wrapped around the face of humanity, relentlessly jamming its blood funnel into anything that smells like money." Goldman makes profit for Gold-man, and appears to have no other role in society whatsoever. It is the most profitable securities firm in history.

One resigning staff member (Fabrice Tourre) described the company cre-ating Frankenstein financial products of no intrinsic value. Others described a culture where ripping off Goldman's clients, or selling them stock which Goldman staff felt had little chance of making a profit, was rife. Traders called securities "crap pools" and "shitty" investments between themselves, as they continued to sell them to their clients.

When the housing boom neared its end, Goldman set about making bil-lions from the collapse of industries it had spent the previous years selling to its customers. It wasn't alone. Everyone was up to it. One department at Deutsche Bank sold its clients sub-prime mortgages, fraudulently packaged together as AAA products, while another division of the bank shorted them, betting that their values would plummet.

The selling of assets in the full knowledge that they are junk is fraudu-lent. People are arrested, tried, and imprisoned for much smaller frauds every day. But the Obama administration told us that the reason for not prosecuting powerful executives was that it was too hard to obtain convictions. That was always certain to be true if no one even tried, and this would in no way have been related to the fact that Treasury Secretary Hank Paulson, the most senior money man in America, was the former CEO of Goldman Sachs.

Once upon a time, even the banking houses could be seen to be playing a role in society, but these days it's hard to see what Morgan Stanley or Goldman Sachs actually do except make money. If you asked the average person in the street what these leviathans, with their well-known names, actually do, you might hear the word money a lot, but otherwise it's hard for most people to define. They don't make anything, and they don't sponsor, grow or support anyone, except their own staff and customers.

Physicists know that the wonderfully immutable laws of physics apply across the known universe, no matter how large the distance or huge the forc-es involved. But at the subatomic level, it appears some of these rules can be discarded by the tiniest particles known to man. Capitalism works the same, but in reverse. At the street-level to which we are most accustomed, the simple laws of supply and demand level the playing field in a way that seems both fair and reasonable. If two sandwich bars open next to each other and offer a similar product, the cheaper one will probably get more customers. If the expensive one produces a clearly superior sandwich, it may be able to gain a clientele with more disposable income, or persuade people to spend more on a quality item. If the product is poor, the people will stay away and the doors will eventually close.

This works for restaurants, carpets, taxis—nearly everything. But the major banking houses of the world have out-grown this natural leveler. They know that there is effectively no competition, and are often their own clients. Banks create their own investment products, and use high-speed algorithms to trade at a pace beyond us mere mortals. Best of all, banks know that their power to lobby the government means that the rules the rest of us play by simply don't apply to them. Flagrant breaking of the law results in the tiniest of punishments, or most often no punishment at all. Ultimately, they also now know that if it all comes crashing down, the government will be there to save them.

What a fantastic world it must be to live in. You work in a company that the government itself guarantees will not be allowed to go bust, and operate in a framework where clearly illegal actions are never, and can never, be prosecuted. This represents a stratified elite within American society, entirely beyond the rule of law.

Effective exemption from the laws of the land positively encourages these huge institutions to continue to act as criminals, safe in the knowledge that they can never be prosecuted. Taken as a whole, the financial crisis of 2008 wasn't a blip or an accident. It was the inevitable outcome of an industry out of control.

The government's bailout offered no incentive for the banks to clean up their act, instead giving them a green light to carry on as before, which is what they have done. In 2015, whistleblower Herve Falciani exposed documents showing that HSBC continued to provide banking services for arms and drug dealers, and helped rich people evade taxes. Falciani was sentenced to five years in prison for breaking arcane Swiss banking secrecy laws. The penalties for HSBC remained far from clear.

Credit Suisse created a handbook on how to launder money called "How to Transfer US Dollar Payments." They distributed the book to their dodgy clients.

Exempt from prosecution or the risk of bankruptcy, Wall Street's tone-deaf reaction to public scorn was mind-boggling to watch. In the space of just months they went from their knees, begging for bailouts to save their sorry skins, to the same bonus practices and trebles-all-round culture that had so revolted the public (who paid the taxes that bailed them out). After momentary lip-service was paid to the appearance of contrition, the old behavior was back, most notably in the obscene sums paid to those at the top. In 2011, as most Americans wages fell or stagnated, and Occupy Wall Street was being harassed on the streets of New York City, top executives enjoyed a pay hike of up to 40 percent in one year, not including dramatic increases in pensions, stock options, and payoffs.

There were voices within US politics that reflected the public outrage, but they were few. The same month that AIG was bailed out, a petition was presented to Hank Paulson with thirty-two thousand signatures, calling for an end to the bonus culture. The petition was organized by a little known Senator from Vermont. His name was Bernie Sanders.

Despite the carnage in 2008, the financial sector rabidly fought against proposed new transaction taxes, aimed at slowing the insane pace of bond, security, and derivative trading. Some taxes were proposed at a rate of just 0.01 percent (one ten-thousandth). All were treated by the industry like an outbreak of botulism.

In late September 2008, Christopher Cox, chairman of the Securities and Exchange Commission (SEC) announced that, to his surprise, the system of voluntary self-regulation placed on Wall Street (at the insistence of Wall Street themselves) had not worked. This may rank among the most blinding statements of the obvious in history, but it illustrates how little regulation had been placed upon banking operations until then. When an industry demands to regulate itself, there is trouble ahead. Yet, unabashed, Wall Street demanded that the first package of bailout money be subject to no congressional oversight or supervision. They wanted the money that would save them, but didn't want anyone to tell them what to do with it. It seems that beggars could be choosers.

The main lesson of the crash should have been that the banks had enjoyed too much regulatory freedom, and that new and stronger regulation was necessary to stabilize the sector and overall economy, to ensure this could not happen again. Of course nearly nothing has been done. Although ring-fencing retail and investment banking arms would be a start, the main issue remains. The banking sector is too big to fail, and thus holds the world to ransom. These leviathans are larger than nation states, and threaten them when unstable.

Ring-fencing won't do it. Lehman Brothers didn't have a retail side, but was so large that its collapse nearly ended modern capitalism.

One of the most heinous sins that Barack Obama was accused of was socialism, yet in practice, America operates socialism for the rich and capitalism for the poor. Huge financial losses by the richest corporations in the land were covered (in effect insured) by the state, and the businesses were saved from bankruptcy, while for the poor it was every man for himself. Tens of millions lost their jobs and were turfed out of their homes, and the government did little or nothing to stop it.

Socialism for the rich, capitalism for the poor. That is how our economies now work. Those at the bottom are subject to the rigors of the free market, and a lost job or failed business venture spells disaster. Those at the top are pampered and protected by the state, profits are privatized (kept) and debts socialized (insured by the government). It's win-win. And it means that there is no incentive for the industry not to act the same way all over again. After the events of 2008, chief executives and chairmen know that in the background is the constant safety net of government intervention if things really go tits up.

When are we going to see these institutions for what they are: the biggest financial criminals on the planet. In the last few years alone, we've had banking houses selling dodgy mortgage securities, betting these would fall, manipulating interest rates, being exposed as the biggest drug money launderers on earth, and bringing the world to its financial knees. Those involved should be prosecuted. Their businesses should be broken up. Fines should come in the billions, not millions. CEOs should be in prison.

America's two-tier justice system now means that the poor (mostly people of color) convicted of low-level, non-violent offences can often face the most staggering jail terms, while those involved in high-level fraud—crimes often affecting millions of people—are routinely excused the inconvenience of even facing legal action for their huge crimes.

The lesson here is quite simple—capitalism as a system fundamentally fails when financial organizations reach a certain size. The rules cease to apply. An entity that is too big to fail is too mighty to regulate, and becomes a crazed gorilla at a tea party. The major houses of Wall Street have been comprehensively shown to be untrustworthy, too much of a risk to society, and often entirely lawless criminals who consider themselves above the law and have been proven to be just that, as huge and systemic law-breaking has been entirely ignored by government.

Just as control of armies, schools, and government are not (and should never be) left to private enterprise, the control of credit ought to be strictly regulated in a society which depends on its free flow in order to function. Banking houses that are too big to fail threaten entire societies. The banks present a much greater and more immediate threat to society than terrorism. They must be broken up into small pieces immediately.

If anything, the calamity of the great financial crisis and collapse of Lehman Brothers illustrated one truism that should be remembered when the next crisis arrives. The money is behind everything. Wall Street and the banks are the ultimate source of power in this world. The dollar pays for the politicians and the media, the politicians write the laws and command the military. Wall Street and the City of London are, ultimately, in charge of everything.

Some Win Big

Michael Lewis' excellent book *The Big Short* told the story of people who saw the crash coming and tried to enrich themselves as the heavens fell. Although the stock market dropped 60 percent between late 2007 and early 2009, some investors bet the farm and chose the right time and method to effectively short the market and ensure that there was money to be picked up at the bottom.

Hedge fund Paulson & Co. bet against the market, and made $15 billion in 2007, as the world around them collapsed. Other individuals also made spectacular sums. Some saw it coming, but got their timing wrong and missed out.

Even large institutions like Goldman Sachs knew there was trouble afoot. As the economy teetered, one division of the company told its clients that all was well, and that perhaps the slight downturn was a good time to buy, while another division bet heavily on a free-fall. Again, plain fraud.

Despite the collapsing markets, it's important to remember that the crash really didn't hurt rich people at all. Some saw their net worth drop, but for the most part the most profound financial collapse since the Great Depression in fact saw the rich get much, much richer.

The number of billionaires worldwide rose by 30 percent between 2007 and 2010. There are about 1,800 of them now. Their combined wealth sits around $7 trillion, more than the GDP of Germany and the UK combined. These days, just over one thousand individuals have a combined wealth of $4.5 trillion, one third of America's GDP. The richest four hundred people in America have more wealth than the bottom 150 million.

The growth in disparity of wealth had been happening for some time. Between 1980 and 2005, 80 percent of all new income went to the richest 1 percent. The crash actually accelerated this process.

Even those closest to the disaster came away unscathed. Daniel Mudd and Richard Syron, the bosses of Fannie Mae and Freddie Mac, left with $9.43 million in retirement benefits. When the Royal Bank of Scotland's share price dropped 37 percent in a year, the Chief Executive was offered a bonus of £1.4 million. Wouldn't it be great to live in a world where you get million dollar bonuses for shrinking your company by a third in just one year?

It didn't have to be this way. Of all places, the small country of Iceland provided the most powerful counterpoint to America's policy of no-blame banking bailouts and business as usual. Iceland took their former prime minister to court for his actions in dramatically deregulating the country's financial sector, setting it up for one of the biggest crashes in Western history. In a short space of time, Iceland's biggest three banks had been allowed to swell from regular national institutions to bloated hyper-banks, with paper values more than ten times the size of the country's GDP. After the crash, bankers were indicted for their behavior, and the nation's constitution redrafted to ensure such insanity could not take place again. Iceland simply refused to pay back its international debt. The entire political system was dismantled.

After the Crash

The immense amount of money now controlled by the banking and financial sectors distorts whole economies. Uncontrolled credit pours into pointless banking activity (take-overs, private equity, financial engineering) that makes banks fortunes simply through the transfer of wealth from point A to point B, rather than the creation of products, jobs and the manufacture of things.

As the world's economies have stagnated, corporate profits have risen dramatically, leaving corporations with vast piles of unused cash, which mostly sits idle. In mid-2016, Apple alone had cash reserves of over $230 billion. They appeared not to know what to do with it.

Bank assets have again swollen to be larger than before the crash of 2008, while we have been told to austerely tighten our belts because of the economic crisis. These are conditions that can only cause continued moribund economic performance at best, and an even more cataclysmic crash at worst.

Nowhere is the hypocrisy of modern capitalism more naked than when it comes to tax. Governments lecture the poor about straitened economic times, while corporations (who make large political donations) secrete their profits in offshore tax havens, and pay staggeringly low marginal rates of tax in the countries where they make most of their profits.

Vast concentrations of wealth present a clear and present danger to the world economy, not least by the owners of that wealth and the political power it provides, further exacerbating financial imbalance by persuading governments to lower taxes and reduce corporate regulations, and robbing people in the host country by paying corporate tax in offshore havens.

Although commerce creates great profits and should deliver subsequent taxes, this needs to be offset against the tax-dodging that actually takes place, and more pertinently the massive sums required to bail banking institutions out when they fail. Despite the huge government bailouts, America's banks consistently failed to meet lending targets to small and medium-sized businesses, which were supposed to kick-start the economy—the stated aim of the government's gifts of money in the first place. Failing to meet targets actually meant refusing to meet them.

While the recovery in the US was slow, that was not the case in the stock market, which boomed after the crash, ending 2013 at all time highs. This may have seemed like good news, but the richest 10 percent of Americans hold 80 percent of the shares (by value), so the stock boom that followed 2008's collapse almost exclusively benefited the rich, and this was reflected by the incredible growth in their net wealth during this period.

Those with money couldn't keep it at the bank; deposits were earning close to 0 percent interest rates. Instead, rich people invested in stocks and shares, and the market went up because of it.

The boom in stock values was also brought about by the increase in corporate profits, and most of those profits in such moribund economic times were achieved by slashing costs. The biggest cost slashed was wages. Globalization meant jobs could be outsourced to China or emerging countries. And so it was that during a time when true economic indicators showed a profound depression, the poor got poorer and the rich made a killing. Just to twist the knife, tax codes written by Republican governments meant that rich people were able to pay around half the tax on their dividends (and other classes of wealth gain) that the rest of Americans pay on their salaries.

US politics is now universally seen as broken, with money such a factor in getting elected that the rich effectively own the government. The idea that conservatism is by nature a better approach to fiscal probity has proven disastrously wrong. Trickle-down economics wasn't a theory that proved flawed, it was a lie, designed to fool us into letting the rich get much richer.

The crash of 2008 was different to those that preceded it, and represents a true existential crisis in modern capitalism. Its repercussions will play out over a generation or more.

The Obama administration's refusal to arrest even one Wall Street banker offered de facto immunity to an industry whose systemic law-breaking ruined millions of lives, and provided a platform from which the rich not only survived but thrived, during the greatest recession since the 1920s.

Governments printed money and massively increased sovereign debt in order to stabilize their economies. Interest rates stayed near zero, yet most economies barely showed anything like the kind of growth that free money should guarantee. Only the large financial institutions and corporations thrived.

In Britain, the banks received tens of billions of pounds in rescue funds from the government, but the bonus culture barely paused to say thank you before resuming. We shouldn't be surprised, as the financial sector provides over 25 percent of the funding for the ruling conservative party.

With the trillions handed out through quantitative easing in America, every unemployed person in the country could have been given a job paying $50K per year. Instead, the number of homeless and those on food stamps soared, while the rich made off with a fortune.

When terrorists struck America, killing three thousand we were told that nothing could ever be the same again, but when the banks of Wall Street brought the world's financial system to its knees, ruining the lives of millions of people, it appeared no changes whatsoever were required, and no one was to blame. Within months, the entire system had regenerated and started again.

Astronomical Remuneration and Wealth

Across Europe and the US, the public have been told that only a collective tightening of our belts can rein in huge national debts, and make our economies balance again. But that's bullshit. People haven't been living beyond their means, the money available has been vacuumed up by the rich.

In the US, the median wage (adjusted for inflation) is only a tiny percentage higher than it was thirty years ago, although the economy is nearly three times the size. The majority of people in America can now only get by through significantly increased work commitments, and the taking on of unpayable debt. In 2013, the median household income remained steady at $51,000 (down 9 percent, adjusted for inflation, since 1999). The difference is at the top. That same year America's top ten CEOs took home at least $100 million each.

The richest people in our society used to include doctors and teachers. These days the top 1 percent is almost exclusively made up of CEOs and people in the financial industry. Finance and banking makes the most profit and sucks up most of the money, but contributes nearly nothing to society's well-being. Its appetite for more money seems infinite.

In 1980, CEOs were paid around forty-two times the average worker (and top tax rates for the rich were 70 percent). Now that multiple is 380. Some companies pay their CEOs more than the company pays in tax. This is unsustainable, unjust, and causes CEOs to act in ways that are out of touch with those that they employ.

The richest one percent in the UK (six hundred thousand people) are worth one trillion pounds and have as much money as the poorest 55 percent of the population combined. The top 10 percent have assets totaling four trillion pounds. 0.28 percent of the people own 64 percent of the land. This did not happen with the other 99.72 percent of the people happily agreeing to it. On the contrary, one million of them (in the sixth richest country on earth) feed themselves via food banks.

Oxfam published a report in 2014, stating that the richest eighty-five people in the world have more assets than the poorest 3.5 billion people combined. Forbes magazine thought that number was just sixty-six. They could all fit on a double-decker bus. The number comes down each year, meaning the ultra-rich are getting much, much richer. A lot of space on the bus might be required for their combined wealth of £1 trillion. Worldwide, the richest one percent have assets worth $110 trillion. That's sixty-five times as much as the poorest 50 percent of humans on the planet.

The Wal-Mart family members have more money than the poorest 30 percent of all Americans—thirty-three million families. The four hundred richest people in the US have as much as the bottom 50 percent—155 million people.

The disparity is such that the rich now need protection from the poor. America employs more private security personnel than high school teachers.

The rich don't just have the assets, they make all the income. In 2010, the richest 1 percent in America got 93 percent of the year's gain in income. In 2009, American bankers awarded themselves $14 billion in bonuses. These institutions would not have existed had it not been for the tax-payer, yet just a year after complete calamity the bonus culture had returned, and bankers took advantage of tax loopholes to screw the people who had just saved their lives.

CEO and top 1 percent income disparity is also a major cause of unemployment. The ultra-high wages paid to those people at the top of large organizations reduces the cash available to employ many more people on normal rates of pay. So the next time you're on hold to a big company and hear the words "all of our consultants are busy," remember that at least in part this is because the CEO of the company is taking home millions, meaning the company can't afford enough people to answer your call.

Unemployment and low wages flow through society like a poisoned river, destroying lives, causing antisocial behavior and costing the state billions in benefits and assistance to the weakest. This is the real cost of that CEO taking home his millions. If a small number of rich people had their wages cut (to figures which still represent a very sizeable income), a much larger group of people could be employed, increasing business productivity and reducing negative impacts on the state and society.

In March 2016, a report from the London School of Economics reported that there would be no negative effect on Britain's economy if CEOs had their salaries slashed. Headhunters interviewed for the report said that for every CEO employed, another hundred individuals could do the job just as efficiently. The headhunters said they were concerned that the massive salaries paid to CEOs had serious implications for the social fabric of the country.

In the UK, bonuses from 2007 to 2015 topped £100 billion, £1,500 for every man, woman, and child in the country. When the EU tried to put a cap on bonuses in 2012 (limiting them to just one or two years' salary, and allowing shareholders the final say), Britain's conservative government opposed the legislation, saying it would damage the financial sector. They even took the EU to court, to protect the ability of banks to routinely award their staff large bonuses, spending British taxpayers' money defending their banker friends.

In a time of profound depression, the richest one thousand people in the UK saw their wealth rise by £155 billion in just four years, enough to pay off the entire government deficit. From 2005 to 2015, these lucky people saw their already considerable wealth double.

Tax Evasion and Offshore Funds

And still it is not enough. The rich have hijacked the political system, rigging the rules in their favor in a vicious cycle of wealth and power, yet despite the fact that taxes for rich people have fallen in twenty-nine of the leading thirty countries in the world since the late 1970s, tax evasion by wealthy individuals and large corporations is now so widespread that it seems impossible to stop.

Around $20–$30 trillion are now stored in tax-free offshore accounts by the richest people in the world. That's as much as the US and Japanese GDP combined. Half of that money is controlled by the richest ninety-one thousand people on earth, just enough to fit inside a large sports stadium. We're not sure of the exact figure of course, as the accounts are designed to be concealed. Given that the money is hidden, estimates are likely to be on the low side. As the world's economy teeters on the edge for want of capital, imagine what just half of that money could do for humanity.

The practice of offshore money-channeling and tax evasion is not on the periphery of business practice, it is very much in the mainstream. The four biggest banks in the UK have 1,200 subsidiaries in tax havens. Many of the tax havens themselves are British overseas dependencies and territories. Britain actively participates in its own fleecing.

These monies, mostly secreted legally and managed by the elite banking houses of the West, won't easily be repatriated to the economies that produced them. The richest people can afford accountants and lawyers who are at the vanguard of tax avoidance. When the day comes that financial calamity or ecological disaster finally strikes, you can be sure that those with the money will prefer the collapse of society to handing back their fabulous wealth in order to help fix the problem. This massive concealment of wealth, depriving struggling nations of tax revenue in the face of impending collapse, presents a clear and present danger to democracy, and to humanity's survival.

In the developing world, money that has leaked out of legitimate econo-mies into tax havens is enough to pay off host nations sovereign debts. Crip-pling debt repayments are most often cited as the premier cause of the poor nations of the world staying poor, so millions live in poverty because a few individuals have made off with all the money. Ever wonder why oil-rich Ni-geria is in such a poor state? Three hundred billion dollars leaving the country in private hands might have had something to do with it.

This staggering build-up of offshore capital should be mentioned every single time we hear statistics about world poverty, or when austerity measures are presented as the only way out of our problems. The fact is there's plenty of money for all—it's just stashed away by a very small number of very rich people. These wealthy individuals, some of whom may be good people with kindly hearts, collectively form a direct threat to the lives of billions of people. No politician dares stand up to them, as has been amply shown over the last thirty-five years. This financial power is augmented by corporate media, the owners of which are within this elite group. Any mention of a tax on the rich is shouted down as abominable socialism, and practically the end of civilization.

Corporations are, if anything, more aggressive than individuals when it comes to tax avoidance. Paying next to no tax allows big businesses to grow to such a size that they are unwieldy, slowing human progress through sti-fling competition, and a danger to entire economies should they collapse. Why does Apple base so much of its business in Dublin, Ireland? Tax avoid-ance. Apple has been so successful in its tax affairs that it sits on enough cash to give $720 to every man, woman, and child in America. And that's just one company.

Boots, Britain's largest chemist, has their head office in Switzerland. In 2013, they were accused of using a legal loophole to avoid £1.1 billion in tax. Google put 80 percent of its profits through Bermuda in 2011, cutting its overall tax bill in half, but Google really isn't a Bermudan company, is it?

Between 2009 and 2012, Starbucks paid no corporation tax in Britain at all, despite having over eight hundred outlets there. How could owning eight hundred busy coffee shops not make a taxable profit? Try answering that with a straight face.

In fact, you would do very well to name a large corporation you know of or deal with that is not putting its affairs into a washing machine of offshore companies, in order to avoid paying tax in the country where you bought the goods.

This is a problem. As benefits and state spending are cut, multinationals turning over billions manage to pay no tax at all, without breaking the law. The British government focuses much attention on benefits cheats, but the real cheats are at the top table, dining with the Prime Minister and laughing all the way home.

We are all unwilling participants in this. The conveniences of modern life are courtesy of business practices that destroy the fabric of the world's economy. The avoidance of paying tax by these companies isn't maximizing shareholder return, or following best business practice, it is robbing the societies in which they operate. Corporate tax avoidance should be a crime, since it robs the public of a government who can afford to offer them the level of healthcare they need, good enough teachers or roads that are safe.

If that's not bad enough, imagine being a local business trying to compete with these multinationals. Their buying power is already enormous, as is their ability to squeeze out competitors, by pricing goods at a loss for periods of time. Your local shop really can't compete with the breadth of products corporations offer. But when they don't pay tax either, it really takes the biscuit.

Corporate tax evasion on this scale is robbery, pure and simple. A crime robbing the rest of the world of a chance to feed, clothe, and educate ourselves.

The Effect on Society

If Reaganomics and neoliberalism (revered as practically the word of God by Republicans) are such a raging success, why do we now face thirty-five years of flat wages, millions in poverty, and a US national debt that can never be repaid?

There can be no debate whatsoever—Reagan's poisonous legacy, tainting America to this day, represents policies that screwed the poor and enriched the wealthy. It's been a disaster for America, causing more imbalance and damage to the country's economy than any other regime, ideology or policy. This destructive process accelerated under George W. Bush and the economic catastrophe he presided over. Sadly, Obama shares some of the blame.

Yet voices questioning the whole damn system remain on the periphery.

The net worth of the middle fifth of American households plunged by 26 percent between 2009 and 2011. America now has more people on or below the poverty line than at any time in its history, with six million more people falling into poverty since 2004. One in six Americans now live in poverty. One in six! That's the highest number ever reported by the US Census bureau. Seventy-six percent of Americans live from paycheck to paycheck. In some parts of America life expectancy has actually declined over the last twenty years.

Low wages, caused in part by the astronomical sums paid to CEOs, also slow the pace of national economies. Flat wages deprive consumer-based societies of consumers, meaning deflation or the running up of unsustainable personal debt, as poor people struggle to keep up with rising costs.

American CEOs take advantage of a loophole in tax law that allows performance related pay to be tax-free, costing the state nearly $10 billion per year, or enough money to provide healthcare for five million children. Would it be unfair to draw a straight line from one point to the other—tax loopholes robbing government of the funds to pay for healthcare, which in turn fails to treat sick kids and inevitably causes the death of thousands of poor children? Would murder be too strong a word?

A Radical Proposal

The financial imbalance in Western democracies is now so pronounced it threatens the very fabric of society. In 2007 and 2008 we came very close to the collapse of capitalism itself, and none of the lessons that should have been learned have been acted upon. Banks are still too big to fail, regulators remain weak, and illegal activity is still regularly exposed in the banking sector (and almost always elicits no criminal charges). All the conditions for a further, more calamitous collapse are there. We will not be so lucky next time. Trillions stashed offshore by very rich people mean that the rest of us live under governments who can't seem to find the money to pay for healthcare, public safety and education. This is a truly radical situation. We can find a way out of it, but it requires radical measures.

Taxing the rich in these times of austerity is so obvious it is beyond absurdity to suggest any other course. The numbers are relentless. In the UK, the top

0.003 percent (the thousand richest people) have assets worth over £414 billion, more than three times the entire UK budget deficit. Their wealth has doubled since the worst economic crisis in living memory, up £261 billion. These one thousand lucky people have a total wealth nearly one-third of Britain's GDP.

Sorry, Mr. Reagan, but there really is no connection between tax cuts and economic growth, nor is growth stifled by increasing taxes on the wealthy. Economist du jour Thomas Piketty has suggested that the top tax rate in the US could be 83 percent and the only people less well off would be the fabulously rich.

Disparity in wealth creates so many societal problems that it has to be radically challenged, for the good of everyone. A glass ceiling of wealth should be created, based on the notion that a certain level of wealth is all that anyone could ever need. One hundred million dollars leaps to mind. Who could claim with a straight face that they can't live on $100 million? I guarantee you someone would. Only forty-five thousand people on earth have that kind of wealth. To have $100 million in assets means you are fabulously, incredibly, stinking rich.

Any assets beyond this glass ceiling should be seized by the state, and quickly distributed among the remaining 99 percent of the population, whose lives would be improved to such an extent that it seems almost impossible to imagine. Moribund economies would take off like a rocket. Most private debt could be forgiven. Huge portions of national debt could be paid off, allowing services to resume without the crippling effect of repayments. Schoolteacher pay could double.

Imagine what a boost to national economies such measures would make. More government investment means more jobs, better infrastructure, more well-educated people becoming innovators, better results for 99 percent of the people—how could that not be an improvement to any society. The rich would benefit too. After the initial pain of losing some of their assets (a reminder, each one still has $100 million), they would live in one of the most thriving economies on earth, and see their personal wealth create a vastly improved country. The rich love to tell us how patriotic they are. This would be the ultimate gesture.

Cancelling personal debt would stimulate the economy many multiples of times more than the measures taken by Western governments since the 2008 crisis. No economist could deny this with a straight face, yet it is the emperor's new clothes, something entirely unmentionable in the arena of accepted thinking.

Some British banks have assets greater than the country's GDP. Given this reality, even outright separation between retail and investment banking (which is not happening) would still leave companies that are too big to fail. Major corporations need to be broken up into more manageable sizes, so their sheer girth does not become so large that their failure would risk bringing down the whole system. Businesses that reach a certain size have, by their capitalistic nature, to start to take decisions that weigh human life against profit, so it is in humanity's best interest to not allow corporations to get to a size where they become essentially psychopathic in outlook.

Glass-Steagall must be reintroduced in America, and other laws need to be written to securely separate retail banking from the riskier side of their operations. If banks wish to have gambling, speculative sides to their business so be it, but they need to be entirely separate from retail banking. Financial institutions also need to know that if their business goes bust, no government is coming to save them.

If CEOs and corporations feel the law does not apply to them, they inevitably act like criminals. If companies, no matter how big, are found to have broken the law, they must be tried by the state, just like everybody else, up to and including Chief Executive Officers.

A minimum level of bank capitalization must be introduced. Really large institutions like Barclays and HSBC still have perilously low capital when compared to their assets—declines of 4–6 percent in some asset prices could leave these businesses underwater again. Runs on banks are incredibly damaging. People panic when they think the bank is going bust and doesn't have their money. This destabilizes entire countries. Well-capitalized banks don't face these issues.

Executive pay must be limited. Paying huge salaries distorts business and entire industries, exacerbates societal issues caused by wealth disparity, and encourages risk-taking by those at the top. Tax rates on very high wages should be substantial. Tax loopholes must be closed. It cannot be impossible to pass legislation making law the idea that people working in one country or making sales there must pay tax there too.

Auditing must be overhauled. The consolidation of the accounting industry over the last thirty years must be entirely reversed. As it is, big accounting firms earn millions by auditing big banks, but they're all different heads on the same beast—the banks that failed in America in 2008 all got clean bills of health from their auditors, some just days before they collapsed. Auditing of larger businesses should be nationalized.

Financial regulators need to be given real teeth, and employ the best people in the industry. Without it the financial world will never respect the rules. Ultimately, a lack of regulation nearly caused capitalism to collapse, and there has been no regulatory revolution since then.

These ideas are, of course, beyond fiction in today's climate, and in many ways our governments are heading in the opposite direction. The media will tell you that it simply cannot be done. That is not true. Radical changes to the regulation of how things work at the top of society have happened before, but it normally takes a calamitous state-level collapse before it occurs to people that there is simply no alternative, and the results are never pretty. The Spanish Civil war was caused by similar conditions to those we see today in America. The French Revolution is an even better example. The rich were so odiously rich, and the poor were so incredibly poor, that it suddenly occurred to them that their country might be improved if they got every aristocrat and cut their heads off.

Given that executing every rich person in the land with a big guillotine, guilty or innocent, is probably something we would rather avoid, it would be to everyone's benefit to begin a process of economic rationalization now, rather than later.

Of course, all hell would break loose. The power of orthodoxy seems inescapable. Despite the mess we're in, suggesting a new approach is treated as radicalism. The newspapers would call any leader who proposed measures like these worse than Karl Marx, but it would be interesting to see if there were riots in the streets. After all, the richest one percent in Britain is just six hundred thousand people. More than three times as many protested the Iraq War in London. And a glass ceiling of one hundred million wouldn't stop enterprise—there are plenty of people in the world who would still strive for success and think one hundred million would do just fine.

This is all basic common sense, yet in the climate of our times seems radical. However, what I believe is truly radical is seventy individuals having as much money as 3.5 billion people. Or a CEO earning 350 times as much as the rest of the people who work at his company. That's a year's salary every day. Or seeing the world's economy on the brink of collapse when there's $30 trillion stashed away. That is as radical a situation as can be. Our system has been abused and broken by rich people with lots of connections, and ideological politicians who couldn't see they were being played for fools. Radical times call for radical measures, and failing to act now is inviting a much more disorderly demise in the near future.

Yet I think nothing, perhaps not even complete collapse and the end of democracy, will pry money's hand from the steering wheel of American society. What the Obama presidency showed us is one constant of US polity—gains in social and civil rights issues (such as gay marriage or the legalization of marijuana) can be achieved if popular opinion evolves and the clamor becomes loud enough, but the economy, and the fundamental rules of how it is run (and who benefits) is a sacred cow, that cannot and will not be affected by the will of the people.

It's my belief that the global financial collapse of 2008 was not just another blip, but the beginning of the end for globalized neoliberal capitalism. Financial institutions that were too big to fail, and rescued with hundreds of billions of dollars in public funds, now carry on as if nothing happened, but soon we face the prospect of countries that are too big to save, and the enormous trauma to the world's financial system that their collapse will cause.

While Wall Street clamors for less regulation and for government to get out of the way, the truth is the opposite. Rebuilding a productive economy requires government intervention to shift the economic center of gravity away from the world of high finance and back to industries that employ people and provide tangible value, like manufacturing and services.

This will be fiercely resisted until a much greater financial collapse will eventually leave us no alternative. By then it may be too late. The collapse of capitalism is not just a risk; it is inevitable the way the world's finances are now structured.

As economist Stewart Lansley has shown, there have only been two times in the last hundred years when the richest 1 percent in the US received more than 20 percent of the nation's income. The first was in the eight years preceding the Great Depression. The second was in the eighteen years before 2007. Actually, there is a third time. We're living through it now.

PART FIVE

OBAMA AND BEYOND

After Barack Obama's inauguration ceremony on January 20, 2009, a TV broadcaster announced, "George Bush is no longer President of the United States," and many in the crowd broke into a cheer, taunting Bush as he took his last presidential helicopter flight over Washington, and away toward Texas. Although there was much hope that America's first black president, an intelligent man who campaigned exclusively on "change," would bring an end to the horrors of the Bush years, for many the cause to celebrate was much simpler—George W. Bush was gone.

Barack Obama took office at a time of extraordinary national turbulence, but although he proved a calm and measured presence in the White House, his soaring oratory was in marked contrast to many of the actions of his administration. There was little real hope that Obama would prosecute those responsible for the lawlessness under Bush, but many expected he would at least close Guantanamo and restore the legal process to American governance.

Instead, Obama bailed out Wall Street without apportioning blame, allowed state surveillance to expand, and accelerated morally dubious aspects of America's (now renamed) War on Terror, including drones and presidential-level assassination. His legacy is the ability for a true political ogre to take full control of America.

Instead of change, Obama codified the state excesses of the Bush era. It seems much of what Bush put in place is now the new normal. For those who love America, its greatness lay in institutions of government that are now in tatters. Bush and Obama have left American democracy grievously, perhaps mortally wounded. Where change was required, Obama gave us more of the same. With America's governance now profoundly dysfunctional or broken, this leads the nation down a dangerous path.

CHAPTER TWENTY ONE

DRONES

Drones are the most dangerous development in warfare since the atomic bomb. Planes without pilots, guided remotely from the other side of the planet and raining death from the skies, only seem a comforting concept when your side are the exclusive owners, and when the victims are far, far away.

It is vital that the public is allowed an open and informed debate about the use of drones, as twenty years from now they will fill the skies above every country in the world, with profound consequences politically, morally, and for mankind's freedom and safety. Yet the military's use of drones is shrouded in state secrecy, and we are once again denied a role in this debate by state apparatus that claims to work to keep the public safe from harm.

Like so much new technology, drones have an enormous capacity to bring benefits to our lives. Drones can deliver supplies and medicine to cut-off communities, or put out forest fires where it's too dangerous for a human pilot. Drones can help in all manner of emergencies. Soon they may drop off your daily groceries. There seems no reason why passenger-carrying drones won't one day let us all take to the skies more conveniently than commercial air travel today.

Right now that seems rose-tinted. The largest drones in operation are owned by the military, and most new technology development is funded and utilized by those in uniform. The Wright brothers brought us holidays in Florida, but they also saw us drop bombs on Hiroshima and Nagasaki.

The first lethal drone strike in human history took place in 2002. Under George W. Bush, America conducted fifty-two drone strikes outside designated warzones. However, in his first two years in office (during which he received the Nobel Peace Prize) Barack Obama more than trebled that number. During Obama's administration we know of over five hundred deadly American drone attacks around the world. Drones are one of the key legacies of the Obama years.

President Obama made the calculated decision that after eight years of George Bush's warmongering, although a war-weary American public would not support the continued presence of significant boots on the ground (and consequent flow of body bags), the war on terrorism offensive could be continued, at little cost in American blood, by using drones above faraway lands, populated by brown-skinned people who we neither see on our televisions nor appear to care about in our hearts.

From one perspective, it's better than the carpet-bombing and chemical dioxin warfare waged against Southeast Asia in the 1970s, but that's hardly a compliment. Drones feel like video games, safe and distant, especially in America where the media never runs footage of consequences which are all too real and all too bloody.

In Pakistan, local informants earn fees of around $5,000 (a fortune in such a poor country) by identifying militants and tagging their cars with GPS monitors, which can then be targeted by Hellfire missiles. But often the desperately poor informants just tag those who they don't like, and death rains down on entirely blameless people, who never stand a chance or get the opportunity to explain their case for clemency from the ultimate punishment.

In Pakistan's border regions over eight hundred thousand people, almost all of whom are entirely innocent, have endured years of the psychological trauma of having armed drones over their skies 24/7. The British Ministry of Defense (in a scarily named document called "British Air and Space Power Doctrine") praised the psychological impact of drones, which they said proved "extremely effective" in exerting influence. Traumatizing an entire region for the crimes of a few is apparently now acceptable.

Civilian body counts associated with drone strikes are skewed, as the US assumes that any male aged between fifteen and seventy (designated of military age) in a combat zone (and the world is a battlefield) is a militant until proved otherwise, a reclassification made specifically to reduce the civilian casualty total. Whether someone is a civilian or a militant is something that's hard to check when the victims are blown to bits by remote-controlled machines thousands of feet up in the sky, guided by someone eight thousand miles away.

Drones also allow the West to violently attack people in areas where fighter jet excursions would not be permitted, or where the consequences of fighters within foreign borders would be much more significant. In 2013, Pakistan's high court in Peshawar ruled that, as no state of war existed between the US and Pakistan, America's drone strikes were international war crimes. Yet US drones continue to operate with impunity over Pakistan. International law is simply ignored by our side.

Making life and death decisions based on informant information and satellite images inevitably leads to mistakes. The Bureau of Investigative

Journalism estimated that from 2004 to 2013, drones killed up to 893 civilians (including 176 children) in Pakistan, 178 in Yemen and 57 in Somalia. I bet you didn't even know we had drones over Somalia.

In 2014, the human rights group Reprieve calculated that US drone attacks aimed at killing forty-one men had killed 1,147 people. That's twenty-eight dead people for every targeted man. Yet in January 2012, President Obama claimed that civilians killed by his administration were not a huge number. Could not the argument be made that the 1,100 innocent victims' relatives and friends might spawn another 41 insurgents? Droning is like playing an evil version of whack-a-mole.

Barack Obama, the constitutional law professor, vetted the secret kill list at weekly meetings dubbed Terror Tuesdays, using macabre CIA baseball cards featuring the condemned target's biographical details, and personally approved each assassination. Individuals often remain on these lists for months at a time, so by definition do not always pose an imminent threat. The government refuses to disclose the legal criteria used to make its targeted killing decisions. Yet few in the press criticized Obama's actions, or pointed out their clear illegality. Glenn Greenwald has said that due process, "once the defining feature of American freedom . . . is now scorned as some sort of fringe, radical, academic doctrine."

Obama's unlawful decisions were themselves only as good as the information they were based on. The US army uses the Orwellian disposition matrix computer database to decide who is a terrorist, what risks they pose and how they should be disposed of.

Drone assassination seems destined to be with us forever. Obama administration officials admitted that the policy of targeted killing, kept almost entirely out of public sight, was likely to extend for at least another decade, but this statement had no value when made by those leaving office in 2016. As drone manufacture expands and technology improves exponentially, what hope is there that our armies will suddenly decide to stop using these new tools as weapons?

Not only has the American public been denied information about drone strikes with which to make informed decisions, officials have routinely lied in relation to America's conduct, and the consequences of its droning program. Civilian deaths have been denied and downplayed by politicians whose statements have been proven to be barefaced lies, yet the media treats their subsequent pronouncements with respect.

No population will support a campaign like this if they are faced with the grisly evidence of their government's actions, so the US media uniformly chooses not to show images of drone strike results, despite these being shown on other national TV networks. There's plenty of evidence on YouTube if you're strong enough to stomach looking. Or perhaps look at the photos of Noor Behram, a journalist from North Waziristan, that show the true costs of when America's drones rain down. Behram's exhaustively collected images include that of a seven-year-old boy covered in bandages, weeping; of a little girl with a broken arm; of a dead ten-year-old boy. These kids look just like yours and mine.

These horrors can't be excused as mistakes. They are inevitable when firing remote controlled missiles using grainy surveillance images as proof of guilt. In parts of Pakistan at least, the world has become one where at any moment a hellfire missile might rip you and your family apart, in a campaign from the skies that by definition can never be won or ended.

Anwar al-Awlaki

Anwar-al-Awlaki was the first US citizen killed by a drone when he was assassinated in September 2011, a killing directly authorized by President Obama, without any form of judicial process or legal oversight. Under Obama, a decision was apparently made that American presidents now have the right to assassinate their own citizens, anywhere in the world, without even charging them with a crime.

A once moderate American Imam with Yemeni background, who became progressively more radical in the decade following 9/11, al-Awlaki had been in regular contact with at least two of the 9/11 hijackers in 2001 (Hani Hanjour and Nawaf al-Hazmi), and followed them from San Diego to the East Coast at the same time that the men relocated. On arrival, he chose to preach in both Washington and the tiny town of Falls Church, which by chance also happened to be the home of four future hijackers and two brothers of Osama bin Laden.

Al-Awlaki's unresolved connection to the players in the 9/11 plot is not in doubt. Even Philip Zelikow of the 9/11 Commission called him a 9/11 loose end.

Al-Awlaki became a well-known face in Washington's Muslim community, and was even invited to lunch at the Pentagon (a building allegedly attacked by his own associates) shortly after 9/11, as part of an outreach between Muslim-Americans and non-Muslims.

In the years following 9/11, al-Awlaki's preaching became more radical, and he came under scrutiny from America's intelligence community. However, evidence of actual wrongdoing by al-Awlaki has remained essentially non-existent, and the Obama administration fought lawsuits that sought to reveal the government's case against him. This may be in part because many suspect al-Awlaki was an FBI asset. For a suspect, he certainly appears to have had a close relationship with his pursuers, entering into an extended series of emails and phone conversations with FBI agents, and on a number of occasions being allowed to travel when he should not have been. At least twice, he was released from custody at FBI instruction.

In 2002, with his arrest seeming likely, al-Awlaki fled the US on a Saudi jet, but remained a relatively peripheral figure until the Fort Hood shootings of 2009 (for which his religious preaching was blamed), and a number of other failed terrorist plots. As al-Awlaki's prominence grew, President Obama authorized the CIA and military to capture or kill him. There followed a years-long game of cat and mouse, with several failed attempts on al-Awlaki's life (all through drone attacks), some of which killed innocent civilians.

Anwar al-Awlaki was finally killed in a successful drone attack on September 30, 2011, in Yemen. Two weeks later his son, Adulrahman, a teenager aged just sixteen (and also an American citizen) was killed in another US drone strike. No reason was given, no apology made, but the boy who had run away from home to look for his fugitive father was marked for death from the skies. Robert Gibbs, Obama's former press secretary, charmingly said that Abdulrahman's death was justified on the grounds that he should have had a far more responsible father. The young man was so thoroughly destroyed by the missile that only the back of his head was able to be identified by a family member.

A 2013 Department of Justice white paper justified the killing of Anwar al-Awlaki, by suggesting that as a high-value target he posed an imminent threat to the United States, but this was widely mocked for its bizarre interpretation of the concept of imminent threat. Al-Awlaki was not a soldier, and had no training in arms or terrorism. Imminent threat, it seemed, could mean just about anything, and was a fig leaf excusing the lack of due process.

When pressed, the US government refused to release their evidence against al-Awlaki, citing the ubiquitous national security. A bill trying to stop the extrajudicial assassination of US citizens only attracted the vote of seven members of Congress.

In 2014, lawyers for the Obama administration cited the 2001 "Authorization to Use Military Force" (AUMF) law as providing the authority to kill US citizens (specifically al-Awlaki) abroad without trial. AUMF was passed just three days after 9/11 (opposed solely and bravely by Congresswoman Barbara Lee) and has proved hugely controversial, as it is so broad and unlimited in scope and reach that it could conceivably be used to justify nearly any kind of action by a US president. No limits on time or geography are contained within the law, and although Barack Obama said that the law should ultimately be repealed, his administration took no action in that regard.

It would be easy to say these assassinations were the result of a political system and army gone entirely mad, or alternately to suggest that in fact these events were not random at all, and that on one level or another even young Abdulrahman was guilty of something that the government knows, which we are not privy to be told. With his intimate knowledge of the alleged 9/11 hijackers, and close connections to the FBI, Anwar al-Awlaki may simply have known too much. But a precedent has been set. The office of the president of the United States now has the authority to assassinate anyone on earth without any legal process whatsoever. Imagine the danger this power poses.

The Double-Tap

Modern terrorism is nihilistic murder without any form of moral code whatsoever. In this sick state of mind it matters relatively little who the victims are, whether friend or foe, so long as the point is made and the balance of power shifted, even a tiny amount, in your favor.

Many of us can imagine ourselves possessed of a murderous rage, given the right circumstance, but the cold-blooded attention to maximizing mayhem marks terrorists out as the most disgusting of our species.

It's hard to choose the vilest of man's crimes from the unfortunate smorgasbord we have at our disposal, but the "double-tap" concept, where one bomb is detonated then another shortly after, in order to kill and maim those who ran in to help the injured, is such a stomach churning abuse of human nature that it almost defies belief.

Or at least it does until you find that our side practices the same tactics. Time and again, US (NATO) forces have rained bombs from the sky on humans below, then followed up with a second attack, killing those who had come to the aid of the initially wounded, or mourners at the funeral of those killed by an earlier drone attack. This has been widely reported in Western media without real critical comment. Despite Barack Obama's monotonous insistence that drones were highly targeted and kept on a leash, the CIA's own reports show dozens of civilians killed in follow-up strikes when they had gone to help drone attack victims. Funeral attacks have been described as using the dead body as bait.

The Obama administration accelerated the use of these tactics, while deriding them as terrorism when employed by others.

Our side's tactics are often no different to an attack on the Red Cross on the battlefield. These are war crimes (UN Special Rapporteur on the promotion and protection of human rights Ben Emmerson described them as such), as defined in the many Conventions to which Western countries were not only the signatories but the architects, back in the days when our victorious side wanted to ensure that such barbarity could not happen again. Now we are the barbarians. We have become that which we profess to abhor.

Through its conduct of a supposed war on terrorism, America is itself often guilty of politically motivated atrocities that amount to state terrorism. Those involved, most importantly those in charge who authorize such tactics, should be tried at the Hague.

Yes, the Taliban, al-Qaeda and ISIS are ruthless murderers, but surely that increases, rather than reduces our need for moral superiority. Instead we launch signature strikes and double-tap attacks in more and more Muslim countries and dehumanize the victims. Operators of drones have called the humans on their screens being ripped to shreds "bug splats."

Drones fuel terrorism, and are often used for terrorism themselves.

When media omission has failed, censorship and the criminalization of news-gathering have taken its place. Journalists trying to document the aftermath of drone strikes face enormous risks, both from the dangers of reaching unstable places and from their own governments.

One missile strike in Yemen that killed many civilians was at first claimed by the Yemeni government. Then Abdul Shayi, a local journalist, visited the area of the strike and reported that the pieces of weaponry on the ground all bore US manufacturing stamps—the strike must have come from a US cruise missile, in a country that was not at war with America.

Shayi was immediately imprisoned and tortured. When Rabbuh Hadi, the president of Yemen, decided to pardon and release the journalist, he received a phone call from Barack Obama, expressing concern as to the release. Once again, America's champion of the free showed his true colors. America wanted to be able to conduct drone strikes in Yemen without declaring war, and without local journalists exposing the fact. So began a US campaign of missiles and murder in yet another Muslim country.

Armed drones have been used by the US in Pakistan, Afghanistan, Iraq, over Iran, Somalia and Yemen, and even above the US-Mexican border. Unarmed American surveillance drones have been used much more widely. No war has been declared in nearly all of these countries. Most of them have said they want the drone strikes to stop, or that they are crimes. America ignores them.

Many strikes in the Middle East come from drones launched from a secret US base, built in 2010, in Saudi Arabia. The *Washington Post* knew about the secret base but decided not to publish the information for over a year at the request of the administration.

In 2013, Barack Obama announced a policy change on the use of drones in signature strikes, requiring that strikes have a near certainty that the targeted terrorist is present before launching attacks, but by 2015 the policy was shown to be a sham, with the White House admitting it had targeted suspected al-Qaeda compounds, rather than individuals, and often didn't even know who they were trying to kill.

It's worth looking again at the logic and morality at play here. Signature strikes are mostly conducted through the collection of hours of surveillance (from a great height), but often do not target a particular person. Instead, the Obama administration marks groups of people for death based on patterns of behavior, such as who and where people meet.

As if the idea of not even knowing who you are killing isn't bad enough, it is easy to imagine any number of circumstances under which this could lead to disastrous consequences for people entirely unrelated to military matters. A poor farmer and his family, for example, whose premises are taken over by Taliban fighters briefly as they move around the country, is hardly in a position to tell the Taliban to leave, but risks seeing his family incinerated due to patterns of movement he has no control over. We wouldn't accept this in the case of a fugitive on the run in rural Montana, why is it any different in Pakistan?

Despite a lack of informed public debate, or perhaps because of it, drones have grown to be a central part of America's arsenal. In 2012 the Pentagon had around seven thousand drones. The number grows each year. Figures are confidential, but most estimates suggest drone pilots now outnumber actual pilots in cockpits. The training is much cheaper. New talent is often sourced from the gaming community.

Drones only feel good because the other side doesn't have them. That will change very soon, and then we will all have cause to be afraid. Drone strikes and assassinations abet America's enemies and alienate its friends, according to former president Jimmy Carter. He believes that America's abrogation of justice and international law means that the US can no longer speak with moral authority.

Although drones can boast a superficially impressive body count, allowing politicians to claim to have killed a large number of bad guys, they serve no strategic purpose, are of dubious morality and legality, and the huge collateral civilian death toll that goes with these imprecise weapons means that one dead bad guy is simply replaced by another. For all the drones over Pakistan, Yemen, and Afghanistan, there is little evidence of a significant impact on degrading America's enemies, nor somehow bringing peace via death from the sky. Public opinion against the US in droned countries is now overwhelming, dramatically increasing the risk of radicalized individuals who seek to do something about it.

Drones over America

Anyone familiar with the sight of America's police forces during civil unrest will know that one significant effect of America's huge military expenditure on wars in Afghanistan and Iraq has been the spare military equipment making its way into domestic law enforcement hands. Modern police look like Robocop, armed to the teeth, often in domestic settings that make them look entirely out of place for their role as civilian law-keepers. Drones are a logical and inevitable progression in the same direction, continuing the blurring of lines between America's civilian peacekeepers and its warmongers.

Perversely, 9/11 opened up the richest market in the world to defense contractors. In the US, the drone business is hugely profitable. The industry lobbies Washington heavily, and is seamlessly integrated with the military industrial complex.

Unarmed drones are already in regular use by America's police forces and the FBI, mostly for surveillance, but there is little legislative barrier (and even less political courage) to stop these drones being weaponized sometime soon. At least eleven states now operate drones for surveillance over US soil. Estimates are hard to come by, but some believe there are already ten thousand police drones in America.

When faced with the question of whether or not the president can carry out drone strikes within the United States, Obama's Chief Counter-Terrorism Advisor, John Brennan, (who became Director of the CIA in 2013) equivocated, saying that the administration had "no intention of doing so." Intentions can change. It took a filibuster speech from Senator Rand Paul to get a straight answer to the question of whether the president can use drones to kill Americans not engaged in combat, in America. Although the answer was a grudging no, a caveat was that the Obama administration had classified al-Qaeda members as engaging in combat even when they were driving down the road or sitting at home.

The FAA Reauthorization Act of 2012 made specific provision for the allowance of a fleet of domestic drones. By 2020 there will be thirty thousand of them above America. Many are now the size of small birds, and all but silent. Tiny assassin drones are being developed that can fly silently inside buildings and explode next to their target, all controlled via iPad. Drones are also being used by corporations, which carries with it the risk of unethical or even dangerous behavior. It was corporations that sold your metadata to the government—imagine the power of having thousands of corporate-controlled airborne vehicles collecting information.

New York State plans to implement a series of high-altitude drones permanently stationed overhead, with cameras so powerful and high-resolution they will be able to make out the haircut of those on the streets below. Soon you may not be able to walk outside in Manhattan without your every move being recorded. This will tie-in with the omnipresent surveillance at ground level.

The use of weaponized drones over US soil is inevitable. Police chiefs already promote the idea of drones deploying non-lethal weapons like Tasers or beanbags in areas where on-the-ground crowd control could be dangerous, and the industry is responding in kind. Predator drones with their weapons removed have already been used for domestic surveillance in the skies above America, but in the future drones will mostly be smaller (but no less deadly), fitting into the trunk of a car or a backpack. The inevitable result, above and beyond lethal use in times of unrest, is permanent surveillance from the skies, first over just the cities but quickly over the entire country.

Weaponized drone use has already arrived on the ground. In July 2016, Dallas police found themselves in a standoff with a gunman who had killed five officers. Although armed standoffs are hardly uncommon, the police in this instance chose a novel way to end the situation—they blew the man up with a bomb attached to a robot. This was the first time a drone had been used to kill an American on American soil, yet the story gained no more coverage than other killing sprees by deranged lunatics. The killing set a precedent—the first time guaranteed there will be a next time, and subsequent drone killings will be less cut and dry. Gradually the bar will be lowered as to when cops risk their lives to arrest someone and when they just send in a robot with a bomb. In the Dallas incident there was no doubt that the man killed was guilty, but a lack of due process means that can't be guaranteed in the future. One day the bomb will accidentally kill someone subsequently found to have been innocent. The use of drones is unlikely to calm civil unrest and will often inflame tensions further. This becomes just another step in the militarization of American police, and their effective separation from the public they serve.

In September 2016, North Dakota became the first US state to legalize the use of armed airborne drones by police. Although this was limited to non-lethal weapons (such as tear gas, Tasers, and rubber bullets), these are not always non-lethal. Few doubt that other states will now legalize armed drones, or that the non-lethal clause will soon be broached, then commonplace.

Israel is the lead exporter of drones worldwide, with 60 percent of the market. The US has 24 percent. Between the two allies, that's 84 percent of the world drone export market. In 2015, thirty-five countries owned drones. The number increases every year. America is leading the proliferation, selling drones to its numerous state friends, many of whom have dubious human rights records. The skies over planet earth will be very different in fifty years time, and there is no guarantee that this will be for the better.

In most wars an overall goal can be defined, and explaining it to the public is important, but drone attacks appear to require no strategy beyond killing endless numbers of bad guys. This seems a doomed imperative, producing yet more bereaved and enraged people prepared to take up the fight against America. If body counts won wars, America would have won in Vietnam.

For some reason we seem able to live with the idea of children in rural parts of Pakistan being terrified of the skies, but drone proliferation means it's only a matter of time before seeing them hovering overhead makes up part of our own daily life. The idea of an armed drone attack against America, launched from foreign shores, seems fantasy, but that will not be the case forever. A foreign force or international terrorist will surely see a drone attack as an easy and risk-free means of killing people without the need for human sacrifice. As we have seen, the attacks of 9/11 may have been the first true drone terrorism.

Drones only offer comfort when we own them and our enemies do not, but that is only a matter of timing. Drone technology has advanced so quickly that the inevitable next step is enemy drones over Western skies, and just as certain will be our launch of counter-drones to combat these. Drone warfare in the skies is as inevitable as tomorrow's dawn unless we collectively choose to stop it, something which there is no evidence to suggest we have the intelligence to achieve.

America sources much of its drone piloting talent from the gaming community, but just as in a video game there's really no reason why one individual should not command a fleet of drones, rather than just one. Serious organizations and serious people are warning us that drone robots (on the ground, rather than in the air) are just a few years away. Ground-based drones (which are unlikely to look like humans) will offer a future president even more ability to wage war without the loss of American blood, but it is far from clear whether the technology allowing us to remotely control an armed vehicle on the ground will avoid similar civilian casualties to those seen through the use of drones in the air. For a soldier on the ground or someone looking at a computer screen, in times of stress and disorder it remains difficult to distinguish between a woman holding a bottle of water and an armed man brandishing a gun.

Putting humans in charge of drones thousands of miles away already poses huge moral and technological issues, but the simple logic proposed by some would be to take life and death decisions away from us faulty humans altogether. Humans get tired or bored, or make mistakes. Many ask how long will it be before a land-based drone robot is empowered to make life or death decisions, independent of its living masters. If this sounds exactly like the plot of a *Terminator* movie, that's because it is, but it's much closer than we may think.

TWENTY TWO

SURVEILLANCE BEYOND THE RULE OF LAW

A sweeping domestic surveillance program was secretly signed into law by President George W. Bush in October 2001, just weeks after the attacks of 9/11. The information collection protocols, codenamed Stellar Wind, rode roughshod over even the rubber-stamping process of the FISA courts, and gave the National Security Agency (NSA) carte blanche to intercept as many phone calls and records as it wanted, from all the major telephone companies. It was entirely illegal, and those involved knew it, but after 9/11 no one was questioning the office of a president who painted his every move in the palette of patriotism. Stellar Wind was just the first in a dizzying array of new legislation that has profoundly changed the relationship between government and citizen, and ripped up the Constitution in the name of defending the public.

NSA

Despite being bigger than the CIA and FBI combined, the NSA used to fly under most people's radar when compared to its more celebrated espionage contemporaries. The NSA's mission specifically focuses on foreign intelligence, but its central role in America's new surveillance state has now come into sharper focus, as the sprawling agency has built the largest and most pervasive spying machine in human history.

Senior members of the Bush administration saw the events of 9/11 as an opportunity to permanently consolidate America's position as the world's only superpower. Militarily the results have been mixed, but controlling the planet through information dominance and ubiquitous surveillance has been much easier.

At the instruction of President Bush, the NSA took programs designed for gathering intelligence internationally and began using them to spy on every single person in the United States, much as army psychologists had reverse-engineered training programs to design torture regimes at Guantanamo. America's intelligence sights were reset, from enemies abroad to everyone at home.

For the most part this was accepted without question by Bush's senior staff, as yet another essential component in America's War on Terror. When FBI director Robert Mueller offered to resign in March 2004 (having decided that the domestic eavesdropping being conducted was profoundly unconstitutional), President Bush refused to accept his letter of resignation, telling Mueller if they didn't do this, people would die. Both men had sworn to uphold the laws of the United States on taking office. Only Mueller was upholding that pledge. And he was the exception.

In Bluffdale, Utah, the NSA has built the world's largest communications storage facility, capable of storing one hundred years of the world's electronic data. They practically had to invent a new word to describe the facility's data storage capability, defined in increments of zettabytes, the amount of data that would fill 250 billion DVDs.

In 2012, the NSA was collecting more than twenty billion communications per day, all available to the entire intelligence community, including the FBI and CIA. The number now is presumably much higher. Most estimates suggest more than twenty-five trillion messages have now been intercepted and stored. Every indication has been given that the data will be retained in perpetuity. Edward Snowden called the facility the greatest tool for repression in the history of man.

The agency has proved very reluctant to provide information on how many people are monitored and what data is retained, even when questioned directly by US Senators. In 2012, when pressed, I. Charles McCullough (the most senior spy agency man in America) told the Senate Intelligence Committee that to reveal the number of Americans who had had their emails and telephone calls intercepted would, and I quote, "violate the privacy" of Americans.

Simultaneous to the US government's vast expansion of its ability to monitor its own citizens was a raft of new legislation aimed at shielding the government from oversight by the same people. This was precisely the opposite of what the founders of the United States set out to achieve when they structured a government system overseen and elected by the public, who would be shielded from the prying eyes of the state. This subversion of the power of the individual and that of government has profound and extremely worrying ramifications, and not just for Americans.

Now, an unaccountable secret body within the US can track every domain you visit. A phone call, a transaction with your credit card, a website browsed—everything. Cell phones are tracking devices. If your phone is in your pocket, the government can find out where you've been. Domains can be cross-referenced, so the NSA can produce a map of your entire life.

This puts the NSA beyond the control of both the public and the government who represent them. The whole basis of democracy has been subverted before our eyes, with barely a whisper of protest.

Public servants serve the public. We should be able to find out nearly everything that they are doing, as they are accountable to us. Private citizens should, with very limited exceptions, be able to keep their affairs entirely private from government, who really only get a look in when criminal behavior is suspected. But this has been completely reversed since 9/11. With each passing year the US government puts in place more draconian measures to protect themselves from public oversight, while engaging in more and more soft surveillance, which is just lazily sweeping everything up, no matter whether there is suspicion of criminality or not. In the eyes of the NSA we are all guilty of something until proven otherwise.

The nature of this problem is easier to understand when we look at recent (but more primitive) surveillance states such as East Germany or Ceausescu's Romania. These countries also had secret police who listened to and intercepted everything. At the time, that meant letters and phone calls, but the goal was the same—control. The Stasi's motto was *know everything about everyone*. They had a file on over one third of East Germany's 16 million citizens. The NSA's approach looks remarkably similar.

Actually, there is a difference. The NSA's data retention powers now dwarf the technical capabilities of any previous regime. And all government surveillance done by "bad" nations previously was very much a government-only affair. These days the NSA works closely with private corporations, who do much of their work, supply their services, and often gain commercial advantage through the illegal use of commercially sensitive information, gained through the surveillance programs.

Just as in East Germany, the awesome power of state surveillance has routinely been used not to protect citizens, but to shield police and the government from oversight and to stifle those wishing to engage in national politics whose views do not represent the mainstream.

Documents released by Edward Snowden showed that only 35 percent of the NSA's resources were used on terrorism. Although a broad approach to national security might be justified, it's hard to understand the rationale behind spying on anti-war protesters, political agitators, civil rights leaders, and trade unions. Or on members of the UN, or foreign political leaders. Or on elected US representatives. All of these have been spied on by the NSA.

There are so many problems with this that it's hard to know where to start, but one of the main ones is that the algorithms and software that the NSA use builds profiles on everyone. They can't possibly hope to identify true bad guys from the huge deluge of information, so key words, names, and places are used to try to identify people who might be doing something wrong. If you stand out, you become a person of interest. And software often can't tell the difference between someone discussing politics and someone planning to overthrow the government. If you legitimately participate in the democratic process by, for example, questioning government policy or protesting, you can be sure that your name will come to the attention of the NSA's programs.

As has been demonstrated a number of times, you don't even need to be actually doing something wrong. The police will probably not burst through your front door if your words are misconstrued, but it has happened. Blameless Muslim Americans have been caught up in terrorism investigations through having said something that rang bells in a computer program, or having innocently used the wrong words in an email. Metadata and the use of algorithms often mean that if you fit a profile, the state can make grave interventions in your life that are entirely unwarranted.

When the public has voiced disquiet at being permanently surveyed, those in charge of the information portals we use have breezily assured us of our safety. But each example was replete with hypocrisy.

The NSA made secret arrangements with companies like Facebook, Google, Microsoft, AOL, Gmail, Skype, and Yahoo to get access to their customers' global communications. Most of these companies denied that they had provided the NSA with information, before it was proven otherwise. When exposed, they all decided to become vocal about how the surveillance programs should be reined in. But not before.

Google's CEO Eric Schmidt famously said in 2009, "If you have something that you don't want anyone to know, maybe you shouldn't be doing it in the first place." I would respond, "Do you mind if we set up a webcam in your bathroom, Eric?" Schmidt reportedly went nuts when CNET published details of his salary and address. It seems he had something he didn't want anyone to know.

Mark Zuckerberg, who gladly handed our Facebook information to the NSA, spent $30 million in 2013 buying the four houses next to his own in Palo Alto, so as to keep away prying eyes. Zuckerberg likes his privacy, but wasn't so concerned about everyone else.

In 2013, British Foreign Secretary William Hague said, "If you are a law-abiding citizen of this country, going about your business and your personal life, you have nothing to fear." That may seem fair, but try telling that to the law-abiding family of murdered British teenager Stephen Lawrence, who were spied on by the police so as to stop their legitimate campaign for justice for his murder. Or to the peaceful British activists who broke no law but were infiltrated for years by police spies, who fathered children with the female activists and then split. Legitimate protest groups now routinely assume that their phones, emails, and other digital accounts are being hacked and monitored by their own government. Law abiding citizens, going about their business, with something very tangible to fear.

American politicians like Dianne Feinstein defended the NSA with glib abandon, only to realize the seriousness of the situation when it became clear that American spy agencies had been conducting surveillance on them too. This has proved the case internationally, with leaders insouciance at America's surveillance only finally being punctured by finding out that they themselves had been on the receiving end. Angela Merkel, Germany's chancellor, was unconcerned about NSA surveillance within Germany until it became clear that they had been tapping her personal cellphone and emails, at which point the issue suddenly rose up her list of priorities.

Much of the NSA's focus has been on Facebook and Twitter, providing as it does a useful amount of specific information about the personal life of pretty much everyone. When we post to our friends on Facebook, we're building a story about our lives that could be used against us.

Despite the US retaining billions of data files per month, we're told that there's simply nothing to worry about, so long as we're not doing anything wrong. But the human experience is broad. Everyone has something. Whether it's a drunken indiscretion, disloyalty to your company, drugs, or an affair; or just some plain old thing which you wouldn't want in the newspaper, we are all of us fallible (leaders and politicians more so than most), and should someone who knew every single thing about you wish to control or destroy your life, they could. That is the power of the NSA's surveillance capabilities.

It's easy to forget that all of this has been justified by the threat of terrorism and the long shadow of 9/11. Because of this nonexistent threat, and a distant event, the NSA holds onto its awesome power and uses this information offensively in cyber warfare, and to give American corporations huge commercial advantage.

For many years the US government expressed concern that Chinese manufacturers of routers and hard drives might be fitting them with surveillance capabilities in order to give Chinese government and industry leaders an ability to spy within the US. Edward Snowden's documents showed that America had hypocritically been doing precisely that. The NSA routinely intercepted routers and servers from companies like Cisco before reaching their shipping agents, implanted backdoor surveillance equipment, and resealed the packages for shipment.

This may have been counterproductive, as the exposure of the NSA's actions and hypocrisy caused concern among American tech companies as to their international viability, given legitimate concerns that US products might be fitted with spying equipment.

Snowden's revelations also showed that the NSA had planted malware in over one hundred thousand computers worldwide, affording them complete monitoring and control capabilities. Data could be mined or deleted on these computers, even when they were not connected to the internet.

It is also highly concerning to note that the NSA has a memorandum of understanding with Israel, allowing the regular sharing of raw intelligence data, including information on US citizens not charged with or even suspected of a crime. This is despite the NSA's own internal documents identifying Israel as one of the most aggressive nations in spying on the US.

Given what we now know is being done by the NSA, America's Fourth Amendment is essentially defunct. The amendment is clear. It reads, "The right of the people to be secure in their persons, houses, papers and effects, against unreasonable searches and seizures, shall not be violated, and no warrants shall issue, but upon probable cause, supported by oath or affirmation." The NSA no longer requires probable cause, and conducts surveillance on their own population in a way that leaves the amendment in tatters. This is something that those who revere the Second Amendment (as a justification for America's lax gun laws) never seem to mention.

What was once considered radical is now completely normal. The NSA holds more power than any elected representative of the people, including the president. They can retain enough data to build a profile on nearly everyone, and our digital lives inevitably contain the seeds of our own destruction.

It's the crux of one of the best arguments against the gathering of mass data. If you gain complete access to anyone's collected digital archive, you can construct some case against them, without exception. 'Twas ever thus. As Cardinal Richelieu put it in the seventeenth century, "If you give me six lines written by the hand of the most honest of men, I will find something in them which will hang him."

Nowhere to Hide

The right to privacy is fundamental to human life, enshrined in Article 12 of the United Nations Universal Declaration of Human Rights. In America this right is disappearing, and the time is fast approaching when there will be nowhere for citizens to hide from their government.

Disney now shares its facial recognition technology with the US government. When you go to Disneyland your photo is taken, and facial recognition technology links photos of your visit to your credit card details. Think it would be bad if Disney shared their data with state intelligence organizations? They already have. The government can find out if you've been to Disneyland.

Facebook and Google use facial recognition technology to tag you in your friends' photos. It's a bit disturbing though; some of the new technology can recognize adults from pictures taken when they were children. Facebook can tell it's you, even if you cover most of your face. This might appear benign, until you realize that these companies have been all too happy to sell mass data to the NSA. Your friends photos can now help build a profile on you, even if you don't have social media accounts of your own.

Across America, facial recognition cameras operate on the streets of major cities, with no law to restrict the building of huge databases. It won't be long before you can't walk through a city in the United States without the government knowing you're there, unless you wear a hat or a fake beard. This may sound funny, but don't forget that the targets are not criminals, they're everyone. Billions of dollars are being spent on biometric identification. Iris-scanners are already used widely. In New York, facial recognition cameras are mounted on lamp-posts at major landmarks. The whole of lower Manhattan is blanketed in security cameras. Cops wear cameras on their hats. These are now believed to be linked to facial recognition technology.

In October 2016, Georgetown Law's Center on Privacy and Technology issued a report stating that half of all adults in America now have their facial features recorded on law enforcement databases. This number was increasing rapidly, year on year. No suggestion of criminality is required, and as always, this disproportionately affects communities of color.

When mass data collection and retention is combined with amazing advances in facial recognition software, it is fair to say that in lower Manhattan, at least, the government knows pretty much every single thing about you. The gap between the intelligence and law enforcement communities has disappeared. America has become a surveillance state.

This staggering destruction of personal privacy is by no means limited in use to stopping bad guys. States have been found to be spying on environmental protesters, supporters of libertarian politician Ron Paul, Senators, even Supreme Court justices. Documentary makers, activists, people with foreign-sounding names—anyone, including lots of people who don't even oppose the government's spying programs, can find themselves the target of domestic surveillance.

Those who speak out, write, or organize dissent find themselves detained at airports, have their laptops seized, or are subject to other rights violations. The unseen effect of this is to stifle dissent, with those who might otherwise protest deciding not to because of the perceived consequences, while those who don't create a nuisance continue their lives unaffected, and often claim that these privacy violations simply don't exist. Mass surveillance by government stifles dissent, as people become fearful of making themselves conspicuous, knowing what could be done, should someone knowing everything about them wish them ill.

Observing the treatment of those who comply with authority and keep their head down is not how a society should be judged. You can gauge societal freedom only by seeing the treatment of those who challenge political orthodoxy.

Have you knowingly edited yourself online? Perhaps been careful not to write an email to a friend or colleague that could later be used against you by some malevolent force? Most of us, since Edward Snowden made his revelations, have quickly got used to the idea that our government is possibly, or probably, able to access our texts, emails, phone records, credit card statements—just about anything—to form a picture of our essentially blameless lives.

The power that this gives agencies such as the NSA is vast. The ability to track and store every digital imprint made by every person in the country gives it the capability to exert mass control over citizens, in a way never before experienced in human history.

What is good for the goose is good for the gander. If governments are keen on destroying all personal privacy in order to make society "safe," their administration and private lives should also be transparent. But that's clearly not happening. The US government takes the opposite approach, hiding and instinctively classifying more and more mountains of uncontroversial government conduct, and working feverishly against transparency. As we give up every moment of our lives to digital spying and data retention, Western governments and politicians put in place legislation that does exactly the opposite, shielding themselves from inspection and oversight. And that's a problem, because they don't want to be held to the same standards as us.

Much less sophisticated regimes such as the Stasi in East Germany found it possible to gain almost total control over their population. Imagine what having access to a person's email, browsing history, texts, and phone data affords the NSA. Try to imagine the power this would provide a government which truly set out to subvert democracy, or one that declared martial law due to a major crisis and started imprisoning those it deemed threats to national security. The danger of giving government the ability to watch everyone, all the time, does not need to be explained.

Mass surveillance gives the NSA more power than the president. Just like Hoover had at the FBI, the NSA now has access to data history on all candidates running for public office. Should one ever emerge who campaigned on a policy of stopping the NSA's surveillance powers, details could be leaked of an email he or she wrote five years ago to a friend, admitting drug use, marital infidelity, or any other frailty that makes us human but can shame and destroy a political campaign. How could you get elected and take down the NSA, now that their surveillance power has put them above and beyond the control of government.

When the *New York Times* discovered in the spring of 2004 that President Bush had, since 2002, been using the NSA to illegally wiretap US citizens, Bush summoned the paper's publisher and editor-in-chief to the Oval Office, and insisted that revealing that his government was spying on Americans would help the terrorists. *New York Times* executive editor Bill Keller spiked the story, and the paper delayed publishing news of the NSA's wireless spying program for more than a year.

Crucially, that delay meant that Americans went to the polls in the 2004 election not knowing about Bush's secret surveillance program, something that would have been a major issue, and which might well have swung the election just the 2.5 percent required toward John Kerry that would have changed the outcome. Rather than being charged with multiple felonies, Bush got a second term in office, allowing the NSA four further years to build their leviathan unchecked.

Edward Snowden said that the *Times'* acquiescence to Bush's demand that the paper censor itself changed history. It represents one of the most important journalistic decisions of this generation, and dealt a huge blow to American democracy.

The *Times* only chose to publish the story in the end because journalist James Risen chose to write a book on the subject, rather than face more frustration at the hands of his employers.

Again and again, the Bush government persuaded the so-called liberal media not to publish details of one story or another on the grounds of national security, actions that amount to state censorship. Covering up important facts about government operations allowed the White House to lie with impunity, and often to continue to break the law without citizens becoming aware of their actions.

Despite domestic spying being a clear breach of the law of the land by the president himself, federal courts ruled that the surveillance program's secrecy was so vital to national security that making a ruling on it would be damaging to the national interest. The circular logic of the new US state meant that crimes couldn't be investigated because they might damage the security of the government who was committing the crimes.

The other major difference to the past is the role of large corporations in state surveillance, whether handing data to the NSA or collaborating with the government in order to spy on protesters and anyone deemed suspicious. This behavior truly subverts the functioning of American democracy, allowing government access to commercial information so as to spy on anyone they see fit, while corporate giants profit from the inside information they receive, use arcane business structures to avoid paying tax, and fleece the countries in which they operate.

It's important to emphasize that keeping Americans safe from terrorism is the seed from which this global surveillance has grown, but terrorism itself kills a very small number of people, and there are a very small number of terrorists and plots. In December 2013, Federal Judge Richard Leon said that the Justice Department had failed to provide a single case in which the use of metadata had stopped a terrorist attack. Although the NSA claimed the programs had stopped fifty-four worldwide terrorist events, it provided no proof, so the essence of their claim was that the NSA says that the NSA's programs work. Judge Leon called the NSA's power almost Orwellian in scope.

A fundamental tenet of American government is that public servants should be held to account by transparency and by an investigative media, but America's media consistently fails in this regard. James Clapper, the Director of National Intelligence who lied to Congress under oath on March 12, 2013 when claiming that the NSA did not collect data on millions of Americans, was only the most recent in a long line of NSA officials who lied on that subject for years. In 2012, NSA director Keith Alexander (whose motto at the NSA was "collect it all") lied to Congress on the same subject. When these lies were exposed by Edward Snowden's leaks, Alexander was allowed to retire quietly. Lying under oath is a felony. Both men should have been arrested, but few in the media even dared to suggest they should be.

Clapper and Alexander felt safe in lying under oath because they knew that there was no chance whatsoever of their illegal actions actually eliciting consequence. They knew that they were entirely beyond the rule of law.

Obama's Failure to Address the Past

When Nelson Mandela and the African National Congress took control of South Africa from the National Party regime that had ruled the country for 46 years, he could easily have had those who committed the worst crimes during the dark days of apartheid arrested, tried, and imprisoned. Clear, ghastly racist acts had been carried out by the state, including widespread torture and murder. Instead, this truly wise and great man established truth and reconciliation hearings, at which those who had carried out crimes were forced to confront their actions and request amnesty from prosecution, while the victims were able to tell their terrible tales and exorcise the ghosts of their past. No one went to prison, but South Africa was able to face up to the appalling truth that had been its recent history. The state had institutionally broken the law, and although individuals were guilty, the nation was able to move forward without a full-scale dismantling of government and the jailing of an entire generation.

Barack Obama's election filled many with the hope that, at the very least, America would face up to its own period of state criminality under the Bush administration. Horrible acts had been carried out by the state, including widespread torture and murder. Instead, the entire thing was just swept under the carpet as if nothing had happened. Those involved accepted no guilt, admitted no wrong, and remain able to use the media to argue their case, denying to this day that they made the wrong decisions or broke the law at all, in spite of overwhelming evidence.

"I was a big supporter of waterboarding," Dick Cheney acknowledged in a television interview in February 2010. When asked about the 25 percent or more of the torture victims that America itself declared had been innocent, Cheney repeatedly said he had no problem with that, and portrayed himself as a patriot for having taken tough decisions to keep his people safe.

Cheney's lack of regret or contrition for his actions could be taken as evidence of his clear sense of certainty that what he did was right. As the years have passed, however, and every new revelation further illustrated the depravity of America's torturers and the ineffectiveness of the program, it feels more and more like Cheney is blustering.

His boss George W. Bush has made it clear on a number of occasions that he approved waterboarding, as well as personally giving the green light to interrogation techniques that clearly constituted torture. Bush also expresses no regret, and says he would do it all over again.

From a moral perspective, this is quite incredibly degrading to America's position in the world. If it's OK to imprison, torture, and occasionally kill innocent people for a cause, how very different is that to the actions of ISIS militants and other Islamic extremists.

The torture regime instituted under the Bush administration violated US federal law. It was a crime, both in US and under international law (the US ratified the Convention Against Torture in 1994). Given that Barack Obama and his Attorney General Eric Holder both said that waterboarding is torture, and torture is a crime under US law, it is hard to understand how these two things don't go together, and why senior figures within the Bush administration, who acknowledge they personally approved the torture programs, are not facing charges for crimes they admit having committed.

Barack Obama failed to bring to justice any single person responsible for the Bush administration's torture regime. While campaigning for president in 2008, Obama often said that although he was against witch-hunts, he would ask his Attorney General to look at any evidence of crimes committed during the torture programs, on the basis that nobody is above the law. However, on taking office Obama changed course entirely, saying that America must look forward as opposed to "looking backward," but that is like arguing that we should not prosecute any crime at all.

Imagine a crime had been committed against you, and the police said not to worry about it, it's best not to look backward. Well that's real nice, but it is not how we treat crime and the law in our society, and it's not the natural state of human affairs. Without justice and resolution, no nation can move forward. Obama's approach chose to ignore wholesale state criminality, and by not acknowledging that crimes even happened, encourages a descent into darkness again the future.

This perhaps explains why Republican candidates in the 2016 election campaign felt so brazen in invoking Bush administration actions to show their toughness. Nearly all the leading candidates said that they would fill Guantanamo with more inmates, and that they would have no problem bringing back waterboarding and torture. Obama's decision to turn his back on state crimes committed under George W. Bush has given future presidents the moral basis (as they see it) to do it all over again. That is the price of ignoring justice.

The office of the president does not command the judiciary. There were plenty of other ways for America's legal system to confront the horrors of the Bush administration. But perhaps no institution failed as spectacularly to live up to its own standards as federal judges.

It could be that the implications are so earth-shattering that they simply cannot be faced. Any legal action would have to include the architects of the torture regime, including George W. Bush, Richard Cheney, George Tenet, and Donald Rumsfeld, as well as the lawyers who drafted the torture memos that provided legal cover for these crimes. Bush and his colleagues also deliberately subverted the US Constitution in order to gain access and control over the personal and private information of America's citizens.

CIA and FBI staff who participated in rendition and illegal detention should be charged, as should those who participated in torture at Guantanamo, Bagram, and elsewhere. Mercenaries who committed crimes while contracted to the US Army in Iraq should face trial. Army psychologists who used their medical training to devise the most effective torture techniques should be arrested, tried, and have their licenses revoked, given their flagrant violation of the ethics of medicine they claim to practice.

This would lead to hundreds of arrests, perhaps thousands. You can see the problem. The CIA's torturers would testify that they received orders and approval from the highest levels of government. This would leave no option but to bring charges against Bush and his senior officials, and as we have seen these men are treasonous criminals who carried out the attacks of 9/11 for their own benefit and killed three thousand civilians for political gain. Charging anyone for the crimes under Bush would lead to the arrest of an entire political generation, and would require facing up to America's darkest fears and the wholesale dismantling of government.

The implications of pursuing justice are beyond imagination, but the alternative is much worse. If America wishes to remain a free society and a democracy, then *fiat justitia ruat caelum*. Let justice be done, though the heavens fall.

There has been no sign of this happening. Barack Obama's government was filled with many who were very close to the Bush administration. His second Attorney General, Alberto Gonzales, authored the initial memo justifying torture for the Bush administration. So, instead of going after the most egregious criminals in America's history, Obama decided to criminalize the journalists who sought to expose the wrongdoing.

CHAPTER TWENTY THREE

WHISTLEBLOWERS AND SURVEILLANCE

If you wish to find out how free your society actually is, it's necessary to look at cases of those who challenge authority. It's all very well sitting in the middle of the enclosure—it's only when you get to the edges that you can feel the steel bars. America's recent treatment of high profile whistleblowers and journalists illustrates just how dangerous it now is to expose wrongdoing by the state.

Obama's War on Journalism

The Obama administration prosecuted more than double as many whistleblowers (under the arcane 1917 Espionage Act) than all previous US governments combined, efforts many described as a war on journalism. Having promised to be the most transparent administration in history, Obama presided over the opposite. His Presidency was intensely secretive and more aggressive in prosecuting whistleblowers than any previous government (including that of George W. Bush). Under Obama, it became a crime to reveal the crimes of the state.

It's worth noting that the Espionage Act was written at the height of the First World War, a time of genuine threat to the United States, when spies held the lives of tens of thousands in their hands and their capture was of vital national importance. This was a far cry from the situation under Barack Obama.

An already cowardly media was further intimidated by the Obama administration's campaign of abuse, threats, and prosecution against journalists acting in ways that previously would scarcely have merited comment.

Fox News journalist James Rosen was prosecuted in 2013 for being a co-conspirator with his source's crimes (in relation to a story about a leak of US intelligence assessments of North Korean state actions). This charge could be laid against every journalist who ever had a source, and represented a significant development in the history of American journalism. The judge in Rosen's case said it was the first time that he had seen this level of taking "ordinary, reasonable, traditional, lawful reporter skills" and claiming they constitute criminal behavior.

Journalist John Kiriakou was sentenced to thirty months in jail for leaking information about waterboarding, while at the same time ex-CIA Deputy Director of Operations Jose Rodriguez promoted his best-selling book *Hard Measures*, which revealed classified details about the same subject. The difference was that one supported the torture regime, the other did not. Those who committed state-sanctioned kidnap, torture, and murder walk free, and the only person to see the inside of a jail cell was the one who spoke publicly about the laws being broken. The judge in the Kiriakou case said she would have given him much more jail time, if only she had been able.

Investigative journalists described an unprecedented climate of fear under President Obama. The aggressive prosecution of whistleblowers led many to fear for their lives, and countless others presumably decided against exposing themselves to such risk.

While treating journalism as a crime, the Obama administration oversaw a period of unprecedented growth in government secrecy. In 2011 alone, more than ninety-two million new documents were classified. This combination of journalists and whistleblowers fearing for their lives if they exposed secrets, and an exponential growth in state secrecy, has degraded American democracy and weakened US society across the board. Without journalists, politicians philander, corporations lie, cheat, and pollute, and the rich break the law with impunity. It is journalism that is there to keep the bastards in line. With federal judges apparently willing to bend at will to the demands of the executive branch, whistleblowers and journalists are often our only chance to expose wrongdoing by the state.

Perversely, this exponential growth in government secrecy all but guarantees huge leaks, whether by whistleblowers or hackers. Digital data storage technology means both now have the ability to steal millions of documents in a short space of time. When Daniel Ellsberg stole the Pentagon Papers in 1969, he took seven thousand papers in forty-seven volumes, painstakingly copied on a Xerox photocopier. In 2001, when Jeremy Hammond of activist group Anonymous hacked into intelligence firm Stratfor, he took five million emails in what appears to have been a couple of hours.

This increases the risk of the release of information that both politicians and responsible journalists would agree should remain secret.

The Obama administration and its Department of Justice (DOJ) sought to intimidate the press on numerous occasions. For example, in 2013 the DOJ secretly obtained two months of phone records of Associated Press reporters and editors. Twenty journalists had their home, office, and cellphones bugged, and every phone call they made for two months was recorded. Imagine the shadow this cast over other American journalists and their confidential sources, when investigating the actions of government, knowing that at any time their phones could be bugged by that same government. This is not the America we have been sold.

The awesome new power vested in government since 9/11 means that no real proof (or even suspicion) of wrongdoing needs to be provided for administrations to pursue journalists like this. Secret FISA courts and grand juries rubber-stamp nearly all applications for phone records. Although the law stipulates that other avenues of investigation by the government must first be examined, this almost never happens.

Governments who monitor and aggressively prosecute journalists and their sources are effectively criminalizing the practice of journalism. In a democracy without a functioning media, especially one with a huge volume of state secrets, the voting public are going to miss out on information that is often pertinent to the running of the country. Making newsgathering a crime subverts democracy. We know without a shadow of a doubt that governments and state officials routinely lie to the public on all manner of subjects. A vigorous and independent press is the only means we have of countering their lies and keeping the public informed. Without that, democracy cannot function.

Criminalizing journalism represents one of the key legacies of the Obama years and presents a terrifying threat to the future of America as a democracy.

The treatment of the bravest whistleblowers during Obama's time in office is illustrative of the huge risks now faced by those exposing state level crimes.

Chelsea Manning

While serving in Iraq as a US army intelligence analyst in 2009, Bradley (now Chelsea) Manning became concerned by the level of wrongdoing she saw, and copied around seven hundred thousand mostly low-level government documents and files, which she handed to WikiLeaks.

Manning's documents included the famous "Collateral Murder" video from July 2007, one of countless, mostly undocumented examples of war crimes committed by America in Iraq and Afghanistan.

The video shows a US helicopter crew massacring unarmed Iraqis and firing on journalists. A van draws up next to the wounded men, and civilians get out and attempt to get the wounded to hospital, before the helicopter opens fire again, having already noticed there are children in the vehicle.

"Oh yeah, look at those dead bastards . . . nice," says the US crewman. "It's their fault for bringing their kids into a battle." But it's not a battle, it's a slaughter on a suburban street, and the unarmed civilians trying to help their mortally wounded countrymen are ripped apart by the most sophisticated killing machines on earth.

After the video's release the pilots were not charged, but Manning was arrested and accused of aiding the enemy. This followed a pattern under the Obama administration in which war crimes were not treated as crimes at all— only breaching the wall of state secrecy that is the lifeblood of the War on Terror was considered criminal. Releasing evidence of state crimes was said to aid an undefined enemy.

After seeing the documents published by WikiLeaks, the Iraqi government said it would no longer grant immunity to US soldiers operating in Iraq. As a consequence, President Obama announced he would be pulling troops out of the country. Chelsea Manning helped end the Iraq war.

Manning could easily have sold the documents for profit, but took not a cent and showed the information to the world because, she said, she wanted worldwide discussion, debates and reforms based on informed public opinion. As such, Manning should be considered a classic whistleblower. But her leaks embarrassed the government, so the full power of the law was arraigned, at the same time that genuine crimes exposed by her leaked documents were entirely ignored. Shooting the messenger is the way in today's America.

Manning's case highlights the lack of distinction now made between real spies (those transporting or selling state secrets to enemies for money) and whistleblowers, who see immoral or often illegal activity within their own government and seek to publicize it for no reason other than transparency, national accountability, and to benefit public discourse.

WikiLeaks, the publisher of Manning's documents, was accused of having blood on its hands, despite officials not being able to cite one case of anyone (except Manning) being harmed by the release of the information.

All this took place under the leadership of Barack Obama, the man who as candidate for president said, "The best source of information about . . . abuse in government is an existing government employee committed to public integrity and willing to speak out. . . . Acts of courage and patriotism . . . should be encouraged rather than stifled as they have been during the Bush administration."

Chelsea Manning saw her countrymen committing clear war crimes and made a brave and ethical decision to show these actions to the world, but instead of investigating the crimes themselves, the US government responded with a litany of charges, one of which carried the death penalty. Before coming to trial, Manning was imprisoned for ten months in intense solitary confinement, treatment that was widely condemned as sadistic and torture. She was made to strip naked at night, to stand naked for inspection on a daily basis, and kept in an 8 x 6 foot cell for twenty-three hours and forty minutes per day. She was woken three times every night because of her alleged suicide risk. Every week psychiatrists reported Manning was in good mental health and posed no risk to herself. Every week they were overruled. A UN investigation called Manning's treatment cruel, inhuman, and degrading.

No official transcript of Manning's trial was released (a measure of the government's comfort with transparency), but one brave citizen managed to make a recording of Manning's final statement. In it, Manning calmly and eloquently recounted her deployment to Iraq, horror at the "war porn" videos she saw, the decision to release the Collateral Murder video to the public, and her hope that the American people would see the horrors that were being conducted on their behalf and demand more ethical behavior.

Although none of the documents released were classified top secret, what Manning had done was reveal lies, corruption, war crimes, and illegal behavior by the world's most powerful country. Because of that she received an unprecedented thirty-five-year sentence. Manning's treatment was meant as a warning to others considering releasing evidence of state-level wrongdoing. No matter what the state does, revealing it now appears to be a crime.

It's important to note here that although the Manning, Julian Assange, and Snowden leaks were large in scale, they were in essence not much different to the constant barrage of leaks that are a mainstay of daily life in Washington. The Obama administration consistently leaked information favoring the president. National security invoked as an excuse for prosecuting whistleblowers is ignored if the leaks favor the administration's goals.

Julian Assange

The man who published Manning's revelations, Australian Julian Assange, remains imprisoned in the Ecuadorian embassy in London, for fear of trumped up allegations that would allow his extradition to a certain life sentence in an American cell.

Despite facing no charge, if Assange leaves the embassy he will be arrested and taken to Sweden to face accusations of rape which the two alleged victims themselves deny happened. One has said on record that Swedish police made up the charges. Even the rights group Women Against Rape have called the allegations a smokescreen.

There is no doubt that if Assange is removed to Sweden he will be extradited to face a grand jury in the US and the rest of his life in a maximum security prison. It's hard to imagine why the British government would otherwise spend millions on round-the-clock policing outside the Ecuadorian embassy in order to arrest one man accused of (but not charged with) rape in Sweden, and unclear what role the snipers on the roof have played in ensuring that there is no escape.

Everyone knows the charges in Sweden are bogus, and a means of expediting Assange's extradition to America, yet no one in office is now brave enough to stand up to the rampaging US state, which demands vengeance against those who transgress the tight lines of secrecy it holds sacrosanct. WikiLeaks did no more or less than any other newspaper, but its exposure of massive crimes by US forces embarrassed a superpower and must be punished. Death threats have been made against Assange on numerous occasions by American politicians. Vice President Joe Biden called him a cyber-terrorist.

Given the treatment meted out to Bradley Manning, Julian Assange is absolutely right to fear for his life. He is alleged to have a forty-two thousand-page FBI file, despite not being charged or convicted of any crime by any country. All of this means that Assange's liberty and life are under a profound and ongoing attack by the nation that prides itself on freedom of expression.

It's noteworthy that America's policy of indefinite detention, as well as its use of manifestly disproportionate prison sentences for non-violent crime, has reduced its moral standing internationally and had a counter-productive effect on the ability of American prosecutors to extradite individuals from many foreign countries, including America's friends. Abiding by their own international and domestic law obligations, key ally states have rightly refused to extradite accused terrorists (often in fact nothing of the sort) to the United States for military detention or prosecution, reasoning that indefinite detention is illegal, and that America's criminal justice system is capricious and vindictive.

When considering the outrage expressed at Assange's ability to evade US justice, it's also worth remembering that America refuses to extradite several high-profile murderers, like Gonzalo Sanchez de Lozada, the Bolivian ex-president wanted by his own country for trial for genocide. What you leak and who you favor defines your treatment.

Edward Snowden

The greatest whistleblower in American history, Edward Snowden's amazing story illustrates both the counterproductive nature of the expanded US security state and the ability of one brave individual to change a nation.

In the wake of 9/11, America's already huge national security apparatus grew incrementally, and with it the use of contractors. The US defense and intelligence sector simply wasn't able to keep up with the huge requirements of its security state. Private companies filled in the gaps, with employees often moving from the public to private sectors and back again as their careers progressed.

Most estimates suggest that the various US government agencies charged with homeland security do business with at least two thousand contracting companies. The million or so private individuals with top-secret security clearance are mostly scattered around these two thousand companies. Around nine thousand of Booz Allen Hamilton employees (Edward Snowden's company) have top secret or higher clearance. This marriage of public and private security may seem like a logical extension of a huge area of government, but it carries with it the risk of another Snowden, and behind the scenes many in government must privately rejoice that the individual they got was such an intelligent and patriotic man.

Edward Snowden managed to copy the largest cache of top-secret documents ever released. Snowden had access to such broad information that he could, had he so chosen, have published the names of every NSA operative (and, it is assumed, FBI and CIA employee and asset) in the world, single-handedly destroying America's spy machine and grievously wounding the state. Instead, Snowden leaked selected information on illegal and secret NSA spying programs, in the hope (much like Manning) that this would assist the American public in deciding the kind of society they want. For this he was attacked, vilified, and condemned as a traitor.

Standard government procedure when faced with embarrassing revelations by whistleblowers is to entirely ignore the facts revealed and go after the messenger. It's vital that the public perceive the whistleblower as a deranged opponent of America whose immoral actions have put lives at risk, and weakened the benevolent state's ability to act morally and keep everyone safe. This approach has been used to some effect for generations, and helps distract the public from the much more real issues often brought up by the leaks. Discrediting the whistleblower was the reason that Richard Nixon had his henchmen break into Daniel Ellsberg's psychiatrist's office—the whistleblower has to be portrayed as an unsafe lunatic.

The furious reaction to Snowden's actions should be viewed not so much through the prism of national security, but as retribution for embarrassing the

US government. It is this embarrassment that explains the zeal with which Manning, Assange, and Snowden, have been pursued.

Both Manning and Snowden were condemned as American traitors, but traitors could have sold the information they had for fabulous sums to America's enemies. Although you have the right to question their actions, it is undeniable that what these two individuals did was release information for no material gain, at considerable risk to their lives and wellbeing, explicitly in the hope that allowing the public to peer behind the veil of state secrecy might allow citizens the opportunity to make informed decisions as to what their governments were doing. One received a life sentence, another locked in a small London embassy and unable to go outside, while the third is in exile in Russia. All have paid a heavy price for no personal gain. Far from traitorous, it's hard to think of actions more heroic. Daniel Ellsberg said he thought Chelsea Manning deserved a Congressional Medal of Honor.

One argument consistently employed by the US government has been that rather than leak information to the press, those within the intelligence community who saw wrongdoing should have reported it to their superiors. But this is a ridiculous suggestion. The superiors were often the architects and biggest supporters of the illegal surveillance and torture programs that whistleblowers sought to expose. Those like Thomas Drake (a senior executive at the NSA) who did exactly that, found themselves flagged, passed over for promotion, and ignored. It was career suicide. There is not one example of someone who raised concerns internally about the excesses of the state and got a fair hearing, resulting in those government excesses being reined in. It's beyond absurd.

Edward Snowden found himself marooned in Russia, of all places, in his quest to find freedom from persecution, for revealing the NSA as an organization completely out of control and beyond the reach of citizen or government. The balance of power, which should be between the electors and the elected is, in Snowden's words, "tipping toward the rulers and the ruled." History is replete with examples of how badly this ends for a society.

However, the digital age is also one where, as governments have enlarged spying programs on their own citizens, whistleblowers' ability to leak (or hack into) government databases has also increased incrementally. There may be more to come in the future from this David and Goliath story.

The story of Edward Snowden adds one interesting angle to that of 9/11. Those who claim that the events of September 11, 2001 could not have been carried out by the US government, simply on the basis that a large number of people couldn't keep a secret like that, are refuted by the NSA programs Snowden unveiled. Huge, sweeping government surveillance programs had been kept entirely secret from public eyes for over a decade, and yet were widely known by the intelligence community, perhaps numbering tens of thousands of individuals. Were it not for Edward Snowden, it is likely that these thousands of people would retain their secrets to this day.

William Binney

William Binney, the former Technical Director at the NSA (where he worked for more than thirty years) has said that it was a matter of days (less than a week) after 9/11 that the NSA decided to begin implementing domestic surveillance programs aimed at everyone in the United States. This has led many to speculate that the NSA had either anticipated the attacks or known they were coming, since there was so little time before these new programs were commenced.

Binney may be the most senior and well-connected of all the whistleblowers who have helped public debate in America over the past few years—a highly placed NSA employee saying that the NSA's behavior has been and is illegal. Binney has also said that the NSA's spying capabilities exceed those of the KGB, Stasi, or Gestapo, and that he believes the NSA retains copies of every single email sent within the United States.

William Binney resigned from the NSA in October 2001 and became a whistleblower, reporting his concerns to both Congress and the Department of Defense. He openly questions the official 9/11 story, and calls for a new investigation of 9/11, an extraordinary statement from someone who held such a senior position at the NSA (and something that has been met with a wall of media silence).

Binney and several colleagues tried to address their concerns about the legality and constitutionality of the NSA's behavior internally. For their efforts, they were stonewalled, sidelined, and intimidated. As a whistleblower, Binney was subject to a prolonged campaign of intimidation, including in March 2007, when a dozen agents raided his house with guns drawn. It's hard to see what other reason there could have been for such a heavy-handed invasion—Binney has never been accused of a violent crime, was naked in the shower at the time, and is a diabetic double-amputee. Not by chance, the raid took place at the same time as Attorney General Alberto Gonzales was testifying on Capitol Hill about the NSA's surveillance programs. The message was clear. We will not allow testimony that contradicts the government's line.

In today's America, the government breaks the law, and the whistleblower is an enemy of the state.

State Surveillance in America

The activities of the US surveillance state are far from limited to just national security matters. When Jeremy Hammond hacked into Stratfor's servers and released five million emails to WikiLeaks, he found that much of the work undertaken by the logistics and forecasting company was on behalf of corporations. Dow was spying on protesters looking into the Bhopal chemical disaster of 1984. Coca-Cola was snooping on PETA activists. This kind of commercial espionage is unlikely to be limited to just one NSA contractor. A leaked 2011 email from Stratfor also confirmed that the US government had a sealed indictment against Julian Assange, something that had been consistently denied.

For the first few years of the War on Terror, most of the egregious measures taken in the name of public safety were all directed overseas, at people who Americans could neither see nor cared much about. But from around 2007 onward, these same measures were turned about face.

What we are seeing through the spread of an entirely unaccountable state security apparatus, keeping everything secret in the name of keeping us safe, is the end of functioning democracy in America, and the beginning of a worldwide security state that is beyond the reach of both citizen and political leader.

To judge the relative danger of any law, ask what processes could be undertaken to review, revise, or revoke it. Mass surveillance in the digital age is a genie that can't be put back in the bottle, and the logic of a war against terrorism means that executive power is only limited by how much of it the president wants. Barack Obama, by most measures a sober and calm figure, nevertheless claimed and exercised the right to assassinate US citizens (and all others, of course) abroad, without charge or trial. His administration equivocated when asked if they believed they had the power to carry out drone assassinations within the United States.

Just imagine how much power this might vest in a "less nice" president, in charge of a country shocked by another terrorist attack from abroad. How different would that look to a police state or a dictatorship? History shows us that awesome power can be fantastically dangerous.

In 2015, Edward Snowden said, "If we do nothing, we sort of sleepwalk into a total surveillance state where we have both a super-state that has unlimited capacity to apply force, with an unlimited ability to know (everything about the people it is targeting)—and that's a very dangerous combination. That's the dark future."

What This Means for American Society

While it's natural to suggest that these sweeping, unprecedented new executive and surveillance powers will be very dangerous if control of the US government falls into the wrong hands, it's just as easy to argue that this has already happened, albeit under that nice Mr. Obama who seemed so human and approachable.

Obama was not the first president to preside over an administration that simultaneously advanced social policy (marriage equality and healthcare in this case) while eroding fundamental civil liberties elsewhere, but in other times Obama's foreign policies and continued shredding of the Constitution would look like a radical and almost revolutionary departure. Obama got away with it because he seemed like a human being, and because almost anyone would have looked good after George W. Bush.

The power of the US government and the NSA doesn't need to fall into the wrong hands—any government with this kind of power will inevitably use it in ways we would not want. What is terrifying is to imagine the US government's capabilities if a true political ogre took it upon themselves to begin the shutdown of democracy. National security measures sold to the public as temporary changes in uncertain times almost always become permanent, and throughout history governments who have loudly claimed the need to protect their societies from frightening external threats have ended up classifying anyone challenging their power as enemies of the state.

The self-serving nature of a war against terrorism, which by definition can never end, means that the drastic increase in domestic and international surveillance, started under Bush and codified by Obama, can and never will be rolled back. Other temporary measures put in place during troubled times in America, such as the Japanese internments of the Second World War, are now a source of embarrassment and shame, but the War on Terror does not fit the model of a true war, and is just a smokescreen to allow the state to do whatever it wishes in the false name of national security. More Americans have died falling in the bath than from terrorism since 9/11. The end does not justify the means.

For all the color-coded terror alerts and media hysteria, the American public still broadly understands this concept. A Pew survey in July 2013 found that more Americans were concerned about the civil liberty aspects of US surveillance measures than were worried about being protected from terrorism. 70 percent of them thought the data collected was being used for purposes other than terrorism prevention.

Privacy is freedom, and freedom requires privacy. Without these you can crush societies. There's no need for a police force when privacy dies. Surveillance doesn't even need to be active; the simple idea that an email or phone call might be being monitored quickly changes the way people interact and communicate. This is why repressive states have always used mass surveillance to control their societies, and it simply doesn't work to suggest that because America is a "good" country, by definition there can be no threat to its citizens. North Korea declares itself a bastion of righteousness, but we all know that ain't so.

A report for the PEN American Center in November 2013 found that 24 percent of those surveyed had deliberately avoided certain topics in emails or phone calls because of concerns over state surveillance. These weren't criminals, but government surveillance had caused the chilling of communicative freedom across the board. Everyone has something they wish to keep private. Just because there are things that you don't want on the front page of the newspaper, it doesn't mean you are doing something wrong.

Bulk data collection does not help prevent terrorism. It creates false leads based on algorithms, uses up precious resources dealing with huge unwieldy sets of information, and assists the bad guys in losing themselves amongst the throng. In fact, bulk data collection damages national security, the opposite of what we have been told.

Americans (and by extension all people on earth) have been denied the right to debate this subject. Perhaps we are indeed happy for our governments to collect this data, trading privacy for security, but as it is we don't know, because citizens have been deprived of informed choice by laws written and interpreted in secret. When "we the people" asked for the right to see what was going on, the government repeatedly told us that there were no mass surveillance programs in place, and when those lies were exposed, we were still denied transparency.

There is going to come a time when "national security" is seen for what it is—a blanket and often false justification invoked by those who simply want to hide very important things from the people they purport to serve.

The actions of the NSA are, for the most part, not about protecting people from terrorism, but a new tool for maintaining America's financial and militarily dominant position in the world, and control over civil society. With a broken media under constant attack, and almost all oversight removed, this presents a very dangerous imbalance of power.

The stated benefits of the NSA's surveillance program need to be balanced against the costs, especially in a society with 45 million people (nearly 15 percent of its population) living below the poverty line, and one that refuses to provide healthcare to its citizens. Domestic security costs have totaled by over $1 trillion since 9/11, but almost all planned terrorist attacks have been by crazed individuals who are, according to a July 2012 report in *International Security* journal, "incompetent, ineffective, unintelligent, idiotic, ignorant, unorganized, misguided, muddled, amateurish, dopey, unrealistic, moronic, irrational, and foolish." This is counter to the state's constant portrayal of terrorists as nimble geniuses, almost superhuman in their cunning evil.

Much the same seems to be the case with so-called radicalized Muslim fundamentalists. Many are far from the devout fanatics pictured in the media, and are often attracted to jihad by both the perceived glamour and excitement, and by their own boredom with life.

For the most part, this is the enemy that America has destroyed its country in order to face down.

CHAPTER TWENTY FOUR

THE STATE OF AMERICAN DEMOCRACY

The Seeds of American Militarism

Vice President Henry Wallace wrote of the dangers of American fascism in 1944 (at a time when fascism was in danger of destroying the world). His words seem just as relevant today:

> "Fascist demagogues claim to be super-patriots, but they would destroy every liberty guaranteed by the Constitution. They demand free enterprise, but are the spokesmen for monopoly and vested interest. Their final objective toward which all their deceit is directed is to capture political power so that, using the power of the state and the power of the market simultaneously, they may keep the common man in eternal subjection."

Wallace was a truly great American. It is history's tragedy that he was denied the presidency.

The term military industrial complex, first spoken by President Dwight Eisenhower on January 17, 1961, was originally to have been called the military-industrial-political-complex, something it truly resembles these days. But perhaps the best expression for the nexus of money, power and death that now dominates the politics of the United States would include the words military, financial, and political, in that the US defense sector and its political patrons are ultimately dominated by Wall Street and City of London financiers.

Nevertheless, the substance of Eisenhower's prophetic words remain. An army industry of "vast proportions" now has America placed on a permanent war footing, so entrenched it's impossible to imagine a president declaring a period of peace. It's an industry that holds Eisenhower's warned of unwarranted influence on government, but perhaps even he would be shocked at the level of militarization that today borders on complete dominance of the mechanics of American government.

While the argument could be made that America's financial prosperity has historically been down to its political and military strength, US society is now so polarized between rich and poor and its politics so manifestly broken, that this view simply doesn't work anymore. Perhaps one of Eisenhower's less well-known statements puts this more succinctly. "The problem in defense is how far you can go without destroying from within what you are trying to defend from without."

Without wishing to mythologize politicians from the past, the present state of America is also perfectly captured in the President's famous "Chance for Peace" speech of April 16, 1953. It needs no embellishment:

> "This world in arms is not spending money alone. It is spending the sweat of its laborers, the genius of its scientists, the hopes of its children. The cost of one modern heavy bomber is this: a modern brick school in more than thirty cities. It is two electric power plants, each serving a town of 60,000 population. . . . [We] pay for a single fighter with a half-million bushels of wheat. We pay for a single destroyer with new homes that could have housed more than 8,000 people. . . . [This] is not a way of life at all, in any true sense. Under the cloud of threatening war, it is humanity hanging from a cross of iron."

Eisenhower was no saint; he oversaw the biggest national buildup of nuclear weapons in history. He could easily be cast as the most dangerous human that ever lived. But he was nothing if not a realist, and his concerns about the growing influence of the defense sector over every other part of American life have been more than borne out.

The Militarization of Police

When taken in combination with the increased surveillance power of the state, the militarization of America's police is a stark and frightening harbinger of the ability for fascism to flourish and be enforced in the United States. America's system of government prohibits the creation of a federalized police force, and forbids military involvement in civilian peacekeeping, but the line has become so blurred as to be irrelevant.

$5.1 billion of military equipment has been transferred to state police as part of a Pentagon program that has only accelerated in the last few years.

Section 1033, a small part of the National Defense Authorization Act, allows the Department of Defense to donate or sell spare military hardware to civilian police forces. Given the trillions spent in Iraq and Afghanistan, there has been a lot of spare equipment to go round.

Armored vehicles, military aircraft, machine guns. There are no restraints on what can be applied for. This has led to rural police forces finding themselves owning mine-resistant vehicles. Morven, a tiny farming town in Georgia without any bodies of water nearby, bought military boats and scuba gear. Ohio police have used armored personnel carriers for law enforcement at college American Football games.

America's police now more often resemble paramilitary troops than a domestic law enforcement agency whose mission is apparently to protect and serve. SWAT team deployments increased 1400 percent between 1980 and 2000. The rate has accelerated further since 9/11. In 2005, there were over forty-five thousand SWAT raids nationwide. SWAT teams now regularly deploy tactics learned from the military, including using flashbang explosive devices thrown when entering properties, to disorientate those inside. In several instances, however, they've had the wrong house, and the flashbangs have landed on or near sleeping children, killing or grievously wounding them. These tactics are, as usual, overwhelmingly deployed in African American communities. SWAT teams and tactics were developed to counter hostage situations and riots, but these days 62 percent of SWAT raids are drug searches, and 79 percent on private homes. Regular citizens sitting around smoking joints at home find their doors kicked down by cops dressed like commandos and throwing disorientation grenades.

For weapons manufacturers and defense contractors, the homeland market has proved a highly lucrative new revenue stream. Vast new opportunities have arisen to profit from keeping Americans "safe" in their own country.

Armored Mobility Inc. aggressively markets body armor that can stop thirty rounds from an AK-47, to protect police and security officers, including those working at elementary schools.

The police often don't have the resources to properly manage these new weapon stocks. Some have made it into civilian hands. Local officers have been found selling police weapons on eBay, or losing stock of deadly weaponry after poor inventory management. The weapons keeping Americans safe are making it to American criminals.

Worse perhaps is that police forces issued with exciting new weapons inevitably feel empowered to use them, no matter how inappropriate that may be to civil law enforcement. A militarized response to domestic disturbances increases the risk of violence and injury. The American Civil Liberties Union has called it "War Comes Home," but residential neighborhoods are not warzones, and should not be treated as such.

"Militarization" of the police is in fact too narrow a description. Every aspect of domestic enforcement has been militarized, right down to University campus security guards. Ongoing gun violence in America merely encourages seemingly benign institutions like shopping centers and schools to employ armed security, who often behave like they've just stepped off a battlefield.

From a broader perspective, this has profoundly worrying implications for American society, especially should a terrorist attack or politician with an agenda cause the state to seek more direct control over its people.

Homeland Security's Transportation Security Administration (TSA), formed just two months after 9/11, now has fifty thousand staff and the power to tightly control all forms of public transportation, aggressively groping air travelers and routinely using drug and bomb-sniffing dogs at airports and train stations. If this is a response to 9/11 and terrorism, why are drug sniffing dogs being used? Perhaps the TSA's training center slogan will assist. "Dominate. Intimidate. Control." This is often achieved by the over-use of strip-searching for routine non-violent infractions—a classic authoritarian harassment tactic, and overwhelmingly used against the black community.

The expression of political dissent has become a dangerous pastime. Non-violent protest is now routinely broken up by police using pepper spray and extreme violence, under the coordination of the Department of Homeland Security, which was formed to protect the public from attack.

Police violence often mirrors political agendas. Despite the media telling us that the Occupy Wall Street (OWS) movement has no message, that is not the case. In fact, OWS's top two agenda items are removing money from US politics and reform of the banking sector, including the reintroduction of the Glass-Steagall Act. So it's easy to see why the police choose to pepper spray and beat small groups of people sitting on the ground and offering no resistance. Particularly in 2011, when the group was highly active on the streets of major US and British cities, the police acted with a brutality that seemed curiously out of kilter with the threat posed by non-violent, rational protesters who clearly constituted no threat to law and order or the safety of the public. Reporters were arrested and removed from the scene of OWS protests in unprecedented numbers, despite having press credentials clearly displayed. During the unrest, the Department of Homeland Security was found to have advised eighteen city mayors on how to suppress the protesters. American cops can now be used as political weapons.

When you see how the world of corporate profit is so tightly bound together with that of national security, it becomes easier to understand why members of OWS who call for major banking reform, and thus threaten the era of unlimited profit (and zero risk, courtesy of government rescues), find themselves treated like rioters setting the streets alight.

All of this police militarization has taken place while violent crime in the United States has been on a slow but steady and unbroken decline for over thirty years. The billions of dollars of taxpayer money spent on weaponry to keep Americans safe is in spite of historically low crime, not because of an increase in violence. Criminologists describe militarization as being a top-down phenomenon, driven from above rather than conditions on the streets below. Ironically, the return home of veterans, suffering from PTSD but highly trained by the military, has been referenced as one reason that the police need to be so highly armed, although the link between PTSD and violent crime is so spurious as to be statistically non-existent.

Police militarization has also drained resources from actually helping US citizens. Since 9/11, the additional money spent on arming the police could have rebuilt post-Katrina New Orleans five times over, and housed every homeless person in New York City. Instead, it's the defense contractors who have profited.

Military tactics abroad have also come home to roost, with evidence in 2016 showing that some American police forces established black sites, where those arrested by police could be hidden from view and from their legal rights. These facilities appear not nearly as awful as those abroad, but surely a straight line can be drawn between the military's operation of sites beyond the reach of law and the practice coming home. Tactics at the black site (Homan Square) revealed in Chicago were eerily similar to those used at America's military sites. People were held beyond the reach of attorneys, beaten, and shackled. There were deaths in custody. Questionable guilt. Some of the detainees in Chicago were lawful protesters. Over 80 percent were black. All had nothing to do with terrorism.

In conjunction with the spectacular growth of its surveillance state, post 9/11 America watches infrastructure crumble and the poor starve in order to face down the nonexistent threat of terrorism. The mechanisms for mass suppression by the police are also now in place.

Incarceration and Race

Sadly, it's impossible to assess the state of American democracy without mentioning poverty. To mention poverty one has to discuss race, and to discuss race is to be obliged to take stock of America's system of mass incarceration. The days of slavery may be gone, but black people in America face a system that for the most part is no less racist, and appears to govern through two entirely separate sets of rules.

Although the presidency of Barack Obama had huge symbolic significance, despite overwhelming support from the African American community, Obama's time in office provided no net benefit to black Americans. Black unemployment was the only sector to have gone up under Obama. For young black men in the US, unemployment has hovered near 50 percent, many multiples that of their white counterparts. The average white American household has twenty-two times the wealth of the average black American home, a staggering disparity.

When you are poor in America, you stay poor. America now has so little social mobility that a child born to poor parents in the US has double as much chance of staying poor as a child born in Northern Europe.

Obama sang "Amazing Grace" at a church service for slain black men and women, and hosted Jay-Z and Beyoncé at the White House, but the tangible benefits to the black community were very hard to find. His focus appears to have been elsewhere. In 2011, Obama became the first president since 1948 not to mention poverty at all in a State of the Union speech.

As with so many of America's current ills, it was the election of Ronald Reagan in 1980 that saw the beginning of an explosion in America's prison population. Reagan and his wife's "Just Say No" campaign promised legislative toughness against drug scourges seemingly sweeping across society, but while the 1980s cocaine blizzard was ingested by both rich and poor, the crime that accompanied its prohibition only devastated poor communities, which meant black communities, and it was this demographic that was sent to jail in record numbers.

We are now more than three decades into an experiment that imprisons more people than Stalin's gulags and disproportionately affects poor and black communities. There are now more black men in America's correctional system (in jail, on probation, or on parole) than were enslaved in 1850. America's jails leave hundreds of thousands brutalized and their lives in ruins, often for non-violent crimes of a much more minor nature than the punishment saw fit. More people, longer sentences, less mercy than any other developed nation on earth.

Felons lose the right to vote, so mass incarceration hugely influences America's voting patterns, given that the poor and minorities overwhelmingly vote to the left of the spectrum. More African American men are disenfranchised than in 1870, when voting rights for blacks were secured.

The costs of incarceration have similarly soared. Some US states now spend more money imprisoning their citizens than they do educating children. Imagine what that means to a society.

The numbers are staggering. 2.2 million people are behind bars in America, that's one in every 110 adults. The United States holds one quarter of the world's prisoners (one third of incarcerated women, worldwide). The human stories behind these horrifying statistics represent a nationwide disaster.

Personal devastation for many has meant enrichment for a few. Private prison companies now earn billions in annual profits locking up their fellow citizens. The privatized correctional industry has made prison in America one of the worst places you could go in the world. Rape and assault are commonplace, riots a regular occurrence, and private prison guards earn 30–40 percent less than their federal counterparts and are poorly trained and ill-equipped to cope, often responding with overwhelming violence to any transgression. Of course, violence by inmates normally leads to their being given longer sentences, so to make your prison a house of animals (with the inevitable results) is actually good for business. G4S, the security and incarceration behemoth, is now the third largest employer in the world, with over six hundred thousand employees.

The devastation of overwhelming poverty, a lack of social mobility, and a two-tier justice system handing out incredible sentences for minor infractions, produces black American social statistics that make you want to cry.

One in three African American boys born after 2001 will go to jail in their life. In 2015, the *Washington Post* reported that one in nine black children in America had a parent in jail. One in fifteen black American men are currently in jail. A black male who drops out of high school is sixty times more likely to find himself in prison than one with a bachelor's degree. Blacks get sent to prison more than whites for the same crimes, and receive longer sentences. Wonder why the black community doesn't trust the cops? African Americans are double as likely to be unarmed as whites when killed by police.

When the small town of Ferguson, Missouri experienced rioting in the summer of 2014, after yet another unarmed black man was killed by a white cop, there were sixteen thousand outstanding arrest warrants in a town of twenty-one thousand people.

It's up to you. Either black people in the US (but not so elsewhere) are genetically criminal, or a variety other factors are the reason for this appalling situation. If you believe the former, please stop reading this book and go and throw yourself into a lake. If you favor the latter view, then we must reluctantly conclude that America remains one of the most racist countries in the world, and practices a form of legal and social apartheid that devastates its ability to function as a democracy, by disenfranchising and keeping down an entire class of people based solely on the color of their skin. Without fundamental change to this dynamic, the rich will remain entirely cut off from their fellow citizens and the collapse of democracy cannot be arrested, because America now wages war against its own poor.

The War on Drugs

Things connect. There are wheels within wheels. Just as climate change is inextricably linked to wealth disparity (the rich people make most of the emissions), America's foreign policies and military machine are often directly joined to its war on drug use and cultivation.

Military equipment is sold to South American governments to help curb the cultivation of plants relentlessly consumed by Americans. In Afghanistan, Taliban fighting against American troops get most of their income from the sale of heroin, consumed on the streets of Western countries. The money spent by addicts in New York paid for the bullets that killed Americans in Kabul.

Narcotics are such a large factor in that country's economy and society that it's impossible to consider the war in Afghanistan without seeing it through the prism of the War on Drugs. Nearly all the heroin in the world comes from Afghanistan. The cultivation of poppies is easy, and conversion of their sap into heroin is not complicated or expensive. It is the illegality of heroin that artificially sends the price through the roof. Afghan farmers would have to be clinically insane not to grow poppies. Without heroin's illegality, the Taliban's primary source of income would plummet, and with it their ability to rule. The war in Afghanistan was lost because of narcotic revenues. The War on Drugs, just like the war on terror, feeds on and regenerates itself.

Richard Nixon launched the War on Drugs in 1971, the year I was born, with an annual federal prohibition budget of $50 million. The war is nearly half a century old and has cost America $2.5 trillion. America's annual counter-narcotics budget is $51 billion, but there's more drugs on the street, they're cheaper and being used by more people than ever before. For a war waged across two generations costing trillions, prohibition has been the most abject failure imaginable, achieving the opposite of its goals.

This "war," which ceases fire whenever society's greatest ingestion killers (alcohol and tobacco) come into view, imprisons the harmless and the sick, empowers the street thug, and enriches the white-collar criminal. It sets in place a vicious cycle where politicians lay claim to ever more draconian measures, filling America's prisons in a battle that cannot be won and is fundamentally against human nature.

The sheer breadth of the war's reach is extraordinary. From the poor farmers of Colombia, Mexico, and Afghanistan, the drug mules risking their liberty for a tiny profit, the millions imprisoned for their role as transporter or casual consumer, law enforcement officers and judicial systems wasting time on non-violent offenders, state funds diverted away from socially beneficial programs . . . all the way to the banks pocketing illicit billions, America's war on drugs is the worst and most devastating social policy of the last hundred years.

Drugs and Money

It's estimated that the global drugs trade is worth $320 billion per year. It's the most profitable large business sector on earth. Worldwide, the war against drug use costs $100 billion per year, over $3,000 every second.

Drug prohibition not only hands criminals huge profits, but has proved an effective means of transferring the social cost of our love affair with narcotics from the (rich) consumers to the (poor) producers, and leaving all the money back in America's bank accounts.

You might think that a country like Colombia, synonymous with coca cultivation (in 2009 it produced 43 percent of the world's cocaine), would at least retain pockets of fabulous wealth, but you'd be wrong. Just 2.6 percent of the street value of the drugs grown in Colombia stays there, with 97.4 percent of the money exiting the country, laundered through Western banks by crime syndicates.

The drug trade in Colombia accounts for a tiny fraction of GDP (around 1 percent), yet represents utter disaster and devastation for its society. Enforcement almost exclusively focuses on the two-percenters, the little guy smuggling pockets of contraband across sovereign borders, and the farmer who chooses the most profitable crop for his land. Colombia is a leading recipient of US military arms and training, despite its record as one of the worst human rights violators on earth. American defense contractors profit from the mayhem. The War on Drugs in South America is really just a war on the poor.

In Colombia, if you want to bank any cash amount over $2,000 you have to provide comprehensive paperwork to prove it's not drug money. Yet the vast profits from trafficking cocaine, almost always in the form of cash, have to be laundered somehow. So while the Colombian government attacks its own citizens with American guns and rockets on the ground, and sprays herbicide made by Monsanto on poor rural farms from the air, billions are laundered through the likes of Citibank and HSBC, almost always without comment or legal consequence.

Michel Chossudovsky's book *War and Globalization* put the matter succinctly:

> "The multi-billion dollar revenues of narcotics are deposited in the Western banking system. Most of the large international banks—together with their affiliates in the offshore banking havens—launder large amounts of narco-dollars. Therefore, the international trade in narcotics constitutes a multi-billion dollar business of the same order of magnitude as the international trade in oil. From this standpoint, geo-political control over the drug routes is as strategic as oil pipelines."

Perhaps this begins to explain part of the reason why Afghanistan was invaded, or why HSBC's recent drug money laundering scandal was so lightly punished. Many of the West's major banking houses are predicated on the laundering of narcotic dollars, and without that source of income might be in peril. This also sheds light on why the war on drugs has not ceased, despite clear evidence that ending the war would have overwhelmingly positive results for mankind.

Let's look at one example to see the profits available and risks faced by those who launder drug money at the top of the chain. Through an investigation that started in 2005, Wachovia bank was shown to be laundering vast sums of drug money, looking the other way while transferring $376 billion from Mexico to the US, mostly in cash, and not flagging one transaction as possibly suspicious. That's just one bank, moving one third of Mexico's annual GDP up to the US. Although Wachovia was caught red-handed and proceedings were instigated, fines and forfeitures totaled just $160 million, 2 percent of the bank's annual profit. Crucially, neither the bank nor any employee had to go to court.

When Martin Woods, Wachovia's anti-money laundering security officer, noticed the huge sums coming in from the Mexican border area and flagged his suspicions, he was told to keep quiet, then fired.

Not only does this story illustrate the huge incentives and almost total lack of risk faced by international drug money launderers, the punishment meted out to Wachovia (when caught) would have, in itself, encouraged other banks to take advantage of the huge rewards and low risk available. Which is exactly what they have been doing. It was widely known that the Wachovia saga was just the tip of the iceberg, and that major international banking houses like HSBC and Citigroup were moving even more staggering sums. The irony is that when these institutions faced their moment of truth in 2008, it was US taxpayers who bailed them out.

It's not just drugs. HSBC has been condemned by the US Senate for laundering money for al-Qaeda. Despite this, it seems that the US incarceration system, with its record number of inmates and disproportionate sentences for small crimes like minor drug possession, has no space for the white collar criminals who launder billions in drug and terrorism money.

In the real world, banks have a responsibility to know their customers, and to ensure that funds being moved around the world within their company are legitimate, and have been legitimately earned. But this is fantasy when the profits are so gargantuan and no individual ever risks seeing a jail cell when they are caught up to their neck in it. As US customs agent and money laundering authority Robert Mazur says, "The only thing that will make the banks remain properly vigilant to what is happening is when they hear the rattle of handcuffs in the boardroom."

The consequences of the banks' dirty deeds are death and mayhem in Colombia, Mexico, and other countries near the US. They are there in the ongoing conflict between America (and its allies) and an Afghan Taliban resistance, funded through the proceeds of opium poppy sales. Perhaps worst of all is the suspicion that were these sources of funding removed, the much threatened banking and financial collapse that came so close in 2008 might finally take place—the bastards might take us down with them.

Large drug manufacturers in supplier countries end up with enormous amounts of cash. Drug dealers don't take American Express. This cash is so enormous as to be useless. It has to be put into a bank and legitimized. So there is plenty of opportunity there, should someone have the will, to put a massive bottleneck in the financing of international drug production and distribution (terrorism has to be mentioned in the same sentence, as the two often operate hand in hand). But with the major banking houses of the world reliant on countless billions flowing back to the West via drug cartels, this bottleneck is never applied, and the drug trade keeps flourishing. A straight line can be drawn from terrorism to drugs, to drug money laundering, to world finance, and, ironically, to senior staff at Western banks snorting these same drugs up their noses after a hard day at the office. The world's leading drug money launderers are on Wall Street and in the City of London.

HSBC provides another illustrative recent example. In 2012, HSBC was found to have been involved in massive money laundering in Iran, as well as with terrorists, organized criminals and Mexican drug cartels. When handing down his judgment in the case, Assistant Attorney General Lanny Breuer pointed out that drug dealers would visit Mexican HSBC branches with hundreds of thousands of dollars in cash each day, neatly wrapped into boxes that fitted perfectly through teller windows. They had measured the windows at the bank, and knew to bring their money packaged at the right size. And yet no one ever thought to ask where they got it. HSBC was working with and facilitating the actions of some of the biggest drug dealers in the world—armed, murderous thugs. Would it be outlandish to say that this makes HSBC one of the biggest money launderers and drug criminals on the planet?

Don't blame HSBC entirely. Everyone was doing it. They just got caught. The $1.9 billion fine they were handed might seem large, but it represented just four weeks company earnings. The shareholders paid the fine and, most importantly, no one at HSBC was prosecuted for wrongdoing.

Compare that to the decades in American prisons being served by tens of thousands of mostly African Americans for non-violent possession of small amounts of drugs. In what light does this cast the morality of the war on drugs? What an insult. How disgustingly wrong.

Rolling Stone's December 2012 exposé of the corrupt injustices played out between rich bankers and poor drug possessors (entitled "Outrageous HSBC Settlement Proves the Drug War is a Joke") questioned how much money the government should have taken from HSBC, and put the inequity succinctly:

> "How about all of it? How about every last dollar the bank has made since it started its illegal activity? How about you dive into every bank account of every single executive involved in this mess and take every last bonus dollar they've ever earned? Then take their houses, their cars, the paintings they bought at Sotheby's auctions, the clothes in their closets, the loose change in the jars on their kitchen counters, every last freaking thing. Take it all and don't think twice. And then throw them in jail.
>
> Sound harsh? It does, doesn't it? The only problem is, that's exactly what the government does just about every day to ordinary people involved in ordinary drug cases."

Large organizations in the US, those too big to fail, are not just treated more leniently by the law, they are effectively immune to it. This exemption from any kind of meaningful relationship with the law has encouraged a level of financial lawlessness never before seen in world capitalism.

Banks that are too big to fail are also too big to prosecute, as was demonstrated by the US Justice Department, who said that despite the clear guilt of HSBC staff they had decided not to charge a single person with a crime, on the basis that a prosecution would have collateral consequences, such as

HSBC losing its banking license in the US. This in turn might destabilize the entire banking system. The Justice Department called HSBC a "systematically important institution," implicitly suggesting that such was its size that it had to be effectively above the law. The *New York Times* called the matter "a dark day for the rule of law."

The vast majority of the profits from drug trafficking, cultivation, and sales are retained in the rich countries of the West that consume most of the drugs. The war on drugs has become a proficient way of exporting death and mayhem abroad and making fabulous, risk-free profits at home. If you ever wonder why common sense hasn't led to reform of worldwide drug prohibition that has so spectacularly failed and destroys the lives of millions of poor people, remember that it is drug profits that prop up the richest institutions on earth. For them we must suffer.

Worse still, the utter hypocrisy of the "war" is clear when one considers that US intelligence agencies not only require the continued illegal drug trade in order to sustain their importance, but connive in the failure of law enforcement. This is particularly so in the case of the CIA, who have for decades imported colossal amounts of cocaine into America to fund their own black-ops. The empty morals invoked as part of this war are viciously circular, and enslave millions.

International terrorism itself cannot exist without the oxygen of money. With organized crime laundering $900 billion per year, terrorist networks are intrinsically linked to the drug trade. The war on drugs provides the money for those we fight in our War on Terror. They are two heads on the same beast.

Drugs and Incarceration

In the 1970s America's prison population was less than five hundred thousand. Now it's more than 2.25 million. In a generation, American justice has become the world's largest mass incarceration program, aimed squarely at the poor and those of color.

America has not had a crime explosion to justify the incarceration during this period, and it's facile and wrong to say that the steady decrease in violent crime has been down to putting all the bad guys behind bars. From 1990 to 2013 violent crime fell across America by over fifty percent. 1.1 million extra people were sent to prison in the same period. However, a number of reports have shown that the reduction in violent crime has been due to a variety of factors, such as improved and digitized policing methods, DNA technology, even improved street lighting. States like California and New York, where the prison population has decreased, have seen faster decreases in crime than those that have locked more people up.

What has happened during this time is that America has profoundly redefined the nature of criminality and the punishment meted out to those who transgress.

African American women's incarceration rates have increased 800 percent, mostly putting away small time drug users and addicts. White women use drugs slightly more prevalently than black women in America, but black women go to prison three times as much. Blacks and whites use marijuana at virtually the same rate, but blacks are charged with possession four times as often.

Drug treatment has been shown to be far more effective than incarceration, and costs the state a fraction as much. Jail has very little reformative effect on offenders. Recidivism (reoffending after release from jail) is rampant. Once you have been to jail in America, you tend to go back again. All this costs the state yet more money. Despite this, America's drug laws remain incredibly punitive.

The punishment for poor (mostly black) people when caught is scandalously harsh. There are simply too many examples to table, but it's not uncommon to hear stories of low-level marijuana dealers with a few hundred dollars of pot getting on the wrong side of the justice system and receiving prison sentences of over fifty years.

The two-tiered approach to law enforcement in the United States is broadly divided between rich and poor, but with such a yawning disparity between the wealth of whites and blacks, justice is seen to be administered very differently along racial lines as well. Nowhere is this more obvious than in the area of narcotics, where white collar bankers routinely use cocaine, and where one head of a major Wall Street bank is widely known to be a daily user of marijuana. When was the last time you heard about an American banker going to jail for drug possession? Google it. It virtually never happens.

In black communities, crack has caused devastation, but much of that has been in relation to law enforcement and incarceration rather than the drug, and despite crack and cocaine having virtually the same chemical make-up, the ratio of the amount possessed in order to trigger outrageously punitive mandatory minimum sentences has for most of the last twenty years been 100 to 1 (Obama reduced it to 18 to 1 in 2010). Blacks caught with coke are punished much more severely than whites.

Over three thousand American prisoners don't even have the opportunity to reform, imprisoned for life for non-violent petty offences that attracted America's insane "three strikes" mandatory sentences. Under these laws (in twenty-eight states), if you were convicted of three low level offences, a life term was mandatory. Even judges couldn't overrule the law. People in America were sent to prison for life for stealing a coat from a shop. Disproportionately, people of color face the harshest sentencing laws on earth. In Louisiana 91 percent of three-strike lifers are black. Eighty percent of those serving these ludicrous sentences had non-violent drug-related charges. In July 2015 the three strikes concept was struck down by the Supreme Court, but it remains to be seen if the overall use of disproportionate sentencing is reduced.

What's particularly strange about the extraordinarily harsh sentencing in the US is that virtually no one seems to think it's a good idea. Judges, police, lawyers, even most politicians all agree that long sentences for non-violent crimes are patently disproportionate and ineffective, particularly in deterring others from crime. Clearly the deterrent hasn't worked. Perhaps the whole policy is bogus.

Drug law enforcement is now routinely used as intimidation by the state against entire communities. African Americans in particular find themselves subject to roadside strip-searches and cavity checks, mostly under the suspicion of minor drug infractions. Black people (often wrongly) suspected of holding even the tiniest amounts of marijuana have found themselves naked on the side of the road with a police officer's fingers in their anus or vagina.

Seven hundred thousand Americans get arrested for marijuana use or possession each year, despite nearly all recent presidents and presidential candidates admitting this common youthful indiscretion. Jeb Bush was not only a smoker, he was a dealer at his school, but as Governor of Florida he presided over a regime that showed no mercy to drug offenders, no matter how minor. Except when his daughter was caught—she got rehab.

Barack Obama admitted in his autobiography to regular pot use, "and a little blow." This shameful, immoral behavior that destroys young lives sadly led to him only being able to forge a successful law career and become president of the United States. Yet he singularly failed to reform America's federal drug laws (while some individual states have taken it upon themselves to decriminalize). It would be interesting to know Obama's opinion on US drug laws in relation to his own career, in that had he been caught smoking just one joint while at school in Hawaii, he surely would not have been able to become president. Despite this, his administration appeared comfortable that thousands of other young lives should be destroyed because of behavior he found so unremarkable.

Drug enforcement and incarceration costs a fortune and ruins far more lives than the drugs themselves. Nowadays, the number of people whose lives are destroyed by drugs is vastly overshadowed by the number of people whose lives are destroyed because of the effects of the illegality of drugs. We regard with shock the dark days in recent history when women were denied equal rights or when being gay wasn't just seen as shameful—it could land you in prison. Yet we're living through another age just as egregious.

Despite the overwhelming evidence of prohibition's failure, and the unarguable flood of logic showing counterproductive results, there seems little that anyone in charge is prepared to do about it. When election time comes and complex issues have to be presented to stupid voters, the slightest hint of political reason and compassion is painted as soft on crime. And so it goes.

The Harm Caused by the War on Drugs

Alcohol and tobacco are by far most harmful drugs in Western society, killing many more than all the illicit drugs combined. Alcohol is a leading factor in child abuse, road deaths, assaults, and hospital emergency admissions. Looking at society with an unbiased perspective, alcohol and cigarettes should both get Class A ratings, and be made illegal immediately.

Yet, just as the War on Terror focuses on the negligible risk of terrorism (to the detriment of real killers like gun laws and a lack of healthcare), Western governments focus disproportionate money, time, and political capital on drug prohibition while ignoring the leading drug killers in their society. In the UK alone, the cost to the state of dealing with people who are drunk and disorderly is £6 billion per year, yet alcohol is pervasive throughout society and barely a word is breathed about regulation. Marijuana policing costs £500 million each year, yet the drug is widely known to cause just a tiny fraction of the social ills linked to alcohol.

The prohibition of drugs puts control of these substances into the hands of criminals, the very last people you would want running a drugstore. The crime and violence that often accompanies illegal drugs is not there because of the drugs themselves, it's there because of the illegality, as criminals fight to control an illicit market that promises outrageous profits and a demand that never stops.

The only time alcohol has been associated with violent crime syndicates was during America's Prohibition era in the 1920s. Alcohol went from an accepted social vice to something controlled by Al Capone and his thugs. Of course, that isn't the case today. As Stephen Downing, the former deputy LAPD chief said, "You don't see Coors and Budweiser distributors shooting it out on the street. That's because alcohol is legalized and controlled and taxed."

Drugs themselves don't cause violence. Half of the planet's opium poppy cultivation is for medicinal use, but we don't see hospitals battling for control of the market.

Those pointing out the harm caused by drug prohibition are not the hippies once so associated with counter-culture. The 2012 International Institute for Strategic Studies report entitled "Drugs, Insecurity, and Failed States: The Problems of Prohibition" concluded that the current law enforcement and prohibition approach is "not only failing to win the war on drugs," it is also a "major cause of violence and instability in producer and transit countries."

On the street, drug illegality means that those wishing to consume drugs buy from dangerous people, and consume things that have no certification. You wouldn't take Nurofen if you weren't sure what was in it, nor drink beer if you suspected it was contaminated with methanol, but that is the roll of the dice that drug consumers have to take.

Almost exclusively, people are killed by heroin because of a lack of regulation. The illegality of this terrible drug means people take it in unsafe ways and don't know what they're getting. Heroin only works if injected, so users never know until it's too late what the purity is. Most die because they got a batch that was more pure than they expected, not less.

In the UK, legislation aimed at banning so-called "legal highs" is always behind the curve, with new compounds entering the market each week. Legal highs are disproportionately taken by poor people who can't afford the real thing. When good quality illicit drugs become scarce or expensive, people take fake ones, and hospital admissions skyrocket.

The worst harm, however, occurs overseas. Supplier and transit countries see their entire societies implode when the drug cartels take over. As the West snorts its way to temporary happiness, Mexico counts the cost, with over 140,000 dead and missing as the War on Drugs becomes an actual war.

Ending the War on Drugs

Prohibition has failed. The current policies, tried and paid for across 45 years, have succeeded only in making toxic narcotics available to nearly everyone, and spawned an entirely parallel worldwide economy controlled by murderous criminals. America has spent $2.5 trillion on the War on Drugs over the last forty years, yet there are more people taking a wider variety of drugs, more often, than at any other time in human history. As the world's economy creaks at the seams, drug law enforcement is a staggering waste of money. Ending the war on drugs would create new industries of a size that would likely change entire national economies.

Forward-thinking countries are often held back from decriminalization by the power of America, which threatens reformers with a variety of measures showing official disapproval. Those that have had the courage to break free (like Portugal), and have decriminalized narcotics across the board, have seen clear and demonstrable improvements in public health outcomes. Ironically, countries now considering the relaxing of national drug laws are often the ones who have suffered the most, such as Mexico and Colombia. The West's drug habits have decimated their societies, yet America still has the gall to lecture these countries on governance.

America fights proxy wars and kills countless poor South American people, ignoring the real problem, which is that so many American citizens want to put white powder up their noses.

Prohibition has made drugs the second biggest industry on earth, after oil. Joaquin Guzman, the Mexican drug lord, has been ranked as the world's fourteenth richest man. Drugs account for 50 percent of the world's organized crime group profits. Taking down their business model and destroying the market through legalization would seem to be of huge benefit.

Further, a regulated and controlled market for drugs would reap enormous tax benefits. Think of the tax revenues and astonishing savings in law enforcement costs, all currently spent on an unwinnable battle. We have tried and failed to control the supply of narcotics around the world. It is time to take control of the demand.

Cigarettes are the poster child for how dangerous substances can be legal, distributed and controlled, without the need for prohibition. We all know that smoking causes cancer, but our society has wisely chosen not to prohibit the sale of cigarettes. These days the product is encircled—cigarettes are expensive, hidden behind counters, covered in warnings and only sold to adults. People don't smoke much on TV or in the movies anymore. Cigarette companies can't sponsor sporting events or advertise. If you want to smoke, you have to go outdoors now. Yet, if you want to smoke a cigarette, you still can. All of the unwanted side effects of prohibition have been avoided, and smoking rates in Western societies have plummeted. Legalizing dangerous drugs can be done, without the sky falling in.

Those calling for a radical overhaul in our approach to drugs have moved from the shadows to the mainstream, and today include the former deputy head of Britain's MI6 and the International Institute for Strategic Studies. More than twenty US states have legalized marijuana in one form or another.

Again, you will notice that this has not been accompanied by the fall of civilization. With the sweeping and startlingly swift adoption of marriage equality, social change is possible even within the US. The benefits of legalizing cannabis would be incalculable.

However, legal pot won't solve the issue. Harder drugs sell for the highest prices and make the most profit, and so cause most of the crime. The full legalization and controlled sale of all narcotics is required. This would not only cut off organized crime at the roots; it would improve outcomes for sick addicts, bring in huge revenues to sovereign governments, pay for vital services for law-abiding people, end the carnage in Mexico and South America, remove the Taliban's funding and power base, and save the world a trillion dollars in law enforcement over the next ten years. It might be the single most important move our societies could make toward a better world.

America must take the lead, as it has been the leader in the worldwide prohibition of narcotics.

The National Rifle Association

The shredding of the Constitution in the years following 9/11 has been selective. Although the Fourth amendment ensuring freedom from undue government oversight has been entirely subverted, the Second amendment, which ensures the right to bear arms, is defended as if touching it threatens the very existence of America.

To the outsider, America's love affair with the gun seems beyond bizarre. The simple link between gun ownership and civilian gun death statistics is so obvious that a child of six could understand it, yet America seems entirely unable to get its hands off guns, and politicians cravenly cling to illogical dogma, even when faced with grieving parents of slain schoolchildren.

There are ninety guns for every one hundred people in the US (a number that is rising and will soon exceed one per head). Eighty-five people a day are killed with guns, and more than double that number injured. America suffers another 9/11, in terms of deaths, every thirty-five days, without fail. America's homicide rate is four to twelve times higher than other Western countries. States with higher rates of gun ownership have more gun deaths than those with lower gun ownership.

Of course, the majority of the victims of America's gun laws are the weakest—the poor, the young, black people. If you're black and under the age of forty-four, the gun is the most likely form that death will take.

Mass shootings in the US are now so commonplace that it is only the most terrible bloodbaths that make the headlines. In 2015 there was more than one mass shooting event (defined as an incident with four or more deaths) per day. You don't need to study social patterns to know that when you have a mass shooting every day, something is very wrong in your society. You can only have so many isolated incidents before this looks more like a pattern than an aberration. More Americans get killed by firearms every five weeks than have been killed by terrorism since 9/11.

Yet, although mass slaughter atrocities make the headlines, the bigger tragedy happens in the everyday murders and accidents that make US troops in Kabul safer than civilians in Chicago. Despite the image of gun violence and crime as being essentially one and the same thing, the overwhelming majority of gun deaths (over 60 percent) in America are suicides. People feeling hopeless who have access to a gun are obviously at much greater risk of self-harm than those who do not. In America, those seeking help often can't find or afford it. The absence of a functioning public health system means that the prison system is the largest mental healthcare provider in the country. If you're not imprisoned, your mental illness is very likely to be left undiagnosed until it's too late. Prison or suicide is no choice at all.

Those living outside of America simply cannot comprehend why there is debate within American society as to whether guns are the cause of all the gun-related deaths. Some issues are complicated, but some just pretend to be. We all know that more guns in society leads inevitably to more gun deaths. The reason Americans don't look at the world as the rest of us do is not that they are inherently different or unable to form reasoned views, it's that gun arguments are framed in such a different way within American society (and there is so much money involved) that people remain fearful, misinformed and adherent to the prevailing message.

The so-called gun debate is really nothing of the sort. Logic debates money, and money wins. But logic can destroy money's case for unrestricted gun ownership in two short paragraphs:

- While the US Constitution is one of the great documents of modern history, it was also written 230 years ago, so while it can remain the backbone of American society, it is necessary to at least interpret its Articles and take note of the world in which we now live, which is somewhat different to the picture in 1787. When, for example, NASA decided to change the space program from rockets to the Space Shuttle, the Constitution was not required, as Thomas Jefferson had little need for governance over space travel. The internet was also not mentioned very much back then.

So although the Constitution is important, it is also important that America writes laws today, to deal with today's issues.

- It is possible to acknowledge the Second Amendment (and its unfortunately rather flowery language in relation to bearing arms) and agree that there are still limits on that sacred right. For instance, even the most staunch NRA member wouldn't want someone to be allowed to walk down Wall Street wearing one hundred grenades on his jacket, or carry a ground-to-air missile launcher near an airport. Clearly that's ridiculous, so the right to bear arms is not meant to allow any US citizen the right to walk around with any kind of weapon he or she so chooses.

Today's lawmakers have the right to prepare laws that acknowledge today's society and to impose restrictions on the bearing of arms, so as to reflect the concerns of the twenty-first century. You and I know that anyone who can do their shoelaces up has to agree with these points, so why are so many Americans unable to at least chart their way through these simple bits of logic. The answer of course, as with so much in US society, is money.

The domestic gun market is worth around $38 billion per year. The NRA acts as representatives of that money, and is one of the most powerful and well-connected lobbyists in Washington. They have politicians in their pockets, so no gun atrocity or sober assessment of statistics elicits a meaningful response. When England had a gun massacre at Dunblane, and Australia at Port Arthur, laws were quickly changed, with demonstrable results. The rest of us see this as simple common sense. But even the slaughter of twenty primary schoolchildren at Sandy Hook could not persuade politicians that guns are a cancer at the heart of America.

The NRA claims to have more than 4 million members, and exerts an extraordinary influence on American politics. Politicians are given ratings by the NRA, based on how they vote in relation to gun laws. Any statement except one unquestioningly supporting Americans unrestricted right to bear arms can be punished. A poor rating in a rural seat can cost a politician their job. Nuance and logic are not allowed. The NRA practices informational Nazism.

It's a recession-proof industry. Gun sales rose 50 percent in the weeks after Obama was elected and continued to rise, despite Obama's total failure to address gun laws in any way. In 2013, 10.8 million guns were manufactured in America, a 220 percent increase from ten years previously. America has 4.4 percent of the world's population, but around 50 percent of the civilian-owned guns in the world. Toddlers kill more people than terrorists.

If gun ownership leads directly to gun deaths (it does), then to cut America's gun-death toll to that of the UK they would need to remove 98 percent of the guns from civilian hands. But every time there is a major mass shooting in the US, the share price of gun manufacturers goes up. People respond to gun crime by buying more guns. Gun ownership per person has gone down, but gun sales are up—people who own guns in the United States own seven of them, on average.

The majority of Americans support tighter gun control, but can't seem to get legislative traction. 85 percent support background checks, 70 percent want a federal database to track gun sales. But the NRA makes sure that these voices are not heard, and if they are, they are shouted down.

In the fifteen years following 9/11 (in which three thousand civilians died), gun deaths in America totaled around four hundred thousand. Which of terrorism and gun legislation do you think should be the priority?

Nothing is inexplicable. The reason why guns so infect American society is money, and money's influence on politics. It is money that stops the War on Drugs being addressed, money that buys off the politicians and distorts America's democracy, and money was the true source of the attacks on 9/11.

Money and American Politics

America has elected the party that raised the largest amount of electoral funds during nearly every single election. This means that the party that the moneyed class wants to win does win. It almost seems pointless to have actual elections.

Despite claiming to have been a grassroots president, 60 percent of Barack Obama's 2008 presidential campaign was funded by big donors. The poisonous effect of money on America's politics can be seen on every level, in every individual and in every decision made.

Members of Congress now spend a huge portion of their time raising money, mostly from donors representing the interests of the richest 1 percent of the population. The average new lawmaker arriving in Washington is expected to spend 40 percent of their time fundraising for the next election. Congressional and Senate representatives consistently vote in line with the interests of those who back them financially. As such they have ceased to be legislators and are effectively employees. In what other sphere of life would we allow the referees to be paid off this way?

Corporations don't even pretend to donate money to match their political views or business outlook. They fund both sides. That way they are hedging their bets on election results, knowing whoever gets in will be beholden to their interests. To call this money "political donations" is entirely false. It's abetting barefaced corruption. Money corrupts America's entire political system.

The modern Republican Party is not some chance meeting of a group of awful, right-wing people who have randomly chosen to espouse the interests of the rich and powerful. America's political structures mean that it is not possible to reach the top without having taken the money of the great and the powerful, and that money makes a puppet of politicians. The system produces the people who promote the system's values. It is money that is the root of the problem.

Powerful players have openly tried to buy American elections before, but their ability to do so, and to influence the entire political agenda, has increased with the sheer volume of money that now greases every palm in Washington.

Perversely, Donald Trump was able to pitch himself as something new, on the basis that because he has so much money, he could campaign for (and would govern as) president, free from anyone's influence. Others have tried to use money, power and the media to buy their way to placing a candidate in the White House.

In 2011, Rupert Murdoch persuaded Roger Ailes, Fox News' legendary president, to send an emissary to Afghanistan to try to persuade General David Petraeus to run for president. The premise was simple. Rupert and Roger said they knew that Petraeus shared their principles, and told him that if he ran he could be guaranteed the full power of Murdoch and Fox's awesome media machine behind him. Or to put it another way, Rupert Murdoch wanted to subvert American democracy and buy a president. Ailes' emissary K.T. McFarland told Petraeus that if he ran, Fox News would be his in-house. Remember that when you next watch America's favorite "fair and balanced" news network.

Despite the undeniably corrosive effect money has had on its democracy, America's legislators have consistently voted to allow money more, not less, influence. In 2010 the Supreme Court betrayed its own people by passing the infamous Citizens United ruling. Five members of that ignoble court ruled that corporations had the same rights as actual people when it came to exercising free speech in the form of spending money to influence politics. Corporations can now use their money, at any time, to run campaigns for and against politicians (disguised as political philosophies), no matter how obvious it is that this leads to corruption. The ruling has already had an enormous upward effect on the total funding now required to wage and win a presidential campaign.

Don't expect the media to tell you that money in American politics is a problem, as all that money spent on political advertising goes into the coffers of the media corporations. They're in on the racket.

Citizens United was a dreadful decision, one of the worst in US legal history. Despite Mitt Romney's statement (when campaigning for president in 2011) that corporations are people, they are not. Corporations don't have legs and walk around. Unlike most people, American corporations retain around $2 trillion in their bank accounts and lobby Washington every minute of every day. They are immensely more powerful than people, have no interest in democracy, and should not be allowed such a baleful influence over it. Allowing corporations to spend unlimited amounts on political interference means politics is for sale. Citizens United should be overturned immediately and the Supreme Court system overhauled, to avoid having such right-wing appointees casting their lifelong shadow over American society.

Membership of Congress and the Senate is now, almost without exception, a gateway to huge personal wealth. Lobbying and consulting fees now swell the pockets of the nation's servants, who make vast profits trading on information that is not yet in the public domain . . . a practice called insider trading, which is outlawed for us common folk. Money has led the country to become a kleptocracy, where the rich and powerful use their influence and power to line their own pockets at the expense of the poor. As the rich get richer, their power to influence politics increases. This has been made flesh with the election of billionaire Donald Trump.

All this would be relatively easy to change. Scrap raising money for elections, let the state contribute funds. Force broadcasters to give free airtime to candidates. Public financing for electoral campaigns would probably be welcomed by many politicians, freed from the endless task of raising money, and the impossibility of matching their actual views with those of their corporate masters.

Change is vital. Congress's approval rating has been at or around 9 percent for many years. In 2013 it was reported to be just 6 percent, lower than used car salesmen, North Korea, or King George during the revolution. The public know their political system is broken. This is not particularly controversial. Eight in ten Americans polled in 2012 agreed that clamping down on corporations and the big money funding US politics was a good idea. Nine in ten agreed that there is way too much corporate money in politics.

As it is, American governance now represents an unaccountable nexus of military, corporate, and financial interests, with politicians the salesmen to a frightened and misinformed public. Removing the money would be one big step towards restoring the public's trust that the referees are not being paid off, and would allow the game to continue according to the rules. But who could gain the power to remove the money, without having first accepted the money required to get that power?

Only a form of revolution can change this.

CHAPTER TWENTY FIVE

AMERICAN FASCISM

Republicans Under Obama

America's early abandonment of a Westminster style of government allowed politicians to enter a brave new world, where cooperation was the only way to get things done. Gone were the British-era days of political parties noisily barracking at each other behind a nominated leader. In America, if something needed to be passed, there was often simply no other way than to reach across the aisle and find an accommodation. This idea served the United States well for generations.

However, after a drift towards ideologically-based conservatism (that accelerated under George W. Bush), the election of Barack Obama marked a line in the sand when the Republican party moved further to the right than ever before. At best, Obama governed like a traditional center-right president, yet during his tenure at the White House, Republicans waged a campaign of political dysfunction unprecedented in US history, blocking nearly every single agenda item Obama produced, even when that meant voting against their own policies.

The bogus Tea Party faction that rose to national prominence after Obama took office pushed Republicans so far to the right that the party began to fracture, spawning freaks like Michelle Bachmann, know-nothings like Sarah Palin, and individuals like Ted Cruz—detested by their own colleagues.

During the Obama years, the more that moderate Republicans had to pander to the crazies, the less the party was able to hold together a coherent narrative. This was made flesh in the form of Mitt Romney, a weak candidate from a tradition of moderate, centrist conservatism, whose loss in the 2012 election was down to his own invidious mission impossible of making peace with the uncompromising Tea Partiers while appealing to the large centrist group of the American population. In the end, it just made Romney seem like he stood for nothing.

This unprecedented obstructionism and political paralysis could be seen most clearly through Republicans' rabid and ongoing attacks on the Affordable Care Act (nicknamed Obamacare), in itself a flawed and timid approach to an obvious healthcare problem (that would be seen as not nearly enough in every other Western country on earth), which was attacked as little less than medical Nazism and possibly the end of civilization itself. Dr. Ben Carson saw his early lead in the 2016 Republican primaries unchanged when he said that he thought that Obamacare was the worst thing to happen to his nation since slavery. Many Republicans seemed to agree. The rest of us just gasped. The crazies were taking over.

As the party lurched to the right, Republican primaries began to resemble an extended run of America's Got Talent. They even allowed someone like Sarah Palin to be taken seriously (for a while). Palin's nomination as the vice presidential candidate probably cost John McCain the Presidency in 2008, but although her vapid quirks made for a chuckle, consider that McCain lost the election by only 7 percent of the vote. The world came close to having Sarah Palin just one heartbeat away from being president of the United States. It should have come as no surprise that celebrity television spawned the rise of Donald Trump as a national political figure. His candidacy was initially treated as just another example of how nuts Republican politics had become. Now the laughter has ceased.

Demographic Time Bombs

Republican opposition and obstruction was not just focused on policy, but squarely on the man. Obama, Republicans told us, was a Kenyan Muslim hardline socialist, hell-bent on destroying the United States itself, and the most radical, divisive and dangerous president in the history of the United States. That's really what they said.

This nihilistic approach dragged America's political discourse into the gutter. It was particularly damaging to Republican electoral prospects with minorities (who are rapidly ceasing to be a minority). When Mitt Romney ran for president in 2012, he achieved a statistically staggering zero percent rating with African Americans.

The increasing racial diversity of America's population grows more of a threat to long-term Republican prospects for power with every year. In 1970, 83 percent of the country identified as white. By 2010 it was 64 percent. The "pale, male, and frail" strategy aimed at Evangelicals and those in the South will not survive the changing nature of America's population. Angry old white men, by their nature, are a dying breed. Republicans have won the popular vote only once in the seven elections from 1992 to 2016, and the broadening palette of American demography lead many to believe that the party is likely to split, or be destroyed as an electoral force, unless it can find a way to more centrist policies.

If we can just hold out long enough, shifts in demographics mean that Texas, which has voted Republican in every election since 1980, will one day soon turn blue. Without the Lone Star state, the Republican party may struggle (under normal circumstances at least) to win any subsequent election.

Changing demography means that the Republican party faces a choice—retain power through any means possible, or lose and die. This merely raises the stakes, given the powers now vested in the office of the president, and with a country that is on the point of collapse.

Falling Behind

Most of us still believe that, despite the dreadful disappointments and betrayed ideals, Barack Obama was still at least a functioning human being with a heart and soul who probably wanted to do the right thing at least some of the time. But if this man, who campaigned exclusively on hope and change, was unable to materially alter the strategic direction of the United States, what chance has anyone got?

Obama's presidency served only to highlight the enormous structural and functional problems within America's politics. Despite his pledges, Guantanamo remained open, drone strikes accelerated, wiretapping and domestic surveillance continued, incarceration rates remained the highest on earth, and the lives of black Americans barely improved at all. Obama promised change, but delivered only stasis. His signature policies on healthcare and marriage equality were, despite the opposition from Republicans, both political free kicks, in that neither affected the state apparatus, and one cost no money. Although these were to be welcomed, the majority of Americans continued to face dire circumstances, despite their residence in the richest country on earth.

In Washington City, life expectancy is lower than in Gaza. In Detroit, infant mortality is similar to that in Syria. Life expectancy for white working class people has actually declined since the financial crisis. Absent a war, social collapse, or plague, this never happens, and is almost exclusively a product of the fact that one third of Americans now live in, or close to, poverty. Most Americans now think it is unlikely that their children will lead a better life than they did. More than a third think America's best days are in the past. The country is in decline.

The shredding of civil liberties and flagrant disregard for the US Constitution has now seen out four presidential terms and two presidents. Once lost, these precious laws and institutions (often paid for with blood) are rarely regained, and leave any country at risk should a tyrannical leader take charge.

Thomas Jefferson said, "In questions of power, then, let no more be heard of confidence in man, but bind him down from mischief by the chains of the Constitution." Jefferson knew the power of a written Constitution, and the risks of abrogating that document in the false name of security.

9/11 marked the start of a takeover of civilian life by military and intelligence agencies, the beginning of the end of American democracy as we know it, and a new age where the concerns of the security state ride roughshod over every other aspect of society. This new state, where dissent and oversight are all but removed, is not built on foundations of freedom and liberty, but on the requirement for ever-more national security measures, destroying the fabric of a great nation in a fight against an unseen enemy that can never be defeated.

America presents itself as playing the role of leader of the free world, a beacon of liberty, the world's good guy sheriff. Yet, morally and institutionally, this is less and less able to withstand scrutiny. Across international boundaries, America is regularly a glaring outlier in world governance and affairs.

Consider that the US has refused to sign the Kyoto accords and leads the world in CO_2 emissions, and can thus be described as the primary driver of climate change. America refuses to even contemplate taking the lead at the International Criminal Court, in the knowledge that some of the world's worst violations of international law are carried out by Americans. America hasn't signed the UN Convention on the Rights of the Child. The only other non-signatory in the world is Somalia. Yes, Somalia. America lectures the world on its values and on human rights while refusing to ratify treaties which the rest of the civilized world regard as the very foundations of law.

America's unflinching support for the state of Israel creates huge amounts of distrust and anger in the rest of the world, which laments the plight of the wretched Palestinians and see Israel as the belligerent aggressor, rather than victim. Again and again, the United Nations votes to censure Israel and America vetoes (with Britain abstaining). When the UN voted against the militarization of space in 2006, the vote was 166 to 1 (with two abstentions). Guess who thinks that space weapons are a good idea?

Obamacare, which has been treated by Republicans as if it was a call for all newborns to be slain, would in most other Western countries be regarded as a very poor first step. Before Obamacare, nearly two-thirds of personal bankruptcies in the US related to healthcare costs. If you got sick, you went broke. Nearly fifty million people had no healthcare insurance, and many with insurance who fell sick found that either their insurance policy was full of holes or that they couldn't pay the 20 percent or more of the medical costs (the copay) that they still had to cover.

Forty-five thousand Americans die each year because they don't have medical coverage. Compare that to the risk from terrorism, and the vast sums spent on preventing another attack.

Modern America's resemblance to a banana republic is more than just sheen. The moneyed class are rescued when their risks don't work out, while the spine of the nation is left to rot. After the 35W bridge collapsed into the Mississippi River in 2007 (killing thirteen people), a review of the nation's six hundred thousand bridges found that twelve percent were structurally deficient. America had chosen to spend money on tax cuts and wars. Its infrastructure had lost a generation of investment.

In the space of a few short years under the last Republican president, America went from the bastion of the free world to a land that allowed indefinite detention, military justice commissions, hidden prisons and prisoners, torture, state-sanctioned kidnap, rendition, surveillance of all its citizens, lost two wars at a cost of trillions of dollars, and waged war on an abstract that by definition can never be defeated. The story of the Bush years is a raw demonstration of the power of fear when used as a political weapon, and how a country can sell its soul when the government attacks its own Constitution—all the while telling everyone they are defending it.

Congress has been poorly rated by the American public for decades, but that trend moved into overdrive after the lies President Bush used to justify the invasion of Iraq collapsed. This is the malaise that gave rise to the Tea Party and Occupy movements, as well as figures like Bernie Sanders and Donald Trump, each diametric political opposites, but all united in their belief that the political establishment needs to be torn down.

This may seem like an attractive concept, but the rise of anti-politics may make us regret what we've wished for. Bernie Sanders held the promise of a change of direction, but his policies really amounted to a return to the "old normal," pre-Reagan days of governance. Donald Trump, however, promised a racist, xenophobic government without precedent in American history. America's anti-politics mood could soon take the nation further from its founding principles than ever before.

Never Ending War

The idea that America is a nation of peace, one that seeks an end to war and violence, is beyond parody. Its entire state structure is now geared toward fighting wars, arming foreign nations, and profiting from a never-ending flow of death profits.

In 2011, the US controlled 78 percent of the global arms sales market—worth $66.3 billion, followed (not closely) by Russia, with just 5.6 percent. Between 2010 and 2011, US arms sales tripled. No other country has a worldwide set of military bases (perhaps a thousand or more), such a powerful army or the willingness to use it so regularly.

The sheer sprawl of US military power is unprecedented in human history. At last count 132 of the world's 190 countries had a US military presence. America is by far and away the world's leading seller of weapons and purveyor of war, and rapidly attaining a position of total dominance in arms sales and military projection. The *Guardian's* Tom Engelhardt put it succinctly, saying that the US is "in a sense, a massive machine for the promotion of war on a global scale."

The circular logic of the military industrial complex means that any proposed cut to military spending is opposed by hawkish Senators from states where firms like General Dynamics and BAE Systems remain key employers.

Yet, the militarism of the United States is not nearly as broadly supported by the public as one might imagine. Poll after poll shows that, except in times of (often manufactured) public hysteria, while general questions about keeping America safe receive broad backing, concepts such as "military force can often create more terrorism than it destroys" are ones Americans are happy to examine and support. Large majorities in polls consistently show that Americans would like military spending cut, think that Iraq and Afghanistan weren't worth the losses, and oppose the bombing of Iran. This is especially true of younger people, who have seen disastrous wars like Iraq and Afghanistan, rather than the elderly generation raised in the shadow of World War II.

The US now seems chronically unable to win the wars it wages, but perhaps that doesn't matter anymore. It could be that the military's true goals, those of control of carbon deposits, worldwide projection of power, and vast military expenditure (enriching those lucky enough to be at the supply end of the chain), are actually consistently met through a world riven by endless war and conflict.

It is a widely held (though entirely untrue) notion that Ronald Reagan deliberately bankrupted the Soviet Union by forcing Russia to spend unsustainable sums in order to keep pace with America's military buildup. Whatever the truth, the US should now think about applying this lesson to itself. The documents we can now access show that Russia never seriously considered invading or attacking Europe or the West. Only Mikhail Gorbachev stopped Reagan's insane nuclear brinkmanship.

Terrorism is a much more convenient enemy than a sovereign nation, where a new leader can quickly lead to rapprochement and peace. The threat of terrorism can never be eradicated, but defeating this paper tiger may ultimately cause America's own downfall.

The Rise of American Fascism

The use of the word *fascist* to describe any society is highly emotive, bringing to mind as it does Nazism, Hitler, and concentration camps. But fascism does not need human ovens and mass extermination; it can be a slow slide into repression and dictatorship, often scarcely noticed day by day. Fascism is often wrought by those who claim to be the most patriotic, and to have God at their side. Novelist Sinclair Lewis wrote in 1936 that "when fascism comes to America, it will be wrapped in the flag, carrying a cross."

Consider the actions of Constitutional law professor, President Barack Obama, widely seen as a moderate and a "return to normality" after the madness of George W. Bush. Yet in eight short years, Obama achieved the kind of CV that puts him near the top of the list of most right-wing administrations in America's history. Mr. Obama:

- Adopted nearly all of Bush's anti-terrorism policies.
- Killed thousands of civilians using weaponized drones over Muslim countries, without a UN mandate, without formally declaring war, and in contravention of the wishes of those countries.
- Launched an unprecedented war on journalism and whistle-blowers.
- Oversaw a huge increase in government secrecy and new laws that were profoundly unconstitutional.
- Launched war on Libya against the wishes of Congress.
- Kept Guantanamo open and failed to revoke the policy of indefinite detention for captives.
- Ran a covert campaign against Iran that could easily have been seen by that nation as an act of war.

- Concluded that the president has the power to assassinate US citizens (and by extension everyone on earth) without charge or due process, including in the US.
- Allowed the NSA to establish the most powerful civilian spying program in human history.
- Oversaw a period of modest to non-existent growth during which the richest people in the country dramatically increased their wealth.

If Obama was a socialist, he was a very bad one. On the contrary, Bush and Obama have left US democracy in tatters. In its place are all the signs of an emerging fascist nation.

There is room for disagreement here. Broad societies are often hard to define with just one word. Given that terms like fascism are so often pressed into the service of disparate political agendas, they are by their nature hard to define. But take a look at Laurence Britt's well-known list of fourteen characteristics of fascist nations. They fit frighteningly well with America today.

1. Powerful and Continuing Nationalism: Fascist regimes tend to make constant use of patriotic mottos, slogans, symbols, songs, and other paraphernalia. Flags are seen everywhere, as are flag symbols on clothing and in public displays.
2. Disdain for the Recognition of Human Rights: Because of fear of enemies and the need for security, the people in fascist regimes are persuaded that human rights can be ignored in certain cases because of need. The people tend to look the other way or even approve of torture, summary executions, assassinations, long incarcerations of prisoners, etc.
3. Identification of Enemies/Scapegoats as a Unifying Cause: The people are rallied into a unifying patriotic frenzy over the need to eliminate a perceived common threat or foe: racial, ethnic or religious minorities; liberals; communists; socialists, terrorists, etc.
4. Supremacy of the Military: Even when there are widespread domestic problems, the military is given a disproportionate amount of government funding, and the domestic agenda is neglected. Soldiers and military service are glamorized.
5. Rampant Sexism: The governments of fascist nations tend to be almost exclusively male-dominated. Under fascist regimes,

traditional gender roles are made more rigid. Divorce, abortion, and homosexuality are suppressed and the state is represented as the ultimate guardian of the family institution.

6. Controlled Mass Media: Sometimes the media is directly controlled by the government, but in other cases, the media is indirectly controlled by government regulation, or sympathetic media spokespeople and executives. Censorship, especially in war time, is very common.

7. Obsession with National Security: Fear is used as a motivational tool by the government over the masses.

8. Religion and Government are Intertwined: Governments in fascist nations tend to use the most common religion in the nation as a tool to manipulate public opinion. Religious rhetoric and terminology is common from government leaders, even when the major tenets of the religion are diametrically opposed to the government's policies or actions.

9. Corporate Power is Protected: The industrial and business aristocracy of a fascist nation often are the ones who put the government leaders into power, creating a mutually beneficial business/government relationship and power elite.

10. Labor Power is Suppressed: Because the organizing power of labor is the only real threat to a fascist government, labor unions are either eliminated entirely, or are severely suppressed.

11. Disdain for Intellectuals and the Arts: Fascist nations tend to promote and tolerate open hostility to higher education and academia. It is not uncommon for professors and other academics to be censored or even arrested. Free expression in the arts and letters is openly attacked.

12. Obsession with Crime and Punishment: Under fascist regimes, the police are given almost limitless power to enforce laws. The people are often willing to overlook police abuses and even forego civil liberties in the name of patriotism. There is often a national police force with virtually unlimited power in fascist nations.

13. Rampant Cronyism and Corruption: Fascist regimes almost always are governed by groups of friends and associates who appoint each other to government positions and use governmental power and authority to protect their friends from accountability. It is not uncommon in fascist regimes for national

resources and even treasures to be appropriated or even outright stolen by government leaders.

14. Fraudulent Elections: Sometimes elections in fascist nations are a complete sham. Other times elections are manipulated by smear campaigns against or even assassination of opposition candidates, use of legislation to control voting numbers or political district boundaries, and manipulation of the media. Fascist nations also typically use their judiciaries to manipulate or control elections.

I find it hard to see how, reading this list, you could not recognize much of America's daily political life and discourse. President Donald J. Trump is the human incarnation of these traits. A perfect fit.

This is not to say that the American public is fascist. Far from it. They twice elected a man like Barack Obama, specifically as a repudiation of the excesses of the Bush era, and are consistently shown to lean further to the left on most issues than their elected officials. The American state, however, has taken a huge surge to the right since 9/11, and sadly its people have been shown to respond well to media and political campaigns warning that the entire country is at risk.

Despite living in times of almost unprecedented safety, peace, and order, Americans have allowed their country to exchange huge and hard-fought societal freedoms in order to gain what their government has sold to them as national security. But fascist leaders don't want to get rid of the bogeyman. They need him to be there, forever, to guarantee their form of social order and continued hold on political power.

The fascist governments of Germany and Italy in the 1930s both came to power legally and democratically. It was only when they gained power that they revealed their true colors. Both also commenced dismantling the mechanics of government legally, telling their people that the measures they were taking were vital to national security because of the crises they faced.

Benito Mussolini once said, "Fascism ought more properly be called corporatism, because it is the perfect merger of power between the corporation and the state." That merger is now complete. When American corporations faced disaster, the state came to their rescue. The NSA's spying programs have been used to gain American corporations competitive advantage. Corporate money now controls America's politicians and the power of corporations and the American state have become one and the same thing. Mussolini's fascist Italy is a model that sadly bears considerable comparison to twenty-first century America.

The NSA's goal appears to be the elimination of public privacy, globally, forever . . . actions that are the very definition of fascism. However, the focus on terrorism is just a convenient excuse for the building of state control structures that threaten the very foundations of the United States. Despite the routine and hysterical exaggeration of the risk of terrorism, the actual chance of an American being killed in a terrorist attack is one in 3.5 million. Bee stings kill many more. More Americans have been killed by falling refrigerators than terrorism since 9/11. Eight times as many people die at the hands of the police than do because of terrorism. Driving a car is a thousand times more risky. But the state now demands that this infinitesimally small risk has to be made even smaller, to the detriment of other measures like universal healthcare that would guarantee thousands of saved lives. This wildly disproportionate focus is the cause of worldwide war, torture, and assassination programs, all of which combine to leave America less safe, and unable to afford to feed or educate many of the people it so strives to defend.

As the huge inequities of American life begin to tear its society apart the government now has the political power, homeland security apparatus, police, and armed forces to forcibly put down its own people. This has already begun to happen, and the American public has got used to daily intrusions by the state that would never have been permitted before 9/11. Authorities themselves admit that most security sweeps are not in response to specific threats. The state now intrudes on daily life in America, wanting to know what you are up to, without suspecting it is a crime.

The internet, potentially the greatest tool for mass information, freedom, and self-expression, is in danger of turning into the most potent weapon for oppression in human history. If you live your life online, the government conceivably knows you better than your spouse. See that camera on top of your laptop? It is no longer paranoid to think that 'they might be watching'.

George W. Bush borrowed more than all other previous presidents combined (then Obama did the same, although he inherited a nation in flames). America's military misadventures have crippled its finances. Even after cuts in 2012, the US Defense budget still made up more than 40 percent of total world military spending—three times as much as China, seven times that of Russia. With an army of 1.4 million active duty personnel, the US is capable of fighting nearly anyone at any time, and a society predicated on war, that has been at war for almost a generation, needs another big one soon.

America has the biggest and most powerful army, the most nuclear weapons, the largest economy, the broadest surveillance powers, and hosts nearly all of the world's main telecommunications hubs. US military bases dot nearly every country on earth, as do secret prisons far from prying eyes. Across government, the army, intelligence agencies, the police force, and in the corporate sector, the pieces are now all in place for the emergence of the most overtly fascist nation the world has seen since 1939. It took a World War to bring down Hitler, but America is much more powerful than Germany ever was.

Jim Garrison, the only man to try someone for the murder of John Kennedy, once said, "Fascism will come to America in the name of national security." The pursuit of this security has left America at the crossroads, a nation on the edge of calamity.

CHAPTER TWENTY SIX

TRUMP

Genesis

It is sometimes hard to locate the genesis of a catastrophe. Most examples of societal breakdown are preceded by a long period of decay, before a moment of truth sets a country on an irreversible downward plummet.

The French Revolution came about after years of costly wars, leading to a government near bankruptcy requiring higher taxes during a time of severe famine, in turn caused by several years of failed harvests. Like America, disparity in wealth stratified French society, and led to intense resentment from the starving masses. This eventually boiled into bloody revolution. A vast gap between rich and poor rips a society apart.

When Hitler rose to power in Germany, he took advantage of a broken nation with weak democratic institutions, and was able to quickly crush all opposition. However, Hitler's rise was made specifically through a populist appeal to make his country great again, after years of reparations (for the First World War) crippled Germany's economy and collapsed its currency. Most people in Germany in the 1930s weren't bad human beings, but they were desperate, and hungry, desperate people are powerfully motivated. That motivation can be harnessed, for good or evil.

The seeds of Donald Trump's 2016 election victory were first sown during the presidency of Ronald Reagan, and his second term in office in particular. Reagan's neoliberal policies (of low taxation, high defense budgets, and the removal of regulation and trade barriers) were continued by George H. W. Bush and Bill Clinton (in one way or another), but it was the events of September 11, 2001 that allowed new President George W. Bush to accelerate the rush to make the rich richer and the poor poorer. Perversely, the financial crash only added more impetus to this national fleecing.

The astonishing collapse of America's huge middle class took place in this post-9/11 world. In 2000, just 33 percent of Americans identified as working class. By 2015 that number was 48 percent, or half of the country. Nearly fifty million people (out of around 320 million) live below the poverty line in the richest country on earth. The economy has barely recovered from the financial crash. Social mobility is at its lowest level ever.

It used to be said that poor Americans just considered themselves temporarily embarrassed millionaires. That perception has changed. The poor know they are staying poor. No one believes the bullshit anymore.

Franklin Roosevelt said in his 1944 State of the Union speech that "people who are hungry and out of a job are the stuff of which dictatorships are made." Huge sections of America's society are hungry and out of a job right now, while Apple (by itself) sits on cash reserves that have come close to a quarter of a trillion dollars. This is the stuff of which dictatorships are made.

Perhaps another quote from the past will help. The Supreme Court Justice Louis Brandeis wrote in 1941 that "we may have democracy in this country or we may have great wealth concentrated in the hands of a few, but we can't have both." Great wealth is now concentrated in the hands of a few. America's democracy is dying.

Neoliberal or supply-side economic policies—enacted by politicians who were acutely aware what the consequences would be—were the direct cause of millions falling into poverty, lower living standards, and a more precarious life for the majority of Americans. A tiny handful of rich people and corporations saw their wealth balloon in a way unimaginable before the Gipper took control of America in 1980. It was these policies, and their social consequence, that were finally rejected in 2016 by an outpouring of populist anger, first with Britain's vote to exit the EU, then shockingly with the election of Donald J. Trump.

The Campaign

Donald Trump's campaign for the Presidency is the political story of our generation. Trump staged an astonishing assault on every level of America's electoral process, vanquishing foes at every turn and staging a hostile takeover of the Republican Party. During the primaries he easily out-gunned low-energy Jeb Bush, scorned "Little" Marco Rubio and ripped flesh from Lyin' Ted Cruz, suggesting that Cruz's father had somehow been involved in the Kennedy assassination and tweeting unflattering photos of Heidi Cruz alongside his own attractive wife.

Whether through political genius or just capturing a moment in time with his bluster (almost certainly the latter), Trump ripped up the rulebook and took America's media hostage with an unrelenting barrage of antics and outrage. Back in 2004, Howard Dean lost his primary bid for the Democratic nomination because he shouted the word "yeah" too loudly at the end of a speech. In 2016, Trump suggested that Fox journalist Megyn Kelly had asked him tough questions because she was menstruating and his numbers barely wobbled.

A gaffe used to be political strychnine. American politicians parsed their words carefully to avoid putting one demographic or another offside. This sometimes left them looking bland. Trump did the opposite. Instead of trying to quell outrage at the things he said, Trump doubled down. When his statements were exposed as lies (often laughable, ludicrous lies), Trump insisted that what he had said was indeed true. His ability to defuse one bomb by exploding another nearby took advantage of a press and public who run on twenty-four-hour news cycles. This political "stick and move" was a new tactic, allowing Trump to say anything with complete impunity. Truth and decency lay slain.

Trump insulted a Gold Star family (who had lost their son in battle), and said that he too had made similar sacrifices through his hard work in the business arena. He said that Muslims should carry identity cards, and when asked how that would differ from Nazi Germany's treatment of the Jews, answered, "You tell me." Trump discussed the size of his penis in a Presidential debate and was caught on tape boasting about sexually assaulting women. Nothing seemed to touch him.

The word unprecedented was used so often it seemed to lose its currency. Trump called for America's archenemy, Russia, to hack Hillary Clinton's emails while she had been secretary of state. He successfully convinced his followers that Clinton was not just a political opponent but a career criminal, perhaps even an existential threat to the nation, and insisted that if he won he would have her imprisoned. Donald Trump was the most radical presidential candidate in American history.

As the election neared, we learned a new phrase for what was happening. We had entered the era of post-truth politics, in which political debate is framed entirely in terms of emotion, rather than fact. This hysteria allowed Trump to tell lies that a six-year-old might regard as a bit much.

Trump said that Hillary Clinton had been fighting ISIS her "entire adult life", and claimed that if Clinton was elected she would let 650 million immigrants into the country in the first week, tripling America's population. In a week.

How would you feel about me if, over dinner, I told you that my new car went six thousand miles per hour, and when you said don't be ridiculous I angrily continued to claim I was right, and then told you another obvious lie in order to obscure the previous one? *Deranged* might be a word you would use. Trump's eighteen months in the presidential race spotlight were an endless stream of the utterly absurd. And still they voted for him.

The fact-checking website Politifact found that 71 percent of Trump's statements were either mostly false, false, or "pants on fire," a rate higher than any other politician they had ever covered (Clinton's number was 26 percent). America's public had either lost the ability to discern truth from lies, or lost the will to care.

Undermining the very mechanics of American democracy, Trump refused to say that he would accept the result of the election if he lost. This wasn't just irresponsible, it was a dangerous threat. Yet, despite this litany of deceit and outrage, a month out from the election Hillary Clinton maintained a small (but consistent) lead. Trump had insulted women, minorities, the LGBT community, the disabled—pretty much everyone except for white men. It would take an extraordinary combination of events for him to have a chance of winning.

Then that extraordinary combination took place.

Election Day

The 2016 election has to be viewed in context. This was not one election gone awry, but the culmination of two generations of electoral sabotage, almost exclusively conducted by Republicans.

The Republican party viewed the 1960s civil rights era (that empowered and enfranchised black and minority communities) as a threat to their ability to gain and retain political power. Most black people in America were poor, and poor people vote to the left of the spectrum. Almost simultaneously to the passing of the 1965 Voting Rights Act, Republicans set about trying to stop minorities from being able to exercise that right.

In every election, and in 2016 in particular, Republicans know that the fewer the number of voters, the higher their chances of victory, so every trick in the book is used to suppress voter turnout. Gerrymandering, widely used by Republican officials, refers to altering county boundaries to favor one party. Voter identification laws have been shown to almost exclusively intimidate and target black communities, and have been pursued with vigor. Even the holding of an election on a working day (a Tuesday) helps suppress the vote, as poorer voters struggle to get away from their jobs and face long lines to cast their ballot. Voting stations have been cut in poor neighborhoods. Lines to vote in rich (Republican voting) areas are much shorter than those in minority communities.

America's huge prison population and vengeful justice system disenfranchise nearly six million felons, who are not allowed to vote. Again, these are mostly the poor and people of color. 13 percent of adult black men cannot vote due to a felony on their record. 88 percent of black voters chose Hillary Clinton in 2016. It's not hard to see that, from a Republican perspective, mass incarceration is a huge electoral assist.

Money has dramatically increased its influence, especially since the Citizens United ruling by the Supreme Court in 2010 that allowed unlimited corporate funds to be spent. In 2000, the total cost of the federal election was $3 billion—by 2016 that figure had more than doubled to nearly $7 billion. In the 2012 election, the candidate with the most money won 95 percent of the time. Although Trump spent less than Clinton in 2016, his appointment of Goldman Sachs bankers immediately after his victory clearly indicated where his loyalties lay. Money has completed its capture of America.

And this is before we take into account the scurrilous litany of dirty tricks that are a regular feature of US Federal elections. This has been the case since the dawn of the Republic, but the pervasive nature of the internet and social media incrementally increased the reach of false information and its influence on voters in 2016.

Online flyers were circulated that read "Save Time Avoid the Line" and advocated voting by text, which is not possible. Automated calls told voters that their ballots wouldn't count. Both instances targeted Democratic voters.

Online, there was an unprecedented tsunami of illegitimate content masquerading as fact: false news. Around three-quarters of online Americans use Facebook. Sixty-two percent of US adults get news from social media (and there are estimated to be eighty-three million fake Facebook profiles). This is a profound change from the days when great newspapers and television broadcasters were overwhelmingly the primary provider of Americans information on current affairs. Although these organizations were owned and controlled by corporations and prone to unquestioningly accepting false government narratives, they also employed real journalists who checked their sources and took measures to try to verify that a story was true. In the Facebook era, there is no such requirement.

Fake news content spiked dramatically as election day neared. Suddenly social media pages were filled with reports that Hillary Clinton had terminal cancer (she doesn't), that the Pope had endorsed Donald Trump (he didn't), or that those investigating Clinton kept being murdered (they weren't). Clinton,

Facebook reports told us, was a pedophile enabler for child-rapist Bill Clinton. The FBI had a criminal investigation into the case. Democrats were paying protesters $3,000 to go to Trump rallies. Tens of thousands of fraudulent ballots for Clinton had been found in a warehouse. She had just weeks to live. The list seemed endless.

Whatever the source of these stories, they overwhelmingly favored Donald Trump, and although it's impossible to gauge their effect on the result of the election, those propagating the falsehoods clearly did so with an intent. The sheer volume of falsity makes it impossible to believe that it all came from a few sick individuals.

This deluge of fake news tied in with the post-truth atmosphere, in which the Republican candidate lied nearly three-quarters of the time. How were Americans supposed to know truth from fiction in such a climate?

Despite this, despite all this, twelve days out from the election Clinton led Trump by an average of nearly 6 percent in the polls. A six-point win would be a crushing. Pollster Nate Silver gave Clinton an 81 percent chance of winning. It still seemed that only a lightning bolt could get Trump across the line.

Then it happened. On October 28, just eleven days from the election, FBI director James Comey announced that he was reviewing additional emails relating to Clinton's use of a personal server. The absurd and irrelevant issue of a minor computing infraction had still managed to dog Clinton's campaign, and was blown completely out of proportion by Trump and social media. It was a non-story. Comey poured fuel on a fire that had all-but gone out. It was an extraordinary decision.

Jim Comey is no fool—he would have been acutely aware that any announcement from the head of the FBI that contained the words Clinton, emails, and investigation, made less than two weeks from an election, would be laden with political ramifications. And he was right. A Politico poll taken just after the announcement indicated that fully one-third of Americans said that the revelation made them much less likely to vote for Clinton. Seven of that 33 percent (who said the Comey letter had an effect on them) were Democrats—nearly ten million voters, proportionately—more than enough to cost Hillary Clinton the Presidency.

In the nine days from Comey's initial announcement to his second letter (two days before the election, in which he said that nothing substantial had been found), Clinton's lead dropped to 2.9 percent, a three point swing in just over a week.

Trump's surrogate Rudy Giuliani intimated that the Trump campaign had known of Comey's surprise in advance. Whether that is true or not, Comey's intervention is one of the most egregious political interferences in an election by a federal intelligence body in American history. Without doubt, it was one of the key factors that handed the country to Donald Trump. A faction within the FBI took a conscious decision to try to affect the outcome of the most consequential election in modern history. The timing of the announcement and retraction left no time for voters to regain their sanity. By itself, this is a bigger scandal than Watergate. Treason might be an appropriate word.

It gets much, much worse.

Russia got involved. Despite evidence that both DNC and RNC servers were hacked, WikiLeaks provided a steady stream of embarrassment to the Democratic party only. Trump openly called for Russia to hack the emails of Hillary Clinton during the campaign (a treasonous call by itself). It appears Russia took up this invitation. However, having openly called for Russia to hack the emails of his opponent while she was one of the top officials in the United States government (actions that would interfere in the election), Trump refused to believe his own intelligence services when they said they had evidence that Russia had indeed interfered in the election. These two positions simply don't go together.

At the time of writing, the CIA have indicated that Russia hacked American political party emails, leaked information designed to damage Clinton only, and were involved in false news production for social media. They may well have hacked voting machines themselves on election day.

Clinton led in nearly ever poll going into the election. Polls had never been this consistently wrong before. Is that not prima facie evidence suggesting that, rather than all the pollsters having been wrong, something else was at play? Princeton professor Andrew Appel showed that Sequoia's voting machines could be hacked in just minutes, despite not being connected to the internet. Europe has broadly banned electronic voting for just this reason. Hacking the machines would have been easy, and increments of alteration could be so small that they did not appear obvious. Hacking could change the overall result from one candidate to another.

Dozens of factors lined themselves up against a win by Hillary Clinton. And so it came to pass. Clinton lost the election because she lost the Rust Belt states of Wisconsin, Pennsylvania, and Michigan. From over 135 million votes cast, Trump's collective margin in these three states represented just 0.056 percent of those who voted. Voter turnout was the lowest in twenty years, but despite all the gerrymandering, disenfranchising, money, voter suppression, lies, fake news, and FBI and Russian interference, Clinton still gained a popular vote margin of around 2.8 million. It was the electoral college that gave Trump the Presidency.

America's arcane electoral college process has meant that the last two Republican presidents have taken office after getting fewer votes than their opponent. In fact, despite the huge obstacles to free and fair elections, Republicans have lost the popular vote in six of the last seven elections. If the individual who gained more votes in each election was made president (as should be the case), the list of Presidents since 1992 would read Clinton, Clinton, Gore, Bush, Obama, Obama and Clinton. The world would be a very different place.

There have been seven hundred congressional proposals to change or get rid of the electoral college system in the last two hundred years, more than any other issue. It never happens. Those in power have no incentive to change the system that placed them there.

A month before the election, Washington newspaper *The Hill* reported that only three in ten Americans believed that the nation's process for electing a new president is functional. This lack of faith in the system is likely to have worsened.

The party of Abraham Lincoln was now led by a buffoonish man-child, with a terrible comb over, dyed hair, and an orange face. Despite the racism, misogyny, lies, thin-skin, and the pussy-grabbing, Donald John Trump was president of the United States.

Trump's Personality

America has had its share of presidential characters. Kennedy's sexual profligacy would have ended his presidency had he lived. Calvin Coolidge used to take a nap each day and change into his pajamas in order to do so. Nixon was such an astonishing crook that journalists covering his election campaign openly debated whether he was actually a human being. But there has never been a president like Donald Trump, unprecedented in his inexperience and mendacity, a lifelong crook who boasts of sexually assaulting women, with a personality disorder rarely seen outside the halls of a psychiatric institution.

Listen to the way he talks. When Trump met the board of the *Washington Post* in March 2016, this is what he said when questioned about the use of nuclear weapons against ISIS:

> "I don't want to use, I don't want to start the process of nuclear. Remember the one thing that everybody has said, I'm a counterpuncher. Rubio hit me. Bush hit me. When I said low energy, he's a low energy individual, he hit me first, I spent, by the way he spent $18 million worth of negative ads on me. That's putting . . . I'll tell you one thing, this is a very good-looking group of people here."

The man is unwell. He's babbling. Trump talks of "nuclear", and "the cyber." His sentences constantly miss words: "I'm automatically attracted to beautiful, I just start kissing them." Beautiful what? Donkeys? When you write down what Trump says on a piece of paper, it's clear that he very rarely forms a sentence that includes a noun, an adjective, and a verb. Trump has some form of mental agitation that can't focus long enough to form a clear sentence. Yet Trump says he has "the best words."

Trump is a fairground barker, a snake-oil salesman, an old-fashioned crook. He successfully convinced poor and poorly educated white Americans that their country was in an existential crisis, and that only he, a billionaire, had their concerns at heart. His business practices suggest the opposite. Trump has consistently cheated his suppliers, choosing not to pay when the work is done in the safe knowledge that he has deep pockets and the best lawyers. His ties are made in China, as is much of the steel he uses to build his gaudy, tasteless towers. His wealth is vastly over-stated. He's almost definitely not a billionaire. His university was a sham, his charity a fraudulent front. Trump has been bankrupt six times. He somehow lost a billion dollars owning a casino. As Trump has railed against the loss of American jobs, he has sourced his business overseas, sent small American companies broke, and gamed the system to avoid contributing any federal income tax for nearly twenty years.

Trump is a lifelong racist. His real estate lessors were found to discriminate against African Americans, telling black applicants that his buildings were full when they were not. When exposed, Trump's business practices did not change. Trump says he likes his accountants Jewish, and thinks that Mexicans are rapists.

Trump has been accused by a number of women of sexual assault. The famous Billy Bush tape confirmed his belief that you can just "grab them by the pussy." Trump has spent his entire life rating women purely on their physical appearance and bragging about his sexual exploits, even going so far as to phone newspapers and claim to be a man named John Barron, a Trump employee, in order to list the sheer number of women that his boss was screwing. That bragging on the bus? That wasn't locker-room talk, it was Trump saying exactly who he is. Trump held cocaine-fuelled parties at his suites, where old rich men were introduced to impressionable young models, some of whom were underage, solely to use power and influence in order to pressure the young women to have sex. Trump has used his position to attack women, subjugate them to his will, and ensure that the victims never get a chance to seek justice for what happened to them.

Forty-two percent of female voters opted for Trump over Hillary Clinton. Statistics suggest that a horrifying one in five American women have been sexually assaulted in their lifetime. This means that some American women had been the victims of sexual assault, saw Trump's antics, recognized him as the same kind of monster that had hurt them, and still voted for him.

We've had fools like Truman and Bush Jr. in the White House before. We've had crooks like Nixon, but there has never been a president like Trump, a genuine and complete fraud, whose lifelong association with the darkest side of New York construction, including criminals, Mafiosi, and thugs, has been criminally under-reported.

We all mold truth to fit our own reality somewhat. Truth can be subjective, but I'm not sure that Donald Trump actually knows what the truth is. His life has been so filled with hubris and bluster that he appears no longer able to recognize the difference between truth and lies. Without the money and the power, Trump would be pitiable—a brash, vain, thin-skinned man who appears to have all the worst characteristics of male human beings rolled into one.

America now has a president who considers "winning" his birthright, is happy to break any rule in order to do so, and will take losing as a personal affront. Trump believes that if he loses, it must be because he has been cheated. A democratic leader faces constant opposition to every effort he makes. Trump is not able to deal with this. Democracy doesn't fit his character at all.

Donald Trump doesn't even want to be president. He has no interest in policy or democratic politicking. He just wants to be called President Trump. America's Constitution and institutions of democracy are just inconvenient obstacles. Given the chance, he will swiftly do away with them. Trump wants to be emperor.

Fascism

President Trump commands a nation with the greatest surveillance powers in history, the largest citizen database in history, and the largest military budget in history. His nation has the largest economy in history, but holds the biggest sovereign debt in history. America has the largest number of foreign military bases in the world, and through the use of drones, missiles, and aircraft, the greatest ability to project power abroad in history.

Because of 9/11, Trump inherited the greatest war and executive powers commanded by an American president in history. Because of 9/11, most of these powers are exercised under a historically unprecedented shroud of state secrecy.

It's not that powers like these are prone to being abused. History shows us that this kind of power is inevitably, always abused by those who rule. And America is now ruled by the trickiest, greasiest political crook in its history, a man who at one moment says the election of 2016 was rigged, then an instant later insists that the result must be respected. Reality is flexible. Truth depends solely on how it benefits Trump. It is very difficult for a man so removed from reality to be removed from power.

Some opine that an unstable character like Donald Trump will be constrained from enacting his most extreme ideas by the strength of America's noble institutions of government. The events of 9/11 defy that notion. The attacks (and the anthrax mailing that followed) demonstrate that in the event of a crisis, America's democratic institutions fail spectacularly. This has been the case throughout America's history, and is true for every democracy on earth. Institutions are just constructs made by fallible human beings. American exceptionalism is a myth. Slavery, segregation, mass surveillance, internment and CIA torture (to name but five) were all enacted legally in the United States. September 11 provides the clearest example of how, when placed under unique stresses and during moments of fear, normally sane democratic institutions cannot stop a ruler who is determined enough to do what he wants.

Trump is a textbook fascist. He fits like a glove. Evil and genius are words that don't need to go together. Trump's personal incompetence presents more of a threat than would a man with talent. George W. Bush demonstrated how an incompetent bumbling fool can, through the people who surround him, still reduce a country to ruins in a few short years.

With so many generals, Trump has put together the most militarized administration in modern history. His cabinet is filled with corporate and Goldman Sachs alumni, their combined personal wealth exceeding one third of US households combined. Trump hasn't drained the swamp—this is the swamp.

Trump has hijacked the party to which he attached himself and taken the very notion of Republicanism to the brink of destruction. He has laid bare the idea that Republicans have any form of moral compass. Senior party figures built their careers promoting viewpoints they claimed as conservative moral positions, but although they reluctantly condemned Trump's racism during the election cycle, in the end they all still voted for him.

Failure to disavow racism is to participate in it, and to continue to support a man whose policies you profess to abhor means you have sold your soul. These people are exposed. They stand for nothing. Republican leaders now know that if they abandon Trump they will be rejected by their own party, and if they stay they are tacitly endorsing his vile statements. This is a classic fascist power-grab.

Trump even convinced evangelical voters that a serially unfaithful, thrice married, sexually-assaulting crook shared their values. If you don't think sexism was a major factor in the election, try to imagine the reaction if Hillary Clinton been married three times and had children with three different men. Religious voters are used as useful idiots.

Trumpist Republicanism

Democracies on a slide into dictatorship experience a tsunami of fear, as one group after another find themselves marginalized, disenfranchised, vilified, and then targeted. This normally starts with the weak, the poor or "others," people with the wrong religion, sexuality, or skin color. Those higher up the social ladder allow this to happen, believing themselves immune.

America's eleven million undocumented immigrants came under unprecedented attack during the Obama administration. Obama deported over two million of them, more than all presidents in the twentieth century combined. Donald Trump has pledged to accelerate this process, starting with the two to three million "criminals" he has somehow identified. A deportation force of up to ninety thousand people is proposed. Homes will be raided in the dead of night, women and children taken against their will, families torn apart. People who have lived in America their whole life will hide in the basement and fear going outside. Those arrested will need to be imprisoned before their deportation, perhaps in camps. There is talk of trains being used to transport people. This may have some historical resonance for you.

When Trump said, "I am the law and order candidate," it was a message specifically aimed at white people. Trump failed to disavow an endorsement from David Duke or to distance himself when the Ku Klux Klan and white supremacists celebrated his victory. As the Republican nominee, Trump offered to pay the legal fees of anyone who beat up Black Lives Matter (BLM) demonstrators protesting at his rallies. Trump's response to the BLM movement was to suggest that it is the police who need more protection, but young black men are nine times more likely to be killed by police than other Americans. The entire legal and judicial system of the United States specifically targets and punishes the African American community. Black people in America have every reason to be afraid of this new law and order president.

Perhaps no group has so much to fear as America's three million Muslims. Trump has made it very clear that he holds the entire Muslim community accountable for every individual within it. With entire nations deemed so dangerous that no citizen can even visit the United States for a holiday, the stigma faced by those even suspected of being Muslim will be enormous. So-called Islamic extremism (which almost always is nothing of the sort) commands a vastly disproportionate focus in America's public life. Remarkably spared Islamic terrorism since that terrible September day, America remains on edge, one fright away from panic. In the event of another terrorist attack within America, the atmosphere is now so hysterical that the president can easily be imagined declaring a temporary period of martial law and a suspension of civil liberties. There would be nothing anyone could do to rein in such an exercise of executive power.

Trump appears to have no moral objection to the return of torture. As a candidate, he said he would bring back waterboarding and a "hell of a lot worse." Given how unlikely it is that President Trump will close Guantanamo, it is fair to now consider whether those who remain there will be imprisoned, without trial, until they die. Perhaps that is the only way America's gulag will finally reach closure.

Under Obama, America saw an unprecedented explosion in right-wing anti-government groups, almost exclusively made up of white men. These groups have clearly been emboldened by the arrival of Donald Trump, and are more dangerous than jihadists (as of 2016, right-wing terrorists had killed more Americans since 9/11 than Islamic extremists). Of course, these groups of men are never called terrorists, simply because their skin is white. For people of color, this is just one more reason to be afraid.

Journalism in the Trump era is once again a dangerous profession. Vilification of the media was a routine part of Trump presidential rallies. On occasions, the abuse aimed at the press gallery was so visceral that they were provided security guards in order to leave in safety. Reporters at rallies were required to take escorts to the bathroom when they left the pen in which they were confined. Trump called the press disgusting and corrupt, despite benefiting from billions of dollars of free coverage during his headline grabbing campaign.

Trump takes criticism personally, and makes a point of going after individuals who he feels have slighted him. Naturally, female reporters have been more ferociously targeted. NBC reporter Katy Tur was singled out three times for personal abuse at Trump's rallies, for an apparent snub a year and a half previously. Trump has called for journalists (who he feels have been unfair to him) to be fired. Fox journalist Megyn Kelly described her treatment by Trump as a relentless campaign. Kelly received death threats from Trump supporters, and was forced to employ armed security guards, even on a family vacation to Disneyland. She stated that she believed the harassment was being directly incited by Trump's senior aide, Dan Scavino.

Muting and intimidating the media is a classic symptom of a fascist leader. Individual reporters are intimidated, and often beaten or killed. Vladimir Putin has presided over precisely this sort of behavior—journalists in Russia know that their life is at risk if they dare upset the leader, and behave accordingly. Many have been killed, most notoriously Anna Politkovskaya in 2006. Much of Putin's power is derived from Russia's pliant media.

Large media organizations can also be targeted. President Trump wants to strengthen America's libel laws so he can go after newspapers. With the power of the state behind him, this is likely to be effective. America's independent media collapsed in the fearful years that followed 9/11—Trump will use times of national insecurity to crush the media. Without a functioning press, there will be little to stop Trump from doing whatever he wants. People won't be told when he is breaking the law. History tells us of the incredible dangers that arise when this happens.

Women should be afraid. Trump hates women. He thinks they are only for decoration, self-aggrandizement and sex. Flat-chested women can never be a ten, and the ones who cross him are pigs, dogs, slobs and disgusting. Trump said that if his daughter was harassed at work she should "find another career."

Trump has clearly indicated that a priority will be overturning Roe vs. Wade. American women may soon need to leave the country to get an abortion. If Mike Pence has anything to do with it that will include in the instance or rape, incest, or risk to the mother's life. Back-alley abortions may again become a part of America's underbelly. Trump has said that women seeking abortions should be punished. This will be just one of a number of measures that will make Trump's presidency a disaster for women's rights.

Again and again, Trump has shown a willingness to denigrate one group, class or race in order to fit the mood of the day. Although he governs for billionaires, it is the white working class who form his electoral base. They have pinned their hopes on him.

For many white working class families, society has fallen apart. Suicide and addiction rates have rocketed since the turn of the century, and increased further since the financial crisis. Life expectancy in many poor white communities has decreased. This never happens in functioning societies. Across America, and in the Rust Belt in particular, the social contract (that a person willing to work can find a decent paying job, that provides enough money to support life's requirements) has collapsed.

Social catastrophe affects young and old. Six times as many retirees in the US live in poverty as those in France. Oxycontin and painkillers have become the lead drugs abused in America, outstripping illegal narcotics. In Montana there are eighty-two prescriptions for painkillers for every one hundred people. Heroin use has never been wider, helped in great part by there never having been so much heroin available, in turn because America couldn't win a war against Afghanistan, one of the poorest nations on earth.

There's plenty of money around, it just never makes it to the pockets of the poor any more. With America's vast GDP the country could (for example) be at the vanguard of solar panel technology and manufacture, as it was with railroads and the automobile. Instead America has chosen to spend trillions on pointless wars, and on bailing out the richest institutions in the world when their business model collapsed.

Faced with desperation, poor white Americans grasped at anything that looked like change, and chose the only brand on offer: Trump. The collective rage of these people when they find that Donald Trump is going to do nothing for them is perhaps the thing we should fear the most. It remains to be seen if this anger is directed internally, or channeled toward some foreign body.

Trump's cabinet picks give no indication of a newfound passion for social justice and reform. Trump's team consists of a secretary for Housing and Urban Development (Ben Carson) who has described fair housing agreements as "communist," a secretary for the Department of Education (Betsy DeVos) who presided over plummeting standards in Michigan, and a climate change denier to head the EPA. Rick Perry (Energy) is just one of a number of individuals who head government departments they have explicitly said they would like to destroy.

Mike Pompeo, hired by Trump to head the CIA, has said that despite existing domestic surveillance powers being the most pervasive in human history, he feels that the US needs "a fundamental upgrade to America's surveillance capabilities."

It's a zoo. Comedian John Cleese suggested that Trump looked like he was assembling the crew for a pirate ship.

Those outside America are right to tremble. The most frightening aspect of Trump's Presidency is his finger on the nuclear trigger. Notwithstanding his inexperience and manifest personality problems, Trump has also often appeared blasé to the awesome power of nuclear weapons (which he describes as "the nuclear"). He said he would be comfortable with the idea of South Korea and the Saudis getting nuclear weapons, and said of America's arsenal, "if we have them why can't we use them?"

Three further potential catastrophes present a clear and present danger to world stability and peace during Trump's Presidency. Climate change, financial disaster, and war.

Climate

In early 2016, 750 experts gathered at the World Economic Forum rated climate catastrophe as the biggest threat to the world's economy. The survey had been done for eleven years, but 2016 was the first time that the Earth's climate had been rated number one by economists (rather than scientists). Those surveyed noted the risk of inter-connections, or the onslaught of further disasters caused by an initial shock, such as mass migration caused by rising sea levels.

This is not a view shared by America's president. Donald Trump famously said that climate change is in fact a hoax, made up by the Chinese to gain competitive advantage. He has called global warming bullshit, and said that in fact the earth is freezing, with "record low" temperatures. This idiotic and childlike view is refuted by overwhelming evidence. Every year is now the hottest ever recorded. The year 2015 was the first since records began that CO_2 in the atmosphere stayed above four hundred parts per million all year (normally the Northern hemisphere summer growth reduces the figure somewhat). We haven't seen CO_2 levels like this in the Earth's atmosphere for eight hundred thousand years, back when humans didn't exist and the oceans were thirty meters higher than they are today. Florida is perilously exposed to limited rises in ocean levels, yet they voted for Trump, like turkeys approaching Thanksgiving.

At the precise moment when dramatic measures could still stop climate change becoming an uncontrollable disaster, Trump wants to remove regulations on drilling and CO_2 emissions. Trump's presidency threatens the ongoing viability of mankind on planet earth. We're genuinely battling for survival now that he's in the Oval Office. Climate change is happening much faster than nearly all scientists predicted. It will blight or end our children's lives. Donald Trump incrementally increases this risk to us all.

We could easily fix the world's emissions problems with political courage and vision. Waging a war against climate change would kick-start the American economy. Solar power more than covers our transportation, domestic and business needs—panels are cheaper, more plentiful, and more efficient than ever before. Breakthroughs in large battery storage technology and pricing are made regularly. But, instead, at this critical juncture we are choosing to do the opposite, digging up and setting on fire ever more of the world's underground carbon deposits at the precise moment that the earth's climate is showing signs of critical breakdown. It's a quite extraordinary situation.

The fact is that until corporate money is removed from America's political process, or until a truly cataclysmic event transforms our world, America's political leaders are always going to respond to any issue by referring to what is best for their paymasters, and corporations are simply unable to see far enough ahead to address issues like climate change. The demands of capitalism make it impossible for them to change course, even in spite of the gathering storm. If the corporations win, humanity is doomed to disaster. At some point we are going to have to make a choice between capitalism and the survival of humanity.

I fear that Trump's election means the battle against catastrophic climate change is lost. Before Trump leaves office, there will be periods when there is no sea ice in the Arctic circle. The oceans will quickly begin to rise. Some countries will cease to exist. Hundreds of millions will be displaced, causing global chaos. We're fiddling while Rome burns. Around the world, armed men fight to defend or take back some small plot of soil from their neighbors, ignoring the relentless numerical doom of four hundred parts-per-million of carbon dioxide in our atmosphere, a number that creeps higher each year. Their priorities are desperately misguided. They should put down their guns and plant seeds instead, but seem unable to see the tidal wave on the horizon.

Money

George Orwell described the genesis of his book *Animal Farm* as having been sparked by a moment in which "I saw a little boy, perhaps ten years old, driving a huge cart-horse along a narrow path, whipping it whenever it tried to turn. It struck me that if only such animals became aware of their strength we should have no power over them, and that men exploit animals in much the same way as the rich exploit the proletariat."

In America, the richest 1 percent own 42 percent of the wealth, while the poorest 80 percent hold just 7 percent. Income disparity is just as bad—the richest 0.1 percent earns more than the poorest 120 million people combined. Such staggering inequality is symptomatic of a society in trouble.

History shows again and again that people will only take exploitation for so long before they take to the streets. Angry populations do have the means of bringing their country under control. Revolutionary France pitted seemingly powerless peasants against the nobility, yet it was the noblemen (and women) whose heads were separated from their bodies, and France didn't stop until nearly all of them were dead.

Around sixty individuals now collectively hold more wealth than the bottom 50 percent of humanity. They have around $1 trillion more in wealth than they did in 2010. For them, this decade-long downturn has been a vintage harvest. This extraordinary wealth disparity doesn't appear to shock anyone anymore, but it's unprecedented in human history. Rich individuals and corporations have stashed a planet-altering $20–$30 trillion offshore, as plain of a "fuck you" to the world's poor as it's possible to give. Multinationals steal money from your children's mouths by taking their profits offshore and paying no tax. Every time you are told there is not enough money to pay for civic services or unemployment benefits, remember that there is around $30 trillion stashed offshore. Hundreds of thousands of people die each year for want of that capital. Offshoring funds is mass murder by asymmetric means.

The stock market boom that followed Donald Trump's election may have seemed like good news, but 80 percent of stocks in America are held by the richest 10 percent of the people. The rich immediately got richer after they elected a billionaire. What do you think is most likely to happen now: this process continuing, or Donald Trump defying seventy years of doing nothing but enriching his own interests and discovering a passion for the poor?

As presidential candidate, Trump railed against Hillary Clinton and global banking elites, but within weeks of the election he appointed a who's who of Goldman Sachs alumni. It's very clear where his priorities lie.

Trump wants to dismantle the Dodd-Frank financial regulation Act of 2010, itself a flimsy attempt to rein in Wall Street excesses. A cascade of regulation will be removed and income taxes slashed. It's going to be a financial free-for-all, and the rich are going to get much, much richer. A lack of regulation and asset bubbles are precisely the conditions that led to the 2007/08 crash. A new and much bigger crash is as inevitable as the rising sun, and when it comes there will be no government that can save us. The implosion of Western banking, and of capitalism, will be nearly impossible to avoid. War will be the outcome.

War

For all of George W. Bush's faults, even after 9/11 he never explicitly demonized minority groups in the US. In fact, Bush pointedly visited a mosque just six days after the attacks. But this time it's different. Trump's candidacy demonstrated that being anti-Muslim and racist can be a political asset, not a liability. The direction to ostracize the Other, whether they are Muslim, gay, or anybody not white and male, is coming direct from the president. This has emboldened those harboring feelings of hatred or intolerance, who genuinely believe that this man is their president and shares their views. These sentiments will be easy to harness when it comes time to demonize a foreign entity.

War will hand Trump unlimited political power and the attending profits for those within the military industrial complex for whom death means money. If you doubt this, take a look at the stock price of defense logistics behemoths such as Northrop Grumman, Raytheon, and Lockheed Martin. All shot up dramatically on the day after the election. Investors aren't fools. Trump means war, and war means profits.

Despite the terrible debts that America faces, Republicans will tell you that the US military budget needs to increase. It doesn't. They will tell you that the navy fleet needs to be enlarged, to counter the rise of China. It doesn't. In fact, the US fleet is larger than the next thirteen navies combined (eleven of whom are allies). China's aircraft carrier is a refurbished old craft bought from Ukraine in 1998. It was originally built to be a floating casino.

It will be claimed that missile defense and weapons in space will keep America safe, when the opposite is true. There is no feasible way to defend America against an attack from thousands of Russian missiles and decoys, coming in at fifteen thousand miles per hour (an attack that is never coming), but a new American missile defense strategy will, with 100 percent certainty, cause Russia to build their own anti-missile defenses, with trillions spent by both sides, crippling their economies and causing impoverished citizens to live in a world that is much less safe.

Trump's team will eventually say that military action in Iran is vital in order to make Americans safe. It isn't. We must call them out for this mendacious, insane lie. National security can no longer be invoked when justifying military intervention in countries (almost always) in the Middle East. America must end its reflexive urge to intervene in other countries domestic affairs.

America has been at war for around 93 percent of its history. The events of September 11, 2001 seem to draw a line in the sand, after which America will never again be at peace. Financial collapse might cause war. War might cause financial collapse. Climate catastrophe will cause both. But America's government and military machine demand wars to feed their vast budget. Trump will get his war. It remains to be seen if he (and those around him) are able to contain it.

Change

First they came for the Socialists, and I did not speak out—
Because I was not a Socialist.
Then they came for the Trade Unionists, and I did not speak out—
Because I was not a Trade Unionist.
Then they came for the Jews, and I did not speak out—
Because I was not a Jew.
Then they came for me—and there was no one left to speak for me.

Martin Niemoller's famous poem was written to illustrate the cognitive dissonance that German intellectuals displayed as their country descended into Nazism. People living under authoritarian regimes often claim that nothing has changed, and even deny that repressive laws are being enacted right in front of them. They give away much of their power freely, in advance. People see what the regime is likely to want and start doing it, for fear of losing their fast-vanishing freedom, and out of conformity. Americans are already prepared for this, it seems. A survey done in 2014 found that a staggering one in six Americans felt that military rule (of their own country) would be a good or very good thing.

Politicians and leaders from the far right of the spectrum almost never voluntarily give up the emergency powers they claim for themselves in times of (real or imaginary) national crisis, and the Republican Party appears to genuinely believe that the US is in a permanent state of existential danger. Now Republicans have all three levers of government. A loss in 2016 might have fractured and destroyed the party. Instead they hold unparalleled power. Democrats may never again gain political control in the United States.

Vladimir Putin is regularly elected with crushing majorities, but no one would call twenty-first-century Russia a functioning democracy. Putin has gamed the system to retain control for eighteen years (and running). It seems that only illness or retirement will end his rule. A question that should always be applied to powerful leaders is this—how easy is it going to be to democratically remove this person from the national stage? Trump has already shown his disdain for the mechanics of America's democracy and for its results (before and after he won). It is abundantly clear that he doesn't think much of elections.

I find it impossible to see how the effects of this presidency cannot end in disaster, the end of American democracy, and an existential threat to the medium and perhaps even short-term viability of mankind on planet earth.

Democrats, progressives and anyone interested in freedom and democracy must wage an unprecedented campaign of intransigence, disobedience, and opposition to every single measure Trump and his group put forward. When Obama was in office, Republicans acted this way. When Bush was president, Democrats tried to play by the rules. We can't afford to play fair in this environment. The rules must be abandoned to save us all.

Impeachment proceedings should start now. Democrats must oppose every word that comes from his mouth. That's what Trump said he would do if Hillary Clinton had won. Noam Chomsky said that there's no point in speaking truth to power, since power already knows the truth. Freedom from tyranny and inequality is not going to be offered from above; it has to be taken by those below. Citizens should get involved, agitate, march, organize, protest, and donate to causes that support liberty and freedom.

The power of technology now hands whistleblowers the opportunity to bring down governments. Edward Snowden said, "I have been to the darkest corners of government, and what they fear is light." Trump will have more than enough skeletons in his cupboard to have him removed from office, if we can just get it done before the institutions of democracy are closed down.

Civil disobedience is a powerful tool. If you don't think you can make a difference, read the story of Gandhi. If enough people simply refuse to do the things they're supposed to, the entire system can be shut down. It needs to be, because very soon it is going to be too late. It is not acceptable to sit back anymore.

As I've stated previously, America is poised to emerge as the most overtly fascist political nation since Nazi Germany, the difference being that America is vastly more powerful than Germany ever was. Broken societies either practice social revolution or elect demagogues. Strong, violent men promising to make their nation great again can seem alluring to those harboring anger about the state their country is in. The results in Germany are well known, the comparison to today's America sadly no longer imprecise. Those who draw parallels with 1936 are missing a trick. It is immensely more dangerous now than then.

In 2017, Americans aged sixteen and under will have lived their entire life in the new normal of an endless War on Terror and under emergency provisions that are destroying the Constitution of the United States. They won't know any different. In two more years they can begin to vote. A generation of post-9/11 kids is coming.

Behind all of this is 9/11. Without 9/11 there would be no Trump. The exposure of the falsity of that event has the power to move mountains. Ask questions. Demand answers.

As for me, I still can't believe this has happened. The seventy years of post-World War Two peace that we've enjoyed is unraveling before our eyes. I've lost hope; hope that we can still find a way out of this. Faith that we have the ability to save ourselves.

CONCLUSION

THE DEATH OF A NATION

When you come to the conclusion that the attacks of 9/11 were orchestrated and carried out by the United States government, it casts a shadow on every aspect of America's political life since that day. Every statement about America's actions or intentions has to be preceded with the words, *given that 9/11 was carried out by the US government*. It's an appalling realization, staining every proud word from America's politicians and covering every noble intention with a shroud of doubt.

The facts surrounding the events of that terrible day are so overwhelmingly contrary to the official story that, once examined even briefly, the entire edifice of falsity collapses like a house of cards. Not only is there evidence showing that the official 9/11 story is entirely false, it's really surprisingly obvious. This in turn illustrates just how astounding it is that a story so full of holes was propagated by the government and media, and swallowed whole by the American public. It's a worrying precedent for what could happen in the future.

Not knowing all the answers to the question of what really happened does not disprove the statement that the official tale is false. We may never know what happened to flight 77 or fully comprehend how explosives can have been placed inside Building 7 at the World Trade Center, but that does not diminish the power of evidence such as the tiny hole in the wall of the Pentagon, the lack of resistance encountered by the collapsing twin towers, the symmetry of Building 7's collapse or the lack of a plane altogether at the official crash site in Shanksville.

As we have seen, for the attacks to circumvent America's sophisticated air defenses, numerous protocols had to be rewritten, circumvented, or stood down. A myriad of war games closely mimicking the attacks were conducted so as to confuse people trying to effect a response. Those at the very head of US government all curiously chose to do nothing as the attacks commenced.

In the end, what was vital was also quite simple—America's air defenses had to fail for a very short period of time, around 112 minutes.

With what we know, it is fair to assume that had the fourth plane struck its target, and the fifth plane (and perhaps more) got off the ground, the attacks might have been incrementally more devastating. From the attackers' perspective, 9/11 can only be judged a partial success. We missed out on the end of American democracy in 2001 quite by chance. We will not be so lucky again.

Nonetheless, the events of September 11, 2001 were an abomination. No matter who you believe conducted the attack, the murder of three thousand civilians was an appalling crime. What it was not, however, was an existential threat to the survival of the United States, or to civilization itself, as has been claimed. When Hutus began slaughtering Tutsis in Rwanda in 1994, they had a 9/11 (in terms of casualties) every twelve hours, for one hundred days. Vietnam experienced perhaps a thousand 9/11s at the hands of the US. Dreadful and bloody events happen around the world with depressing regularity. What was unique on 9/11 was that America was the victim, and it was America's response that changed the world.

Senior members of the Bush administration, heavily implicated in the attacks themselves, openly spoke of 9/11 being a blessing in disguise, and something that had silver linings. Having published a political wish list, only achievable in the event of a new Pearl Harbor, the attacks provided them with the justification to carry out precisely what they had hoped for. Any crime investigation starts with the question of who benefits, yet those who would on any rational basis have been the prime suspects were also running the country, and thus beyond suspicion. George W. Bush and his cronies were able to hand trillions of dollars to oil, defense and logistics contractors, as well as to the US military, and preside over a Ponzi-style financial boom that made the rich richer, then bail the entire banking industry out when it collapsed, ignoring the plight of millions of their impoverished citizens. 9/11 allowed them to do all this.

The Bush administration left behind a mortally wounded nation in smoldering ashes. They should be judged the worst government America ever had.

The murky tales of un-Islamic and idiotic behavior by the alleged attackers, Saudi spy liaisons, stock market activity showing foreknowledge, and American spy agencies clearly ignoring vital clues, all add to the impression of an attack that was widely known and anticipated, and allowed to happen by those whose jobs were specifically to stop such an event.

Many of America's closest state allies appear nefarious at best. Israel's government clearly had foreknowledge of the attacks and may well have played a part in carrying them out. Saudi Arabia provided nearly all of the alleged attackers, yet President Bush chose to secretly fly out bin Laden family members and Saudi royals, and smoked cigars with the Saudi ambassador at the White House just forty-eight hours after the attacks, thumbing his nose at those who died in the most offensive manner imaginable. It seems power, money and international relations were quickly adjudged more important than the American civilians that Bush said he served.

The inquiries into 9/11 were not worthy of the name, staffed by insiders and set on clear courses to avoid embarrassing questions and come to preset conclusions. The twenty-eight pages kept secret from the world for fourteen years showed that the Saudi government provided financial and logistical support to some of the alleged hijackers, and would have known that 9/11 was coming in advance. This calls into question whether America's relationship with Saudi Arabia is indeed so warm and friendly. I suspect that most who read these pages will suggest that, far from remaining friends, America should declare war on the Saudis. The earth-shattering ramifications need not be spelled out.

The attacks of 9/11 are the direct cause of the disintegration of Iraq as a state, the ongoing catastrophe in Afghanistan and the war in Syria. 9/11 is the genesis behind an American economy that has recovered more slowly than at any time since the Great Depression. 9/11 provides the justification for the immense power now held by the NSA and America's executive office—power that is unprecedented in the nation's history and provides a clear and present danger to the survival of American democracy.

What would it mean for the relationship between East and West if it became common knowledge that rather than an attack by nineteen Arab men funded by a Saudi, the events of 9/11 were in fact an act of self-sabotage by the leaders of the largest Christian nation on earth, men who wore their faith on their sleeve, who decided to murder three thousand of their own citizens in cold blood in order to profit from war and death elsewhere. 9/11 was in fact a declaration of war on the oil-rich nations of the world by America, and the single most treasonous act of betrayal in human history. This realization has the power to change our entire understanding of world events, and will force us to reinterpret every major development since 2001. There will be no alternative but to disband the government, jailing many of those who led it in the last few years, and to build an entirely new mechanism of governance to avoid any danger of a repetition or escalation. The heavens would fall.

America has a choice to make, between liberty and what the government will describe as security, which in fact is nothing of the sort. No government can possibly claim to keep each and every one of its citizens safe from violent attack all of the time. While it is true that one dead body is a tragedy too many, every country has to balance societal safety with individual liberty. Free societies are vulnerable, and the only way to fully shore up the risks is to close down the freedoms.

Nothing can be done to stop the violent actions of a deranged lunatic (although America should note that not allowing people to heavily arm themselves reduces the carnage significantly). Groups who espouse terroristic actions are almost always separatists, minorities, or people who feel their society has wronged them. Although terrorism is an abomination, these groups often have some form of political point, and if governments choose to stop attacking them for a moment, they can be negotiated with. The idea of negotiating with terrorists is often scoffed at, but Tony Blair did just that with the IRA, and the concessions his government made ended a terrorism movement in Northern Ireland that had run for generations. It can be done.

Despite the horror of 9/11, terrorism (especially in the Western world) is rare, and remains one of the most unlikely ways to die. A focus on reducing salt in people's diets would save many more lives, as would encouraging them to take a morning walk. Yet the focus on the negligible threat of terrorism to the exclusion of all other rational concerns has allowed the NSA to weld the tools of totalitarianism onto American democracy, with surveillance powers that closely resemble those of hated regimes that came before. As American politicians loudly proclaim the freedom of their society, they have ripped their precious Constitution to shreds in the name of keeping their people safe.

There are matters on earth that truly threaten humanity; matters often ignored by our focus on much less weighty affairs. The rise of antibiotic-resistant bacteria threatens an unstoppable pandemic. A collapse of the West Antarctic ice sheet (which appears underway) would raise global sea levels to an extent that would leave hundreds of millions homeless and submerge Manhattan and Miami. In the short term, a war with Iran, a climatic disaster, or nuclear mishap all truly threaten worldwide devastation. Yet America focuses its huge financial and military resources on defending its population from phantoms in a war that serves only to regenerate itself. Not only does America's war against terrorism offer no guarantee of safety (and in fact increases the risk of global terror), it distracts us from addressing these truly pressing concerns for the viability of mankind on earth.

You only have to look at the leverage that Donald Trump took from the San Bernardino shootings of December 2015 to understand how highly-strung the American public now feels. In that terrible instance, a seemingly normal couple returned to a work function and killed fourteen people. It was an appalling tragedy, but in no way a statistical outlier in America's grim daily toll of mass shootings, nor any more tragic than the 123 people who die per day from a lack of healthcare, or the eighty-five people who die per day because of America's gun laws. Yet Trump built much of his campaign around the threat of Islamic terrorism and Muslims in general, even threatening to ban all Muslims from entering the United States.

As terrorist strikes take place around the world, often at a rate of one every two days, America has stayed remarkably clear from Islamist violence. Yet Republicans focus relentlessly on demonizing Muslims and misrepresenting Islamic terrorists as people who just *really* hate freedom.

This disproportionate hysteria leaves the American electorate at severe risk of a paroxysm should another attack take place. It doesn't need to be an earth-shattering spectacular from the skies like 9/11; four men with Kalashnikovs can change the course of an entire nation. Imagine the overreaction that an Islamic terrorist attack on the US would engender in the instance of a president under pressure to prove his security credentials. America's population is now so indoctrinated and cowed by the concept of terrorism, that in the event of another major attack, the government would not have to impose tyrannical measures on its people; the people would demand them for their own protection.

Middle Easterners and Muslims would be incarcerated in scenes similar to those of the Japanese internments of World War II, perhaps hundreds of thousands of them. An entire section of America's society would fear walking the streets. Islamic Americans might tell you that day has already come.

Edward Snowden has said that in intelligence communities, terrorism is known as a cover for action, provoking an emotional response that allows politicians to authorize programs that the public wouldn't normally tolerate. Fear engenders tyranny, which in turn breeds conformity. To the authoritarian leader, terrorism can be used to consolidate political power and control a frightened population. The Bush administration conducted a spectacular attack in 2001 and got away with it. There is nothing to stop equally dangerous American leaders from even more tyranny in the future. Looking at the state of the Republican Party, can you truly say that another devastating terrorist attack on the United States under a right-wing president might not set in place measures that would qualify as dictatorship?

In the dying days of World War II, the SS in Berlin let river water into the subway tunnels where frightened citizens were hiding. We are all in this together. Crumbling empires have a habit of taking their people down with them.

Senator Frank Church, investigating America's intelligence agencies in 1975 (and shocked at the power of the NSA), gave a warning that forty years later sounds astonishingly prescient.

"The National Security Agency's capability at any time could be turned around on the American people and no American would have any privacy left, such is the capability to monitor everything, telephone conversations, telegrams—it doesn't matter. There would be no place to hide. If a dictator takes over the United States, the NSA could enable it to impose total tyranny, and there would be no way to fight back." Church would be appalled by the intrusion of the NSA and its surveillance programs on Americans today. His worst fears are not in our future, they are right here, right now. The NSA now has the power to turn America into the most sophisticated, pervasive and repressive surveillance state in human history.

One of the great lessons of history is that seemingly inviolate institutions and ideas can, often quite quickly, be vanquished or destroyed when the right moment comes. Most of America's great social programs of the twentieth century were launched under Franklin Roosevelt, not because he was an especially humanitarian person, but because he faced a country in open revolt during the Great Depression. Desperate times saw desperate measures.

FDR also allowed the Great Depression to play out, abandoning failed institutions and leaving financial dead bodies everywhere, giving him the opportunity to bring in strong new laws that kept the banks healthy and fit for purpose for decades to come.

America faced a similar situation in 2008—an overwhelming depression, interest rates at zero, and vast untapped human potential through unemployment. This neatly combined with the dawn of extraordinary new technologies that could transform human affairs. Recession and climate change could have met in the middle, with a short and long-term payoff for all humanity.

As it is, Obama spectacularly blew it, and with the exception of the limp Affordable Care Act, we've got very little to show for his eight years in office. All that is left to debate is whether Obama lacked the courage or the power to implement the change on which he had campaigned. Globalization, which is as much an implied threat as it is a system, leaves politicians cowering and gives corporations power much exceeding that of sovereign governments. There is no global or political authority with the power of the financial sector, which means they are a law unto themselves. Politicians are just window-dressing for the totalitarianism of the markets.

America's extraordinary, perhaps unprecedented, dominance of world affairs makes it look like a leviathan that could never be challenged. But like every great beast, America has an underbelly of profound weakness. The limitations of its military have been rudely demonstrated by failures to decisively win wars against minnows such as Afghanistan and Iraq. At home America is a divided nation, its population experiencing levels of poverty not seen since the 1930s. Political institutions are deadlocked and seem unable to make any meaningful contribution to progress. Government is weighed down by the highest debt in recorded human history. In 2008, America's financial system nearly collapsed.

The most powerful nation on earth is the sick man of the West.

It has often seemed that political change in America was not possible. Both sides presented equally unattractive and often indistinguishable visions for the future. That is no longer the case. While the Democratic Party can on occasions seem uninspiring, the Republican Party (when not tearing itself apart) offers a vision of devastation. Republicans want to tear up the nuclear agreement with Iran. Republicans don't believe climate change is even real, let alone manmade. Republicans want to repeal Obamacare, seemingly for the casual cruelty it will inflict upon those who finally have medical coverage. The right of the party is now considerably further right than they were under the administration of George W. Bush. To call them fascists is not hyperbole.

9/11 enabled an entirely new direction for US political policy. We are now through the looking glass. The election of Donald Trump has inflicted what is perhaps a mortal blow to American democracy, and is likely to precede a period of world war, vast homegrown terrorist outrage, American democratic collapse, dictatorship, and the end of the free world as we know it.

The world changed, we were told, because of 9/11. America claimed the right to preventive and preemptive war, unilateral aggression, and disregard for any international law that gets in the way, solely to protect itself from another attack. But all of this was a facade. The government of the United States attacked its own people on September 11 and is capable of doing so again. 9/11 was an inside job. This reality is so shattering that only the complete dismantling of America's political system can stop its progression towards totalitarianism.

The rise of Donald Trump to the office of president of the United States of America alerted the world to the fact that the foundations of American society are shaking; but in truth the story was less about Trump and more about a nation that is coming apart at the seams.

Had Trump not been in a position to mount his attack on America's political establishment, another angry white man would eventually have taken his place. Trump is not a demagogue genius harnessing otherwise moderate people; he is emblematic of Americans' frustration at the inequities of their society. The world should hold its breath as America decides how to resolve the problems its society faces. Reform and a return to moderation remain possible, but to the right lies calamity. The very future of our species will be defined by this decision.

End

After two hundred thousand or so words, allow me an indulgence. A now silent voice has helped to make things clear in my life. He may strike a chord for you, too. Thank you for reading this book and enjoy these last few words:

"The heavens parted, God looked down and rained gifts of forgiveness onto my being, healing me on every level, psychically, emotionally, physically, and I realized our true nature is spirit, not body, and that we are eternal beings and God's love is unconditional, and there's nothing we can ever do to change that. It is only our illusion that we are separate from God, or that we are alone. In fact, the reality is, we are one with God and he loves us.

Now if that isn't a hazard to this country . . ."

Bill Hicks, *Rant in E-Minor*.

BIBLIOGRAPHY

Ahmed, Nafeez Mosaddeq. *The War on Freedom: How and Why America was Attacked September 11, 2001*. California: Tree of Life Publications, 2002.

Ahmed, Nafeez Mosaddeq. *The War on Truth: 9/11, Disinformation, and the Anatomy of Terrorism*. Massachusetts: Olive Branch Press, 2005.

Ahmed, Nafeez Mosaddeq, *The London Bombings: An Independent Inquiry*. New York. The Overlook Press, 2006.

Ali, Tariq. *The Clash of Fundamentalisms: Crusades, Jihads and Modernity*. London: Verso, 2003.

Arendt, Hannah. *The Origins of Totalitarianism*. California: Harcourt, 1973.

Baker, Norman. *The Strange Death of David Kelly*. England: Methuen Publishing, 2007.

Baker, Peter. *Days of Fire: Bush and Cheney in the White House*. New York: Anchor, 2014.

Boyle, Francis. *Tackling America's Toughest Questions: Alternative Media Interviews*. Atlanta: Clarity Press, 2015.

Brand, Russell. *Revolution*. London: Century, 2014.

Briody, Dan. *The Iron Triangle: Inside the Select World of the Carlyle Group*. Australia: Wiley, 2004.

Brzezinski, Zbigniew. *The Grand Chessboard: American Primacy and Its Geostrategic Imperatives*. New York: Basic Books, 1998.

Burke, Jason. *The 9/11 Wars*. London: Penguin Books, 2011.

Bush, George W. *Decision Points*. New York: Crown Publishers, 2010.

Chatterjee, Pratap. *Halliburton's Army: How a Well-Connected Texas Oil Company Revolutionized the Way America Makes War*. New York: Nation Books, 2009.

Chomsky, Noam. *Failed States: The Abuse of Power and the Assault on Democracy*. Australia: Allen & Unwin, 2006.

Chomsky, Noam. *Power and Terror: Post-9/11 Talks and Interviews*. Canada: Seven Stories Press and Little More, 2003.

Chomsky, Noam. *9/11*. New York: Seven Stories Press, 2001/2002.

Chomsky, Noam. *Hegemony or Survival: America's Quest for Global Dominance*. Australia: Allen & Unwin, 2003.

Chossudovsky, Michel. *War and Globalisation: The Truth Behind September 11*. Canada: Global Outlook and the Centre for Research on Globalisaton (CRG), 2002.

Clarke, Richard. *Against All Enemies: Inside America's War on Terror*. New York: Free Press, 2004.

Coll, Steve. *Ghost Wars: The Secret History of the CIA, Afghanistan and Bin Laden, from the Soviet Invation to September 10, 2001*. London: Penguin, 2004.

Dubose, Lou. *Vice: Dick Cheney and the Hijacking of the American Presidency*. New York: Random House, 2006.

Edmonds, Sibel. *Classified Woman — the Sibel Edmonds Story: A Memoir*. Self-Published, 2012.

ElBaradei, Mohamed. *The Age of Deception: Nuclear Diplomacy in Treacherous Times*. New York: Picador, 2012.

Ferguson, Charles. *Predator Nation: Corporare Criminals, Political Corruption, and the Hijacking of America*. New York: Crown Business, 2013.

Ferguson, Charles. *Inside Job: The Financiers Who Pulled off the Heist of the Century*. London: Oneworld Publications, 2012.

Fleischer, Ari. *Taking Heat: The President, the Press, and My Years in the White House*. New York: William Morrow, 2005.

Freeman, Steve, and Joel Bleifuss. *Was the 2004 Presidential Election Stolen? Exit Polls, Election Fraud, and the Official Count*. New York: Seven Stories Press, 2006.

Gerges, Fawaz. *The Rise and Fall of Al-Qaeda*. England: Oxford.University Press, 2011.

Giuliani, Rudolph. *Leadership*. New York: Hyperion, 2002.

Gottfried, Paul. *Leo Strauss and the Conservative Movement in America*. Engand: Cambridge University Press, 2013.

Greenwald, Glenn. *No Place to Hide: Edward Snowden, the NSA and the Surveillance State*. New York: Henry Holt & Company, 2014.

Griffin, David Ray. *The New Pearl Harbor: Disturbing Questions About the Bush Administration and 9/11*. Massachusetts: Olive Branch Press, 2004.

Griffin, David Ray, and Peter Dale Scott. *9/11 and American Empire: Intellectuals Speak Out*. Massachusetts: Olive Branch Press, 2007.

Griffin, David Ray. *The Mysterious Collapse of World Trade Center 7: Why the Final Official Report about 9/11 is Unscientific and False*. Massachusetts: Olive Branch Press, 2010.

Hasen, Richard. *The Voting Wars: From Florida 2000 to the Next Election Meltdown*. Connecticut: Yale University Press, 2012.

Hayes, Stephen. *Cheney: The Untold Story of America's Most Powerful and Controversial Vice-President*. New York: Harper Collins, 2007.

Heppermann, Christine. *Bush v Gore: The Florida Recounts of the 2000 Presidential Election (Landmark Supreme Court Cases)*. Minnesota: Abdo Publishing, 2012.

Isikoff, Michael, and David Corn. *Hubris: The Inside Story of Spin, Scandal, and the Selling of the Iraq War*. New York: Broadway Books, 2007.

Jenkins, Simon. *Mission Accomplished? The Crisis of International Intervention*. London: I.B. Tauris, 2015.

Jones, Stephen. *Others Unknown: The Oklahoma Bombing Case and Conspiracy*. New York: Perseus Books Group, 1998.

Lewis, Michael. *Liar's Poker*. New York: W.W. Norton & Company, 2010.

Lewis, Michael. *The Big Short: Inside the Doomsday Machine*. New York: W.W. Norton & Company, 2011.

Lewis, Sinclair. *It Can't Happen Here*. Doubleday, Doran and Company: New York, 1935.

Lippold, Kirk. *Front Burner: Al Qaeda's Attack on the USS Cole*. New York: Public Affairs, 2013.

Litvinenko, Alexander, and Yuri Felshtinsky. *Blowing up Russia: The Secret Plot to Bring Back KGB Terror*. New York: Encounter Books, 2007.

MacQueen, Graeme. *The 2001 Anthrax Deception: The Case for a Domestic Conspiracy*. Atlanta: Clarity Press, 2014.

Mamdani, Mahmood. *Good Muslim, Bad Muslim: America, the Cold War, and the Roots of Terror*. New York: Harmony, 2005.

Mann, James. *Rise of the Vulcans: The History of Bush's War Cabinet*. New York: Penguin Books, 2004.

Mayer, Jane. *The Dark Side: The Inside Story of How the War on Teror Turned Into a War on American Ideals*. New York: Anchor, 2009.

McDermott, Terry. *Perfect Soldiers: The 9/11 Hijackers: Who They Were, Why They Did It*. New York: Harper Perennial, 2006.

McDermott, Terry, and Josh Meyer. *The Hunt for KSM: Inside the Pursuit and Takedown of the Real 9/11 Mastermind, Khalid Sheikh Mohammed*. New York: Back Bay Books, 2013.

McDonald, Lawrence, and Patrick Robinson. *A Colossal Failure of Common Sense: The Inside Story of the Collapse of Lehman Brothers*. New York: Crown Business, 2010.

Meyssan, Thierry. *9/11 The Big Lie*. London: Carnot Publishing, 2002.

Morris, Charles. *The Two Trillion Dollar Meltdown: Easy Money, High Rollers, and the Great Credit Crash*. New York: Public Affairs 2009.

National Commission on Terrorist Attacks. *The 9/11 Commission Report: Final Report of the National Commission on Terrorist Attacks Upon the United States*. 2004.

Ottaway, David. *The King's Messenger: Prince Bandar bin Sultan and America's Tangled Relationship with Saudi Arabia*. London: Walker Books, 2008.

Owen, Mark, and Kevin Maurer. *No Easy Day: The Firsthand Account of the Mission That Killed Osama bin Laden*. New York: Dutton 2014.

Peters, Gretchen. *Seeds of Terror: How Drugs, Thugs and Crime are Reshaping the Afghan War*. New York: Thomas Dunne Books, 2010.

Piketty, Thomas. *Why Save the Bankers?: And Other Essays on Our Economic and Political Crisis*. Massachusetts: Houghton Mifflin Harcourt, 2016.

Piketty, Thomas, and Arthur Goldhammer. *Capital in the Twenty First Century*. Massachusetts: Belknap Press, 2014.

Pilger, John. *The New Rulers of the World*. London: Verso, 2016.

Ricks, Thomas. *Fiasco: The American Military Adventure in Iraq, 2003 to 2005*. London: Penguin, 2007.

Ridgeway, James. *The 5 Unanswered Questions about 9/11: What the 9/11 Commission Report Failed to Tell Us*. New York: Seven Stories Press, 2005.